INTELLIGENT SUPPORT SYSTEMS FOR MARKETING DECISIONS

INTERNATIONAL SERIES IN
OPERATIONS RESEARCH & MANAGEMENT SCIENCE
Frederick S. Hillier, Series Editor Stanford University

Weglarz, J. / *PROJECT SCHEDULING: Recent Models, Algorithms and Applications*
Sahin, I. & Polatoglu, H. / *QUALITY, WARRANTY AND PREVENTIVE MAINTENANCE*
Tavares, L.V. / *ADVANCED MODELS FOR PROJECT MANAGEMENT*
Tayur, S., Ganeshan, R. & Magazine, M. / *QUANTITATIVE MODELING FOR SUPPLY CHAIN MANAGEMENT*
Weyant, J. / *ENERGY AND ENVIRONMENTAL POLICY MODELING*
Shanthikumar, J.G. & Sumita, U. / *APPLIED PROBABILITY AND STOCHASTIC PROCESSES*
Liu, B. & Esogbue, A.O. / *DECISION CRITERIA AND OPTIMAL INVENTORY PROCESSES*
Gal, T., Stewart, T.J., Hanne, T. / *MULTICRITERIA DECISION MAKING: Advances in MCDM Models, Algorithms, Theory, and Applications*
Fox, B.L. / *STRATEGIES FOR QUASI-MONTE CARLO*
Hall, R.W. / *HANDBOOK OF TRANSPORTATION SCIENCE*
Grassman, W.K. / *COMPUTATIONAL PROBABILITY*
Pomerol, J-C. & Barba-Romero, S. / *MULTICRITERION DECISION IN MANAGEMENT*
Axsäter, S. / *INVENTORY CONTROL*
Wolkowicz, H., Saigal, R., & Vandenberghe, L. / *HANDBOOK OF SEMI-DEFINITE PROGRAMMING: Theory, Algorithms, and Applications*
Hobbs, B.F. & Meier, P. / *ENERGY DECISIONS AND THE ENVIRONMENT: A Guide to the Use of Multicriteria Methods*
Dar-El, E. / *HUMAN LEARNING: From Learning Curves to Learning Organizations*
Armstrong, J.S. / *PRINCIPLES OF FORECASTING: A Handbook for Researchers and Practitioners*
Balsamo, S., Personé, V., & Onvural, R./ *ANALYSIS OF QUEUEING NETWORKS WITH BLOCKING*
Bouyssou, D. et al. / *EVALUATION AND DECISION MODELS: A Critical Perspective*
Hanne, T. / *INTELLIGENT STRATEGIES FOR META MULTIPLE CRITERIA DECISION MAKING*
Saaty, T. & Vargas, L. / *MODELS, METHODS, CONCEPTS and APPLICATIONS OF THE ANALYTIC HIERARCHY PROCESS*
Chatterjee, K. & Samuelson, W. / *GAME THEORY AND BUSINESS APPLICATIONS*
Hobbs, B. et al. / *THE NEXT GENERATION OF ELECTRIC POWER UNIT COMMITMENT MODELS*
Vanderbei, R.J. / *LINEAR PROGRAMMING: Foundations and Extensions, 2nd Ed.*
Kimms, A. / *MATHEMATICAL PROGRAMMING AND FINANCIAL OBJECTIVES FOR SCHEDULING PROJECTS*
Baptiste, P., Le Pape, C. & Nuijten, W. / *CONSTRAINT-BASED SCHEDULING*
Feinberg, E. & Shwartz, A. / *HANDBOOK OF MARKOV DECISION PROCESSES: Methods and Applications*
Ramík, J. & Vlach, M. / *GENERALIZED CONCAVITY IN FUZZY OPTIMIZATION AND DECISION ANALYSIS*
Song, J. & Yao, D. / *SUPPLY CHAIN STRUCTURES: Coordination, Information and Optimization*
Kozan, E. & Ohuchi, A. / *OPERATIONS RESEARCH/ MANAGEMENT SCIENCE AT WORK*
Bouyssou et al. / *AIDING DECISIONS WITH MULTIPLE CRITERIA: Essays in Honor of Bernard Roy*
Cox, Louis Anthony, Jr. / *RISK ANALYSIS: Foundations, Models and Methods*
Dror, M., L'Ecuyer, P. & Szidarovszky, F. / *MODELING UNCERTAINTY: An Examination of Stochastic Theory, Methods, and Applications*
Dokuchaev, N. / *DYNAMIC PORTFOLIO STRATEGIES: Quantitative Methods and Empirical Rules for Incomplete Information*
Sarker, R., Mohammadian, M. & Yao, X. / *EVOLUTIONARY OPTIMIZATION*
Demeulemeester, R. & Herroelen, W. / *PROJECT SCHEDULING: A Research Handbook*
Gazis, D.C. / *TRAFFIC THEORY*
Zhu, J. / *QUANTITATIVE MODELS FOR PERFORMANCE EVALUATION AND BENCHMARKING*
Ehrgott, M. & Gandibleux, X. / *MULTIPLE CRITERIA OPTIMIZATION: State of the Art Annotated Bibliographical Surveys*
Bienstock, D. / *Potential Function Methods for Approx. Solving Linear Programming Problems*

INTELLIGENT SUPPORT SYSTEMS FOR MARKETING DECISIONS

Nikolaos F. Matsatsinis
Technical University of Crete

Yannis Siskos
Technical University of Crete

KLUWER ACADEMIC PUBLISHERS
Boston / Dordrecht / London

Distributors for North, Central and South America:
Kluwer Academic Publishers
101 Philip Drive
Assinippi Park
Norwell, Massachusetts 02061 USA
Telephone (781) 871-6600
Fax (781) 871-9045
E-Mail: kluwer@wkap.com

Distributors for all other countries:
Kluwer Academic Publishers Group
Post Office Box 322
3300 AH Dordrecht, THE NETHERLANDS
Telephone 31 786 576 000
Fax 31 786 546 474
E-mail: services@wkap.nl

Electronic Services <http://www.wkap.nl>

Library of Congress Cataloging-in-Publication Data

A C.I.P. Catalogue record for this book is available from the Library of Congress.

Matsatsinis, Nikolaos & Siskos, Yannis/ INTELLIGENT SUPPORT SYSTEMS FOR MARKETING DECISIONS

ISBN 1-4020-7194-9

Printed on acid-free paper.

Printed in the United States of America.

Contents

Preface vii

PART I - Marketing Decisions 1

1 Decision Analysis and Support 3

2 The Structure of Marketing Decisions 21

3 Strategic Marketing Decisions 61

PART II - Intelligent Support Systems 83

4 Information Systems 85

5 Decision Support Systems 111

6 Advanced Decision Support Systems 171

7 Intelligent Decision Support Methods 221

8 Intelligent Decision Support Systems in Marketing 273

9 New Product Development Methodology 339

10 Analysis and Design of MARKEX 367

11 Applications in Marketing 403

References 423

Index 509

Preface

The recent collaboration of Multicriteria Analysis, Decision Support Systems and Artificial Intelligence in Marketing, has yield particularly significant results in strategic marketing decisions, especially in decisions related with new product development and formation of penetration strategies. The aim of this book is to cover the gap of international literature concerning these results.

The first applications of Artificial Intelligence in Marketing appeared in 1986, with the publishing of the work of Choffray and Chapin, and Rangarwamy, Burke, Eliashberg, and Wind. These research efforts have focused, on one hand, on the pure scientific direction (type of logic process, knowledge structure, etc) and on the other hand on the support of marketing decisions, which has been developed more extensively. In this book, the effort is to record and analyze current operational intelligent marketing decision support systems. Furthermore, the proposed multicriteria methodology for new product development decisions approaches the entire process as a process of integrating new product development decision-makers with intelligent decision support systems.

An early attempt involved the design of a new methodology for market analysis and new product design, proposed by Matsatsinis and Siskos, based on the study of consumer behavior. This methodology has been implemented by an intelligent decision support system, named MARKEX, and has been successfully applied to a series of real world market surveys for new product development. The developed system combines the ability to manipulate effectively qualitative and quantitative data through the system's marketing models. The implementation of the methodology is accomplished by using several forecasting, data analysis, multicriteria analysis, and branch choice models.

Throughout this book, the following subjects are studied:

- The theoretical background required for the development of Intelligent Decision Support Systems in Marketing, such as decision theory, marketing decisions, multicriteria decision analysis, information systems, decision support systems, intelligent decision support methods.
- Current trends of Intelligent Decision Support Systems in Marketing and short presentation of some characteristic systems.
- A new multicriteria methodology for new product development and formation of market penetration strategy, based on the analysis of consumer's behavior.
- The implementation of this methodology, through an Intelligent DSS.
- The procedures followed for knowledge elicitation, acquisition, and representation of the system's knowledge bases as well as for the development of a heuristic brand choice model.
- Fundamental issues of modern technologies such as intelligent agents.
- The system's multicriteria methodology and function through the presentation of a real-world application concerning the development of a new product.

As innovative points of this book, the following may be considered:

- The proposed multicriteria methodology for new product development decisions and choice of market penetration strategy, based on the qualitative study and analysis of consumer's behavior.
- The development of an Intelligent DSS that implements the above mentioned multicriteria methodology.
- The presentation of the essential scientific background in which the multicriteria methodology and the system are based on.
- The analytical presentation of all the utilized models.
- The analytical presentation of the system's knowledge bases concerning the choice of data analysis method, the assessment of firm's financial status, and the choice of brand choice model.
- The presentation of a heuristic algorithm for brand choice model selection.
- The presentation of the results of a survey on existing IDSSs in marketing.
- The presentation of current trends in the development of web-based DSSs and other modern technologies such as intelligent agents, neural networks, heuristics, etc.
- The presentation of real-world cases of new product development decisions, in which the methodology and the system where applied.

In addition to the above, the book differs from other books, also in the following points:

- It focuses on a certain category of DSSs, namely on IDSSs .

- It studies their application and function in a single portion of marketing, which deals with the development of new products based on the study of consumers' behavior.
- The book examines the application of multicriteria decision analysis for qualitative analysis of data, consumers' behavior analysis, criteria analysis, and market simulations.

In the first part of the book (Part I – Chapters 1, 2, and 3) the basic concepts of multicriteria analysis theory, marketing decisions and strategic decision making in new product development situations are examined.

Part II, presents basic concepts from the fields of information systems (Chapter 4), decision support systems (Chapter 5) and intelligent decision support methods (Chapter 7). In Chapter 6, specialized categories of DSSs, such as multicriteria DSSs, web-based DSSs, Group DSSs, Spatial DSSs, etc, are presented. Chapter 8 studies the current situation in IDSSs in Marketing, formed trends, and short presentation of some typical systems of this category. In addition, a list of IDSSs in Marketing along with their most important features, which is the result of an extensive survey, is presented.

Part III, begins with the proposed multicriteria methodology for new product development (Chapter 9). Chapter 10 presents the analysis, design and development of the Intelligent Decision Support System that implements this methodology. This chapter also presents the system's models and knowledge bases. Finally, in Chapter 11 the methodology and the function of the system are presented through a real-world application concerning the development of a new product.

I

PART I. MARKETING DECISIONS

Chapter 1

Decision analysis and support

1. INTRODUCTION

The continuous and enormous increase in the complexity of organizations renders the decision making almost an impossible task to be managed by individual decision makers and generated the necessity for more efficient and effective administration and management procedures. In order to satisfy these requirements new scientific fields have emerged or expanded like management science, operational research, applied economic sciences, behavioural sciences, etc. The evolution of these research fields led to the systematic and scientific analysis and handling of administrative and managerial problems.

This immense development of new methodologies and expansion of existing scientific fields was augmented by the contribution of the:

- Rapid progress of computer science in hardware and software, and
- Evolution in communication and network technologies.

The vast complexity of decision-making problems resulted in the expansion and augmentation of the role that humans play in the decision-making processes. The shift of focus from models and numbers to human decision makers led, in the beginning of 70's, to the emergence and flourishing of a new scientific field known as Decision Science.

The goal of the decision science is to study all the factors and procedures that can direct to a desirable decision. Decisions are reached through the elaboration of a set of highly complex processes, which aim at studying and extensively analysing the consequences of the decision alternatives and then at synthesizing the goals and intentions of the involved parties in order to find a commonly acceptable solution.

The term decision denotes the group of actions (thoughts, judgments, etc) taken by an individual or a group in order to choose a certain action through a set of alternative choices. In order to be able to talk about decisions we have to assume that the decision maker is able to choose at least between two alternatives. When only one alternative exists then we cannot consider the problem of making the decision, since the choice is mandatory by default. The possibility not to take any action (i.e. do nothing) is regarded as an alternative choice.

According to Simon (1960) the decision making process is composed of programmed and non-programmed decisions. In the same spirit, Keen and Scott-Morton (1978) and Keen (1980), point out three types of decisions: (1) structured, (2) semi structured, and (3) unstructured or ill-structured decisions.

The structured framework includes the decision problems in which:

- The process that is followed for making the decision is always the same.
- The decision task is explicitly defined, and
- The input data as well as the results of their process are specific.

In contrast, unstructured decisions share some different properties:

- The process of reaching to the decision is always different, depending on the particular decision task, and
- The objective of the decision making process, the input data, and the results are not explicitly defined.

In the case of semi structured decision-making situations, some elements of the process are well structured and explicitly predefined where as some other are rather vague in the beginning of the process.

According to Keen and Scott-Morton (1978) and Keen (1980), decisions that fall into the structured framework can be reached from computer systems without the necessity of the participation and active involvement of a decision maker. Semi structured decision-making situations can be handled by the cooperation and interaction between the decision maker and a computerized system. The main point of difference from the structured decision making situations is that in this case, decisions are made by the human decision maker and not by the system solely. Finally, unstructured decisions are considered those that can not be structured and solved in a specific and predefined manner or those that yet can not be included into the structured decision making framework.

However, if we accept, that decision making is an exclusive attribute of human thinking and judgment then we conclude that the first categorization of the decision making processes in structured (Keen and Scott-Morton, 1978) or programmed (Simon, 1960) can not be accepted as a single class of decisions since there is no human intervention in making these types of decisions. Consequently, decision-making processes can be categorized in two distinct classes: semi structured, and unstructured decisions as already explained earlier.

2. THE DECISION SUPPORT PROCESS

According to Simon's famous model (Simon, 1960), the decision making process followed by a single decision maker can be divided in three district phases:

1. Intelligence phase: The opening phase of the decision process includes the quest of situations and circumstances for which a decision can be made.
2. Design phase: The design phase includes the investigation, analysis, and development of the complete set of alternative actions or decisions.
3. Choice phase: In the final phase, the selection of the right decision is accomplished among the set of alternative actions or decisions.

If these three phases of the decision making process are structured the problem is considered as completely structured. In the adverse situation where none of the decision-making phases is structured the problem belongs to the unstructured case. Finally, if some phases are defined and some others are unstructured then we face the case of a semi-structured problem. The third phase (choice) also includes the tasks related with the implementation of the decision. Because of its high importance, many authors regard that the implementation of the solution is a fourth independent phase of the decision process (*Figure 1*).

Anthony (1965) defines three overall categories of decisions, which include all the potential managerial activities:

- Operational control, which corresponds to the efficiency and effectiveness of performing specific tasks.
- Managerial control, which has to do with the acquisition and efficient utilization of the necessary resources for achieving the goals.
- Strategic planning, which refers to long-range goals and the corresponding resource allocation strategies.

Table 1 adopted from Turban (1993) presents the combination of Simon's (1960) and Anthony's (1965) ideas as these were perceived by Gorry and Scott-Morton (1971).

2.1 Intelligence phase

In the beginning of the intelligence phase, we seek to find possible problems in the environment, which demand the taking of a decision. Then, we investigate to find out if each particular problem is an actual and autonomous problem and not a part of a more general one. Then we have to explicitly determine each problem and define its degree of importance so as to a priori know the priority that is set for the solution of the problem on behalf of the enterprise. Each problem is classified into one of the predefined categories (structured, unstructured or ill-structured problems) and it is then decomposed, if possible, into partial sub problems. The intelligence phase ends with the recording of the problem.

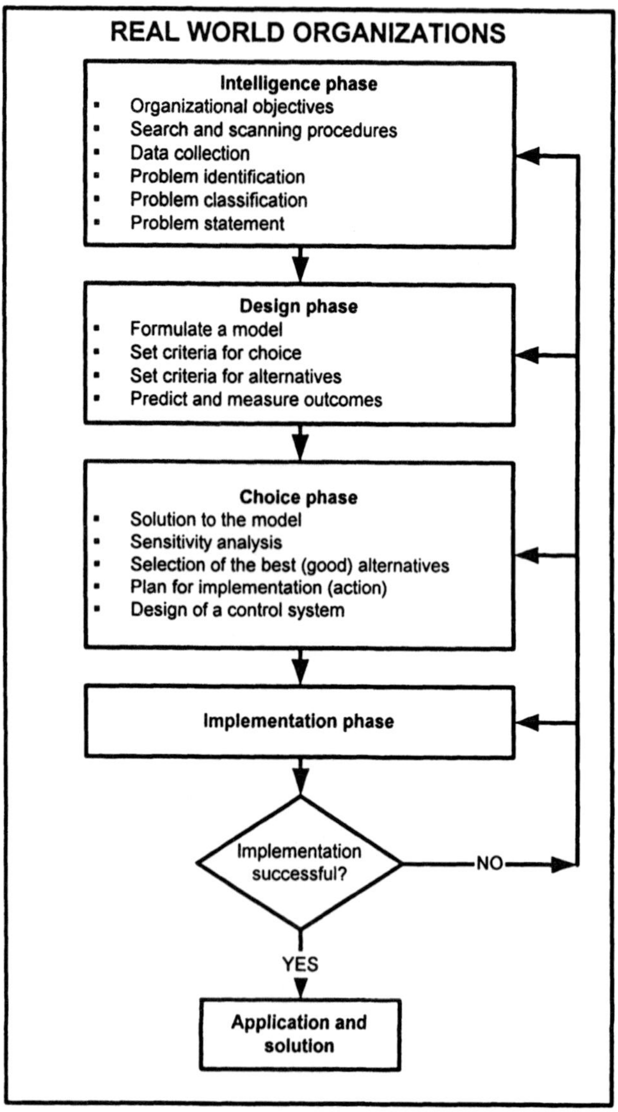

Figure 1. Decision making process (*Source*: Sprague and Carlson, 1982)

Table 1. Decision Support Framework (*Source*: Turban, 1993)

Decisions	Operational Control	Managerial Control	Strategic Planning	Support needed
Structured	Accounts receivable, Order entry	Budget analysis, Short-term forecasting, Personnel reports, Make-or-buy analysis	Warehouse location, distribution systems	MIS OR and Management Science models
Semi structured	Production scheduling, inventory control	Budget preparation, Credit evaluation, Project scheduling	New product design, new product planning	DSSs
Unstructured	Approving loans, buying software	Negotiating, buying hardware.	R&D planning, new technology development.	DSSs, Expert Systems

2.2 Design phase

The phase of problem design begins with the exhaustive study of the problem in an attempt to achieve an ample comprehension of it. Then we attempt to find all the possible alternative actions. The elaboration and analysis of these actions lead to the evaluation of the solutions, which in turn will be tested in order to find out if their implementation is feasible. One of the most significant sections of the design phase is the process of modelling the problem. Problem modelling defines the process of formulating a model that can efficiently represent the state of the problem. This model is then tested and validated.

2.3 Choice phase

The choice phase includes the tasks of searching, evaluating, and finding of the appropriate solution of the model. The search of the solution can be either goal-driven, or data-driven, or a combination of them.

- Data-driven search: In this case, we attempt to reach some conclusions that approach our goals based on the data on hand.
- Goal-driven search: In goal-driven search, we start the procedure from the assigned goals or from the goals that we seek to achieve and search out for facts that can sustain or reject these hypotheses.

The techniques that are used for the search depend on the selected decision models. Optimisation models use the analytical search techniques and the exhaustive implicit search techniques (*Figure 2*) while the descriptive models use either partial implicit search techniques or heuristics methods (*Figure 3*).

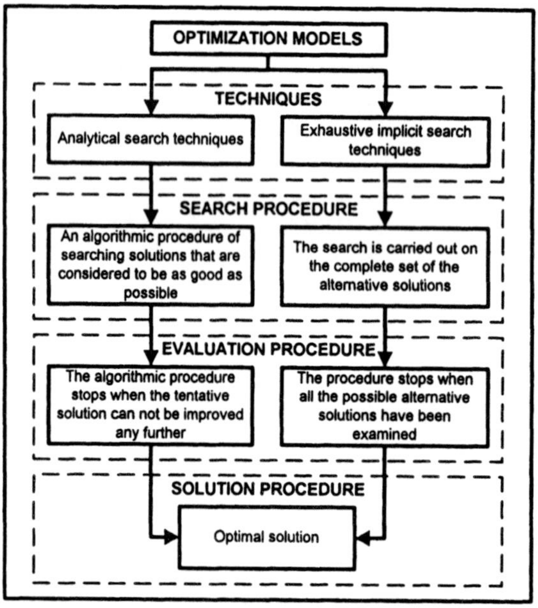

Figure 2. Solution search in optimisation models.

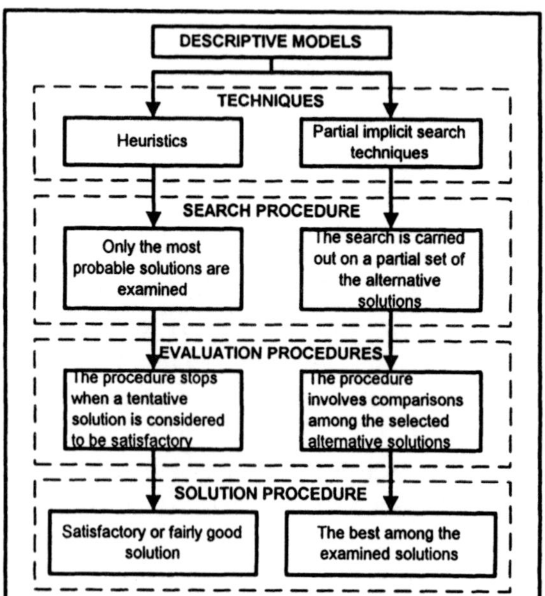

Figure 3. Solution search in descriptive models.

- Analytical search techniques. They are mainly used for solving structured problems. They follow an algorithmic search procedure, which examines if a tentative solution can be further improved. If there is no possibility of improving the tentative solution then the current tentative solution is proposed as the optimal one and the search is completed.
- Exhaustive implicit search techniques. These techniques examine all the alternative solutions and the best among them is the proposed solution.
- Heuristics. Occasionally, it is very important to find a satisfactory approximate solution even if this is least effective from the optimum one. The disadvantage of obtaining an inferior solution is compensated by the reduction in the necessary search time. In this case, we use our empirical knowledge (rules of thumb) or any other background knowledge and restrict the search in the alternative solutions that can provide us with a satisfactory solution of the model with higher probability (Zanakis and Evans, 1981; Pearl, 1984).
- Partial implicit search techniques. In partial implicit search, only a certain fraction of the set of the alternative solutions is examined. The examination is carried out until the best solution, from the examined set of possible solutions, is found.

2.4 Implementation phase

In this phase, we proceed to the implementation of the proposed solution. If the results are satisfying then we are in the position to assume that all the tasks carried out in the preceding phases were properly handled. If on the other hand, the results are not stimulating then we have the ability to repeat and revise some components of the preceding tasks until we end up with a satisfactory result.

3. MULTICRITERIA DECISION ANALYSIS

Most of the existing operational research models exhibit a significant disadvantage. They attempt to find solutions on the decision problems based only on a one-dimensional analysis. They propose solutions that take into account entirely one criterion. On the other hand, the typical real decision making environment involves a set of parameters and factors that have to be taken into account in order to find a solution and reach a decision. The need to find solutions on decision-making problems and at the same time preserve the multidimensional nature of these problems prompted for the need of evolution of Multiple Criteria Decision Analysis (MCDA) methods.

Because of the existence of multiple and often conflicting evaluation criteria, multicriteria problems belong to the family of low structured decision making problems. Accordingly, the number of criteria and the complexity of their interrelations, affect the preference system of the decision maker, which in turn is characterized by a low structure degree. Consequently, the decisions belong to the semi-structured category, a fact that generates the necessity for supporting the decision maker with the development of appropriate multicriteria models.

Despite the fact that the fundamental ideas of multicriteria analysis were already established from the 18th century (Bernoulli and Cramer) the development of a theoretical background and axiomatic foundation for multiple criteria decision problems began two centuries later with the work of von Neumann and Morgenstern (1944) and Savage (1954). The rapid evolution of this branch of the operational research field commenced after the accomplishment of the first MCDM conference in 1972 in the University of South Carolina (Cohrane and Zeleny, 1973; Fishburn, 1970; 1972; Keeney and Raifa, 1976; Evans and Steuer, 1973; Zeleny, 1974; Roy, 1968; Jacquet-Lagrèze and Siskos, 1982).

Different approaches in the decision making process resulted in the development of two major schools in multicriteria analysis, the American, and the French school.

The American school or Multiple Criteria Decision Making (MCDM) accepts the existence of a value system that represents the preferences of the decision makers towards a set of decision alternatives. MCDM is mainly expressed by Fishburn (1970), Keeney and Raifa (1976), Saaty (1990), Keeney (1992), French (1993), von Winterfeldt and Edwards (1993). According to the MCDM framework, the preferences of the decision maker towards the decision alternatives are considered in the formation of a value system. This value system, which satisfies a set of conditions, guides the decision maker to the selection of the most satisfying solution.

The French school or Multiple Criteria Decision Aid (MCDA), is mainly expressed by the ideas stated in Roy (1976; 1985; 1990), Bouyssou (1984); Jacquet-Lagrèze and Siskos (1982); Vincke (1992). The fundamental points of the MCDA framework are (Roy, 1990):

- In general, more than one decision makers are involved in the decision making process. In many real-world problems the decision maker does not really exists as a person truly able to make a decision. Usually, several people (actors or stakeholders) take part in the decision process and share different opinions.
- The objective of multicriteria analysis is not to point out to the decision maker better solutions but rather to lead the decision maker to the

selection of a satisfying solution through a process of progressive understanding and improvement of his/her abilities and knowledge.

According to Roy (1975; 1990), the general modelling framework in multicriteria analysis is determined by the following four successive and interactive stages:

1st stage: Decision objective.

Each problem is decomposed in a finite or continuous set of alternatives, actions, decisions, $A = \{a_i, i = 1,2,\ldots,n\}$. The set of alternative actions can be characterized as:

- Fixed, if no modifications of its composition are allowed during the decision making process.
- Revisable, if during the decision making process the structure of the set can be revised.
- Comprehensive, if every element contained in A exclude all the others.
- Fragmented, if the results of the analysis involve only a certain part of the set A.

In the accepted set of actions the decision maker defines a certain problematic, which can be altered during the decision making process. According to Roy (1985) the analyst may choose among four reference types of problematic:

- The *choice* of one and only one alternative from the set A of alternative actions.
- The *sorting* of the alternative actions into classes (groups) that share some specific attributes.
- The *ranking* of the alternative actions from the most to the least preferred.
- The *simple description* of the actions and their consequences in a language that can be fully conceivable by the managers.

2nd stage: Analysis of elementary consequences.

Each alternative action can be analysed according to a set of attributes or a cloud of elementary consequences (Roy, 1985).

The analysis of the cloud of elementary consequences of each alternative action guides the analysts to the choice and modelling of a consistent family of criteria $F = \{g_1, g_2, \ldots, g_m\}$ that will be used in order to evaluate the alternatives and reach the final decision. The criteria are modelled using real functions $g_j : A \to R$, $a \to g_j(a)$, where $g_j(a)$ is the evaluation of the action a according to the *j-th* criterion. The true criteria should fulfil the following conditions:

- They should preserve monotonicity and be consistent with the individual preferences:
  - $g_j(a) > g_j(b) \Leftrightarrow a \succ b$ i.e. action a is preferred than action b (preference relation)

- $g_j(a) = g_j(b) \Leftrightarrow a \sim b$ i.e. action a is indifferent to action b (indifference relation)
- They should be exhaustive according to the limitations in the available information
- They should avoid redundancy (non redundant)

At this point, we have to define the notion of multicriteria evaluation table: Assume that we have n decision alternatives and m criteria. These evaluations can be represented by a multicriteria evaluation table as shown below. Each element *ij* of this table represents the evaluation (score) $g_j(a_i)$ of the alternative a_i with respect to the *j-th* criterion.

		Criteria			
		g_1	g_2	....	g_m
Decision alternatives	a_1	$g_1(a_1)$	$g_2(a_1)$	....	$g_m(a_1)$
	a_2	$g_1(a_2)$	$g_2(a_2)$	....	$g_m(a_2)$
	...	...	...	....	...
	a_n	$g_1(a_n)$	$g_2(a_n)$	....	$g_m(a_n)$

Figure 4. Multicriteria evaluation table

3rd stage: Formation of decision model or model of behaviour.

This stage involves the aggregation of the criteria by applying a specific model of holistic preferences. This model is used for the comparison of the decision alternatives belonging to the set A of actions.

4th stage: Elaboration and implementation of scenarios.

In the last stage of the process, the analyst attempts to find answers in the decision maker's questions ("what-if" scenarios) in order to better support the decision making process.

Multicriteria decision-making is mainly characterized by four theoretical research streams, which will be detailed in the subsequent sections.

4. MULTIOBJECTIVE MATHEMATICAL PROGRAMMING

The theory of multiobjective mathematical programming deals with mathematical programming models, mostly linear ones, with m objective functions. For example, a multiobjective linear programming model can be stated as follows:

$$[\max]\ g_i(\mathbf{x}) = c_{i1}x_1 + c_{i2}x_2 + \cdots + c_{il}x_l, \quad \text{for} \quad i = 1,2,\ldots,m$$

under the constraints:

$$\mathbf{x} \in A = \{M\mathbf{x} \leq \mathbf{b}, \mathbf{x} \geq 0\},$$

where A is the decision space, and $M, \mathbf{b}$ are matrices of size $k \times \ell$ and $k \times 1$ respectively

There are three types of methods according to the mode of articulation of the decision maker's preferences during the application of the method: (1) no articulation of the DM's preferences, (2) a priori articulation of the DM's preferences, and (3) interactive articulation of the DM's preferences. Most of the modern methods are interactive ones allowing the decision makers to judge the solution that the method proposes at each iteration and to stop the procedure when the decision makers believes that the solution is satisfactory (see for instance, Goicoechea *et al.*, 1982, Hwang and Masud, 1979; Hwang and Yoon, 1981; Zeleny, 1982; Steuer, 1986).

4.1 Multiattribute utility theory

Multiattribute Utility Theory-MAUT originally evolved in the 60's from the work of Adams and Fagot (1959), Yntena and Torgerson (1961), Miller and Starr (1969) and others. Roy and Vincke in 1984 expressed the axiom of global and transitive comparability that explores the properties of a preference system so as these can be expressed by a certain utility model. In addition, these properties suggest a methodological framework for estimating utility functions (Huber, 1974; Keeney and Raiffa, 1976; 1993; Fishburn, 1972; 1977; Vincke, 1985; French, 1993).

Multiattribute utility theory is founded on two basic assumptions:

- All the possible actions can be compared to each other. There is no possibility that two actions are incomparable, and
- The preferences of the alternative actions are transitive.

The reasoning of evaluating alternatives by using a value system, heavily "facilitates" the decision makers, which are generally used in utilizing quantitative evaluation systems. Despite the wide acceptance of the method some researchers pointed out some weak and sensitive points (Stewart, 1992). Hence, there are some objections even on the two basic assumptions of the multiattribute utility theory. Indeed, there is always a possibility in some problems where the decision maker is unable to compare two actions or even he/she wishes to use different rationale for which he prefers the action a_k over action a_i and action a_i over action a_r.

The decision, according to the prior defined problematic, is reached with the assessment of a real valued function, called value or utility function, such as:

$$\forall a_i, a_i \in A$$

$$U(a_i) > U(a_j) \Leftrightarrow a_i \succ a_j \text{ (preference)}$$

$$U(a_i) = U(a_j) \Leftrightarrow a_i \sim a_j \text{ (indifference)}$$

In general, the global value or utility function has the following form:

$$U(a) = U\left[g_1(a), g_2(a), \ldots, g_m(a)\right], \quad a \in A$$

There are many methods and techniques that are used for the estimation of the exact form of the value or utility function. The most widely used function form is the additive one:

$$U(a_i) = \sum_{j=1}^{m} p_j u_j(g_j(a_i)), \text{ with } \sum_{j=1}^{m} p_j = 1$$

The real valued functions u_j, $j = 1,2,\ldots,m$ are called marginal value or utility functions defined on each criterion separately and are supposed to be normalized between 0 and 1; p_j is a positive weighting factor of the *j-th* criterion. We shall briefly examine two methods in the following sections.

4.1.1 Conjoint Scaling – The lock-step procedure (Keeney and Raifa (1976; 1993)

According to this method, the value to be assessed is the following:

$$\mathrm{U}(\mathrm{a}_j) = \sum_{j=1}^{m} u_j(g_j(a_j))$$

$$u_j\left(g_{j^*}\right) = 0,\ u_j\left(g_j^*\right) = 1, \text{ for } j = 1, 2, \ldots, m,\ \alpha \in A$$

and $g_j(\alpha)$ are increasing functions for each alternative action.

The algorithmic procedure includes the following steps:

Step 1:

$$U(g_1^*, g_2^*, \ldots, g_m^*) = u_1(g_1^*) = u_2(g_2^*) = \ldots = u_n(g_m^*) = 0$$

Step 2:

One criterion g_{11} is selected arbitrarily for which it is assumed that $u_1(g_{11})=1$.

Step 3:

The decision maker is asked to appoint values to the remaining $m-1$ criteria $g_{21}, g_{31}, \ldots, g_{m1}$, in order that

$$u_2(g_{21}) = u_3(g_{31}) = \ldots = u_m(g_{m1}) = 1$$

Step 4:

The decision maker is asked to specify the values of the m criteria $g_{12}, g_{22}, g_{32}, \ldots, g_{m2}$, so that

$$(g_{11}, g_{21}, g_{3*}, \ldots, g_{m*}) \sim (g_{1*}, g_{22}, g_{3*}, \ldots, g_{m*}) \sim (g_{1*}, g_{2*}, \ldots, g_{m2})$$

resulting in

$$u_1(g_{12}) = u_2(g_{22}) = \ldots = u_k(g_{m2}) = 2,\ k=1, 2, \ldots, m$$

The process of step 4 is repeated until the final assessment of the points of the marginal utility functions.

Step 5:

Based on the assessed points $g_{jk}, u_j(g_{jk}), k = 1, 2, \ldots, m$, the functions $u_i(g_j)$ are constructed by graphical approximation.

4.1.2 The midvalue splitting technique (Keeney and Raifa, 1976; 1993).

This method assesses a utility function of the following form:

$$U(a_i) = \sum_{j=1}^{m} p_j u_j(g_j(a_i)), \text{ with } i = 1, 2, \ldots, n \text{ and } j = 1, 2, \ldots, m$$

where

$$u(g_{j*}) = 0, \; u(g_{j}^{*}) = 1, \; p_j \geq 0, \; \sum_{j=1}^{m} p_j = 1, \; \alpha \in A$$

$g_j(\alpha)$ are increasing functions for each alternative action.

Step 1:

The decision maker assesses the value functions of the criteria by specifying a point g_{jr} in the interval $[g_{j*}, g_j^*]$, for which he is willing to yield the same quantity of value to the two generated intervals. This point is assigned the marginal value $u(g_{jr}) = 0.5$

This process is then repeated with two new subintervals in order to find the points $u(g_{jk})$ and $u(g_{jl})$ to which the marginal values $u(g_{jk}) = 0.25$ and $u(g_{jl}) = 0.75$ are assigned respectively, and so on until we come up with enough points in order to draw the value function of the criterion.

Step 2:

The weights of the criteria p_j are calculated according to the following procedure. The decision maker is presented with m vectors $b_j = (g_1(b_j), g_2(b_j), \ldots, g_m(b_j))$ and is asked at first to order them and then to compare them in pairs, thus changing the vectors to become equally preferred by him. From these vectors the following system of equations is derived, which is then solved in order to calculate the weights of the criteria:

$$\sum_{j=1}^{m} p_j u_j(g_j(b_j)) = \sum_{j=1}^{m} p_j u_j(g_j(b_i)).$$

4.2 Outranking methods.

The theory of outranking methods has been inspired by the work of Roy (1968) with the development and application of the ELECTRE family methods. Since then, ELECTRE methods have been applied in several types of problems such as behaviour analysis (Roy, 1985; Roy and Bouyssou, 1993), engineering and infrastructure investment (Rogers *et al.*, 2000), etc. Outranking methods are based on the idea of binary preference relations that evolve through the pair wise comparisons of the alternative actions.

The methodology that is followed, in general, by the outranking methods can be realized in three stages:

- Formulation of the problem and modelling of the decision maker's preferences.

- Construction of the trivial or fuzzy outranking relations between the alternative actions.
- Exploitation of the outranking relations according to the prior defined problematic.

Outranking methods accept the possibility of incomparability between two alternative actions, where the decision maker does not want, cannot, or does not know how to compare the alternatives.

We define as the outranking relation, $(a_i \; S \; a_j)$, the binary relation S between two alternative actions a_i and a_j, if a_i is considered to be at least as good as a_j. All the possible binary relations are presented in *Figure 5*.

In the presence of pseudo-criteria (criteria defined by means of two thresholds, a preference threshold and an indifference threshold) the model leads to fuzzy outranking relations.

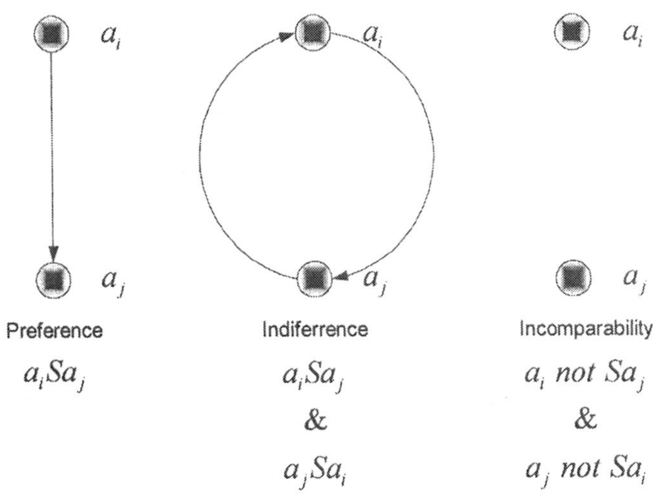

Figure 5. Binary preference relations

The most well known representatives of methods that are based on the concepts of outranking relations are those that belong in the general ELECTRE family of methods, which are aggregation rules of both the roles played by the criteria, the concordance and the discordance:

- ELECTRE - ELECTRE I (Roy, 1968)
- ELECTRE II (Roy and Bertier, 1971, 1973)
- ELECTRE III (Roy, 1978; Skalka *et al.*, 1992; Vallèe, 1994)
- ELECTRE IV (Roy and Hugonnard, 1982; Roy, 1985; Skalka *et al.*, 1992; Vallèe, 1994)

- ELECTRE Is (Roy and Skalka, 1985)
- ELECTRE TRI (Yu, 1992)

4.3 Disaggregation approaches

This methodology uses ordinal regression models in an attempt to approach the reasoning of the decision makers through an aggregation-disaggregation procedure. With this procedure the analyst is able to infer an analytical model of preferences, which is as consistent as possible with the DM's global preferences on a small set of reference actions (past choices, pair wise comparisons, ...). Hammond *et al.* (1977) used such a regression model in order to develop an interactive system for the analysis of the DM's preferences, named POLICY. Later, Jacquet-Lagrèze and Siskos (1982) introduced an ordinal regression model, the UTA method, while in 1983 Siskos and Yannacopoulos presented an improved variant of the original UTA method, the UTASTAR method.

In contrast to the reasoning followed by the majority of multiple criteria analysis models, that the decision is determined through the aggregation of the criteria, the aggregation-disaggregation approach accepts that the decision and the criteria are progressively elaborated into the time, as shown in *Figure 6*.

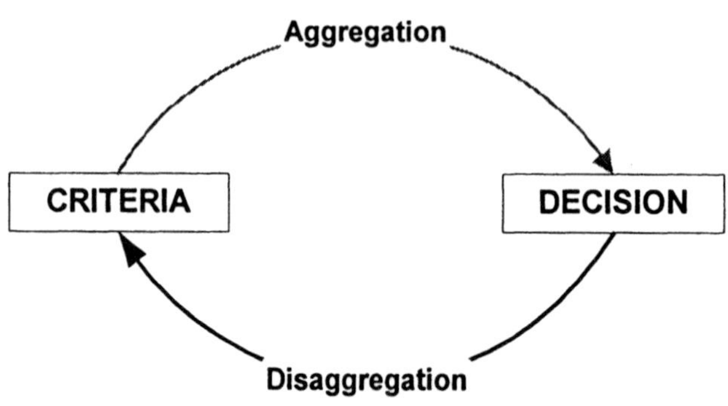

Figure 6. Aggregation-disaggregation approach

This new approach contributes towards the conception of a new reasoning for decision aid. In essence, it deals with the known problem of inferring a model of preferences from a real-world decision. The procedure, of attempting the acceptance of a preference model through a repetitive interaction between the model and the decision maker, is graphically shown in *Figure 7*.

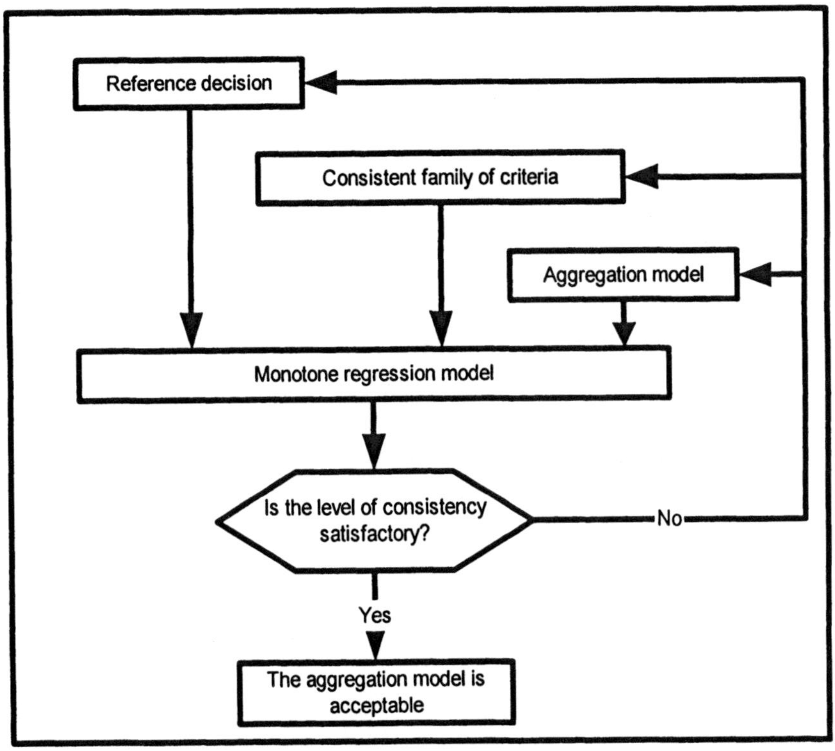

Figure 7. Iterations and interaction between the DM and the model

In the case where the decision maker is unsatisfied with the consistency degree between the model and his preference system i.e. the case were the results of the model and the preferences of the decision maker do not match, he/she is able to address new questions about:

- The consistency of the family of criteria (absence of key criteria, selection of more appropriate indicators of their impact, etc).
- The validity of the reference decision (non rational).
- The model used for the aggregation of the criteria (over simplified).

When the decision maker considers that the degree of consistency is satisfactory then the multicriteria preference model is accepted and it can be extrapolated on new sets of decision alternatives.

Apparently, it is not possible to analyse in depth the theoretical aspects of the Multiple Criteria Decision Analysis in the short limits of this introductory chapter. Our intention is to provide the reader with some key information on the benefits of MCDA methods and the pluralism of methods and techniques contained in this field. For a more comprehensive and detailed study of the foundations of the MCDA the reader can resort to Fishburn, (1970; 1972); Keeney and Raifa, (1976); Zeleny, (1982); Roy,

(1985; 1989); Keeney, (1992); Vincke, (1992); French, (1993); and von Winterfeldt and Edwards, (1993); Stewart and van den Honert (1998); Triantaphyllou, (2000); Jacquet-Lagrèze and Siskos (2001); Deb, (2001).

Chapter 2

The structure of marketing decisions

1. INTRODUCTION

Today's philosophy of marketing, places the customer-consumer in the center of consideration of the enterprises, while at the same time strives to achieve two goals:

1. To satisfy in the best way the needs of the consumer, and
2. To increase the profits of the enterprises.

The market is no longer characterized as product orientated but rather as consumer oriented. Marketing pays more attention at the consumer, at his needs and desires, which it tries to satisfy by the development and production of suitable products and services.

There are several definitions of the term "marketing". Each one displays an aspect of the overall notion whereas the whole set together describes the term. Following, we will cite some of the most representative definitions that have been presented for the term "marketing".

> Marketing is defined as the set of business activities, which aim at the discovery, prediction, and satisfaction of the needs of the consumers and the attainment of the objectives of the enterprise (British Institute of Marketing).

> Marketing is a social and managerial process, which allows individuals and groups to obtain anything they need and desire through the creation and exchange of products and values (money) with other individuals or groups (Kotler and Armstrong, 1987; Kotler, 1994).

The term "marketing-management" is best described by the definition adopted by the American Marketing Association. According to this definition:

> Marketing-management is the process of planning and realization of promotion, pricing, and allocation strategies of ideas, goods, and services aiming at the generation of commercial transactions that satisfy individuals or groups of individuals (McCarthy and Perreault, 1990; Linneman and Stanton, 1991; Kotler, 1994).

The majority of marketing decisions are heavily depending on the existence of multiple criteria such as prices, market shares, sales, profits, etc. Therefore when discussing about marketing decisions we should always have in mind that we are actually facing multicriteria marketing decision making situations (Starr and Zeleny, 1977; Zionts, 1978; Zoltners, 1981).

Information necessary for the marketing managers comes from several external and internal sources (Table 1). This information is used in order to give competitive advantages to an enterprise and is managed and processed by marketing information systems.

Leeflang and Wittink (2000), in their view of the future of building models for marketing decisions, propose a new marketing model and suggest some contributions models. The proposed model is as simple framework of six steps that describes the role that a customers plays for an enterprise (*Figure 1*).

2. A REVIEW OF MARKETING PROBLEMS AND DECISIONS

Marketers, during the decision making process, are receives of internal and external information. The various types of internal and external data are presented in Table 2.2, adopted by Marshall, 1996.

A marketing problem stems from an internal or external change in the status of an enterprise and corresponds to the observed gap between the assigned objectives of the enterprise and those that are finally achieved.

The detection of the problem's existence should be followed by its classification with respect to the type of the problem and its importance before the attempt of the decision maker to proceed in the search of a solution. The importance of this classification is supported by the following arguments:

- All the problems are not equally important or share the same priorities
- Identical problems usually have common solution approaches.

Table 1. Information needs (Marshall, 1996)

Typical External Environment Information Needs	Related Marketing Strategy and Mix Elements	Typical Internal Environment Information Needs
Competitors	Target markets	Inbound logistics
Market Shares	Segments	Suppliers
Products	Size	Internal prices
Cost structures	Characteristics	Storage costs
Industry structure		
Technology	Product design	Operations
Product related		Manufacturing costs
Production		Inventories
Communication		Finished goods
Information systems		Flexibility
		Rework costs
Customers	Distribution systems	Outbound logistics
Purchase patterns	Sales force	Shipping costs
Demographics	Type of outlets	Storage costs
Psychographics	Transport logistics	Shipping costs
Product requirements	Warehousing	
Satisfaction		
Economic	Promotion plans	Sales
Employment trends	Advertising media	Product sales
Economic projections	Ad content	Salesperson commissions
Disposable income	Sales promotions	Geographic area
Interest rate trends	Public relations	Wholesaler
Exchange rates		Retailer
		Commissions
Political	Pricing plans	Customer service
Legislation	Prices	Costs
Treaties	Financial terms	Requests
Elections	Channel margins	Complaints
Regulatory agencies		
Judicial rulings		
Social and cultural		
Roles/values		
Religions/belief systems		

We already have categorized the decision problems into programmed and non-programmed decisions according to Simon's fundamental ideas (Simon, 1960). In the same fashion, we can classify the marketing problems into tactical problems, which approach the programmed problems, and strategic problems, which come closer to the non-programmed problems of Simon (Nylen, 1990). Strategic problems, when compared to tactical problems, are much more important for the decision maker.

Howard (1963a; 1963b) proposed another classification of marketing decisions in which three distinct categories are mentioned: routine, limited solution, and extended solution problems (Robinson *et al.*, 1967; Howard *et al.*, 1975). According to Drucker (1967), marketing problems can be partitioned into general (programmed) and specific (non-programmed) ones, whereas somewhere between them assigns problem that result by their combination.

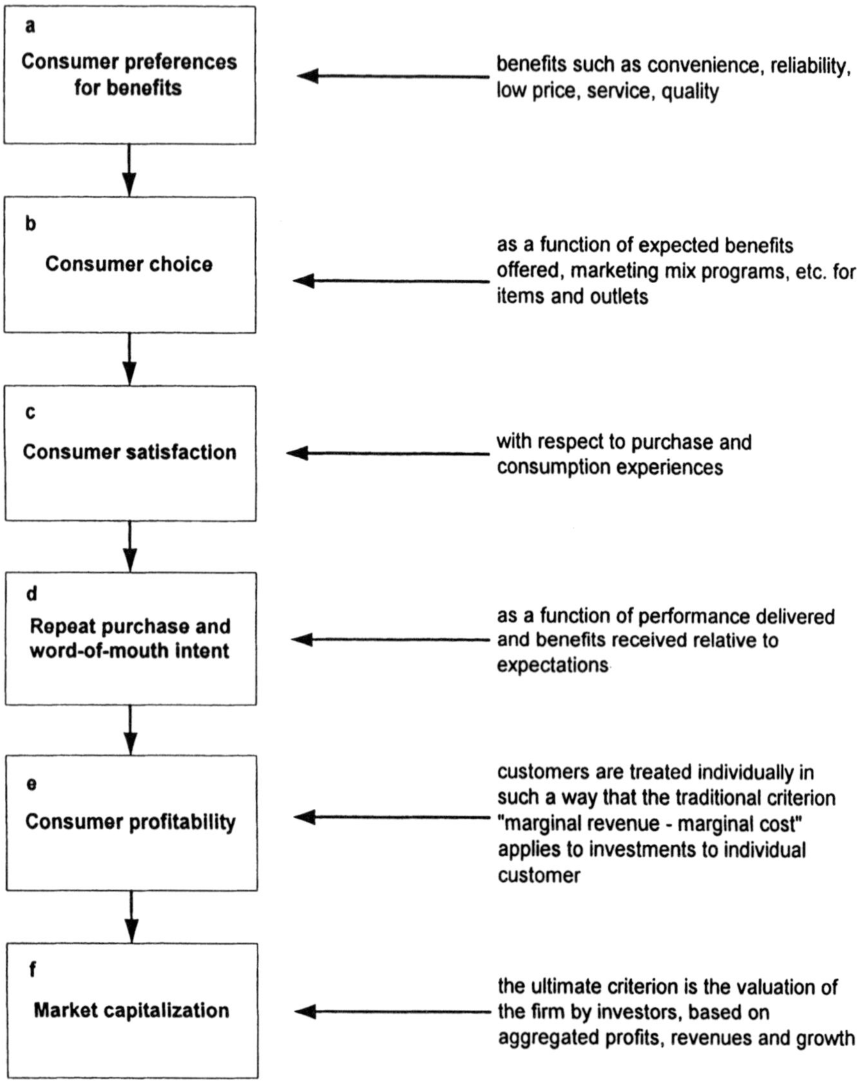

Figure 1. A framework presenting the role that customer plays (*Source*: Leeflang and Wittink, 2000)

The emergence of a problem obviously calls for its solution, a fact that generates the need for making a decision. Marketing decision-making can

be thought as a process that consists of the following actions (Drucker, 1954):
1. Determination of the marketing problem.
2. Problem examination.
3. Determination of alternative actions.
4. Choice of the most appropriate solution.
5. Implementation of the selected solution.

Figure 2 presents the decision-making processes in strategic and tactical marketing problems.

Table 2. Types of internal and external data (*Source*: Marshall, 1996)

Marketing Decision Making	
Internal Data	External Data
Customer service data	Marketing environment data subscription
Service records	services
Customer complaints	Government
Help-line	Private
	On-Line
Outbound logistics data	Single-source data services
Finished goods inventory records	Panel data services
Warehouse inventory records	Scanner data
Shipping records	
Production and operations data	Market research projects
Production schedules and delays	
Production costs	
Rework and modification records	
Quality control records	
Inbound logistics data	Business partners
Bids received	EDI
Purchasing and accounts payable systems	Sales data
Receiving system	Order data
Raw materials and parts inventory	Inventory data
system	
Sales and marketing data	
Marketing lead and prospect data	
Sales commission records	
Quotation system records	
Order entry systems	
Accounts receivable system	

The vast majority of marketing decision-making involves problems of strategic nature. The emphasis in strategic problems is devoted firstly in the understanding of the problem situation and then in the planning of the appropriate actions that could aid the coping of this situation. Complex problems require complex solutions. Decisions in strategic marketing problems exhibit unusual difficulties because these types of problems are complicated, dynamic, usually present interactions among each other and frequently their causes are very difficult to be perceived by the decision maker. When a marketing problem is determined then it can be decomposed in partial sub-problems. This function results into better examination and analysis of the problem, a fact that has an important positive impact in the improvement of problem comprehension. The procedure is followed by the planning of the actions that should be carried out in order to cope with the specific marketing problem.

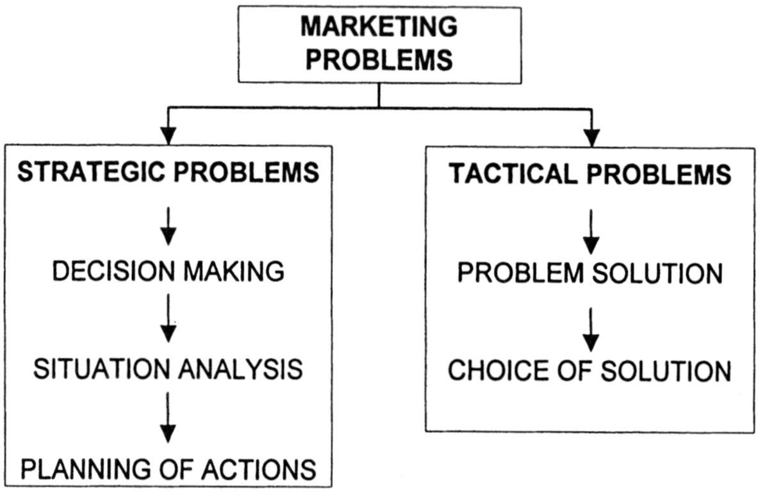

Figure 2. Marketing problems (*Source*: Nylen, 1990)

3. CHARACTERISTICS OF MARKETING PROBLEMS

Table 3 shows the main attributes of the non-programmed strategic marketing problems (Nylen, 1990).

4. DECISION MAKING PROCESS IN MARKETING

During the last years, descriptive models seem to play a constantly increasing role In the process of marketing decision making, in comparison to prescriptive (normative) models (Zoltners, 1981; Nylen, 1990) (*Figure 3*).

The emergence of a problem generates the necessity of making a decision. Most certainly, the decision maker faces more than one alternatives (actions) from which he has to choose the one that is considered the best. The choice of the actions is based on the determination, comparison, and evaluation of the expected results of the alternative decisions.

Table 3. Attributes of strategic marketing problems (*Source*: Nylen, 1990)

Attribute	Description
Hidden	Normally we are not able to detect the problems themselves but some of their indications.
Complex	They characterize the complexity of the problems, in the solution of which, a large number of variables have to be taken into account.
Interactive	The above variables are, as a rule, dependent of each other. A variation in one of them has a certain impact on the remaining ones, and so forth.
Competitive	There is a high level of interaction among similar organizations. Consequently, when an organization triggers a variation in a certain feature of the market (price, new product, promotion, distribution networks, etc) this affects the competitive companies and generates their reaction.
Occasional	Each decision should be addressed to the particular prevalent market status. Therefore, an analysis of the market status prior to the making of a decision is essential, a fact that requires the existence of the necessary information.
Uncertain	The information required for the analysis and understanding of the market status, incorporates a certain portion of uncertainty.
External	These are the problems that are generated by external factors. In order to be solved the enterprise should make an appropriate marketing decision.
Dynamic - Urgent	Marketing decisions should be immediate in order to prevent the deterioration of the problems. Marketing problems are dynamically evolving. Their timely confrontation requires the existence of prompt and complete information. These two characteristics are incompatible, since complete information requires time-consuming processes (market surveys, etc). Therefore, decision makers prefer to make decisions using the available incomplete information, instead of waiting to obtain complete information when the problem will probably get worst.

In general, the results involve predicted sales, market shares, profits, etc. The decision makers are able to use marketing models in order to help themselves in the determination of the expected results and finally in the choice of the most appropriate decision.

5. BASIC MARKETING DECISION MODELS

Leeflang and Wittink (2000), argue the past, present and future in the development of models for marketing decisions. In their chronological approach, model building in marketing is divided in the following eras:

1. 1950–1965: An era characterized by the direct application of existing operations research OR and management science MS methods to marketing problems.
2. 1965–1970: An era characterized by the adaptation of models to fit marketing problems.
3. 1970–1985: In the third era of implement able models there is an increased emphasis on models that are acceptable representations of reality and are easy to use.
4. 1985–2000: In this era, models are increasingly implemented, and there is an interest in marketing decision support systems.
5. 2000–: In the recent era, the changes in technology stimulate the growth of new exchange systems, and there is an opportunity and a need for new modeling approaches.

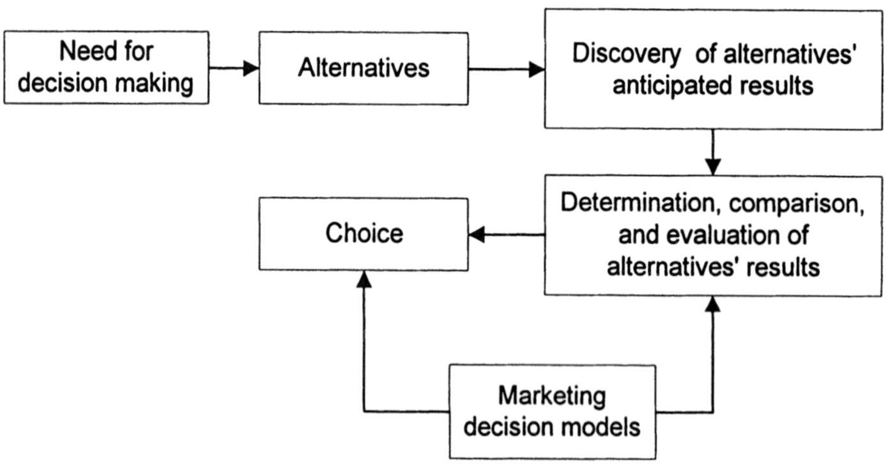

Figure 3. Marketing decision making process (*Source*: Zoltners, 1981)

According to Little (1970), it is very hard to find good models, however the process of properly defining their parameters is even more puzzling. There are many factors such as, the strain imposed by the competition, the existence of multiple objectives, uncertainty, environmental influence, lack of information, etc that have a certain effect on them and thus contributing in their complexity. Naert and Leeflang (1978) examined the results of the application of marketing models in ill-structured problems and reached to the conclusion that despite the fact that these models cannot yield exhaustive solutions they cannot be regarded to be totally useless.

Research on marketing and management science resulted in the formation of a variety of marketing models, which aim at supporting the decision makers in their attempt to determine and comprehend the situation of the market as well as to anticipate the results derived from the application of alternative decisions.

Descriptive models attempt to thoroughly and reliably represent the examined situation such as the behavior of the market, of the consumers, of the competitors, etc.

Hulbert (1981), in an investigation of the research efforts concerning the development of descriptive models, found out that the majority of them pays attention to the solution of tactical (structured-programmed) problems rather than strategic (non-programmed) problems. Thus, the majority of research studies mainly involve marketing decision making situations concerning the solution of partial sub-problems such as pricing decisions, sales forecasts, means of advertisement, new product development, etc. The findings of this research, about the methods of decision making in marketing, can be summarized in the following points:

- Past decisions play a vital role in a significant number of models (Lindblom, 1959; 1965).
- Decisions are reached in consecutive phases and not instantaneously.
- The rules that are followed for making the decision are rather simple and in general, they do not follow the theoretical principals and procedures.
- Important marketing decisions are reached through the collaboration of a group of people rather individual decision makers.
- Forecasting models are applied in order to predict the impact of the implementation of different decisions or actions like the prediction of market shares for new products, products' sales etc.

Descriptive marketing decision models (Hulbert, 1981) have been developed, among others, for making pricing decisions (Cyert and March, 1963; Howard and Morgenroth, 1968; Farley *et al.*, 1971; Capon and Hulbert, 1972; 1975; Farley *et al.*, 1978; Hulbert, 1981; Kotler, 1994), advertising (Marschner, 1967; Rados, 1970; 1972; Fleck, 1973; Capon and Hulbert, 1975; Lambin *et al.*, 1975; Sissors and Petray, 1976; Capon and Scammon, 1979; Hulbert, 1981; Kotler, 1994), products (Massy and Savvas, 1964; Levitt, 1972; Montgomery, 1975; Capon and Hulbert, 1975; Hulbert, 1981), forecast (Cyert and March, 1963; Staelin and Turner, 1973; Capon and Hulbert, 1972; 1975; Capon *et al.*, 1975; Farley *et al.*, 1971; Farley *et al.*, 1978; Hulbert, 1978; 1981).

Normative models are used at the final stage of the decision making process in order to aid the decision makers in the choice of the most suitable decision alternative. Zoltners (1981) used the taxonomy, exhibited in *Figure 4*, to portray the descriptive models.

Theoretical models. Theoretical models are mainly used in the development of normative theory, in the ability of making decisions through the acquisition of experience, in the search of an optimal solution for problems that cannot be exhaustively defined in mathematical terms (Zoltners, 1981). Generally, these are descriptive models and usually support decision-making strategies that can be easily generalized (Dorfman and Steiner, 1954; Kotler, 1971). Theoretical models are usually applied in order to efficiently represent with mathematical terms the behavior of the market.

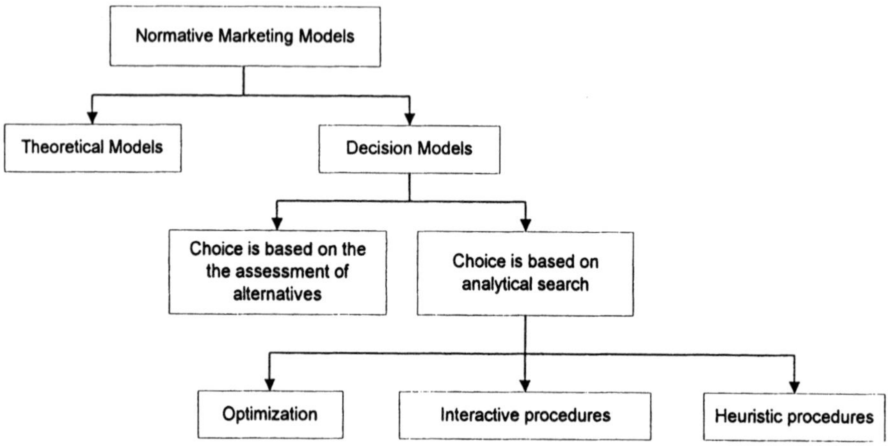

Figure 4. Taxonomy of normative models (*Source*: Zoltners, 1981)

Decision models. In contrast to theoretical models, decision models support the provision of particular solutions in specific decision problems and are mainly addressed to the analysis and solution of real world problems (Morin, 1963; Little and Lodish, 1969; Aaker, 1975; Zoltners, 1981). Decision models are used in order to foresee the results of the alternative decisions, as if these were actually implemented. Thus, in the beginning one has to define the results of all the alternative solutions and then to assess and compare them (*Figure 3*)

Alternatives' evaluation decision models. These models are a sub-category of decision models that are mainly used in the determination of alternative marketing strategies. An example that falls into this category is the ADBUDG model (Little, 1970). ADBUDG is used for designing the advertising strategy based on the results of comparing alternative budgets of different market situations.

Analytical search decision models. Analytical search decision models provide the ability to exhaustively search for the desired decision through a set of potential decision alternatives. The analytical search is accomplished through the following procedures (Buzzell, 1964; Little and Lodish, 1969; Lodish, 1971; Geoffrion, 1975; Zoltners *et al.*, 1978; Zoltners and Sinha, 1980).

Optimization procedures. They aim at the exhaustive examination of the decision alternatives in order to find the optimum solution.

Interactive procedures. With the interactive procedures, we content ourselves with the finding of a solution that is very close to the optimal one. Today, in decision-making, it is almost unanimously accepted the concept of finding a satisfactory solution rather than finding any optimal solution (Nylen, 1990).

Heuristic procedures. With heuristics we can achieve a satisfactory solution, which also may be the optimal one. Heuristics use rules of thumb in order to approach the desired solution.

6. CONSUMERS' BEHAVIOR ANALYSIS

The effectiveness of all the followed marketing strategies is determined the moment when the consumer decides to buy or to reject a product. Therefore, marketers are heavily interested in extensively studying the behavior of the consumers during the process of making a purchasing decision.

The theory of consumer behavior consists of the composition of ideas and aspects of various scientific fields such as microeconomic theory, psychology, sociology, etc. Today, one of the main components and considerations of strategic marketing planning is the examination of consumer's behavior due to the following reasons:

- In the rapid increase of the number of new products as well as in the large number of their failure to gain the confidence of the consumers,
- In the smaller life cycle of the products,
- In the improvement of the consumers' protection terms and legislation,
- In the environmental consequences,
- In the change in the philosophy of marketing (production-product),
- In technological advancements in the fields of computer science, data analysis, marketing, etc.

The theory of consumer behavior investigates the process that is followed in consumer decision-making. It is concerned with the study of human behavior during the phases of purchase and use of products and services. It attempts to provide answers to questions such as what, why, how, when, from where and how often the consumers buy.

The study of consumer behavior, among others, helps the experts in marketing as well as the consumers themselves to:

- Be aware and to comprehend the needs of the consumers as well as the motives in purchasing decisions,
- Identify the complexity of the decision making processes,

- Investigate and identify the opportunities and the threats for an enterprise,
- Identify the real needs of the consumers and to develop and produce new products that meet those needs and thus minimizing the risk of failure,
- Improve the market segmentation techniques by following criteria of identical behavior and positioning of the product in the right market segment and thus improving the possibilities for its acceptance, etc.

7. CONSUMER'S DECISION-MAKING PROCESS

The possession of detailed and in depth knowledge about the procedure followed by a decision maker in making a purchasing decision is extremely useful to the decision makers that hold the responsibility for planning the marketing strategy of a product.

It is more than obvious that the presence and use of a variety of models is more than necessary in order to represent the numerous types of consumer behavior and efficiently satisfy the set of managerial objectives. Various behavioral patterns have been identified that describe different approaches during the purchasing decision making process such as economic, passive, cognitive, and emotional man.

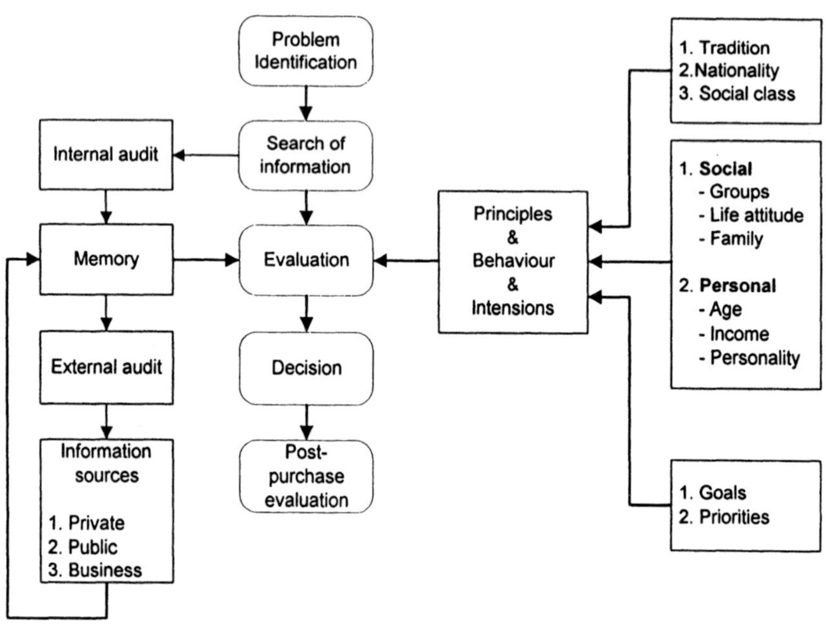

Figure 5. Model of individual purchasing decision process (Hill Nigel, 1996)

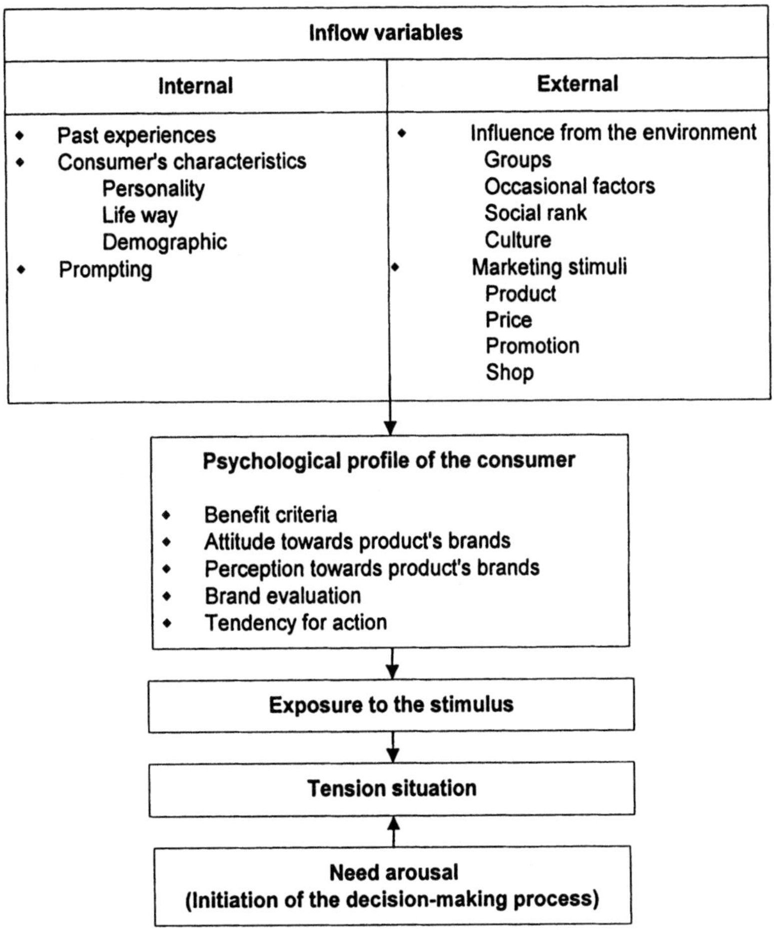

Figure 6. Need arousal process (*Source*: Assael, 1992)

According to Kotler's opinion (Kotler, 1994), the research should focus rather in the study of the purchasing process than in the purchasing decision itself.

Figure 5, displays the five consecutive stages of the decision making process (Kotler, 1994; Lilien *et al.* 1992; Assael, 1992; Hill Nigel, 1996).

Identification of the problem. The process of purchasing a product initiates with the ascertainment that a need is in existence (need arousal) as shown in *Figure 6*. Need arousal stems either from the creation of a motive or from information that comes from internal or external sources (advertisement for example). As soon as the consumer conceives the existence of the problem he moves towards its solution and decides for the type of product that is able to satisfy his specific need.

On the other hand, the enterprises seek to find the circumstances under which the consumer discovers the existence of a need. Thus, they seek to find what kinds of needs can be generated, what was the cause of their generation, and in which fashion the consumer directed to a certain product.

This stage is modeled by the Stochastic Models of Purchase Incidence and by the Discrete Binary Choice Models.

Search of information. The solution of the problems, on behalf of the consumers, is made through the processing of the available information, which stems either from internal and external sources. Initially, the consumer searches for pre-existing information, opinions, attitudes, perceptions in identical problems that he was forced to cope with during the past. If the information is not sufficient then the consumers turn to external sources of information. Frequently, external information can be provided to the consumer even if he did not choose to seek for it in order to change his former perceptions. As external sources of information can be considered the other members of the consumer's family, friends, various experts, advertisements, salespersons, etc. The percentage of the impact of these sources varies according to the type of the product, the character of the buyer, and the circumstances under which such a decision is made. The information that is gathered by the consumer is stored into his mind as personal knowledge, opinions, and attitudes. The effectiveness of a decision made by the consumer is improved when the quality of the gathered information is improved. In contrary, the effectiveness of consumer's decision is decreased when the volume of collected information increases (Keller and Staelin, 1987). The behavior of the consumers is also affected by factors such as the consumer's sex (Meyers-Levy and Maheswaran, 1991), the mode in which the information is presented to the consumer (Levin and Gaeth, 1988), the available decision time (Hauser *et al.*, 1993), the age of the consumer (Moorman, 1990; Cole and Balasubramanian, 1993), etc.

Depending on the intensity of the stored need, the consumer enters one of two states:

- The first is called "heightened attention" where the individual becomes alert to information bearing upon the needs and its gratification.
- Under conditions of more intense need, the individual enters the second state, the state of active information search, where the consumer seeks information from personal, commercial, and public sources.

An enterprise should be aware of the information sources used by the consumer and the importance assigned by him to each one of them in order to be able to influence his final decision. Thus, it should seek information on where the consumer became aware of the product or brand for the first time, which information followed and the importance assigned by the consumer to each one of his information's sources.

This stage is modeled by the Individual Awareness Models, the Consideration Models, and the Information Integration Models.

Evaluation of alternatives. Initially the consumer is able to choose a certain product among the total set of products of the market. After the stage of information, this set of products is reduced to a smaller set known as the awareness set. These products are evaluated according to the initial purchasing criteria of the consumer and some of them are preferred and form the consideration set of products. The collection of additional information results in a further reduction of this set to the choice set of products, i.e. the products among which the consumer will make his final decision. At this point, the consumer arrives at the most crucial phase where he has to process all the available information and proceed to his final decision. The products that managed to enter the choice set are evaluated by the consumer according to a family of criteria that, according to the latest scientific approaches, are determined by the knowledge and the rationality of the consumer. Thus, each product is decomposed, in the point of view of the consumer, to a set of criteria. The consumer assigns greater importance to the criteria that better meet his needs. Consequently, if we have an explicit knowledge about the importance of the criteria, assigned implicitly by the consumers, then we can proceed to a segmentation of the market into groups of consumers that share the same opinion on the set of criteria. Here, we have to emphasize on a delicate point, namely the distinction between the terms "salient" and "important" criteria. According to Myers and Alpert (1976), important criteria are the criteria in which the consumer assigns their true value, when the consumer is unbiased by any external influences. Thus, the measurement and explicit knowledge of the importance of the criteria is what really interests an enterprise or an individual decision maker.

Implicitly, the consumer assigns to each criterion a utility function. This function describes the level of expected satisfaction of the consumer that corresponds to each alternative assessment (subdivision) of the criterion. If we combine the assessments of the criteria that hold the maximum assigned utilities, then we can form the ideal product for each consumer. Consequently, the expected utility value from the products of the market will be equal or less than the utility value assigned to the ideal product. The presence of multiple products that are evaluated by the consumer according to a specific set of criteria, introduces the concept of multicriteria decision making on behalf of the consumers (Green and Wind, 1973; McAlister, 1979; Saurais and Siskos, 1980; Siskos, 1982; Siskos, 1984; Matsatsinis and Siskos, 1999).

An important challenge stems from the above assumption for an enterprise: "Does the ability of having explicit knowledge on the multicriteria evaluations of a consumer, permits an enterprise to predict which product will be the choice of the consumer?"

If we exclude from consideration the particular situation where there is explicit preference towards a product then in order to find some answers to the above question we have to use a variety of different models (Fishbein, 1967; Myers and Alpert, 1968; Green and Wind, 1973; Miniard and Cohen, 1981; Kotler, 1994).

Some authors regard that this phase is contained in the previous phase of information search (Nylen, 1990).

The process of the evaluation of the alternatives has two phases:

- Initially the consumers establish their perceptions about the features of the alternative products and form their opinions, and
- Based upon these opinions, they must decide about their attitudes towards the products under consideration by expressing their preferences.

This stage is modeled by the Perceptual Mapping models and Attitude Models – Compensatory and non-Compensatory.

Purchase decision. Up to this point, the consumer goes over the phase where he expresses his intention to purchase a specific product in the decision of making the purchase. Between those two phases, numerous imponderable factors or even the position of other individuals towards the consumer's decision may intervene and alter the final decision of the consumer (Fishbein, 1967; Bauer, 1967; Taylor, 1974; Sheth, 1974; Gafin and Torrance, 1981). Furthermore, the intention of the consumer is affected by random changes in the expected factors such as the unavailability of the product for example.

The consumer seeks to find the product to be purchased by a subset of the available products in the market (Hawkins *et al.*, 1992 –*Figure 7*). This happens because it is almost impossible for the consumer to have exhaustive knowledge of all the products of the market, all the brands are not available at the same time, the consumer for some reasons rejects some brands, etc.

It is well known that every purchase, when its effect is not certain, includes in some extend a certain risk. The enterprise should conceive the factors that could cause feelings of risk to the consumers, because of their purchases, and provide them with all the available information attempting to reduce their impression on the undertaken risk.

Models that are used for this stage are the Multinomial Discrete Choice Models and the Markov Models.

Post purchase consumer behavior. After the purchase of the product follows the phase where the consumer uses the product and gains experiences from it. The consumer implicitly compares the benefit that he receives from the use of the product with the expected benefit from its purchase. This comparison directs him to the evaluation whether he is satisfied and in what extent, by the purchase of the product (La Barbera and Mazursky, 1983; Day, 1984; Kotler and Mantrala, 1985). At this phase, the behavior of the consumer is determined by the degree of his satisfaction. A satisfied consumer will most probably proceed to the purchase of the same product in the future where as at the same time he will talk positively about this product, influencing other consumers that still are in a previous phase of the purchase process (Bayus, 1985). In contrast, a dissatisfied consumer has a, small or extensive, defective influence on the product (Hirschman, 1970; Day and Landon, 1977; Rogers, 1983; Gilly and Hansen, 1985; Kotler, 1994). The enterprises should always use the degree of usage of their products and the degree of the satisfaction of the consumers, in order to realize at the proper time the reactions of the consumers and implement suitable marketing strategies.

Appropriate models for this stage are the Variety Seeking Models, the Satisfaction Models, and the Communications and Network Models.

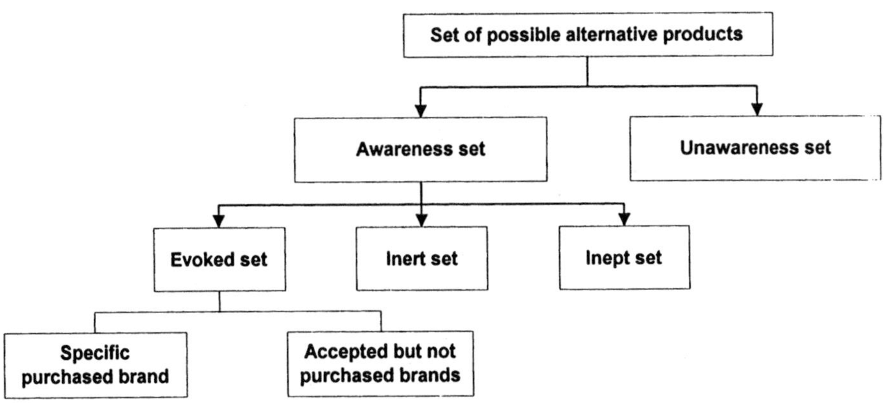

Figure 7. Choice procedure (*Source*: Hawkins *et al.*, 1992)

Level of involvement. The second major dimension along which we classify consumer behavior is the level of involvement that the consumer has with the decision process.

Consumer decisions vary by level of involvement. Low-involvement decisions, such as the purchase of a detergent, involve little effort and can thus be described by relatively simple models. In this case, the consumer follows a limited information search (Kapferer and Laurent, 1993; Flynn and Goldsmith, 1993). In contrast, the consumer attempts to collect as much information as possible in high-involvement decisions, such the purchase of a car. High-involvement decisions require considerable effort and accordingly more complex models.

Figure 8 displays the differences between high and low involvement consumer behavior (Beatty and Kahle, 1988; Assael, 1992).

In case of (a) and (c), there are large differences between the brands whereas in case of (b) and (d) there are only minor differences between them.

High-involvement	Low-involvement
Cognition Attitude Behavior	Knowledge Behavior Attitude

Figure 8. Consumer behavior in high and low-involvement cases

High-involvement	Low-involvement
Complex Decision-making or Brand Loyalty (a)	Variety Seeking (c)
Discordance Reduction or Attribution (b)	Inertia (d)

Figure 9. Involvement of consumer with the product (*Source*: Assael, 1992)

Diversification dimensions for models. Except from the dimensions that classify and assign the models into different categories there are also dimensions that differentiate between these models:

1. **The Breadth of Phenomena Addressed.** This dimension refers to the degree to which a model unifies theories in mapping the whole or a part of a decision making process. More specifically, this dimension refers to how many of the decision-making stages a model spans.
2. **The Level of Aggregation.** A dichotomy in consumer behavior models exists depending on whether the unit of analysis is the individual or groups of individuals.

3. **The Level of Detail of the Model.** Ideally, a model would have the following properties:
- Identification and measurement of all major variables making up a behavioral system
- Specification of the fundamental relationships between the variables
- Specification of exact sequences and cause and effect relationships
- Permission of sensitivity analysis in order to explore the impact of changes in the major variables.

For the sake of parsimony, most consumer behavior models only attempt to do a portion of this job. Thus, models are classified according to the level of detail that follows in this procedure.

8. FACTORS AFFECTING CONSUMER'S BEHAVIOR

The consumer, depending on his special characteristics, reacts to the external motives and by following the decision-making process makes his final choice. Consequently, the importance of the personal characteristics of the consumer, in the formation of the final choice, is extremely high. Therefore, it is almost requisite to examine these factors more exhaustively (*Table 4*, Maslow, 1954; Boyd and Levy, 1967; Coleman and Rainwater, 1978; Derrick and Linfeld, 1980; Kassarjian and Sheffet, 1981; Tybout *et al.*, 1981; Mitchell, 1983; Schiffman and Kanuk, 1983; Coleman, 1983; Price and Feick, 1984; Moschis, 1985; Brinberg and Plimpton, 1986; Kotler, 1994).

Table 4. Factors that influence the behavior of the consumer.

FACTORS			
Cultural	Social	Personality	Psychological
Culture	Reference groups	Age and life cycle	Motives
Subculture	Family	Profession	Perceptions
Social classes	Roles and situations	Financial position	Knowledge
		Life style	Beliefs and attitudes
		Personality	
CONSUMER			

The possible factors that exhibit some influence on a consumer and lead him to the choice of product may include: motives, attitudes, learning procedures, knowledge, interpersonal reactions characteristics, personality, etc. Each individual, as he grows older, constantly receives influences from his environment that shape his consumer behavior. Another essential factor is the acquired education, which in turn affects the consumer habits. Thus, the study of these factors independently as well as the examination of their interrelations, requires the close analysis of all the parameters of the market.

Figure 10 depicts the factors that affect the behavior of the consumer, according to Chisnall (1985), who adds economic factors to the above.

9. A TYPOLOGY OF CONSUMERS' ATTITUDES

We have already encountered the successive steps of the decision making process of a consumer (*Figure 7*). Numerous individuals intervene in this process either directly or indirectly. Therefore, before proceeding to the examination of the decision process, it would be helpful to examine the roles of the various individuals that somehow participate in it. In addition, it would be contributive to examine the various types of purchase behavior of the consumers. According to Kotler (1994), we can classify these types in the following five categories:

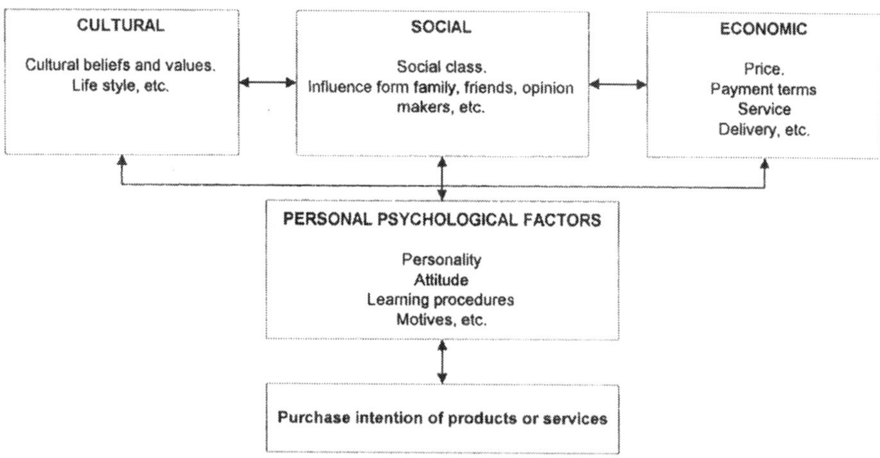

Figure 10. Factors that influence the behavior of the consumer (*Source*: Chisnall, 1985)

1. The individual that recommends the purchase of a product or a service.
2. The individual that affects, because of some special knowledge, personality, position, etc the making of the final decision (leader)
3. The individual that makes the final decision if the purchase will be eventually completed, what will be purchased, how it will be purchased, from where it will be purchased, in which quantity it will be purchase, etc.
4. The individual that makes the purchase.
5. Finally, the individual, which will use the product.

In the case where this product is purchased again, there is a feedback to the previous procedure and evaluation of the utility of the product, before the making of the decision to purchase the product again.

A complicated decision and a decision with high cost for the consumer, implies that many people will be involved in the process and a lot of discussion and deliberation will be devoted to the process prior the making of the decision. We can detect four types of consumer behavior (*Table 5*), depending on the complexity of a purchase decision and the diversification that is observed between the participating products (Howard and Sheth, 1969; Howard, 1989; Assael, 1987).

A consumer exhibits a complex purchase behavior, when he is going to purchase a product that:

- He considers expensive.
- He is not well aware o f the product
- There exists high probability risk to loose his money (e.g. stocks...)
- He is not well informed for this group of products as well as for the diversification among them (e.g. personal computers...)

Table 5. Types of purchase behavior (*Source: Assael, 1987*).

	Large complexity	Small complexity
Significant diversification among the products	Complex purchase behavior	Variety search purchase behavior
Negligible diversification among the products	Discordance that attenuates the purchase behavior	Out of habit purchase behavior

The consumer reaches his purchase decision through the formation of an opinion about the products, initially attempting to find information on the group of products and afterwards by attempting to find existing differences among them.

An enterprise that disposes of such products should inform the consumer about the common characteristics of these products and afterwards should stress the relevant advantages of its products while at the same time should take care to inform the consumer for the high prestige that the company retains in this branch.

A consumer exhibits a variety search behavior when he frequently switches a product brand, not because he is dissatisfied with the product, but for variety search reasons (e.g. shampoos...)

An enterprise that is the leader of the market should be interested in reinforcing the utilization of its products out of habit by imposing its dominance on the shelves of the shops. On the contrary, smaller companies should oppose on the former strategy of larger companies, by attempting to impose the search of variety of products through making some offers to the consumers such as lower prices, free samples, larger quantity with the same price, promotion of the idea of testing something new, etc.

Discordance that attenuates the purchase behavior exists when the consumer is confused with his decision because of the lack of diversification among the products of the market. In this way, he is directed to the purchase of a product, under uncertainty, based on some criterion (price, convenience of the purchase due to time restrictions, place, tenders, etc). After the purchase, the consumer acquires experience using the product and attempts to confirm the correctness of his choice. This leads him to gain an opinion and shape an attitude towards the product.

The enterprises should turn on the encouragement of positive the opinion of the consumers about their choice, by reducing the discordance that is observed between the "expected benefit of the consumer from the purchase of the product" and "what did he finally obtained"

The consumers exhibit out of habit purchase behavior when there is no complexity in the market or diversification among the products. In this case, the consumers do not have to search and concentrate any information about products falling into this category neither to evaluate them according to a family of criteria. They are merely passive receivers of the information that is provided to them through the advertisement. The consumers, initially, establish their need for purchasing a certain product (real need or implicitly evoked). Then they establish an opinion through passive acceptance of the information submitted to them and finally they proceed to the purchase of the product. In any case, there is no evaluation of the product at all. In addition; the consumers do not become attached to any of these products.

The enterprises that sell products of this type should attempt to use as motives the price and sales promotion efforts in order to urge the consumer to test their product. The objective of the advertisement should be to render the consumer capable of remembering the product at the time he makes the purchase. Therefore, the advertisement should mainly focus on subjects-symbols that the consumer can easily relate with the specific product. The most appropriate means of providing such simple, repetitive messages that contribute towards the passive information is the television (Krugman, 1965). However, some times the enterprises attempt to change the type of behavior of the purchaser, in order to boost their sales, by transferring their products to the category of high complexity.

10. SURVEY OF CONSUMER BEHAVIOR

Schiffman and Kanuk (1994) suggested a procedure for conducting a survey for determining the behavior of the consumers that is displayed in *Figure 11*.

As we can observe in *Figure 11*, the process starts with the resolution of the objectives of the survey. The next step involves the situation analysis i.e. the gathering and examination of all the available secondary information. In the exploratory phase there is an attempt, through discussion with experts in the field, to determine a representative market (subset of products) and the family of criteria that are used by the consumers in order to evaluate and finally choose the products of the market.

The process continues with the design and development of initially a pilot questionnaire and then a final questionnaire that is used for the conduct of the market survey and the collection of the necessary secondary information.

After the collection of the results of the survey follows the analysis of the data, the synthesis of the results, and the generation of the final reports that discuss the proposed marketing plan and the strategies to be followed.

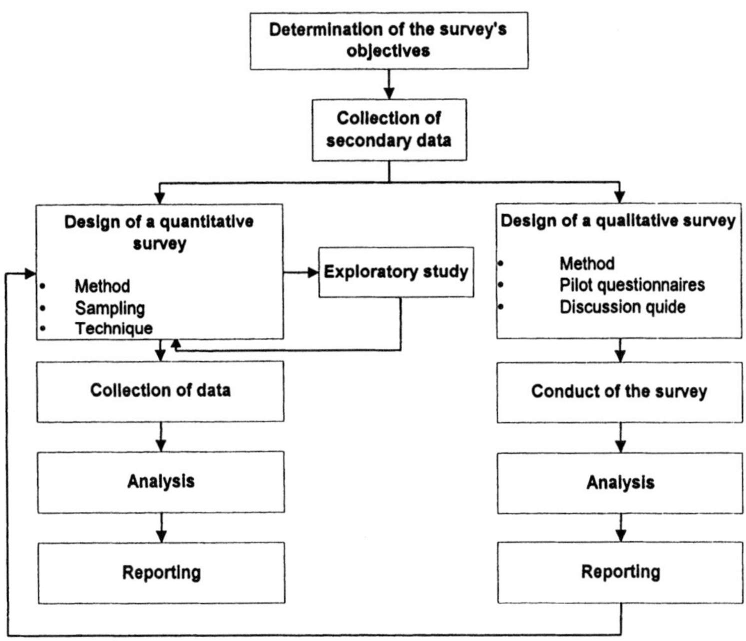

Figure 11. Process of consumer behavior survey (*Source*: Schiffman and Kanuk, 1994)

11. DECISION MAKING MODEL OF A CONSUMER

Kotler (1978, 1994) proposed an overall behavior model based on the relation between motive-reaction (*Figure 12*).

The incentives, stemming either from marketing or the environment, affect the consumer and trigger his or her choice decisions concerning the purchase of a product, a brand, a salesperson, the purchase timing, etc. As Kotler (1994) reports, the important thing for the decision-makers is to be aware on what lies between the rendering of incentives and the purchase decision.

An important category of marketing models is those attempting to describe the behavior of the consumers during the choice and purchase processes of a product. The understanding of consumer behavior results in the improvement of the marketing decisions through the application of suitable marketing models that attempt to reflect the variations of consumers' behavior. The theory of consumer behavior can be considered as a simplified, abstract representation of the reality, which is used by us in order to understand the complex human behavior of the consumer (Karmarck, 1983; Howard, 1989). This representation is accomplished through the aid of behavior models developed during the last four decades, which vary in the complexity and in the orientation (Alexis and Simon, 1968; Russ, 1971; Bettman, 1970; 1974; Haines, 1974; Payne and Ragsdale, 1978).

The development of a model initially requires the determination of the parameters of the market and then the assessment of their effects and possible interrelations in order to avoid ambiguity and subjective judgments. Due to the dynamic nature of the market, models should constantly be tested and revised.

The basic functions of the behavior model include the following:

The formation or the selection of such as model, before the actual implementation of the necessary survey, ensures the collection of all the requited data and, hence, the construction of lengthy questionnaires.

Behavior models result in the simplification of the results of a survey by permitting the proper combination of the answers to the questions, and, hence, ensuring that only relevant and analyses will be performed.

In addition, behavior models aid in the reduction of the gap, observed between the report on the results of the market survey and the making of the final marketing decision.

Consumer behavior theory aids, first, in the collection of the required data from consumers, then in the analysis of those data, and finally in the representation of the results with some appropriate manner.

Zaltman and Wallendorf (1983) expressed the opinion, that a sound consumer behavior theory should meets the following ten attributes-criteria:

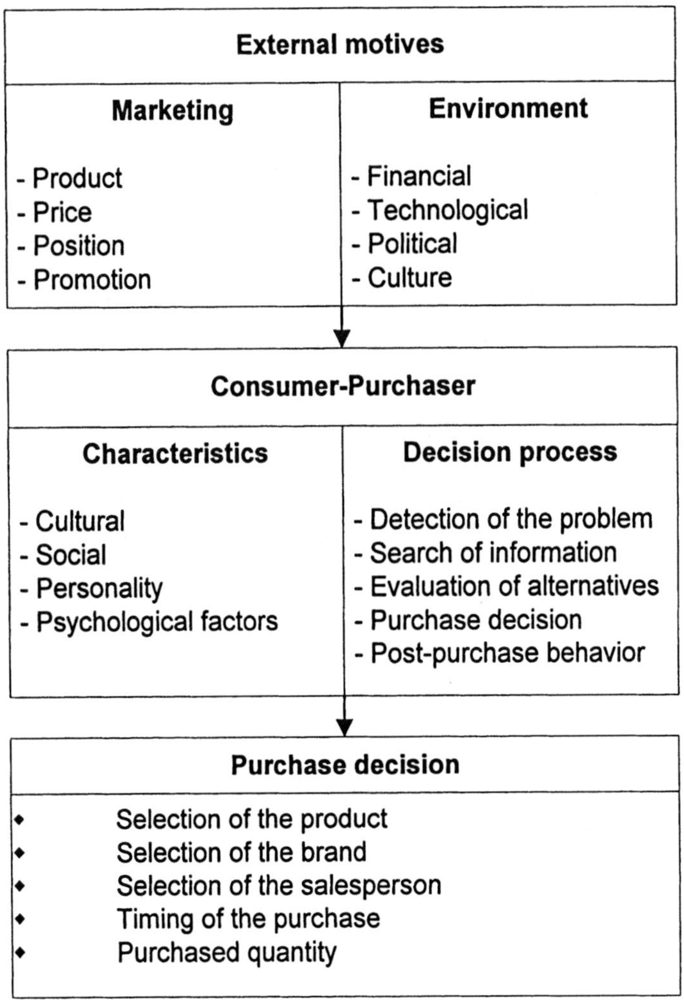

Figure 12. Model of behavior (*Source*: Kotler, 1994).

1. The theory should explain, on one hand, how the consumers buy, and on the other hand, to predict which consumers will buy.
2. The theory should join prior unrelated knowledge areas.
3. It should be simple enough, thus, if it is conceived then to be applicable in practice.
4. The test of the theory should be feasible in order to allow for checking its validity.

5. The theory should be supported by existing data, to check if the facts verify the result of the theory. If the verification is negative, the theory should be modified until it is supported by the existing data. If this is in not possible the theory should be rejected.
6. Any theory should be general enough in order to be applied in as many cases as possible.
7. It should have a heuristic form to allow the integration and incorporation of the generated knowledge.
8. It should be internally consistent.
9. It should be authentic; otherwise, it has nothing to offer in the existing knowledge.
10. Finally, the theory should be plausible.

Later, Howard (1989) added one more attribute (Howard, 1963a;b; Howard and Sheth, 1969):

11. The theory should be applied in the planning and scheduling of a marketing strategy.

The first models that appeared were the monadic models, which were developed to satisfy certain needs in specific scientific fields (Psychoanalytic model, The 'black box' models, Perceived risk model, etc). These were later enriched by other scientific areas and we arrived at the development of multivariable models (Lunn, 1971; Chisnall, 1985).

Numerous consumer decision models have appeared in the marketing literature (Andreasan, 1965; Nicosia, 1968). Among them, the most accepted ones are the Bettman model (1979), the WW model (Webster and Wind, 1972a; b), the EKB model (Engel *et al.*, 1978; Engel *et al.*, 1986), the Howard and Sheth model (1969), the Howard and Ostlund model (1973), and the CDM model (Howard, 1989).

Howard's model (1989) provides a systematic explanation of the process followed by a consumer when he or she makes the purchase. In addition, according to the model the actions of the consumer are predictable (*Figure 13*). Another advantage of the model is it simplicity, which provides safety regarding the results and ensuring at the same time their generality. In addition, the model takes into account competition situations. The validity of this model has been tested on real-world application. The objective in the design of the model was to operate as an MIS, providing the ability of developing marketing strategies with its use.

12. CUSTOMER'S SATISFACTION

Lately, the enterprises have increasingly come to understand the tremendous importance of investigating a very exceptional parameter of marketing-management, namely the satisfaction of the consumers. Numerous studies indicate that there is a strong link between customer satisfaction, customer retention, and profitability.

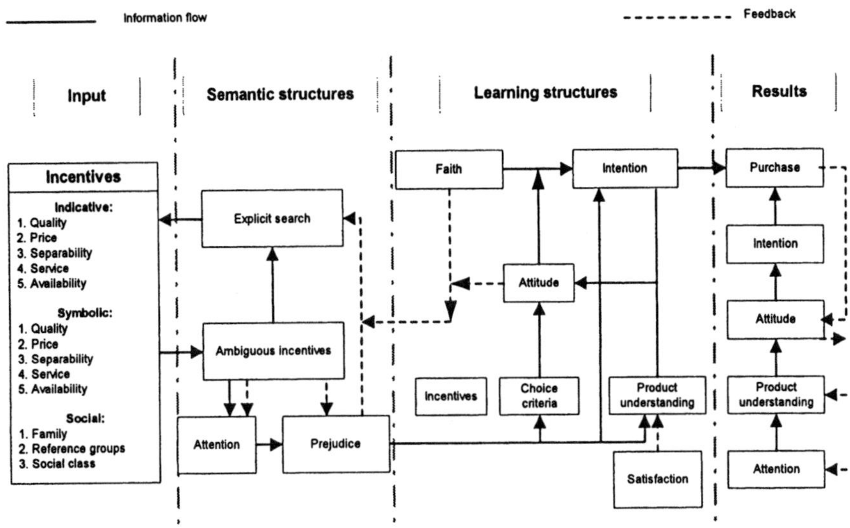

Figure 13. Model of consumer behavior (*Source*: Howard and Sheth, 1969; Howard, 1989)

Customer satisfaction has therefore become the key operational goal for many organizations. They have invested heavily in improving performance in areas that make a strong contribution to customer satisfaction, such as quality and customer service. However, before proceeding in further investigation of this factor, it would be useful to give a definition of customer satisfaction. According to Hill (1996), customer satisfaction is customer's perception that a supplier has met or exceeded their expectations. The author believes that the key word in the above definition is "perception". Customer satisfaction is in the consumer's mind and may or may not conform to the reality of the situation. Therefore, customer satisfaction measurement is about measuring how customers perceive their satisfaction from the products or services of their suppliers.

The average business losses between 10 and 30 per cent of its customers each year, but they often don't know which customers they have lost, when they were lost, why they were lost, or how much sales revenue and profit this customer decay has cost them (Hill, 1996). Most companies have traditionally placed a lot more emphasis on winning new customers rather from worrying about customers they are losing.

The fundamental reason for customer decay is clearly their dissatisfaction. The theory of "service gaps", which resulted from a considerable amount of research on this area in recent years, attempts to explain the causes of the dissatisfaction of the consumers. The overall gap, which results in a dissatisfied customer, is the gap between expectations and experience. Yet, the root cause of consumer dissatisfaction can easily be tracked back to one of five earlier gaps, promotional, understanding, procedural, behavioral, and perception (*Figure 14*).

The Promotional Gap. The origin of the problem can often be tracked to the company's marketing communication. In their eagerness to win customers, by selling the benefits of the product or service companies can very easily create expectations in the mind of customers that will be difficult to fulfill. A common example is the sales person promising a delivery date to secure an order without first making absolutely certain that the date can be met.

The Understanding Gap. The next possible problem area is that the managers of the organization do not have an accurate understanding of consumer's needs and priorities. If they do not really know what is important to customers, it is extremely unlikely that the organization will take the necessary actions to satisfy the requirements of the customers however much emphasis it places on quality and service.

The Procedural Gap. Even if we assume that the organization does have a full understanding of what matters to customers it will still fail to deliver customer satisfaction if it has not translated customer's expectations into appropriate operating procedures and systems.

The Behavioral Gap. Sometimes organizations have clear procedures which are well matched to customer's needs and priorities but do not achieve a consistently high level of customer satisfaction because staff are insufficient trained or disciplined to follow the procedures to the letter at all times.

The Perception Gap. It is possible that gaps 1-4 do not exist but the customer surveys still show an unacceptable level of dissatisfaction. This is because customer's perception of the performance of your organization may differ from reality. A customer who is dissatisfied by any reason in the past will form a negative attitude towards the organization, and it may take considerable time and much experience of good personal service before that perception is modified.

As shown in *Figure 14* any of the five gaps can result in the overall Service Quality Gap that leaves a customer dissatisfied.

A large portion of consumer's satisfaction from a product or a service is formed prior to the making of the purchase. Customers form their expectations concerning the benefits of a product or a service before the actual acquisition of it. Consequently, the actual benefits of the purchase of a product or a service are always compared to the expected ones. For this reason, the proper measurement of consumer satisfaction requires the detailed understanding of the ways used by the customers to evaluate and reach a purchase decision.

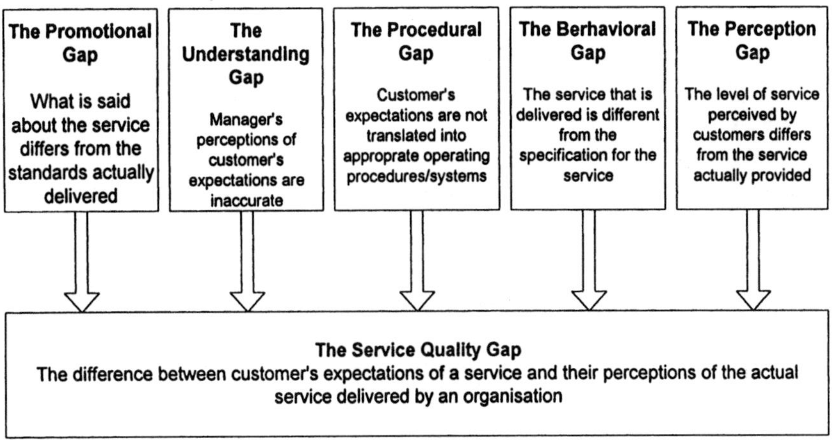

Figure 14. Service gaps (*Source*: Hill, 1996)

These decision processes differ whether they regard a lonely customer or they are ones that are more complicated. In paragraph 2.7 we presented they sequence of stages that lead in the purchase decision of a consumer.

Still, in many case, the information search does not stop here, that is the information that is stored in the memory of a consumer is not considered to be sufficient for making a decision. Thus, the consumer turns into the search of external information. External information sources can be classified into personal sources (e.g. the opinion of a friend), public sources (e.g. Yellow Pages), and commercial (e.g. advertisement).

With the process of information search, the consumer has finally formed a set of alternatives. The next stage of the decision making process involves the evaluation of these alternatives. The evaluation process can be affected by three significant factors:

1. The principles of the consumer,
2. His behavior, and
3. His intentions.

The principles or beliefs of a consumer are based on the tradition, the nationality, and the social class. The principles, which include the social, political, or religious beliefs, that characterize each consumer, shape in large extent the final decision.

Another important factor is the behavior or the attitude concerning facts, products, or services. Attitude can be modified more frequently than the beliefs as it is directly affected by the family, the social groups, the lifestyle, the age, and the financial state.

In addition, consumers have goals, priorities, and ambitions that attempt to fulfill. These factors are often reflected in their purchase decisions. Thus, the evaluations of the alternative purchase decisions are jointly affected, sometimes in a smaller and sometimes in a larger extent, by the factors mentioned above.

The next step in the decision process is the decision itself; even of this decision is merely something more than an "intention". That is, in some cases and especially in large purchases (e.g. a car purchase), the customer might change his initial preference, despite the fact that this has been its optimal choice for a long time. An additional factor in this level is the risk that consumer associated with his purchase. The risk is higher for expensive purchases where the knowledge of the consumer about the product is minimal. Consequently, the consumer finds it difficult to choose among the alternatives. With high levels of risk are also associated decisions that will affect the credibility of the consumer in the opinion of third parties. Some consumers are hesitating in general, but all the consumers are undecided in some purchase occasions.

The final stage of the process is the post purchase evaluation. Some consumers are fully satisfied from the accomplished purchase and some others are satisfied in some extend. Despite the level of satisfaction (maximum, intermediate, or minimum) the consumer will remember it and will always affect by it in similar future decisions. Some purchases, especially the expensive ones, increase the level of alternatives' evaluation in future purchases. Doubts are expressed by the purchasers when they perceive that some of the rejected alternatives finally possess the features that could fulfill their requirements. Thus, they are influenced by the advertisement of alternative products and investigate the choice of another alternative. It is as if they want to convince themselves that, without any doubt, they have made the right choice from the employed set of alternatives.

In this case, it should be best for enterprises to support the choice of their customers by persuading him that he has made the best possible choice. An advertising strategy that can help in this direction is the appearance of customers that are completely satisfied by the company's products and at the same time present the advantages and benefits of the product. Consequently, the deletion of post purchase hesitations is of great importance because else they can lead to customer dissatisfaction.

Among the main research streams, which deal with the problem of customer satisfaction are the marketing science, total quality management, consumer behavioral science, econometrics models, statistical methods, and graphical methods.

The modern approaches in marketing put the consumer and the satisfaction of his needs and requirements in the center of their interest. A simple method for the assessment of customer satisfaction if the decision made by a consumer for the purchase or non-purchase of a product. This is accomplished by the analysis of the results of market surveys, which aim at the determination of the loyalty of a set of customers towards a specific brand (Cadotte *et al.*, 1987). The mathematical marketing models associate the satisfaction of the customer with the market shares or the volume of sales of an enterprise (Olshavsky and Miller, 1972).

According to the definition, Total Quality Management, is the set of activities and methods adopted by and enterprise, which aim at the satisfaction of customers and at the same time at the activation of all the dynamic of the enterprise, with the lower feasible cost (Business Week Guide, 1994). Thus, it is more than obvious, that the objective of Total Quality Management is the satisfaction of the customers. Towards this goals various models are developed that measure the opinions, the desires, and the satisfaction degree of the consumers. The conclusions of the measurements are translated into adjustment of products and services supplied by an organization but also into adjustment of its mechanism in order to satisfy its customers.

Consumer behavior analysis focuses its attempt in the development of behavioral models that interpret the satisfaction of the consumers through the overall analysis of the purchase process, as this has been presented in the later paragraph.

The approach that uses econometric models examines the relation between the performance variables of the enterprise that are depended on the consumers (quality of products, customer's satisfaction) and traditional accounting performance variables (market shares, profit margin).

From a different point of view, statistical methods exhibit the problem of arbitrary codification of qualitative variables. Thus, statistical approaches usually yield different result depending on the followed codification.

Finally, another class of customer satisfaction measurement methods is the graphical data representation methods such as the histograms and the probability diagrams. These methods are based on the answers of the consumer on a specific questionnaire, which attempts to estimate the difference between the optimal and the actual level of customer's satisfaction on a specific attribute of the examined product or service (Dendy *et al.*, 1990).

All the above approaches are consumed mainly in the recording of the factors that affect the satisfaction of the customers; yet, they put lower importance in the determination of the degree of customer's satisfaction. The majority of these methods use data collected from surveys involving the customer's satisfaction from one product or service. Usually, the questionnaires do not contain the parameter of importance that is assigned by a customer to each factor or criterion, thus disregarding valuable information.

In these two shortcomings, attempt to find answers a model presented by Siskos *et al.* (1998), which is based on the principles of multicriteria analysis and belongs to the broader category of preference disaggregation models (§ 1.3.4). This model of customer's satisfaction measurement attempts to examine and analyze the multicriteria behavior of a set of customers, provided the multicriteria preferences of them are known.

The main objective of the model is to aggregate the opinions of the customers into a function, by assuming that the global satisfaction of the customer depends on a set of criteria or variables that is expressed by the features of a product or a service (*Figure 15*). According to the model, each customer expresses his judgment about the product or the service, i.e. his global satisfaction and his satisfaction concerning each criterion.

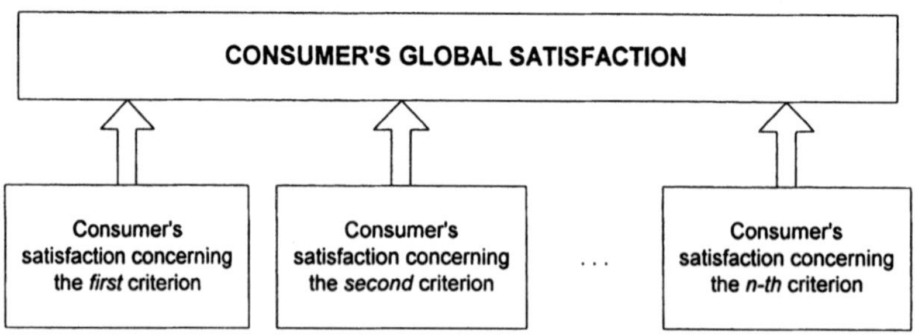

Figure 15. Aggregation of consumer's preferences

The model estimates the global and partial satisfaction functions, Y^* and X_i^* respectively, based on the evaluations of the customers, Y and X_i. The method follows the general principles of constrained regression analysis, using linear programming techniques for its solution (Jacquèt-Lagreze and Siskos, 1982). The basic equation of the linear regression analysis has the following form:

$$\tilde{Y}^* = \sum_{i=1}^{n} b_i X_i^* - \sigma^+ + \sigma^-$$

$$\sum_{i=1}^{n} b_i = 1$$

where

$\tilde{Y}^*$: estimation of the global satisfaction function, Y^*

σ^+, σ^- : overestimation and underestimation errors respectively

b_i : positive criteria weights

The formulation of the linear problem is the following:

$$
\begin{cases}
[\min]F = \sum_{j=1}^{M} \sigma_j^+ + \sigma_j^- \\
\text{s.t.} \\
\sum_{i=1}^{n}\sum_{k=1}^{x_i^j - 1} w_{ik} - \sum_{m=1}^{y^j - 1} z_m - \sigma_j^+ + \sigma_j^- = 0 \text{ for j} = 1,2,\dots,\text{M} \\
\sum_{m=1}^{\alpha^j - 1} z_m = 100 \\
\sum_{i=1}^{n}\sum_{k=1}^{\alpha_{il}^j - 1} w_{ik} = 100 \\
z_m \geq 0,\ w_{ik} \geq 0\ \forall \text{ m,i and k} \\
\sigma_j^+ \geq 0,\ \sigma_j^- \geq 0 \ \text{ for } j = 1,2,\dots,M
\end{cases}
$$

where M denotes the number of customers and n the number of criteria.

In order to reduce the order of the linear program the following transformations took place:

$$z_m = Y^{*m+1} - Y^{*m} \text{ for m} = 1,2,\dots,\alpha\text{-}1$$

$$w_{ik} = b_i X_i^{*k+1} - b_i X_i^{*k} \text{ for k} = 1,2,\dots,\alpha_i\text{-}1 \text{ and } \text{i} = 1,2,\dots,\text{n}$$

The next stage of the method involves the post-optimality analysis to check for the stability of the model. Finally, the mean global and the mean partial satisfaction indices are calculated by the formulae:

$$S = \sum_{m=1}^{a} p^m y^{*m}$$

$$s_i = \sum_{k=1}^{a_i} p_i^k x_i^{*k}$$

where S is the mean global satisfaction index, s_i the mean partial satisfaction indices for the *i-th* criterion, p^m the frequency of consumers that belong to the y_m satisfaction level, and p_i^k the frequency of consumers that belong to the x_i^k satisfaction level.

The application of this model allows for the calculation of the weights of the criteria b_i and in the calculation of the mean indices of global and partial satisfaction. This feature distinguishes the above model, with all the other approaches applied to the problem of consumer satisfaction measurement.

The discussion on customer satisfaction has demonstrated the tremendous importance of the understanding of customer's behavior and accordingly of the measurement of customer's satisfaction for an organization. As a conclusion, the most important advantages of the measurement of consumer's satisfaction are:

1. The most secure method of improving the competitiveness of an organization is to provide the customers with what they really want. The analytical measurement of customer satisfaction is the only method of measuring the performance of an organization in this vital section.
2. It is more profitable to build an organization by preserving its current clients (or by reducing the customer decay) rather than seeking new customers.
3. Market surveys related with the consumer satisfaction provide an invaluable tool for conserving the focus of an organization to customer satisfaction. Some guidelines should always be followed in market surveys; the two most important is the use of a professional methodology and the selection of the appropriate sample of customers.
4. Full understanding of the needs and priorities of consumers provides the standards for the majority of managerial decisions. Business that better satisfy the needs of the customers, with regard to their competitors, are able to increase the prices of their products, because the majority of customers are willing to pay more money for a product or a service that fully meets their demands.
5. The most powerful motive in doing anything in business is that it will increase profitability. Measuring customer satisfaction, and acting appropriately on the results, will increase profitability. The surest route to success for most organizations (in both the private and public sector) is to "do best what matters most to customers".

13. BRAND CHOICE MODELS

The study of consumer behavior is accomplished by the aid of sociology for the external influences of the consumer and by the aid of psychology for his internal influences. The various models differ among them in the weight that each one attaches to the influence of the external environment and in the internal processes. The vast variety of models is essential in order to cover for the numerous forms of consumer behavior. According to Lilien *et al.* (1992), the models of consumer behavior could be categorized according to the phase of the decision making process and according to the level of complexity of the purchase decision. The complexity of a decision affects all the phases of the decision process and determines the factors that will affect the attitudes and behavior of consumers. Consumers initially form their perceptions and then determine their preferences. The behavior of the consumers is formed not by the actual features of a product but according to consumers' personal perceptions about them. Thus, while the features of a product remain actually the same, yet each consumer follows his personal point of view and forms different opinion about them. In the case when some consumers share similar opinions, we have a group of consumers that belong to the same market segments with similar behavior. To these consumers we can address with appropriate marketing strategies.

Fishbein (1967) and Lancaster (1966), even if they were motivated by the psychology and economy fields respectively, agree that consumers always relate a product with a set of attributes. Thus, in each category of products corresponds a series of attributes that are important for this category. Each consumer assigns to the attributes of a group of products different levels of importance. We could exploit this fact to proceed to market segmentation into segments that will consist of consumers with similar attitude.

Hauser and Urban (1978) proved that the utility theory of Von Neumann and Morgenstern (1947) is consistent with the descriptive models that deal with the consumers' decision making. In these models, the preferences and the final choice result from the comparison of the products of a "market" according to a family of criteria, thus making possible the modeling of their relation by using a utility function of Von Neumann and Morgenstern (1947). This fact implies that descriptive utility theory can be used to study the behavior of consumers (Hauser and Urban, 1977; 1979; Eliashberg, 1980). According to the utility theory a product A will be preferred to another product B iff the expected utility from A is greater than the expected utility from B:

$$U(A) > U(B)$$

Consumers, based on their perceptions, shape their preferences. By the use of models a utility function is assigned to the consumers, that determines the expected, by them, utility from the purchase of a product. The utility function describes the evaluation of a product according to a set of attributes-criteria. The importance of the criteria and accordingly their impact to the utility values are different for each criterion. The weights, assigned by a consumer to the criteria indicate their relative importance. The knowledge on how the importance of the criteria ranges over a set of consumers is an invaluable piece of information for new product development decisions. Through a process of comparisons and assessments of a set of products, the consumer formulates its attitude by expressing his preferences. These preferences can be expressed by the ranking of the products. Consequently, having the evaluations and the expressed preference of the consumers on a set of products we attempt with the aid of models to estimate the purchase probability of each product by the particular consumer. By extending this estimation to a representative set of consumers, we can calculate the purchase probabilities of each product, in this representative market, and subsequently to estimate their market shares.

13.1 Process oriented models of consumer choice

In the context of this chapter we have already encountered and carefully examined the various phases of the decision making process of a consumer. For each of these phases, miscellaneous appropriate consumer choice models have been formulated. Al these models are based on two basic assumptions:

1. Maslow's hierarchy of needs, according to which the needs are classified in a hierarchy and the consumers firstly satisfy the needs belonging to the top of the hierarchy and afterwards those that belong to lower levels of the hierarchy.
2. The McClelland's principle, according to which the needs evolve through a learning process i.e. the consumer gradually discovers and learns his needs.

In order to proceed to the estimation of the purchase probability of a product during the stage where the consumer detects a certain need, a variety of models has been developed such as the stochastic models of purchase incidence and the discrete binary choice models - binary probit - binary logit etc (Zaltman and Wallendorf, 1983; Ben-Akiva and Lerman, 1985; Hauser *et al.*, 1983; Hauser and Urban, 1986; Coursey, 1985; 1988; Bodnar *et al.*, 1988; Gessner *et al.*, 1988). Both types of models are based on the hierarchy of needs and in the assumption that those needs are gradually obtained. In general, the binary nature of these models stems from the existence of two cases, purchase or non-purchase (expected utility from the purchase of the product and expected utility from the non-purchase of the product).

Other types of models have been developed in order to calculate the purchase probability of a product when the consumer is at the stage of information search. In general, models used for this situation belong to one of the following types.

Models of brand awareness. The consumers become aware about a product either by their own initiative either passively. According to Rossiter and Percy (1987), the term awareness signifies that the consumer should have the ability to identify the specific product among the set of the rest product in the same category so as to proceed to its purchase. Obviously, the advertisement plays a significant role in all these models (Blattberg and Jeuland, 1981; Mahajan *et al.*, 1984; Leckenby and Kishi, 1984).

Models of consideration. These models are used for the calculation of the probabilities of only those products that the consumer has selected from a broader category and seeks further information for them. These products constitute the choice set i.e. the final set of products from which the consumer will make his decision. Models of this category have proposed, among others, by Narayana and Markin (1975); Day and Deutscher (1982); Gensch and Svestka (1984); Fotheringham (1988); Hauser and Wernerfelt (1990), Roberts and Lattin (1991), Shocker *et al.* (1991).

Models of information integration. These models are applied to consumers that are aware of the products of the latter category (Hagerty and Aaker, 1984; Meyer and Sathi, 1985; Oren and Schwartz, 1988; Roberts and Urban, 1988).

In general, two methods are used to model the behavior of the consumers during the stage of attitude formation and evaluation, the compositional methods and the decomposition ones. The former are mainly based in the use of factor analysis models (Jöreskog and Sörbom, 1979; Shocker and Srinivasan, 1979; Hauser and Koppelman, 1979; Hauser and Shugan, 1980; Long, 1983; Hauser, 1984; Srinivasan *et al.*, 1989; Urban and Hauser, 1993) while the latter in nonmetric multidimensional scaling (Carroll and Chang, 1964; Klahr, 1969; Green and Rao, 1972; Harshman *et al.*, 1982; Holbrook *et al.*, 1982; McKay and Zinnes, 1986; DeSarbo and Rao, 1986; Moore and Winer, 1987; DeSarbo and Hoffman, 1987; Malhotra, 1987; Elrod, 1988; Katahira, 1990).

In the stage of preference and attitude formation of the consumers, we try to initially investigate and then realize the existing relation between the perceptions and the attitude of the consumers (Hughes, 1974). The attitude of an individual towards a product is determined by the way that individual feels about the product. Accordingly, the attitude determines the way he will react when he will enter the purchase phase. The majority of the existing models presume that the attitude of an individual is determined by his evaluations on a set of criteria. The weight that is assigned to each one of the decision criteria indicates the importance of the criterion according to the consumer. If we regard that the weaknesses of the products in some criteria are compensated or not by the high/low values of other criteria then we have the case of compensatory and non-compensatory models respectively. As compensatory models are considered those that assume that the weak points of a product in one of the criteria can be balanced by the prospect of another criterion. Each consumer evaluates the product according to a family of criteria and based on these evaluation determines the priority rank. Typical compensatory models are those developed by Fishbein (1963); Wilkie and Pessemier (1973); Lutz and Bettman (1977), the extended Fishbein's model (Fishbein and Ajzen, 1975; Wilson *et al.*, 1975; Bearden and Etzel, 1982), and the loyalty model (Bass and Talarzyk, 1972; Mazis and Ahtola, 1975; Green and Srinivasan, 1978; Shocker and Srinivasan, 1979; Horsky and Rao, 1984).

The non-compensatory models assume that the consumers do not choose a model by using the whole set of criteria but only those that are considered more important. Consequently, the weak points of a product in some criteria are not balanced by the potentiality of the rest (Nakanishi and Bettman, 1974). In the family of non-compensatory models belong, among others, the conjunctive models, the disjunctive model, and the lexicographic model (Bettman, 1979; Lynch, 1985; Johnson and Payne, 1985).

Arriving at the purchase phase, we have to point out that is very likely the consumer not to purchase the product that is ranked as first in his priorities but a product that exists in a lower position. This situation might happen if the most preferred product is not available at the time of the purchase. Other reasons are that the family of criteria, upon which the consumer is based in order to evaluate the products, is incomplete or even when the products that form the market are not representatives. Models that are used in this phase is the constant and random utility models (Luce, 1959; 1977; Axelrod, 1968; Allaire, 1973), the multinomial Logit model (McFadden, 1976; 1980; Punj and Staelin, 1978; Gensch and Recker, 1979; Chapman and Staelin, 1982; Berkowitz and Haines, 1982; Guadagni and Little, 1983; Louviere and Hensher, 1983; Louviere and Woodworth, 1983; Gensch, 1984; 1985; 1987; Bunch and Batsell, 1989), and some hierarchical choice models such as the nested Logit model (Tversky, 1972; McFadden, 1978; 1991; Ben-Akiva and Lerman, 1985; Dubin, 1986; Hauser, 1986; Dalal and Klein, 1988; Manrai and Sinha, 1989; Bechtel, 1990).

Many other models, finally, have been developed in order to predict the behavior of the consumer at the phase where the consumer already has purchased the product, (McAlister, 1982; McAlister and Pessemier, 1982; Rogers, 1983; Biehal, 1983; Bearden and Teel, 1983; Latin and McAlister, 1985; Latin, 1987; Westbrook, 1987; Singh, 1988; Tse and Wilton, 1988; Simonson, 1990).

13.2 Stochastic models of consumer choice

Probably, the use of a stochastic brand choice model should be more beneficial if we take under consideration the prevalent uncertainty because of the simplifications, the lack of variables, and the existence of numerous errors that enter into the various stages of calculations (Lilien *et al.*, 1992). The stochastic models can be classified into Purchase Incidence models (Morrison and Perry, 1970; Ehrenberg, 1972; Schmittlein and Morrison, 1983; Wagner and Taudes, 1986; Schmittlein *et al.*, 1987; Morrison and Schmittlein, 1988; Ehrenberg, 1988; Wellan and Ehrenberg, 1990), Brand Choice Models (Kuehn, 1962; Montgomery, 1969; Massy *et al.*, 1970; Ehrenberg, 1972; Wierenga, 1974; Lilien, 1974a; Bass *et al.*, 1976; Horsky, 1976; 1977; Kalwani and Morrison, 1977; Kalwani, 1979; Jeuland *et al.*, 1980; Leeflang and Boonstra, 1982; Bass *et al.*, 1984; Kahn *et al.*, 1986), combination of brand choice and purchase timing (Lilien, 1974a, 1974b; Zufryden, 1978; Jeuland *et al.*, 1980; Dalal *et al.*, 1984; Givon and Horsky, 1990). They are mainly applied to purchase decisions with low levels of involvement and focus on the random nature of the brand choice process rather providing a deterministic interpretation

Given the multicriteria evaluations of a consumer, according to a consistent family of criteria, for a set of representative products that form the "market" and a set of brand choice models, our goal is to initially detect the preferences of the consumer and the importance assigned by him to each criterion and then to calculate the choice probability for each product of the market. This is accomplished by a set of brand choice models for new products that are based on the utility theory of Von Neumann and Morgenstern (1947); Keeney and Raiffa (1976); Keeney and Lilien (1987); Hauser and Urban (1979); Eliashberg (1980).

Chapter 3

Strategic Marketing Decisions

1. INTRODUCTION.

The term "strategic marketing decisions" describes the set of activities of an enterprise that are oriented to the consumers (Fletcher, 1990). Terms such as business politics, strategic market planning, strategic marketing, business strategy, will be included, from now on, in the term "strategic marketing decisions". By speaking more generally, we could say that the importance of various strategies varies according to the nature and the market position of each enterprise.

When we refer to marketing decision-making, usually we imply the product specific decision-making. However, an enterprise should make decisions that take into account the whole set of products produced by it along with their interrelationships. Decisions that involve the drawing of guidelines and the long-term marketing planning can be described by the term "strategic market planning process".

2. STRATEGIC MARKET PLANNING PROCESS

The objective of strategic marketing is to determine, on one hand, the markets that can be supplied by the enterprise and on the other to determine how to succeed in preserving the competitive advantages in those markets (Nylen, 1990).

The successful implementation of this process requires an answer to the following questions (David, 1986):

- Who are we?
- Who do we want to become?
- Which is the best way of becoming what we want?
- Which are our superior points and drawbacks?
- How can we take advantage of our capabilities and fight down out weak points?
- Which are the major opportunities and threats in our area?
- In what way can we take advantage of our opportunities and avoid the threats?
- What are the actions of our competitors?
- Which are the capabilities and the shortcomings of our competitors?
- In what way will the competitors react to our strategies?
- How much vulnerable are we to the strategies of our competitors?
- How much vulnerable are our competitors to our own strategies?

The possibility of finding answers to the above questions gives competitive advantages to the enterprise. *Figure 1* presents the process that should be followed by an enterprise in its attempt to go over from current *state* to the desirable one.

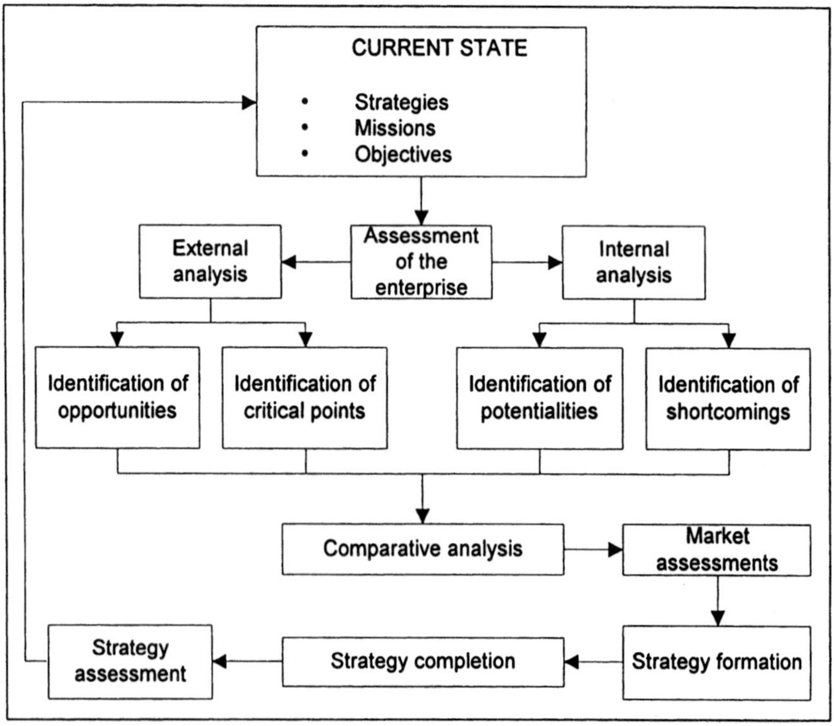

Figure 1. Strategic marketing process (*Source*: David, 1986)

The matching process is normally accomplished by the variation of some marketing mix parameters (c.f. §3.4), such as the improvement of one product, the modification of its packaging, etc. These actions are placed among the attempts of the enterprise to obtain comparative advantages against its competitors. According to Wiseman and Macmillan (1984) the attempt of an enterprise to achieve competitive advantages against its competitors will succeed if the enterprise is substantially improved in the following three strategic goals:
- suppliers,
- consumers, and
- competitors.

The strategic planning process provides the decision maker with an approach that facilitates vital marketing decision-making concerning specific products. Marketing plans for specific products should determine the target market as well as the positioning of them. In addition and parallel to the planning of existing products, the enterprise should carry out tasks for planning the development of new products.

3. DEVELOPMENT PROCESS OF A NEW PRODUCT

According to Kaärkkaäinen *et al.* (2001), the valuation of the customers' needs is a very critical factor concerning the successful development of new products. Customers' need assessment for the development of new products is a systematic effort of gathering and valuation of these needs. On the basis of the conclusions inferred by the precedent process, the attributes of the product are determined so as to cover the demands of the consumers. Kaärkkaäinen *et al.* (2001), have divided customers' need assessment into six phases (*Figure 2*). As depicted in *Figure 2*, there is continuous interaction between the phase of customers' need assessment and the phase of new product development in order to implement the strategic program of the firm and the attainment of the goals set. The success of the new product development should be predicted by the elaboration and evaluation of the information collected through the study of consumers' needs. Once the new product enters the market, it is necessary to collect information about the customers' satisfaction from the use of the product. This information supports the continuous re-design and improvement of the features of the new product in order to possibly fulfill the varying demands of the consumers.

When a product is regarded as a new product? Which are the criteria that help us to determine whether a product is new or not? A lot of discussion has been devoted on this problem but practically a product is new when the consumer considers it so. To consumers, as new products are considered those related to new usage or demand new ways of purchase (Nylen, 1990).

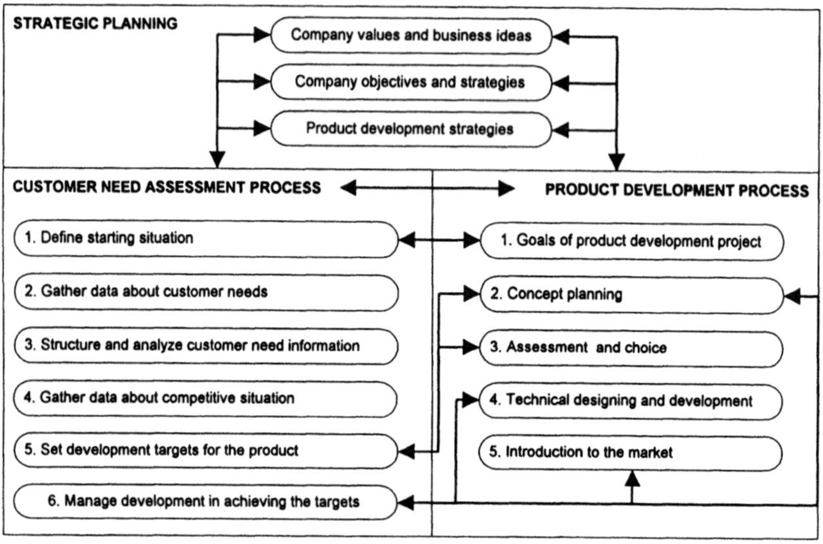

Figure 2. The links between customers need assessment, product development processes and strategic planning processes (*Source*: Kaärkkaäinen *et al.*, 2001)

On the other hand, enterprises consider as new products those that are new for the enterprise or those that result from modifying the attributes of existing ones (e.g. modification of packaging) or those produced in a new production line, etc. According to Ahituv *et al.* (1998) the most important reasons that will render the new product development process harder over time include:

- The increase of the new product development cost and of the raw material supplies
- The increase of competition due to the globalization of the market.
- The rapid rate of technological changes.
- The change in communication methods and means along with the development of electronic commerce.
- The change in purchase habits.
- The attenuation of products life cycle.
- Changes in the international legal system, etc.

Booz *et al.* (1982), in a market survey among 700 companies found out that these companies spent 31% of their profits in developing new products. O'Connor (1986) mentions that before reaching 2000, USA companies are about to spend 50% of their profits in products, aged less than five years.

According to Ali *et al.* (1993), this tendency is originated by technological advancements, the shorter life cycle, the more intense competition, etc.

Table 1 summarizes .the primary reasons that lead to the failure of the new products, according to a study of Booz *et al.* (1982).

Table 1. Reasons of new product failure (*Source*: Booz et al, 1982)

Cause of failure	Reported failure percentages
Inadequate analysis of the market – for example unsuccessful definition of the market or of its size	45
Problems or defects of the product	25
Inefficient marketing strategy – for example ineffective positioning, pricing strategy or promotion of the product	25
Cost higher than the one anticipated	19
Tough reaction of the competitors	17

The new product development process aims at the transformation of ideas into product concepts that will have a certain sense to the consumer. The general approach adopted, deploys the original idea into several alternative concept forms and evaluates each concept by presenting analytical descriptions and profiles to consumers that participate in specialized market surveys. The results of these market surveys are then used by the experts in order to estimate the customers' satisfaction from the use of the new product. The experts attempt to evaluate the idea of the new product under development before this enters into mass production and subsequently the market.

The development process of new product, which begins with the conception of the idea and ends with the development of the appropriate marketing strategy, is briefly examined in the following sections (Finklin, 1983; Takeuchi and Nonaka, 1986; Nylen, 1990; Fletcher, 1990; Urban and Hauser, 1993).

Generation-birth of a new idea. In a well-organized enterprise, the conception of an idea about the development of a new product is not a random event; it is based on programmed actions (Levitt, 1966; Von Hippel, 1982; 1985; Nylen, 1990; Fletcher, 1990; Urban and Hauser, 1993). Through market surveys suitable markets for the introduction of the new product are tracked. In addition, the enterprise should record and realize the needs of the consumers to design a new product that will cover them as much as possible. By using appropriate techniques, it is possible to determine the importance of attributes of a group of products, according to the consumers' opinion, by explicitly asking them to express their preferences. With the recording of the attributes of the existing products and with the measurement of the consumer's satisfaction level by them, it is possible to detect existing gaps in the market that could be covered by the creation of new product. In addition, the enterprise should consider studying the competitive products.

Exhaustive examination of the ideas. Normally there are a large number of generated ideas concerning the new product development. These ideas should be exhaustively examined in order to determine the ones that really worth the investment of money and resources (O'Meara, 1961; Hamilton, 1974; Nylen, 1990; Fletcher, 1990). Ideas that concentrate the higher probabilities of success should be promoted. The judgment of the success probabilities of each new product development idea is based on a set of criteria with different importance (size of the market, developing market or not, life cycle of products, past experience, complementary to existing products, etc). In the formation of the set of criteria, the enterprise should take into account factors that lead to the failure of the new products (Cooper, 1979; Calantone and Cooper, 1981).

Furthermore, in this phase of the development process, we can integrate the examination phase of the idea by the consumers, before blocking the resources of the enterprise for the new product development. This test is accomplished by exhibiting to the consumers a prototype of the product along with relevant existing products in the market. This attempt aims at the prediction of the consumers' purchase intention against the new product as well as the prediction of its expected sales by using scientific methods.

Examination of the enterprise. In this phase, we proceed with the evaluation of cost and profit probability from the developing of the new product aiming at making the decision whether the enterprise should proceed to the development of the new product or not. This analysis has the form of state analysis, as exhibited in *Figure 3*. (Stevenson, 1976; Day *et al.*, 1979; Rothschild, 1979; Nylen, 1990). It should include, among others, the identification of:

- Competitive products,
- Competitor's adapted marketing strategies.
- Potentiality of the market.
- Prediction of the new product's sales.

Development and test of the new product. The product, which until this moment was merely an idea, begins to realize according to the results derived in the previous courses of action. It would be beneficial to aid the scheduling of the entire development processes by appropriate techniques such as PERT (Program Evaluation Review Technique), CPM (Critical Path Analysis) (Dusenbury, 1967; Dean and Chaudhuri, 1980; Cooper, 1988; Fletcher, 1990). Each stage of the development process should be evaluated and checked before proceeding to the next. Examinations of this type involve the test of the technical capabilities of the product, its production possibility, the safety provided by its use, etc. Furthermore, consumers should also participate in the tests in order to express:

- Their opinion on the attributes of the product.
- Their preferences on the existing products and on the new one, and
- The purchase probabilities of the products included in the survey.

Miscellaneous models have been developed in order to predict the sales of new products. Authors that suggest models of this type are, among others, Hamburg and Atkins (1967); Ehrenberg (1972); Urban (1970; 1975); Assmus (1981); Lilien and Kotler (1983); Taylor (1984); Hisrich and Peters (1984).

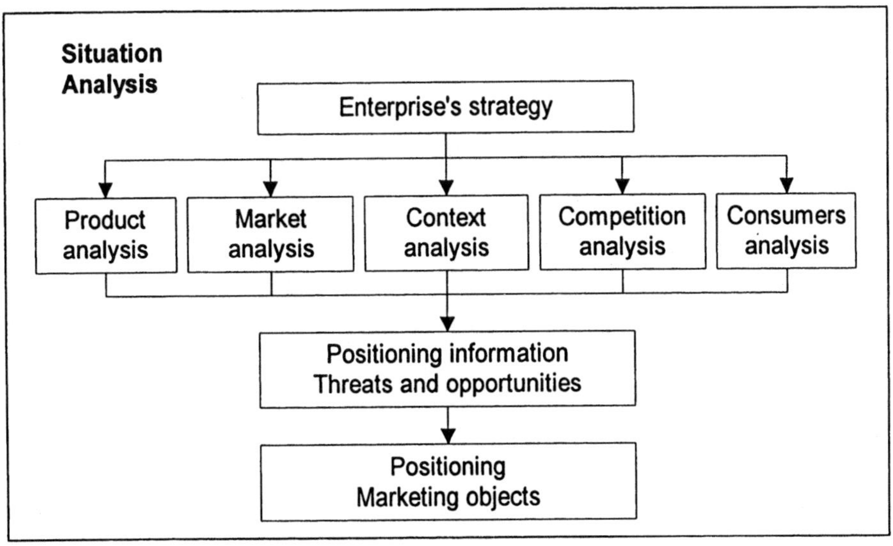

Figure 3. Situation analysis (*Source:* Nylen, 1990).

Development of a marketing strategy. The goal here is to determine a marketing strategy that combines the results of the situation analysis, of the positioning operations and the product marketing mix.

Introduction process of the new product into the market. This process consists of three stages, according to Nylen (1990), in each one of which certain determinative decisions should be made.

a) **Market survey pre-tests.** This stage is usually adapted in place of the marketing test because it is less time consuming and inexpensive. The pre-test aims at the examination of the introduction strategies of the new product. First, in this stage it should be decides whether the market survey protest will be eventually carried out and then which will be the utilized technique. The available techniques are:

1. **Sales variations tests:** The product is evaluated by a group of consumers in an artificial market situation in order to measure the acceptance level of the new product and the inclination of repeating its purchase.
2. **Laboratory market tests:** It is a market simulation in which, responses of a group of consumers against advertisement messages, purchase bids, and other parameters, are measured. Furthermore, in this stage we measure the purchase and test intentions of the new product. Suitable models are used to carry out those measurements, which combine data on the attitudes, intentions and purchase in order to predict the results of the new product entry into the market.
3. **Controlled market tests:** These tests exhibit lower levels of credibility, high cost, and more time consuming with respect to the former ones. They are much like the traditional market tests except the fact that in this case the market has a very small size.

b) **Marketing tests.** Marketing tests are the most comprehensive ones permitting the evaluation of the entire components of the marketing plan for the introduction of the new product. These tests ensure a safest prediction of the results of the new product's introduction, and provide information concerning the improvement of the marketing plan prior to the launching of the new product. Other measurements, that take place during this phase, are dealing with the effectiveness of advertisement, the reaction of the remaining products, as well as any other information regarding the marketing mix. In addition, all the alternative strategies are examined and their expected sales and marketing shares are predicted (Klompmaker *et al.*, 1976; Tauber, 1977; Narasimhan and Sen, 1983). As drawbacks of marketing test, we can mention the involved high cost and the resulted time loss in the introduction of the new product (Cadbury, 1975).

c) **Launching.** A product might be launched in the entire market or in some specific segments. Along with the launching decision the enterprise should at the same time make decisions about the introduction time of the new product into the market and the breadth of its launching

Dissemination and acceptance processes. After the launching of the product, the product becomes accepted and it is gradually purchased by the consumers. It has been proved by researches that, consumers that buy the new product at the same periods, share common attributes. The enterprises design a different marketing policy for each one of these categories, except the last one. The duration of the acceptance period depends on the category of the product. *Figure 4* displays the categories of consumers and their percentages whereas their characteristics are briefly discussed in the following sections.

- **Innovators.** It is the smaller group but they are open minded, educated, social, and with relative financial convenience. Financial convenience depends on the type of the product (car, clothes, food...) and consists an attribute that differentiates innovators into those that would like to buy but they are not able to do so, because of financial reasons, and those that want and can buy.
- **Early adopters.** They are the opinion leaders and the acceptance of the product by them entails its success. Early adopters are kept informed about new products, relatively young, educated and with high social position.

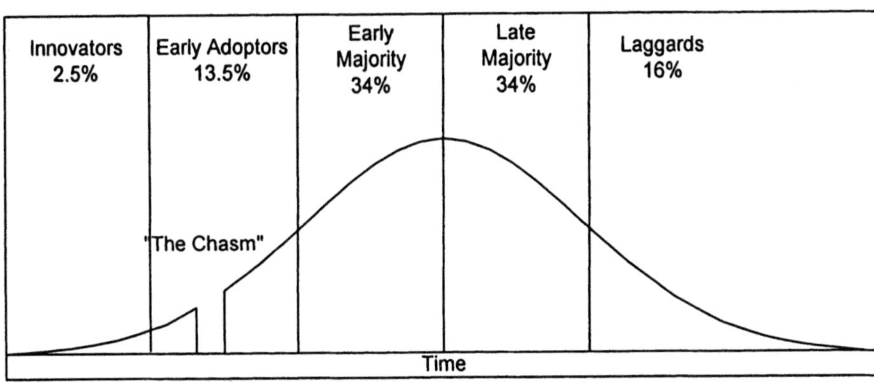

Figure 4. Product's adoption process (*Source*: Rogers, 1983).

- **Early majority.** The acceptance of the new product results due mature thinking and influence of consumers that belong in the former category. These are older individuals, educated ones, and with high social position.
- **Late majority.** This is the second larger group of consumers, the members of which confront cautiously a new product and accept it after detailed consideration and influence of other individuals. These are older people, of average education, financial capabilities, and social position.
- **Laggards.** These are cautious and mistrustful individuals, old, unsociable, with modest financial capabilities and social position. They are the lasts to accept the new products almost before their redraw from the market.

The consumer should pass through a certain process in order to accept a product, which is composed of the following stages (Siomkos, 1994):

- Awareness.
- Comprehension.
- Attitude.
- Legitimization.
- Trial.

- Adoption.

The duration of each stage but also the exact timing a consumer passes through each one of them, until he accepts or rejects a product, vary accordingly.

4. THE MARKETING MIX

Marketing mix is a concept that it is considered to correspond to the planning of the marketing components of a specific product (Borden, 1964). According to Kotler (1994), marketing mix is the set of marketing tools used by an enterprise to achieve the objectives of the adapted marketing in the particular marketing segment. Marketing mix is composed of two types of variables: controllable and uncontrollable ones.

Controllable variables are those associated with the components of a product's marketing plan while the uncontrollable ones are related with the market environment in which the product will be launched. The controllable variables are widely known under the 4-P term: Product - Promotion - Price - Place (McCarthy and Perreault, 1990). The uncontrollable ones are the purchase behavior of the consumer, the behavior of the market, the behavior along with the position of the competitors, and the behavior of the state. Each one of these variables is subdivided into other variables.

The marketing mix development follows the following steps:

- **Situation analysis.** Situation analysis attempts to investigate the available resources of the enterprise, the needs of the consumes, the characteristics of the market, the competition conditions, and the tendencies of the environment (social, economic)
- **Positioning.** Positioning requires the results of situation analysis in order to make possible the market segmentation, the selection of the specific market segments in which the product will be introduced and the determination of the manner the product will compete the existing ones. Positioning signifies the drawing of the image of the enterprise in such a way that the consumers belonging to the specific market segment to understand and appreciate its position in relation to its competitors (Kotler, 1994). The necessary information for the positioning of a product is related to the characteristics of the segment, the attributes of the product, and the attributes of the competitors (Aaker and Shansby, 1980; Neal, 1980; Ries and Trout, 1980; Nylen, 1990, Urban and Hauser, 1993).
- **Marketing mix development.** The results of the former two steps are used here in order to take those decisions that are related to the design of the product, its prices, its means of distribution, and its promotion.

During the marketing mix, process miscellaneous decisions are made about several partial points.

- *Figure 5*displays the criteria used to take the partial marketing mix decisions (Nylen, 1990).
- **Results.** The results of marketing mix application are represented by financial terms.

The present *state* of markets internationalization posses some serious problems and gives rise to questions regarding the followed global marketing mix, which has to be tackled in a different manner (Baker, 1985; Quelch and Hoff, 1986; Leoniades, 1986; Douglass and Graig, 1986; Clark, 1987; Fletcher, 1990). Thus, some enterprises apply the same marketing independently of the country, others diversify partial marketing mix variables depending on the target country, and others follow the same marketing for groups of consumers that share similar attributes independently of the country of origin.

Consumers' behavior	Needs: Consumer's decision making process, positioning
	Purchase behavior: Classification of commodities
Competition	Market structure: Competitive market structure and product's life cycle
	Competitive positioning: State analysis and positioning
Means-Resources	Product's attributes: State analysis and positioning
	Enterprise resource: Market strategic planning
	Budget constraints
Strategic directions	Strategic planning and strategic objectives
Commerce	Requirements: Choice of wholesalers and retailers
Environmental	Economic, social, cultural, tendencies, etc.
	Technological changes
	Regulating requirements

Figure 5. Criteria of *marketing* mix decision-making (*Source: Nylen, 1990*).

5. PRODUCT LIFE CYCLE

When a new product enters the market, it begins its life cycle that ends up with its "death". *Figure 6* displays a typical product life cycle whereas *Table 2* and *Table 3* indicate corresponding characteristics and strategies for each stage of the product life cycle (Day, 1986; Fletcher, 1990).

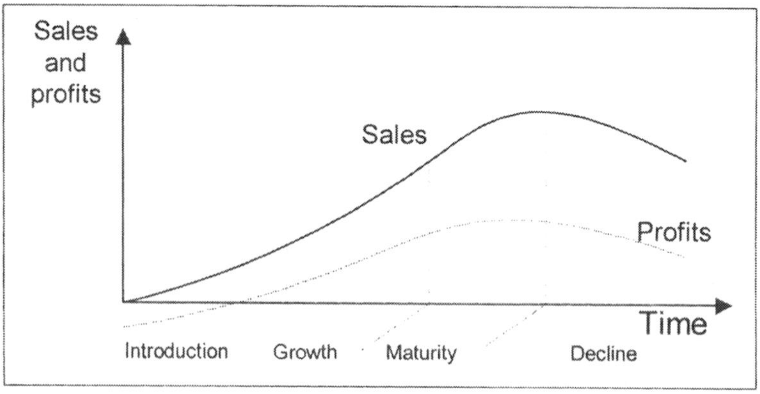

Figure 6. Typical stages in the sales and profit cycles (*Source*: Fletcher, 1990).

Table 2. Characteristics of life cycle (*Source*: Fletcher, 1990).

Characteristics	Introduction	Growth	Maturity	Decline
Sales	Low	Rapidly rising	Peak sales	Declining
Costs	High	Reducing fast	Lowest	May rise depending on market share
Profits (per unit)	Negative	Highest/unit in cycle	Average for industry	Declining
Customers	Innovators	Early adopters	Early and middle majority	Laggards
Competition	Few	Growing number of imitators	Shakeout causes declining numbers	Further decline

Table 3. Strategies of life cycle (*Source*: Fletcher, 1990).

Strategies	Introduction	Growth	Maturity	Decline
Overall objective	Create awareness and trial. Product design critical	Market share penetration	Protect share manage for profit. Emphasize competitive advantage	Reduce expenditures and harvest
Product	Basic	Offer product extensions, features, and services.	Diversity of brands and models	Phase out weak items
Price	Cost plus	Competitive pricing	Match or beat competitors	Reduce or maintain to keep profit margins
Distribution	Selective	Build more	Intensive and	Selective

Strategies	Introduction	Growth	Maturity	Decline
	distribution	intensive coverage	extensive	eliminating high cost outlets
Communications	Create awareness	Simulate wider interest through trial sales promotions	Stress brand differences and benefits	Phase out

Along with the above displayed "traditional" life cycle there is a large variety if different forms of product life cycles depending on the type of the products, the adapted marketing strategy, the approach method, etc (Buzzell, 1966; Cox, 1967; Wasson, 1976; Enis *et al.*, 1977; Abell, 1980; Swan and Rink, 1982; Schultz and Rao, 1986; Nylen, 1990; Norton and Bass, 1992; Urban and Hauser, 1993).

As we already mentioned, the life cycle of the products has become shorter. One of the main causes of this fact is the rapid advancement in the information technology areas, which has a heavy impact on the re-evaluation of the adopted marketing strategies (Qualls *et al.*, 1981). Enterprises are compelled to engage in research and development of new products. The appropriate combination of the several research and development phases along with the life cycle of products is of strategic importance to the survival of the enterprise and the attainment of profits (Levitt, 1965; Fletcher, 1990).

6. STRATEGIC MARKETING DECISIONS

The management of an enterprise has reached a decision by choosing among the proposed alternatives. The problem of choosing a new product with attributes A against another product with attributes B can be described as:

> "Allocation of the resources to the alternatives which will maximize the benefit contribution (value) of the resulting program to a firm given a set of alternatives (projects and proposed projects) which require common scarce resources" (Baker, 1974).

Ali *et al.* (1993), present a non-exhaustive taxonomy of various methodologies that attempt to solve the problem (*Figure 7*). In addition, the authors propose a game-theoretic model to obtain insights into the project selection problem taking into account competitive reactions to a firm's choice of project development strategies and technical uncertainties associated with project completion times (Ali *et al.*, 1993).

Strategic planning is related with the creation and the assessment of the alternatives in order to choose the overall strategy. According to Clark

(1992), the analysis of the decision-making process that is related with the strategic marketing planning is composed of four steps:
1. Analysis of the context.
2. Determination of the plan direction.
3. Determination of the plan strategy
4. Implementation of the strategy.

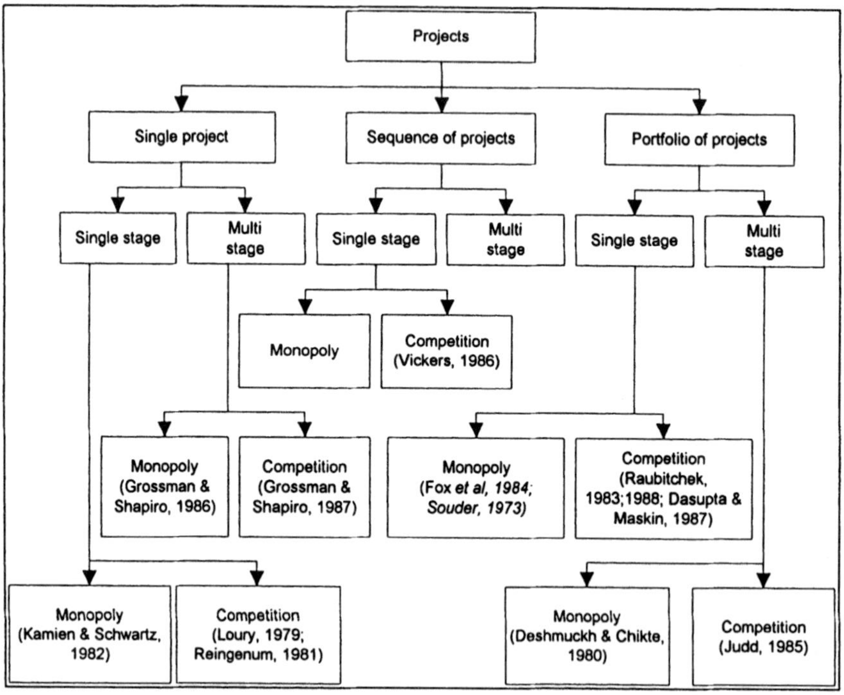

Figure 7. Taxonomy of project selection problem (*Source*: Ali *et al.*, 1993).

The process of marketing strategic planning has certain characteristics such as complexity, ill-structured nature, uncertain and incomplete knowledge, and diversified specialization. The selection of the overall strategy requires the contribution of several departments of the enterprise, such as the human resource management, the financial management, the marketing management, the research and development and the production management. Therefore, marketing strategic planning is considered as a process of distributed decision making.

A new perspective in the process of marketing strategic planning arises from the collaboration of decision aid and distributed Artificial Intelligence fields (chapter 8 §5.2).

7. EVOLUTION OF THE AGRICULTURAL MARKETING

The rise of real consumer income during the post-war period, the increase in the production capacity of the industry, the high degree of product specialization, the expansion of international trade and other factors have resulted in the transformation of markets from product-oriented to consumer-driven. The focus of marketing has experienced several phases, from a commodity phase (agricultural products, manufactured goods, services) to institutional (producers, marketing intermediaries), to functional (buying, selling, promoting, distributing, pricing) to managerial (analysis, planning, organizing, controlling) and to social (market efficiency, product quality, social impact) (Kotler, 1972).

Ritson and Hutchins (1991), identify five overlapping phases in interpreting the factors that influence the changing patterns of food consumption during the period 1940-90: war-time austerity and rationing, return to 'normal diets', effect of income growth, price instability and the "consumption" revolution.

Up to the early post-war period, the evolution of agricultural marketing was similar to that of general marketing theory. Since then, it has developed somewhat differently from mainstream theory. Several reasons have been proposed to explain what has prevented agricultural marketing from using the multidisciplinary approach followed by marketing, thereby keeping its individuality, the two predominant ones being: Marketing is mainly concerned with business decisions and objectives, while agricultural marketing has been developed primarily as a policy subject concerned with governmental intervention (Bateman, 1976).

The structure of farming consists of thousands of small businesses where individual farmers have little contact with the final consumer, and are characterized by a limited capacity to manage the agricultural marketing mix (Meulenberg, 1986; Ritson, 1986).

7.1 Agricultural marketing mix

Special product characteristics. Compared to industrial products, agricultural products are distinguished by their biological nature, bulk and perishability. While other industries processed and adapted their products to consumer wants and needs, agricultural output was considered finalized and ready to be processed for consumption. External factors such as weather and susceptibility to diseases and pests have significant effects on the output and quality of agricultural produce, whose attributes of taste, aroma, color, age, shape, moisture, nutritional value and chemical composition define their quality. The sorting procedure, in which agricultural products are classified according to standardized grades, differentiates them from industrial products. Top grades are processed directly to the consumer, whereas lower ones are treated as raw materials.

A competitive disadvantage is often created in domestic markets with respect to the supply of similar agricultural products from abroad, which can mainly be attributed to limited production capability and quality deterioration. A lesser variability in the quantity and quality of agricultural produce can be ensured by quality control and special post-harvest methods. The similarity of appearance of agricultural products supplied to the market often creates confusion and difficulties for consumers who prefer product differentiation adapted to a balanced and nutritious diet. Quality, taste, convenience, nutrition, wholesomeness and value are the main attributes that the consumers look for in food products (Senauer, 1989).

Price formation of agricultural products. As Kohls and Uhl (1990), point out, the forces affecting agricultural prices can be identified as: supply, depending on farm production decisions, weather, disease, harvested acreage, and food imports; demand, determined by income, taste, preference, demographic factors and exports; food marketing sector, based on value-adding activities, cost behavior and procurement strategies and government policies, through price support, supply control, trade or other general policies.

Among the factors influencing the agricultural prices are periodic expansions and contractions in supply, seasonality of demand and production and consumption patterns. Both economic and behavioral concepts must be taken into account in agricultural product price formation, as prices follow the general pattern of inflation and deflation. Farm prices have always been the focus of agricultural marketing. Low farm prices are considered to be associated with the inefficiencies created by the channel distribution system, resulting in government intervention by establishing institutions such as marketing boards, leading to policy orientation in the marketing of agricultural products.

Promotion of agricultural products. A great proportion of the food industry budget is allocated to product promotion and advertising, in order to develop awareness and perception among consumers in the expectation of further demand expansion for a product.

Several studies (Goddard and Amuah, 1989; Liu and Forker, 1988; Powers, 1989), examine the effectiveness of generic and brand promotional programs for oranges, liquid milk, oil and fats. A positive relationship with the consumption effect has been revealed. Overall, the promotion of highly differentiated products has been more effective than the one of generic products.

Kohls and Uhl (1990) report that two marketing strategies are frequently followed by food firms: (1) product differentiation, seeking to find a product's unique features which set it apart from its competitors; increased brand loyalty with a less elastic demand is expected and market segmentation, concerning the development of unique product variations that will be better perceived by different consumer classes and market segments.

Agricultural product design and promotion are based on distinct factors such as attributes of the particular variety, possible health effects and region of origin. Promotional strategies and activities in general should pay great attention to the nutritional content and to the overall product contribution toward a healthy diet. Capewell and Penn (1986) report that studies conducted in the UK indicated that while few consumers are health addicts, many are becoming aware of the link between diet and health, although this feeling is weaker amongst the elderly and low income earners. Petroni (1991) identifies an increase in consumer preference, which has recently been created for natural foods without ingredients that can affect the organoleptic properties of the product or harm health.

A significant difference has been distinguished by Frohn (1991), in the EU countries in food advertising distribution between the two large media groups. In Portugal, Greece and Italy, electronic media prevail, while in Denmark, The Netherlands, Germany, France and Great Britain, printed media are the prevailing forms of advertising.

Distribution. Baker (1990), distinguishes four routes usually utilized for channeling, distributing and delivering fresh agricultural products to the consumer: (1) producer - consume; (2) producer - retailer - consumer; (3) producer - wholesaler - retailer - consumer; and (4) producer - broker/agent - wholesaler - retailer - consumer.

At the farm level, the sale of the raw products either to agricultural cooperatives or to food processing companies is mainly based on factors such as available information, convenience and price. At the food processing stage, a study of European companies showed that the production of greater technological value is necessary to respond to the changing needs of the consumer; in fact a general ageing of the population is occurring in the major industrialized countries as well as an increasing sensitivity towards food quality and safety (Petroni, 1991).

Food retailing has significant effects on food wholesaling, processing and farming. The relationship that exists between processing, wholesaling and retailing is complex, interdependent and concentrated. The highly competitive retail environment coupled with the demand for high quality produce has contributed to the changing nature of the business relationship between retail buyers and fresh produce suppliers (Knox and White, 1991). To control factors such as timing, delivery, price, quality, packaging and own-labeling, food retailers have often reached back to the beginning of the marketing distribution channel. According to Davies (1990), retailers have become far more proactive in their dealings with suppliers and in their control over distribution. Their role is that of a product marketer for the supply chain.

Transport and storage procedures are also part of the food marketing distribution system; both occur at each stage. While the transport function creates both time and place utility, storage creates only time utility. The bulk, perish ability and production characteristics of agricultural products require transport and storage facilities equipped with new technology. Transportation and storage are of great importance in agricultural marketing since raw products are seasonally produced but consumed throughout the year.

Certain agricultural regions are characterized by the fact that a large percentage of the local agricultural production is controlled, processed and marketed by cooperative organizations.

7.2 The implications of EU integration on the marketing of agricultural products

For the agricultural sector, the Single European Market implies the free movement of goods, the eventual elimination of barriers to trade, common prices and effective health protection legislation. For supply, a greater potential for new market development is expected, and for the consumer greater product choice and price range. A common agricultural strategy was implemented through the Common Agricultural Policy (European Documentation, 1987) to increase productivity to ensure a fair standard of living for the agricultural community, to stabilize markets, to assure the availability of supplies and to guarantee reasonable prices for consumers. The CAP's ability to achieve the objectives of the Treaty of Rome and to adapt to the constantly changing circumstances has been subject to considerable criticism.

A study of the EU fresh fruit market (Martinez and Quelch, 1991) revealed that European markets differed significantly in per capita consumption, taste and preference for varieties, sizes, quality and color. There is a broader distinction between consumers in Mediterranean countries, where excellent quality fruit is produced, and where there are strong preferences for size and quality, and the Northern European consumers with less demanding tastes. A similar conclusion was reached by Henson and Loader (1991) in examining food consumption patterns in Europe, recommending a predictable split between Southern and Northern countries.

Organic products: a new market prospect? A recent demand has risen for agricultural products produced either organically or without the use of synthetic chemicals (Lampkin, 1990; Ophuis, 1991). Community regulations legislate the production, preparation, marketing, labeling and inspection of organic products, thus improving their credibility in the eyes of consumers and helping these products achieve a more distinctive profile (Council Regulation, 1991). Different names have been adopted in different parts of the world for organic products: some of the common ones are biological, natural, ecological and alternatively - produced products.

The Euro consumer: a possible reality or a myth? The new marketing environment of the single European market is a challenge for many food marketing firms, an opportunity for a greater product and market development; others regard the business merger wave and the constantly increasing market power of the main wholesale and retail associations as a threat to their survival. Exogenous factors such as health, environment and resource use are of great importance to most European consumers. Therefore, special effort is awaited by the agribusiness firms for these factors to be integrated in their marketing approach. The use of biodegradable packaging, for example, is one of the many required.

Consumer wants and needs are the focus of marketing strategy. Preferences and trends in the EU are difficult to predict. Henson and Loader (1991) concluded that the Euro consumer does not yet exist but distinctive segments across the continent do and that consideration should be paid to identifying and servicing them. A similar conclusion for the Single European market was reached by Uhl (1991), who tested a hypothesis of market convergence for the EU and the US.

A slow but continuous homogenization of European markets was predicted by Martinez and Quelch (1991). The free movement of workers, easier travel across borders development and an increasing concentration of pan - European television and other media, are among the factors that may indicate further similarities among European consumers.

7.3 Research background

Research methodologies in agricultural marketing are mainly based on:

1. Statistical, econometric and data analysis methods;
2. Network, causal, multidimensional, heuristic and behavioral modeling.

A typology of relative key studies is presented below:

Statistical methods. The most common statistical techniques used are frequency distributions, cross tabulations, ANOVA, factor analysis and discriminant analysis. All were used in a market segmentation study conducted on behalf of the International Olive Oil Council (IOOC) in 1990 in the United States of America.

Cluster and factor analyses were employed in an effort to group the EU countries and identify the variables contributing toward consumption similarities. This study, by Henson and Loader (1991), showed that groups of EU countries had certain consumption similarities for specific food products. The groups were West Germany - Denmark, Portugal - France - Italy, Greece - Spain and France - UK - Portugal.

Factor analysis was applied in a study to establish beer drinkers' attitudes to certain aspects of the beer market and revealed two factors by which drinkers perceive beer: masculinity and experience, and physical and social effects (Ness, 1986).

The same procedure was also used in a survey examining the role of health and environment as product attributes, their relationship to other product characteristics and their mutual relationship in the perception and preference of food products using a conceptual model for health and environment as product attributes (Ophuis *et al.*, 1992). Perceived product quality was composed of the position of a product with respect to a number of quality attributes.

The Kolmogorov-Smirnov technique and the McNemar test were used in a study examining the main factors affecting the export marketing of Cyprus wines in the UK (Morgan and Sarris, 1991). Consumer perceptions and attitudes toward taste, purchase cost, labeling, packaging, reputation and chemical composition were studied.

The analysis of variance (ANOVA) method was used in a survey to evaluate the level of agreement/disagreement with attitudinal statements related to food choice (Marshall *et al.*, 1992).

Econometric methods. The basic relationship of retail demand to generic advertising of processed grapefruit and the movement of grapefruit juice prices were examined by Lee (1981). An estimate of retail demand for grapefruit juice was based on the advertising effect on the consumer.

A switching regression analysis was performed to examine the effect of a coupon promotional program on coupon redemption behavior by the Florida Department of Citrus (Lee and Brown, 1985).

A study by Menkhaus *et al.* (1988), identified factors with a significant impact on consumer purchase and reorder decisions of a branded low fat fresh beef product. An estimation of logit functions relating the probability of beef purchase and reorder decisions to consumer demographic characteristics, meat purchase behavior factors, beef product characteristics, and post-usage test product appeal was made.

Non-linear squares, Box-Jenkins' procedures and Gauss-Newton numerical methods were employed in a study conducted by Liu and Forker (1988).

An empirical analysis of the Canadian fats and oils market (butter, margarine, shortening and vegetable oils) determined the own and cross commodity effects of advertising expenditures on each good (Goddard and Amuah, 1989). The model was based on a two-stage optimization process, which assumed that consumers allocated their budgets in two stages: determination of aggregate consumption of fats and oils, and determination of consumption of individual fats and oils.

According to Lee *et al.*, (1989) advertising impact occurs in two forms: a necessary exposure required before a consumer decides to buy, and a sales impact for an extended period of time. The restriction that the consumer faces is the selection of goods and services best satisfying his needs and wants within his budget restriction.

The two-stage least squares (TSLS) method was used in a study of demand response to weekly advertising of fresh California - Arizona navel oranges (Powers, 1989).

Multiple regression and Box-Jenkins time series techniques were employed in a study with respect to factors affecting the demand for olive oil, the examination of the effect of price and income elasticity and consumer price forecasting (Escribano and Mili, 1990).

To estimate a demand system for meats in EU countries, an econometric model, the linear approximate almost ideal demand system was utilized (Canali, 1991).

Network modeling. Total cost in an agricultural marketing system is the sum of production, handling, processing, transportation and storage costs. A study by Garcia-Diaz *et al.* (1982) compared the minimum-cost constrained network flow models with the standard linear programming, transportation, and transshipment models. Special attention was paid to the efficient integration of the physical, spatial and temporal aspects into the network model.

A causal model. A causal model of food store patronage behavior was used by Meulenberg and Steenkamp (1991), which assumed that patronage is a function of the distance to a store and its image. The latter was assumed to depend on price, product quality, assortment, service and atmosphere.

Multidimensional modeling. Multidimensional measurement and analysis procedures are appropriate for determining the major attributes through which food products are perceived by consumers and for examining the existing relationships between these attributes and consumer preferences (Wierenga, 1980). The attributes that a consumer takes into account with agricultural and food products are both physical (nutritional value, health impact) and psychological (social status, side effects).

In the same way, multicriteria analysis and data analysis models (principal components and correspondence analyses) were jointly used to analyze the choice behavior of wine and olive oil consumers in different European countries (Baourakis, 1994).

The multidimensional scaling technique was used by Ness (1986) to produce a perceptual map displaying the position of the various brands with respect to certain attributes. This technique was employed by the IOOC (1990) to determine and design an optimal message strategy in the US market.

A heuristic model. The Danish Ministry of Agriculture undertook an extensive research consumer study as part of its attempt to enhance consumer choice in the food market through assessing product characteristics of organically versus conventionally grown foods and to provide information for the design of campaigns for organic foods (Grunert and Kristensen, 1992). A heuristic two-part model was designed: the micro, with value - attitude - behavior / hierarchy and socio-economic conditions, and the macro, representing the market situation.

Behavioral modeling. Tuorila (1987), examined consumer behavior and behavioral intention in relation to different types of milk focusing on: subjective experience related to a shift from one milk type to another; overall liking of non-fat, low-fat and regular-fat milks; the use of the Fishbein model is in predicting consumer behavior and beliefs and evaluations.

II

PART II. INTELLIGENT SUPPORT SYSTEMS

Chapter 4

Information Systems

1. INTRODUCTION

It is very important to acknowledge that due to constantly and rapid changes in the market environment decision makers should possess at the right time the right information in order to arrive at the most appropriate decisions (Gale, 1992). Effective decision making within an enterprise calls upon the existence of on time and valid information (Schewe and Smith, 1980), thus providing additional advantages to any company against its competitors (Lewis, 1990). In their presentation, on the awareness of the information consequences, Garvin and Bermont (1983) state that every problem in an enterprise is in fact an information problem. Davis (1987) recognizes the underlying constraints for the decision makers, in the information process and problem solution, the variety and complexity of the required information, along with the existence of cooperation problems among decision makers and analysts regarding the determination of the information requirements. He proposes a gradual approach, consisting of five steps, in order to determine the information requirements for the development of a strategy.

Today's market conditions forces decision-makers to become more competitive through the improvement of their decisions (Kotler, 1994). Moreover, the need for effective decision-making is the factor that maximizes the importance of the need for information (Schewe and Smith, 1980). Inadequate or inaccurate information may lead to improper decisions and consequently to other substantial damages for the company (waste of time, waste of money, increase of cost, etc).

The value-importance of information is assigned by the decision maker who utilises this information (King, 1977; 1978; 1988), thus information should be treated as an important company asset (Eccles, 1991). Benefits resulting by the utilization of information through information systems should be related to the improvement of the company in decision-making and strategic tasks rather in the cost reduction and the improvement of company's efficiency.

In 1979, Myers *et al.* observed the wide gap between the vast volume of the available information and the small degree of its daily utilization. A substantial number of researchers have since then worked on this phenomenon (Ferris, 1979; Kroeber and Sprague, 1980; Fletcher, 1983; McLeod and Rogers, 1985; Johnston and Woodward, 1988; Oasis, 1989). Most of the devoted research involved the study of information systems' use as a similar equivalent term with information, rather that the study of information itself. A global conclusion of these studies is that in order to avoid this gap, the importance of the information should be accepted by the company prior to any attempt of its elaboration through information systems. The ideas of information diffusion and management, have been extensively elaborated by a significant number of researchers, among them: Albaum (1964), Ackoff (1967), Tricker (1971), Mintzberg (1971; 1975), Allen *et al.* (1979), Nonaka and Nicosia (1979), Piercy (1980, 1983), Pfeffer (1981), Piercy and Evans (1983), Davis and Olson (1985).

In general, the information available to the decision makers exhibits a number of problems and obstacles. According to Kotler (1966; 1994) the most common and significant problems involve:

- Validity of the acquired information.
- Non-existence of adequate information.
- Existence of redundant information.
- Diffusion of the information within the numerous departments of the company. This fact stresses the required efforts to solve even small and rather simple problems.
- Concealing of information from various company employees due to the existence of mistakes.
- Important information usually arrives too late.

This fact directs the companies to the necessity, on one hand, to develop and operate an information system, and on the other hand, to establish an appropriate infrastructure in order to conduct market surveys. Besides, Kotler has pointed out the importance of the use of computer systems since 1966. Usually, the process of the market survey is used by information systems as a technique for information gathering about specific products (Montgomery and Weinberg, 1979). According to Cox and Good (1967), the use of management information systems results in the improvement of the information quality, thus aiding the decision makers in:

- The control and assessment of the planned activities and decisions, which they can compare with those actually made, because of the application of the marketing information systems.
- The marketing planning process.
- In the decision making process with the provision of forecasting models of the application results of the possible alternative decisions, in order to choose the most applicable among them.

McLeod (1993), proposed a model that could be used in the management of the various information resources (computer hardware and software, information specialists, users, facilities, databases, information) of an enterprise (*Figure 1*). The information resources management (IRM) model presents the effects of all the different users (executives – users) on the management of information resources.

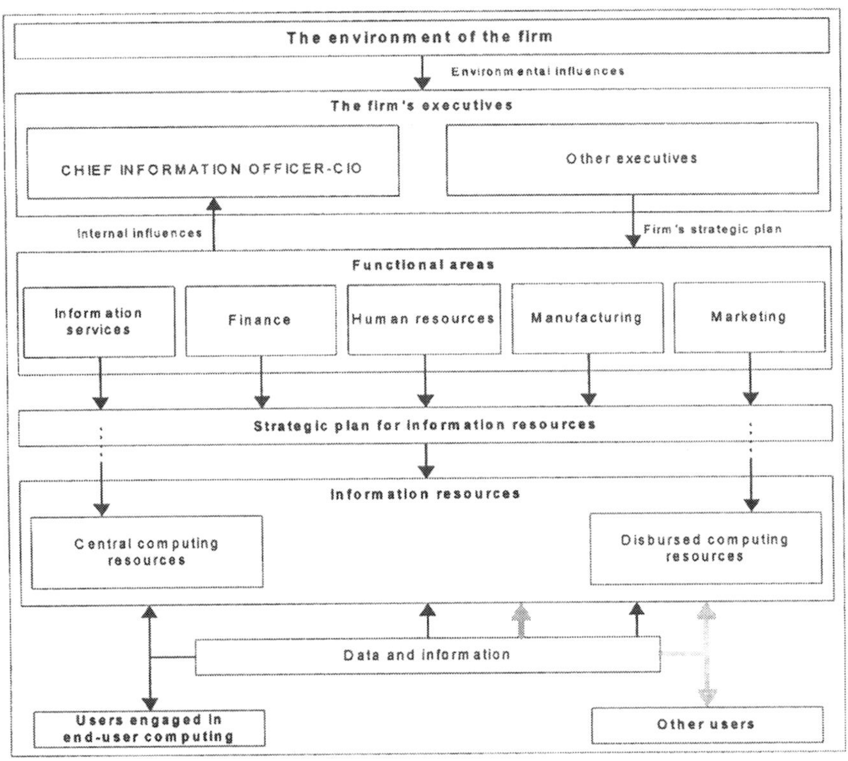

Figure 1. The information resources management (IRM) model (*Source*: McLeod, 1993)

We may broadly define as an information system (*Figure 2*) a set of media of information collection, storage, processing, analysis and diffusion aiming at the attainment of a certain goal. An enterprise may encapsulate numerous different types of information systems, such as:

- **Stand-alone.** Information systems, which are developed and operate separately in order to implement certain tasks.
- **Grouped.** Information systems that operate basically as stand alone units but also are able to work jointly and support each other in order to implement a certain task (output data of one system can be transmitted as input day to another system).
- **Networked.** Information systems that operate in a network environment following the client-server architecture.

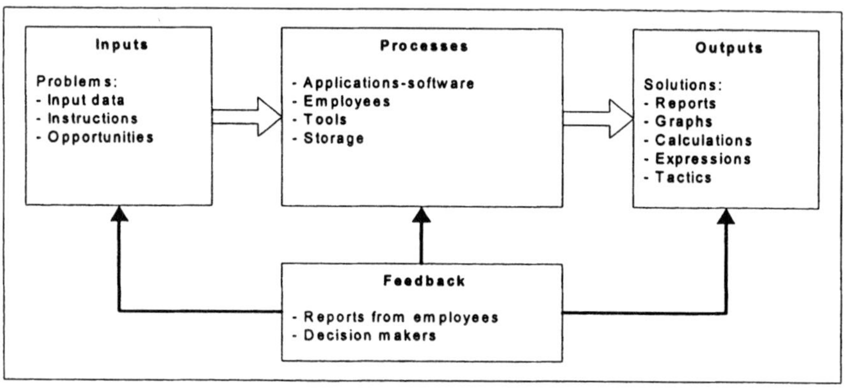

Figure 2. Information system (*Source*: Turban *et al.*, 1996)

Even if the above definition encapsulates all the types of different information systems, in practice it is accepted that the term information system refers to computer-based information systems only.

Thus, we define as computer-based information systems those information systems that use computer technology (hardware and software) in order to support their users in the implementation of their tasks and goals.

The term information technology is usually related to the technological aspect of information systems (hardware, software, databases, CD-ROMs, CD-RECs, printers, etc), whereas as some times it is also used as an equivalent term for information systems or for the group of information systems of an organization or an enterprise.

2. THE STRATEGIC ROLE OF INFORMATION SYSTEMS

The majority of businessmen and managers considered that information systems are indispensable for the support of the operations and functions of an enterprise, but they do not exhibit satisfactory results in important business tasks such as: market shares, profits, development of new entrepreneurial initiatives, etc. This opinion changes, day by day, and now it is considered that the role of information systems is to provide competitive advantages to the enterprises. However, this point of view cannot generate, in any case, the certainty that each enterprise that develops and uses information systems achieves a priori the anticipated results in the implementation of the target goals. The principal cause of failure stems from the fact that the developed information systems are adapted to the underlying outdated organizational structure of the enterprise and solve current problems. The attainment of competitive advantage with the help of information systems is related with the reorganization of management operations and procedures within the company's environment as well as with the increase in the utilization of specialized information systems (DSSs, EISs, ESs) of high level executives-decision makers in order to solve specialized problems.

Annual surveys, held under the supervision of Datamation (a specialized journal on information systems), showed that during the last years, the most significant role of information systems is to support the organizations in their effort to:

- Increase of productivity (reduction of cost, increase of effectiveness).
- Quality improvement.
- Formation of competitive advantages.
- Structure and formation of the company's strategy.
- Reorganize and recreation of the company mechanically.
- Reach better and more effective decisions.
- Respond directly to the customers' demands and to changes within the company or its environment.
- Receive a large volume of data.
- Creativity improvement and innovation promotion.

3. COMPONENTS - STRUCTURE OF INFORMATION SYSTEMS

The term software engineering was originally introduced in two NATO conferences in 1968 and 1969 in an attempt to organise in a collective manner the production of software related products. Constantine, one of the pioneers in structured software design, developed a hierarchical decomposition method. His worked inspired many other researchers like Yourdon and Constantine (1975); DeMacro (1978); Constantine and Yourdon (1979); Gane and Sarson (1979) who wrote their books on structured analysis. Until then the existing methods only covered a part of the software life cycle phases. The structured analysis method (DeMacro, 1978) was initially applied in systems' analysis and design but soon the method expanded and covered all the phases of the life cycle. Since then, new techniques have been developed, all of them grounded upon in the above original ideas. In general, there are two types of system integration, technical and functional integration (Hale *et al.*, 1989; Brooks, 1989).

Technical integration is divided into three types:

1. Vertical integration of information systems.
2. Horizontal integration of information systems.
3. Project integration.

The goal is to improve the effectiveness by an overall reengineering of several functional procedures, thus providing the enterprise with additional competitive advantages (Benjamin and Scott-Morton, 1988; Clemons and Row, 1991). In the following sections two types of operational integration are described:

1. Vertical integration of functions.
2. Horizontal integration of functions.

The term compatibility denotes the measure of logical correlation between the tasks carried out by the users and the modules of the information system used for the completion of these tasks (Johnson, 1989). In essence, compatibility represents a measure of the information system's quality design.

Project integration is especially suitable for the development of information systems, because usually users of information systems employ many of their subsystems, guiding the developers of the systems to seek for the provision of a better level of service and more benefits by the system's usage (Sääksjärvi and Talvinen, 1993).

4. THE SYSTEM LIFE CYCLE

The software products also have a life cycle that begins with the apprehension of a new idea for the development of a new product and reaches until the moment of its retraction from the market or from its cut-off. In addition, the life cycle also includes all the activities necessary for the development, operation and maintenance of the system.

Numerous software development models have been elaborated aiming at the description of the various stages of the software life cycle (Yourdon, 1989; Norris and Rigby, 1992), such as:

- The waterfall model (Royce, 1970; Boehm, 1984; IEEE, 1983; Rook, 1986).
- The spiral model (Boehm, 1988).
- The stepwise refinement and iterative enhancement model (Wirth, 1971).
- The prototyping model (Agresti, 1986; Carey, 1990; McLeod, 1993).
- The operational model (Zave, 1984).
- The automatic programming model (Agresti, 1986; Stahl, 1986; Parnas, 1985).
- The software reuse model (Davis *et al.*, 1988).

These models, in general, describe broad categories of software development bypassing detailed references to specific cases. In fact, software development models cover the general principles of software development, whereas the development and maintenance of a software product are adapted to its development conditions (company, users, development team, existence of managers, expertise of the analysts, underling hardware, etc). Techniques stemming from the software technology science are applied in each development phase.

Table 1 below presents the main activities of the information systems' life cycle.

Table 1. Information systems' life cycle phases

Phases	Activities	Documentation
Requirements' analysis	Assessment of users' requirements Feasibility study Determination of user's demands Preparation of tasks planning	Users' requests Suggestions and cost estimation Feasibility study Requirements' analysis Project planning
Requirements' analysis	Assessment of users' requirements Feasibility study Determination of user's demands Preparation of tasks planning	Users' requests Suggestions and cost estimation Feasibility study Requirements' analysis Project planning

Phases	Activities	Documentation
Logical design	Preparation of general design specifications Clarification of users' demands	Functional description Data requirements documentation
Actual design	Preparation of detailed design specifications Determination of subsystems Design of the database structure	Specifications of system and subsystems Specifications of databases Program specifications
Program design	Program codification Test of program modules Modules documentation	Program documentation
System integration	Test of subsystems modules System's tests Users' training Data conversions	Test planning Report on test results Users' manual
Installation and operation	System operation Maintenance of the new system System's appreciation	Operations' manual Maintenance manuals Assessment report

5. SYSTEMS' PLANNING, ANALYSIS, DESIGN, IMPLEMENTATION AND USE

The development of information systems emphasizes on the following points:

- The acceleration of information systems development
- The use of 4th generation languages, which support graphics, data base management system, interaction capabilities, queries submission- answers, report generators, data dictionaries, word processing, reusable code, software development library, data access security, etc.
- The development of prototypes for the experimental test of the applications during the conductions of tests. A prototype is a software product that is developed within short time and includes all the basic functions of the final product. It is used in order to perform the necessary checks, track down the errors and examine possible additional requirements and functions. The improvements are then applied to the system and the procedure is repeated until the construction of the final product.
- The use of structured development techniques for the development of applications by CASE (Computer-Aided Software Engineering) tools. These tools in combination with structured data analysis techniques aim at

the automation of development of large-scale and complex information systems.

- Development of applications using Object-oriented programming techniques and languages.
- Development of open architecture systems. It aims at the independency of data, logic and procedures. The developed applications will be independent from the development platform, easy to modify and integrate with other applications.

5.1 Structured system's analysis-design

A system is developed in order to cover the needs and requirements of an enterprise, an organisation, etc. Thus, initially the objective goals of the system under development should be defined. The first phase of the system's development process is the determination of the system's requirements (specifications). During this process the requirements of the system are recorded, analysed and determined. This enables us to obtain a description of the system's possibilities in order to check whether the system satisfies its development goal. The requirements of the system to forms and types of information and the respective functions-processes that produce or transform the information are determined in this phase. In addition, other non-operational issues are clarified such as the validity and security of the provided information, the factors that affect the function of the system, and so on.

During the system's design phase the functions-processes are transformed in order to facilitate the easy implementation of the system with the available hardware and software tools. This allows the determination of the modules that perform specific functions-processes such as the way of data management, of user-system communication, and other functions.

A more thorough study of the available methods and tools used for the specification of system's requirements and for system's design can be found in IBM, 1974; DeMacro, 1978; Gane and Sarson, 1979; Yeh, 1982; Alford, 1985; Ross, 1985; Whitten *et al.*, 1989; Yourdon, 1989; Sommervill, 1992.

5.2 Development tools

In order to develop software of a certain quality according to the principles of structured analysis it is necessary to use appropriate tools. Thereby, the graphical representation of the system's functions and reasoning are accomplished by using the following tools (Yourdon and Constantine, 1975; Myers, 1975; Gane and Sarson, 1979; DeMacro, 1978;

Yourdon, 1989; Gibson, 1989; Norman and Nunamaker, 1989; McCusker, 1991; Lindholm, 1992):
- Data Flow Diagrams – DFD.
- Data Dictionaries – DD.
- Structure Charts – SC.
- Data Structure Diagrams – DSD.
- Data flow diagrams.

For a more detailed examination of these tools see Yourdon, 1989; Whitten *et al*, 1989; McLeod, 1993.

6. COMPUTER-BASED INFORMATION SYSTEMS (CBIS)

A flashback to the evolution of Information Systems shows that the first computers were designed to calculate formulae for scientific and military application during, and immediately after, the Second World War. The first business application appeared in the beginning of 1950. McLeod (1993), used the term "computer-based information systems (CBIS)" to describe the five application categories that use computers (*Figure 3*). Bocij *et al.* (1999) use the same term in order to differentiate these systems by paper-based IS. Today the term Information System implies only computer-based Information Systems.

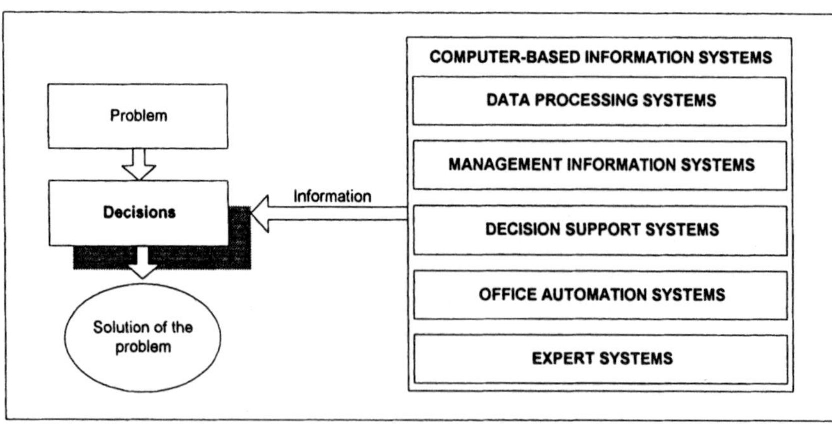

Figure 3. Computer-based information system model (*Source*: McLeod, 1993)

Figure 4 presents the main categories of information systems according to Alter (1992; 1999); there are also some intermediate types of systems that result by the cooperation and interaction of the main categories

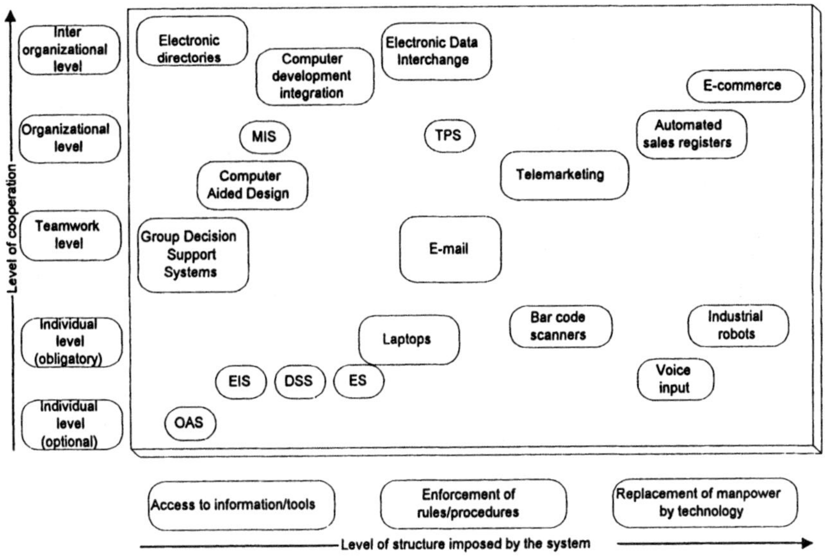

Figure 4. Main and intermediary categories of information systems (*Source*: Alter, 1992)

The decrease of the computational cost and the simultaneous increase in the capabilities of computer systems justified the use of information systems in solving business and managerial problems. A new generation of information systems, following the first generation of Data Processing Systems, appeared in the 60's. These were systems that specified, organized, summarized and reported information in regard to the decisions in operational areas. Such systems were named "Management Information Systems (MIS)", and they are primarily characterized by their capability to produce periodical reports, such as daily lists of workers and work hours, weekly sales reports of the products, monthly expenditure reports, etc (McLeod, 1997).

Initially, Management Information Systems had a historical accession; they described events once they had occurred. Later MIS were used in order to forecast trends and to support ordinary decisions. In the beginning, MIS were typically used by middle level managers, yet their use soon expanded even further with the course of time. Nowadays, MIS reports include specialized statistical reports and many other sophisticated types of information.

In the beginning of 70's advances in computer science and networking enabled the communication among computers. New applications of computers appeared, such as for example the development of on-line booking systems. Systems that employed the capabilities of computer networks and supported the daily tasks found in an office are known as Office Automation Systems (OAS).

Decision Support Systems, appeared almost at the same time. The main goal of DSSs is to support managers in the decision-making process of complex ill-structured or unstructured problems (Holsapple and Whinston, 1996; Sauter, 1997)

The employment of multicriteria decision analysis in the modelling and solving processes of complex decision problems generated a new category of systems, called Multicriteria Decision Support Systems (Siskos and Spyridakos, 1999). Such systems have been used in solving a variety of decision problems in various application areas such as the agricultural sector (Baourakis *et al.*, 1995; Siskos *et al.*, 1995; Siskos *et al.*, 1996; Matsatsinis *et al.*, 1995; Baourakis *et al.*, 1996; Yakowitz, 1997; El-Swaify and Yakowitz, 1998; Hayashi, 2000; Siskos *et al.*, 2001), financial applications (Zopounidis *et al.*, 1997), etc.

In the middle of 80's appeared the first commercial applications of systems that employed Artificial Intelligence techniques. Among them the so-called Expert Systems (ES) were of particular interest. Expert Systems use knowledge in order to identify problems, to suggest solutions, or train personnel.

Executive Information Systems that appeared in the late 80's were designed to support the special information needs of executives. Since most decisions require the cooperation of several decision makers Group Decision Support Systems, were developed in order to support groups in complex decision making situations (Matsatsinis and Samaras, 2001).

Another type of systems appeared in the beginning of 90's. The main characteristic of these systems is their ability to learn. Such systems as the Artificial Neural Networks –ANN, Machine Learning, Intelligent Agents, etc found many applications in the solving process of specialized problems (Matsatsinis *et al.*, 1998, Matsatsinis and Samaras, 1998).

A particular category of information systems is the Geographical Information Systems - GIS). A GIS is a decision support system that encompasses spatial related data in a problem-solving environment (Cowen, 1988; Mennecke, 1997). The systems that arise by this integration are called Spatial Decision Support Systems - SDSS) and were developed in order to support the decision making process in complex spatial problems (Leung and Shatin, 1997).

Table 2 presents a taxonomy of information systems depending on the information and support they provide to the users.

Strategic decisions are made by high-level managers that are supported by EISs or DSSs. Managerial decisions are made by middle-level managers that are mainly supported by MISs where as ordinary decisions are made by special managers or operators that are supported by TPSs. The cooperation and interaction of all these systems is a very usual phenomenon. Actually, in most cases all these systems coexist and operate under a common form (environment); they are discriminated by the particular tasks that they perform, i.e. the intent of their use. For example, the development of an MIS can be based upon an existing TPS; an EIS can be developed by the incorporation of existing and operational TPSs and/or MISs (Millet *et al.*, 1991; Millet and Mawhinney, 1992).

Table 2. Support of Information Systems

Information System	Supports
Transaction Processing Systems – TPS	Central activities
Management Information Systems - MIS	Managers that make decisions in the operational level of a company
(Office Automation Systems – OAS	Secretarial needs
Group Support Systems – GSS	People that work collectively for the attainment of a goal
Decision Support Systems – DSS	Specialized managers and users
Executive Information Systems – EIS	Members of the strategic management level
Intelligent Support Systems - ISS	Managers included in the first two levels of the hierarchy or internal specializes consultant that need support on critical issues from Artificial Intelligence techniques.

According to the above, the various types of information systems may operate either as independent units or as complete inter-supported systems. The basic elements determining these kinds of collaboration are the needs of the enterprise, the development time, the cost and the needs of the users.

Thus, in a long-time operational enterprise, we may have:

a) Systems with specific characteristics that operate autonomously and serve specific needs; these systems, independently, receive input data and produce final results.
b) Integrated interrelated systems that consist of Transaction Processing Systems (TPS), Management Information Systems (MIS), Decision Support Systems (DSS), and Executive Information Systems (EIS). Systems of this type cover either the needs of a single enterprise or the needs of a group of enterprises with uniform activities. The modes and methods of cooperation and interrelation among the various types of information systems vary from case to case (*Table 3*), are constantly evolving and enhancing with the new advances in hardware and software technologies, especially in the field of computer networking.

The various information systems are classified by their developers into certain categories. Mcleod (1993) in an attempt to clarify the concepts of MIS and DSS argues that the key dissociation between the two types of systems depends on who uses the system and for which purpose. We can generalize this approach to state that the motives that lead to the development of a system are not of such importance. What is really important is wherefore the system is used. The use of a system is what determines the characterization and classification of the system; not the system's actual capabilities since these as a rule are not fully exploited by the users and they are known only to the members of the development team.

Table 3. Information systems support to managers

Support	System categories	Types of systems
Executives – General Managers	Strategic Systems	Executive Information Systems (EISs)
Special Scientists – Specialized staff	Support of Executives	Decision Support Systems (DSSs) Expert Systems (ESs) Artificial Neural Networks (ANNs)
Managers	Management Systems	Management Information Systems (MISs)
Line managers – administrators	Operational Systems	Transaction Processing Systems (TPSs)
Personnel	Office Automation and Communication Systems	Office Automation Systems (OASs)
Supported by	Internal and external information Databases	

7. MARKETING INFORMATION SYSTEMS

The classical organization of enterprises around activities and functions (marketing, manufacturing, finance, human resources, etc.) guided the development of operational information systems oriented to each function (McLeod, 1993). Each functional information system makes use of the various types of information systems. Thereby, a marketing information system may contain MIS, DSS or ES subsystems, depending on the attended users. In this section, we will analytically study one of the available categories of information systems, the Marketing Information Systems (*Figure 5*).

Kotler (1966) was the first to point out the importance of using computers in marketing. The first definition of MkIS was given by Cox and Good (1967). The MkIS are an effective tool for the conversion of raw data into useful information (O'Brien *et al.*, 1995). An MkIS can be thought as a set of procedures and methods for the analysis and presentation of information that is to be used in decision-making.

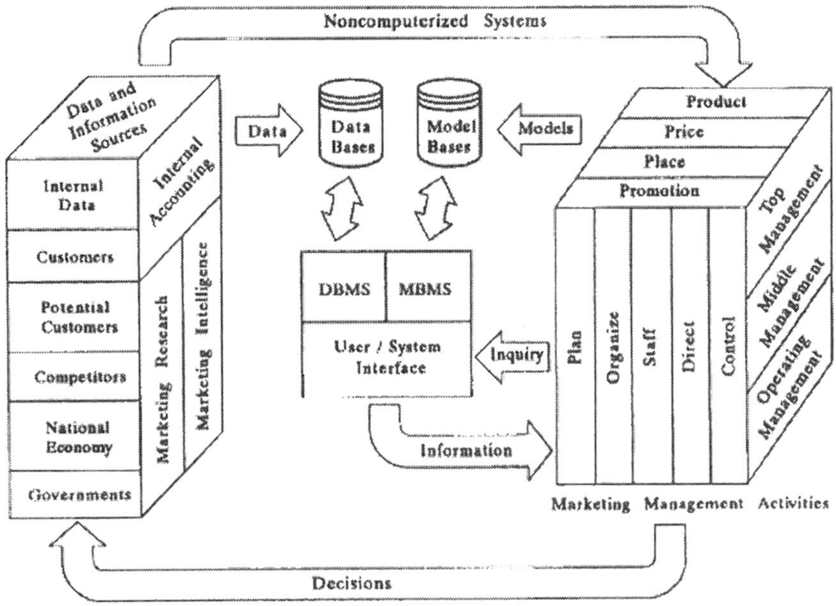

Figure 5. Framework of a Marketing Information System (*Source*: McLeod and Rogers, 1985)

Several surveys on the use of Marketing Information Systems have been carried out in the past (McLeod and Rogers (1985); Berry (1983); Mentzer *et al.* (1987); Li, McLeod and Rogers (1993); Li, (1995). Some of the conclusions of Li's study are the following:

- Marketing managers need computers in order to retrieve, store and process the data.
- The majority of the enterprises gather a large amount of data concerning their customers. Also, enterprises gather information about their competitors and their potential customers.
- Middle-level managers are the regular users of MkIS.
- MkIS are used to support the planning and control operations.
- Most of the resources of MkIS are consumed to support decisions related with the prices and the products.
- The software contained in the MkIS includes models, spreadsheets, conventional/third generation programming languages and database management systems.
- Statistical analysis software, logic programming languages, and expert systems shells are only used occasionally.

The early computer applications in marketing management appeared at the beginning of 1960 (*Table 4*), with the first studies on the use of mathematical models in marketing (Frank *et al.*, 1962; Buzzell, 1964). This was followed by the development of Marketing Information Systems (Brien and Stafford, 1968; Amstutz, 1969), the development of decision calculus (Little, 1970; Lodish, 1971) and the application of econometric modelling (Parsons and Schultz, 1976; Naert and Leeflang, 1978). During the last decades, several applications of Marketing Decision Support Systems have appeared in the literature (Kotler, 1971; Little, 1979; Van Bruggen, 1992).

Table 4. Evolution of computers' use in marketing (*Source*: *Wierenga, 1992*)

Time	Type of systems
1960	Marketing Models
1965	Marketing Information Systems
1970	Decision Calculus
1975	Econometric Modelling in Marketing
1980	Marketing Decision Support Systems
1990	Knowledge Based Systems in Marketing

7.1 Components

A marketing information system (*Figure 6*) is configured by people, suitable equipment and procedures, which aims at the collection, sorting, analysis, evaluation and distribution of on time and proof information to the decision makers. Nylen (1990) defines marketing information systems as interactive systems consisting of procedures and methods that systematically handle the collection and process of information and the generation of reports in order to support the marketing decision-making. Little (1979), stresses on the use of models and therefore employs the term marketing decision support systems. According to Marshall and LaMotte (1992) and Marshall (1996), we refer to marketing information systems like a comprehensive and flexible, formal and ongoing system designed to provide an organized flow of relevant information to guide marketing decision making.

Marketing decision-makers require information about the evolution of issues related with the marketing context (markets, goals, channels, competitors, public relations and macroeconomic possibilities) in order to perform analyses, planning, integration and control. For these reasons, the management of marketing information through the corresponding information systems has become one of the most vital issues for effective marketing (Sääksjärvi and Talvinen, 1993). Marketing information systems may be thought as tools for the conduction of market surveys, planning, analysis of alternative actions, reporting, budgeting and control (Vandermerwe and Carney, 1987; Higby and Farah, 1991). The marketing information system weighs the information needs of the decision-makers, processes and produces the necessary information and supplies these information on time to the decision-makers. The processing of information is performed by the four subsystems of the marketing information system, which are described below.

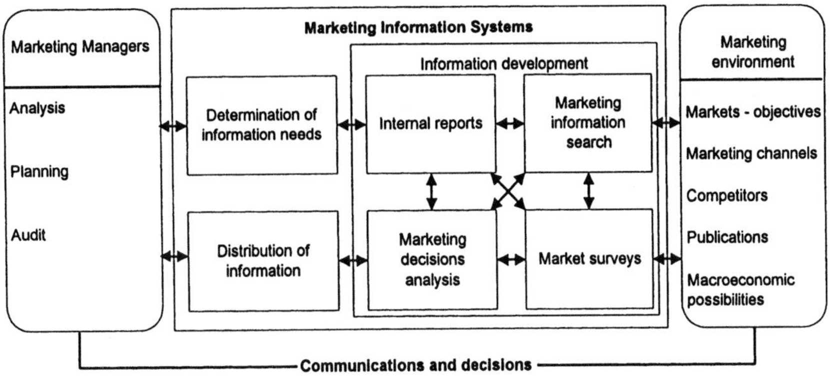

Figure 6. Marketing Information Systems (*Source*: Kotler, 1994)

1. **Internal reporting subsystem.** This subsystem includes all the information that lie within orders, sales, products' cost, products' quality, inventory, cashing, payments, and any other type of reports that circulate within the enterprise. These information are scattered in the various departments of the enterprise. The subsystem is responsible for the gathering and processing of this information.
2. **Marketing information search subsystem.** This subsystem consists of a set of procedures and means used by the decision makers for their daily information about the current evolutions of the external marketing environment. Thereby, the decision-makers are able to catch on the actions of the competitors or the needs of their consumers and make on time decisions.
3. **Market survey subsystem.** Apart from the secondary information acquired by publications, books, etc., an important type of information is the primary information that may be acquired by gallops, sales forecasting or advertisement effectiveness studies. This information is acquired through the conduction of market surveys. The term market survey denotes the systematic planning, collection, analysis and formulation of the results related with a specific marketing problem of the enterprise. They are primarily conducted for analysing the market shares, analysis of sales, study of the market trends, analysis of the characteristics of the market, study of the pricing policy, etc. The

evolvement of market surveys and the improvement of their effectiveness has been substantially supported by the fast evolution of information science, the development of suitable techniques for the construction of questionnaires, the employment of operational research, data analysis methods, other mathematical models, etc.

4. **Marketing decision analysis and support.** This subsystem consists of a statistical models database (descriptive statistics procedures, data analysis models) and of a decision models database (pricing models, consumer behaviour models, product design models, etc). With the additions of these two databases the marketing information system is upgraded to a Marketing Decision Support System (*Figure 7*).

Speaking more generally, we may state that all the marketing information systems consist of:

1. The information collection module. The information is acquired from:
   - External sources (secondary sources, competitors, distribution channels, interesting markets, etc).

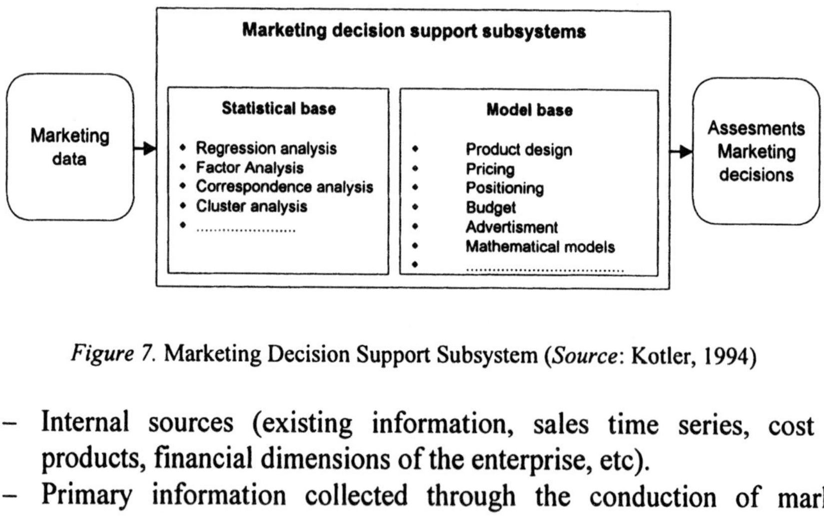

Figure 7. Marketing Decision Support Subsystem (*Source*: Kotler, 1994)

   - Internal sources (existing information, sales time series, cost of products, financial dimensions of the enterprise, etc).
   - Primary information collected through the conduction of market surveys.
2. The information processing module consisting of:
   - The database management subsystem in which the data is saved. Prior to the storage, data should be codified in order to allow the effective elaboration of the information by the system.
   - The statistical processing subsystem (descriptive statistics, data analysis methods.
   - The marketing models management subsystem.
3. The user-marketing information system interface subsystem, which is used for the presentation to the decision maker of:

- General reports on the existing data.
- Answers to the questions posted by the decision-maker (what-if).

Martell (1988), supports that Marketing Information Systems (MkIS) should be considered as components of Management Information Systems (MIS). A marketing support system may constitute the component of a more general information system or a component of a decision support system. (Fletcher, 1990). On the other hand, Moriarty and Swartz (1989) presented an integrated marketing system, which they described as marketing and sales productivity system rather than marketing information system. The difference is that marketing information systems handle all the issues, functions and tasks related with marketing, whereas the other type of systems handles only partial tasks. Other systems of the same type have also been presented by Fletcher *et al.* (1988); Proctor, (1991); Burns and Ross (1991), and Sisodia (1992).

According to Marshall (1996), a simple MkIS (*Figure 8*) consists of the following five components:

a) The internal environment.
b) User interface.
c) Databases.
d) Applications software.
e) Administrative supports.

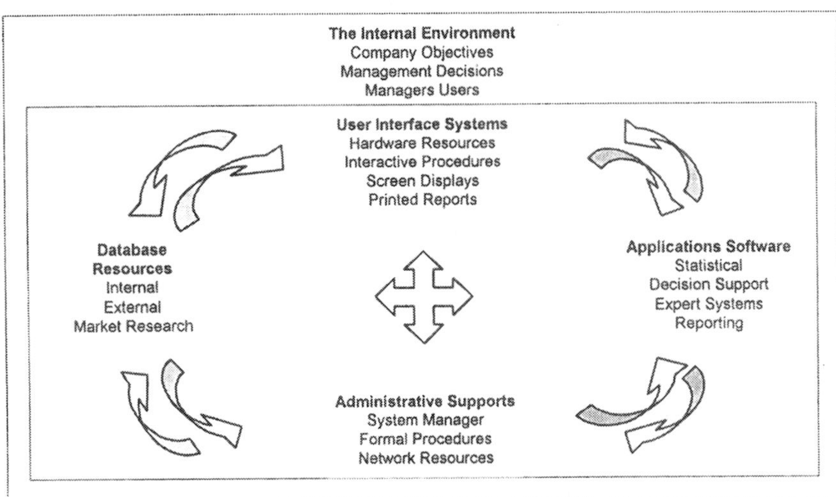

Figure 8. MkIS components (*Source*: Marshall, 1996)

8. ELECTRONIC COMMERCE – EDI – VIRTUAL ENTERPRISES

Electronic commerce is a process that gives the opportunity to companies to maximize their performance with the minimum possible cost. However, the most important fact is that potential customers are able to purchase the available products or services of the company / organisation from any geographic location.

Electronic commerce, the application of which slips the narrow borders of a country and spreads universally, is heavily favoured by today's information intense society and in general by the propensity of societies to converge to commonly accepted standards. The growth and evolution of electronic commerce depends on the following:

- The growth of electronic market
- The formation of confidence climate.
- The involvement of the technology.
- The inter functionality of services and the interconnection of networks.
- The establishment of uniform structural and juridical framework.
- The amplification of the interest of potential users
- The continuous support.

With the wide spread of Internet, which is the basic operation media for electronic commerce services, several critical issues arise, which concern the support of automated processes that will handle, through the Internet, the computer-to-computer communication minimizing the human intervention and the adoption of mutually accepted methods for electronic payments.

Of course, the integrated and really broad solutions that result from using Electronic Commerce services require a suitable technological environment. The Intranets, the various networks within each enterprise that are used for sharing data, applications, and other information systems resources have been proven to increase the overall efficiency of the enterprise; in addition the use of networking technologies improves the collaboration, reduce the bureaucracy, accelerate the processes and are the first step to adopting Electronic Commerce.

Today, Electronic Commerce services that are provided in the Internet are primarily restricted to retail commerce services. However, retail commerce services consist only a small fraction of the services that can be supported by Electronic Commerce, such as legal, financial, credit, accounting, medical, citizen support services and many others. However, an important volume of commercial or banking transactions are currently dispatched by private networks and value added networks, which mainly support business-to-business data exchange. Even though these systems provide several safety processes their use obstructs the expansion of

Electronic Commerce over the Internet, because the latter has a business-to-consumers spirit.

One of the most important issues is to preserve the security feeling of the parties that are involved in each transaction of Electronic Commerce. Since all the transactions and the exchanges of documents are automatically handled by computers, private and confidential data should be safely kept out of sight of possible unauthorized intruders.

According to Ahuja (1996), the success of Electronic Commerce on the Internet faces two risks:

1. The lack of significant amount of sales.
2. Problems related with legal and network security issues.

Welz (1995) cites that likely by the year 2000, 2/3 of the Internet users in USA will consist of consumers and only 1/3 of companies and academic users. The author argues that an additional reason for the small number of on-line business is that clearly Internet is not a medium exclusively devoted to the enterprises; however Internet can play an amplifying role of retail commerce. Currently, almost 20 million people have Internet access, a number that is going to rise dramatically in the near future.

However, the use of Internet for Electronic Commerce requires the solving of some problems, namely:

- Lack of efficient security, despite the fact that several security standards have been proposed and developed.
- The majority of protocols/standards do not encompass additional features to provide the support and quality of the security services, which they offer
- Even today, it is difficult for the typical consumer to find the products and services that are supplied in the Internet, despite the fact that browsing in the World Wide Web is a task that can be handled by the majority of consumers through modern browsers. The availability and continuous expansion of search engines may be the solution to this problem.
- There are no mechanisms to reserve the copyrights.
- There is a significant lack of uniformity.

The existing insufficiencies are discouraging, in a certain extent, especially the small-middle enterprises, to adopt e-commerce services. In particular, current laws cannot encourage small-medium enterprises to use e-commerce since e-commerce is characterized as open-systems platform and each organization has adopted measures and standards that are particular to each country or geographic location (Mitrakas, 1995).

There are several international organizations that have been established in order to study the legislation of electronic data interchange such as the TEDIS (Trade EDI Systems) in Netherlands, the EDIFORUM in Italy, the

EDI Association in Great Britain, the American Bar Association in USA, the EDI Council in Canada, and the Electronic Commerce Organization in Australia.

The technology of open-networks, the continuous progress of information technology and telecommunications, have shaped a new communication environment that favour the rapid expansion of electronic exchange of messages and the evolution of e-commerce, which today is identified with EDI. These factors set up the platform on which the e-commerce is based on. On the other, the roots if electronic data interchange are traced to the initiatives of the National Information Infrastructure and Defence Information Infrastructure in USA. The idea of commercial exploitation of on line information and telecommunications systems was born with the development of large-scale systems by CompuServe in USA and by MiniTel in France.

In order to guarantee the safety of the transactions and the open and straightforward exchange of information several specifications have been developed (*Table 5*). Typically, secure electronic commerce through Internet, requires the existence of the following three components (Ahuja, 1996):

a) Internet & Web services
b) Security services
c) Electronic commerce applications

Table 5. Issues related with security in e-commerce

Requirement	Security principle	Technology
Determination of user's identity	Identification	UserIDs
Verification of user's identity	Authentication	Passwords ή Certificates
Protection of confidential data	Confidentiality	Encryption (ISO 7498-2)
Verification of data intervention during the network transfer	Data Integrity	Message Digest
Verification of the message's source	Source Authentication	Digital Signature (ISO 7498-2)
Confirmation that the sender sent the message and the recipient received it	Non repudiation	X.509 Certificates

It is not an overstatement to say that Electronic Data Interchange (EDI) is the most important and most prominent application of the new systems in information communication. EDI is defined as the exchange of structured information through installed computer applications among different organizations (companies' departments, companies, etc), using predetermined standards.

Another definition describes EDI as a technology for exchanging business documents between organizations through computer systems, using a prescribed and computer processible standard (form). It is considered as a form of technology that can support only the communication of information with a higher level of structure, that is a dialogue form among computer systems, in theory without requiring human interference. The automatic transfer of information requires the structure of information in some pre specified form according to some rules, so that computers can identify and use any type of transferred information, with the least possible human interference.

The main reason for the limited spread of the EDI technology in the early phases of its development was the inability to clearly define the standards necessary for the exchange of information. However, today the problem has been effectively solved with the emergence of quality assurance standards.

Despite the fact that EDI is a relatively recent technology, it has already provided substantial benefits to companies, business branches (for example industrial sector) and also to the functional and organizations of the state. It can be thought as an opportunity to exchange messages electronically and to replace the vast volumes of business paperwork and also as a novel form of business activities and communication with the form of electronic commerce. This is why EDI is called by many people as «commerce without documents» or «communication without documents» and constitutes the shortest communication path between collaborative organisations in now days.

From an organisational point of view, EDI can be seen as a cooperation technology among organisations. From a technological point of view, the type of the informational interdependence of the related organisations is the heaviest factor that affects the ability to adopt and successfully apply EDI as a medium that enhances and supports collaboration (Doukidis *et al.*, 1993).

Recently, due to the presence of factors such as the time pressure for decisions and actions, the complexity of the rapid market changes and the existence of global competition, many organizations collaborate with other organizations or individuals, thus creating new corporate forms called virtual enterprises. However, we should not confuse the notion of virtual enterprises with the traditional consortiums or other forms of corporate collaborations. Virtual enterprises exhibit a significant number of differences when compared to past forms of corporate cooperation. First, the goal of the collaboration is focused on the development and production of a specific product or a project. They are very flexible and in most cases, they have a very short life cycle. Virtual enterprises are primarily based on capabilities rather than historical affiliations or cost relations. Finally, virtual organizations are far more complex. It is very common phenomenon, virtual; organizations to consist of companies that are parts of global networks of virtual alliances that include customers and competitors or companies that provide research, design, production, marketing, and other supporting services (Grenier and Metes, 1995).

The same notion of Virtual Organizations is described in the literature also by the terms Virtual Organizations, Virtual Corporations, or Strategic Networks.

A Virtual Enterprise is a short-lived network of independent companies or departments of the same company that includes suppliers, manufacturers, marketers, and customers, which are connected by computer technology in order to communicate and share capabilities, cost and market shares. Each independent company or department contributes to the network's efforts according to its especial capabilities. An important feature of the network is the complete lack of any type of hierarchy structure or the existence of a very flat hierarchy that is focused on the functionality of the value chain. The Virtual Enterprise is represented to the outside world by the network manager, which is the person responsible for the connection of the partial skills and capabilities. Internally, the network may be organized and managed according to guidelines provided by the management and administration principles either by a co-operator in chief, the network manager, a leading committee, or the technology of computer science itself (for example: workflow systems, GroupWare, executive information system, etc). (Erben and Kersten, 1997; http://www.virtual-organization.net).

The International Association of Virtual Organizations, IAVO, reports that the roots of the Virtual Enterprises spring from the rapid development of telecommunications, commenced at the end of the last decade. Basically, a Virtual Enterprise is any business group, society, institution, governmental party or any other entity, the existence of which depends-partially or entirely- on the progress of the telecommunications, and mainly on the progress of network technologies such as Internet. In other words, the idea of developing Virtual Enterprises was based on the rationale that organizations no longer need central support services in order to implement their processes and that the activities of their members will not be reduced because of the dispersed geographic nature of the network.

We could summarize the factors that impelled the vast and rapid progress of the Virtual Enterprise under the following:

- The rapid progress of the electronic technologies that facilitates the digital, wireless transmission of text, video, and voice.
- The steep flooring of computer networks.
- The progress in telecommunication technologies that allows the organizations to efficiently respond to their customers, reduce their cost and allow their employees to provide their services from their homes (Yager, 1997).

Actually, a Virtual Enterprise is a network with nodes that represent a particular service. This service may be provided by an individual, or a group of people or even a company. The skills and knowledge of the entire nodes result in the ability of the organisations to respond to its obligations. More likely, a Virtual Enterprise employs a small number of employees. They are the heart and the soul of the organisation and in many case its financiers. They ensure the coordination of the partial activities and set the goals and standards. The small number of employees renders the existence of a central administrative service unnecessary. On the contrary, much of the required work could be actually accomplished at home. Computer technology permits the dispersions of the nodes anywhere in the world and together permits them to operate at different times.

We could summarize the basic characteristics of a Virtual Enterprise under the following:

- They constitute very flexible forms of collaboration.
- In terms of cost, they are efficient and effective.
- They are established and winded up continuously.
- They take advantage of informatics with innumerous ways.
- They motivate their employees or their co operators to versatile develop their professional and labour activities.
- They are decentralized.
- They are based on a dynamic network of suppliers, vendors, and clients.
- They reduce the production cost but increase the necessary coordination cost.
- They abolish the concept of space and time in the work.
- Their operation is based not on the existence of a strict hierarchy but on the acknowledge skills and knowledge of the nodes.
- The existence of members and infrastructures that are continuously adopted to different situations.
- The management is based on the mutually undertaking of responsibilities and not on the observance of assignments.
- The search for efficient methods of working and not the keeping of pre specified procedures.
- The addition or the suppression of nodes depending on the current needs and requirements.

There are at least five conditions, imposing the formation of Virtual Enterprises:

1. Today, organizations need to balance between innovative organizational structures, which require a networked approach, and structures that ensure the complete coordination of actions, which require a strict structured approach. Many existing organizations base upon structures of the second type than on structures that follow the networked approach.

2. Labour is increasingly related with knowledge and the process of information rather that the production of material products. Even, in production the important thing is the way the product is delivered to the customers and not the way it is produced or manufactured.
3. Knowledge can be efficiently exploited only when there is a wide basis of experts with different viewpoints, expertise, age, knowledge, education, and culture.
4. Responsibilities and also the interconnection of the various responsibilities become increasingly complex. The variety of the business environment continuously increases by the support of the novel technologies and communications. There is a plethora of alternatives; simplified solutions can no longer be applied to the business problems.
5. The role of managers changes from that of the "boss" to that of the facilitator, of the instructor, of the mentor or the advisor that makes efforts to impart knowledge and experience (Skyrme, 1997).

Chapter 5

Decision Support Systems

1. INTRODUCTION

In the beginning of 70's, the notion of "Decision Support Systems" (DSSs) appears in the science literature, signifying a new perception of the role that computer systems can play in decision making procedures. The interpretation of the term is not always the same. The different point of views, from which researchers perceive and describe DSSs, have lead to the formulation of various definitions of the term DSS itself.

Little (1970) defines a decision support system as a set of procedures for data and reasoning management, which aim to aid managers in the decision-making processes. Such a system is considered to be successful if it is simple, robust, adaptive, complete, easy to use and equipped with a nice user interface.

Keen and Scott-Morton (1978) gave the following classic definition: "DSSs combine the intellectual abilities of humans with the abilities of computer systems in order to improve the quality of the decisions made. DSSs are computer-based systems that are used in order to support decision makers in ill structured problems" (see also Alter (1977) and Huber (1980)).

In the beginning of 80's Bonczek *et al.* (1980), Moore and Chang (1980) and Keen (1980), introduced three additional definitions of the term DSSs based on the perception on what the system really performs and how a DSS accomplishes its objective (*Table 1*).

According to Sprague and Carlson (1982), a DSS is a set of procedures, which with the help of a computer aim at the expansion of the decision maker's cognitive space regarding the confronted problem. The above definition has been extended by Andriole (1989), Sage (1986; 1991) and Adelman (1992), to the following final formulation: "Decision support systems are interactive computer-based systems (software) which use analytical methods such as decision analysis, optimisation algorithms, etc, in order to develop appropriate models that will support decision makers in the formulation of alternative solutions, the resolution of the reactions amongst them, their representation and finally in the choice of the most appropriate solution to be implemented."

Table 1. Characteristics of DSSs definitions.

Definition	Based on
Little (1970)	System's operation and the characteristics of the communication between the user and the system.
Keen (1980)	System's development procedure.
Bonczek *et al.* (1980)	System's components.
Moore and Chang (1980)	System's utilization and capabilities.

According to Zeleny (1982), the role of DSSs is to extend the capabilities of decision makers so that the solutions proposed by them become better over time and not to propose solutions that are better than those solutions that decision makers can understand.

The above point of views on DSSs reflects Simon's ideas, already expressed in 1960, on the ways to approach decision problems. In his book Simon states that in fact the scepticism on the choice of a solution between a satisfactory and an optimal solution is not important considering that an optimal solution cannot be specified, therefore we should simply focus on the quest of a feasible solution. Actually, the cognition and skills of the decision makers are limited therefore we should try to expand their cognitive space and extend their abilities so that to improve the quality of the decisions they make

By using a DSS one tries to improve the quality of information on which a decision is based on whereas the system provides a number of alternative solutions rather than one simple solution. This helps the decision makers to understand in depth the nature of the problems and accordingly to improve their decisions.

Various scientific fields contribute to DSSs development. The theoretical framework in decision analysis, which is considered to be critical in order to design useful and original approaches for the selection of the most appropriate decision, is provided by the scientific field of Management Science/Operations Research (MS/OR). Behavioural and cognitive science participates with the study of the ways people and organizations process information and make decisions. Computer science provides the necessary hardware and software DSSs development tools. Finally, the Management

Information Systems (MIS) field provides the design and operation database management tools.

DSSs support all the different phases of a decision making procedure, according to Simon's model (Simon, 1960), which is presented in §4.2.1 (Figure 4.1), contrary to Management Information Systems which support only the intelligence phase) and management science which mainly supports the choice phase and partially the design phase. Expert systems, which will be discussed later in this chapter, provide support to all the phases (Sprague and Carlson, 1982; Turban, 1993).

The main justification for having difficulties in establishing a globally accepted definition on DSSs is probably the fact that these systems combine together three different concepts (Keen, 1987). Hence:

- The concept of "decision" is related, on one hand, to non-technical operational and analytical aspects of DSSs, and on the other hand, with the selection criteria of their applications.
- The concept of "support" focuses on the integration and comprehension of the ways people operate and act as well as on finding ways to help them.
- Finally, the term "system" focuses on the technical expertise of design and development.

Each one, of the already expressed definitions, approaches more effectively one of the above concepts and therefore a lack of balance is observed amongst them. As a result, none of them is completely representative of what a DSS actually stands for.

Keen (1987) stresses that the development of DSSs during the next decade should follow the following objectives:

- The broadening of scientific cognition
- The research, and finally
- The application.

Eom and Lee (1990) presented a state of the art on DSSs applications between 1971 and 1988 while in 1993 Eom *et al.* examined the existence of a semantic structure between the various DSSs types using factor analysis. Also, by using cluster analysis Eom (1999), studied the changes and trends in the field of DSSs by examining bibliographic references in two periods 1971-1990 and 1991-1995.

According to Jelassi (1986), there are five DSSs generations in terms of the computer systems technology, their completeness, their autonomy, and the communication method between the user and the system.

- **The first DSSs generation** is characterized by the existence of a single multicriteria method, the system's user interface is poor and the structure of the databases is highly depended by the problems in which the system is used. Thereby, in order to solve new problems the reprogramming of some of the system's modules is necessary.

- **The second DSSs generation** is characterized by improvements at the database design and at the related management subsystem.
- **In the third DSSs generation** a dialogue base and a dialogue management subsystem has been added in order to improve the communication between the user and the system. The communications subsystem is responsible for managing the procedure selection screens, for managing the data management dialogues and for the visual presentation of the system's results to the user.
- **In the fourth DSSs generation** a model base and a model management subsystem has been added. These systems integrate a variety of models and also appropriate mechanisms for generating new models.
- **Finally the fifth DSSs generation** adopts techniques stemming from the field of Artificial Intelligence in order to improve the user-system communication and to provide appropriate consultation to the user in the selection of the best-fit model that will be used in the problem solving procedure.

Despite the fact that the use of a DSS, in general, improves the quality of the decisions, numerous problems arise by the utilization of the systems on various organizations and companies. According to researches conducted from time to time (PCWeek, December 1994; Financial Times, April 1996), the principal causes of failure are related to:

- The difficulty of the decision makers in finding analytical models capable of describing their problems.
- The difficulty of the users in managing the models and other tools that are continuously increasing
- The fact that Decision Support Systems are application specific while they utilize specific input/output formats to each application.

According to the studies of Eom (1989) and Eom and Lee (1991), research in the field of DSSs is mainly focused on Multicriteria Decision Support Systems, Group Decision Support Systems, model managements, system design, and implementation.

We have already mentioned marketing information systems and to their analysis and support subsystem, as described by Kotler (1994). In the next paragraph, we will more closely examine the marketing decision support systems (MkDSSs).

In general, MkDSSs consist of the same components as the DSSs. The main features, fundamental to a marketing decision support system, are similar to features of a DSS (Montgomery and Urban, 1970; Little, 1979; Sprague, 1980; Van Bruggen, 1992), while their difference lies on the way the primary information is acquired. In marketing decision support systems primary information is obtained through market surveys and in some extent

by using appropriate marketing models. According to Little (1970; 1979), Urban and Hauser (1993) these models should be:
- Simple.
- Robust.
- Easy to control.
- Adaptive to new conditions.
- Complete on importance issues.
- Easy to communicate with. An important factor that contributes to this goal is the development of continuously evolving use-MkDSS communication systems.

Marketing models with MkDSSs may represent (simulate) the responses of the market to the various actions of the decision makers. By this way decision makers and marketers are able to prefigure the reactions of the consumers before actually try to push a product in the market. Thus, the decision makers examine closely the effects of numerous decision alternatives in order to choose the most perfectly suited.

Data used by MkDSSs, derive from various sources (internal – external – market surveys, etc). It would be useful here to mention some information sources, which are not self-evident, like (Urban and Hauser, 1993):
- Technocratic assessments made by experts regarding pricing policies, advertisement, etc.
- Results obtained by testing products by the consumers in order to realize their consuming responses. These tests should also be carried out with simulations of market's reactions.
- The results obtained by performing statistical analysis to the historical data available to the enterprise.

The main application scopes of MkDSSs, which coincide with those of marketing management, are according to Little, 1975a; Fletcher, 1990; Nylen, 1990; Urban and Hauser, 1993:
- Strategic marketing planning, which pertains to the allocation of the company's resources so as to allow the company to obtain and preserve competitive advantages.
- Marketing planning, which pertains to various partial actions (e.g. design and development of a new product), that are placed among the company's strategic planning.
- Marketing decision-making.
- Control and evaluation.

Here we could add as a fourth possible application of these systems the study, control and prediction of the reactions of the company's competitors

Van Bruggen (1992) examined the effectiveness of the application of MkDSS, as this was perceived by the decision makers. In general, his conclusion was there are positive results by the use of MkDSS. However, the efforts devoted on the development of such systems do not keep up with their seeming importance. One of the main reasons is the appearing difficulties in the formatted knowledge representation due to the nature of the reasoning used and the experience of the experts in the marketing management area (Leith, 1986; Moutinho and Paton, 1988; McDonald and Wilson, 1990; Curry and Moutinho, 1991).

2. CHARACTERISTICS OF DSSS

According to Sprague and Carlson (1982), the most important characteristics of an effective DSS are the system's ability to:

- Support the decision-making procedure of semi structured or ill structured decisions.
- Support one or more phases of the decision-making procedure (intelligence, design, choice and implementation).
- Combine the co-action of models, databases and techniques for the presentation of the results.
- Emphasize to simplicity and easiness of use, flexibility and adaptability.
- Interact with other operational information systems.

The above characteristics are also the main points of difference on regard to other systems, such as Management Information Systems (MIS). Because of the different opinions expressed on what actually the term Decision Support System stands for, it is preferable to cite the characteristics and the capabilities of such a system than to adopt one of these definitions.

- The use of a DSS use improves effectiveness rather than efficiency.
- DSSs are developed in order to provide support to all management levels not by overriding and substituting the decision maker but by aiding the user who is in complete control of the system during the whole decision making procedure.
- They support groups of people (Group Decision Support Systems) or individuals (DSSs).
- They provide support to all the phases of a decision-making procedure.
- DSSs are flexible and adaptive.
- They are mainly used to provide support to semi structured or unstructured decisions.
- They are user friendly
- They are flexible to easily adaptable to possible changes.

The utilization of a DSS leads to an improvement of the decision maker's decisions and also to the generation of new user demands, which by turn leads to the improvement of the system itself. The development and improvement procedure of a DSS is continuously repeated in relation with the system's use.

We should emphasize here on the clear distinction between efficiency and effectiveness. By using Management Information Systems (MIS) one tries to improve efficiency where as Decision Support Systems augment the effectiveness of the decision making procedures. Decision Support Systems do not substitute Management Information Systems yet they try to complement them in order to aid the decision makers so as to improve their effectiveness.

According to Holsapple and Whinston (1996), a DSS should have the following characteristics (*Figure 1*):

- A DSS contains knowledge relating with specific points of view of the decision maker about his/her environment. These points of view concern the ways to complete various tasks, which conclusions are acceptable in various cases, etc.
- The system is capable of acquiring and maintaining various types of knowledge apart from descriptive knowledge.
- The system is capable of representing the knowledge on an ad hoc basis with numerous customized ways apart from standard reports.
- The DSS is capable of choosing a subset of the accumulated knowledge and to generate new knowledge in order to use during the procedures of problem identification and/or solution.
- It has the ability to interact with the user enabling the user to choose and manage knowledge.

3. DSS ARCHITECTURES

The architecture of a DSS refers to a general framework that identifies the substantial elements of a DSS as well as the interrelationships among them (Holsapple and Whinston, 1996).

Of the available development architectures of a DSS's components connection mechanisms the most well known are those suggested by Sprague and Carlson (1982), Bui (1987), Thierauf (1988) and Turban (1988). According to these the functions of a DSS come under three independent components. This resolution was suggested as necessary in order to more effectively maintain the system, design and develop it in a more simple way, and check its accurate operation. After the piece-by-piece structure of these components, we continue with the integration of the system by constructing connection mechanisms for the individual components. The suggested architectures will be discusses in the sections below.

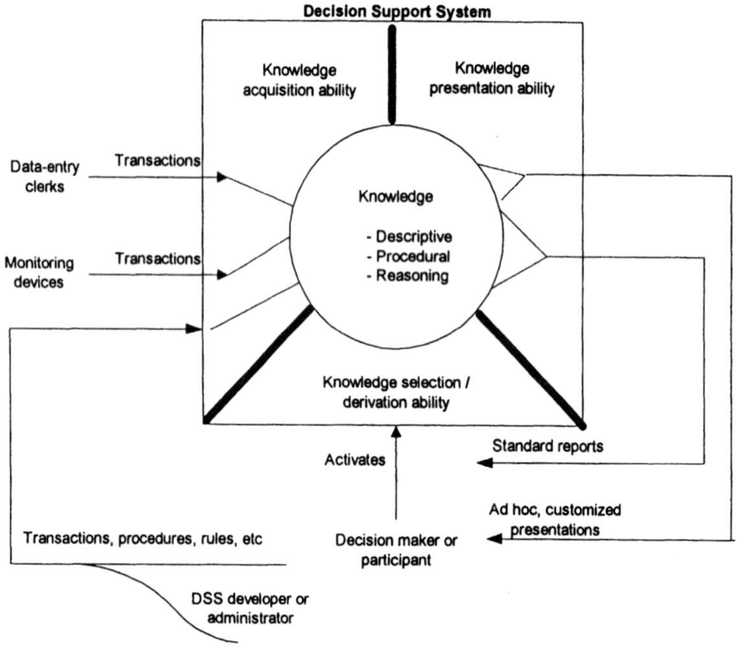

Figure 1. Typical DSS (*Source*: Holsapple and Whinston, 1996)

Network architecture. Network architecture allows different dialogues and models components to share the same data. They also support the convenient addition of new components even if these have been developed in different time, from different people using different programming languages (*Figure 2*).

In order to integrate each dialogue and management components into a DSS, the development of an additional communication component is required. Also, in order to integrate each database into a DSS, the suitable improvement of the corresponding communication components that will use the database is required. Each dialogue or model component requires a communication component. The structure of the network architecture is base on the fact that the relation between the communications component and the other system's components is one to many and also in that multiple communication components are able to communicate together with the same component. It is possible to create different variations of this architecture, as for example, the operation of a single communication component for dialogues and models components, etc. The GMIS system (Donovan, 1976; Donovan and Jacoby, 1977) represents a good example of network architecture.

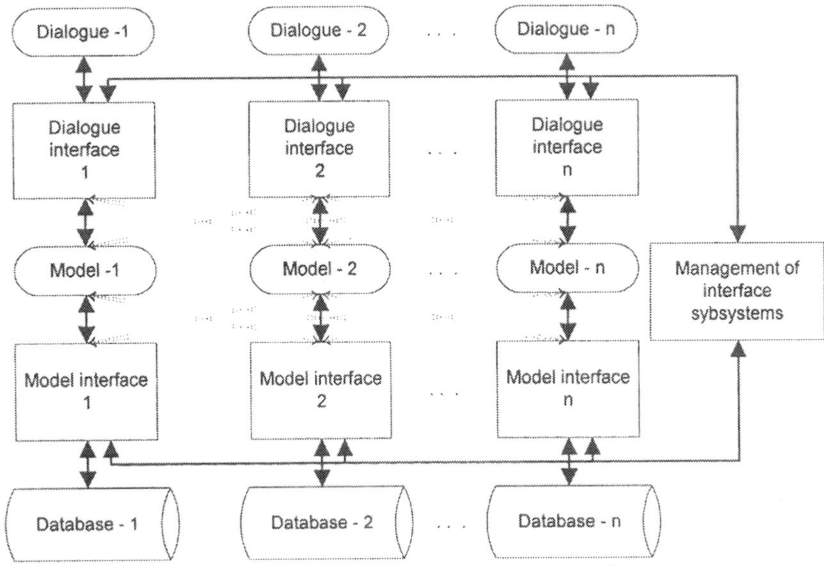

Figure 2. Network architecture

Bridge architecture. The objective of this architecture is to reduce the number of required communication components and also to maintain the ability of extending the DSS by adding new components. The bridge architecture (*Figure 3*) provides a common communication component or a common set of communication components, known as the bridge component, which intervenes between the local dialogue-modes components (single user) and between the common models and databases components. The bridge component performs the same synchronization functions and the same formatting conversions as the communication component in the network architecture, yet it reduces the necessary number of communication components and incorporates their management functions. New components, developed in order to get incorporated into a DSS with bridge architecture, should connect to the bridge component. These points should always be under close consideration when designing and developing such systems. A good example of bridge architecture is the IDAMS system (Erbe *et al.*, 1980).

Sandwich architecture. In sandwich architecture (*Figure 4*) the various models of the system share the same dialogue and database components. The transmission of data between the models components is accomplished by the common databases component while the control of information transmission between the various models is carried out be the dialogue component. Each new model component, in order to be incorporated into a DSS with sandwich architecture, should be able to get connected with both other common subsystems. An example of sandwich architecture system is the REGIS system (Joyse and Oliver, 1977).

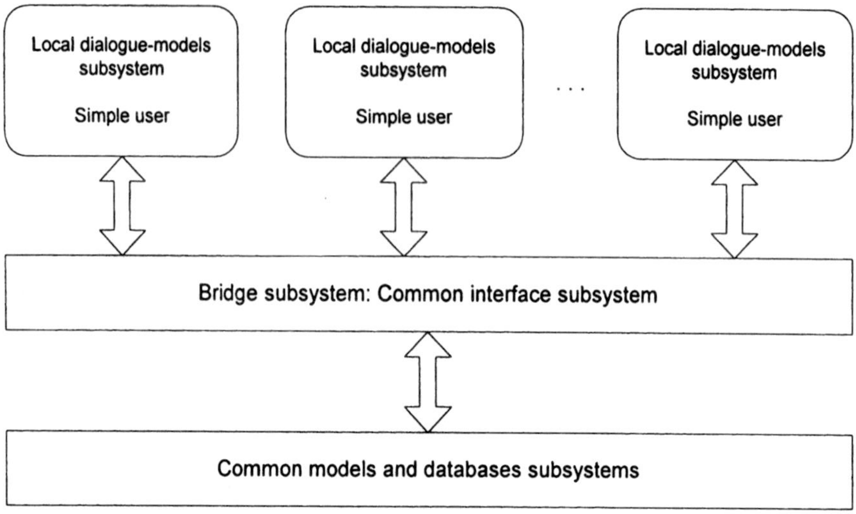

Figure 3. Bridge architecture

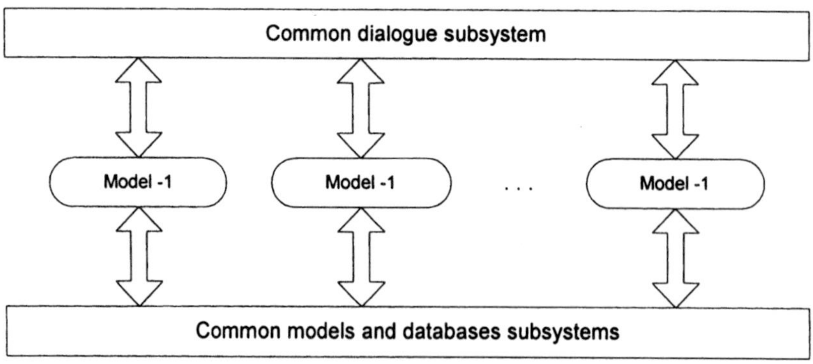

Figure 4. Sandwich architecture

Table 2 contains the most significant advantages and disadvantages of the above-mentioned architectures.

Table 2. Advantages – disadvantages of DSSs architectures

Architecture	Advantage	Disadvantage
Network	Easy to add new components Tracking of the communication components	The existence of multiple dialogue subsystems reduces the convenience of learning the use of the DSS

Architecture	Advantage	Disadvantage
	code resulting in simplification of maintenance and expansion tasks Flexibility in the components distribution	Performance reduction due to the formation of communication queues Operating system dependency Reduction of reliability and stability due to the existence of multiple communication modules
Bridge	Simplicity of implementation procedures Easy incorporation of different types of models components	Performance problems
Sandwich	Allows the incorporation of existing decision support tools Easy learning of the new tools	Limited components control Able to operate only to the same operational environment

Holsapple and Whinston (1996) believe that the above architectures cover only a fraction of DSSs capabilities and for this reason they represent only a special case of their proposed general DSS framework (Bonczek *et al.*, 1980; 1981; Dos Santos and Holsapple, 1989). According to their framework, illustrated in *Figure 5*, DSSs are comprised by four concepts:

1. A language system (LS), which consists of all the input messages of the DSS.
2. A presentation system (PS), which comprises by all the output messages of the DSS.
3. A knowledge system (KS), which consists of knowledge storage spaces and maintained by the DSS.
4. A problem-processing system (PPS), which is the core component of a DSS and which identifies and solves the problems that are placed during a decision-making procedure.

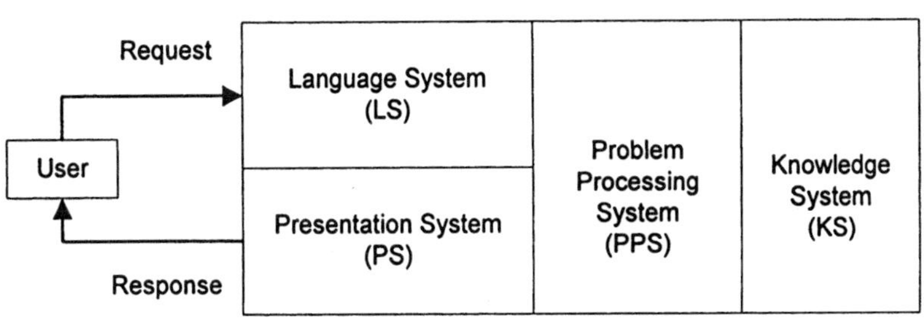

Figure 5. A general DSS framework (*Source*: Holsapple and Whinston, 1996)

This framework contains the bottommost critical and fundamental concepts found in every DSS. There are specific DSSs that use various knowledge manipulation techniques (databases, text, spreadsheets, knowledge bases, models, etc). A decision maker is able to use either various DSSs each of which has a different knowledge manipulation technique or a single DSS, which has multiple knowledge manipulation techniques. *Figure 6* illustrates a compound DSS according to Holsapple and Whinston (1996).

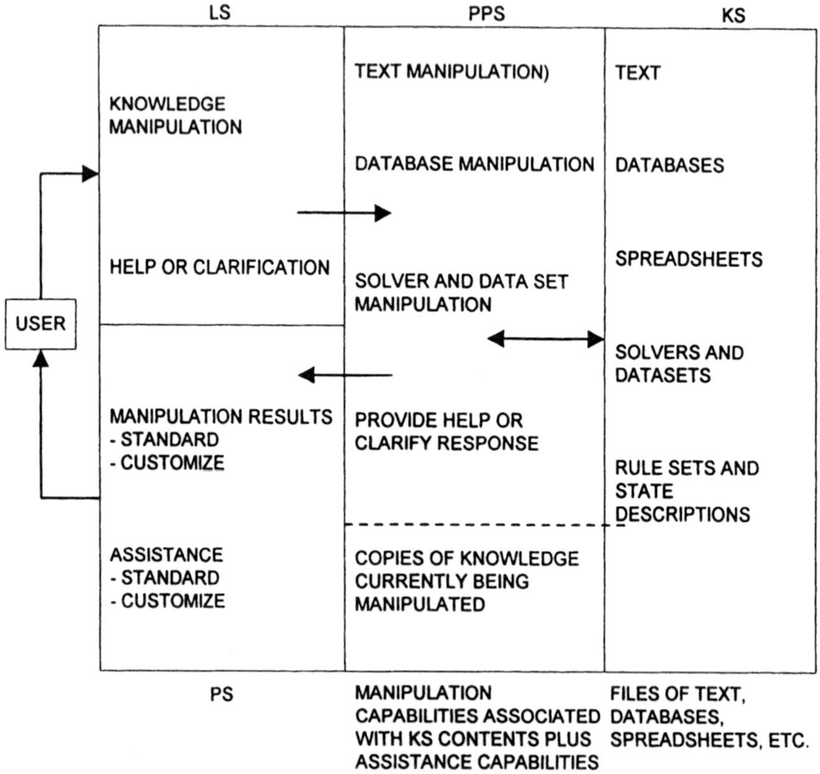

Figure 6. A compound DSS (*Source*: Holsapple and Whinston, 1996)

4. STRUCTURE

An operational decision support system (*Figure 7*), in general terms according both above-mentioned architectures, is comprised of the following modules:

1. Decision maker-user.
2. User-system communication.
3. Data management.
4. Model management.

As it is clearly observed the decision maker is considered to be a section of the system's operation.

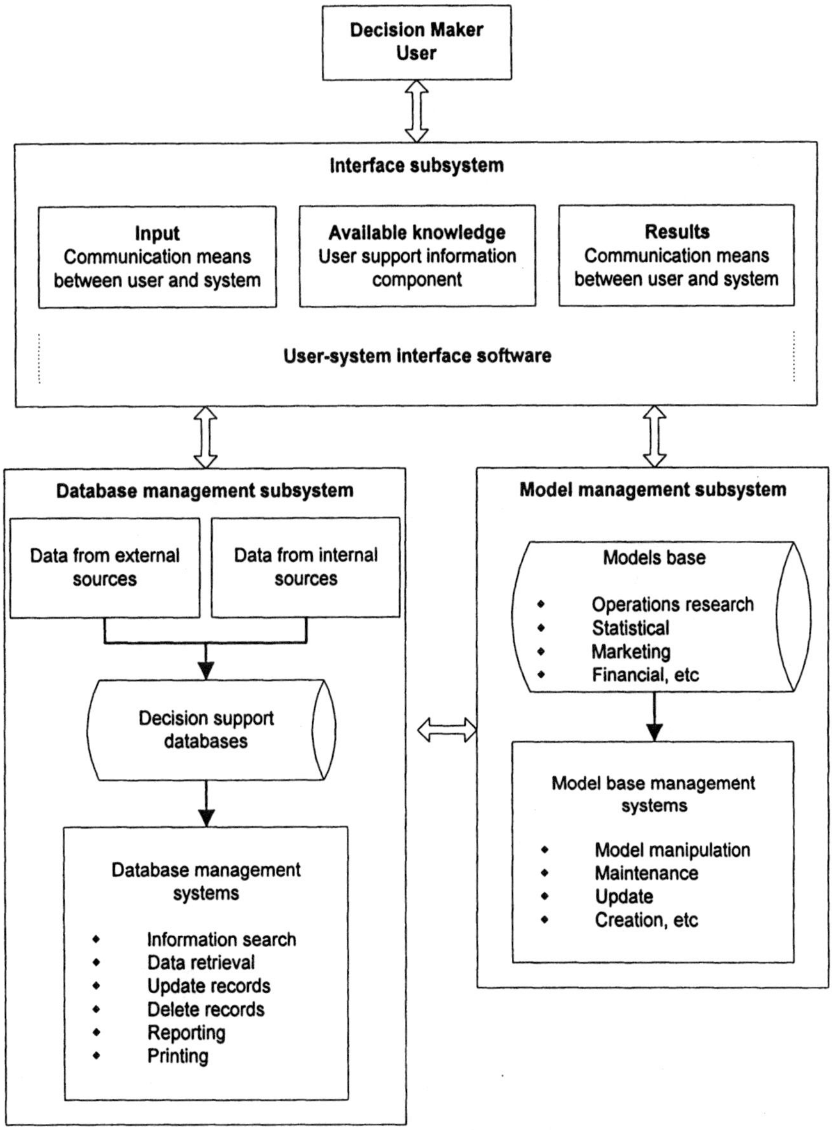

Figure 7. Components of a Decision Support System

Turban *et al.* (1996), believe in the existence of an additional module, referred as the knowledge management subsystem. This subsystem is able either to support the remaining subsystems either to act as a self-contained subsystem providing knowledge in order to solve partial problems. Systems that are equipped with such capabilities are classified as intelligent DSS and are examined more carefully in a following chapter of this book.

4.1 User - Decision Maker

The user of the system is not considered as a specific person that holds a certain position or has a determined level of knowledge or skills. In addition, we do not explicitly know if he is the final decision maker or an expert user of the system or simply someone who participates in the process. However, in general, people who design and develop DSSs should always bear in mind two major DSSs users, the decision makers and the experts in the system's application area.

4.2 Interface Subsystem

A human- computer interface is a vital component of a computer system with the help of which a user interacts with the system in order to complete a certain task and receives reports with the results of these tasks. According to Terveen there are two types of interfaces: a direct one, with which the user inputs information and data into an application (DOS and UNIX applications), and a world, through which the user contacts the visual representation of the system, which he is able to manipulate directly (Windows and other similar graphical environments).

This module consists of the set of means that intervene between the user and the system, thus ensuring the communication between them. The user interface subsystem is considered to be the most important part of a DSS (Sprague and Carlson, 1982), because the user in order to perform any of the desired tasks has to contact the system through the user interface subsystem. According to MacLean (1986) the user interface module of a DSS has two basic dimensions, the ergonomic (appearance, intensity of illumination, colours, position, size, etc) and the communication between the computer and the user. The communication is accomplished by interactive human-computer dialogues. According to Bennett (1977) the following modules comprise the communication subsystem:

a) **User-system means of communication module.** It contains all the available means that the user can use in order to communicate with the system. Examples of such communication means are the keyboard, the mouse, the scanner or optical reader, the joystick, etc.
b) **System-user means of communication module.** This module is used by the system in order to «reply» to the user. System's output is of vital importance in order to effectively support the decision maker. Typical

means of communication used by a system in order to present the results are the screen, the printers, the plotter, etc.

c) **User information module.** Should the user be able to operate the system and exploit all its capabilities requires continuous information in order to increase his effectiveness.

Human Computers Interaction - HCI studies the understanding of how humans use a computer system so as to design systems that can better supply user's demands and needs (*Figure 8*).

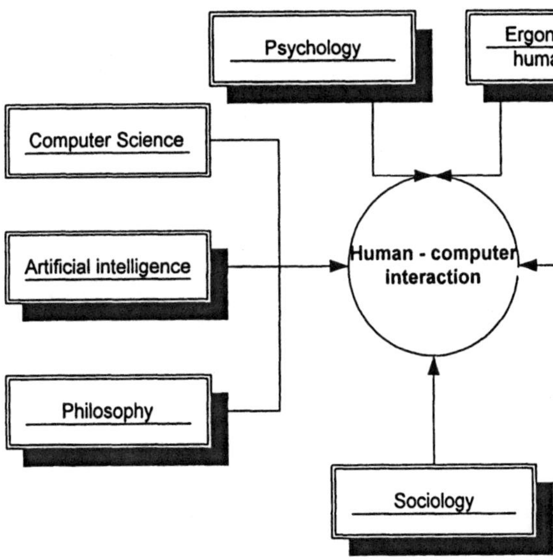

Figure 8. Inter-scientific contribution in the development of human computer interaction systems (*Source*: Preece, 1993)

The user contacts and learns a program-application through its communication system. As a communication system of a software program we consider all the contact points of the user and the specific software. The user is completely unaware of the system's structure, its algorithms, its programming techniques, the structure, organization, and processing procedures of its databases. Therefore, the opinion of the user towards the software depends primarily by its communication system and much less by the perfection of its algorithms' design and development.

Some of the capabilities that the system provides are the following:

- Ensures the communication between the user and each component of the information system (databases, models…).
- Allows the input, processing, and transformation of data, by creating different database structures
- Generates reports that show and print the results.

- It has two or three dimensional graphical capabilities and use of multimedia enhancements.
- Provides user aid and support capabilities as well as other possibilities on learning the user how to use the system
- It can operate in different forms depending the user.
- Ensures the communication between the users in a network environment.

Factors that affect human-computer interaction and should be examined carefully are presented in *Figure 9.*

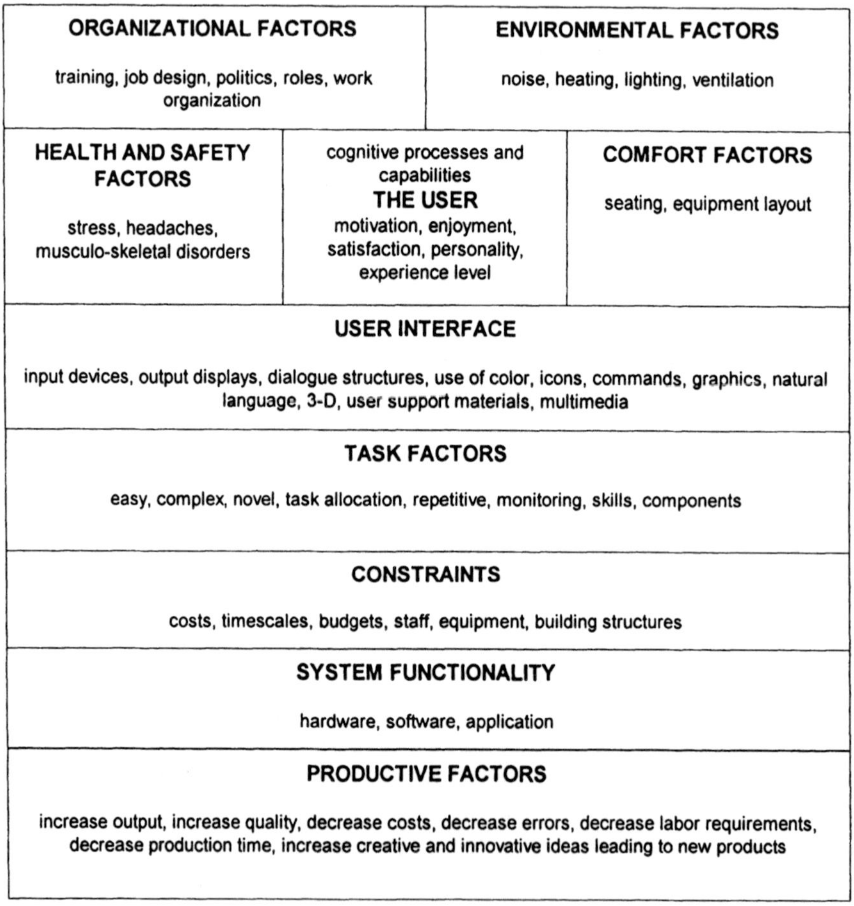

Figure 9. Factors of human computer interaction (*Source*: Preece, 1993)

4.2.1 Types of Communication Systems

Communication between the user and the system is provides by using different forms of communication, such as:

Command line: The input into the system of the desired actions is made by typing certain commands that follow certain syntax from the so-called command line. Each command has a specific result.

Selection menus. The user is able to select a single action by a group of possible selections-commands. Frequently, the menu includes also submenus of allowed actions. Also, there are menus that are selected by clicking one of the «mouse» buttons.

Queries and answers: The communication between the user and the system is accomplished in an interactive way. Some times the system asks the user when it needs supplemental information in order to turn into some actions while other times the user submits queries to the system (what-if, etc).

Natural language processing: It is one of the most intense research fields of Artificial Intelligence. The objective is to develop systems where the questions of the user to the information system as well as the system's answers will be addresses into natural language.

Use of forms and objects: Forms are comprised of various fields in which we can input or change data or select from pre-specified values. A form can also contain images, buttons, or other objects that are activated by clicking the mouse and perform certain actions. All the recent programming languages offer object oriented programming capabilities, providing objects (buttons, images, properties, etc.

4.2.2 Communication Systems with Graphical Capabilities

Recently, the development of new Graphical User Interfaces – GUIs provides the users with the ability to control complex commands and actions through objects.

The basic components of such communication systems are: the windows, the icons, and the tools. Windows are stand alone parts of the screen and can be regarded as independent screens. Each window contains a part of an imaginable surface of a text or an application. Through the windows environment the user can work together in different applications and watch the side results in different windows. He also is able to transfer data, images, figures, and results among the various applications that are executed in different windows. Today, the user is able to see in the screen, text, figures, reports, and graphical results exactly as it will be printed (What You See Is What You Get - WYSIWYG).

4.2.3 Visual Interactive modeling (VIM) and simulations

The employment of modern systems' graphical capabilities in the procedure of interactive decision making and into the representation of the results of operations research, financial, forecasting, marketing, etc models, led to the development of the so-called Visual Interactive Modeling. The development of these techniques was inspired by attempting to solve a series of classical operations research problem, as stated by Dando and Bennett (1981). By using Visual Interactive Modeling the decision makers able to intervene into the decision making procedure, to change data, constraints, assumptions, and to receive, in real time, the results of the application of the utilized models.

According to Hurrion (1986), Visual Interactive Modeling stands for a general term that describes the interaction capabilities of operations research models, which incorporate animation, visual dynamics and graphical representation. He believes that these techniques significantly improved the communication between the systems and the decision makers and also the deeper understanding of operations research models.

By the term Visual Interactive Modeling we consider the procedure of producing and utilizing a visual interactive model in order to recognize problems that are important to the decision maker. The visual interactive system consists of three basic components: a mathematical model, a display in which the state of the model appears, and interactions, which permit changes in the state of the model (Bell, 1986; 1991). Turban and Carlson (1989), consider that visual interactive decision-making is a technique that uses graphical representations, generated by a computer system, in order to interactively signalize the effect of different decisions. Lembersky and Chi (1984), define that Visual Interactive Modeling technique provides an interactive, visual - and not numerical – simulation of the actual decision scenario including the effects of the decision made.

A visual interactive model combines significant (non-trivial) images and easy to use interactions in order to help user's creativity and deep understanding of the problem. By boosting a procedure of "creation and control", facilitates easy learning (Belton and Elder, 1994). According to Bell and O'Keefe (1987), visual displays help the user to understand the behavior of the simulation model

Kirkpatrick and Bell (1989) report a survey conducted by visual interactive models' designers in which 74% of the respondents replied that the understanding of the model on behalf of their clients was improved at least to a small extent by using Visual Interactive Modeling. The same percentage also replied that also the understanding of the modeling technique and its result was significantly improved by Visual Interactive

Modeling. In addition, the survey indicated that 65% of the people replied that the solution they have reached differs significantly from the one that they would have found without using Visual Interactive Modeling, however without indication of the higher quality and performance of this solution. Finally, 88% believed that using VIM helps into the acceptability of the model.

The experience of Bell and Parker (1985) in the installation of visual interactive models led to the conclusion that the intelligible environment, supplied by VIM, can increase the caviling of the decision maker into the solution procedure of the problem. It is self-evident that if the decision maker is able to watch the way a model functions and behaves in a more transparent way then accordingly he/she will be able to better understand the model itself and find out in what extent the model corresponds - or not - to his/her actual needs. An essential advantage of VIM is that it helps the problem analyst to head directly on to the heart of the problem (Bell, 1986; 1991)..

Hurrion and Secker (1978) claim that owing to the fact that users are able to monitor the model in action, they may contribute towards the acceptance and validation of the model, because by this way the use of user's knowledge and expertise becomes attainable in contrast to the case where the analyst would not communicate and cooperate with the user. They also state that VIM improves the model's validity even if the user is not involved during the approval of the model. They support that visual and interactive capabilities are combined in order to allow the analyst to proceed with the model one stage at a time, monitoring the progress and the model in order to verify that the model behaves correctly at actual situations.

The survey on simulation of Crooke and Valentine (1982) details the advantages of Visual Interactive Simulation (VIS), in the augmentation of validity and authentication for both the analyst and the user.

Clients' confidence is a key point in order for a change to occur. If clients do not feel certain for the applied methods or the solutions found it is quite possible to hesitate to apply the changes proposed by the model or the OR method. Hurrion and Secker (1978), state as a factor that contributes positively to the confidence of the clients, their involvement in the validation and acceptance procedures of the models. Interaction, along with the visual contact, plays a very important role for the model's acceptance by the user.

Also, o Bell (1985b) concludes that an essential advantage of VIM is the self-confidence that decision makers acquire exactly because they personally approve the model.

An interactive model allows the dynamic change of priorities (Hurrion and Secker, 1978). They believe that a constant allocation system of priorities in a simulation model is sometimes an oversimplification of the reality because in real situation decision are made in order to change the priorities whenever there is a large burden in some areas of the system. Therefore, is seems logical to use the same dynamic rules in a model of the system.

The interaction of the user, as a result of the simulation process, allows the inclusion of the decision into the simulation. Thus, a large number of systems can be modeled with higher accuracy level (Bell and O'Keefe, 1987). In fact, the user may be incorporated into the model. Decisions that are really hard to be made by the model may be reported to the user during the simulation (O'Keefe, 1987).

VIM, through its supported multiple interface, improves the communication among the user, the analyst, and the model (Hurrion, 1986). It is more than a simple communication between the model and the analyst or between the model and the user. The application of VIM improves the interface of the analyst-user, acting as an interpreter between different cultures.

Animations that are produced during the modeling process is a very useful communication tools between the developer of the model and the user in order to validate the model responds in practice, which in turn increased the confidence towards the model (Porter, 1991).

Communication is also an important factor during the implementation process. By the time a decision maker has accepted and solution derived by an OR method this should be carried effectively to the entire organization. The VIM model can effectively play the role of sound communication kernel, improving the communication among the different organization levels (Porter, 1991).

Lembersky and Chi (1984) presented the way a visual interactive model can be used in the training of wood processing employees. The goal was to increase the profit of the company by training employees in making decisions as close as possible with the decisions of dynamic programming algorithm. They report that the supervisor easily understood the usefulness of the dynamic programming algorithm.

A number of researchers propose that VIM allows the confrontation of new problems that else would not come under the operations research techniques. Bell (1985a), states that management friendly VIM models overcome a basic difficulty in the application of operations research in the solution of executive management problems, namely the stage of identifying the decision maker's criteria. If the decision maker is granted the possibility to participate in the procedure of finding the solution then the need for explicitly identifying these criteria might be inferior.

As already stated, the use of VIM possibly increases the possibility of applying an operation research solution. Gravel and Price (1991), report a case where they devised a solution to a problem by using a non VIM simulation, yet they were unable to persuade the head of the organization to proceed in the application of this solution. Then they developed a visual interactive simulation in order to demonstrate the advantages of the solution and this in fact convince the director to approve the implementation of the solution.

According to Bell (1985a), some VIM advantages are not of vital importance to the decision maker or even the quality of the decision itself, yet they are associated with the objectives of the operations research services provider. He states that visual interactive models may increase the prestige of the operation research service provider and by this way to increase their application scope.

The application of VIM in a certain problem does not guarantee the automatically attainment of all or some of the aforementioned advantages. As with most of the existing techniques there are effective and non-effective ways of applying VIM models. According to Bell (1986; 1991), the attainment of these advantages requires a certain effort on behalf of the developer of the model.

The survey of Kirkpatrick and Bell (1989) showed that studies that used VIM usually last longer than studies that used some other technique. However, this seems to be conversely in proportion with the expertise of the model developer (the bigger the expertise the lesser the time required for the completion of the study). In fact, some of the participated people replied that studies with the use of VIM models last less time. Everett, (1984), stating his long life expertise with the VIM models, reports that time and care of details are necessary for the visual results of the model. Some of Kirkpatrick and Bell's survey participant pointed out that the complexity of the software (necessary for the attainment of the visual and interactive capability) was the cause of the increase of time necessary for the development of the model and of the errors made during the development process.

Bell (1986; 1991), in his report on the conclusion of Kirkpatrick's and Bell's survey, notes that some of the people asked reported that one of the disadvantages of VIM, according to the users, is the tension of unquestioning acceptance of the results. Perhaps, if a "traditional" method, with less convincing presentation capabilities, was used then the users probably would be more interested in asking further details about the way the solution was derived.

These models are classified into two categories, the static ones allow the visual presentation of their application results, and the dynamic models, which visually present the whole evolution process, and intermediary results.

Increase in the use of VIM models in decision making processes arises by the their utilization by the decision makers and the obtainment of their confidence through the understanding of the operation of the models.

The decision maker may submit questions of "what...if" type and monitor the application and the results of the new assumptions. Visual models cause the decision maker to directly work with them interactively rather than to work with some mathematical model with the help of some analysts. Visual models do not behave like "black boxes" in which we input some initial values and then simply take the final results. In visual models we have the ability to observe and monitor all the intermediary stages. In addition, visual models are much more tangible than the quotation of data tables and results.

Visual interactive simulation is an accessory possibility by which the decision makers may visually monitor the evolution of simulation by interacting with simulation models.

Bell and O'Keefe (1987), concisely report in their survey on Visual Interactive Simulation – VIS, that VIS is popular because it allows users to comprehend the model and play an active role by using it and making numerous experiments.

The procedures and the results of simulations (chapter 9, §6, and chapter 11, §2.4) are graphically presented. Figure 11.12, shows an example of the graphical control used for changing the multicriteria evaluations in order to formulate different scenarios. Scenarios are applied, based on brand choice models, simulating the behaviour of the consumers and estimating the market shares of a group of products.

4.2.4 Multimedia – Hypertext

The multimedia technology allows us to overcome the barriers of text and data by combining different communication media like, sound, text, animation, video, graphics, and thus providing advanced interface and communication systems.

Hypertext and hypermedia. Multimedia applications usually have hyperlinks within a text. A hyperlink is a special word, image or command button which if clicked by the user it guides to another section of text or another page. It us usually served to reveal details specific to a certain subject. With hypertext we can move or navigate into text, or databases in order to access data. Links may also guide to other links with different subject. Hyper medias connect not only text but also other communication media like sounds, graphics, animation, video, etc. The advantage is that the user is not supposed to know the physical location of data but he simply chooses the right links by which he is guided to the eligible subject.

Multimedia pages. Multimedia applications are composed by "pages". A page is a set of available information and may contain buttons, text, images, sound, video, etc. The pages that constitute a multimedia application are interconnected by hyperlinks and form a multimedia book.

Video. The video is a sequence of pictures that are displayed with high rate in order to give the impression of movement. In order to correctly display a video the rate should be set to 25 pictures per second. Thus, it is normal even for a small video to have vast storage requirements.

Sound. Even a personal computer has the ability to record and reproduce sounds with the help of specific software, a sound card and a microphone. Subsequently, these sounds can be inserted in a multimedia page.

Display. With a video adapter and a high-resolution monitor a multimedia application is able to draw high quality images.

Compact Disk. It is a disk with high storage capacity that contains digital data or music and is read by a laser beam. The rapid development of technology led to the introduction of many typed of CDs:

- Compact Disk Audio (CD-Audio) is the most popular form of high quality sound storage and reproduction. The quality of sound is not affected even after thousand times of reproduction.
- Compact Disk Interactive (CD-i). It signalises an interactive computer system with sound and video that uses a CD as storage media.
- Compact Disk – Read Only Memory (CD-ROM). A CD that stores digital data but it can be "written" only once. Its storage capacity is more than 650 MB.
- Compact Disk Recordable (CD-R). While normal CDs cannot be updated, CD-Rs can be written again and again by using special equipment.

4.2.5 Systems Based on Virtual Reality

The ability to use three-dimensional (3-D) graphics is one of the most desirable tools on behalf of all the people involved in some type of design process (*Figure 10*). Of course, still remains the problem of drawing three-dimensional graphics in two-dimensional displays. The solution to these problems seems to be the employment of virtual reality. As virtual reality we may consider the technological environment that provides artificial sense of space. The user "believes" that moves or works in a "real" three-dimensional space while in fact the display still remains two-dimensional. Through this virtual reality group of users-decision makers may communicate, cooperate and interact. The abilities to work and operate in such environment are continuously expanding, as the development of communication systems with virtual reality capabilities is one of the most dynamic developing scientific areas.

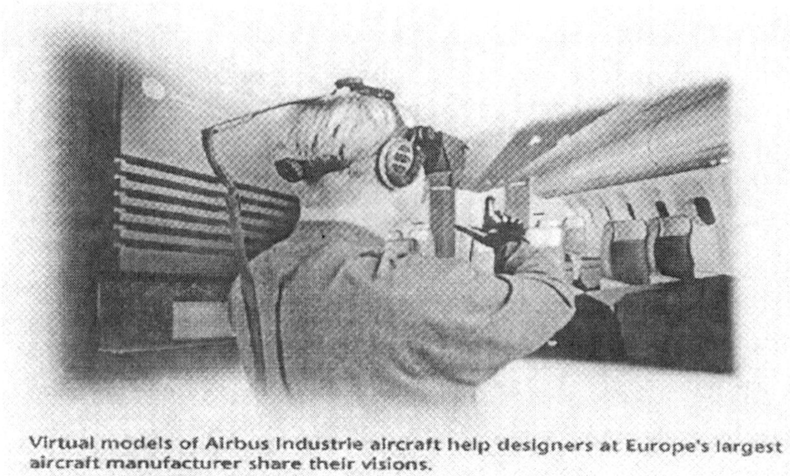

Figure 10. Use of virtual reality (Silicon graphics)

4.2.6 User Interaction via Natural Language, Recognition and Understanding.

The ability of communication between the user and the computer system in natural language, as for example in English, is called natural language processing. In simple words, this means that typing command or selecting them from a command menu is substituted by oral commands. These commands are interpreted and then executed by the computer system. This requires the existence of knowledge-intelligence on behalf of the computer.

4.3 Data base Management Subsystem

This module is a software program that handles the systematic storage, retrieval and maintenance of data. A Data Base Management System (DBMS) handles the users' information needs entirely without preoccupying them with the data handling details.

4.3.1 Data Management

Gray (1996), describes six generations of data management methods, presented in *Figure 11*.

As already mentioned, information casts power to companies. Companies are more and more independent from the information that they possess. Yet, they should be able to obtain the relevant information when needed, in whichever point of the company needed, and in the desirable format. The information in order to become useful should firstly get organized, stored, and properly managed. Responsible for the organization, storage, processing and management of the information and data are the database management systems.

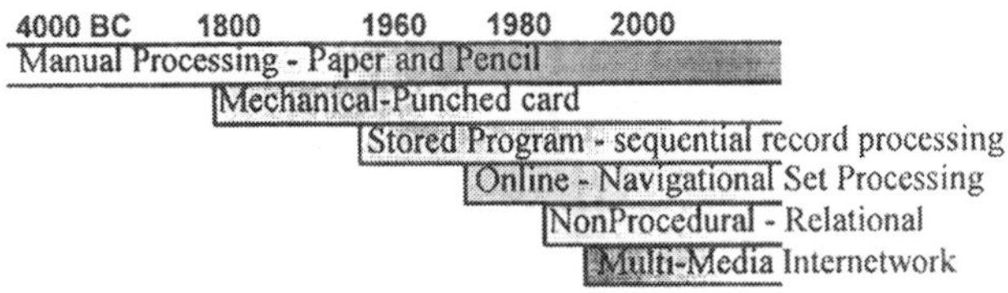

Figure 11. The six generations of data management, evolving from manual methods, through several stages of automated data management (*Source*: Gray, 1996)

The organization of the information can be handled either through files or through databases. In simple words, as a file we consider a set of uniform records that are relevant with a certain subject (person, object) whereas as database a hyper set of related files.

A Data Base or Data Bank is a collection of digital stored data, organized in such a way so as to allow various applications to easily utilize and update its contents but not necessarily define its structure or its contents.

In a database, data are stored in hard disks, floppy disks, tapes or other magnetic storage media. It also contains a number of application software that process these data with all the possible ways (updates, modifications, searches, etc). Finally, there is a group of users that communicate directly with the database through terminals and have the ability to perform any data process (using one of the above methods).

So, a database contains data that can be used by more than one user and most important, data that correspond to each user can possibly overlap with several ways with those of other users. The software that handles the management of the database is called Database Management System

In order to store the data, these are organized hierarchically in files, records and fields (elements). A file is considered to be a collection of uniform logical records that are relevant with a certain subject. A records is a set of fields that are related with a certain object or action. Fields are the smallest unit of data storage. A field can be further subdivided into sub fields that correspond to the same data unit.

Records are divided into two types, logical and physical. The length of a logical record matched the length of its fields. A physical record consists of a group of logical records stored together. The number of logical records that comprise a physical record is called blocking factor.

The database technology allows us to process the data of an organization or a company in an overall and uniform manner. It removes the obligatory dissociation of data in application or user oriented files and allows their exploitation with a way that is most appropriate for the users

Data management involves the following activities:

- **Collection.** Assembly and reformation of the required data in order to obtain the proper format for input into the system.
- **Verification.** Check and verification of data compatibility and integrity according to the established rules.
- **Organization.** Data are organized so as to accomplish storage requirements and users' needs.
- **Storage.** Storage of data in peripheral magnetic media.
- **Security.** Data are protected by storage media failure, improper operations – records, and unauthorized user access.
- **Retrieval.** Data retrieval ability from authorized users
- **Maintenance.** During the operation of a database new records ore fields are added and existing records or fields are deleted or changed. In addition, frequently the reorganization of the files is required.

4.3.2 Data Bases

The databases are part of the systems' database management module (Agrawal and Bell, 1990; McLeod *et al.*, 1990; Kroenke, 1995). Data derived by internal and external sources are saved into a set of distinct files that form the databases of the system. During the storage procedure one attempts to avoid the replication of common data in order to save space. The database components provide the ability into several users to use the same data at the same time.

The objective of the database management subsystem is to:

- Update the system's databases by adding, changing, and deleting records.
- Relate data that come out of different sources.
- Grand the ability to retrieve data from databases.
- Provide the ability to perform composite manipulation of the databases.

Thus, we can state that the data stored in a database are integrated and shared.

As a database or data bank we consider a collection of organized, shared and useful information that are stored in physical peripheral units and which can be processed by various DSSs.

The presentation of a general architecture that will cover all the different cases exhibits significant problems given that there are essential divergences among the various database management systems. A wide accepted architecture of database management systems was proposed in 1975 by

ANSI/SPARC - Study Group on Database Management Systems (*Figure 12*) and consists of three levels:
1. The external level
2. The conceptual level
3. The internal level.

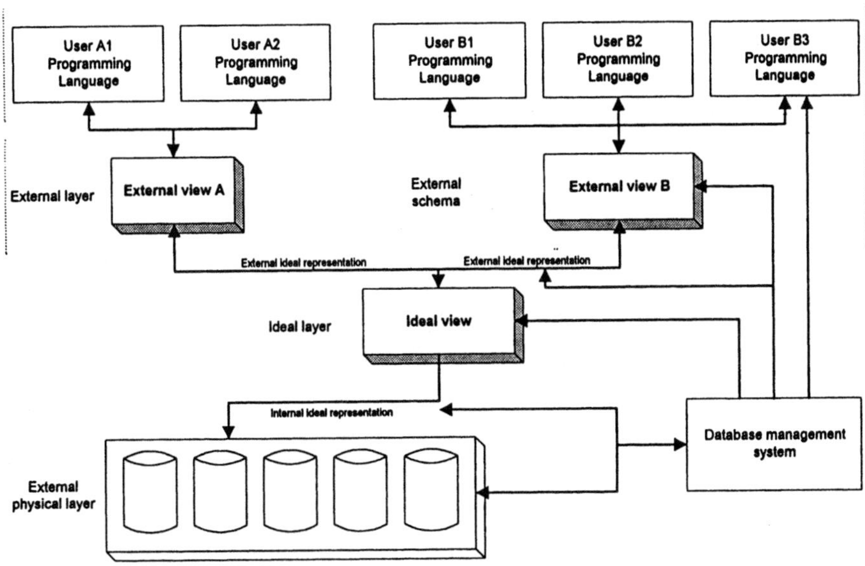

Figure 12. Architecture of database management system

Each user "sees" only a fraction of a database – the external level. The entire group of users "view" the whole database – the conceptual level-, while data are stored only once – internal level.

A central characteristic of database architecture is that conceptual model intervenes between the users and the actual organization of the data, which are stored in the magnetic data media, thus providing a view of the database, as this is perceived by the user. For example, users view a database as if it contains data about the clients and the products of a company, without getting occupied about the way these data are organized and stored.

The conceptual model constitutes a description of the information that is important to the users as well as of the relations that exist among them. This description is independent of the other characteristics of the system used. The design of the conceptual model is one of the most crucial steps in the development of a database management system.

In general, users are not interested for the entire conceptual model but only for a specific part of it, which is relevant with the application workspace that each time the user employs. Also, several times users are interested for a combination of the conceptual model's components. For these reasons, usually users do not communicate directly with the conceptual model but with sub models of data that are subsets of the conceptual model adapted to the needs of the various users' groups. So, users view segments of the information system database while the system administrator view the entire database.

The third level of a database system's architecture is associated with the physical files of the computer system where that data and their relevant information are stored. Usually, data are stored in hard disks because data structures that are used in this level (lists, trees, etc) require direct access. We also have to note that the level of physical files is the only one in which the data are stored while the remaining levels contain only description of the data.

The entire architecture of a database system relies in the Data Base Management System, DBMS, which contains all the necessary software. The DBMS, undertakes, with the collaboration of the operating systems and the remaining basic software of the computer, all the procedures of checking, processing, etc necessaries for the operation of the database system, as for example the processing of queries, the searching of data, the organization of data into files, the processing of the mapping definitions among the various levels, etc.

The users of the database management system can be either application programmers, either terminal users with limited or zero programming background like salesman, executives, managers, and others. Their communication with the system can be established by two ways. The first employs the exclusive use of a special language that permits the easy communication with the database and does not require any special programming background (Query Languages, Data Manipulation Languages). The second form of communication is accomplished by the use of a special language (host language) in combination with custom programming languages like Visual Basic, Cobol, RPG, PL/1, FORTRAN, C, etc. Each user owns a workspace where all the data required for the communication with the database is located.

Important elements to the decision-making procedures are those of data warehousing and on-line analytical processing (OLAP) technologies. The requirements for decision support regarding the databases differ than those of the traditional on-line transaction processing applications.

4.3.3 Data Bases Systems (Conceptual models)

The various database systems differ substantially among them in the type of the logical models they support, the format of the language used for the communication with the users and in the organization of the physical files. The most frequently used structures in the database management systems are the following (Codd, 1970; 1974; CODASYL, 1971; Neat and Traunik, 1986; Courtney and Paradise, 1988; Kroenke and Dolan, 1988; Turban, 1993):

1. The relational model.
2. The hierarchical model.
3. The network-CODASYL model.

This classification is based exactly on the format of the included conceptual models and in subsequently on the information structures they support. Even if, as it has been pointed out, all three categories of database management system can eventually support all the information structures either directly or indirectly, it is a fact that each type of conceptual model better supports certain structures than others. In the following sections we will examine each category of database systems.

Naturally, each type of database organization model exhibits some advantages and some drawbacks. A major advantage of the relational model is the help that offers in the convenient design of the conceptual model and the simple facilitation of operation concerning the users of the system. On the other hand, the relational model fails to provide specific solutions to the problem of a database implementation. As a result, while in theory the relational model is one of the most exciting in practice, and compared to the other two types of organization, only few systems are commercially available.

The implementation of hierarchical system is relatively easier since these systems are grounded on hierarchical organization structures of the physical files, which are known and have been studied for a long time and do not exhibit serious problems. The drawbacks of the hierarchical systems include the difficulty in the conceptual design of the database (for example difficulty in the representation of N to M relationships), the introduction of complexity into the system, problems with database update, etc. However, despite these disadvantages, a large number of systems that follow the hierarchical model have been developed.

Network type systems are the most widely acceptable. Of course they are inferior to the relational systems regarding the facilitation they provide in the conceptual design of the system but, on the other hand, they provide more satisfactory solution regarding development issues.

An essential measure of effectiveness and usefulness of each of the above three categories is the abilities they offer not only in the manipulation of data but also in the support in the manipulation of the three basic categories of logical relationships, found in an actual operating environment (1 to 1, 1 to N, N to M).

4.3.4 Topology of databases

Database systems are classified into three distinct categories according to their physical location:

1. Centralized.
2. Distributed
3. External databases.

The term centralized indicates databases that are stored in a single physical location. Access on these databases is accomplished through the central computer system, in which the databases are connected, that is responsible for their management.

In the distributed type, identical copies of the databases (called replicas) are stored in different storage media that are interconnected in different points into a computer network. Conceptually, the data of a distributed database belong to the same information system however these are stored in different physical storage media. If a user changes the contents or the structure of the database then all the available database copies are updated in order to reflect the most recent changes. It is possible to split the database into fraction that may be stored in different location depending on the needs of the users and the applications. *Figure 13* presents the structure of a distributed database management system.

As external databases are considered those that are not part of the company's information system but are located in other dependent locations and in general are commercially exploited. The communication with these databases is accomplished by phone lines, modems, international networks, etc.

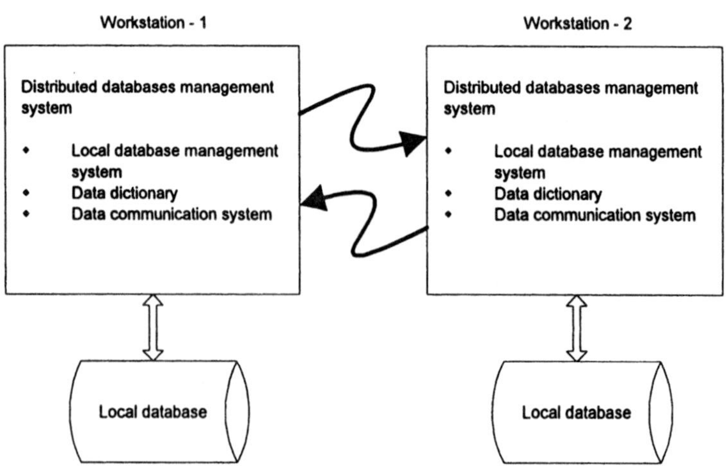

Figure 13. Distributed databases

Most of the up today database systems are developed in order to store only alphanumeric data. Therefore, a problem arises when one wishes to employ more rigorous data types like images, sounds, etc.

In this case, we turn into the principles of object-oriented programming. An object-oriented database allows as to analyse the data by emphasizing to the natural relationships amongst objects. A system of this type encounters a group of data along with their structure as a single object.

4.4 Modelling and Model Base Management Subsystem

A fundamental feature of a DSS is that the system offers a set of models in order to analyse a modelled representation of the reality rather than reality itself. A model is a simplified representation or an abstract expression of the reality. Primarily because reality itself is too complex to be represented precisely and also because a large part of the complexity is not relevant with the essence of the specific problem. The subjects of reduction (simplification) and representation are quite hard to be achieved in practice because these two notions contradict each other. Thereby, a model should be complex enough to capture the essence of each specific case but also it should not be more complex than necessary (Marshall, 1996). In the case of marketing models, the representation of the reality involves the marketing tasks of the firms and their environment. By using models, we are able to perform laboratory experiments that simulate the reality and in consequence we reduce the cost.

The model base contains a set of models that fall into one of the following main categories: strategic, statistical, operation research, marketing, data analysis, financial, forecasting, etc (Mitchell *et al.*, 1991).

The management tasks of the model base are handled and supported by the model base management subsystem. According to numerous scientists, model management is a persistently increasing modern science field (Konsynski, 1983; Applegate *et al.*, 1986; Blanning, 1989; Baldwin *et al.*, 1991; Muhanna, 1993; 1994; Konsynski and Dolk, 1994). For a review of model base management systems, the reader should recur to Blanning (1993).

The major functions of the model management system according to Yeo Gee Kin (http://www.comp.nus.edu.sg/home/staff/yeogk/public_html/index.html) are:

- Creates models easily and quickly, either from scratch or from existing models or from building blocks.
- Allows users to manipulate the models so that they can conduct experiments and sensitivity analysis ranging from "what-if" to "goal seeking".

- Stores and manages a wide variety of different types of models in a logical and integrated manner.
- Accesses and integrates the model building blocks.
- Lists and displays the directory of models for use by several individuals in the organization.
- Tracks models, data, and application usage.
- Interrelates a model with appropriate linkages through the database.
- Manages and maintains the model base with management functions analogous to database management: store, access, run, update, link, catalogue, and query.

The objective of the model base management subsystem is to relieve the user from the storage and processing tasks of the system's model base, in the same way that the data base management subsystem saves the user from the storage and processing tasks of the system's data base (Blanning, 1993). According to him, three are the most important subject of the model management:

1. The structure of the model base, which, in accordance with the database management subsystem, may follow the relational (Blanning, 1984) or the network model (Kotteman and Dolk, 1988; Eck *et al.*, 1990; Chart and Krishnan, 1990; Van Hee *et al.*, 1991). A more recently developed attempt involves structured modelling (http://www.anderson.ucla.edu/faculty/art.geoffrion/home/sm.htm; http://www.comp.nus.edu.sg/~yeogk/course/ic432/ic432.html) which provides a framework not only for the formation of models but in addition for the documentation of the model base (Dolk, 1988), development of reusable model components libraries (Geoffrion, 1989), and object oriented model management (Lenard, 1987; Tung *et al.*, 1991; Lazinny, 1991).
2. The objective of the model base processing, which is carried out even with techniques stemming from the Artificial Intelligence filed, is to facilitate the communication between users and models, to integrate various models or parts of the models, to support the users in formulating models or parts of models, and finally to support the users in the representation of the models' results (Blanning, 1987; Elam and Konsynski, 1987; Van Nee and Lapinsky, 1988; Liu *et al.*, 1990).
3. The organizational environment of the model base management subsystem, in which also Artificial Intelligence methods are utilized (Blanning, 1987; Marsden and Pingry, 1988; Weber *et al.*, 1990; Cohen and Sproull, 1991; Huber, 1990).

4.4.1 Models and Modelling Process

Problem modelling defines the process of formulating a model that can efficiently represent the state of the problem. The process consists of the tasks presented in *Table 3*, which are further discussed in the following sections.

Table 3. Modelling tasks

Model's components
Model's structure
Determination of selection principles
Generation of decision alternatives (actions)
Prediction of results
Measurement of results
Scenarios

The basic components of a model along with some examples are depicted in Let us briefly examine the various components of a model.

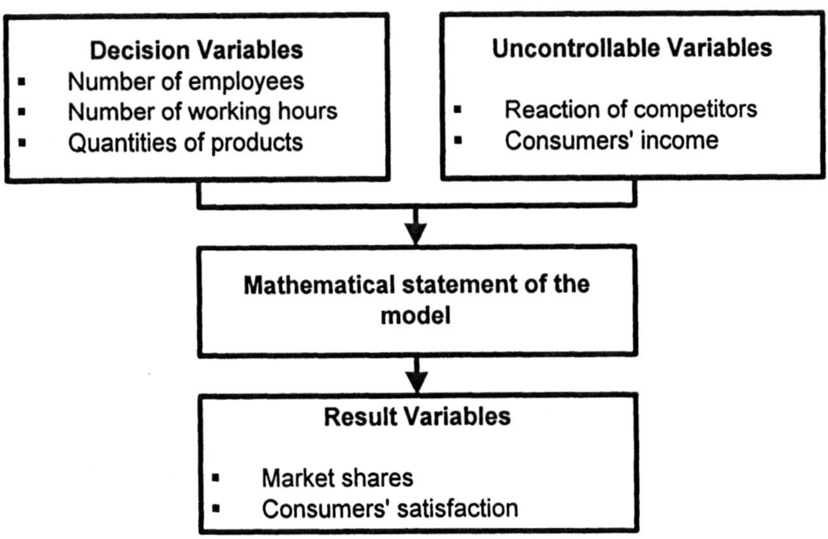

Figure 14. Model's components (*Source*: Turban, 1993)

Decision variables: They describe the alternative solutions of a problem and represent the unknown quantities of the problem. We seek to determine those values of the decision variables that lead as close as possible to better solutions.

Uncontrollable variables: These are the variables of the problem that cannot be controlled by the decision makers. They are used to impose constraints in the solution of the problem.

Model's structure. The components of a model are tied together by sets of mathematical expressions such as equalities and inequalities.

Determination of choice principles. The choice principle is related to the procedure that will be followed in searching a solution for the problem. There are two options in the search of a solution; either we will choose to find a satisfactory solution or we will pursue an optimal solution for a particular criterion. The two most considerable selection principles are the monocriterion and multicriteria optimisation models (linear programming, dynamic programming, etc) and the descriptive models (forecasting models, simulation models, etc).

At this point, one has to determine the criteria that will be used in order to pick the final solution. Recall that the final solution will be selected among a set of possible solutions that will be derived as results from the selected model.

Generation of decision alternatives (actions). The decision alternatives are generated either as a result of the application of the selected model or as a result of the model's application in previously determined alternative solutions. We have to emphasize that the solution that is obtained from the model is not a unique solution for the problem itself. The solution of a problem provided by a model belongs to a set of possible solutions.

Prediction of results. In order to choose a certain solution among the set of alternative solutions provided by the model, these have to be evaluated according to predefined criteria. This implies that the results of each solution should be already known. But the results of each solution cannot be explicitly defined prior to the actual implementation of the solutions. Therefore, we have to make certain predictions of the results of each alternative solution.

The obtained decisions are reached:

a) With complete certainty, when the decision maker is provided with all the necessary information for every single decision alternative. This speculation implies that the decision maker is able to determine and choose the best alternative.
b) With a certain probability when the decision maker examines the alternative solutions, that each shares a certain possibility to occur. The lack of complete information, or the existence of incomplete information, for each decision alternative prevents the decision maker of evaluating the consequences of his/her choice. Consequently, the decision maker is not able to select the "best" alternative and he/she has to evaluate the expected results (consequences) of the selection of each alternative. The

evaluation procedure can then in turn lead to the selection of the "best" solution.

c) With uncertainty, when the decision maker has to evaluate situations where some results are expected for each alternative solution. In this situation, the amount of information available to the decision maker is minimum.

Measurement of results. The value of an alternative solution is usually expressed in the same units that are used for expressing the assigned goals and objectives. If the value of an alternative solution is expressed in some other terms then the results are usually converted to units that have been used in the determination of the goals.

Scenarios. We use the term "scenario" to describe each procedure that has to be followed in order to render feasible the examination of each possible decision. Scenarios provide answers in questions of type "What will be the results if...". The number of the scenarios to be examined is not predefined or constrained. It is determined by the extent and depth of the decision maker's analysis and his willingness to explore and investigate the results of different decision actions. A typical strategy is to examine at least three different scenarios: one that is considered as the worst scenario, one that is considered as the possible optimum, and one that represents a mixed situation.

4.4.2 Models and Methods Management System

Despite that the title indicates a similarity with the database management system, yet the resemblance between the two systems is quite small. Difficulties that are encountered during the development of model base management systems, basically can be grounded to the following considerations:

- Multiformity and special requirement of the models.
- Existence of different methods required for model management.
- Necessity for a uniform management fashion.
- Different expertise of the users regarding the selection of the most appropriate to each case model
- Format and type of the input data.
- Presentation format of the derived results.
- Interpretation of the results.

The complexity of the model base management systems grows with the addition of new models into the system. Thus, a management system should provide:

- Direct selection of the model from expert user and suggestions for model selection or even automated model selection in cases where the users have limited or non-existing knowledge on the specific type of models.
- Enrichment of the base by the addition of new models.
- Ability to test alternative scenarios.
- Ability to use in parallel several models and compare their results.
- Selection of groups of data, by filtering the available data, in order to apply the numerous models.
- Presentation of intermediate and final results of the application of the model.
- Feedback of the models' results into another models.
- Exploitation of the presentation capabilities of the results, base on what is referred in chapter 5 about communication systems.
- Operation of model in group decision-making environments where groups of individuals use the same models in order to achieve a common goal.
- Analysis and interpretation of results in order to support expert users.

Now we shall focus on two DSS frameworks, which are responsible in a great extent for the formulation of the DSS research during the last decade. Each one provides a basic concept regarding the design of the DSS structure as well as in the planning of the software tools that will be used for its development.

The SC (Sprague and Carlson, 1982) framework consists of three partial modules, as thoroughly presented in *Figure 15*.

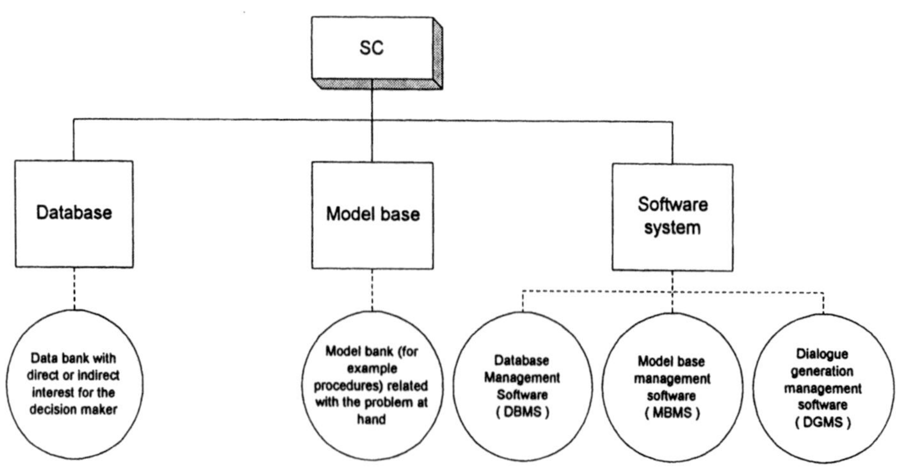

Figure 15. The SC framework (*Source*: Sprague and Carlson, 1982)

1. The DGMS determines which requests the user may submit to the DSS and which responses the system will return.
2. The DBMS is the software used by the database in order to manipulate data (read, write, update, etc).
3. The MBMS provides the necessary functions in order to create, manage, and use the model base.

The BHW (Bonczek, Holsapple, Whinston, 1981) framework also consists of three partial components, as shown in the figure below.

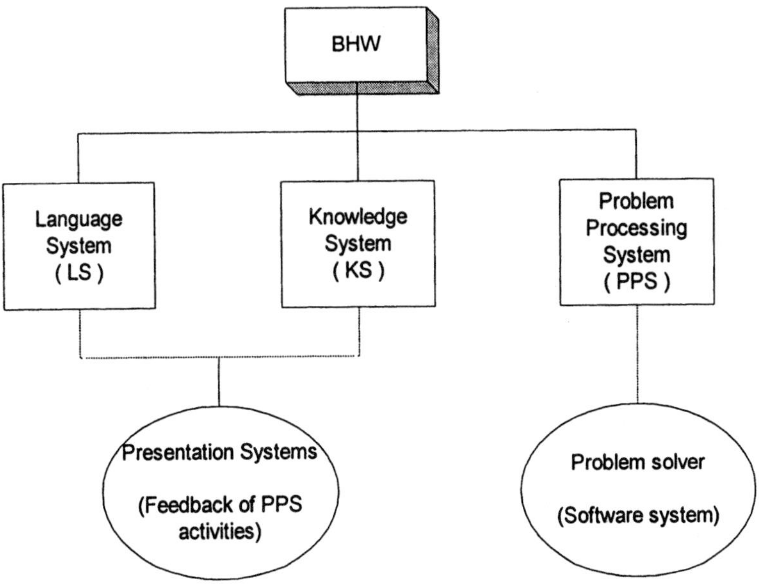

Figure 16. The BHW framework (*Source*: Bonczek, Holsapple, Whinston, 1981)

Today, research activity is focused on the following points of concern:

a) Software tools and in which way these can satisfy the needs of a DSS developer for higher degree of flexibility, and
b) Dynamics of problem resolution, that is, study of what occurs within the DSS when the user requests data that require a certain analysis.

4.4.3 Simulations

The capability o perform simulations of several situations is one of the most powerful tools in the hands of the decision makers. Simulations attempt to emulate reality. They allow us to control situations by performing trial runs in different input data.

In general, the simulation procedure includes the following steps (Turban, 1993):

- The decision makers are called to face a specific problem.
- Comprehension of the problem, determination of its parameters and inspection if simulations are required or possible.
- Formulation of a new simulation model or selection of an existing one.
- Check of the applicability of the model in simulating the specific state of the examined problem.
- Acceptance of the simulation model.
- Planning of the scenarios that will be examined by the application of the model.
- Implementation of the simulations and receipt of partial results.
- Comparison and evaluation of the alternative results. If the decision makers are not satisfied by the derived results then we return in a previous stage of the process.
- If the results are satisfactory then the simulation procedure is completed.

4.4.4 Heuristics

Heuristics are non-algorithmic methods that are capable of solving difficult problems, in which algorithmic methods fail to give satisfactory solutions. According to Reeves (1995), a technique is characterized as heuristic when it gives nearly optimal solutions with moderate computational cost, yet without the ability to ensure optimality or feasibility of the obtained solution or at least determine the distance between the obtained solution and the optimal one. In general, heuristic methods do not use an analytical methodology or algorithmic procedures for the search of the solution but they are driven towards the solution by partial practiced control from external factors. In other words, heuristics are partially driven random optimisation methods (Mars *et al.*, 1996). In their review, Zanakis *et al.* (1989), report the existence of more than 500 of such methods applied in specific or more general problems. Some of them, as for instance the genetic algorithms, exhibited a rapid progress because they achieved to provide satisfactory solutions in many situations and also because they were developed as general solution methodologies of representative problems.

Heuristics, as exhibited in *Figure 17*, are related by a bi-directional relationship with Artificial Intelligence, a fact that indicates that frequently the two methodologies help and support each other. In addition, heuristics are used in expert systems either as subservient elements for rule generation, either as optimization and search mechanisms. Computation intelligence is an important category of heuristics techniques. The term encapsulates the three widely known methodologies, neural networks, evolutionary computation, and fuzzy logic. Besides the above category of method, a variety of other heuristic methods have been presented in the literature, which can be classified in techniques that may be used in a general category of problems and to those that are applied exclusively in solving specific problems.

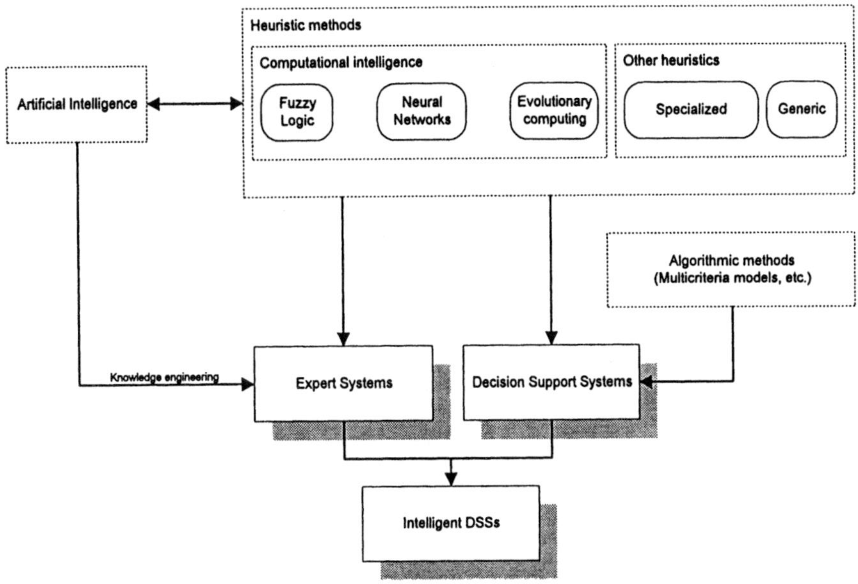

Figure 17. Interaction of Artificial Intelligence and heuristics

5. THE DEVELOPMENT PROCESS

Analysis and planning tasks are more than difficult subjects in the development of large scale, complex DSSs, especially when systems are designed in order to support several diversified functions and operations of an enterprise.

The first stage in the development of large scale DSSs, called the Decision Support Analysis –DSA phase, includes the processes of planning, user requirements assessment, problem diagnosis, management orientation and determination of priorities.

The DSA approach encapsulates five different subjects: structured interviews, decision analysis, data analysis, technical analysis, and management orientation (http://www.mstnet.com/mstnet/articles/wp_ds/wp_ds.html).

A vital point is the involvement in the analysis procedure of the managers-users, in order to trace their decision-making procedures. This assertion implies that emphasis should be given in the user-system interface in order to offer procedures that match with the standard procedures of the managers. The methodology to be followed should be familiar with the managers' decision-making procedures and should determine priorities that might improve those procedures. Analysis of managerial activities should be relevant with manager's individual goals and also with the goals of the entire company, that is with the more important success factors of the managers (Rockart, 1979).

Analysis should unmask information for the improvement of special professional activities, the satisfaction of current performance, the improvement expenditures and the amount of technological and operational risk that is associated with the suggested alternatives.

The Decision Support Analysis was designed so as the DSS achieves rapidly the results described above. There are five basic elements of the DSA approach: Structured interviews with managers, decision analysis, data analysis, technical analysis and management orientation. These procedures and their respective expedient results are presented in *Figure 18.*

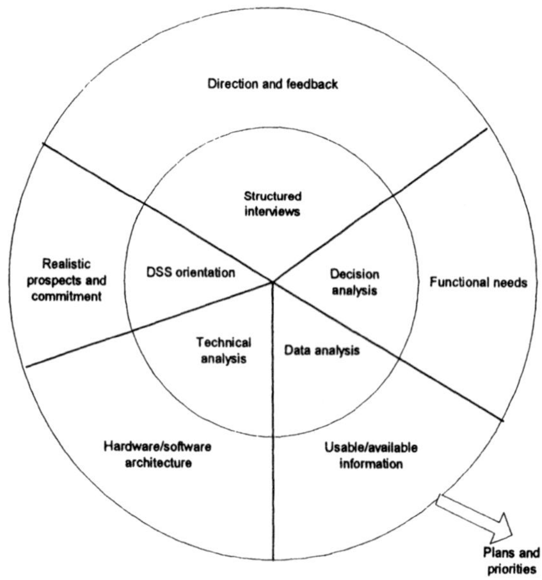

Figure 18. Procedures and results of DSS assessment needs (*Source*: http://www.mstnet.com/mstnet/articles/wp_ds/wp_ds.html)

Such an approach has been studied and developed by the "Image Tec" company, in order to present the entire process flow. It is oriented mainly on the design of large scale industrial DSSs, in environments where the user's community includes multiple managers in different professional operations (*http://www.mstnet.com/mstnet/articles/wp_ds/ wp_ds.html).*

The importance of analysis in the development of classical MIS And TPS applications is well established. As reported by Boehm (1973), in a new system more errors are recorded through analysis failures, than through design, implementation or installation failures. Shooman and Bolsky (1975) found that errors in the analysis process have a higher cost in order to be fixed and also heavier consequences in the effectiveness of the system those errors that occur during design or implementation. McKeen (1983), found that extra time spend in the analysis, resulted in time and cost reduction during the implementation and also higher user satisfaction with the final system. Developers of classical systems now recognize the importance of analysis and devote much more time and effort in this process. Their objective is to thoroughly pre-describe the entire system. However, DSSs development typically follows a different approach. DSS analysis follows a plan that contains the special tasks to be followed and also the order in which these will be carried out. A recent survey on DSSs applications shows that design is considered significant from both users and DSSs developers. Still it is not always performed effectively (Meador *et al.*, 1984). The first step in this procedure, the Decision Support Analysis, includes the identification of:

a) Applications of high priority.
b) High level of operation demands for these priorities.
c) Characteristics and information requirements.
d) Correct basic approaches in user's needs requirements, including system's architecture and detailed technical requirements, and
e) User orientation in DSSs concepts and their relevance with support of users' tasks.

The first four sections are used to guide the evaluation and choice of software and the design and development of the prototype.

The successive development stages of a DSS are presented in *Figure 19*, which is a composition of the works of Keen and Scott-Morton (1978) and Meador et a1. (1984).

Development and implementation plan. Initially, the systems' development objectives and the key decisions are determined. The decision maker, in order to reach a decision, should be supported in this decision by the system, which will provide him with all the necessary information in order to accomplish this task.

Investigation of the development possibility. This stage involves an exhaustive investigation of the user requirements and demands and also of the available resources and means, the previously acquired experience and the current situation on the relevant research field.

Analysis. In this phase the most promising development approach of the task is analysed and determined along with the required means for the integration of the system. The term means encapsulates the workgroup, the technical means, the financial resources and organizational subjects. Keen and Scott-Morton (1978) propose the determination of ideal information supply models for key decisions.

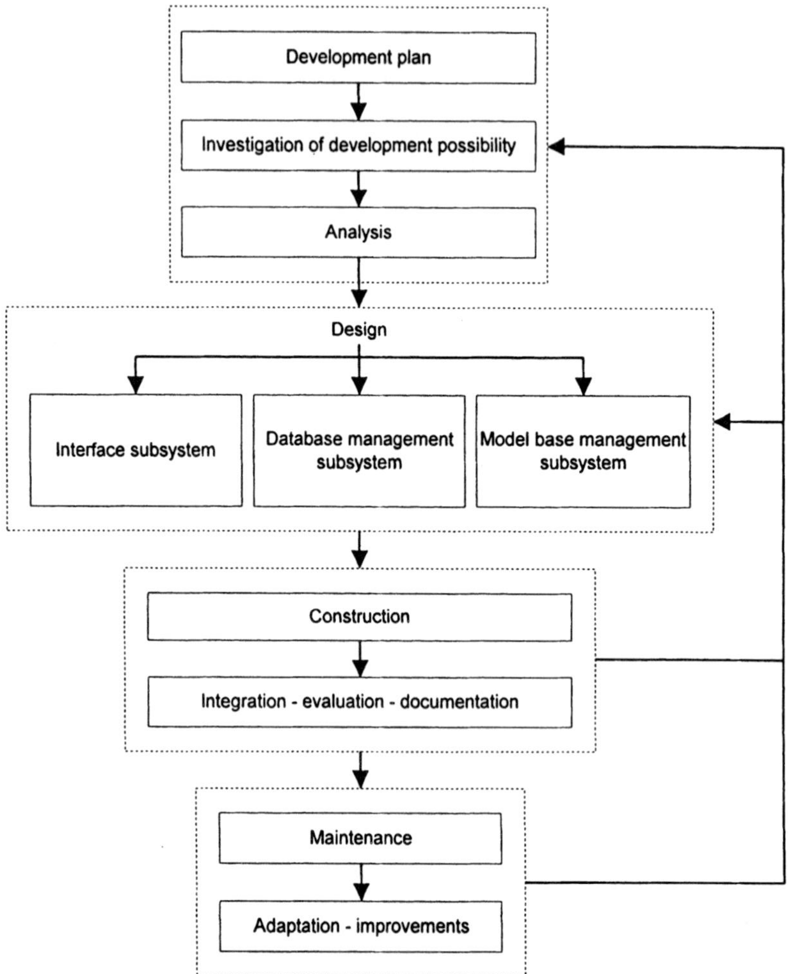

Figure 19. DSS development stages

Design. In the design phase, details associated with the structure, the characteristics, and the various system's components are designed and determined. As exhibited in *Figure 19*, the operation proceeds with the design of the three subsystems (dialogue-communication, database and model base management) as well as with the establishment of the interrelationships among them.

Implementation. It is the actual programming implementation of the previous task. The implementation phase also includes test of the system's proper functionality and possible supplemental improvements.

It should be noticed that frequently due to the fact that decisions are much too complicated users, on the one hand, do not clearly know which tasks the system should perform and, on the other hand, the members of the workgroup are not able to understand precisely the needs of the users. Therefore, in the first development stage, a prototype of the system should be implemented rather than the complete system itself, which will be then tested and evaluated by the user-decision maker, before stepping into the complete implementation of the system (*Figure 20*). The prototype is a rough approach of the system, yet it includes all the necessary characteristics of the complete system.

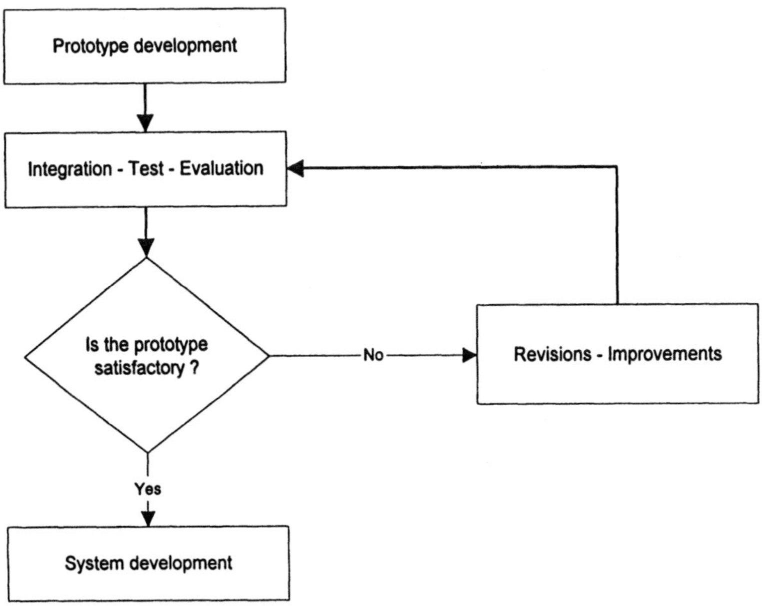

Figure 20. Prototype development process

Integration. The system at this stage is installed in its working environment. However, prior to the initiation of the system's full operation, it is necessary to run the validation and verification tests. The validation test is used in order to check the suitability of the selected algorithms. In other words, we examine if we have indeed create the correct system for the problem. Verification is necessary in order confirm that the various functions and processes of the system have been implemented according to the system's design (Ruttman, 1980; Sprague and Carlson, 1982; Riedel and

Pitz, 1986; Rouse, 1986; Andriole, 1982; 1986; 1989; Adelman and Donell, 1986; Adelman, 1992). Possible declinations lead to the revision of the system and to reiteration of the remaining necessary tasks. This process is repeated continuously until the system fully satisfies the needs of the user-decision maker.

Documentation. A very important task, which usually is neglected, is the documentation process. Documentation is very important not only to the maintenance of the system but also to the system's development process. For example, the documentation of the system's specifications is uses in the process of system's overall design while the documentation of the overall design is uses in the detailed design and implementation activities. Documentation should progress along with the overall development of the system otherwise it will remain unfinished or will not be available when needed during the development process.

Next, the system's capabilities are officially presented and demonstrated to the executives of the enterprise. Then the users are trained to both theoretical and practical aspects of the system.

The final step is the deployment of the system to all the necessary workstations and the beginning of its operation. It should be noted that the system should be accompanied with the necessary operation manuals. Also, the system should be able to give instructions, regarding its use, to the users.

Maintenance. It involves the continuous support of the system by its developers concerning problems that may occur during the "life" of the system.

Adaptation-improvements. During the operation of the system new needs may rise to its users-decision makers or possibly some new characteristics (new methods, etc) should be added into the system or any other kind of additional change might considered to be crucial. System's development team should then have to adopt the system to the new demands. Thus, some single tasks or a series if tasks should possibly be repeated

6. TECHNOLOGY LEVELS

Systems that have been already developed and have the above characteristics us for their development three technology levels (Sprague, 1980). Each of these is used by people with different level of technological background. Also, the use of some of these depends on the type and objectives of the systems that are called to implement. (Turban, 1993).

- **Specific.** These systems are called Specific Decision Support Systems and were developed in order to cover the needs of a specific decision or of a specific decision making procedure as well as of special combinations of models, databases, presentation techniques and other special tasks.

- **Generators.** In the second level are classified software systems that help us to develop a system of the previous level (specific), easily, quickly and with low cost. These systems are called Decision Support Systems Generators. Some well-known systems of this category are Lotus 1-2-3, Excel, Symphony, Framework, GADS (Geodata Analysis and Display of I.B.M), and others.
- **Tools.** In the lower level are software tools or utilities that are used for the direct development of specific systems or generators. It is possible some parts of the developed system to be made by generators and some others by the help of special tools.

The development of specific systems with generators results in the skip of possible financial barriers as well as in the reduction of the time needed. The process of developing specific systems or generators by using tools is generally a more time and money consuming process. In the entire system development process special hardware is utilized.

7. DSS IN MARKETING

As already discussed in chapter 4, §8 the actual use of MkIs is to support marketing decisions. A marketing decision support system is a coordinated collection of data, systems, tools and techniques with supporting software and hardware by which an organization gathers and interprets relevant information from business and environment and turns it into a basis for marketing action (Little, 1979).

MkDSSs, where developed to aid the decision making process of strategic marketing (Moormann and Lochte-Holtgreven, 1993; Wilson and McDonald, 1994; Li, 2000b). Even if the DSSs have proved that are reliable in giving competitive advantages to the enterprises, still there are evidence that several enterprises have been disappointed by their use. The main reason is the complexity of the problems related with the development of marketing strategies as well as the rapid changes of the external environment parameters. Some other reasons are the inherent uncertainty, the limited information, and the limited abilities of the systems to use qualitative data (Amaravadi *et al.*, 1995; McDonald, 1996; Li, 2000b). We should always have in mind what Eisenhart states (Eisenhart, 1990): If you put MkDSS in the hands of lousy decision makers you get lousy decisions.

Nevertheless, in the effort to face the various problems, several techniques have been used. Respectively, several systems were developed by adopting these techniques. *Table 4* lists the strengths and weaknesses of different computer systems, which were developed for aiding the strategic marketing processes (Li, 2000b).

Table 4. Strengths and weaknesses of various types of computer-based systems for developing marketing strategies (*Source*: Li, 2000b)

Type of System	Function	Strengths	Weakness (es)
Marketing Information Systems (MkIS)	Regular planned analysis and presentation of information	Widespread, therefore familiar; information mainly about the past	'Mechanical'; expensive; can result in information overload
Decision Support Systems (DSSs)	Providing data and models to support unstructured problem solving	Can explore many options quickly; calculates quantitative decisions	Mainly quantitative; cannot handle missing data or situations requiring expertise and experience
Executive Information Systems (EIS)	Data retrieval, information handling and business models for senior executives	Information handling and presentation; specifically aimed at senior management; easy to use	As for DSSs, but these weaknesses are more severe for executive decisions
Expert System (ES)	Making/advising on decisions in a specific domain	Can share expertise of others; enables consistent decision making	Only works within very narrow, well structured domain; human expert(s) needed for system to be built
Artificial Neural Network (ANN)	Forecasting; recognizing patterns in data	Can cope with noisy or incomplete data	No explanation facilities
Fuzzy Logic	Making/advising on decisions in a specific domain	Can use imprecise input; output may be either fuzzy or precise	Membership functions and rules specified manually, therefore slow; still experimental

Studies, carried out in USA (Boone and Kurtz, 1971), revealed that only 33% of Fortune 500 companies were using MkDSS. In 1985, McLeod and Rogers discovered that about 75 % of Fortune 1000 companies were using such systems. Another study (Higby and Farah, 1991) showed that 91% of marketing managers were using MkDSSs. Buttery and Tamaschke (1995), studied the use of MkDSSs on 708 Australian companies. They found out that only 58 companies were using a MkDSS, a fact that indicates that the wide acceptance of these systems has not been achieved yet.

A comprehensive study (Hewson and Hewson, 1994), of the application of sales and marketing information systems in the UK, reveals that most MkIS in the UK support sales management (93%), sales productivity (85%), and direct mail (85%). Very few MkIS support market analysis, competitor intelligence and campaign management. Similar findings were reported by Wilson and McDonald (1994). Xu (1999) studied 55 UK marketing managers in computer and financial industries. He examined the current practice of the strategic function of marketing, and the application of information systems in supporting the strategic function. These studies suggest that the current MkIS focus on the operational process of sales and marketing. The marketing strategic functions, such as external intelligence, strategic events/issues, position mapping, strength/weakness/strategic opportunities/threats/(SWOT) analysis, have been significantly neglected.

One of the findings of Xu's study (Xu, 1999) is the gap, which exists between the current practice of marketing strategic function and the support of information systems. Assessing the existing support function of information systems in the context of strategic marketing will help identify the areas for further strategic application. As marketing strategic function is centered on external contact, and is essentially different from marketing operational function, a MkIS application matrix for mapping out the current application is suggested in *Table 5*.

Table 5. Strategic application of marketing (*Source*: Xu, 1999)

	Internal	External
Strategic Support	Trends Monitoring	Market Positioning
	Effectiveness monitoring	Competitors, Mapping
	Strength/Weakness	Benchmarking
	New Product Development	Opportunity/Threats
		Environmental Scanning
Operational Support	Sales Promotion	Market Research
	Advertising	Direct Marketing (databases, internet)
	Product Pricing	
	Sales Force Management	Contact Management
		Public relations

By taking under consideration the findings of his research, Xu (1999), suggests a model for the future design of MkIS (*Figure 21*). This model embodies managerial vision and knowledge as a part of the system; it also emphasizes marketing environmental scanning and strategic decision support tools as the unique functions of a strategic-oriented MkIS.

Wierenga and Oude Ophuis (1997), after studying data from 525 companies in Netherlands, proposed a conceptual framework of the factors that affect the adoption, use and satisfaction των marketing decision support systems.

According to van Bruggen and Wierenga (2000), three key issues are important for MMSSs in order to be successful:

1. A demand-oriented approach towards the development and implementation of MMS's.
2. A contingency-based assignment of MMS's to a marketing problem situation not every system is suitable for every marketing decision.
3. Awareness of factors beyond the systems itself that are critical to the success of MMSS.

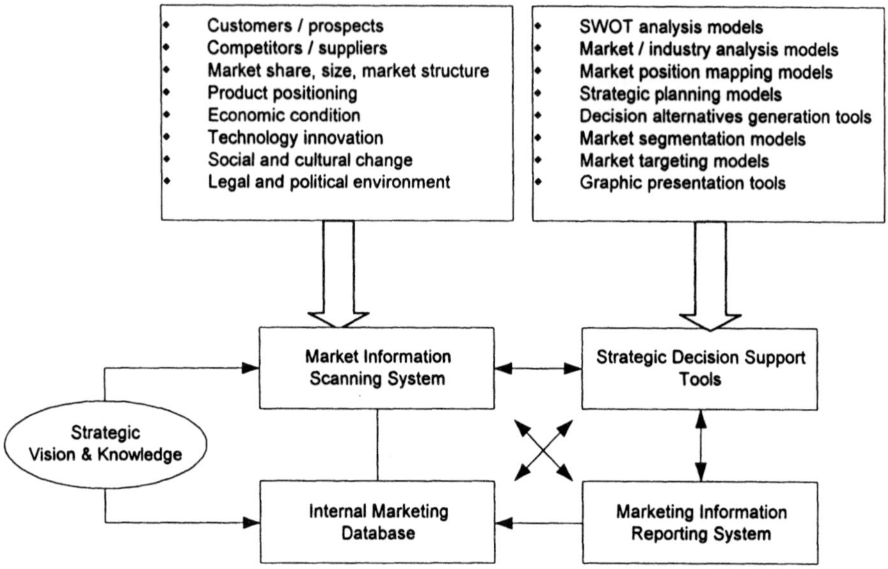

Figure 21. A strategic-oriented MkIS (*Source*: Xu, 1999)

Wierenga and van Bruggen (2000), adopt the term marketing management support systems in order to describe existing information systems in marketing and classify these systems in eight different types:

1. Marketing models consist of mathematical representations of marketing problems that aim at finding optimal values for marketing instruments. The philosophy underlying these systems is that it is possible to find an objective best solution.
2. Marketing information systems aim at the storage, retrieval, and statistical analysis of data. By means of manipulating quantitative information, marketing information systems assist marketers in analyzing what has happened in the market and determining possible causes of events.
3. Marketing decision support systems provide marketers with the opportunity to answer 'what-if' questions by means of making simulations. Marketing decision support systems put a large weight on the judgment of the decision maker, rather than on searching for the optimal best solution.

4. Marketing expert systems capture the knowledge from a marketing expert in a specific domain and make this knowledge available in a computer program for solving problems in the domain. Like marketing models, expert systems take a normative approach in searching for the best solution for a given problem.
5. Marketing knowledge-based systems describe a broader class of systems than marketing expert systems. They obtain their knowledge from any source, not just from human experts but also from textbooks, cases, and so on and can use a wide range of knowledge representations methods. Unlike marketing expert systems, marketing knowledge-based systems do not focus on finding a best solution but emphasize the reasoning processes of decision makers.
6. Marketing case-based reasoning systems focus on the support of reasoning by analogies. Analogous thinking is a way of solving problems in which solutions to similar past problems are taken as a starting point for solving a current problem. Marketing case-based reasoning systems make cases available in a case library and provide tools for accessing them.
7. Marketing neural networks are systems that model the way human beings attach meaning to a set of incoming stimuli, that is, how people recognize patterns from signals. Based on this principle, a large supply of algorithms is available now that we can recognize patterns in data.
8. Marketing creativity support systems are computer programs that stimulate and endorse the creativity of marketing decision makers.

The above classification generates some problems, unless it is a recording of the historical evolution of these systems. The use, by some authors, of new terminologies in order to describe existing systems and the introduction of different systems' categories create more confusion than solutions. By assigning new names, new categories of systems are created. The creation of new categories requires new definitions that can classify the systems. This fact generates confusion and vagueness to the definitions and to the segregation between new and existing categories of systems.

The above-suggested classification sets a number of questions. Is the concept of Marketing Management Support Systems a broader concept that Marketing Information Systems or is it the opposite? Are Marketing Models computer-based or simply theoretical models? If they are indeed computer-based then where do they differ from Marketing Decision Support Systems? If they are theoretical models then how can they be classified in Marketing Management Support Systems, since when they will be implemented they will be computer-based and accordingly should belong to the MkDSSs category? The Marketing expert systems, Marketing knowledge-based systems, Marketing case-based reasoning systems and Marketing neural networks are merely subcategories of Intelligent Marketing Decision Support Systems. The DSSs that incorporate data mining in which category do they fall? Are MkGDSS a subcategory of MkDSS?

According to the international standards in Information Systems, the Marketing Information Systems consist a broader concept from Marketing Decision Support Systems. The use of Artificial Intelligence techniques and their integration creates a new group of systems, the Intelligent Marketing Decision Support Systems, which also are classified in the broader concept of MkIS. A business Information System may contain a MkIS, which in turn may contain several MkDSS or IMkDSS, which are applied to the solution of various marketing problems.

In *Table 6*, we present an indicative alphabetical listing of MkDSS, while in the next section we will thoroughly examine the MUSA system.

Table 6. MkDSS software

System's name-Company-Authors-www address	Product description – application scope
ADBUDG – Little (1970)	It predicts market shares for given advertising budgets.
ADVISOR 2 – Lilien (1979)	A system for modelling the marketing mix for industrial products.
AlphaBlox Analysis Suite - http://www.alphablox.com/	Using AlphaBlox Analysis Suite you can quickly and easily deliver custom Web-based analytical applications that accommodate the diverse information and analysis needs your users, customers, and suppliers.
Apollo Software Suite - http://www.infores.com/ http://www.infores.com/public/prodserv/AB/apolo70.htm http://www.infores.com/public/prodserv/	The Apollo Suite ensures consistent execution of category management and new product launches at the shelf. All Apollo components can be adapted to fit specific retail or sales force needs.
ASSESSOR – Silk and Urban (1978)	The system is designed to estimate the sales potential of new packaged goods before they are test-marketed.
Brio.Enterprise, Brio.Report, Brio.Portal - http://www.brio.com/non-secure/Products/Products_-_Brio_ONE.html	Integrates query, analysis, and reporting capabilities for the Internet, intranet, extranet, and client/server environments. Combines push and pull server technology for automatic query processing and report distribution, zero administration, and dynamic query over the Web Enables developers to build dynamic, customized analytical applications to capture intellectual capital and best practices Optimizes IT resources and existing legacy environments

System's name-Company-Authors-www address	Product description – application scope
	Supports queries to relational, multidimensional, and operational databases Incorporates information from multiple data sources into one document for side-by-side, relational analysis Scales to meet growing enterprise needs without increased impact on IT resources Leverages database and Internet security protocols
Burke & Associates, Inc. - http://burkesystems.com/Software.htm	Maintenance Management Decision Support System
Business Objects - http://www.businessobjects.com/products/index.htm	Several products
BVAR (Bayesian vector auto regression) – Jiang, Klein and Pick (1998)	A marketing category management system: a decision support system using scanner data
Cosmic Solutions Trade Marketing Solutions - http://www.cosmic-solutions.co.uk/trmksol.htm	Retail Fixture, Design Space Planning, Direct Profit Profitability, Promotion Evaluation
CrossGraphs®- http://www.belmont.com/	It is a software tool that helps you visualize, understand, and report complex, multidimensional data in analysis databases and data warehouses.
DecisionPoint® - http://www.dpapplications.com/main.cfm?p=b0400	
Demand Solutions - http://demandmgmt.com/products.html	Sales and Operations Planning Forecast Management
DSS Vendors - http://dss.cba.uni.edu/DJP/Companies.html	A list of DSS vendors
DynaMight - http://ds-dataset.com/Dyn_Marketing.html	The Marketing Suit: DynaStrat, DynaTact, DynaRep
EXMAR - http://www.exmar.com/main.htm	It assists companies for developing their Strategic Marketing Plans.
Expert Choice Inc. - http://www.expertchoice.com/software/	Expert Choice for Windows is a multi-criteria decision-support
IMS Health - http://us.imshealth.com/intersite/default.asp	IMSView is a Windows-based decision support system that lets users select, retrieve, display, manipulate, and analyze sales and marketing data Sales Performance Service™ used in order to take advantage of opportunities in promotion, market segmentation, and micro marketing.
Informix Red Brick Warehouse - http://www.informix.com/informix/solutions/dw/redbrick/rbw_datasheet/	It is an open, relational database designed specifically to meet the requirements for single-subject or departmental data marts.

System's name-Company-Authors-www address	Product description – application scope
HELM - http://www.codework-it.com/eng/homee.html	The system is countless and provide effective support to different classes of people: financial analysts (budget revision, foreign currency conversions, consolidation,), accountants (cost allocation, study of past performance, elimination scenarios,), and product managers (analysis by product line, by distribution channel, by region, by responsibility,)
Jiang, Klein, Pick (1998)	A marketing category management system: a decision support system using scanner data
Lumina - Analytica® - http://www.lumina.com/software/aboutanalytica.html	A system for developing business models
MAPLAMOD – Bloom and Stewart (1977)	An integrated marketing planning system.
MARKSTRAT 3 - http://www.markstrat.com	Analysis of model planning in marketing processes
Marketing category management system - Jiang, Klein and Pick (1998)	It is a prototype system, which allows users to manage the complex models and scanner data to make forecasts in an interactive fashion.
MUSA – Grigoroudis and Siskos (2001)	Customer satisfaction measurement
National Decision Systems - http://www.natdecsys.com/home.html http://www.natdecsys.com/prodlst.html http://www.natdecsys.com/products.html	List of products
NEWPROD – Assmus (1975)	The design and implementation of a new product model.
NEWS – Pringle *et al.* (1982)	A decision-oriented model for new product analysis and forecasting.
Optimal television programs – Kelton and Stone (1998)	Optimal television schedules in alternative competitive environments.
PATHMOD – Weber and Dholakia (1998)	It is a decision support system, which can help managers to utilize their market knowledge and experience to develop more effective market share growth plans in mature business markets.
PERCEPTOR – Urban (1975)	A system for product positioning.
PETAPS – Davis and Sundaram (1995)	It is a prototype decision support system for consumer product marketing and promotion.
PowerCenter, PowerMart - http://www.informatica.com/products/	Within an enterprise decision support solution, PowerCenter is responsible for extracting data from operational sources, enriching it for decision support, cataloging it for use and re-use, and delivering it to powerful business intelligence and analytic applications.

System's name-Company-Authors-www address	Product description – application scope
Priceman - http://acnielsen.com/products/tools/priceman/	A successful category management program focuses on all aspects of your business: product assortment, merchandising, promotion and pricing.
PROMISE - Jun Lee, Chang Lee (1999a; 1999b)	It is a distributed DSS approach to coordinating production and marketing decisions
SAS - http://www.sas.com/	
SCAN*PRO – Wittink *et al.* (1988)	It provides brand managers with an understanding of the impact of promotional activities.
System for the Analysis and Simulation of Marketing (SASM) – Nuzzolo *et al.* (1995); Crisalli (1999)	It used to assist decision-making for corridor operative marketing plans for long-distance railway services.
TRACKER – Blattberg and Golanty (1978)	An early test market forecasting and diagnostic model for new product planning.
The A/S response model – Rao and Miller (1975)	A system for advertising/sales response functions.
A System of Promotional Models – Rao and Lilien (1972)	
ZS Associates - http://www.zsassociates.com/maps/maps.html	MAPS
ZS Associates - http://www.zsassociates.com/expertise/dss.html	EvaluMap

7.1 The Multicriteria Satisfaction Analysis System – MUSA

The MUSA for Windows system implements MUSA methodology (MUlticriteria Satisfaction Analysis), a multicriteria preference disaggregation model proposed by Grigoroudis and Siskos (2001). The main objective of the method is the aggregation of individual judgements into a collective value function assuming that client's global satisfaction depends on a set of n criteria or variables representing service characteristic dimensions.

This assumption of a value or treelike structure is presented in *Figure 22*, and it is also mentioned as 'value tree' or 'value hierarchy' (Keeney and Raiffa, 1976; Keeney, 1992). It should be noted that the number of layers might not be uniform across a value hierarchy.

The multicriteria model evaluates a set of marginal satisfaction functions in such a way that the global satisfaction criterion becomes as consistent as possible with customer's judgements. The required information is collected via a simple questionnaire in which the customers evaluate provided service, i.e. they are asked to express their judgements, namely their global satisfaction and their satisfaction with regard to the set of discrete criteria. A predefined ordinal satisfaction scale is used for these customers' judgements. This way, the evaluation of customer's satisfaction can be considered as a multicriteria analysis problem.

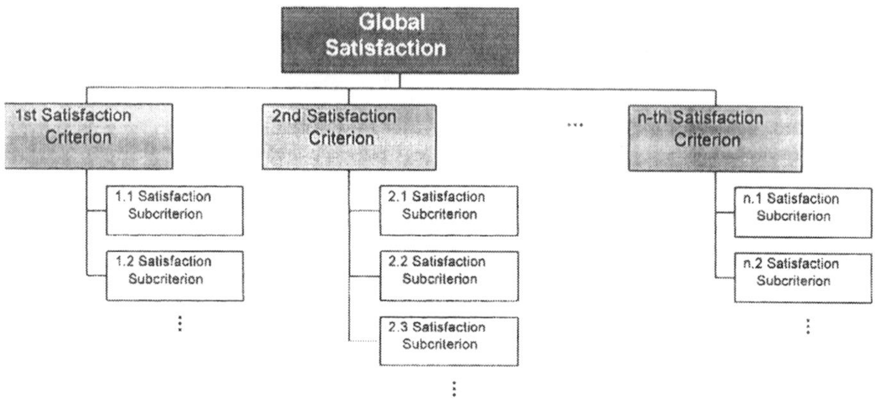

Figure 22. Hierarchical structure of a customer satisfaction problem

7.1.1 Method

The MUSA method assesses global and partial satisfaction functions Y^* and X_i^*, respectively, given customers' judgements Y and X_i. It should be noted that the method follows the principles of ordinal regression analysis under constraints using linear programming techniques (Jacquet-Lagrèze and Siskos, 1982; Siskos and Yannacopoulos, 1985; Siskos, 1985). The ordinal regression analysis equation has the following form:

$$\begin{cases} \widetilde{Y}^* = \sum_{i=1}^{n} b_i X_i^* - \sigma^+ + \sigma^- \\ \sum_{i=1}^{n} b_i = 1 \end{cases} \qquad (1)$$

where: $\widetilde{Y}^*$ is the estimation of the global satisfaction function, Y^* and X_i^* are the partial satisfaction functions (normalised in 0-100), σ^+ and σ^- are the overestimation and the underestimation errors, respectively, and b_i is the weight of the i-*th* criterion.

According to the aforementioned definitions and assumptions, the customers' satisfaction evaluation problem can be formulated as a linear program in which the goal is the minimisation of the sum of errors under the ordinal regression equation (1) for each customer, and the normalisation constraints for Y^* and X_i^*.

The preference disaggregation methodology includes also a post optimality analysis stage in order to address the problem of model stability. Exploring the polyhedron of near optimal solutions, which is generated by the constraints of this particular linear program, the final solution is obtained.

Finally, the MUSA method assesses a series of helpful indices (i.e. average satisfaction indices, average demanding indices, etc.) in order to analyse customer satisfaction in detail (see also §4). A detailed presentation of the MUSA method can be found in Siskos *et al.* (1998) and Grigoroudis and Siskos (2001).

7.1.2 Data management

The input and output data files that are used by MUSA system have a very simple format because they are basically text files (ASCII files). This means that they are fully compatible with almost all application programs, and may be accessed through:

- Spreadsheets,
- database management systems (DBMS), and
- text editors and word processing packages.

Through this way, MUSA data may be read from an external text file or they may be entered directly to the program. The output data file is also saved in a text format so that the user may use it to perform any kind of complementary analysis with other software packages.

The information required to create the MUSA data files refers basically to the definition of the variables of the model and it consists of:

- title of the problem,
- number of customers, number of criteria, and number of sub criteria per criterion,
- global, criteria, and sub criteria satisfaction scaling (number and titles of satisfaction levels), and
- main data table (customers' judgements).

Figure 23 presents example data for a pilot customer satisfaction survey concerning a radio station. The figure shows that for this particular example, global satisfaction depends upon a set of 4 criteria, while a 5-point scale is used for global as well as for partial satisfaction measurement. It should be noted that the main data table consists of ordinal data, and for this reason the displayed numbers represent coding for the defined satisfaction levels.

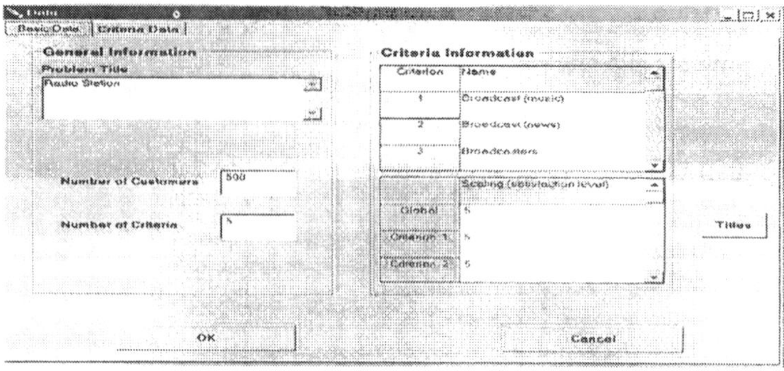

Figure 23. Data management in the MUSA system

7.1.3 Presentation of results

The MUSA system provides basic descriptive statistical analysis based on the calculated frequencies (*Figure 24* and *Figure 25*). Available results consist of global criteria and sub criteria satisfaction frequencies, and they give a general view of the customer satisfaction data.

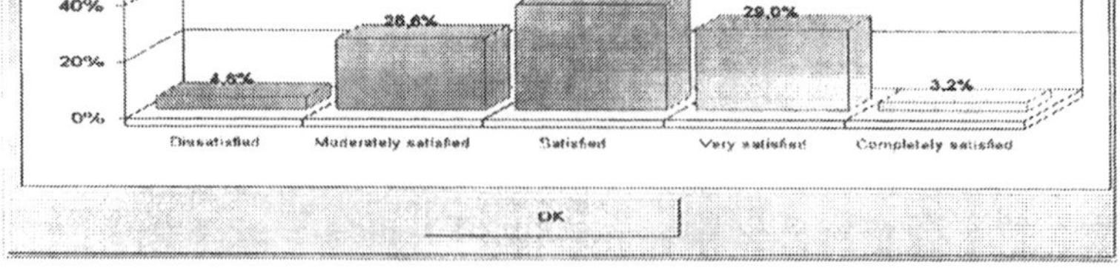

Figure 24. Descriptive statistical analysis

The system includes also global and partial explanatory analysis in order to perform in depth customer satisfaction analysis (*Figure 26*, *Figure 27*, and *Figure 28*). Global analysis focuses on the overall satisfaction results, while partial explanatory analysis gives a detailed view on specific satisfaction dimensions (criteria/sub criteria analysis). The main results provided by the MUSA system consist of:

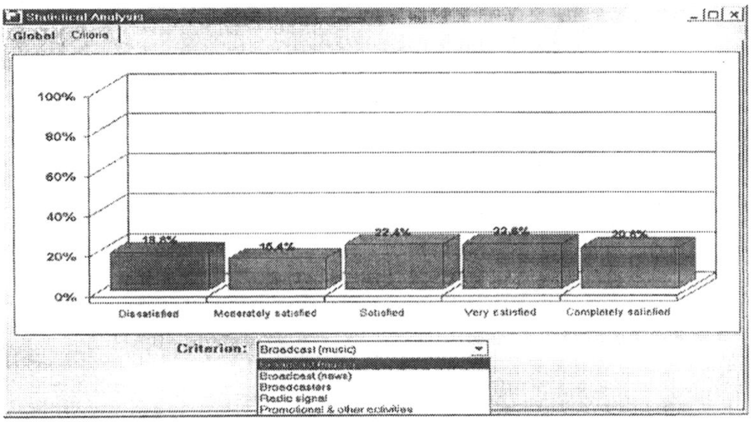

Figure 25. Descriptive statistical analysis

- **Value functions:** they show the real value (in a normalised interval 0-100) that customers give for each level of the global or partial ordinal satisfaction scale.
- **Criteria weights:** they represent the relative importance of the assessed satisfaction dimensions.
- **Average satisfaction indices:** they show in the range 0-100% the level of customers' satisfaction; they can be considered as the basic performance norms.
- **Average demanding indices:** these indices are calculated according to the shape of global and partial value functions, which indicate customers' demanding level.
- **Average improvement indices:** they represent the improvement efforts and they depend on the importance of satisfaction criteria and their contribution to dissatisfaction as well.
- **Additional diagrams:** similar to SWOT analysis, they combine the previous average indices in order to provide a series of strategic or decision maps, like:
- **Action diagrams:** they indicate which satisfaction dimensions should be improved.
- **Improvement diagrams:** they determine the output/extent of improvement efforts.

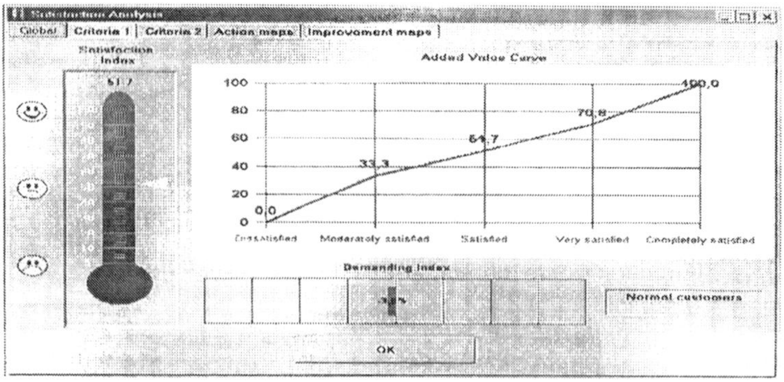

Figure 26. Global satisfaction analysis

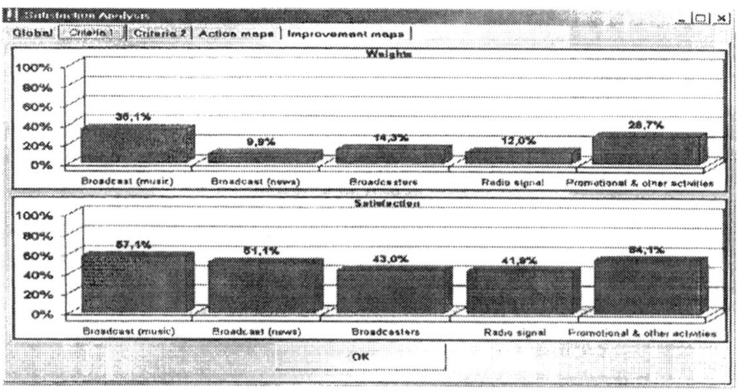

Figure 27. Partial satisfaction analysis

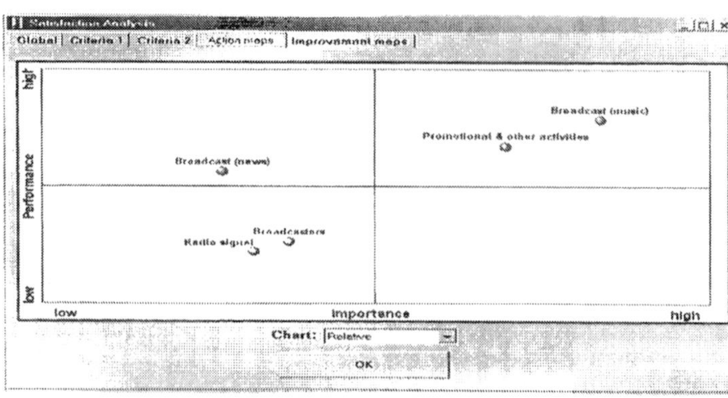

Figure 28. Action and improvement diagrams

7.1.4 Concluding remarks

The main advantage of the MUSA system is that it fully considers the qualitative form of customers' judgements and preferences, as expressed in a satisfaction survey. This way the collected information is not arbitrarily quantified. Other advantages of the system include the following:

The provided results are focused not only on the descriptive analysis of customer satisfaction data but they are also able to assess an integrated benchmarking system. This way they offer complete information set (value functions, criteria weights, average satisfaction indices, etc.) which is sufficient enough to analyse the satisfaction evaluation problem in detail.

A significant effort has been devoted in order for all the provided results to be easily and directly understood. For this reason the indices' sets are assessed in a normalised 0-100% interval.

The implementation of the system in satisfaction evaluation problems refers mostly to customers or employees of business organisations. Siskos *et al.*, (1998); Siskos *et al.*, (2000b); Mihelis *et al.* (2001), Grigoroudis, *et al.* (1999a), and Grigoroudis, *et al.* (1999b), present several real world applications of this type. Furthermore, satisfaction evaluation problems may refer to any human activity or social field like evaluation of educational systems (Siskos *et al.*, 2000a), voters' satisfaction, shareholders' or investors' satisfaction, expectations and needs of a labour market, or benchmarking for business organisations.

Chapter 6

Advanced Decision Support Systems

1. INTERACTIVE DECISION SUPPORT SYSTEMS

The stride in the field of information technology along with the low maintenance cost and usage independence of has lead in the development of more flexible and effective DSSs that operate in an interactive communication environment between user and system. This new DSSs generation was labelled by Courbon *et al.* (1977, 1979) as "Interactive Decision Support Systems (IDSSs)". Systems of this type utilize the judgment and expertise of decision makers in order to guide them in decision-making through a trial and error procedure. The role of IDSSs is a continuous effort of gradual approach of the decision maker's way of reasoning through his interaction with the system (*Figure 1*).

2. MULTICRITERIA DECISION SUPPORT SYSTEMS

Multicriteria DSSs comprise a DSSs subcategory since they exhibit the main characteristics of a DSS, as these have been described in the previous chapter, provided that at least one of their supported models stems from the multicriteria decision analysis field (see Chapter 1).

In the following section we will try to present, in shortness, some Multicriteria Decision Support Systems by recording and analysing several characteristics like their structure, their architecture, the methodologies used, and some applications. The necessary information was acquired by bibliographic inquiries and from the actual application of the systems, courtesy of their developers.

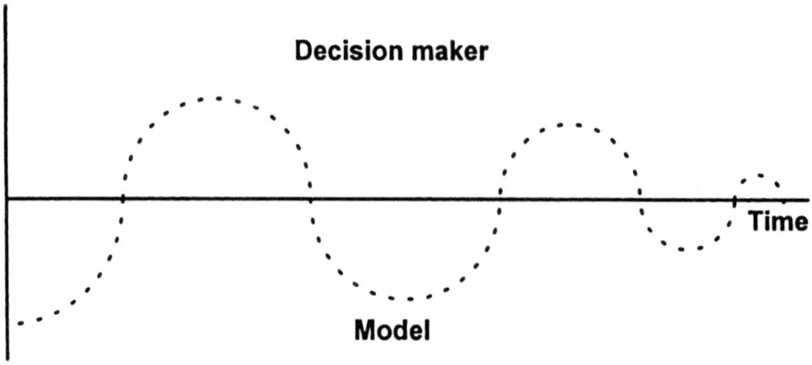

Figure 1. *A*pproach between the decision maker and the model

ELECTRE family. The ELECTRE systems employ the methods of Outranking Relations and are among the earlier developed systems (http://lamsade.lamsade.dauphine.fr/english/software.html).

- The ELECTRE I system (Roy and Skalka, 1985) is classified in the first generation of these systems characterized by its relatively primal dialogue subsystem.
- The ELECTRE III-IV system (Skalka *et al.*, 1992) is classified as third generation system as they use hierarchical selection screen and special worksheets in order to manipulate data. They have been developed for DOS environment with the help of BASIC. There is also a later version of ELECTRE III-IV, developed in WINDOWS 3.1 (Zielniewicz, 1994; http://www.lamsade.dauphine.fr/logiciel.html).
- The ELECTRE Is system is a generalization of ELECTRE I, that uses pseudo criteria in its modelling process in order to choose a single or a group of alternatives. It has been applied to the SEMA Group, Air France, Direction Generale des Postes, Ministere de l'Environnement, Centre National d'Etudes Spatiales, and elsewhere (Roy and Skalka, 1985).
- ELECTRE TRI (Yu, 1992)

MINORA. The MINORA (Multicriteria Interactive Ordinal Regression Analysis, Siskos *et al.*, 1993) is a multicriteria interactive decision support system with a wide spectrum of supported decision making situations. The core of the system relies on the multicriteria Utastar method (Siskos and Yannacopoulos, 1985), an improved variant of the original Uta method (Jacquet-Lagrèze and Siskos, 1982). The goal of the method is to assess/infer certain additive utility functions that minimize the deviations from a specified preference structure of the decision maker (reference ranking). The system employs a trial and error procedure that aim at the resolution and improvement of the consistency between the judgment policy of a decision maker and the additive utility model. Perfect consistency is achieved when the higher utility value corresponds to the top of the ranking and utility values progressively fall to the bottom of the ranking (*Figure 2*). The existence of actions with high order and low utility value or actions with low order and high utility value are considered as decision maker's overestimation and underestimation errors respectively.

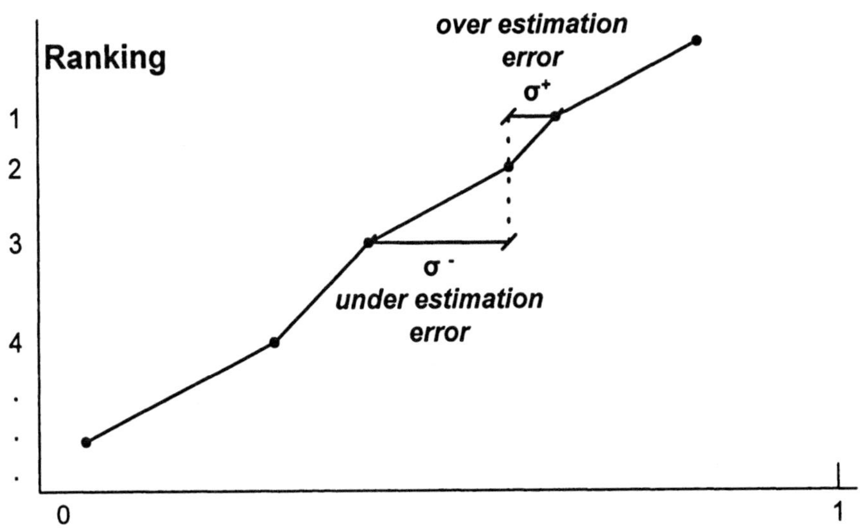

Figure 2. Monotone regression curve

The MINORA employs a dialogue procedure between the decision maker and the system in order to resolve any existing inconsistencies. During this dialogue procedure, the decision maker may accept to upgrade or downgrade reference actions, in other words the decision maker is able to modify his judgement policy. In addition, the decision maker has the possibility to revise the model itself by changing either the criteria modelling or the marginal criteria utilities (trade off analysis). Finally, the system employs two indices for measuring inconsistencies, the F index which is the sum of positive and negative horizontal deviations around the regression curve and Kendall's τ that measures in a scale between -1 and 1, the quality of regression between the decision maker's and the model's rankings.

The Minora system supports five different types feedback in order to deal with overestimation and underestimation errors:

- **Type 1 feedback.** The decision maker does not accept the suggestions of the model and revises the modelling of the decision criteria.
- **Type 2 feedback.** The decision maker accepts the suggestions of the model and changes accordingly the weak order of the actions (his judgment).
- **Type 3 feedback.** The decision maker does not accept the suggestions of the model, yet he decides to change the marginal utilities of the evaluation criteria (their weights) by performing a trade-off analysis.
- **Type 4 feedback.** When the compromise between the decision maker and the model is not possible, the development and employment of a different reasoning model of the decision maker is required.
- **Type 5 feedback.** If there is consistency between the user and the model, the model is extrapolated to the entire set of alternative actions. If the results of the extrapolation procedure do not satisfy the decision maker then the entire modelling of the problem should be reconsidered and re-examined.

This repetitive process of trial and error drives the decision maker to learn and understand the model that explains his preferences and allows him to alter the model when inconsistencies appear between the model and his preference structure. This learning procedure is the most essential feature and the great advantage of the MINORA system.

Based on the MINORA system Siskos, Zopounidis and Pouliezos (1994) developed an integrated decision support system for the financing of enterprises on behalf of a financial organization. The managers of the bank evaluated companies of the same or different branch regarding their status, their competitiveness, and future development, by using quantitative profitability criteria and qualitative criteria associated with the management level.

In addition, the MINORA System was applied on an actual decision making situation by the French financial organization SIPAREX (see Siskos and Zopounidis, 1987). SIPAREX is among the companies that fund the equity capital of fully developed companies, which in general are not introduced in the stock market. The employment of the system supported the decision makers to construct an evaluation model of the enterprises combining qualitative and quantitative criteria that compound their expertise and background knowledge.

The Institute of Geologic and Mineral Studies of Greece used the MINORA to map the landslide trend in Greece (Hatzinakos et al, 1991). Twenty-three Greek regions were ranked in terms of their geological solidity in order to specify the factors and their weights that affect this phenomenon.

With the extrapolation of the evaluation model in a representative set of regions the impression of the landslide trend in Greece was enabled.

Hurson and Zopounidis (1997) used the MINORA in a survey concerning the evaluation of portfolios. They evaluated several portfolios considering criteria reflecting the profitability and the risk of the stocks. Then they proceed with a combination of the ELECTRE TRI system (Yu, 1993), MINORA (Siskos *et al.*, 1993) and ADELAIS (Siskos and Despotis, 1989). With the first two systems, they ranked the stocks in a descending order by using evaluation criteria of stocks' profitability and risk. Then from this ranking of the stocks they formulated the optimal portfolios by using the multiobjective linear programming system ADELAIS (Siskos and Despotis, 1989). Cosset *et al.* (1992) used MINORA to rank order countries by assessing their credit worthiness based on financial, economic, and political criteria.

PREFCALC. The PREFCALC system (Jacquet-Lagrèze, 1983) also employs the UTA method but with a different adaptation philosophy than MINORA. The linear functions of marginal utilities of the criteria are estimated both implicitly and explicitly.

In the explicit method, the user rates the criteria by determining the weights that correspond to the $u_i(g_j)$ values of the alternative actions. The system assigns an arbitrary non-linear global utility function in which a series of decision maker's feedback actions are performed. When the decision maker accepts the global utility function, he is able to modify locally the marginal utilities through repetitive interactive procedures.

In the implicit method, the decision maker expresses his preferences in a reference set of alternative actions that are evaluated by a certain number of criteria. Then with the employment of suitable linear programming techniques, the marginal utility functions of the criteria are estimated and the error function between the model and the decision maker. The search of post optimality solution is accomplished by a heuristic method.

The PREFCALC system was developed in 1983, a fact that renders the software a bit primitive concerning the management of the database and the dialogue subsystem as well as the extraction speed of the results. Yet, the system remains a user-friendly and operational multicriteria decision support system that meets a large number of applications. A Windows version has been developed in LAMSADE. Finally, Beuthe and Scanella (2001) developed the MUSTARD system, which also works in case of uncertainty about the evaluation of actions. The system was applied to evaluate transportation projects in Belgium.

The PROMETHEE system. The PROMETHEE (Preference Ranking Organization METHod for Enrichment Evaluations) system is based on the homonymous method originally developed by Brans and Vincke, (1984;

1985) and Brans *et al.*, (1986). According to the method, given a multicriteria problem:

$$\text{Max } \{g_1(\alpha),\ldots,g_n(\alpha) \;/\; \alpha \in A\}$$

where A is a finite set of actions, $g_i, i = 1 \ldots n$, with n the number of the evaluation criteria that need to be optimised.

Through the PROMETHEE methods the above multicriteria problem is solved in the following stages:

a) The development of an outranking relationship on the set A of the alternative actions.
b) The exploitation of this relationship in order to solve the examined multicriteria problem.

The PROMCALC system. PROMCALC (Brans and Mareschal, 1989) employs the multicriteria methods PROMETHEE I, II, IV that are based on the theory of outranking relations and GAIA analysis that applies principal components analysis techniques.

The PROMCALC system is an integrated 4th generation system and has been developed using Turbo Pascal for DOS environment. A major advantage of the system is the high degree of interaction between the user and the system with simultaneous process and presentation of the results.

AIM. The AIM system (Lofti *et al.*, 1992) was developed in order to support less complicated problems. Thus, the system offers some aid in order to investigate the entire set of alternative actions and the comprehension of certain points of the problem.

The decision maker expresses his preferences by assigning maximum and minimum criteria values, the form of the criterion utility function within a set of 15 available choices, and a goal level for each criterion.

Initially, the system classifies the alternative actions by eliminating values that lie outside of the bounds of the criteria. Then the alternative actions that are more close to the preferences of the decision maker are selected through a goal value for each criterion. The alternatives are weak ordered in terms of the goal values and the objective weights are evaluated as expressions of the distance between ideal and goal values. Finally, the alternatives are evaluated and the existing dominance relationships are presented in the entire set of alternative actions.

The system has been developed by using Quick Basic and employs work sheets and tables in order to present the results. The use of the system is quite simple but it is not advisable in actual complicated problems because it does not meet the actual nature of problems.

VIDMA. The system was developed by Korhonen and Laakso (1986a; 1986b) in order to determine a subset, as small as possible, of the actions that approach the desires of the decision maker. This is performed by the employment of a reference direction that is calculated by the Wierzbicki function, and an approximation selection function of the reference subset.

1st step. The criteria to be minimized or maximized are selected. The weight w_i of a criterion g_i is calculated according to the formula:

$$w_i = \begin{cases} \dfrac{r_i}{\left|\max_i\left(r_i^* g_i\left(a_j\right)\right)\right|} & \text{if} \quad \max_i\left(r_i^* g_i\left(a_j\right)\right) \neq 0 \\ r_i & \text{if} \quad \max_i\left(r_i^* g_i\left(a_j\right)\right) = 0 \end{cases}$$

where $r_i^* = 1$ when the criterion i is maximized, and $r_i^* = -1$ when the criterion i is minimized.

2nd step. The goal levels on the criteria $g_i(s)$ are determined. The reference direction is defined by the vector that begins with the current selection and ends with the target point.

3rd step. A subset of alternatives is determined with the employment of multiobjective linear programming.

4th step: The results are graphically presented to the decision maker who selects the solution that best meets his preferences. The corresponding criteria values define the new target point and steps 2 and 3 are repeated. The repetition stops when an acceptable subset of alternatives has been determined.

A weakness of the employed methodology, as pointed out by the developers themselves, is that during the procedure of repetitive interactive actions one can drop to circular situations that could not lead to convergence. The system was developed using Turbo Pascal and offers graphical capabilities for the presentation of the partial and intermediary results. It has been applied in actual multicriteria decision support systems evaluation problems.

The ELECALC system. The system, developed by Kiss *et al.* (1989), combines the outranking relation ELECTRE II with the aggregation-disaggregation approach in order to rank order the alternatives. The aggregation-disaggregation approach is used for the determination of the concordance $(c1, c2)$, discordance $(d1, d2)$, and indifference (v) thresholds and for the determination of the criteria weights. The ranking of alternatives is performed by ELECTRE II.

The use of system is quite complicated and is not suggested for the naïve user. In addition, the system requires a large volume of information from the decision maker, which results in the reduction of its reliability and in inability of control in large-scale problems. It has been developed using C, assembly languages, and Quick Basic.

The EXPERT CHOICE system. The system (Selly and Forman, 1985) uses Saaty's (1980) well-known Analytical Hierarchy Process. AHP is a theory of measuring the subjective distance among the various criteria, which can be qualitative or quantitative. It is based on the principle that in order to make some decisions, the expertise and knowledge of the decision makers are as valuable as the information they use. The method lets the decision makers to model a complex problem with a hierarchical structure, which shows the relations among the goal, the criteria, the subcriteria and the alternatives.

In order to apply the AHP method, four steps should be carefully followed:

1. Decomposition of the problem and formation of the hierarchy.
2. Assignment of priorities.
3. Composition.
4. Sensitivity analysis.

According to Forman (1996), these steps could be analyzed in more details by incorporating them to seven descriptive stages of the process.

The FINancial EVAluation (FINEVA) system. The FINEVA system (Zopounidis *et al.*, 1996) is a multicriteria DSS for the evaluation of companies' performance and viability. The structure of the system is based on a combination of a multivariate statistical method (principal components analysis), of an expert system and of a multicriteria method to derive objective and completed evaluations as possible. It also has the ability to classify companies in groups according to the respective associated business risk, based on some reference standards and by using the multicriteria UTASTAR method (Siskos and Yannacopoulos, 1985, Jacquet-Lagreze and Siskos, 2001).

The FINEVA was applied on a sample of 156 Greek companies (Zopounidis *et al.*, 1997), which belonged in the portfolio of a major Greek bank. The objective of the application was to examine and analyse the credit risk of these companies. The evaluation of the credit risk was performed by the employment of 15 financial ratios (profitability, solvency, and management performance ratios).

Initially, the expert system was used in order to difference companies in very satisfactory, satisfactory, fair and non-satisfactory ones according to their performance. Nevertheless, in order to determine the competitive level among the enterprises, considering also the credit capability of the bank, the

UTASTAR method was employed. The bank's experts in credit analysis defined a weak order of the companies that was then inputted into the system in order to assess an additive utility model that matched the preferences and policy of the experts. The form of the model and its derived results were judged as satisfactory by the experts of the bank.

The FINancial CLASsification (FINCLAS) system. The FINCLAS (Zopounidis and Doumpos, 1998) system differs to FINEVA in that it does not contain an expert system in its structure. The current form of the system is adapted in encountering problems of credit risk evaluation. The basic advantage of the system is its flexibility, which allows the easy adaptation and expansion of the system in dealing with other financial sorting problems (selection of investing projects, portfolio selection and management, and others).

Through the user-friendly interface system, the decision maker can easily communicate with the system. In addition, the interface (or communication) system facilitates the smooth communication between the system's data and model base. The database contains financial data that can be extracted by the basic financial statements and qualitative information. The model base of the system contains more than 30 financial ratios (profitability, solvency, liquidity, management performance), and also the differential balance sheet, the financial table, the linear regression method, and the method of sales percentage, thus providing support to the decision maker during the determination of the companies' basic financial attributes.

The FINCLAS system was applied in the prediction of business failure using data from the survey of Dimitras *et al.* (1996).

The MIIDAS (Multicriteria Interactive Intelligent Decision Aiding System) system. The MIIDAS (Siskos *et al.*, 1999) system is an integrated 5th generation system. Its basic structure consists of the dialogue, models, and data subsystems and corresponding expert subsystems. The system was successfully applied to the job evaluation problem for a Greek Telecommunication company (see, Spyridakos et al, 2001).

3. DISTRIBUTED DECISION SUPPORT SYSTEMS (WEB-BASED DECISION SUPPORT SYSTEMS)

Frequently, decisions are characterized by the high degree of complexity and thereby it is necessary to break the original problems into partial problems each of which will be handled by different groups of experts. In this case, we face a Distributed Decision Making (DDM) situation. According to (Ching, 1988) DDM is a decision making process in which the participating people own different specialized knowledge, execute different specialized task, and communicate with each other through a computer environment, which aims at the support of the entire process.

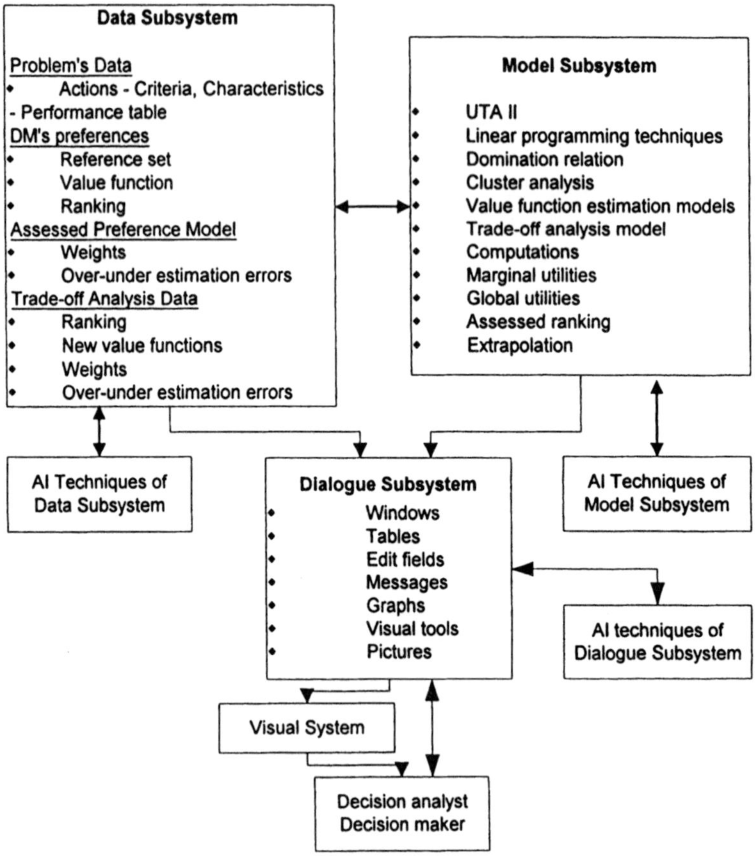

Figure 3. Structure of MIIDAS (*Source*: Siskos *et al.*, 1999)

On the other hand, Information Systems are increasingly characterized by the on line and real time information capabilities. Through the availability of real time information companies improve their competitiveness since immediate information offers the decision makers the ability of immediate response to the competitors' actions (http://cism.bus.utexas.edu/). Most of the current information systems provide such capabilities that can be characterized as distributed on-line systems. The appearance, on the one hand, of inexpensive PC's and workstation systems and, on the other hand, the interconnection of the companies through Internet - World Wide Web (WWW) provides the opportunity of distributed systems development. In addition, Electronic Commerce and Electronic Data Interchange increase the effectiveness of companies operation. In these networked systems with real time online information capabilities (inter- and intra-organizational), the use of distributed artificial intelligence and intelligent agents becomes increasingly common.

The rapid development of such systems and their adoption from more and more enterprises has led numerous academic research centres and enterprises to dispose resources on the development of distributed DSS. With Internet, decision makers are continuously updated on possible new tools thus avoiding the problem of "reinventing the wheel". For a decision maker it is desirable to have the ability to match various scattering tools along with various data contained in them without dealing with details on the installation of these to his computer. In other words, it is vital to have convenient access to tools and data that are installed in remote computer systems. This is exactly the idea that Jeusfeld and Bui (1997) tried to implement. Substantial effort has been devoted to the development of systems to support teamwork (Sriram *et al.*, 1989; IEEE Computer Journal, 1993; Huang *et al.*, 2000). Recent studies indicate the constantly increasing role that Internet-based systems play (Huang and Mak, 1998; Erkes *et al.* 1996). The use of World Wide Web (WWW) with its inherent hypertext capabilities, as an operation medium of distributed decision support systems, resolves many communication problems and is inclined to institute a new appearance standard of communication systems that use the Internet (Goul *et al.*, 1997). Goul *et al.* (1997), face the spread of the DSSs within the Internet as an innovative medium for:

- The facilitation of search and usage of newly developed DSSs.
- The immediate evaluation of the new systems by receiving the reactions by their use.
- The promotion of larger DSSs diffusion through training and learning.

We will now examine in more detail a first approach in the development of distributed decision support systems (Jeusfeld and Bui, 1997), which is based on exploiting Internet resources.

The goal of these systems is to allow users (decision makers, analysts, etc) to exchange information and exploit data, models, and tools (DSS processors) that are scattered in the network. Users may belong to different company sections (geographically dispersed) or in different cooperating companies.

Figure 4 shows a simplified representation of the proposed network. In the figure, three cities are connected through Internet. The orthogonal nodes represent tools (DSS processors), that is, software programs that process the information that is associated with a decision. The cylindrical nodes represent the repositories. The repositories contain all the information required for tracking down the requested tools in the network. Repositories are usually materialized as data or knowledge bases, each of which is devoted in a specific area or a specific goal.

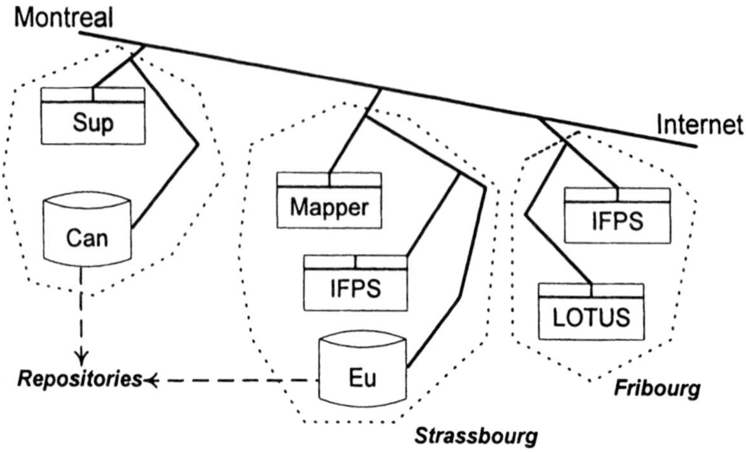

Figure 4. Architecture of the proposed DSS (*Source*: Jeusfeld and Bui, 1997)

Each repository employs it own names because users are interested in numerous and different DSS tools. In addition, with this, one achieves higher "security" on the data since the data and tools of repository are available to all the users that have access to the specific repository.

The system may continuously expand with the addition of new DSS processors. As mentioned above, the goal of repositories is to provide the users with information on new available tools in the network and to facilitate the installation of these tools. The sequence of required tools for the search and installation of a DSS processor in the domain of a user is the following:

- The user addresses a repository searching for suitable DSS processors that may facilitate the solution of his problem and chooses a specific DSS tool.
- Then the repository is requested to commence the installation procedure of the tool to the user's domain.
- The installation procedure is transferred to the user's machine and executed (if possible).

The proposed system adopts two modes for the convenient and secure exchange of data. The fist one considers the adoption of common data format while the second one the employment of URLs (Uniform Resource Locator) (http://www.w3.org/hypertext/WWW/Addressing/

URL/URL.TOC.html) in order to determine the location in the Internet of the DSS processors and data.

The adopted data exchange standards is the OEM format (Papakonstantinou *et al.*, 1995). It is used because it nests the type of the object in the object itself, that is the structure of the object can be directly extracted from the representation of the object itself. Therefore, the structure of an object can be directly extracted by its representation. Obviously, each network node, which contains data or tools, should be capable of receiving call from remote nodes and to activate the suitable DSS program, which in turn should be able to call remote HTTPD Servers (which it can achieve by the help of the libwww library. Both the calls made by remote nodes and the arguments of these calls should follow the OEM format.

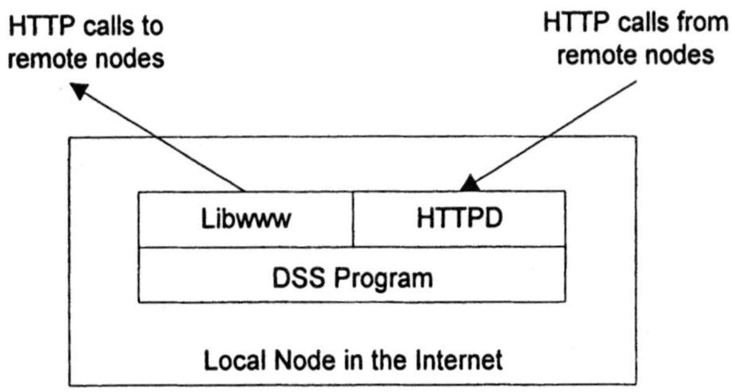

Figure 5. Representation of a DSS processor connected to the WWW (*Source*: Jeusfeld and Bui, 1997)

The idea in which such a system is based on is the exploitation of the existing Internet infrastructure, the protocols used by Internet (http) and the mechanisms through which the communication among remote computers is achieved. Thus, by exploiting the existing Internet infrastructure we may gain access to data, models, and tools that are dispersed in the network.

Figure 6 presents a framework for the development of a Distributed Intelligent Executive Information System. DIEIS) (Chi and Turban, 1995). The development of a DIEIS goes far beyond the standard development procedure of a simple EIS, since the system integrates elements that come from Distributed Artificial Intelligence, DAI (Chapter 7, §10).

In the case of Distributed Problem Solving (DPS) we focus mainly on the nature of the problem and to the multi-agent environment that will be used for its solution. An essential factor that should be considered when intelligent agents are used in solving a problem is the adoption of an efficient coordinating mechanism among the agents.

A high-quality coordination mechanism can be a factor to the faultless cooperation among the agents and in return the intelligence and consequently the effectiveness of the system of agents as a whole will be superior to the aggregate of each partial agent intelligence and efficiency.

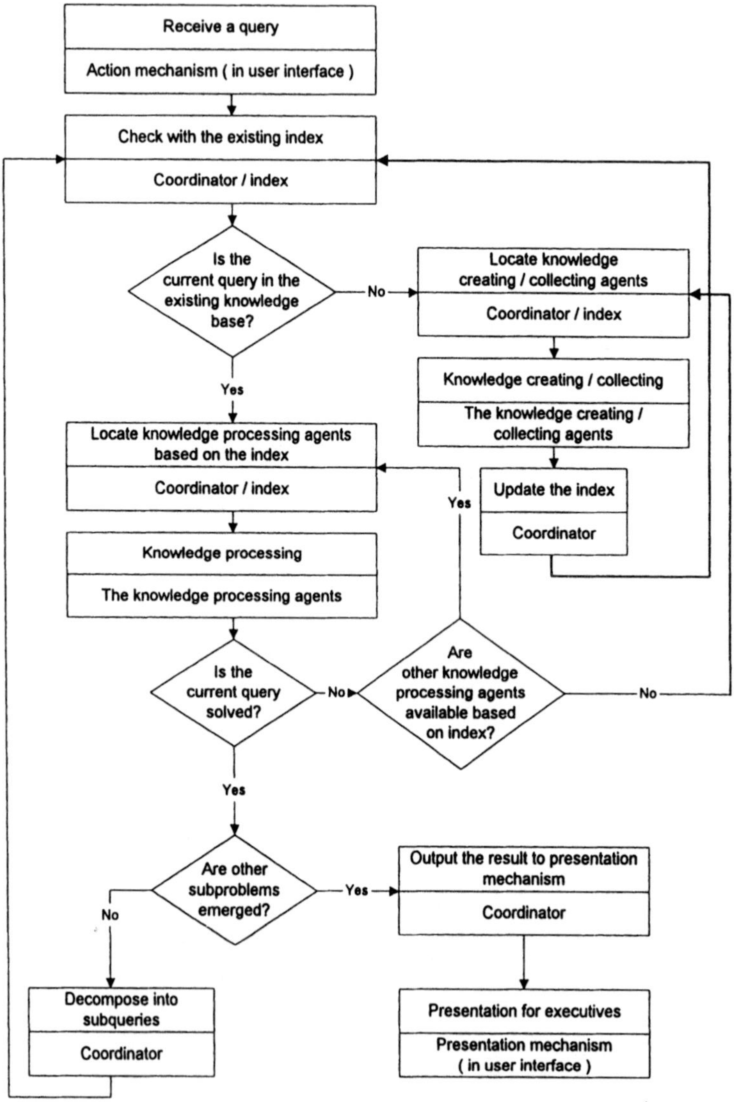

Figure 6. Generation and process of information in the proposed DIEIS (*Source*: Chi and Turban, 1995)

4. GROUP DECISION SUPPORT SYSTEMS

Group decision-making is among the most important and frequently encountered processes within companies and organizations in both public and private sectors. The majority of real-world decision-making problems involve multiple decision makers. However, the comprehension, analysis and support of the process becomes intensely difficult due to the ill-structured, dynamic environment and the presence of multiple decision makers each one of them having his or her own viewpoint on the way the problem should be handled and the decision to be made. Choi *et al.* (1994) point out four properties of group problems which render them hard to attack: (1) they are social problems not mathematical or scientific ones, (2) they are difficult to satisfy all constraints and requirements, (3) they are more difficult to set model than single problems, and (4) there are few methodologies to verify fairness, a concept that is closely related to the aggregation of preferences (Sen, 1970).

Developments in multicriteria decision making methodology and the increasing popularity of computerized MCDM methods have provided management scientists with a set of tools that can be used in solving problems with multiple criteria for a single decision maker. However, most decision situations need to be tackled collectively by a group of people rather than an individual decision maker (Turban, 1988). Therefore, the effectiveness of MCDM methods when used by multiple decision makers remains unproven. Practical preference aggregation methods are necessary to extend the existing MCDM methodology and computing methodology to support group decision problems (Iz, 1992).

The overall characteristics of Group Decision Support Systems (GDSS) have been articulated by a number of researchers. According to Huber (1984) a GDSS is a set of software, hardware, language components and procedures that support a group of people engaged in a decision-related meeting and its major function is to support the three common group activities-information retrieval, sharing, and use. DeSanctis and Gallupe (1987) define GDSS as interactive computer-based systems that combine communication, computing, and decision support technologies to facilitate formulation and solution of unstructured problems by a group of people. Bui and Jarke (1986) define co-operative group decision making as a problem-solving process in which:

a) There are two or more persons, each characterized by his or her own perceptions, attitudes, and personalities
b) Who have recognized the existence of a common problem
c) Attempt to use the system (GDSS) to reach a collective decision.

Several GDSS classification schemes have appeared in the literature. DeSanctis and Gallupe (1987) propose a 3-level GDSS taxonomy based on the systems' functions. Level 1 systems are basically communication media providing technical features (such as procedures for voting and ranking) aimed at removing communication barriers between group members. Level 2 systems provide decision modelling and group decision techniques (such as multiattribute utility methods, brainstorming and Nominal Group Technique) aimed at reducing uncertainty and "noise". Level 3 systems are more sophisticated and can include experts' advice in selecting and arranging the rules to be applied during the decision making process.

Bui and Jarke (1986) and Jarke (1986) proposed four attributes to characterise the decision environment:

1. Spatial distance (local or remote).
2. Temporal distance (meeting or mailing).
3. Commonality of goals (co-operation or negotiations)
4. Structure of the process (democratic or hierarchical).

Jelassi and Beauclair (1987) describe three GDSS configurations:

1. Face to face as well as well as non-face-to-face interactions.
2. Synchronous or asynchronous sessions.
3. Close or dispersed proximity configurations.

Teng and Ramamurthy (1993) present a functional taxonomy of GDSS. They argue that the GDSS concept is based primarily on two dimensions: (1) group process support, and (2) problem content support. Content support is described as the extent to which a computer-based system is capable of providing support to its users in addressing the substantive issues in a specialized domain while process support refers to the system's ability to support or influence proceedings in a group meeting. In the proposed two-dimensional taxonomy, there are four levels of process support: (1) no process support, (2) communication support, (3) process structuring support, (4) and intelligent process support, and four levels of content support: (1) no DSS support, (2) conventional DSS support, (3) DSS for decision analysis, and (4) knowledge-based DSS.

The obvious problem when multiple persons are involved in a joint decision problem is the fact that each individual has his/her own perception of the problem and accordingly to the decision outcome. Therefore, in such an environment the conflict between the members of the group is not a seldom situation. This conflict is referred as interpersonal conflict (Bogetoft and Pruzan, 1991), and may arise due to the presence of numerous factors such as different values and objectives, different criteria and preference relations, lack of communication support between the members of the group, etc. Roy (1996, pp. 274) encapsulates the miscellaneous factors leading to conflict under the term "distinct value systems" e.g., different ethical or ideological beliefs, different specific objectives, or different roles within an organisation. Whatever the origin of the conflicting value systems, they usually affect the evolution of the decision process in ways that were not expected in the outset.

Multiple criteria decision aid (MCDA) methods may be a useful tool in coping with such interpersonal conflicts where the aim is to achieve consensus between the group members or at least attempt to reduce the amount of conflict by concessions. Bogetoft and Pruzan (1991) argue that, in the planning context which is a typical group decision making situation, even if formalised multiple criteria analyses is not an integral part of a decision process at least even simple multiple criteria thinking can make considerable contributions in conflict resolution. In their opinion, the lack of a multiple criteria framework becomes even more evident when considering the systemic conflict notion i.e. the value conflicts that arise between those who make decisions and those parties who are affected by these decisions.

A number of decision methodologies in the group decision-making context have been presented in the multicriteria decision aid literature. A comprehensive list of existing group decision-making methodologies and synthesising mechanisms can be found in Hwang and Lin (1987). Jelassi *et al.* (1990) review formal models for group decision and negotiation, discuss relationships, similarities, and differences between group decision-making and negotiations, and describe some examples of conceptual frameworks and actual implementations of group decision and negotiation support systems. Jelassi and Foroughi (1989) review negotiation theories used as the basis for designing NSS and provide a comprehensive survey of existing software in the area of computer-supported negotiations. Iz and Gardiner (1993) perform an extensive survey and analysis of the MCDM techniques and related Group Decision Support Systems (GDSS) that have been tested in co-operative decision-making situations. A rather broader survey of Group Support Systems is reported in Kraemer and King (1988) and Davison (1995). A comprehensive collection of papers devoted to the synthesis and analysis of group support procedures and software can be found in Bostrom et al. (1992) and Jessup and Valacich (1993) despite the fact that they do not explicitly examine the problem under the multiple criteria decision aid framework.

Technology can support group work in four ways: (1) structuring group processes, (2) supporting communication, (3) providing enhanced information processing, and (4) providing modelling capabilities (Bostrom et al, 1992). Bui and Jarke (1986) argue that Multiple Criteria Decision Making methods provide an elegant framework for three important GDSS tasks: (1) representing multiple viewpoints of a problem, (2) aggregating the preferences of multiple decision makers according to various group norms, and (3) organising the decision process. MCDM provides a simple but structured framework for controlling the decision making process while the simplicity of MCDM outputs makes it easier to communicate, co-ordinate and aggregate individual analyses in the group decision making process (Bui, 1987). Jarke (1986) states that MCDM methods can serve as formal tools for preference surfacing, preference aggregation, negotiation, and mediation, both in co-operative and in non cooperative decision situations. Noori (1995) recognises that from a practical point of view, conflicting objectives often exist among the group members due to interpersonal differences and goal incongruities. The multiple criteria process of a GDSS is, therefore, the crucial aspect of the system because it provides a structured and integrated framework for alternative and criteria assessment and solution compromise.

However, a problem arises when aggregating the preferences of a group of individuals to construct a joint decision model. It is well known that none of the techniques of aggregation of preferences currently known in the literature can satisfy all five conditions imposed by Arrow's Impossibility Theorem (Arrow, 1963). Despite the impossibility of defining an axiomatic fair group solution without resorting to dictatorship, MCDM methods possess a number of advantages for the group decision context (Bui, 1987). By their nature, they integrate multiple views of the problem, using quantitative as well as qualitative criteria. The interactive nature of many MCDM methods allows easy revisions of individual or group problem representations and opinions. In addition, MCDM methods support democratic as well as hierarchical (or bureaucratic) group decision models.

The combination of various aggregation techniques could be used as an attempt to reduce the impact of the lack of a perfect group technique (Bui, 1987). However, this approach assumes a high level of expertise of the users and may lead to difficulties and inconsistencies due to aggregating results obtained by utilising different theoretical principles and theoretical assumptions (Lewandowski, 1989). Choi et al. (1994) argue that a good technique for group problem solving is one that can absorb as many options as possible, build well-formed conceptual model and derive an objective solution.

Multiple Criteria Decision Making is one of the most dynamic areas of research oriented towards the understanding and support of decision making in general, and in group decision making and negotiation in particular (Jelassi *et al.*, 1990). MCDM provides a framework for group decision and negotiation support that may be oriented around the spaces where individuals can make decisions, in which the decisions can be evaluated and compared by an individual or by the group.

From a methodological point of view, one can argue that all known group decision-making processes consist of four elementary stages:

1. An initialisation stage, where the general rules of the decision process to follow are determined. Critical variables of the process such as the set of decision alternatives, the set of the evaluation criteria, the power coefficients of the group members, the rules that settle the successful or unsuccessful end of the process are usually determined in this stage.
2. A preference elicitation stage, where each individual group member states (explicitly or implicitly) his or her preferences on the decision alternatives. Applying a single decision-maker multicriteria method this preferences are transformed to an aggregated measure (a utility function for example) that reflects the individual's point of view on the decision outcome.
3. A group preference aggregation stage, where a synthesising mechanism is used in order to derive a tentative collective decision, by absorbing (in some way) the individual opinions.
4. A conflict-resolution stage, in which an effort to reach consensus (unanimous agreement) or at least attempt to reduce the amount of conflict between individual opinions is performed, usually by group interaction through information exchange or by guiding the process to a previous stage (problem reconsideration). Roy (1996, pp. 274-275) states that in situations with conflicting value systems it is essential to try not to dictate a decision but rather aid in clarifying the various issues and impacts. Kersten (1987) argues that a system should not press decision makers to make concessions but, on the other, should actively participates in negotiations by using available information and generating solutions for all or some decision makers.

Multiple Criteria Group Decision Support Systems have emerged just in the last decade, almost twenty years after the introduction of the multicriteria scientific domain. Kersten (1985) presents NEGO, a two-stage interactive procedure of individual proposal formulation and negotiation leading to compromise based on the generalized theory of negotiations' formulation by Kersten and Szapiro (1986). In NEGO, the negotiating process is a process of contracting and expanding sets of alternatives. Negotiations are carried on in the decision and/or objective spaces, since individual and joint rationality are not assumed, thus providing a more general concept than the utility concept. It is assumed that the set of alternatives is a convex polyhedron defined by a set of hard constraints. Negotiations begin by defining individual optimal alternatives for each decision maker along with aspiration levels. NEGO exerts pressure on decision makers through evaluating their concessions. It compares concessions made in two consecutive iterations and advises that all decision makers are getting closer to a consensus. It also compares concessions made by all decision makers taken together and advises if the whole group is getting closer to a consensus while moving from one iteration to another.

Bui and Jarke (1986) and Bui (1987) present Co-oP a co-operative multiple criteria group decision making system, one of the most well known and best-documented implementations within the multiple criteria - multiple decision makers context. Structure communication between the group members is achieved through interactive multiple criteria methods. Co-oP follows a procedure of six steps: (1) problem definition, (2) group norm definition, (3) prioritisation of evaluation criteria, (4) individual selection of alternatives, (5) group selection of alternatives, (6) consensus seeking and negotiation. It can be used either for the ranking of alternatives using the Analytic Hierarchy Process method (Saaty, 1980) or for selecting one, and only one, best alternative among many, using the ELECTRE method (Roy, 1968). The Co-oP group model bank contains four techniques for preference aggregation: (1) additive ranking, (2) multiplicative ranking, (3) the sums-of-the-ranks approach (Borda, 1781), and (4) the sums-of-the-outranking-relations approach. Co-oP embodies an algorithm, the Negotiable Alternative Identifier (NAI) algorithm, which is based on a triplicate operation concept, expansion-contraction-intersection. NAI is used in order to support decision makers to analyse individual differences when techniques of aggregation of preferences fail to identify unanimity. The algorithm attempts to help the members of the group measure their degree of flexibility regarding their individual assessment of preferences by examining their distribution of preferences among alternatives. It is based on the observation that cardinal ranking of alternatives is a function of two factors: (1) the intensity of preferences can be affected by the total number of alternatives being evaluated, and (2) the distribution of marginal difference among alternatives is rarely uniform. The objective of the extraction operation is to reassess individual preferences by locating possible areas of compromise. The extraction operation yields a subset of comparatively satisfactory alternatives. Given this subset the contraction operation attempts to identify those alternatives that might exhibit a stronger preferential distribution than others might. The intersection operation derives one or more collective solutions that may not be necessarily unanimous but essentially acceptable by all group members.

MEDIATOR [Jarke *et al.*, 1988; Shakun, 1988; Shakun, 1991), is a Negotiation Support System based on Evolutionary Systems Design (ESD) (Shakun, 1988) and database-centred implementation. ESD visualises negotiations as a collective process of searching for designing a mutually acceptable solution. Participants are seen as playing a dynamical difference game in which a coalition of players is formed if it can achieve a set of agreed-upon goals. In MEDIATOR, negotiations are supported by consensus seeking through exchange of information and, where consensus is incomplete, by compromise. In the proposed negotiation setting, a human mediator supports group negotiations and he in turn is supported by the negotiation support system, MEDIATOR. The mediator assists in consensus seeking by aiding the players to build a group joint problem representation of the negotiations-in effect, joint mappings from control space to goal space (and through marginal utility functions) to utility space. Individual marginal utility functions are estimated by applying the UTA method (Jacquet-Lagréze and Siskos, 1982). For the group representation, MEDIATOR uses a common set of dimensions, the union of the individual player dimensions, to define group control, goal, and utility spaces. Players can arrive to a common coalition utility function through exchange of information and negotiation until players' marginal utility functions are identical. In addition to exchanging information and negotiating to expand targets, players can consider the use of axioms to contract the feasible region. Numerous applications of the systems are reported by Shakun (1988).

An interactive procedure for group decision-making problems based on the aspiration theory (Tietz and Barbos, 1983) is proposed by Kersten (1988). He argues that rationality rarely occurs in real-world decision problems and hence it is impossible to determine a group utility function. Therefore, approaches based on the aspiration theory that shift the determination of compromise on the basis of iterative and changing input of decision makers should be used. The proposed method does not require a definition of utility functions or a ranking of alternatives, and it aims at supporting the decision process in a group setting and not solving a group decision problem. In addition, he presents the configuration of a distributed GDSS called Group Decision Support 1 (GDS1), based on the aforementioned procedure.

The PLEXSYS system, described by Dennis et al. (1988), and its descendant GroupSystems (Nunamaker *et al.*, 1991) encompass, among other, an Alternative Evaluator tool, which provides multicriteria decision-making support. With Alternative Evaluator, the group rates each alternative on a 1-10 scale for each criterion. Alternatives can be examined under flexibly weighted criteria to evaluate decision scenarios and trade-offs. Criteria can be considered equally important, or can be assigned different weights.

Lewandowski (1989) describes the decision theoretic framework of Selection Committee Decision Analysis and Support (SCDAS), a group decision support system for selecting the best alternative from a given, finite set of alternatives, based on the satisfying framework (Wierzbicki, 1982).

Each individual group member specifies two levels for each objective outcome. An aspiration level that is interpreted as a reasonable (or satisfactory) value of a given objective outcome and a reservation level which is interpreted as the lowest acceptable level for a given objective outcome. The main emphasis of the system is on structuring the decision process, which is assumed that consists of several well-defined stages. A number of indicators are computed for supporting the process and assessing disagreement for aspiration and reservation levels. Individual evaluation of alternatives is performed by assigning evaluation scores for each attribute to each alternative. An order-representing achievement function (Wierzbicki, 1986) is used to aggregate scores given by an individual group member of various attributes of an alternative and then to rank the alternatives according to their achievement values. A final ranking of alternatives for the entire group is computed by the average achievement values for each alternative.

Vetchera (1991) employs multiattribute utility theory, in order to develop a general framework for group decision support that combines the reduction in cognitive strain provided by individual views with feedback processes. The term feedback signifies changes in the preferences of a group member so that they more closely reflect the other group members' preferences as perceived by that member. He argues that feedback from the group to individual opinions, in spite of the complexity increase in the information structure of the system, is very important for the ongoing support of a joint decision since it leads to possible changes and reconsideration in the expressed preferences of the decision makers. Introducing an additional attribute containing information about the other group members' preferences result in preference modifications. The process starts with individual evaluations based on individual views of the problem, which contain only part of the attributes and equivalence classes of alternatives. The GDSS constructs a common problem representation for the group containing all alternatives and attributes in full detail. It then maps the individual evaluations onto this representation. Using these representations, the system then constructs for each group member an aggregated view of the other members' opinions. A joint decision is reached when all these views are identical. The aggregated views are then transmitted back to the group members, who modify their evaluations and provide information about their modified opinions.

Iz and Krajewski (1992) propose extensions in three single decision maker procedures for multicriteria problems based on interactive multiple objective linear programming (MOLP) techniques. The authors elaborate the Group Naive Search (GNS), an extension of the weighted-sums approach, the Group Step Method (GSM) an extension of the Step method (Benayoun et al., 1971) and the Group Goal Programming Method (GGPM) an extension of the Interactive Sequential Goal Programming Method (Masud and Hwang, 1981). Each original MCDM method has been augmented with a preference aggregation component in order to capture the preferences of multiple decision makers. The three methods were tested with a controlled laboratory experiment involving student subjects, which indicated that the unstructured approach failed to compete successfully with the other two more sophisticated methods in terms of the most measures used.

Carlsson et al. (1992) describe Alicia & Sebastian, a system for formalizing consensus reaching within a set of decision makers trying to find and agree upon a mutual decision. They view group selection as an algebraic operation on a set of alternatives whereas consensus as a topological measure of some metric distance between the same set of alternatives. The system uses the Analytic Hierarchy Process (Saaty, 1980) in order to model the preferences of each decision maker. The general idea for consensus seeking is to "contrast" decision makers into an acceptable consensus area, by advising peripheral decision makers to adjust their preferences in order to approach some centre of the rest of the decision makers. The coordinator (who runs the Alicia) must first set up the meeting. All the decision makers start Sebastian and wait for the meeting to be initialised by Alicia. After this, the decision makers perform their personal ranking of the alternatives and send these to Alicia. Alicia calculates the current consensus degree and if a decision has been reached, informs the decision makers and close the sessions. If this is not the case, a "Sebastian" (a decision maker with a peripheral opinion) is appointed by Alicia and he receives information on how to change his ranking in order to improve consensus. If the Sebastian refuses to change his/her ranking, he is automatically excluded from the process. When Alicia receives the new ranking or is informed that Sebastian refuses to change the ranking, a new consensus is calculated, and if necessary, a new Sebastian is appointed. If too many decision makers are cut off, Alicia will inform the decision makers that a decision cannot be reached and will close the session.

Dyer and Forman (1992) argue that the Analytic Hierarchy Process (Saaty, 1980) is well suited for group decision-making, offering numerous benefits as a synthesizing mechanism, in group decisions. They describe four ways that AHP can be applied to the common objectives context: (1) consensus, (2) voting or compromising, (3) forming the geometric means of individuals' judgements, and (4) combining results from individual models or parts of a model. Finally, they discuss four applications of AHP in group decision situations.

Quaddus et al. (1992) present an application of decision conferencing to strategic planning for a voluntary organization from Western Australia. The modelling of the problem was based on the multiattribute utility theory (MAUT). They used a system called HIVIEW, which is built around a variation of the Simple Multiattribute Rating Technique (SMART) (Edwards, 1977).

Vári and Vescenyi (1992) describe their experience with 26 conferences, associated with 23 decision tasks, and facilitated between 1985 and 1990. The decision to be made included a variety of issues: (1) tactical problems like competition, investment and R&D, (2) organisational strategy like survival or challenge, and development, and (3) inter-organisational strategy and negotiation. In all the evaluation problems (except from one case) they used additive multiattribute utility models (MAUT) to evaluate projects in terms of multiple criteria, including costs, risks, and benefits.

Iz (1992) propose two Group Decision Support Systems based on the Interactive Weighted Tchebycheff procedure of Steuer and Choo (1983). Both systems are designed for solving co-operative group decision problem, in that a unanimous agreement is assumed among the group members regarding the set of problem objectives. The goal (decision task) involves finding an efficient solution, which yields an achievement level for each objective acceptable by all members of the group. The first GDSS aggregates decision makers' individual rankings of the efficient solutions from the Tchebycheff method into a group ranking by solving a pure network model suggested by Cook and Kress (1985). The second GDSS embeds the Tchebycheff method in the Analytic Hierarchy Process (Saaty, 1980). Pair wise comparisons are made by each decision maker at two different levels. First, the objectives in the problem are compared in pairs with respect to the overall objective of finding a group compromise solution, and next, the alternative solutions generated by the Tchebycheff method compared in pairs with respect to each objective. The individual rankings determined according to AHP are then used to find the consensus ranking solution to the multiobjective problem. Both systems have been tested by a controlled laboratory experiment. The findings of this experiment indicate that the system that used the AHP in aggregating preferences failed to compete successfully with the first system which used a less sophisticated ranking procedure in terms of use and the length of the time required to reach consensus. The fact that the examined group decision problem involved only three objectives and that only five efficient solutions were considered at each iteration could imply that the AHP may perform even less successfully when there are more objectives and more solutions to be considered for pair wise comparisons.

Colson and Mareschal (1994) introduced JUDGES, a descriptive Group Decision Support System for the co-operative ranking of alternatives. The system uses graphical representations to provide the decision makers with a clear view of their consensus and disagreements with the help of four Group (Visual) Decision Aids (GDAs) components. GDA1 addresses the problem of detecting similar or dissimilar opinions through a clustering of the individual rankings. GDA2 uses box-plots in order to describe more deeply the distribution of the various opinions. The structure of these box-plots is analysed by GDA3 for consensus seeking. Finally, GDA4 is used for defining and simulating various sets of rules for collective preferences (strong or weak preference, non-preference, indifference or conflict). The basic input data consist of the ranking of the alternatives according to the preferences of each individual decision maker and the decisional power of the decision makers, determined by numerical weights. A pair wise group preference relations system is constructed, defining seven group preference relations: (1) collective strong preference, (2) collective strong indifference, (3) collective conflict, (4) collective non-preference, (5), collective weak preference, (6) collective unclassified relation, and (7) collective refusal relation. This preference relation system is used to analyse the amount of consensus or conflict between individuals' opinions.

Choi et al. (1994) discuss the applicability and practicality of the AHP (Saaty, 1980) in group decision making for a new provincial seat selection in South Korea. Their experience indicated that AHP forms a strong group support tool because its fair and rational hierarchy contributes to understanding the group problem and reducing the gap between conflicting groups. However, they argue that the method cannot guarantee the validity of the decision model. Another problem arises when the hierarchy is too complex or there are too many alternatives for evaluation. In addition, the large number of pair wise comparisons had a strong negative influence to the consistency of the evaluations and the continuous attention of the group members. Finally, they found that it is difficult to keep the mutual exclusiveness of the hierarchy in order to guarantee the reliability of the results.

Teich et al. (1995) present the Resource Allocating Multiple Objective Negotiation Approach (RAMONA), a Negotiation Support System for use in a negotiation involving agricultural income policy. RAMONA develops Pareto Optimal solutions in two party (a party consists of one or more individuals) group decision-making problem with conflict between parties. The system can act as a mediator assisting the parties directly or assist a human mediator in negotiations. RAMONA uses a two-phased method. In the first phase, the parties sequentially answer questions to identify several points on the contract curve or Pareto Optimal frontier. In the second phase parties work out an agreeable solution on that curve. It is designed for negotiations involving multiple issues where conflict exists on every issue, in other words the parties are opposed on every issue. The main advantage of the RAMONA procedure is that it provides a quick and easy approximation of a contract curve without eliciting value functions from the parties involved.

WINGDSS (Cśaki et al., 1995a, 1995b) is a group decision support software intended to aid one or more decision makers, from different fields but with a common interest, in ranking a predefined set of alternatives that are characterised by a finite set if criteria or attributes. In WINGDSS, criteria are hierarchically arranged into a tree. One starts with the most general criterion, which corresponds to the root of the tree, and gradually decomposes it into criteria that are more specific. The leaves represent the criteria, which can be evaluated independently of each other. Criteria are classified into two categories. Those that are evaluated independently of the decision makers are referred as factual data while others that may be evaluated depending on the decision makers' subjective opinion are referred as subjective criteria. The system has a built in function editor and compiler to define functions or rather small procedures in order to evaluate an alternative at each criterion. The importance of any leaf or higher-level criterion is expressed by assigning to them preference weights by the decision makers. Starting from the lowest level of the criterion tree the combination of the preference weights and scores at the leaves results in scores at higher-level nodes. This calculation proceeds to the root of the tree where the final score to each alternative (according to a certain decision maker) is determined. The final score of an alternative during the individual decision process is calculated as the arithmetical (or the geometrical) mean of preference weights and individual scores attached to the criteria.

In the group decision process, for each alternative, a group utility is calculated on the criterion tree. Every decision maker is assigned with a certain voting power at each criterion i.e. at each node of the criterion tree in order to incorporate the different priorities and the expertise of the decision maker. First group weights are calculated by aggregating the weights at each node. Then for each alternative the group qualification at the leaves is computed by calculating the aggregated qualification at each leaf criterion. The group utility is the result of the arithmetical or the geometrical mean of the aggregated qualification values with the aggregated weights (proceeding from the leaf level towards the root). In addition, a sensitivity analysis of the results can be performed in order to analyse the impact of certain decision parameters (individual preference structure, the voting power of the decision makers) on the result.

Salo (1995) develops an interactive approach for the aggregation of group members' preference judgements in the context of an evolving value representation. The method supports several aggregation methods (consensus seeking, normative synthesis, and weighting of individual models), simultaneously. It allows individual group members and coalitions to enter both decomposed and holistic judgements, which are translated, into constraints on the parameters of the joint preference representation. The individual and joint preference representation models can be organised hierarchically as a tree of which the group members' individual value trees form the highest-level branches.

Stanulov (1994, 1995) presents the DIchotomic Matrix multiple Criteria Optimisation (DIMCO) method (or the "dichotomy-cut" method), an outranking approach for individual and group decision-making. He also describes the structure and some applications of the Universal Decision Assistance System (UNIDAS 2), which helps the users in constructing workable decision models of human behaviour by means of the aforementioned method.

Noori (1995) presents a conceptual design of a group decision support system, named NTech-GDSS, developed to guide management through the process of new technology evaluation and adoption. The proposed decision process is a network of relationships among three levels of decision hierarchies: (1) "firm-specific decision criteria analysis" level, (2) "judgement-based alternatives ranking" level, and (3) "performance analysis" level. NTech-GDSS integrates three separate and independent decision models. The decision criteria analysis model structures the decision modelling variables into a company internal audit that assesses the current status of the firm, the need for new technology, and where the technology will have the greatest impact. The alternatives analysis model ranks the technology alternatives with respect to the lowest level of sub criteria defined. A variation of the AHP method (Saaty, 1980) is used to assign weights to the alternatives and to synthesise this information in order to determine the final scores for the alternatives considered. Finally, the performance evaluation model provides an approach for measuring productivity. The system supports both pooled interdependent and sequential interdependent decision situations. In the former mode, decision makers unite to form a homogeneous group and the decision problem is solved collectively and simultaneously while in the latter mode group members address the problem at different times and consider the decision from different angles (Bui, 1987). In the sequential interdependent mode, a weighting set is assigned for the decisions of each individual in the group and the system consolidates the individual decisions into a collective decision based on the weights provided.

A prototype system named Group Work Environment (GWE) is discussed by Ngwenyama et al. (1996). They proposed a set of techniques and an approach to support the facilitator in building consensus during group decision-making. Their procedure is divided into a three-phase process: (1)

pre-evaluation, (2) preference elicitation, and (3) data analysis and reporting. The pre-evaluation phase encompasses three basic activities: (1) selecting the alternatives for evaluation, (2) determining the evaluation criteria, and (3) determining the threshold for agreement. The preference elicitation phase is concerned with ranking the alternatives and providing comparison data. This preference data is then analysed within the data analysis phase, where the goal is to identify possible coalitions, problematic decision alternatives, and individuals whose preferences may serve as a position around which consensus could be negotiated. The decision makers specify their cardinal preferences, using a scale to state their preferences between a pair of alternatives (Saaty, 1980). Using the numeric vectors, three consensus indicators are derived: (1) the group strong agreement quotient, a measure of the level of agreement in the group, (2) the group strong disagreement quotient, a measure of the level of disagreement in the group, and (3) the group strongest disagreement indicator, a measure of the breadth of opinions in the group. Analogous indicators are calculated for each individual decision makers in order to measure the position of each individual relative to the group. The procedure was applied in decision-making situation in which a committee of twelve senior faculty members of a major American business school were required to evaluate a set of five applicants, and nominate one candidate and an alternate for the position of dean (Ngwenyama *et al.*, 1996).

Hämäläinen et al. (1991) introduce preference programming as a group decision support technique in the application of an energy policy problem. The concept of preference programming was also applied in a case study with Finnish politicians (Hämäläinen and Leikola, 1995) and in traffic planning (Hämäläinen and Pöyhönen, 1996). The basic feature of this method is that intervals of numbers include all the opinions within the group. The width of the preference interval is then a measure of the disagreement within the group. Thus, the discussion is directed to attributes, which have the widest preference intervals and the negotiation proceeds as the members of the group re-evaluate their statements and decrease the widths of the preference intervals. The progress of the negotiation requires interaction between negotiators, and the outcome depends on the concessions, which the negotiators are willing to make. The whole process is enabled on-line through the group decision support software, HIPRE 3+ Group Link (Hämäläinen and Kettunen, 1994). Preference programming can be applied using two different procedures (Hämäläinen and Pöyhönen, 1996). In the first procedure each individual member elicits a value model of his or her own, then these individual prioritisations are combined into a group interval model and finally the group continues the negotiation and attempts to reduce the disagreements on the ranges of preference statements until a dominating alternative is found. In the second procedure the group starts to negotiate with a common group interval model which originally does not include any preference statements, i.e. the intervals are at the beginning as wide as possible and then the group members attempt to reduce the preference intervals until again a dominating alternative is found.

Barzilai and Lootsma (1997) apply the Multiplicative AHP (Lootsma, 1993), a variant of the original AHP (Saaty, 1980), to arrive at a joint decision, by incorporating the relative power of the group members. They assign a weight coefficient to each member of the group and use these power coefficients in the logarithmic least squares whereby they analyse the pair wise comparison matrices.

Rangaswamy and Shell (1997), present NEGOTIATION ASSISTANT, a Negotiation Support System that enables negotiators to analyse their own preferences and provides a structured negotiation process to help parties move toward optimal trades. The system, by several utility assessment techniques, helps the parties disaggregate their own preferences and priorities in order to better understand them. Preference assessment is based on a combination of simple additive utility functions (Keeney and Raiffa, 1991) and conjoint analysis techniques. Parties negotiations are achieved through a depersonalised computer network environment. By providing a post-settlement option, the system helps parties identify Pareto-superior settlements, where at least one party is strictly better off, and neither party is worse off.

Miettinen et al. (1997) develop a method for exploring the weighting space in the context of outranking methods, especially ELECTRE III (Roy, 1978). The purpose of the method is to aid decision makers in problems, in which they are not willing (or able) to express their preferences explicitly, and where the data is imprecise. The method studies the weighting vectors resulting in the choice of a certain alternative as the best, with the ELECTRE III method, where a minimum-procedure is used in the exploitation of the outranking relations. This procedure allows the decision makers to contrast their own values to the computed weights. In addition, the procedure provides the minimum and maximum values of each weight, which allow a certain alternative to be ranked as the best in the ELECTRE III method.

Matsatsinis and Samaras (1997) present a group decision-making method using the aggregation-disaggregation approach. They apply the UTASTAR method (Siskos and Yannakopoulos, 1985) to construct a decision model for each individual group member and a collective satisfaction measurement model (Siskos *et al.*, 1998) in an attempt to measure the group members' satisfaction on the collective decision. Structured guidance to consensus achievement is accomplished through information exchange and process redirection. The method can be applied in both democratic or hierarchical decision making i.e. the decision makers may share an equal or unequal weight on the decision outcome. Although the method exhibits interesting features concerning the development of group decision support system, its applicability in real-world decision-making situations remains unproven.

Belton et al. (1997) present a different approach in collective multiple criteria decision-making. They propose the employment of problem-structuring methods (stemming from operational research and systems in the U.K.) for an accurate (or at least satisfactory) definition of the problem joined with multicriteria methods that can be applied in the evaluation procedures of the decision task. In their research, they applied the SODA (Strategic Options Development and Analysis) approach (Eden, 1990), using the COPE software for cognitive mapping, and V·I·S·A (Belton, 1985) for multiple criteria evaluation based on multiattribute value functions. They conclude that that it is possible to combine these two approaches to provide useful decision support in decision conferencing.

Cśaki et al. (1998) describe a method, based on criterion trees, for decomposing a group decision model with decision tables. Instead of complete evaluations (the case where each decision maker accomplishes an individual evaluation on the alternatives), they propose the aggregation of weights and scores into a group weight system and group score matrix, expressing this way the whole group's judgement on any single score or weight. They argue that by decomposing the group decision problem into a basic multicriteria problem (a problem with two-dimensional structure) conflicts among the group members can be resolved in a much easier way because they are presented on not so complex issues such as weights or evaluations of the alternatives with respect to a certain criterion instead in the ranking values of alternatives.

Several others, most attractive and promising, approaches have emerged by joining multicriteria decision aid theory with concepts originating from Artificial Intelligence. NEGOPLAN (Kersten *et al.*, 1988; Matwin *et al.*, 1989) uses an artificial intelligence approach to help evaluate the participants' positions and model negotiating strategies. Negotiations are visualized as a two-stage process. In the learning stage, participants formulate their first proposals while in the interaction stage they exchange proposals and make concessions, reaching either a compromise decision or a deadlock. In NEGOPLAN decision problems are assumed to be hierarchically decomposable i.e. the representation of the decision problem has a hierarchical structure. The structure of the representation may change when there are changes in the perception of the problem, or in the state of the environment or the opponent.

Sycara (1990, 1991) discusses Persuader, a Negotiation Support System that simulates hypothetical labour-management negotiations. The system integrates Artificial Intelligence concepts and techniques, such as frame-based representations and case-based reasoning with graph search and use of multiattribute utilities to come up with a methodology and mechanisms to enable intelligent machine agents to automatically compute and propose problem restructuring during simulated negotiations. Problem restructuring is proposed as a way to remove deadlocks in negotiations, a process of dynamically changing the structure of the negotiation problem to achieve movement towards agreement. Four types of problem restructuring are supported by the PERSUADER system: (1) introduction of new goals, (2) goal substitution, (3) goal abandonment, and (4) changing the reservation prices of the negotiating parties. The system employs four models of problem restructuring:

1. Case-Based Reasoning, which consists of retrieving from memory and adapting previous compromises of similar disputants.
2. Situation Assessment, which represents and recognizes negotiation problems in terms of their abstract casual structure
3. Search of agents' goal graphs to determine interrelations amongst goals of an agent
4. Persuasive argumentation and in particular generating threats and promises, in order to change the beliefs and behaviour of the negotiating parties.

Espinasse and Pauner (1995) describe NegocIAD, a prototype Negotiation Support System based on multicriteria models of negotiation and developed according to a multi-agent architecture from Distributed Artificial Intelligence (DAI) theory. They describe a multicriteria framework, inspired by the Promethee method (Brans *et al.*, 1984), allowing, for a group of decision makers, to apprehend a process of negotiation. Their experiments with the prototype showed that the multicriteria approach coupled with the multi-agent architecture is a worthwhile and operational effort. However, the conceptual framework associated to their multicriteria negotiation method proved too poor to define a relevant support to the negotiation process (Espinasse et al., 1997). In a subsequent effort (Espinasse et al., 1997) they revised their framework, focusing on the definition of assistance dedicated to the mediator. The aim is to provide assistance tools to the human mediator to help him understand conflict situations and to better manage the negotiation process and to permit the human mediator to delegate a part of these tools to an artificial intelligent mediator.

In the same framework, Wong (1994) presents a logical, qualitative problem-solving scheme for cooperative knowledge-based systems that uses social choice theory as a formal basis for making join decisions and promoting conflict resolution. The proposed scheme consists of three steps:

a) The selection of decision criteria and competing alternatives
b) The formation of preference profiles and collective choices
c) The negotiations among agents as conflicts arise in group decision making.

An examination of the literature (which is neither exhaustive nor complete) reveals that group decision making and negotiation problems constitute a challenging area for multicriteria decision aid scientists. Two are the most important aspects in the contribution of the multicriteria decision aid theory to group decision making problems. Firstly, MCDM methods provide the ability to define a joint framework for process structure and information exchange and thus reducing the unstructured nature of the problem. In addition, the utilisation of MCDM methods results in the expansion of the group members' learning ability. Using multicriteria methods each individual is able to explore his own value system from multiple viewpoints and in addition to learn and modify his/her perceptions by obtaining knowledge of the other group members' preference structure, goals, criteria, intentions and beliefs. However, the applicability of current multicriteria group decision aid methodologies need to be extensively tested in real-world decision making situations so as to measure their importance and contribution in group decision making.

An attractive and most promising approach seems to be the one that combines the benefits of multicriteria formalism with tools from Artificial Intelligence. Perhaps the most well suited approach in the group decision context is the combination of multicriteria decision aid and multi-agent theory. Multi-agent theory attempts to model a group of interactive artificial and human agents in order to find solutions to complex ill-structured problems. Thus, considering this description becomes evident the close relationship between group decision making, multicriteria decision aid and multi-agent theory.

5. EXECUTIVE INFORMATION SYSTEMS - EXECUTIVE SUPPORT SYSTEMS

A study conducted by the Research Centre for Information Systems at MIT revealed that almost one third of the major American companies have already installed or proceed to installation of some type of EIS. The study also proved that half of these systems were directly employed by executives. The results of MIT hold with the findings of another survey that was conducted in 1985 by the Personal Computing journal. More recently, the trend to move, through re-organization or staff decrement, several executives has extended the need for EIS development. Lower level managers now undertake more responsibilities and they ask for the services of an EIS. Traditionally, EIS were developed as computer based programs used in large scale computer systems. Their objective was to consolidate data in a single key stroke for people that should make decisions but at the same time were completely compute naïve users. The first developed programs obtained information from financial systems of large scale computers and they simplified it in order to represent graphically performance ratios. These systems were developed in order to emphasize in divergences between forecasts or budgets and finally achieved results. The systems where operated by financial advisors, marketing advisors and chief executives. The objective of the traditional EIS was to provide immediate graphical representation of the performance of sales or the performance of statistical market surveys (http://mtiac.hq.iitri.com/MTIAC/pubs/eis/eis1.htm#1.1). The goal was to develop software applications that could address the information needs of executives. Typically, an EIS does not store the entire company's data but only those that are needed in the support of executive/manager level decisions.

An EIS is constructed to represent summary data of the entire environment of the company, yet at the same time the system allows the examination of sections that require more caution. An EIS represents data in a concise format in order to facilitate managers to check the qualitative data obtained by endogenous and exogenous factors. Most EIS can also present summary information in order to aid decision making and accessory information that support detailed data. Details become available to the user through a data tracking technique, known as "drilling down", which describes the process of providing step-by-step a higher level of detailing. «Drilling down» through data permits an executive to solve problems by analysing a situation from top to bottom and going through more details. The result is a more improved inspection of the problem and subsequently in more improved decisions.

In summary, we may state that the objectives of Executive Information Systems is to:

a) Reduce the amount information that is directed to the executives,
b) To ensure the valid and up to date access on this information, and
c) To help the executives to focus on the critical points of the problem at hand.

An EIS has several characteristics that make it different by other information systems (*Table 1*). A successful EIS reduces the necessary reports as it continuously keeps the executives updated by providing qualitative information.

As typical objectives of an EIS, we may consider the advanced internal audit and the communication. Most EISs emphasize on the sections of the company the encounter a certain difficulty.

Table 1. Typical characteristics of an Executive Information System-EIS (*Source*: http://mtiac.hq.iitri.com/MTIAC/pubs/eis/eis1.htm#1.1)

Characteristics	Description
Usage degree	High, consistent, without necessity for technical assistance
Required computer literacy background	Minimum-it should be easy to learn and use
Adaptability	High-it should reflect the decision making style of each executive
Primarily usage	Spotting, check
Decision support	High management level - unstructured
Data support	Internal and external sources
Performance capabilities	Text, tables, Graphics, sound and video
Concentration of graphics	High, depending on the presentation style
Data access rate	It should be high and provide fast responses

Watson *et al.* (1997) studied the numerous factors that generate the necessity for EISs and ranked them from the most to the least important.

a) External factors

- Increased competitiveness
- Rapid changing environment
- Need for more activity
- Need to access external databases
- Increase of state regulations.

b) Internal factors

- Need for up to date accurate information
- Need for improved information
- Need to access operational data
- Need for ready situation updating or for different situations
- Need for increased effectiveness
- Need to identify past trends
- Need to access collective-group databases
- Need for information that is more accurate.

An EIS allows access in both external and internal information of a company. Both information types play an important role to executives' decisions. External factors, such as the trends of the economy and competitors' actions, should be merged with internal data. Typically, the successful development of an EIS requires the inclusions of both internal and external factors.

As with all information systems, EISs exhibit certain advantages and disadvantages.

a) Advantages

- It is simple in order to be easily used by high level executives.
- The necessary operations do not require extended computer expertise.
- It provides up to date, concise information for the company.
- It offers a better understanding of the information.
- It filters data in order to save time.
- It offers a system for improved information tracking.

b) Disadvantages

- It has limited operations and can not perform complicated calculations.
- It is difficult to determine in qualitative terms the benefits and justify the application of an EIS.
- Its use might result on information overload of the executives.
- The system might be difficult to manage
- It is difficult to keep data up to date.
- Usually the data refreshing requirements are underestimated.
- It exhibits data security problems
- It might lead to less secure and invalid data.
- The application cost is quite large for small companies.

Some of the characteristics that are different between DSSs and EISs are:

- DSSs were developed as support tools addressed to middle or lower level managers. While both types include modelling capabilities and database systems, the presentation modules are typically less advanced in a DSS. This is due the fact that DSSs were designed in order to support decisions to the lower management level and on whereas an EIS emphasizes in supporting decisions in the higher management level exclusively.
- While both EIS and DSS are designed in order to support and improve the decision making process the type of the decision made by an senior executive differ from the corresponding type of a middle level manager. The EIS can be thought as a system that provides information that aid the formation of intelligent queries. These queries may then be forwarded to a DSS. A detailed analysis can be performed by an analyst with the help of a DSS, however this detailed analysis can not be performed by a chief executive.
- The goal of an EIS to allow executives to become familiar with the entire company and not only with a certain section of it. A DSS usually provides detailed information in order to aid the analysis of problems related with a certain section of a company.
- In an EIS, external data that may be retrieved from on-line databases and internally generated data are examined by the EIS only when this is required. That is the EIS emphasizes in the amalgamation of external

data during the decision making procedure whereas the DSS pays limited attention to this point.

- While each type of system tracks and reports the status of certain activities, the level of details provided to a certain problem by each type of system is quite different. An EIS primarily provides summary information and allows the provision of additional details through the incorporation of the "drilling down" capability. The DSS on the other hand will try to ensure all the details that are necessary for the analysis of the problem.

Despite the differentiations though, both types of systems have their advantages and drawbacks and the selection of an EIS or a DSS depends on the level and the form of the analysis required on each case.

- The first generation of EISs was primarily aimed at the determination of problems and the detection of "opportunities'. However, in a very short time it became evident that these systems should expand and obtain decision support capabilities. Thus, the next generation of EISs was developed and these systems are known by the name Executive Support Systems (ESSs). EISs provide mainly information whereas ESSs offer additional decision support capabilities.

According to Watson *et al.* (1997), the term EIS and ESS may be considered identical in most cases, however they consider that an ESS may contain one of the following capabilities:

- Support for electronic communication (email, conferencing…)
- Data analysis capabilities (spreadsheets, DSS…)
- Organization tools (electronic calendars…).

6. SPATIAL DECISION SUPPORT SYSTEMS

A GIS is decision support system, which is rendered with the incorporation of spatial-related data in a problem-solving environment (Cowen, 1988). On the contrary, Devine and Field (1986) expressed the opinion that a GIS is simply a form of a Management Information System that allows the representation of general information in charts.

The capabilities of Geographic Information Systems (storage, analysis, and management of spatial information - http://www.geog.ubc.ca/courses/klink/gis.notes/ncgia/UNIT59; http://www.gis.com/whatisgis/index.html) cover the needs for spatial information necessary for decision-making processes. Consequently, the capabilities of a GIS (Mennecke, 1997) are incorporated into Decision Support Systems. The new systems that result by this cooperation are called Spatial Decision Support Systems (SDSSs). Frequently, decision makers that encounter a complicated spatial problem have several and conflicting goals in the problem solving process. A large number of analytical techniques have been developed in order to aid the decision makers to solve problems of this type by using multiple criteria.

Spatial Decision Support Systems (Densham *et al.*, 1995) were designed to support the decision making process in complex spatial problems, i.e. they constitute the product of cooperation between Geographic Information Systems and Decision Support Systems. SDSSs provide a framework for integrating database management systems, analytical models, graphical representation capabilities, and special decision makers' knowledge.

SDSSs were designed to offer to the user a decision-making environment that enables the analysis of geographic information by a flexible fashion. SDSSs were developed in parallel with DSSs yet their evolution in comparison with the evolution of DSS was delayed for 10 or 15 years.

However, the design, development, application and usage of SDSSs are based on the philosophy of DSSs. Geoffrion (1983), suggests that the SDSSs have the following characteristics:

1. They were designed to support ill structured problems where the goals of the decision maker and the problem itself can not be specifically determined.
2. They are equipped with a user interface with multiple capabilities and easy to use.
3. SDSSs offer to the user the possibility to combine analytical models and data in a flexible fashion.
4. Aid the user to search for possible solution by using the system's models in order to generate a series of feasible alternatives.
5. They are easily adaptable to the needs of the user and provide him with new capabilities.
6. They allow a repetitive solution of the problem, i.e. the decision maker may follow different paths and not a single predefined way of solving the problem.

Because of the complicated nature of spatial problems, SDSSs should offer additional capabilities and functions in order to:

- Provide the necessary mechanisms in order to input the spatial data.
- To allow the presentation of complex spatial relationships and structures that reside within the spatial data.
- To include analytical techniques that are unique to spatial and geographic analysis.
- To present the results by using a variety of spatial forms like charts and other more special forms.

As already stated the development of SDSSs was based on the philosophy of DSS (http://wwwsgi.ursus.maine.edu/gisweb/spatdb/

urisa/ur94015.html). Among the several DSS frameworks, the one proposed by Sprague (Sprague 1980, Sprague and Carlson 1982) was adopted in the spatial field. There are three technology levels included in the framework proposed by Sprague (*Figure 7*).

In the lower level, the toolbox of the SDSSs is located, which includes the software and hardware. In the second level, we find the SDSS generator. The generator is a set of compatible modules of software and hardware that may easily be shaped to produce a specific SDSS, which is the third level of the framework. When the needs of the decision maker change then additional modules may be added to the specific SDSS by the generator or if there are no modules then these must be gathered by the SDSSs' toolbox.

Sprague's framework contains five functions, three of which correspond to the three technology levels (the toolbox, the generator, and the specific SDSS). The toolsmith develops new software and hardware tools for the SDSS's toolbox, the technical supporter adds new capabilities or components to the generator, and the builder shapes the specific DSS. The fourth function is the mediator who communicates with the system where as the fifth function id the decision maker who is responsible for the development and implementation of the proposed solution. Note there are five functions and not five people, i.e. one human may accomplish more than one functions.

The decision maker determines the analyses to be performed and uses the system's results to evaluate the tentative solutions. If the decision maker wishes he might explore other folds of the problem and this action may require the addition of new capabilities in the SDSS.

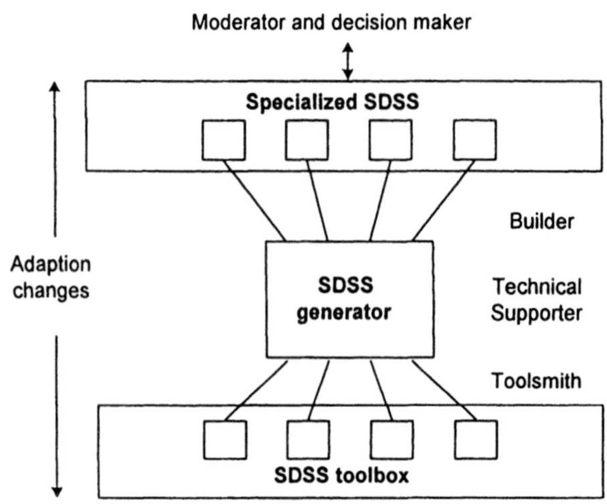

Figure 7. The framework of Sprague (*Source*: Sprague, 1980)

This procedure of system's adaptation and evolution is accomplished quickly during the decision making process. The readjustment procedure increases the flexibility and usefulness of the SDSS to the decision maker.

6.1 Structure of SDSSs

Armstrong and Densham (1990), designed and architecture structure for SDSSs. Their proposed structure is comprised by five software modules, the database and model base management systems, the display and report generators, and the user interface (*Figure 8*). Each module offers a set of operational capabilities. In *Figure 8* the five software modules are represented by boxes. The first four modules are included in the user interface because the communication with the user is exclusively performed by the user interface. The flow of data and information among the modules are represented by the connecting arcs.

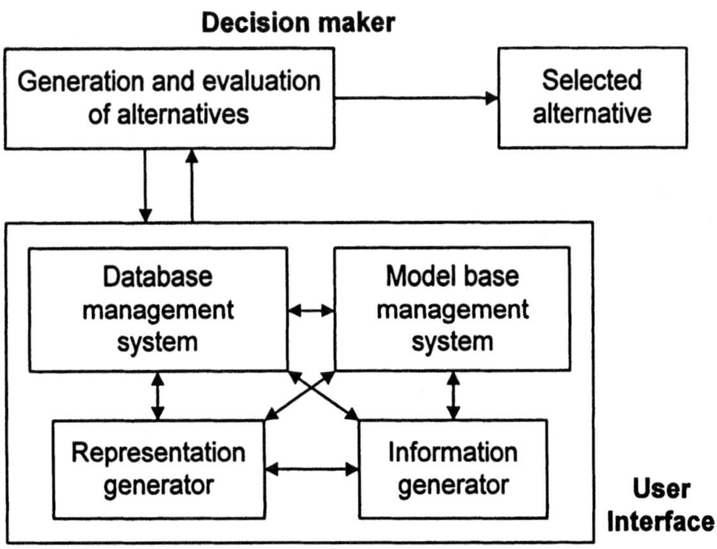

Figure 8. Architectural structure of SDSS (*Source*: Armstrong and Densham, 1990; Densham, 1991)

The results of the system are presented to the decision maker and the decision maker proceeds with their evaluation. A solution may be accepted by the decision maker or if it does not become acceptable, it may be used for determining further analyses.

There are a large number of GIS applications that are specified each time by the particular needs of the users (Maguire *et al.*, 1991; Clarke, 1997;

http://www.gis.com/software/index.html; http://www.bts.gov/gis/; http://www.geo.ed.ac.uk/home/giswww.html; http://www.ibrae.ac.ru/~mkanev/eng/Geostat_GIS.html; http://www.soi.city.ac.uk/~raper/gislinks.html; http://www.baylor.edu/grass/; El-Swaify and Yakowitz 1998; Mennecke, 1997; Contini *et al.*, 2000; Tang *et al.*, 2001; Booty, 2001). Suggestively, out of a large number of possible applications, we mention the following:

- Energy
- Agriculture – irrigation
- Land usage
- Socio-economic studies
- Transportations
- Risk management
- Environment
- Business

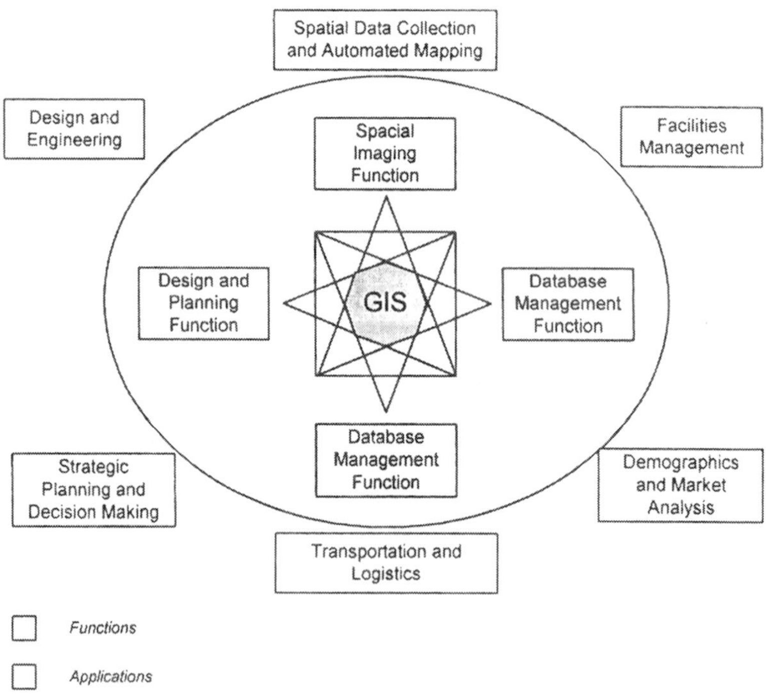

Figure 9. GIS Functions and Applications (*Source*: Mennecke, 1997)

Applications of SDSSs with the employment of MCDM have been developed for the determination of the best spatial location for an alternative according to a predetermined set of criteria (Carver, 1991; Pereira and Duckstein 1993; Tkach and Simonovic, 1997; Chen *et al.*, 2001). Applications of GIS technologies for decision making facilitation in water sources management (http://h2osparc.wq.ncsu.edu/; http://www.ce.utexas.edu/prof/maidment/gishyd97/library/library.htm; Walsh, 1993; Simonovic, 1993; Leipnik *et al.*, 1993; Watkins *et al.*, 1996; Fedra, 1997; Cambruzzi, 1999), have been reported to situations such as:

- The use of GIS in searching for suitable sites for the disposal of radioactive waste in the UK with the aid of multi-criteria evaluation techniques (Carver, 1991).
- The improvement in decision making concerning water resources management with the help of a GIS that cooperated with an Expert System (McKinney and Maidment, 1993).
- Pereira and Duckstein (1993) in order to evaluate potential habitats for the endangered Mount Graham red squirrel applied the Compromise Programming technique within a GIS.

Most of the GIS usages are related with support data analysis and decision making (Mennecke, 1997). A framework of this new category off SDSSs is provided by Mennecke (1997) (*Figure 10*).

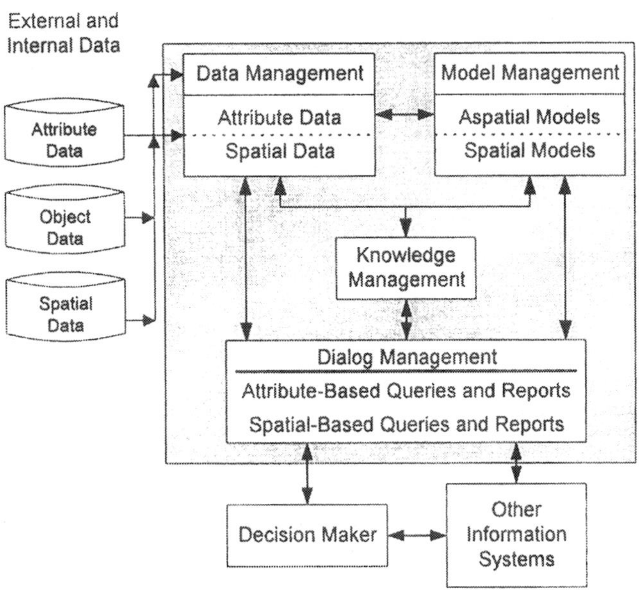

Figure 10. A Conceptual Model of a Geographic Information System Used for Decision Support (*Source*: Mennecke, 1997)

Recently, the development of advanced network technologies (Internet - WWW) permitted the design and development of Spatial Decision Support Systems that operate within Internet (http://www.ccg.leeds.ac.uk/vdmisp/publications/ paper1.htm) (*Figure 11*). Continuously, new web sites are presented with specialized SDSSs that can be operated remotely (http://www.regis.berkeley.edu/index.html, http://imlab9.landarch, uiuc.edu/~eslarp/egrets/index.html, http://www.digimap.ac.uk:8081/, http://www.gisnet.com/gis/notebook/webgis.html).

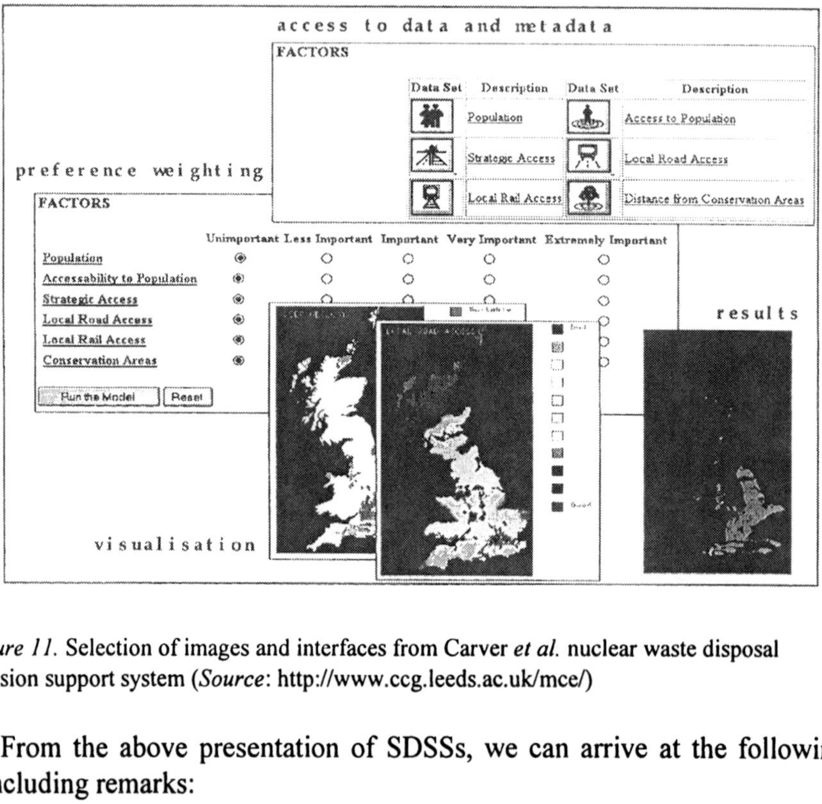

Figure 11. Selection of images and interfaces from Carver *et al.* nuclear waste disposal decision support system (*Source*: http://www.ccg.leeds.ac.uk/mce/)

From the above presentation of SDSSs, we can arrive at the following concluding remarks:

- The SDSSs field has a rapid expansion trend, which is certain to continue in the following years.
- One of main limitations of the SDSSs spread was the cost of the required equipment, which usually was to high for the common user (individual or organization). However, new computer systems with more powerful hardware and software components are now at the disposal of the decision makers, in prices that can be paid by most of the users.
- The training of the users in the SDSSs distinct features was in the past a time consuming process. In addition SDSSs could only be operated by users with high level of expertise and specialty. Modern systems, with

user-friendly interfaces and exploitation of the World Wide Web graphical representation capabilities overcome this problem and allow even computer naïve users to operate them without problems.

Thus, SDSSs seem to have very prominent perspectives in the near future.

7. DATA WAREHOUSES

A data warehouse is a decision support environment that utilizes stored data from several different sources; this data are organized and presented as information to the decision maker in order to aid the decision-making (Singh, 1998). Inmon (1996) defined a data warehouse as the database that is characterized by subject orientation (contains information that concern the company's executives), non-volatility (data cannot be changed after their importation to the data warehouse), time dependency of the data and the sorted and integrated form of its information. According to Simon (1998), a data warehouse is a database that contains read only data records and its purpose is to support decision support systems.

Consequently, data warehousing describes the management of data and the use of technology for its process and analysis whereas data warehouses are special databases that contain suitably processed data that come from the operational databases of the enterprise; this data is used in order to support the decision maker or to support a Decision Support System.

There are some strong differences between the classic databases and the data warehouses. Clearly, according to the definitions, data warehouses contain read only data. Further, data in the data warehouse is the result of properly processed data of partial databases; hence databases and data warehouses contain completely different types of information. In many cases, this data represent structured information and not only a recording of simple facts and elements as in the case of typical databases.

Chaudhuri and Dayal (1997), surveyed data warehousing and OLAP technologies and present a typical data warehousing architecture (*Figure 12*).

A small-scale application of a data warehouse is the data marts, which play the role of a small data warehouse or in other cases are part of a data warehouse. Many enterprises develop several data marts, which are then joined or nested in an integrated data warehouse application.

According to Inmon (1993), who is considered as the pioneer of data warehousing, there are four specific attributes that govern the basic structure of a data warehouse:

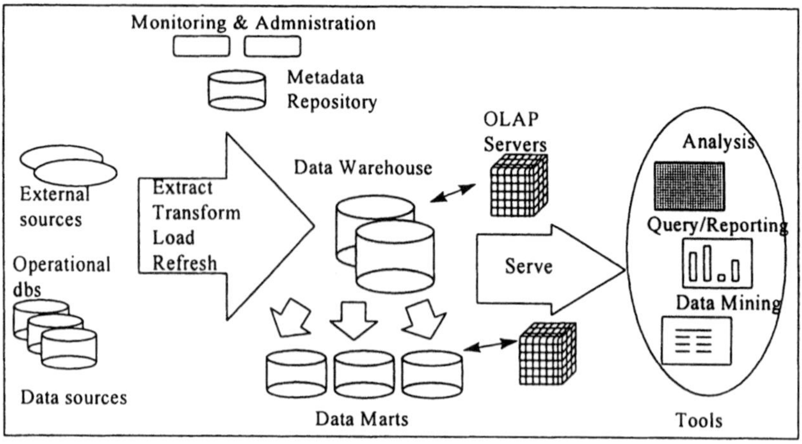

Figure 12. General data warehousing architecture (*Source*: Chaudhuri and Dayal, 1997)

1. **Subject oriented:** The warehouse is built around all the existing applications of the operational data. Not all the information in the operational database is useful for a data warehouse, since it is designed specifically for decision support whereas the operational databases contain information for data-to-day use.
2. **Integrated:** In an operational data environment it is possible to find many types of information being used in a variety of applications, and some application will be using different names for the same entities. For example in one application the gender could be codified as m and f (male and female respectively) whereas in a second application these could be expressed a 1 and 0, for male and female respectively. However, in a data warehouse it is essential to integrate this information and make it consistent; only one name must exist to describe each individual entity.
3. **Time dependent:** A data warehouse contains information collected over time, which implies there must always be a connection between the information in the warehouse and the time it was entered. This is one of the most important aspects of the warehouse as it relates to decision-making, because information can then be used for comparisons and forecasts.
4. **Non-volatile:** Data in a data warehouse is never updated. Thus data can only be loaded from other databases such as the operational database, as only the latter can be updated, changed, or deleted. This means that a data warehouse will always contain historical data; the user can only access this data but is not allowed to alter it any way.

A data warehouse retrieves data from several heterogeneous environments and then transforms and stores it according to a collective model. The transformation and the modification take place each time an update of the data warehouse is required. The information that describes the transformation and storage model is called metadata. The metadata is the form in which the end user perceives the data contained in the data warehouse.

The appropriate selection of information is what makes the data warehouse capable to respond rapidly to the queries posted by the users. The information that is eventually stored gives the ability to the end user to find important information, by executing complex multidimensional queries. For example, the user is able to query the data warehouse for the bestseller product and in which way its sales are related with the distribution of the population and with the seasons. This kind of information if very critical to the decision makers in order to lay out the marketing strategy of the company and achieve the desired goals.

An essential advantage from the use of data warehousing is the increase of the decision maker's productivity through the integration, conversion and integration of operational data; the decision maker has the ability to approach the available data in a totally different way. In short, the benefits of data warehousing are manifold for an enterprise, and are related with:

- Tracing of new market trends.
- Reduction of the cost of new products and increase of the market shares.
- Determination of the most suitable marketing strategy, by promoting the best strategies and improving those that are inferior.

Data warehousing is the first necessary step to manage the vast amount of information. It is an integral part of several commercial Management Information Systems; its significance is even heavier for Decision Support System since it has the ability to manage without difficulty Terabytes of information.

Furthermore, data warehousing is necessary due to the requirement for fast process of data and extraction of information. Existing information systems provide, to a certain extend, this ability to the user but on the other hand they some times entrap the user due to their inability to:

- Manage historical data.
- Give access to data from different operational databases.
- Provide the ability to retrieve information through queries.
- Provide full support for decision-making (support for decision support systems).

7.1 Structure of data warehouses

A data warehouse has a specific structure. There are different levels and structural elements (*Figure 13*).

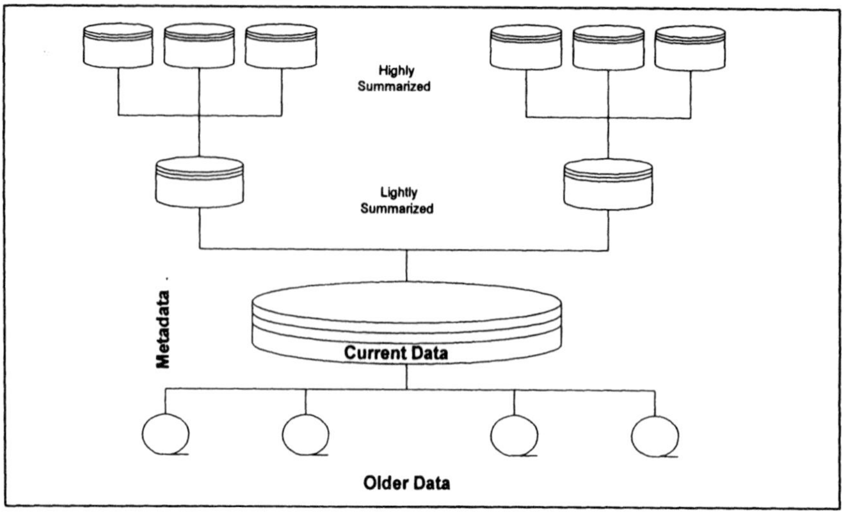

Figure 13. The structure of a data warehouse

According to the figure above, a data warehouse consists of:

1. The current data.
2. The older data.
3. The summarized data.
4. The metadata

Current data is the principal component of a data warehouse. Current data have the following characteristics:

- It represents the most recent facts that at the same time have a certain importance.
- Its volume is very large and is stored in the lower storage levels.
- Storage disks are used for the storage of current data so as to promote their accessibility. However, this renders the management of current data a very complex task especially because of its vast volume.

Older data is the data that is not used frequently. Because of their occasional use, usually it is held in common speed hard disks or in many cases after some time it is deleted permanently.

Summarized data is classified in two categories according to the requirements of their processing and their storage ability:

a) Lightly summarized data, which is the result of data processing that did not yield large amount of information. This type of data is usually stored in storage disks.
b) The highly summarized data, which is compact and easily accessible. It is stored in the primary units of the data warehouses.

Summarized data is only stored only when this type of data can be used frequently. In other words, when summarized data is produced and the possibility to use it is small, then this data is not stored in the data warehouse at all.

The metadata is a very important element of a data warehouse. In setting up a data warehouse the end user and the administrator must have access to all the information in the tables and the attributes. This means that they have to know a number of things, such as where the data is located, what data type or format it is in, where the data is from and to whom the data belongs, etc. For these reasons, another database containing so-called metadata is needed, which describes the structure of the contents of the database. In a complex database environment, adequate metadata is indispensable, since it determines the structure of both the operational data and the data warehouse. Meta data is used by end users for querying purposes as well as by the data manager for structuring the management of a database site. In most cases the metadata is placed elsewhere from the other elements of data warehouse, because metadata does not contain data from the operational databases.

7.2 Categories of data warehouses

The designer of a data warehouse has the discreet ability to choose and shape his distinct features for the application; however he should always have in mind the requirements of the enterprise. Hence, the applications of data warehouses are classified into two major categories:

a) Host-based warehouses: Their management is accomplished through Information Systems or traditional systems.
b) LAN-based Warehouses: They are cooperating with a local network, that is they primarily support a small group of users, and their management is accomplished either through the local network or through the main computer.

Another classification of the data warehouses is based on the location and the source of the data stored in the warehouse. According to this classification there are five types of data warehouse systems:

1. Operational data warehouses.
2. LAN-based workgroup data warehouses.
3. Multistage data warehouses.
4. Stationary data warehouses.
5. Distributed data warehouses.

8. OLAP SYSTEMS

As the amount of information stored in a data warehouse increases, the mining of useful information gets harder and harder. Therefore, an important question is how to exploit the data stored in increasingly larger and more complex databases without increasing the required response time. The use of the well-known client/server architecture gave the enterprises the possibility to utilize specialized servers in dealing with specific data processing problems. However, the client server model cannot adequately handle the multidimensional nature of the questions that usually managers ask. It was necessary to develop a more centralized representation structure capable of storing the operational information in a suitable form that could support its direct access. At this point appeared the OLAP systems.

On Line Analytical Processing (OLAP) is a relatively new term and many times it is confused with Decision Support Systems. But, OLAP is the step that immediately follows the simple scrutiny and presentation of the data; it is also one step before the development of an integrated decision support system.

OLAP systems are evolving very fast. They are applied to organizations that aim at the maximization of their business value through the utilization of their vast volumes of data. This data comes from the various departments of the enterprise or the organization, from databases and data warehouses, and from several other external sources. The processing, analysis and presentation of this data is not a trivial case, especially when the purpose of the data analysis is to reach critical decisions for business plans. In the past, these decisions were based on the intuition and the expertise of the decision makers rather that the on the analysis and processing of the data. Today, systems, which are capable of analyzing such amounts of data and "produce" information, are invaluable.

Codd *et al.* (1993), was the first to set the requirements of an OLAP system:

- Multidimensional representation of the information.
- Accessibility.
- Client/server architecture.
- Multi user support.
- Flexible reports and response.
- Uniform response time
- Unlimited number of dimensions and levels of hierarchy.

A decision maker in order to reach a certain decision needs to process the amount of available data and to place complex questions in order to investigate the several parts of the problem. According to Singh (1998), OLAP systems are a type of software systems that aid the analysts, the managers and executives in the direct access of data and in the multidimensional process and analysis of this data.

All the issues that concern an enterprise are characterized by their multidimensionality. For example, sale can be examined in terms of the period made, the area and the product. Information of this nature is called multidimensional and such relationships cannot easily be analyzed when the table has the standard two-dimensional representation. Instead multidimensional tables should be used, the analysis of which requires the use of particular tools. OLAP systems are characterized by the dynamic multidimensional analysis of the data; at the same time they provide the user with problem modeling capabilities and also with the ability to extract the lowest level and most detailed data and calculations. Within an OLAP system the user can place "what-if" questions, apply and test several scenarios.

As with the data warehousing applications, metadata is a very crucial element in the operation of OLAP systems. Metadata is used to represent hierarchical relations, important information for the transformation of the data, factors related with the analytical procedures, etc. Metadata contains all the necessary information for the connection of the different pieces of an OLAP system and for its operation.

Multidimensional viewing is the way the user communicates with the system. It is adopted according to the needs and requirements of the user. Thus, accountants use multidimensional viewing through spreadsheets; executives require simple and comprehensive forms; marketing analysts use graphical representations where as others use the data analysis information through other programs or through programming languages such as Visual Basic, Java, C, etc.

The capabilities of the computer systems is a very restrictive factor in the development of OLAP applications, since they require huge computational power for the support of the various models for the processing of data and the representation of the results.

An OLAP application should have the following characteristics:

- It should include mathematical, statistical and analytical models such as distributions, percentages, regressions methods, etc.
- It should be able to join and relate the numerous data (original and elicited ones).
- It should support "what-if" questions and analyses.
- It should have the ability to response instantly and support the rapid elicitation of results.
- It should function easily and fast.
- It should be able to manage large amounts of data.

These characteristics represent also the requirements for the design and development of an OLAP environment.

The data used by an OLAP application come either from internal sources of the enterprise (operational databases) or several other external sources. However, the need for multidimensional analysis and processing puts the data warehouses as the central source of data for OLAP systems. The data warehouses contain in one place (centrally) and under summarized form all the required data for the creation of multidimensional spaces that are used by the OLAP systems.

Chapter 7

Intelligent Decision Support Methods

1. INTRODUCTION

The effort to create machines with some sort of intelligence began almost 100 years ago with the ideas of Babbage (1884) as shown in *Figure 1*. In 1950, Alan Turin, the "father of Artificial Intelligence" (Barr and Feigenbaum, 1981), presented the famous Turing test, which gives an answer to the question if a machine is able to think as a human being (Rich, 1983). Turing not only developed a simple, general and non-arithmetic computational model, but he also supported that computational models could possibly behave with a way that could be deemed "intelligent". In 1950, Shannon supported that someone could play a game of chess with the help of computer and in 1955 he proved his idea by developing a chess program while, later Samuel (1963) developed a checkers program. Wiener (1948), founder of cybernetics, contributed by recognizing the similarities in functions of humans and machines. In overall, the actual goal of this effort was to understand and find a solution on how to embody in a computer the ability of human beings to think and rationalize (Durkin, 1994). The term "Artificial Intelligence" was used for the first time by John McCarthy (1963; 1969; 1977; 1980; 1995) during a conference held in Dartmouth College (1956).

The Conference in Dartmouth College is considered as the beginning of the revolution in the area of Artificial Intelligence. Among the participants to the conference were Minsky, Simon, and Newell, which along with McCarthy were the pioneers in AI topics. In this conference, McCarthy presented the LISP (List Processing Programming Language) programming language, the most well known tool to manipulate concepts (rules, commands, names), where as Newell and Simon presented an AI program called Logic Theory (Newell and Simon, 1958; 1972; Durkin, 1994), which is one of the earlier programs known for automatic theory proving.

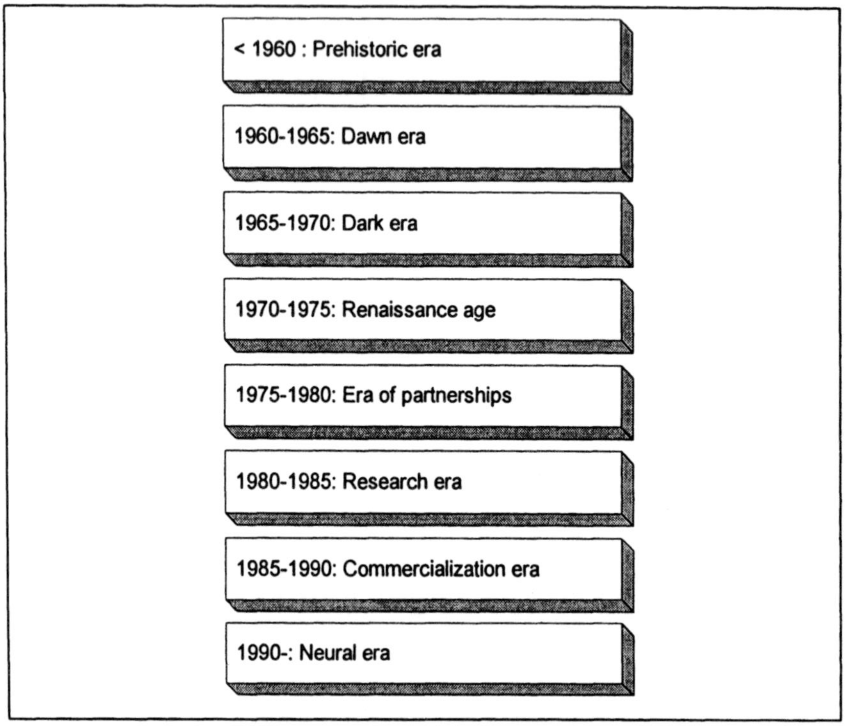

Figure 1. Evolution of Artificial Intelligence

The initial enthusiasm generated excessive expectancies concerning the easy and fast creation of intelligent computers. This early phase is known as the dawn age, characterized by the fact that a large number of scientists believed that within ten years computers would be as intelligent as humans are. One of the most ambitious projects of this time regarded the development of the General Problem Solver (GPS) by Newell (Newell and Simon, 1958; 1972; Newell *et al.*, 1962; Ernst and Newell, 1969; Newell, 1991). GPS was a general problem solving technique and was developed in order to solve many and various problems that varied from games to symbolic representation. The GPS is the first known effort to disjoin the problem solving methods from the knowledge of the problem.

Unfortunately, the results were not those originally expected, and the resulted disappointment and scepticism led to the replacement, sometime between 1970, of the initial euphoria by the modest ascertainment that the development of intelligent programs that would be able to solve real-world problems was a rather difficult challenge. This point of view was expressed by Lighthill (1972), who suggested that Artificial Intelligence should not be considered as a distinct field of information science and that an intelligent computer is the natural continuity or the result of combined efforts in the fields of automation and computer science (Rich, 1983). However, even during this difficult period, there were some steps towards the evolution of AI such as the development of two programs, the ideas of which are used even in nowadays in the development of expert systems, for solving the geometric analogy problem and the symbolic integration problem respectively.

An era of lightness is followed, as a rule, by a dark age and vice versa. Thus, during the dark age there was no substantial progress and everybody were in search of something that could solve all the problems.

The flash that guided the researchers towards the right direction was the DENDRAL program, the implementation of which commenced in 1965 at the Stanford University, after a request from NASA, and aimed at the chemical analysis of the planet's Marsh soil (Winston, 1979). This pioneer work guided the AI researchers to discover that the intelligent behaviour of a system that is called to solve a problem does not primarily depends on the solving methodology of the problem but mainly on the required knowledge in order to solve the problem. The emphasis on knowledge guided Feigenbaum to accept that "power lies within knowledge" and to define the process of creating systems of such type as knowledge engineering (Durkin, 1994), giving rise to the concepts of knowledge based systems and expert systems. The revolution had begun. So, since each dark age is followed by a renaissance, during the following years (1970-75) systems that started to attract the interest begun to develop. Main representatives of this period are the most successful systems PROSPECTOR (Duda *et al.*, 1979a; Buchanan and Duda, 1983), XCON (Kraft, 1984) and MYCIN (Shortliffe, 1984; Buchanan and Shortliffe, 1985).

From 1975 till 1980, a period known as the age of partnerships, the AI scientists begun to cooperate with scientists from other areas (Cercone and McCalba, 1984; Tuthill, 1990). This cooperation resulted firstly to the increment of the number of the scientists engaged and then to the egression of AI from the academic laboratories and to the introduction of it in business research laboratories and to the gradual commencement of developing applications that involved real-world problems. Within the following years a large number of major research projects were developed. Among them, the top project was the decennial project concerning the creation of fifth generation computers, initiated in 1981 at Tokyo by the Japanese government, an idea that was overwhelmed by the USA and European governments as well as by the companies themselves. The European Commission's ESPRIT program shares the same philosophy.

The next age could not be anything else than the commercialisation age, where a large number of companies and researchers are working on the development of Artificial Intelligence systems that attempt to solve real-world problems. Among them, stand the expert systems and natural language comprehension systems.

The current age is characterized by studies and research on the development of sixth generation computer systems, which are related, with the behaviour of the human brain (neural intelligence) and the molecular intelligence (Winston and Shellard, 1990). Already, the first practical results have been presented with the development of neural networks.

2. EXPERT SYSTEMS

Expert system is probably the most well-known application field of Artificial Intelligence. Expert systems are software programs that combine the knowledge of experts and attempt to solve special problems by emulating the reasoning procedures of the experts.

The development of expert systems began in the late 80's. During this period the efforts of AI scientists were turned to the development of the general-purpose problem solver, proposed by Newell and Simon (1972) in their effort to create an "intelligent computer". However, the finding of general methodologies that would solve any problem was impossible because of the different nature and complexity of the various problems and the large volume of the required knowledge (Naylor, 1993). But, methods that aimed at the solution of specific and particular problems were exploited and resulted in the development of expert systems. In their pioneer paper, Newell and Simon (1958) developed the idea of a system that could model some forms of human problem solving procedures by using production rules. The transition from general-purpose problem solving programs to specific-purpose solving process programs occurred in the middle of 60's with the development of DENDRAL by Feigenbaum at the University of Stanford. The observation that the knowledge required for carrying out special tasks is of higher level that the common knowledge used till that time in the development of AI systems, contributed to the rapid development of ESs (Goodman *et al.*, 1991). From the beginning of 70's started the development of such systems that required the process of large volumes of specialized knowledge. The power of an ES lies mainly on the knowledge that has been incorporated into the system rather than in the utilized knowledge representation formalisms or the inference mechanisms.

From the beginning of 80's the development technologies of ESs, which up to that time were kept into the academic community, began to utilized in order to develop commercial applications (R-1, XCON, XSEL, CATS-1, and others). At the same time efforts were initiated in order to develop special tools that could help and contribute towards the faster development of ESs (EMYCIN, AGE, KAS, EURISKO, M.1, EXSYS, and others), which firstly appeared in the market in 1983.

The rapid evolvement of ESs was enormously supported by the existence of current needs in the market in which ES could provide a solution. The continuously increased necessity for specialized advises in all the levels and the lack and cost of specialized staff forced the companies to invest large amounts of money and resources in the development of expert systems.

Just as with AI definitions, there is available a plethora of existing definitions on the term expert system. Each proposed definition depends on the angle by which ES are approached by each scientist (Turban, 1992; 1993). In general the definitions can be classified to those that are based on what an ES does and to those that are grounded on how an ES performs its tasks. We will quote some of these definitions in the following sections.

According to Feigenbaum (1982) an expert system is an intelligent program which in order to solve a problem that is considered difficult enough so as to require substantial experience for its solution, uses special knowledge and inference procedures. The necessary knowledge along with the inference procedures may be thought as a model of the experience of the most qualified experts in the field.

Hayes-Roth (1984), states that the knowledge-based expert systems, or as he briefly calls them knowledge systems, use human knowledge in order to solve problems that normally require human intelligence to be solved.

An expert system is a program that, on the one hands deals with real-world complex problems which require the presence of an expert and on the other hand it solves these problems by utilizing a computation model of expert's reasoning, arriving to the same results with an expert facing a similar problem. An ES attempts to capture sufficient knowledge from the knowledge of an expert so as to solve with expert way the problems (Weiss and Kulikowski, 1984).

In the next year, Sell defines an ES as a system based on knowledge that simulate the thinking of an expert in order to solve important problems in a distinct field.

Hart (1986) views ESs as programs, which perform tasks usually performed by experts. Expert systems incorporate the knowledge of experts and also their ability to utilize this knowledge in order to solve the problems. These programs are bounded by the types of task that they can perform but release their specialization on the approach of suitable problems. In expert systems the knowledge is codified, thus generating powerful tools.

According to Kumara (1986) an ES is a tool able to conceive the special knowledge of problem and by intelligently using this knowledge of this particular field is able to suggest alternative actions.

Curry and Moutinho (1991) define expert systems as programs that attempt to represent the knowledge of an expert in a certain field. These systems offer knowledge and expertise and are able, by using reasoning, to provide advises or to make decisions justifying how they were guided to those advises or solutions

Doukidis (1988), Doukidis and Paul, (1992), by combining what an expert system does and in which way, define an expert system as a program that aids the user by providing information on a specific field. The system accomplishes this by handling information related with a certain area, which are provided by a series of "experts" in this area. Another important feature of an expert system is that the system has the capability to explain and justify the methods that are utilized by it in order to provide the information.

It is quite interesting to concentrate to the development rate of expert systems' applications. During the 70's, when researchers focused on the development of intelligent programming techniques, only a small number of systems were developed, in contrast to the situation observed in ′80's, where the development of expert systems was rapid, because of the better comprehension. According to Walker (1996), the impressive development rate of expert systems can be thought as an indicator of their acceptance by the industry, companies, and research centres (*Figure 2*).

According to Jayaraman and Srivastava (1996), ESs have already been successfully applied in production and management. The authors examined the literature in order to record existing expert systems in the areas of production and management. They established a taxonomy of these systems and also detected some advantages and drawbacks.

Figure 3 presents the number of systems developed for different application areas (Walker, 1996). In 1986, according to a study conducted by Waterman, the majority (30%) of the expert systems' application where concentrated in the field of medicine. The diagram shows that the medicine field is still an attractive application area for expert systems developers. The most important findings of the Walker's study regard the applications of expert systems in the industry and business sectors. The Waterman's study showed that only 10% of the expert systems' applications where in the industry and business sectors where as the more recent study of Walker indicates that more than half (60%) of the expert systems' applications involve industrial or business applications. Thus, the diagram clearly proves that expert systems have matured and are acceptable by the production sectors.

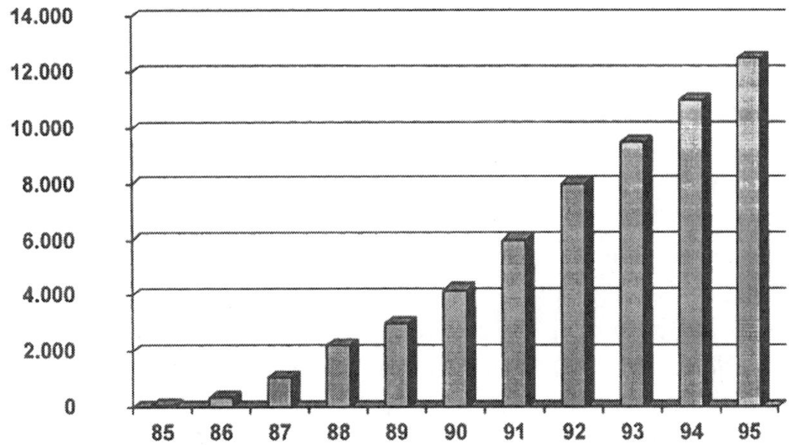

Figure 2. Development rate of expert systems (*Source*: Walker, 1996)

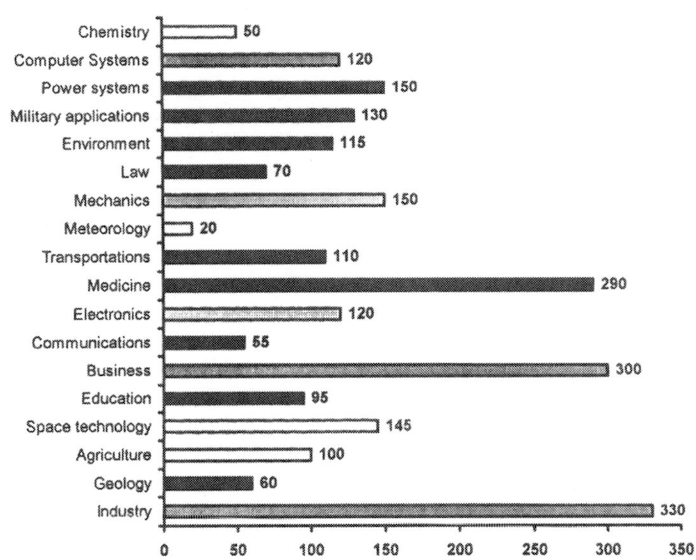

Figure 3. Expert systems in various application fields (*Source:* Walker, 1996)

2.1 Structure of Expert Systems

Each expert system has two views. The first view is the one perceived by maker of the system, during the phases of development and knowledge induction whereas the second one is the one perceived by the user during the system's operation.

A typical operation procedure of an expert system is initiated by a user's request for consultation. Then the ES uses its inference engine in order to manipulate the rules contained in the existing knowledge base. If the system has questions about some facts then it addresses the user for additional information. These facts along with others that result during the various intermediate operation stages of the ES are stored in the working memory. The process continues until the system reaches a final conclusion. The resulted conclusion may be the consultation to the initial query or the system's statement that a valid result can not be reached because of the lack of adequate existing knowledge to complete the requested task.

In the following sections we will examine with more details the numerous components of a representative expert system, as this is presented in (*Figure 4*).

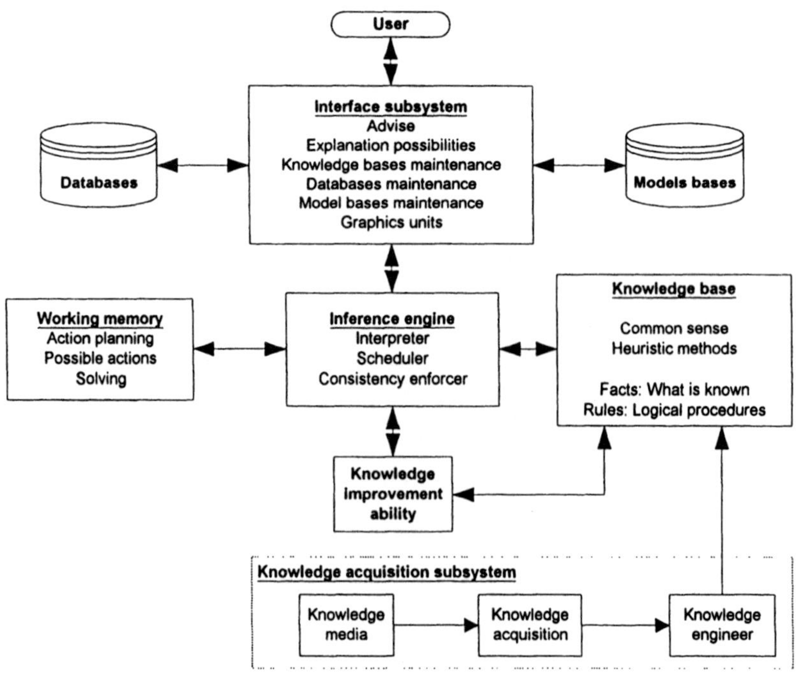

Figure 4. Structure of an expert system

2.2 User interface

The user of an expert system may be a member of the following categories of people:

- **Client.** The user is a non-expert that uses the ES because he needs its advice. With the use of the system he may improve the quality of the decisions he makes.
- **Student.** In this case the user employs the ES in order to increase his knowledge on a particular subject. Here, the system plays the role of the tutor.
- **Expert.** An expert uses the system in order to obtain a second opinion on a decision or to find assist in inconsequent tasks or finally because he wishes to follow the reasoning, through the observation of the gradual steps followed by the system, in order to arrive at a certain conclusion.
- **Developer.** The person uses the system in order to control it, to improve it and to augment the knowledge already contained in it.

Through the user interface subsystem and with the help of various graphic screens, in order to achieve better performance, the user contacts the system with natural language. Also, the user is able to maintain the various knowledge, data, and models bases, which are necessary for the proper operation of the system. Finally, the system's tips are presented to the user through the user interface subsystem. The user is able to exploit the explanation capabilities and receive answers to the following questions:

- How did the system arrive at a certain conclusion?
- Why were some alternative answers rejected?
- Which is the process used by the system in order to arrive at the final conclusion?
- Why did the system prompt for some questions in its attempt to find way to the final question?

2.3 Inference engine

The heart of an ES is the module known as the inference engine. The inference engine has the responsibility of managing and controlling the knowledge that is stored in both the knowledge base and in the working memory for the formulation of conclusions. The main parts of the inference engine mechanism are the interpreter, the scheduler, and the consistency enforcer.

- The **interpreter**, known as the rule interpreter in the majority of systems, handles the execution of the selected actions by applying to the knowledge base the respective rules in order to produce new knowledge. This is accomplished by the application of statistical methods or pattern

matching methods. Based on those methods it assesses the information stored in the knowledge base to discover the suitable rules.
- The **scheduler** handles the system's control strategy. The tasks of the scheduler include the supervision of the execution order of the various tasks and the calculation of the results derived by the application of the rules in light of the data priorities or other criteria of the defined arrangement of actions (agenda). Essentially, the scheduler decides when and in which order the data of the knowledge base will be used. It contains assessment knowledge in order to evaluate the alternative search paths and also control knowledge in order to be able to coordinate its various functions. In many cases it is necessary also to include in the scheduler, knowledge specific to particular problem.
- The **consistency enforcer** attempts to maintain a consistent representation of the presented solution.
- The **working memory** is the space used by the inference engine either to place the necessary information of the current problem or to store intermediary results of the problem solving process. As shown in the above figure, the following three types of decisions are stored in the working memory:
- **Action planning.** It relates with the way of solution of the current problem.
- **Possible actions.** It is a catalogue of the possible actions.
- **Solution.** It contains the alternative assumptions and actions that the system has carried out till now.

2.4 Knowledge acquisition subsystem and Knowledge base

The knowledge acquisition subsystem consists of the knowledge media of the application field and of the knowledge engineer who attempts to elicit, concentrate, codify and convey the knowledge – expertise of a field into a certain knowledge base of an ES. The knowledge sources, except for one ore more filed experts, may include knowledge found in the international bibliography, special field journals, results of special surveys, databases, and other.

The knowledge base contains two basic elements, the facts and the rules. Facts refer to the status of the problem and to the corresponding theory. Rules, govern the exploitation of the existing knowledge for the solving of the current problem. Frequently, instead of using standard rules, some other rules, called heuristics, are employed. Heuristic rules contain special knowledge on the methodology of effective and efficient solution of special and complex problems as well as any other relevant information.

2.5 Working Memory

The working memory contains all the information that either regards the current problem or result from the system. Information that is derived during the working process is called context. The working memory is the component of the expert system that contains the facts of the problem that arise during the usage of the program (Durkin, 1994). The user, during his cooperation with the expert system, enters in the working memory information relevant to the current problem. The system combines this information with the existing knowledge allocated into the knowledge base and extracts new facts.

Next, it imports the new facts into the working memory and the pattern matching procedure proceeds. Finally, the system arrives at a certain conclusion, which by turn is imported into the working memory. In many cases, the expert systems utilize combinations of information sources such as information that come from users, databases, working sheets, and others (Nebendahl, 1988).

3. KNOWLEDGE ENGINEERING

3.1 Users – Experts - Knowledge engineering

We hope that the reader has already understood the importance of knowledge in ESs. As knowledge, we may regard a collection of special facts, procedures and rules. Some of the types, of the typical knowledge used in expert systems, are presented in *Figure 5* (Fikes and Kehler, 1985). All the actions related with the knowledge fall in the scope of knowledge engineering (Feigenbaum and McCorduck, 1983) whereas the experts that work on this field are called knowledge engineers. Knowledge engineering (*Figure 6*) also contains the collaboration of domain experts with the knowledge engineer in order to codify the knowledge of the experts and to clearly define the logical procedures used by experts to solve a real-world problem. Many times, the utilized knowledge is ill structured and vague. The development process of an expert system and the collaboration of the expert with the knowledge engineer force the expert to find several ways in order to express his knowledge and way of thought more clearly (Goodman *et al.*, 1991).

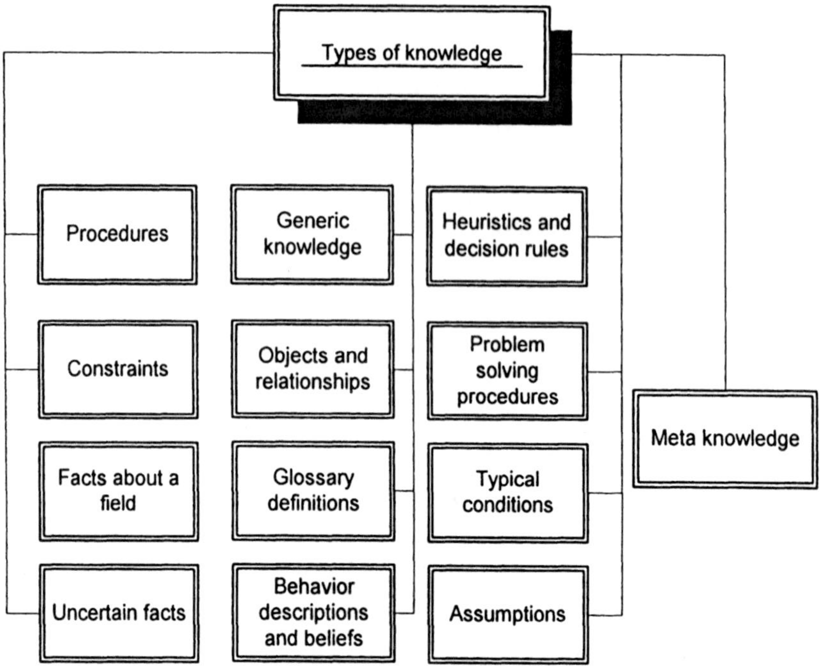

Figure 5. Types of knowledge

The knowledge engineer should pay attention to the dissociation of the knowledge structures from the control mechanisms. In addition, the ES should have the capability of explaining what it has performed, why, and how.

Another, significant problem, except for the problem of knowledge elicitation, is to find out how to represent the acquired knowledge in order to allow for the function of the ES's inference engine. We will discuss this subject with more details in the following sections.

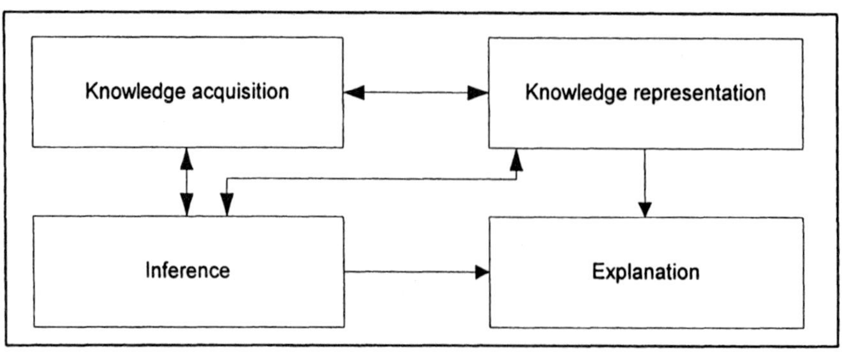

Figure 6. Activities

3.2 Knowledge acquisition

The complexity of the knowledge acquisition process is mainly due to the existence of several information sources and to the existence of different types of knowledge (Boose, 1985; 1986c; 1989; Shaw and Gaines, 1986; Wright and Ayton, 1987; Johnson and Johnson, 1987; McGraw and Harbison, 1989; Brute and Blount, 1989; McGovern *et al.*, 1991). An important factor of the knowledge elicitation process is also the necessary cost related with the acquisition of the knowledge (Dos Santos and Mookerjee, 1993).

3.2.1 Knowledge acquisition process

Figure 7 presents the four main stages of knowledge acquisition (Doukidis and Whitley, 1988). The first stage involves the selection of the problem to be solved, then the determination of its main characteristics, and finally the clarification and determination of the utilized concepts and relations for the knowledge representation (Hayes-Roth *et al.*, 1983; Hayes-Roth, 1984; Turban, 1993). The knowledge elicitation stage, from one or several experts, initially involves the knowledge elicitation and then the knowledge acquisition, during which, the elicited knowledge is organized and represented by the knowledge engineer to a suitable form in order to be available for use by the developing expert system. During the integration stage the acquired knowledge is incorporated into the ES, since it has already been shaped suitably in order to enable its usage by the ES.

The knowledge acquisition process also includes the necessary checks related with the evaluation, validation, and verification of the acquired knowledge (O'Keefe *et al.*, 1987; Marcot, 1987; Nguyen, 1987; Parsaye, 1988). Also the primary characteristics of the system are determined and finally the utilized concepts and relationships for knowledge representation are clarified and established. Many authors consider this final task as an independent stage of the whole process (Hayes-Roth *et al.*, 1983; 1984; Turban, 1993).

The various stages interact through the reconfiguration, redesign and improvement tasks of the developing system. The system is under the continuous and close monitoring and evaluation of the expert or the experts the knowledge of which was used in the system's development process.

A substantial factor in the development of an ES is the necessity of the presence of multiple experts. The involvement of multiple experts is imposed mainly by reasons related with the expansion of the proposed solution to the problem or by the necessity to increase the possibilities of different logical approaches. The cooperation of multiple experts also exhibits some problems such as those arising by the expression of opinions-evaluations of the experts, in which the knowledge engineer is responsible to find solutions (Boose, 1985; LeClair, 1985; Nii, 1986; 1989; Mittal, 1985; Shaw and Gaines, 1986; Alexander and Evans, 1988).

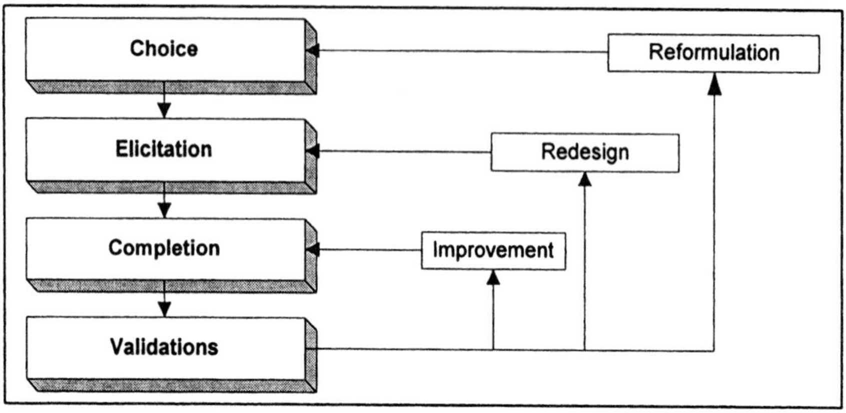

Figure 7. Phases of knowledge acquisition (*Source*: Doukidis and Whitley, 1988)

3.2.2 Knowledge elicitation methods

According to Wielinga *et al.* (1990), knowledge may be elicited by using one of the following fashions:

1. **Manual knowledge elicitation.**
   a) Non-recorded knowledge (Waterman and Newell, 1976; Ericsson and Simon, 1984; Boose, 1986b; Hart, 1986; Abdul-Gader and Kozar, 1990).
      - Personal interviews (Hart, 1986; Wolfgram *et al.*, 1987; Hoffman, 1999; McGraw and Harbison-Briggs, 1989; Agarwal and Tanniru, 1990).
      - Monitoring of the way an expert works during the problem solution process (Newell and Simon, 1972; Ericsson and Simon, 1984; Wolfgram *et al.*, 1987).
      - Completion of special questionnaires or description by the experts (Wolfgram *et al.*, 1987).

   b) Recorded knowledge
      - Knowledge from databases, books, scientific journals, etc (Rothman, 1988).
2. **Computer-aided knowledge acquisition.**

The knowledge may be elicited by using special computer programs and the procedure may be accomplished either by complete absence of the expert

or by small participation of the expert (Quinlan, 1983; 1984; 1986; Gale, 1986; Cronan *et al.*, 1991; Turban, 1993; Deng, 1993).

a) Automated rule induction. By this methodology, we attempt, with the help of specific computer programs, to generate rules by processing a multitude of examples of the specific field of knowledge so as to induce by the specific cases (examples) more generalized cases (generic knowledge) (Michie, 1984; Liang and Turban, 1993).
b) Auto-intelligence. These systems initially attempt, by their interaction with an expert, to acquire the necessary knowledge for the solution of a particular problem and then they process this knowledge suitably and finally generate the respective knowledge base (Parsaye, 1988).

3. **Interactive knowledge acquisition.**

By this method, the knowledge engineer in order to elicit knowledge uses a combination of manual methods and special computer tools. Some of these tools are the communication systems, the explanation provision systems, the expertise transfer systems, the knowledge base control systems, etc (Freiling *et al.*, 1985; Boose, 1986; Diederich *et al.*, 1987; Gaines, 1988; Boose and Gaines, 1990; Gaines and Compton, 1992; 1994).

3.3 Knowledge representation

The knowledge elicited by the expert should be organized and represented in an appropriate manner so as to become as tangible as possible by the ES and the expert himself. The knowledge that is related with the solving procedure of the specific problem is more generic (it is bounded with the solution procedure of other problems as well) and it is allocated to the inference engine of the ES whereas the knowledge that is related with the specific problem is specific and therefore it is stored in the system's knowledge base.

3.3.1 Representation methods

The choice of a specific way to represent the knowledge of a certain problem is an important task considering that it defines whether the reasoning of the expert will be satisfactory approached. Therefore, a suitable method to both the specific knowledge and the specific problem should be selected.

Although, the representation methods exhibit major differences amongst them, they share two common characteristics:

1. They are implemented with the help of one of the existing programming languages, and

2. They use the facts and knowledge contained in them, in their effort to seek reasonable conclusions with the help of special search and pattern-matching techniques of the inference engine to the ES's knowledge base.

The various knowledge representation methods are categorized to the descriptive or declarative representation methods, which are used for the representation of facts and statements, and to the procedural representation methods, which are used for actions and procedures. Known declarative representation methods are the logic, the frames, the semantic networks, the rules and the scripts, whereas respectively procedural methods are the procedures, the subroutines and the rules. The declarative methods describe knowledge without establishing any relation with the way used for the manipulation of the knowledge and they represent it as facts, contrary to procedural methods which contain apart from the specific knowledge and knowledge related with the way to manipulate this knowledge and they represent it as program. In the ESs with declarative knowledge representation, the specific knowledge is separated by the control knowledge rendering the system more transparent.

In the procedural representation, the largest part of the knowledge is represented with the form of special procedures related with specific problems and which are activated through other procedures. Among them, there is a special category of procedures, called demons, which are activated when a condition holds. The implementation of the procedural form of knowledge representation is quite simple, it provides high representational capabilities but it is characterized by the reduced transparency. It uses simple forms of mechanisms for inference. However, because of the high degree of opacity and the existing interaction among the procedures, the maintenance and knowledge revision tasks are rendered quite difficult.

The procedural knowledge representation form is mainly used jointly with the declarative form in order to face specific problems. Each one of the existing methods represents more efficiently some particular types of knowledge. Therefore, in order to achieve the more efficient representation of a certain problem, it is not practical to discuss the exclusive enforcement of a specific method but rather to find the more efficient way to combine the available representation methods.

The decision to use one of the above representation methods should also take into account the differences in the inference mechanisms used by each form of knowledge representation.

3.3.2 Production rules

The early systems were developed by Newell and Simon in 1972 in order to describe the human knowledge. In this type of systems, knowledge is represented by rules with the following form:

IF
  conditions (assumptions)
THEN
  actions (conclusions)

The above form implies that when the conditions are true then presumably the actions are true and vice-versa. Similarly, when the conditions are false then it is implied that the actions are false and vice-versa. This logic is known as modus ponens (Harmon and King, 1985).

According to Curry and Moutinho (1991) the characteristics of the rules are the following:

- The syntax of the rules should contain limited text with clear meaning and should be tangible to every stage of operation.
- The rules may be represented by complex structure or by interconnected groups of rules.
- Their manipulation and appropriate processing requires the use of special programming languages, such as Lisp, Prolog, etc., of various shells, or of specific software in order to handle the system's «reasoning» procedures.
- The knowledge used also holds qualitative dimensions.
- They provide the ability of automated knowledge acquisition from examples or cases (perhaps the most well known method into this category is Quinlan's ID3 algorithm Quinlan (1986).

The rules are used for the outline of heuristic problem solving procedures. The conditions of the rules are very clearly stated and this reduces the interaction among them. Each rule describes a certain knowledge case and thus the represented knowledge is characterized by independence and high level of transparency. The rules are used for the representation of both the declarative and procedural knowledge.

During the development of an ES, two types of rules are generated depending on the type of knowledge that they represented. The declarative knowledge rules are those that provide the knowledge for the problem whereas the procedural rules contain the knowledge for the way to solve the problem. The first ones constitute the knowledge base where as the latter are contained in the inference engine. There is also another type of rules, called the metarules that contain knowledge necessary for the handling of the other two types of rules as well as the handling of the metarules themselves. The metarules are also contained in the inference engine.

Production rules exhibit the following advantages and disadvantages:

a) **Advantages**

- They have a "natural" form of knowledge representation, simple syntax and the understanding of the represented knowledge is very convenient.
- The rules are independent.
- It is easy to modify the rules.
- The development and completion of the knowledge base can be progressed gradually.
- The inference procedure and the explanation provision are relatively easy.
- The have the ability to represent uncertain situations.

b) **Disadvantages.**

- They present difficulties in the representation of generic knowledge regarding concepts and objects.
- It is difficult to represent complex knowledge because of the required large number of rules.
- It is difficult to understand the overall algorithm.
- Limitations to the solution search because of the large number of rules.

3.3.3 Formal logic

The formal logic method of knowledge representation checks only the relations among statements (Goodman *et al.*, 1991). The method does not consider the content of the statements but only checks the soundness of their syntax. It uses simple forms of syntax and therefore it is characterized by clearness and precision. However, it presents certain inability in the understanding of the concepts contained in the statements and also requires complex heuristic methods in order to deal with problems of uncertain reasoning. The formal logic method is mainly used in theoretical aspects of Artificial Intelligence and also underlies the operation of the Prolog programming language. The most well known methods for writing formal logic statements are the prepositional and predicate logic.

3.3.4 Object-Attributes-Value

The triplets and frames are considered as partial cases of semantic networks. So, the link Object-Attribute may be thought as a "have" link whereas the link Attribute-Value is regarded as an "is" link (*Figure 8*).

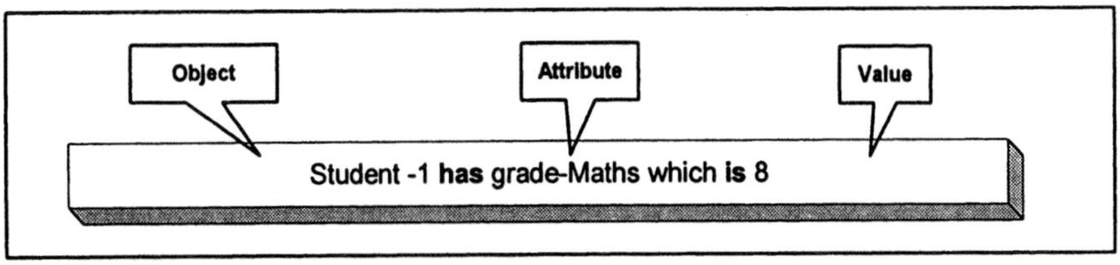

Figure 8. Object-Attribute-Value triple

In predicate logic the resulted conclusions are added to the existing ones without permitting the revision of the knowledge (monotonic knowledge).

The Value prescribes the specific value of an object's attribute.

3.3.5 Scripts

Scripts are descriptions of specific deterministic chain facts. Because of the hierarchical sequence and the interconnection of the facts it is possible to predict facts or to assume that they have took place (plausible assumption) if in the selected script subsequent facts have occurred. By nature, scripts are able to provide explanation on the various facts. Scripts can only represent facts.

3.3.6 Multiple representation

Actually, in most cases it is not recommended to use a single representation technique but rather to use in parallel several different techniques. So, each technique is used to represent the knowledge of a fraction of the total knowledge of the system. In this case, the problem, which arises, is that the different techniques have to work together and also that knowledge represented by one techniques should be able to be handled by the others (Kunz *et al.*, 1984; Drake and Hess, 1990).

An example of such a hybrid representation is the knowledge representation by the combination of frames and production rules, attempting too exploit the advantages of the two methods (Thuraisingham, 1989).

3.3.7 Non monotonic reasoning

Systems that use non-monotonic reasoning are able to revise the existing knowledge in the light of new information (Reiter, 1978; 1980; Doyle, 1979a; 1979b; McDermott and Doyle, 1980; McCarthy, 1980; Rich, 1983; Reinfrank *et al.*, 1989; Rich and Knight, 1991). On the contrary, systems that use monotonic reasoning simply accept the new facts without checking their impact to the existing knowledge. Another type of non-monotonic reasoning systems are those that proceed to plausible assumptions when attempting to solve a problem, which they revise in cases of failure.

3.3.8 Reasoning under uncertainty

Until now, we regarded only two-valued facts, i.e. facts that are either true or false. But in reality, in most cases, people face facts that are characterized by uncertainty, relativity or incomplete information (Lemmer and Kahal, 1988; Clark and Krause, 1993). Therefore, it is vital to use inference techniques that are able to process uncertain data and knowledge (Magill and Leech, 1991). In the rule-based systems, uncertainty is represented with the help of certainty factors - CF.

IF «evidence E»
THEN «hypothesis H» CF(E,H)
Where:
E is the evidence (fact, condition)
H is the hypothesis (conclusion), and
CF(E,H) is the certainty factor of the specific rule

Two problems arise when dealing with uncertainty (Cortes-Rello and Golshani, 1990):

1. How to measure the degree of imprecision and how to calculate the certainty factors for imprecise situations?
2. How to propagate the uncertainty to the construction of conclusions in order to achieve better conclusions despite the ambiguous determination of some rules.

Several methods have been proposed for the management of uncertainty (Grzymala-Busse, 1991; Magill and Leech, 1991). Among them, the most custom to applications are the fuzzy logic with the employment of fuzzy (Zadeh, 1965,1978; 1979; Yager and Zadeh, 1992; Lowen and Roubens, 1993), the probabilistic Bayesian reasoning (Duda *et al.*, 1979b; Andersen and Hooker, 1994), the theory of evidence or belief functions theory (Dempster, 1967; Shafer, 1976; 1981; 1986; 1987; Voorbraak, 1996), and the rule value technique (Naylor, 1983). A review of the above methods can be found in Zadeh (1986), Bhatnagar and Kanal (1986), Neapolitan, (1987), and Lee *et al.* (1987).

3.4 Inference

The solution of a problem is in fact the search of a solution within a field of possible states. The solving process of a problem is depicted in *Figure 9* (Frenzel, 1987; Turban, 1993).

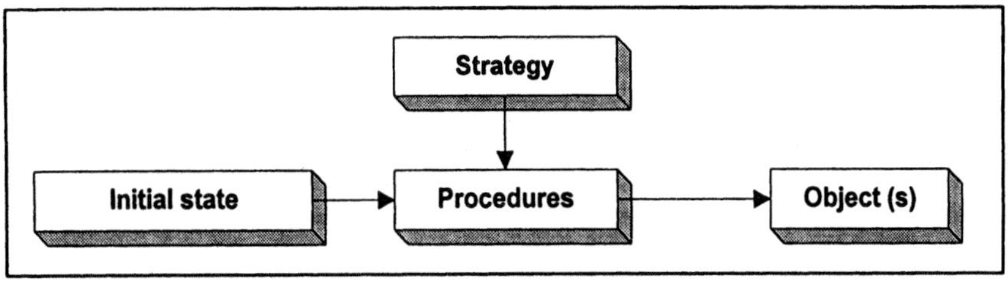

Figure 9. Solution process (*Source*: Frenzel, 1987; Turban, 1993)

During the attempt of goal seeking and according to the selected control strategy the procedures act on the data of the problem's initial state. Both the control strategy and the search methods are heavily related with the utilized method of knowledge representation.

The graphical representation of the set of possible solutions and of their interconnections can be achieved either by the use of a search graph or by using a search tree (*Figure 10*) (Benchimol *et al.*, 1987; Turban, 1993).

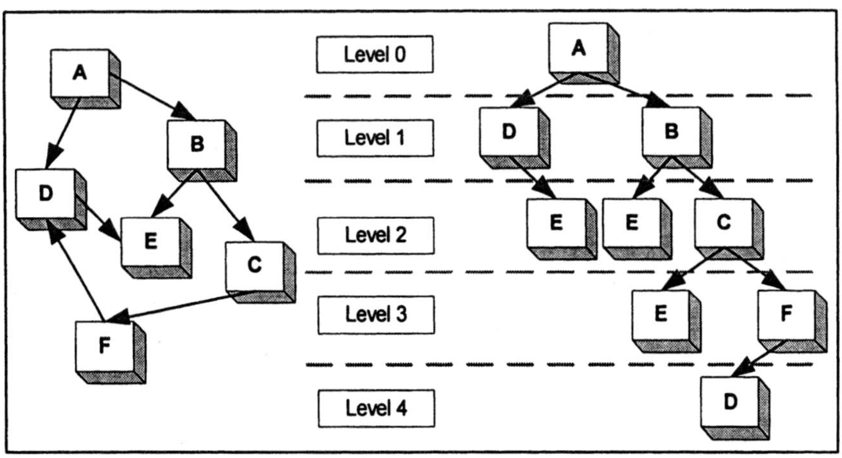

Figure 10. Graph and search tree (*Source*: Turban, 1993)

The following sections are devoted to the presentation of some of the most prevailing search techniques (Rich, 1983; Benchimol *et al.*, 1987; Rich and Knight, 1991; Turban, 1993).

3.4.1 Depth-first search

The search progresses from top to bottom and from left to right (*Figure 11*). The search begins from the root of the tree and continues with the examination of the most left node of the next lower level (A-B). This procedure is repeated until the examination of the final node (A-B-C-D). If the goal is not attained, the search returns to the father node (D-C) and proceeds to the check of any unvisited paths of the father node. If there are no unvisited paths then the search returns to the immediately precedent node and this procedure continuous (back tracking).

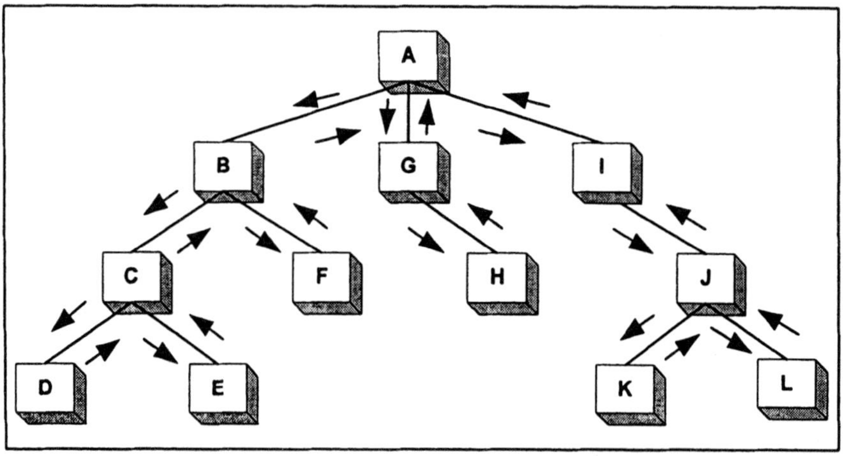

Figure 11. Depth first search process (*Source*: Turban, 1993)

3.4.2 Breadth-first search

In breadth-first search, all the nodes of a tree level are examined before proceeding to the next level (*Figure 12*). The procedure starts from the root of the tree and moves downwards searching from left to right (A-B-G-I-C-F-H-J-D-E-K-L). As in the case of depth-first search, this method will find a solution howsoever. The disadvantage of the method is that when the depth of the tree is too high then the number of the nodes to be examined increases exponentially. This fact has a certain heavy impact on both the memory requirements of the system and also on the time needed to finish the search. Therefore, the method is unsuitable when there is a large number of paths with high depth. One solution would be to pose some limits on the search depth.

Another drawback of the above two methods is that although a solution is a hundred percent detected, yet it is not known if this is the solution with the shortest path or the unique solution to the problem.

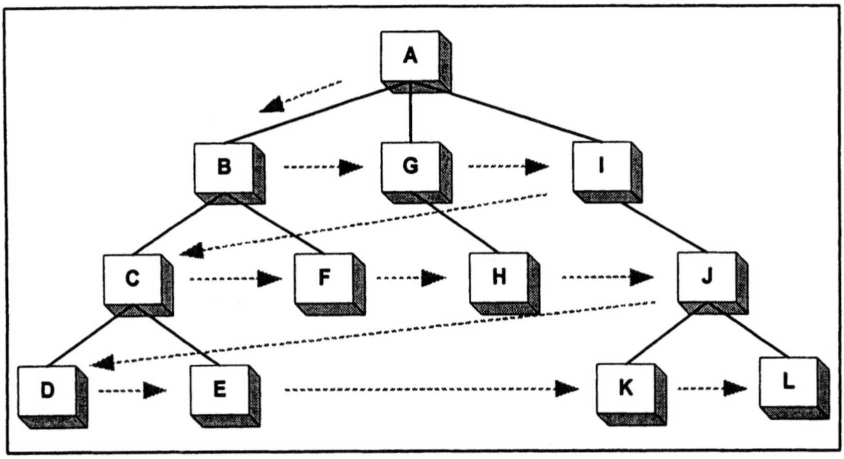

Figure 12. Breadth first search process (*Source*: Turban, 1993)

3.4.3 Branch and bound search

The problem of finding the shortest path of the two previously examined search methods is solved by accepting the distance of the path as a criterion for choosing the best solution. With the brand and bound method the search does not stop with the finding of the first path that leads to the goal but it continuous until it detects the shortest of all the available paths. By this way, the system "remembers" the shortest, till that point, path. If, during the execution of a search, the length of the path becomes longer than the respective length of the shortest path the search stops and the particular path is rejected. During the search the path to be examined is the one with the shortest length.

3.4.4 Heuristic search

Heuristic search techniques (§5.4.4.4) attempt to improve the efficiency through a supervised search so that the path that each time is selected for examination is more possible to lead to a solution (Lenat, 1982a; 1982b, 1983a; 1983b; Rich, 1983; Doukidis, 1988; Rich and Knight, 1991; Turban, 1993). Heuristic search cannot guarantee the finding of a solution in all the cases and also the solution found is not necessary the optional solution to the problem. However, even experts when examining a problem do not necessarily find the optimal solution but only a satisfactory solution (Simon, 1981). This of course is not true for problems that necessary require the finding of the optimal solution.

There are several generic heuristic algorithms but also special algorithms can be constructed in order to solve a specific problem.

3.4.5 Best-first search

The best-first search method is a generic heuristic algorithm. The method attempts to combine the positive attributes of the depth and breadth first search techniques. The selection of the optimal node, through the set of the developed nodes, is based on a certain heuristic evaluation criterion. Then, the selected node is expanded in order to generate its descendants. If one of the descendants nodes is the solution the search is terminated otherwise the new nodes are added to the set of the existing nodes. The heuristic evaluation criterion is applied to the newly formed set of nodes in order to trace the optimal node. This procedure is repeated until the finding of a solution. Each time the new possible solution is compared to the existing, till that point, solution. The heuristic evaluation criterion is suitably adopted according to the examined problem each time.

A well-known algorithm for the selection of the optimal node is the A* algorithm (Hart *et al.*, 1968; 1972; Gelperin, 1977; Martelli, 1977; Rich, 1983). The algorithm is applicable to graphs with nodes jointed with disjunction and not with conjugation (OR type graphs) in order to avoid the repetition of search to similar branches (Tzafestas, 1988).

Some problems are solved by reducing them to sub-problems (problem reduction) that are described by graphs with nodes jointed either by conjugation or by disjunction (AND-OR type). This heuristic search can be performed by special algorithms, such Nilson's AO* algorithm (Nilson, 1971; Rich, 1983) and the algorithm of Chang and Slagle (1971). In order to cope with more specialized problems, several other search techniques have been developed such as the MINIMAX algorithm, the Alpha Beta pruning algorithm, the cooperative algorithms, the nearest neighbor algorithm (Rich, 1983; Tzafestas, 1988; Kriketos and Pastras, 1989; Rich and Knight, 1991).

In many problems where the solution should fulfill certain constraints, special constraint satisfaction algorithms are applied, regardless of the utilized search method.

3.4.6 Inference strategies

In the process of solution finding we may move towards two directions regardless of the utilized search technique. The first alternative is to move from the initial state towards the final state and the second one is choose the exactly reverse way. These are the two strategies followed in inference procedures. The decision of which strategy will be selected is depended on the type of information available and on the desirable goal. It is important to mention that in some special cases it is possible to use the two strategies together. This method is known as bi-directional reasoning.

Another feature of these strategies is their ability of backtracking. Backtracking signifies the ability of the method to return to previous states when the search fails. Both strategies use the same rules, but of course with different manner.

3.4.6.1 Forward reasoning or chaining

Forward reasoning starts from the available data and attempts to result into conclusions. It is, therefore, a data-driven approach. The search starts with the formation of the first level of the inference tree by using the forward reasoning strategy (Rich, 1983; Benchimol *et al.*, 1987; Rich and Knight, 1991; Turban, 1993). The root of the tree is the initial information (the hypothesis of the rule: IF hypothesis Then conclusion). Then, the next level of the tree is generated. Initially, all the rules with left-hand sides that match the information of the root are discovered. Then, the right hand sides of these rules (the conclusions) are located as nodes of this level. The process is repeated for each node of the precedent level in order to construct each following level of the tree. The process stops when the goal of the search is attained.

During the reasoning process, the desired goal is not considered at all, and therefore there is a chance to be guided to mistaken directions and not to end with the desired result. This problem is resolved with the help of heuristic methods.

3.4.6.2 Backward reasoning or chaining

The strategy in this case, attempts to prove the truth of a hypothesis by seeking evidence of its validity or non-validity. It starts from the subject of research and attempts to prove this by resulting to self-evident facts. Therefore, it is about a goal-driven approach, which uses a reverse course than the previous case (Rich, 1983; Rich and Knight, 1991; Turban, 1993).

The process starts with the creation of the search tree root in which the goal to be verified is located. Then, from the knowledge base, all the rules with right hand sides (conclusions) that match the information of the root are discovered. The nodes of the next level are generated by locating to them the left-hand sides (hypotheses) of the precedent rules.

The search process does not take into account all the data of the problem. The user may be asked to intervene if the available information is not adequate or if the system cannot result to any conclusions.

4. DEVELOPING EXPERT SYSTEMS

The development of expert system is not a standard and absolute sequence of successive actions followed by all the makers. Each expert system has its unique particularities and each group of developers follows its own practices in the development procedure. Several researchers have proposed from time to time various analysis methodologies for the systems (Davis, 1974; Mandell, 1979; Liebowitz, 1984; Silverman, 1984, 1985; 1987; DeSalvo, 1987; Turban, 1993, and others). In *Figure 13*, the successive development stages of a typical ES are presented.

4.1 Application problems of expert systems

The most significant problem in the development of an expert system is the acquisition of the appropriate knowledge and the representation of this knowledge with the help of a certain language that will render it use realizable (Gale, 1986c; Curry and Moutinho, 1991).

The subjective nature of reasoning and expertise poses major problems to the necessity of standard representation of knowledge (see for example Leith, 1986). This is the main reason for the limited application of expert systems in the field of marketing and strategic decision making (Moutinho and Paton, 1988; Dubelaar *et al.*, 1991). On the other hand, this fact represented a cognitive challenge for scientists and researchers (Curry and Moutinho, 1991).

We also have to consider the fact that the user always has to realize and understand the reasoning used by the expert system in order to reach a certain conclusion.

4.2 Development process

The time-consuming and extremely complex development process of an expert system is characterized by two critical factors: the involvement of several people that come from various and different specialties and the need for decisions concerning financial, social and technical aspects.

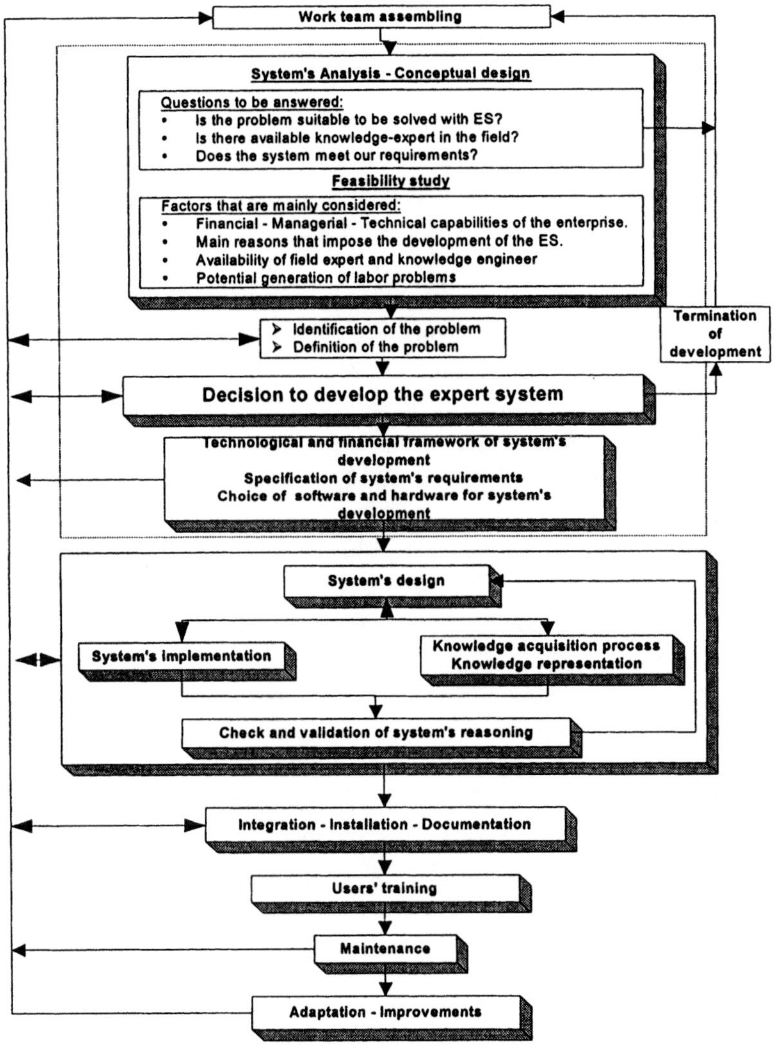

Figure 13. Development stages of expert systems

The first issue to be addressed is the choice, through the set of problem concerning an enterprise, of the particular problem that has the highest priority to be solved. According to Waterman (1985), the study for the choice of the appropriate problem should consist of the following three stages:

- Necessary requirements. Seven requirements are placed in total that should be fulfilled in order to render possible the development of an ES.
- Justification. It is comprised of four preconditions, whereof at least one should be hold, in order to justify the development of the ES.

- Appropriateness. Waterman proposes three factors that should be considered in the judgment whether a problem is suitable or not to be developed in an ES.

Turban (1993) added to the above, some additional necessary requirements and justification preconditions of the ES development.

Various sequences of questions, which follow a standard format, have been developed that attempt to establish if a certain problem is suitable to be solved through its development in an ES. Sagle and Wick (1988), have developed such a questionnaire in which a weighting system is used. The Expert One software package (Human Edge, Palo Alto, CA) offers such a sequence of questions, which, depending on the provided answers, consults the user whether the development of an ES would favour the solution of the problem. Prior to these tasks, a more general study should involve the identification of the problems or tasks for which the ESs are more appropriate (Van Horn, 1986).

This work may be assigned to the work group that monitors the development process of the ES. The work group consists of members of the management and of expert scientists (experts in finance, in informatics, knowledge engineers, etc).

Then, the system's development group should proceed to the analyses task, where the following issues should be examined intensively:

- Whether the particular problem is suitable to be satisfactory coped with the use of expert systems.
- If there is available knowledge in the problem's application field (experts, literature, etc).
- If the system corresponds and satisfies the specifications that are placed by the company.

If something of the above cannot be satisfied, then the development works of the system are interrupted, either permanently or the current problem is redefined or some other problem for solving is selected.

In the whole development process of an ES, the domain expert and the knowledge engineer play the most substantial roles. The work of the knowledge engineer may be defined as the art to link the principles and tools of the Artificial Intelligence research so that these can provide solutions to rough application problems, the solution of which requires specialized knowledge (Feigenbaum and McCorduck, 1983). Moreover, the technical aspects of knowledge elicitation, representation and suitable use in the construction and explanation of reasoning are part of the knowledge engineer's responsibilities and among the most vital problems in the design of knowledge based systems. In order to complete his work, the knowledge engineer should be equipped with knowledge, which may be obtained from experts, books, databases, reports and various other sources (Klein, 1990). Some problems that may arise herein are:

- Who is in charge of choosing the experts or in general who chooses which sources of knowledge are appropriate for the particular application?
- What kind of stimuli will be provided to the expert in order to ensure his cooperation?
- Which are the necessary characteristics of the expert (Goyal *et al.*, 1985; Shanteau, 1986)?
- What should be done when the problem requires the presence of multiple experts (Alexander and Evans, 1988)?
- How is the quality of the expert's judgment measured and under which circumstances is this evaluated (Bolger and Wright, 1994)?

When, the potentiality of developing the expert system for the solving of the problem has been investigated the development process continues with the system's conceptual design and the conduct of its construction feasibility study.

The conceptual design of the system provides a general idea for the system, its purposes and prospective abilities. Some of the parameters, considered in the feasibility study of the system, are the following:

- The financial, managerial and technical capabilities of the company, such as:
- System's development cost
- Expected benefits for the company from the ES development
- System's maintenance cost
- Organizational structure of the company
- Operation of the system in a network environment
- System security of operation
- Availability of hardware and software
- Compatibility with existing systems
- The availability of both a domain expert and a knowledge engineer
- The reasons that enforce the development of a certain ES and not of another
- The potential effects of the ES operation to the labour relations
- The system's time scheduling
- Various other constraints (e.g. legal).

The accomplishment of these tasks lead initially to the identification and determination of the problem and then to the decision to proceed to its implementation or to interrupt the development process.

Then, the technical and economic framework of the system's development along with the requirements set by the company for the system's operation are determined. The decisions to be made involve the following issues:

- The choice and perhaps the provision of the hardware in which the ES will be installed and operate (Graham, 1988).
- The choice and perhaps the provision of suitable software tools for the development of the ES. (Goyal *et al.*, 1985). Several methodologies concerning the evaluation of the software have appeared in the literature (Holsapple and Whinston, 1987; Harmon *et al.*, 1988; Adelman, 1992);

The development process continues with the analytical design of the system in which scientists from the field of information science, the knowledge engineer and the domain expert participate and cooperate. In the beginning, a small-scale system (prototype) is developed, which contains all the basic parts of the ES but only a small and representative fraction of the elicited knowledge (Redin, 1987; Cholawsky, 1988). The development of the prototype provides certain significant advantages, such as:

- The check of the proper function of the system's various components,
- The check and evaluation of the system's knowledge bases, and
- The system's demonstration to all the interested parties in order to allow for their comments and propositions.

If a problem occurs, then some of the precedent tasks are repeated, after the necessary corrections. If the system passes all the tests then the development proceeds to the system's integration.

The integration of the system can be thought as a process that evolves from the initial stages of the ES's development till the system's installation (Lucas and van der Gaag, 1991). The integrated system is tested and evaluated during its development and also during its operation in its real working environment (Dickson and Powers, 1973; Swanson, 1988; Smith, 1988). Several problems may arise during the integration of information systems (Alter, 1980; Lucas, 1981; Meredith, 1981; Dickson and Wetherbe, 1985). When the system takes its final form, it is installed to its working area while together its documentation is completed.

The proper and complete training of the users is an issue that should be closely considered. Users that are not thoroughly familiar with the capabilities and the functions of the system resume a negative attitude towards the system and this might lead to its gradual inactivation. The implications of such an action are catastrophic for the further development of future expert systems within the particular company or within other related companies. In such a case, the impression that is always left is that the system and not the users should be blamed for the inactivation of the system.

Each system should exhibit flexibility and adaptability to possible arising demands. A system should be considered as a living organism that should be able to adapt in the best way to the demand of its users. The system's maintenance is caused by the appearance of certain problem during its operation phase. In fact, the last stages of maintenance, adoption and improvement do not finish without the termination of the operation of the ES.

4.3 Tools

The software tools used for the development of ESs include the following (Benchimol *et al.*, 1987; Price, 1990; Turban, 1993; Durkin, 1994):

- Conventional programming languages (e.g. C, Fortran, Pascal, and Basic) and artificial intelligence oriented programming languages (for example Lisp, Prolog)
- Shells and environments (e.g. 1st CLASS, ESE, Nexpert, Level5, ART, Level5 Object, Visual Rule Studio, Jess, etc)
- Special aiding tools that are used in the implementation of the ES's various components except for the knowledge base, which can be developed with the help of shells also.
- Hybrid systems that are comprised of aiding tools and programming languages. They provide the ability to develop shells or special ES more rapidly (e.g. ART, KEE, Nexpert Object).
- Special expert systems that address specialized subjects

Shells and specialized expert systems may be developed by the use of tools. For the development of specialized ESs may be used either tools or shell, which are developed by the use of tools (*Figure 14*).

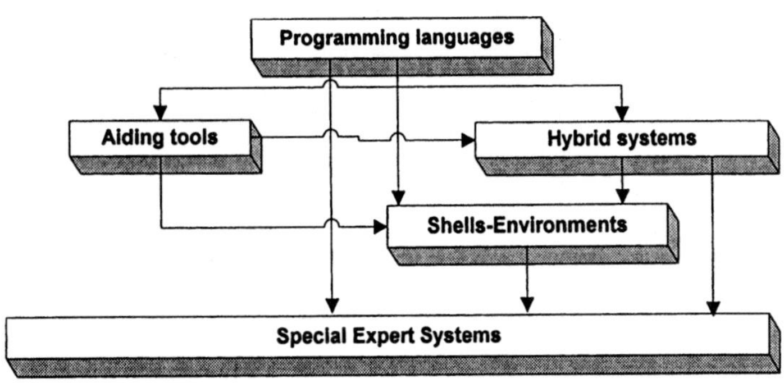

Figure 14. ESs development tools and technology levels

The figures below present the percentage of applications that were developed for different platforms and with different programming tools (Walker, 1996).

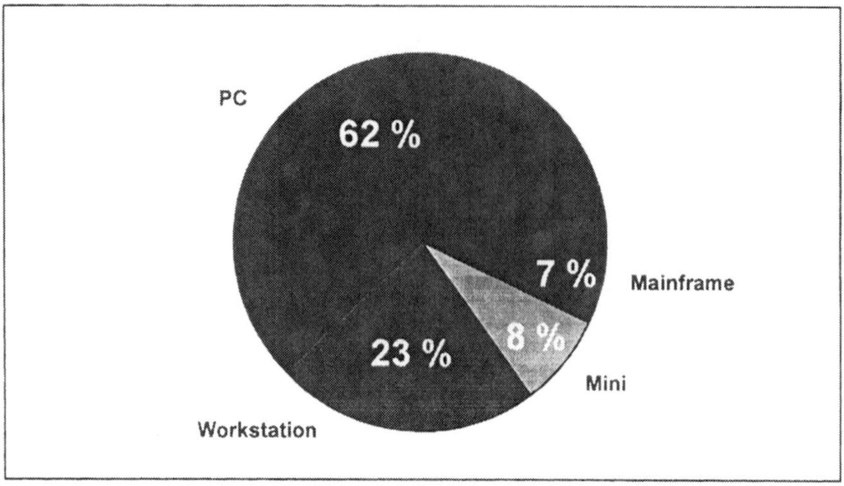

Figure 15. Platforms used in the development of expert systems (*Source*: Walker, 1996)

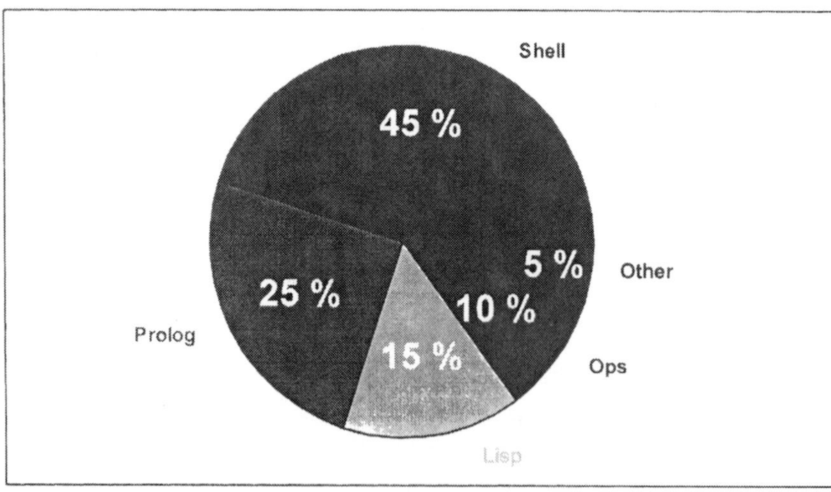

Figure 16. Programming tools used in the development of expert systems (*Source*: Walker, 1996)

As it can be observed by these charts the majority of the systems are developed for PC environments by employing shells.

5. MACHINE LEARNING

The ability of learning is one of the fundamental characteristics of intelligence developed by humans. The field of machine learning, which employs characteristics and methodologies of both cognitive psychology and artificial intelligence, studies the computational procedures that are used by humans and machines in the implementation of the learning process and develops new technologies that help the comprehension of this process. Despite its unique essence, machine learning is comprised by two major sections that are placed among broader scientific fields.

- The researchers of machine learning can not deny the fact that a large portion of machine learning studies the representation of knowledge and the organization of memory, two subjects that are cognitive fields of artificial intelligence and cognitive psychology.
- Learning can appear to whichever function requires intelligence, whether this is related with diagnosis, planning, natural language, mechanical control, or anything else. Thus, one may view machine learning as a field of research and development.

5.1 The use of machine learning in expert systems

Expert systems were developed in order to support or replace human experts. Several real world applications of expert systems have been presented in the literature in various fields such as accounting, finance (Zopounidis, Matsatsinis, Doumpos, 1996; Sintos, 1996), marketing (Matsatsinis, 1995) and manufacturing-production systems (Chandler, 1990; Meziane *et al.*, 2000). There is also evidence that in many cases they perform equal or much better than humans and may be a very useful tool in decision-making.

The development process of an expert system includes, as already discussed earlier, the stage of knowledge acquisition and elicitation by the experts, the stage of knowledge representation and organization, the stage of knowledge storage in some knowledge base and then the application of a certain inference engine mechanism in order to make a decision. In the majority of systems the phase of knowledge acquisition plays the most important role in their performance. Knowledge acquisition includes the elicitation, analysis, and interpretation, of the experts' knowledge and in a subsequent stage the transformation of this knowledge in a form suitable for process. All these tasks are the responsibility of knowledge engineers. Their role is very important in the development process of an ES, as they are the linchpins that join the reasoning and knowledge of the experts with the requirements in the codification of knowledge of every system. There is a series of specialized techniques that are used in the process of knowledge elicitation from the experts, such as structured interviews and protocol analysis. The experts formalize their knowledge with the help of those techniques and the knowledge engineers embody this knowledge into the system.

A major problem that arises by following the above-described approach is that frequently the experts are having difficulties in expressing their knowledge precisely. The acquisition of knowledge may be proved as a very time consuming process that frequently leads to non-complete structures of knowledge. In order to overcome these problems, several scientists have proposed an alternative approach that exploits the inference mechanisms for the construction of decision rules by existing data (past decisions) (Quinlan, 1986). The knowledge engineers collect data from past decisions, identify with the help of experts the most important attributes that affected those decisions, and employ an inference methodology in order to produce a set of decision rules. The core of this approach is the induction algorithm that receives a data set as input and produces as output a set of «If-Then» rules that are able to interpret the existing data set. Comparing to the traditional approach, inductive learning or learning by examples, generates more consistent rules and renders the learning process more independent from the experts.

5.2 The rule induction process

Machine learning algorithms aim at the generation of a set of rules through which we may arrive at a decision. In order to induce the rules there are certain elements that have to be introduced as data into the algorithm.

The **independent characteristics** fully describe each case. They express the attributes that are possessed by each case and on which their classification to a certain group will be realized. The number of characteristics is only limited by the volume of available information for the entire case of the problem. As the volume of the available information grows larger the more the independent attributes of the cases for which we have information and the more accurate the set of rules produced by the end of the algorithmic procedure. Similarly, proportionally increases the probability of correct evaluation and classification of future cases that will appear in the specific problem.

In order to produce rules, information on the values of the attributes for all the examined cases should be available. Therefore if there is a certain attribute, which value is missing for the majority of cases, we have to exclude it from the examined attributes. Similarly, if there is a certain example (case) in the learning set with many attributes with missing values then this case should be excluded from the set of learning cases. In any case, the learning set should be complete. If this is not true, then the analyst should render the set complete by removing some cases or attributes.

The independent attributes should have either symbolic or numerical values, reflecting the qualitative or the quantitative components of each case. Qualitative independent characteristics are usually expressed by symbolic representations, as these allow the analyst to precisely impress the series of information that express qualitative dimensions. In reverse, quantitative characteristics are expressed by their values, as absolute values characterize them unconditionally.

The **dependent attribute** is the subject of research of the machine learning algorithm. The process of the independent attributes result in the production of the rules that will be subsequently used in the evaluation of new cases. The produced rules examine the independent attributes of each case and determine the value of the dependent attribute, thus assigning the case to one of the available (predefined or not) classes. The dependent attribute is always expresses by a qualitative scale that represents the classes in which the set of the examined set is split. When the algorithm is executed in order to produce the rules, the value of the independent attribute is known for each case so as to render possible the induction of conclusions. In contrary, when the algorithm is executed for the evaluation of new cases based on the produced rules the dependent attribute is the subject of research and that which has to be determined for each examined case.

In general the rules produced by machine learning algorithms have the following form

$$\text{If } \left(X \ \alpha \ V\right) \text{ then } \left(Y \ \beta \ C\right) \text{ with probability } \left(prob \ \gamma \ P\right)$$

where

X	One of the independent attributes of the problem
V	A cut off value for the specific independent attribute of the problem
Y	The dependent variable of the problem
C	A value for the dependent attribute of the problem
P	A probability value
α,β,γ	Relational operands that can take the values $\leq, \geq, <, >, =$

As an example consider the following rule:

If

(Temperature $\geq 30^0$ C)

then

(Weather = Sunny)

with probability

(prob $\geq$ 0.95)

The goal of machine learning is the production of rules of this type that are able to represent in the most efficient way the knowledge contained in the data and to provide the ability to predict the value of the dependent attribute of each new case.

Each rule has three basic parts:

1. The first part contains the comparison relation between the independent variable and a cut off value.
2. The second part is the determination relation of the independent variable.
3. In the third part, the probability for the second part to hold while the first part already holds is defined. In some cases, the third part may not exist, depending on the function of each algorithm.

In order to produce rules, each machine learning algorithm should be able to specify:

- The independent variable X, the value of which will be examined by the rule.
- The cut-off value V, of the independent variable.
- The C value, which the rule will assign to the dependent variable, when the each time comparison condition of the independent variable is true.
- The probability P, which is related with the rule and states the expectancy of this rule to hold.
- The three relational operands α, β, γ, which define the type of relation among the parts of the rule.

6. ROUGH SETS

The starting point of the rough set philosophy is the observation that objects may be indiscernible in terms of descriptors. Rough set theory was established by Pawlak in 1982 (Pawlak, 1982; 1991) since then rough sets have been applied in several fields (Slowinski, 1992; Pawlak, 1997), such as the assessment of viability of the firms (Slowinski and Zopounidis, 1995).

Intuitively, a rough set is a set of objects, which, in general, cannot be precisely characterized in terms of the values of the set of attributes. In this case, the only sets that can be characterized precisely in these terms are lower and upper approximations of the set of objects. As we will see later, the lower approximation is related with the group of objects that can be classified in the examined set with complete certainty where as the upper approximation includes the objects the belong to the set of objects with a certain probability. Using a lower and an upper approximation of a set one can define an accuracy and a quality of approximation. These are numbers from interval [0,1] that define how exactly one can describe the examined set of objects using available information.

6.1 Original information and basic relations

The original information required by rough sets, consist of:

- The dependent attribute.
- The number of different classes of the dependent attribute.
- The independent attributes
- The number of different classes of each independent attribute
- The training set.

Rough Sets can only handle nominal (also called categorical or qualitative information). If the problem requires the use of cardinal (also called non-nominal or quantitative) data then these should be translated into some nominal terms. This translation involves a division of the original domain into subintervals and an assignment of nominal terms to them. The boundary values of subintervals are called norms. They usually follow from conventions, habits or subjective assessments. The analyst and the decision maker define the translation process, which is not prescribed for each problem.

Some terminology is required in order to present the rough sets theory. A fundamental notion in the theory is the notion of information system, which is a finite table rows of which are labeled by objects whereas columns by attributes and the entries of the table are attribute-values. Thus, an information system, or else known as knowledge representation system in the theory of rough sets, can be viewed as a collection of objects described by values of attributes. Each row in the table represents the information about an object.

Formally, an information system S is understand as the 4-tuple:

$$S = \langle U, Q, V, f \rangle$$

where

U is a finite set of m objects,

Q is a finite set of n attributes,

$V = \bigcup_{q \in Q} V_q$ and V_q is domain of the attribute q,

$f:U\times Q\rightarrow V$ is a total function such that $f(x,q)\in V_q \; \forall q\in Q, x\in U$ called an information function.

Let $S=\langle U,Q,V,f\rangle$ be an information systems and let $P\subseteq Q$ and $x,y\in U$. The objects x and y are indiscernible by the set of attributes P in S iff $f(x,q)=f(y,q) \; \forall q\in P$. Thus every $P\subseteq Q$ generates a binary relation on U, which is called an indiscernibility relation, denoted by $IND(P)$. The indiscernibility relation is an equivalence relation for any P. Equivalence classes of $IND(P)$ are called P-elementary sets in S and consists of the objects of U that are indiscernible by the set of P. The family of all equivalence classes of relation $IND(P)$ on U is denoted by $U/IND(P)$.

6.2 Approximation of sets

Let $P\subseteq Q$ be a set of independent attributes and $Y\subseteq U$ a set of objects. Three approximations of the set of objects Y can be defined as follows:

P-lower approximation is the set of all elements of U that can be with certainty classified as elements of Y. Formally, this set is described as:

$$\underline{P}Y=\bigcup\left[X\in U \mid P:X\subseteq Y\right]$$

P-upper approximation is the set of elements of U, which can possibly classified as elements of Y. Mathematically is represented by the formula:

$$\overline{P}Y=\bigcup\left[X\in U \mid P:X\cap Y\neq 0\right]$$

P-boundary approximation, is the set of elements of U which cannot be certainly classified to Y using the set of attributes P only, thus

$$BN_P(Y)=\overline{P}Y-\underline{P}Y$$

Set $\underline{P}Y$ is the set of all objects from U, which can be certainly classified as elements of Y, employing the set of attributes P whereas set $\overline{P}Y$ is the set of objects from U which can be possibly classified as elements of Y, using the set of attributes P.

Accuracy of approximation is used in order to express numerically how a set can be defined using a set of attributes. With every set $Y\subseteq U$, an accuracy of approximation of set Y by P in S or, in short accuracy of Y, is defined as:

$$\alpha_P(Y) = \frac{card(\underline{P}Y)}{card(\overline{P}Y)}$$

The coefficient

$$\gamma_P(Y) = \frac{\sum_{i=1}^{n} card(\underline{P}Y_i)}{card(U)}$$

is called the quality of approximation of partition Y by the set of attributes P, or in short quality of classification. It expresses the ratio of all P-correctly classified objects in the system.

6.3 Reduction and dependency of attributes

This is the major goal of the rough set theory, namely to reduce the attributes, in such a way that the reduced set of attributes provides the same quality of classification as the original set of attributes.

The minimal subset $R \subseteq P \subseteq Q$ such that $\gamma_R(Y) = \gamma_P(Y)$ is called Y-reduct of P and denoted by $RED_Y(P)$. An information system may have more than one Y-reducts. The intersection of all Y-reducts is called the Y-core of P, i.e. $CORE_Y(P) = \bigcap RED_Y(P)$. The core is a collection of the most significant attributes in the system. If one attribute belonging to the core is neglected then the information accuracy of the system is reduced.

To compute easily reducts and the core the rough sets theory use the notion of discernibility matrix (Skowron *et al.*, 1991). Let $S = \langle U, Q, V, f \rangle$ be an information system and let $P \subseteq Q$. The discernibility matrix $M(P)$ is a $m \times m$ matrix with entries c_{ij} defined as:

$$c_{ij} = \left[q \in P : q(x_i) \neq q(x_j) \mid i, j = 1, 2, 3, \ldots, n \right]$$

Thus, entry c_{ij} is the set of all attributes that discern objects x_i and x_j. The discernibility matrix assign to each pair of objects x and y a subset of attributes $\delta(x, y)$ with the following properties:

i) $\delta(x, y) = 0$

ii) $\delta(x,y)=\delta(y,x)$

iii) $\delta(x,z)\subseteq\delta(x,y)\cup\delta(x,z)$

It is easily observed that the core is the set of all single element entries of the discernibility matrix:

$$CORE_Y(P)=\left[q\in P: c_{ij}=q\right]$$

Every discernibility matrix $M(P)$ defines uniquely a Boolean discernibility function. Let each attribute $q\in P$ is assigned a binary Boolean variable $\overline{q}$ and let

$$\sum\delta(x,y)$$

denotes Boolean sum of all Boolean variables assigned to the set of attributes $\delta(x,y)$. Then the discernibility function, which is virtually the Boolean product of all the entries of the discernibility matrix, is defined by the formula:

$$f(P)=\prod_{(x,y)\in U^2}\sum\delta(x,y)$$

By employing the absorption law $(x+y)\cdot x=x$, and by multiplying all the constituents we get a simplified form of the discernibility functions. The result enables us to define the core, which consists of the single constituents of the final product.

7. NEURAL NETS

Neural networks are information-processing systems. In their more generic form, they can be represented as "black box" devices, which receive input and produce some type of output. A typical neural network consists of layers that each contains a collection of processing elements, called neurons. Each neuron receives inputs, executes a predetermined mathematical operation, and produces a single output. Each neuron functions entirely independently by all the other neurons. The neurons are connected together by links that are multiplied by a certain weight. For simplicity, the connections are known in the literature as "weights". The weight values are determined by the learning function of the neural network and their adjustment implies the ability of the neural network to learn. Therefore, it can be stated that that the weights are the memory elements of a certain neurons layout that along with the input contribute to the production of the output. Consequently, the underlying functions of a neural network are the learning process (adjustment of weights) and the information retrieval process with the utilization of the existing weights (Sanchez-Sinencio and Lau 1992). According to Freeman and Skapura (1991), the key characteristics of the neural networks are:

- They have a linear correspondence of input and output. This feature enables neural networks to learn non-linear relations of inputs and outputs directly from the training data.
- Generalization. Neural networks can easily provide solutions, provided that they have trained appropriately, to completely unknown environments for them.
- Adaptability. Neural networks are able to automatically adjust their weights in order to improve their behaviour.
- Error tolerance. Because of their parallel structure, neural networks can in many cases successfully handle the partial loss of their structural elements.

7.1 Neurons (Processing elements)

As already mentioned, neurons are the elements of the network that undertake the process of the information. Neurons should fulfil two substantial attributes (Wasserman, 1989):

1. Their function requires only local information that is all the information needed by each neuron is acquired by its inputs only.
2. They produce a single output value. This value is transmitted through the connections to the other neurons or it becomes part of the system's output

These two characteristics allow the neurons to work in parallel.

There are many mechanisms for the derivation of the output of a neural network. Among them, the most prevalent is the linear combination, which is described by the following formula:

$$y_j = f\left(\sum_{i=0}^{n} x_i \cdot w_{i \cdot j}\right)$$

The neurons functions, referred as activation functions or input output functions in the literature, receive as input a certain relation type (usually linear combination) and produce an output that resides in a predefined field of values. The most important type of relation is the linear function, where the produced output has the following form:

$$f(x) = a \cdot x$$

7.2 Training of neural networks

One of the most important attributes of the neural networks is their ability to learn. More specifically, in the neural networks terminology, learning is defined as the change in the values of the weights that aim at the gradual apprehension of the information, which later is available for retrieval. Several learning algorithms have been developed, which are classified in the following categories (Lin and Lee, 1996):

- **Supervised versus unsupervised learning.** A neural network has been trained by a supervised algorithm when in order to find the weights both the vectors of input and desired output are required. These two vectors are known in the literature as training pair. Usually the training of a neural network requires the utilization and test of several such pairs of vectors. During the training process, an input vector is applied and the output of the network is calculated. The output is compared to the output vector and the difference (error) is computed. Then, according to some algorithm, the weights are changed in order to minimize the error. The whole process is repeated until the output of the network satisfies the desirable specifications. Contrary to the above, the training of a neural network with unsupervised algorithm is accomplished when the presence of the output vector is not required for the adjustment of the weights. In the unsupervised case, the weight adjustment algorithm adjusts the weights so as the outputs produced by input vectors that do not differ significantly are the same. By this way, similar inputs that produce the same output are grouped in classes. Unsupervised algorithms are used, in general, for problems where the solution is not known a priori (e.g. forecasting problems).
- **Structural versus temporal learning.** A learning algorithm is structural when the response of the neural network does not depend by the precedent inputs and outputs. In the opposite occasion the learning algorithm is temporal. The majority of learning algorithms fall into the structural category.
- **Off-line versus on-line learning.** The majority of learning techniques are performed off-line, that is the network is trained to provide solution

prior to each actual use. A typical example of off-line learning algorithm is the well-known back propagation algorithm. When the training of the network is completed, the computed weights for each output are preserved and the network is ready to operate in practice. The disadvantage of off-line learning is that the network stops to learn from the point that is used for information retrieval. In order to overcome this drawback, several on-line algorithms have been developed, by which the network can be trained to handle new situations at any time. However, on–line algorithms do not provide satisfactory solutions to hard problems.

8. FUZZY SETS

The idea of fuzzy logic was originally introduced in 1965 by Zadeh, as a general representation of the phenomenon of vagueness. Fuzzy logic theory can be thought as generic mathematical consideration of the classical set theory. In a classic non-fuzzy set, an element of the universe can either belong or not to the set. This means that the membership of the element is fully defined. A fuzzy set is a generalization of the classical set in the sense that the degree of membership for each member is allowed to take values within the interval (0,1). This fact renders fuzzy sets to be highly flexible to practical problems (Zimmerman, 1995; Ross, 1996).

According to Lin and Lee (1996), the basic characteristics of the fuzzy sets are:

1. Fuzzy systems are characterized as numerical model free systems. They can evaluate a function without its mathematical description.
2. They have the ability to improve their performance in uncertain and consequently non-prescribed environments.
3. They have the ability to evaluate samples of a function, through which they can describe the function.
4. They are characterized as structured estimators. They combine the theory of fuzzy sets with rules and by this way they are guided to the result.
5. Their function presents a lot of common points with the methods of artificial intelligence rendering them suitable for applications of artificial intelligence.

9. DATA MINING

Simply stated, data mining refers to extraction or “mining” knowledge from large amounts of data. It has been characterized as the key to the process of Knowledge Discovery in Databases-KDD, which is the non-trivial extraction of implicit, previously unknown and potentially useful knowledge from data. It is also closely related with data warehouses, since data warehouses hold the data that is to be used by data mining techniques. Data warehouses, OLAP applications and data mining techniques all are fresh and very exciting applications in Management Information Systems and Decision Support Systems.

At the first international conference on KDD in Montreal in 1995, it was proposed that the term "KDD" be employed to describe the whole process of extraction of knowledge from data whereas the term "data mining" should be used exclusively for the discovery stage of the KDD process. Thus, data mining is considered as a single stage in the whole knowledge discovery process. As it can be observed in *Figure 17*, KDD is not a new technique but rather a multidisciplinary field of research; machine learning, statistics, database technology, expert systems, and data visualization all make a contribution.

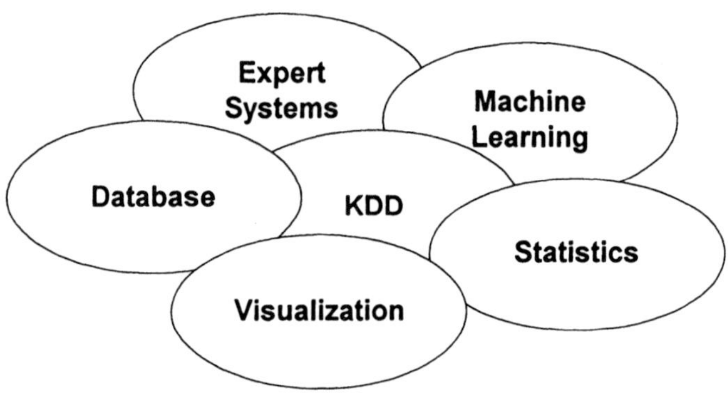

Figure 17. Multi-disciplinary nature of data mining (*Source*: Addriaans and Zantige, 1997)

Data mining was first discovered and deployed in USA, which is clearly ahead of Europe in this regard; its use in European organizations and enterprises is quite recent. However, data mining is considered to be among the "hottest" areas of interest in information science.

Singh (1998) defines data mining as the search of previously unknown but valuable information from large databases. This information is then used to support decision-making.

Addriaans and Zantige (1997), state that data mining is not so much a single technique as the idea that there is more knowledge hidden in the data than shows itself on the surface. Therefore, data mining is the attempt to extract hidden knowledge, new rules and unexpected structures and facts from large databases.

The majority of authors and researchers adopt similar definitions; many authors regard the terms data mining and KDD as synonymous.

Data mining or knowledge discovery in databases is the process of collecting useful information from data. This process includes more than a few methods like data characterization, data discrimination, classification, cluster analysis, association analysis, etc (Frawley *et al.*, 1991).

Data mining is the search of relations and attributes that exist in large databases but remain hidden due to the vast amount of data. These relations represent valuable information on the entities contained within the database (Holsheimer and Siebes, 1994; Holsheimer *et al.*, 1996).

Data mining is the automated process of extracting useful information from large databases. The most important algorithms employed in the stage of data mining include decision trees, inductive learning, association rules, neural networks, and case-based reasoning. Depending on the amount and quality of the available data, data mining techniques can create great commercial and business opportunities for an enterprise. Valuable information can be discovered related with the forecasting of market trends and the behavior of consumers, the detection of possible clients, the discovery of relations between services and products, etc. Wherever large data sets exist, there is the possibility of discovering interesting new applications.

According to Sprague and McMullen (1993), information can be categorized to the following categories:

- Information registered in internal databases (personnel data, customers data, suppliers data, etc).
- Information registered in external databases (competitors sales data, statistical data, stock market data, etc).
- Unstructured data that comes from internal sources and consists of almost anything (documents of any type).
- Unstructured data that flows from external sources and also consists of documents of any type, reports, thoughts, new ideas, etc (governmental sources, financial and business information, etc).

The knowledge discovery process consist of the following six stages (Addriaans and Zantinge, 1996):

1. Data selection, where data relevant to the analysis task are retrieved from the database.
2. Cleaning, to remove noise and inconsistent data.
3. Enrichment, where multiple data sources may be combined.
4. Coding, where data are transformed into forms appropriate for mining.
5. Data mining, where intelligent methods are applied in order to extract data patterns.

6. Reporting, where visualization and knowledge representation techniques are used to present the mind knowledge to the user.

The fifth stage, data mining, is the most interesting part since it is the phase of real discovery of data.

10. DISTRIBUTED ARTIFICIAL INTELLIGENCE AND INTELLIGENT AGENTS

The collection, choice, evaluation, and utilization of information to support decision makers along with the coordination of knowledge acquisition with the efforts dedicated in solving problems of information resources and decision making systems, has been proved an increasingly critical procedure (Sycara and Zeng, 1996). Intelligent software agents are capable to respond exactly to these requirements (Rao and Georgeff, 1993; Sycara and Zeng, 1994; Wooldridge and Jennings, 1995). The concept of agent signifies a person that acts on behalf of another in order to achieve the goals that have been set to him or her.

Figure 18, presents an abstract view of an agent. The agent receives inputs from his environment and generates actions that affect this environment. In most cases, an agent does not have complete control of his environment; in the best case, the agent will have partial control, i.e. will be able to affect the environment. This means that the same action performed by the agent will possibly have completely different results if it is to be performed under different circumstances. In many cases the result will be miles away from the anticipated one. Thus, agents should be ready to handle their possible failure in most of their potential action environments, which under any circumstances cannot be considered as deterministic.

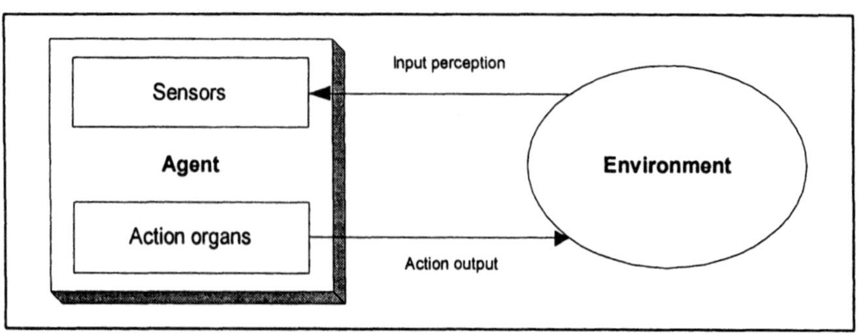

Figure 18. An agent interacting with his environment (*Source*: Multiagent Systems, MIT Press, 1999)

Intelligent software agents are programs that act on behalf of their users, gathering and filtering information online from various sources, aiming at the satisfaction of the user needs. Some have described intelligent agents as "Objects that Think". These thinking "objects" in their effort to satisfy the demands of their user they interact with him, with other «objects», and with the available resources. However, agents have properties that are not contained in "objects", such as beliefs, commitments and goals. Agents can work alone or to cooperate with others in a co-operative society, communicating with each other by exchanging messages.

Agents are here to stay, not least because of their diversity, their wide range of applicability and the broad spectrum of companies investing in them. As we move further and further into the information age, any information-based organization, which does not invest in agent technology, may be committing commercial hara-kiri (Nwana, 1996). In *Figure 19*, we may observe the dynamic of this rapid developing area.

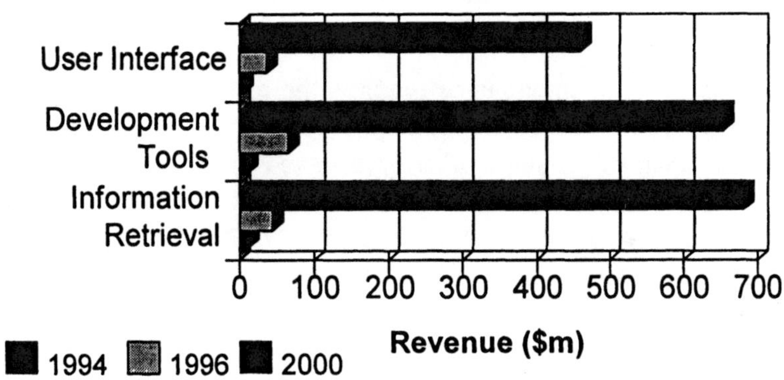

Figure 19. Market potential for software Agents (Ovum, Intelligent Agents, the new software revolution - White Paper -http://www.ovum.com/)

But, what is an agent anyway and what concepts are contained in it or ascribed to it? We will cite some of the definitions given by several researchers.

An agent is a software that does things, that probably a user would do if he had the time (Janca, 1995).

A piece of software that performs a given task using information gleaned from its environment to act in a suitable manner so as to complete the task successfully. The software should be able to adapt itself based on changes occurring in its environment, so that a change in circumstances will still yield the intended result.

Intelligent agents are defined as the modules of a multiagent system, which by turn is defined as a loosely coupled system of problem solvers that cooperate in order to solve problems that go beyond the capabilities of a single solver. These solvers are the intelligent agents (Durfee *et al.*, 1989).

Intelligent agents are computational systems that reside in complex dynamic environments in which they possess capabilities of perception and autonomous action, thus perceiving a set of goals and tasks, for the attainment of which they are designed. These agents can take various forms with regard to the nature of their environment (Autonomous robots-software agents, Knowbots – Interface agents) (http://agents.www.media.mit.edu/groups/agents/; http://pattie.www.media.mit.edu/people/pattie/)

Intelligence is the degree of reasoning and learned behaviour: the agent's ability to accept the user's statement of goals and carry out the task delegated to it (Gilbert *et al.*, 1995).

A minimum level of intelligence requires the existence of a number of preferences, possibly under the form of rules, with the addition of interference mechanism or some other type of reasoning that acts on these preferences. A more advanced level includes a user model or some other type of cognition concerning the desires of the user and the planning of the available resources in order to achieve these desires and goals. There are also systems with learning capabilities, which are adapting to their operational environment according to the available resources and the goals placed by their users. These systems play the role of "assistants" since they are able to examine new relations, links or concepts in order to satisfy their users' needs (Björn, 1996).

According to a significant number of researchers, the term agent bears the notion of a digital system with specific characteristics-attributes (as those mentioned earlier) but also is implemented with concepts that are generally used for humans. For example it is quite common to characterize an agent by conceptual notions such as knowledge, belief, affection, commitment, while recently emotional agents have appeared in the literature.

The basic characteristics of a software system that signify it as an intelligent agent are:

- **Autonomy.** Intelligent agents resume action whenever they intend it and not necessarily when they receive an execution order. They possess the ability to check the status of their environment and also to observe the interaction of the user with the system in order to judge if it is necessary to commence the execution of a certain task.

- **Mobility.** Agents have the ability to move, and respectively to action and to other systems beyond the particular system in which they are installed. This ability of theirs is particularly boosted by the cooperation and the social behaviour that the agents should exhibit. Prior to the execution of procedures in a remote computer environment, permission is required, which is granted after the communication and cooperation with the respective agents (White, 1994).
- **Rationality.** An agent should be characterized by rationality and intelligence with regard to the decision it makes and the way it is planning the achievement of the goals. Intelligence and rationality are primarily based in dynamic rules but also grow with experience. A fundamental ability for an agent is to be able to learn either by its user either by other agents (Galliers, 1994).
- **Adaptability.** It is essential for an agent to be able to adapt its way of action, learning, and behaviour to the various hardware and software platforms, in which it will be called to operate, as well as to the demands and to the special characteristics of its user.
- **Reactivity.** Agents perceive their environment (which may be the natural world, a user through a graphical user interface, a collection of other agents, the Internet, or all of these combined together) and react to its changes within a rational time. This feature implies that agent may spend their time mostly in a condition of sleep, waiting for a motive of activation (the incoming of an electronic message perhaps).
- **Proactivity.** Except for their reaction behaviour to external stimuli (reactivity), agents are able to focus on the attainment of goals and to get prepared for this, basing their judgment to the status of their environment also. So, for example when an agent finds out that its user searches certain software in the Internet, which requires a large space for installation, it takes care of the defragmentation of the hard disk beforehand.
- **Social behaviour.** Agents communicate with each other as well as with users, usually through special languages, like the KQML. This behaviour is quite important because it allows the support and aid among the agents and also allows them to learn by the other agent's experience.
- **Collaboration.** An agent should not accept and carry out assignments without performing any check on them. It should always consider the fact that users make mistakes, forget critical information, or even supply fuzzy information. For example a certain command may lead to conflicts among the assigned goals. An agent should check the possibility of such

conditions either by directly asking the user either by structuring models of users (Eichmann, 1994).

- **Goal orientedness.** An agent is capable of handling complex high-level tasks. Decisions concerning which tasks will be divided into subtasks (and to how many), or in which order some of the tasks will be executed in order to move towards the attainment of the goals, are made by the responsible agents.

According to Gerson (1976), coordination of the intelligent agents in a multiagent system is the process by which each agent perceives its actions and the (prospective) actions of the other agents aiming at the compact operation of the community.

Lesser and Corkill (1987), refer to the coordinating process, which aims at the reservation of the following points:

- All the partial sections of the global problem are contained in the activities of at least one intelligent agent.
- All the intelligent agents interact with a certain way so that their activities are incorporated into a single integrated solution.
- In which way the above can be acquired with the available computational power and resources.

Jennings (1996), from the angle of the architecture of multiagent systems, states the following reasons that render the coordination of the intelligent agents necessary:

- The actions of the intelligent agents are interdependent. This means that the job of a certain intelligent agent might presuppose the completion of the job of another agent. For example, if we have two agents, one responsible for digging and the other responsible for loading, then obviously the latter will start to work after the completion or at least the partial finishing of the excavator's job.
- There are global constraints that must be satisfied. This implies that the agents' tasks have certain time limits or that intelligent agents have limited response time to external stimuli or that they have restrained bandwidth.
- No one has the necessary ability, resources, and information to solve the entire problem. This is self-evident because otherwise we would not a multiagent system but a single problem solver case.

Figure 20, in which the three types of agent: interface, task and information agents are presented, shows the distributed architecture of the RETSINA system proposed by Sycara and Zeng (1996), which follows the general philosophy of BDI, proposed by Rao and Georgeff (1993).

According to Gilbert et al. (1995) the agents' technology is applicable to:

- Systems and Network Management
- Mobile Access / Management

- Mail and Messaging
- Information Access and Management
- Collaboration
- Workflow and Administrative Management
- Electronic Commerce
- Adaptive User Interfaces

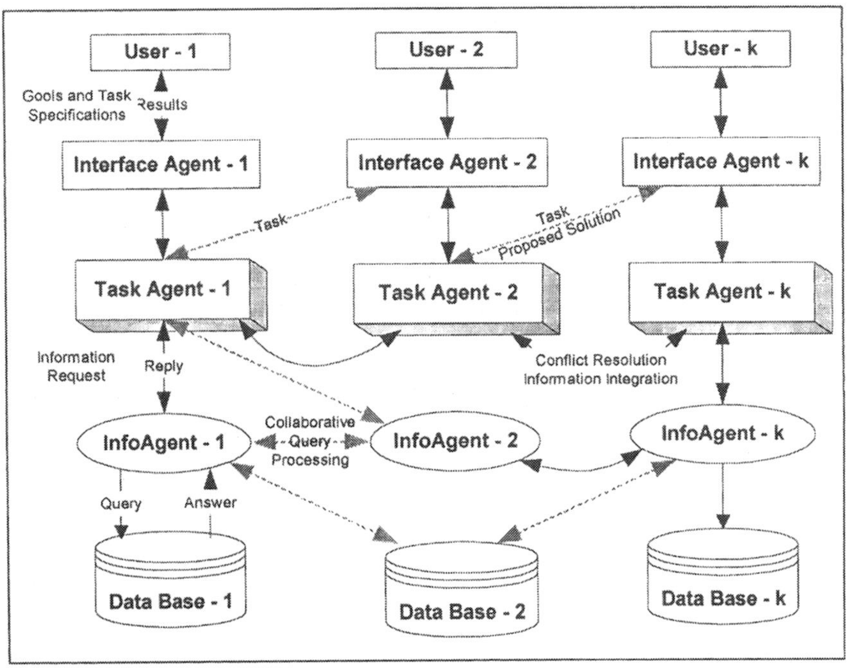

Figure 20. Distributed system architecture (*Source*: Sycara and Zeng, 1996)

Considering the above, intelligent agent could be classified in the following major categories:

a) **Network agents.** Apparently, the basic characteristic of this category is their space of action.
b) **Interface agents.** They are the software agents that primarily aim at the facilitation of the communication of the user with the various interfaces.
c) **Generic agents.** These are intelligent agents that undertake the solution of problems in dynamic and complex environments and recreational agents.

Intelligent agents can also be classified to three groups according to their ability to solve problems (Krin and O'Hare, 1996; O'Hare and Jennings, 1996):

a) **Reactive agents.** This type of agents is able to send or receive messages reacting to changes of his environment or to messages send by other agents.
b) **Intentional agents.** This agent is synchronized with other agents by exchanging information regarding their beliefs, their goals or actions and is able to judge its intentions and beliefs, to plan its actions and to realize its plans.
c) **Social agents.** The social agent has to maintain its models and judge the knowledge contained in them (intentions, commitments, expectations, prospective reactions and hypothetical behaviours) in order to be able to make decisions and plan its actions based on these models.

Some examples of agent-based systems include the following:

- Pleiades (http://www.cs.cmu.edu/~softagents/pleiades/)
- Retsina (http://www.cs.cmu.edu/~softagents/retsina.html)
- Kasbah (http://ecommerce.media.mit.edu/Kasbah/)

More about agent-based systems and their applications in marketing will be presented in chapter 8 §5.2.

Chapter 8

Intelligent Decision Support Systems in Marketing

1. INTRODUCTION

In this chapter, we examine a recent class of systems that have the ability to process data and then by using reasoning to transform them into opinions, judgments, evaluations, and advises. With these systems the capability of reasoning is added to the functionality of the DSS, thus giving the ability to provide advises to specialized problems. Their focus is to support their users into the problem solving process rather than to substitute humans in decision-making. This new type of systems is the result of the cooperation of expert systems and decision support systems. The role of the ESs is to provide their heuristic reasoning and explanatory capabilities while DSS contribute with their analytical procedures and data management (Ford, 1985; Turban and Watkins, 1986; Henderson, 1987; Doukidis, 1988; Holtzman, 1989; Moore, 1992; Turban, 1993).

Several names have appeared in the literature in order to describe this new type of systems, such as Knowledge-Based Decision Support Systems - KB-DSS (Klein and Methlie, 1990; Guida *et al.*, 1992; Liberatore and Stylianou, 1993), Intelligent Decision Support Systems - IDSS (Holtzman, 1989; McGovern *et al.*, 1991; Gottinger and Weimann, 1992), Knowledge Based Management Support Systems (Doukidis *et al.*, 1989), Expert Based Systems (Goul and Tong, 1987) and Expert Support Systems - ESS (Van Weelderen, 1991; Van Weelderen and Sol, 1993). As intelligent Decision Support Systems we define systems (software) that provide information and methodological knowledge (field knowledge and decision methodology knowledge) through decision analytical models (users and systems), data and knowledge bases, aiming at the support of the decision maker into effective decision-making in complex unstructured problems (Klein and Methlie, 1990). The scientific background of these systems is presented in *Figure 1*.

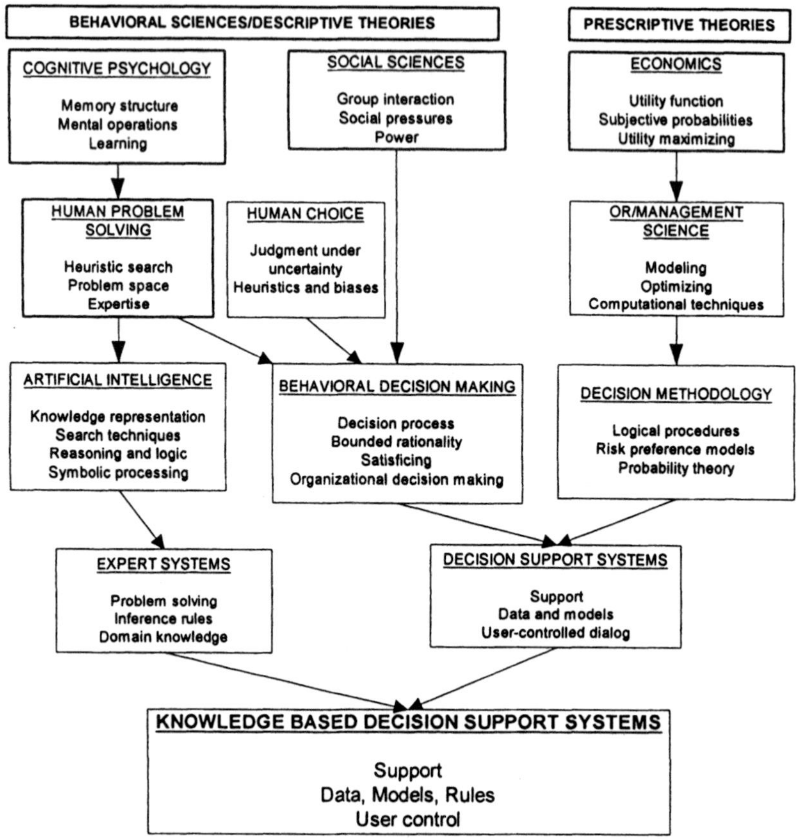

Figure 1. Scientific background of knowledge-based DSSs (*Source*: Klein and Methlie, 1990)

The first studies and work on the integration of the technologies of ES and DSS where presented in the proceedings of the NATO Conference Advanced Study Institute on Decision Support Systems Theory and Application, held in Italy, on 1985 (Holsapple and Whinston, 1987). Previously, Zannetos (1968) referred to the oncoming usage of Artificial Intelligence to Management Information Systems, but not to the DSS. Sprague (1980) introduced some concepts of Artificial Intelligence by recognizing the need for the existence of a dialogue subsystem between the user and the DSS. Within the next year, Bonczek *et al.* (1981) proposed a new framework of DSS development, including the subsystems of knowledge, language, and communication. Hawgood (1985), referred to the necessity of developing DSS adapted to the characteristics of the specific user-decision maker, a proposition that introduces the idea of storing specialized knowledge related with the personal solving way of certain problems (heuristics) and with the personal point of views of the decision maker. A little later, Smith (1986) defined as Expert Database Systems, those used for the development of applications that require knowledge-driven elaboration of the allotted information. To the integration of ES and DSS have also been referred, among others, Kowalik (1986), Lee and Lee (1988), Teng *et al.* (1988), Turban and Watson (1989), Kohout *et al.* (1992), Turban (1993).

It is widely accepted that today the complexity of the decision-making procedures is persistently increasing. The confrontation of the problem and the effective support of the decision maker require the extraction of applicable knowledge from experts and the suitable representation and storage of this knowledge into the DSS. The stored knowledge should contain, apart from the expert's knowledge, and knowledge on the objectives of the decision-maker (Suranjan, 1986). The knowledge representation techniques in the Knowledge-Based DSS stem from Artificial Intelligence and vary according to the type of the problem to be solved and to the characteristics of the systems' operations (Doukidis *et al.*, 1989).

Some theoretical differences between DSS and ES have been pointed out by Pfeifer and Luthi (1987) and Kurstedt (1987). Doukidis (1988), in a study that involved 67 ESs, established that the concepts of semi-structured tasks, decision support, and effectiveness, that stem from the field of DSS are completely applicable to ESs. Differences regard the problem space and the methods used to deal with the problem.

Within the context of this book, we shall equivalently use all the above terms under the more general label of Intelligent Decision Support Systems, in order to ascribe decision support systems that employ methods of Artificial Intelligence and utilize knowledge acquired from several different sources (experts, literature, etc) and not from a single source only (Luconi *et al.*, 1986; Rangaswamy *et al.*, 1989).

2. IDSSS DESIGN AND DEVELOPMENT

2.1 Introduction

Several studies (*Table 1*) have shown that enterprises turn to the development of intelligent DSSs by their belief that the system can play significant role in the their future. An additional motivation for the development of intelligent support systems is the belief that the system will provide larger degree of consistency and correctness in decision-making. This can significantly improve productivity and give competitive advantages to the enterprise and accordingly increase its market shares. *Table 1* presents the mean values of the most important reasons that lead an enterprise to the development of an intelligent DSS, on a Likert scale from 1 (not important) to 5 (very important).

Table 1. Motivations leading to the development of an intelligent DSS (*Source*: Byrd, 1993)

Motivation	Mean
Encouragement by senior management	3.21
Comprehensive feasibility study	2.26
Improvement in customer service	3.25
Believe important for the future	4.16
Potential reduction in work force	2.31
More consistency in decisions made	3.71
More timely business reporting and decisions	3.25
Improved productivity	4.04
Improved competitiveness and market share	3.70
More accurate business reporting and decisions	2.95
Education and training	2.55
Providing ease of access to corporate data bases	2.38
Reduction of workers doing routine tasks	2.53
Workers free to do more creative work	3.44
To improve managerial work	2.53

In general the design and development of IDSSs follows the guidelines of DSSs and ESs development. As soon as the development of the system is accepted the next step involves the determination of system's actions (what the system should do) and also determination of its development specifications. It is important to avoid details in the specifications determination phase so as to avoid placing constraints to the system designer. Specifications should be complete and explicit. They should include, at least, the system's objectives and limitations (*Table 2*); in the opposite case the system might fail to attain its objectives because these were not explicitly clarified (Ince, 1990; Patridge and Hussain, 1994). System's specifications come from several different sources such as the end user, the system's analyst, the knowledge engineer and the domain experts that contribute to the knowledge acquisition phase.

Table 2. Factors included during the specifications determination phase (*Source*: Patridge and Hussain, 1994)

Factor	Involves
Output	Format
	Content
	Availability

Factor	Involves
	Response time
	Retention time
Processing	Inference mechanism
	Inference rules
	Approach to knowledge acquisition
	Approach to knowledge representation
	Uncertainty management approach
	Programming language/shell/ environment to be used
Input	Sources
	Media
	Procedures
	Validity checks
Back-up	Items needing back-up
	Procedures
Security	Define unauthorized access
	What is to be controlled?
	Control of access
	Procedures
	Auditing
	Internal or external or both?
Maintenance	When to maintain?
	When to redevelop?
	Mechanism to maintain
Personnel	Specification of domain experts
	Number
	Who?
	Training
	Who?
	What?
Testing	Approaches to testing
	Content of testing
	Who performs the testing

Blair, Debenham and Edwards (1997), investigated and compared technologies used for the design of intelligent decision support system. According to this study (the results of which are illustrated by *Figure 2*) the most common design methodologies for IDSSs are the following:

- Expert-based systems methodology - EBS (Goul and Tonge, 1987)
- Intelligent decision systems methodology - IDS (Holtzman, 1989)
- The MEDESS methodology (Van Weelderen, 1991)
- Visual interactive modelling methodology - VIM (Angehrn and Luthi, 1990)
- Text analysis approach – TAA (McGovern, Samson and Wirth, 1991)
- Knowledge-based DSS methodology - KBDSS (Klein and Methlie, 1991; 1995)

ID	Description	EBS	IDS	MEDESS	VIM	TAA	KBDSS
K1.	Investigate class of decisions	Few	Yes	Few	No	No	Few
K2.	Knowledge elicitation	Existing	Yes	Existing	No	Existing	Existing
K3.	Multiple knowledge sources	No	No	No	No	No	No
K4.	Decision maker and expert	Yes	Yes	No	Yes	No	Yes
K5.	Circumstances and preferences	Yes	Yes	No	Yes	No	Yes
K6.	Uniform analysis approach	No	No	No	No	No	No
K7.	Decomposition and abstraction	Few	Few	Few	Few	Few	Few
K8.	Four decision making phases	No	Yes	No	No	No	Yes
K9.	Graphical models	Yes	Yes	Yes	Yes	Yes	Existing
K10.	Languages for describing	No	Existing	No	Existing	Existing	Existing
K11.	Validation and verification	Yes	Few	No	No	No	Few
C1.	Easy transition	Yes	Yes	No	Yes	•	Yes
C2.	Decomposition and abstraction	Few	Few	Few	Few	•	Few
C3.	Normalisation	No	Few	No	No	•	No
C4.	Uniform approach for modelling	No	No	No	No	•	No
C5.	Graphical model	Yes	Existing	Yes	Existing	•	Existing
C6.	Rich language for knowledge	No	No	No	No	•	No
C7.	Knowledge independent from use	No	Yes	No	No	•	Yes
C8.	Support for risks and uncertainties	No	Yes	No	No	•	Yes
E1.	Easy transition	Yes	Yes	Yes	Yes	•	Yes
E2.	Selection of algorithms	No	No	No	No	•	No
E3.	Decision analytical techniques	No	Few	No	No	•	Few
E4.	External model	No	No	No	No	•	No
E5.	Functional operations	No	No	No	No	•	No
I1.	Internal model	No	No	No	No	•	No
I2.	Ease of transition	No	No	No	No	•	No
I3.	Defining operational constraints	No	No	No	No	•	No
I4.	Deciding what should be deduced	No	No	No	No	•	No
I5.	Support risk and uncertainty	No	Yes	No	No	•	Yes
I6.	Decision analytical techniques	No	Few	No	No	•	Few
I7.	Deciding language to implement	No	No	No	No	•	Few
R1.	Searching for components	No	No	No	No	No	No
R2.	Understanding components	No	No	No	No	No	No
R3.	Interconnection of components	No	No	No	No	No	No
R4.	Modifying components	No	No	No	No	No	No
R5.	Evaluating component feasibility	No	No	No	No	No	No
R6.	Support all development phases	No	No	No	No	No	No
U1.	Usability before functionality	No	No	No	Yes	No	No
U2.	Representation schema	No	No	No	Yes	No	No
U3.	Defining collaboration	No	No	Yes	Yes	No	No
U4.	Decomposition and abstraction	Few	No	No	Few	No	Few
U5.	Manipulation of interface	No	No	No	Yes	No	No
U6.	Rules for visual language	Few	No	No	Yes	No	Few
U7.	Ease of transition	Yes	No	No	No	No	Yes

Figure 2. Comparison of design methodologies (*Source*: Blair *et al.*, 1997)

The completion of system's design is followed by the implementation of a prototype, a miniature of the complete final system, which contains the basic components of the system as well as representative sections of the knowledge bases under development. The key goal of developing a prototype is to facilitate the on time detection of possible omissions and faults or to test the right development and operation of the system. Fault detection facilitates the taking of appropriate measures in order to correct the system's shortcomings. If the prototype operates successfully the development team proceeds with the implementation of the final product.

After the system is implemented the functional tests of the system are carried out; these involve checking separately the correct function of each subsystem's components before checking the function of each subsystem taken as a whole. Next, the overall function of the system is inspected by the knowledge engineer, the experts employed in the development of knowledge bases, and the end-users.

Then the tasks of validation and verification are carried out (Chapter. 5 §5). The final two phases are the system's documentation and the training of the end-users. If the system successfully passes all the tests then it is installed in its final location.

Table 3. Allocation of responsibilities during the development of an intelligent DSS (*Source*: Patridge and Hussain, 1994)

Phase	Prime responsibility	Support staff
Problem identification	User and corporate staff	Consultant (?)
Feasibility study	Management appointee	Domain expert Consultant Systems staff
User specification	User	Domain expert
Design	Knowledge engineer	Domain expert
Implementation		
Knowledge acquisition subsystem	Knowledge engineer	Domain expert
Inference engine	Knowledge engineer	AI programmer
User interface	Knowledge engineer	Specialist in human factor and psychology 3GL programmer
Testing		
Knowledge	Domain expert	Knowledge engineer
System	Domain expert	Domain expert consultant Knowledge engineer

The introduction of an intelligent DSS should be studied very carefully in order to substantially help users in their tasks, since usually the installation if the IDSS stimulates organizational changes, which include the adaptation and training activities of the users. The introduction of an intelligent DSS in any organization produces additional organizational changes, besides the known implications caused by the introduction of any information system, due to the use of DSSs as well as the use of Artificial Intelligence techniques. Additional problems appear regarding the training of the employees because of innovative concepts inherent in intelligent DSSs, such as original methodologies, knowledge bases, different problem solving and decision support tools like multicriteria analysis, data-mining, intelligent agents, neural nets. Developers should explicitly state to the users, from the beginning of the development process, that intelligent DSS aim at supporting their users in decision-making and not at replacing human decision makers with computer systems (Klein and Methlie, 1995). During the training phase the objectives of the system should be clearly explained. Also, the specific decision-making process that is followed by the decision-makers prior to the introduction of the system should be investigated. Furthermore, the operation of the system should be thoroughly analysed, the models contained should be exhaustively explained and also a typical application of the system should be demonstrated to the users. Demonstration allows participants to analyse in detail selected cases of decision-making and solve them with the assistance of the system, while at the same time users are able to pinpoint differences and advances from the unsupported (manual) decision making process.

The phase of supporting the newly developed IDSS begins after the installation of the system (improvement and maintenance tasks). Improvement tasks include supply of solutions in possible newly presented requirements of the enterprise or of the users. Maintenance operations are mainly due to the appearance of problems during the operation of the system (*Table 3*).

2.2 System development tools

In the development of an intelligent DSS several tools are applied such as common programming languages (Pascal, Visual Basic, C++, Delphi, ...), or Artificial Intelligence languages (Lisp, Prolog, ...). Several alternative methods have been adopted in order to overcome the difficulties in the development of IDSSs (lack of time, unfamiliarity or finding difficult to learn and use programming languages, etc.), such as (Patridge and Hussain, 1994):

- *Programming environments.* These are integrated development environments that support one or possibly more programming languages along with supporting software (editor, debugger). Examples include the Lisp environments MacLisp and InterLisp, as well as the Prolog environments.
- *Intelligent DSS development shells.* A shell is a ready-to-run software that contains at least the inference engine and interface capabilities with other tools or programming languages. Shells require only the development of the appropriate knowledge bases and their integration with the remaining system's modules, according to the specific requirements of the shell. Shells are fast and easy to use; therefore they constitute a very attractive alternative. However, there is the possibility that they cannot match the requirements of the problem at hand. For example, the inference mechanism or the knowledge representation method used by a certain shell may be inappropriate for the particular problem; in this case the shell or the problem or both of them should be modified. Some well-known shells that have been used for the development of intelligent DSSs are: 1st CLASS, ESE, Nexpert, Level5, Level5 Object, M4, EXSYS, Jess, Visual Rule Studio, etc.
- *Toolkits or development environments.* Development environments bear the advantages of a shell but they provide more flexibility than shells in the use of the inference mechanism as well as in the use of the adopted knowledge representation technique. For example regarding the

knowledge representation a development environment provides more than one representation methods along with appropriate graphical tools that render the environment user-friendlier. The problem with the development environments is their price. They are expensive to buy and maintain; also, sometimes they require more sophisticated (therefore more expensive) hardware and operating system. Examples of such development environments are the ART, KEE, and Goldworks.

Table 4 presents a comparison among the various types of intelligent DSSs development tools.

Table 4. Comparison among the various types of intelligent DSSs development tools (*Source*: Patridge and Hussain, 1994)

Tools	Advantages	Disadvantages and limitations
Languages	General purpose Very flexible Produces custom-made products High-performance product	Not easy to use Requires programming skills Time-consuming and slow to produce Product needs a lot of debugging and testing May need specialized hardware
Environments	High programmer productivity	Specialized mix of language and support software Needs debugging and testing May require specialized hardware May not "fit" problem
Shells	Proven solutions (already debugged) Easy to use Available off-the-shelf Little (if any) new resources and training needed Often maintained and updated by vendor Shorter implementation period	Inflexible knowledge representation and inference mechanisms Poor for prototyping Good for "special" purposes May not "fit" problem well
Toolkits	Very flexible and powerful Good for rapid prototyping	Can be very expensive Can be difficult to use May need specialized hardware and operating system

Intelligent DSSs development environments are the most well suited choice regarding the development of an intelligent DSS (Klein and Methlie, 1995). The choice of the most appropriate development environment is based on several criteria, such as:

- Support of graphical user interface.
- Support of report generation. The ability to support the interactive generation of reports that are able to include text, tables, and graphics.
- Modelling language.

- Determination of forms. The inclusion of forms for data input and check is essential.
- Database management system. It should have the ability to interconnect with the most common DBMSs.
- Knowledge base. An important feature is the available possibilities of using different methods for knowledge representation.
- Toolbox. The inclusion of appropriate economic, statistical, forecasting, data analysis, operations research, marketing, etc. algorithmic libraries.
- Platform (hardware and operating system). It concerns the specific platform for which the development environment is available (for example Windows 3.1, 95, 98, 2000, NT Windows, Unix, Linux, ...) as well as the platforms currently used by the enterprise.
- Supplier reliability and support.
- Price of the development environment and total installation and operation cost.
- Existence of qualitative documentation

2.3 Development problems of intelligent DSS

According to Alter (1992), some of the problem that appear during the development of intelligent DSSs, are classified to the following categories:

- *Technical problems.* Technical problem are divided in hardware problems, software problems and technical design problems. The typical hardware problems are described by insufficient power of the CPU, limited memory capacity and limited external storage space. Software problems originate from the fact that implementations of development environments are available only for specific operating systems.
- *Data related problems.* These are divided in two categories. The first category is related with the kind of the data. In this case data may be inaccurate or measured and structured in the wrong way or may not even exist. The second problem category is related with the source of the data.
- *Conceptual problems.* These problems are related with issues concerning the end-users and also with the modelling process and the software employed. In regard to users, usually systems designers are overoptimistic regarding the willingness and the ability of the users to operate the systems. In order to overcome these problems, the extensive training of the users in solving real-world problems with the help of the systems is required. Also designers should always check if the users have the time and the motivations to use the system. Conceptual problem related with the modelling process come from the attempt to use existing models that are incompatible with the specific cases confronted by the decision makers.

- *Human-related problems.* This category includes problems that arise by the fear of users in operating such systems. Such a problem arises when analysts are afraid of being replaced with DSSs. The issue here is to investigate whether the difficulty in accepting the system comes from the users or from actual technical problems of the system itself. Usually, employees do not use the system because they cannot perceive in which way the system will help them to solve or simplify their daily tasks; or because they are not willing to learn how to use the system; or finally because they see no advantage in changing their custom way of work.

Table 5 presents some finding of a survey conducted by Byrd (1993). Byrd surveyed 74 knowledge engineers from private organizations to examine empirically the state of expert systems in these organizations. The respondents classified each of the issues as to how important each was to successful implementing ESs in their organization on a Likert scale from 1 (not important) to 5 (very important).

Table 5. Important issues that appear during the development of an intelligent DSS (*Source*: Byrd, 1993)

Issue	Mean
Finding a willing and able expert	4.52
Communication between knowledge engineer and expert	4.45
Fear of loss of control by organizational personnel	3.04
Fear of loss of jobs by organizational personnel	2.78
Improper introduction by top management	3.63
ES shells not robust enough	2.69
Lack of knowledge engineers	3.15
Difficulty in specifying certainty factors	2.47
Knowledge of specialized AI languages lacking	2.73
The overall cost is too high	2.76
The time for a successful implementation is too long	3.08
Validation of ES is too difficult	2.69
Development of explanation facility is too difficult	2.30

According to Byrd's survey the most important problems include the finding a willing and able expert and the communication between knowledge engineer and experts. Other important issues are the way the system is introduced in the company, the availability of knowledge engineers, the time required for the implementation of the system, and the fear of loss of control by organizational personnel.

3. INTELLIGENT DECISION SUPPORT SYSTEMS

3.1 Intelligent Interfaces

First of all, we have to point out that it is completely different to discuss about intelligent interfaces and about intelligent systems with a simple interface (http://www.sics.se/~annika/ii_links.html; http://www.cs.wpi.edu/Research/airg/IntInt/academic.html#intint). In the first case, we speak about the utilization of intelligent techniques in order to refine the cooperation between the user and the system. Thus, the system may contain knowledge for its functions and knowledge regarding the aid and information of the user. On the contrary, an intelligent system should produce intelligent information. A basic approach on how far an interface can be considered intelligent can be found in the discussion of Birnbaum, Horvitz, Kurlander, Lieberman, Marks, and Roth (1997; http://www.merl.com/reports/TR96-28/).

Nevertheless, which exactly are the reasons that render necessary the development and operation of intelligent interfaces? In short, we can mention the following (Sullivan and Tyler, 1991):

- To facilitate the work of the users so that they feel more comfortable and more intimate when they work with an application.
- Nowadays, as the number of new users increases dramatically, a large number of people are forced to use applications and functions, which they do not know or understand. This fact leads to the necessity to support users though intelligent interfaces.
- The use of applications in radical or specialized cases by knowledge workers or by special users (nuclear station software, space program software, medical software, military software, etc) generates the necessity to support users through intelligent interfaces with multimedia capabilities, knowledge of the functionality, of the capabilities and of the results' presentation possibilities of the system.
- The expansion of the complexity of the applications, caused by the need to cover the demand for more and more sophisticated requirements of the users, leads to the necessity of developing intelligent interfaces in order to guide the users.
- The increase of the available information generates confusion to many user categories that are usually perish in vast volumes of information, being unable to figure out which information is the one required. The finding of the necessary and appropriate information can be handled by intelligent interfaces that are adapted to the needs of their users.

According to Patridge and Hussain (1994), the interface of an intelligent DSS includes the following too:

- The front-end interface for accessing the knowledge base. This interface is addressed to those who are in charge for the system development. During the development phase both the knowledge engineer and the domain experts from whom knowledge is acquired should be able to use appropriate supporting tools to interfere, edit and structure the acquired knowledge. The tools that are provided by the front-end interface are the following:
  - *Editor.* It is used for the construction of the database; also checks the consistency in the syntax of the rules.
  - *Automatic bookkeeping.* This tool records new entries and changes applied to facts and rules contained in the knowledge base.
  - *Screen editor:* This function is activated by the user interface and checks the form and contents of the display presented to the user.
  - *Check of knowledge base consistency.* When new knowledge is added to the existing knowledge base, its compatibility with presented knowledge is checked
  - *Tracing.* It is a fault editing process.
  - *Break package.* This tool has the possibility to interrupt the program in certain places, in order to allow the examination of the variables' values at these points.
- The back-end or end-user interface, for access to the inference mechanism. Its is used by the system's end-user who requires not only the advice of an expert but also explanations that are to be given interactively. This interface consists of:
  - Input/Output functions. Input/Output operations allow the user to query and modify the knowledge base. Questions should be part of a sequence of non-stop interactions where experts' answers and suggestions to a query lead to the next question, until the user is completely satisfied. Interaction can be performed in several different ways:
    - Menu driven guidance. According to this method user makes a choice through a set of predefined alternative choices.
    - Command oriented. User inputs a command or directive to elicit the desired reaction of the computer system.
    - Based on natural language. Commands are given in natural language form instead of a programming language form.
    - Customized. Interface structure and further details have been designed especially for a particular user or as a small group of users.
  - Explanation and justification. A most important attribute of intelligent DSSs is their ability to explain the reasoning that is followed at each point. System suggestions are presented to the user

through the interface. The aid the system offers should be possible to adjust to the requirements of the end user, depending on the user expertise to the operation of the specific system.

Intelligent interfaces are structured by the following modules (http://cs.wpi.edu/Research/airg/IntInt/intint-outline.html):

- The user model.
- Multimodal communication.
- Plan recognition.
- Dynamic presentation.
- Natural language.
- Intelligent help.
- Interface adaptability.

Some intelligent interfaces are briefly presented below (http://www.ntt.co.jp/COLING94/mark.html; http://www.ai.sri.com/~cheyer/papers/mmap/mmap.html):

XTRA (Allegayer *et al.*, 1989) and CUBRICON (Neal and Shapiro, 1991) are both systems that combine complex spoken input with mouse clicks, using several knowledge sources for reference identification. CUBRICON's domain is a map-based task, making it similar to the application developed in this paper. However, the two are different in that CUBRICON can only use direct manipulation to indicate a specific item, whereas our system produces a richer mixing of modalities by adding both gestural and written language as input modalities. It incorporates speech input and output, natural-language text, graphics, and pointing gestures by the user. The objective of using IntInt techniques in this system is to "simplify operator communication with sophisticated computer systems."

PAC-Amodeus (Nigay and Coutaz, 1993) systems such as VoicePaint and Notebook allow the user to synergistically combine vocal or mouse-click commands when interacting with notes or graphical objects. However, due in part to the selected domains, the natural language input is very simple, generally of the style ``Insert a note here."

TAPAGE (http://www.ai.sri.com/~cheyer/papers/mmap/mmap.html) is another system that allows true synergistic combination of spoken input with direct manipulation. Like PAC-Amodeus, TAPAGE's domain provides only simple linguistic input. However, TAPAGE uses a pen-based interface instead of a mouse, allowing gestural commands.

SAGE (http://www.cs.cmu.edu/afs/cs/project/sage/mosaic/sample.html): This program creates intelligent data-graphics. The intelligent interfacing is in determining the best way to display a set of data so that the data is readable and understandable.

CHORIS: This system is designed to enable a wide range of users to interact effectively with varying types of complex systems. Its main strength lies in its knowledge of these complex systems.

UCEgo: the intelligent component of UNIX Consultant. This natural language system helps the user solve problems encountered while using UNIX.

IIFS: The Intelligent Information Fusion System (http://sdcd.gsfc.nasa.gov/ISTO/AIS/ais.html): This effort focuses on the development of an intelligent user interface based on expert systems, natural language query processors, object oriented data representation and data visualization, that allow the user to identify, select and access desired data and supporting information and knowledge in the context of a research or subject domain from an advanced information management system. To effectively monitor, analyse, and understand space and Earth science requires technological developments in an end-to-end intelligent information fusion system. This is primarily due to the enormous size and complexity of the data that will be generated. This requires bold futuristic thinking in many areas of new and emerging technologies logically fused together to form an efficient and effective intelligent information fusion system

The COURT System (http://www.cs.wpi.edu/Research/airg/Court/): The COURT system was developed by Jon Kemble for his WPI CS MS thesis as an intelligent interface for the TENNIS computer network ease of service evaluation project (Kemble, 1994). It uses a presentation description language to control the display of multi-attribute data. The language allows the grouping, naming and association of the raw data provided. It also allows features to be attached to the data. The system interprets and annotates the data, under control of the description language, and then displays the data using general presentation principles, expressed in a rule-base, guided by the annotations. The system is able to produce a credible version of Minard's `Napoleon's March' graphic (Tufte, 1992).

3.2 Intelligent Data Bases Management Subsystems

Recent advancements in the fields of artificial intelligence, object-oriented programming, and hypermedia as well as the requirement for immediate information led to the development of intelligent databases for managing information (*Figure 3*).

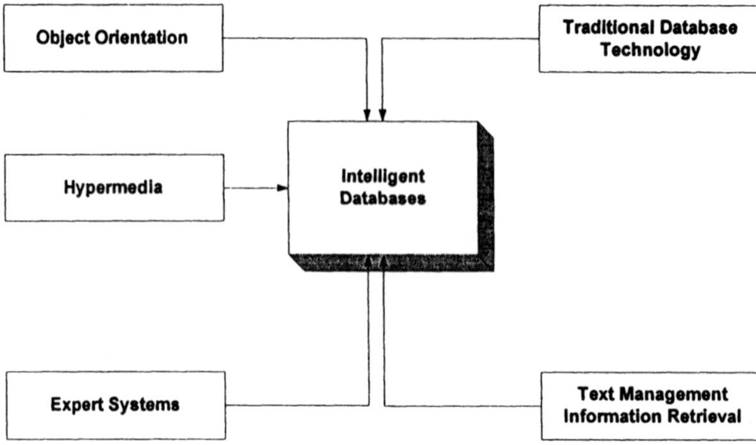

Figure 3. Contribution of scientific fields in intelligent databases (*Source*: Parsaye *et al.*, 1989)

According to Parsaye *et al.* (1989), the general architecture of an intelligent database consists of three levels (*Figure 4*).

High Level Tools	• Knowledge discovery • Data Integrity • Quality Control • Hypermedia Management • Data Presentation • Decision Support • Data Format Management • Intelligent System Design
High Level User Interface	• Multimedia • Personal Databases • Note Taking • Navigation Tools • Object Editing • Semantic Editing
Intelligent Database Engine	• Inference Engine • Database Compiler • Rule Manager • Transaction Manager • Explanation Manager • Multimedia Manager • Meta-data Manager

Figure 4. General architecture of intelligent databases (*Source*: Parsaye *et al.*, 1989)

In the future databases will become more complex and larger and in addition will encompass Artificial Intelligence techniques (Bertino *et al.*, 2001). *Figure 5* illustrates an example of an intelligent database where input data come from standard databases, from expert systems knowledge bases as well as from recently acquired knowledge. There are also tools like data dictionary and concept dictionary that give the ability to users to associate values with characterizations (tall - between1.80 and 1.90 m). The intelligent database is connected with an intelligent database machine, while access is performed through an intelligent interface, to which queries can be placed with several different ways (natural language, voice call, etc) (Patridge and Hussain, 1994).

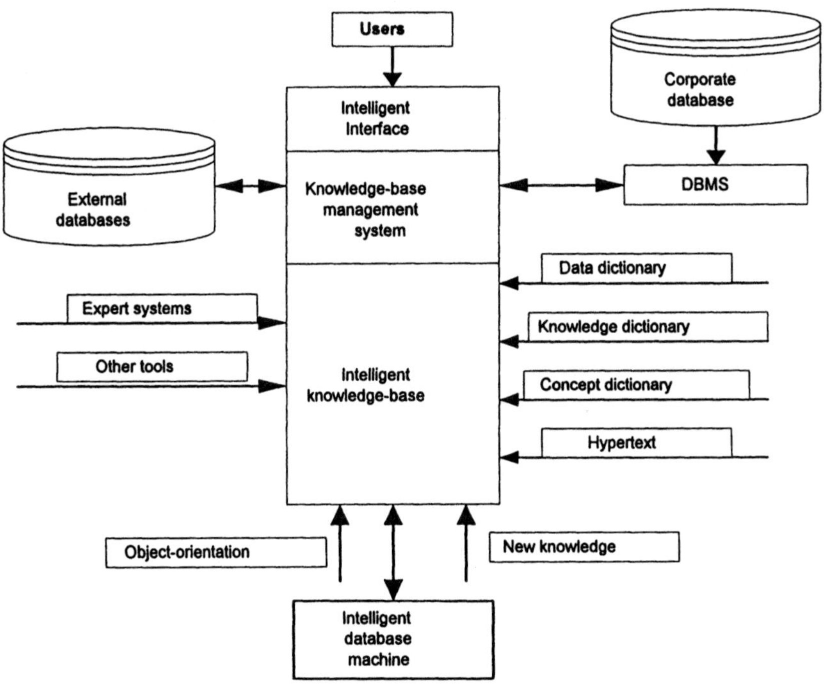

Figure 5. Intelligent database (*Source*: Patridge and Hussain, 1994)

According to Harmon and Sawyer (1990), the examination and determination of the relationships of the database and the ES requires the following steps:

- Decide whether the database access is necessary. The reasons that lead to the decision of connecting the ES and DB are the following:
  - Maintenance of the knowledge bases with the help of the DBMS.

  - Increase of efficiency by the operation of coactive knowledge and databases.
  - Existence of data that are used together by other applications or other users.
- Decide which will be the role of the ES and the DBMS. The cooperation of the ES and DBMS can be:
  - Bilateral: The two modules cooperate as two independent units. The cooperation can be either loose coupling either tight coupling. In the loose coupling case, the ES contains additional knowledge about which data are necessary to it and proceeds to the retrieval of the particular sections of the database that are necessary for the operation of the system, creates a temporary DB and assumes its management. Should the data contained in the temporary DB modified then the main DB should also be updated. In the second case of tight coupling, the DBMS is nothing but the medium for managing the necessary information where as the ES is nothing but a simple user of the DB. The ES should contain knowledge about:
    - When it will address to the DBMS, requesting data-information retrieval, or storage.
    - Which data are required in each case.
    - In which way the retrieval of the data will be performed.
    - Which specific form should the data have in order to be usable by the ES as well as the possible data conversions required in the cases of retrieval and storage? In general, the ES is responsible for the data management.
  - By integration of the ES into the DBMS. A form of this category is when the ES intervenes to the systems and facilitates the communication between the user and the DBMS. In addition, an ES could check the validity of the DBMS operation as well as the validity of the data contained in the DB. Another function can be the conditionally activation and execution of specific operations. Besides, an ES can process the data of the DB and keep certain records about them (e.g. statistical process, etc). Also, data mining algorithms could be integrated in order to recognize certain patterns and similarities in data sets of the DB.
  - By integration of the DBMS into the ES. This integration provides a very powerful tool, mainly for the creation of either programming languages (e.g. Prolog) either of development shells for ESs.
- Preparation of data access. As already mentioned, an ES that uses a DB, should have the following possibilities: file access, file conversion to various suitable formats for the support of the ES, data conversion to suitable formats, data abstraction and data integrity.

- Connection with the DB. There are two possibilities of connection: by incorporating commands of the DBMS to rules and by attaching a database sourcing to an attribute.

Finally, a novel category of Intelligent Data Base Systems is formed by the development of agent-based systems (Marakas, 1999). The increased requirements of those systems in representation, modelling, control of shared and distributed knowledge, and management of several different data types issues raise new challenges for farther research.

3.3 Intelligent Model Base Management Subsystems

According to Kwon and Park (1996), two are the most important issues in Model Management Systems: the representation and management of models.

By taking into account what is contained in §5.4.4, we can further mention several other situations that are favoured by the cooperation between the AI and MBMS fields (Blanning, 1987; Elam and Konsynski, 1987; Marsden and Pingry, 1988; Van Nee and Lapinsky, 1988; Liu *et al.*, 1990; Huber, 1990; Weber *et al.*, 1990; Cohen and Sproull, 1991; http://www.comp.nus.edu.sg/~yeogk/course/ic432/ic432.html).

- In the aid of the user during the model building process in order to formulate the most suitable model.
- When the model themselves contain knowledge (model agents, heuristics, etc).
- When the utilized models stem from the field of AI (fuzzy sets, theory of evidence, ...) or are used in order to generate knowledge (machine learning, data mining, neural nets, rough sets, etc).
- Manipulation and choice of models with the use of knowledge (§10.2.7).
- Interpretation and management of the result derived by the application of the models.

A variety of knowledge representation schemes such as semantic networks, first order predicate calculus, and production rules have been used for model representation and management.

The development of agent based systems technology and their use in the development of IDSS has provided new dimensions and perspectives in the use of intelligence in IBMS (Matsatsinis et al, 1999).

4. IDSSS IN MARKETING

In 1997, a mail questionnaire survey was undertaken by Li (2000b), in 900 large companies in the UK, to explore managerial requirements for computer-based support and current status of information systems in support of marketing strategy development. According to the responses from the 104 marketing directors and managing directors of these companies, 86 companies reported currently using computer-based system to support the development of marketing strategy. Of the 86 companies, the most common computer-based support is provided by database systems (91,7 %) and spreadsheets (90,5 %). Nearly half of the 86 companies (48,8 %) reported currently using marketing information systems. Moreover, executive information systems were used by 25% and 15,5 % were using DSSs. But only 6% of the 86 companies reported currently using expert systems in the support of marketing strategy development (Li, 1999).

Moreover, according to the 86 British companies, most systems fail to provide even moderate help for the following five types of requirements:

a) Help couple strategic analysis with managerial judgment.
b) Provide strategic analysis assistance.
c) Help strategic thinking.
d) Cope with uncertainty and fuzziness.
e) Help understand the factors that affect marketing strategy development

This lack of success has led to the fact that greater number of 55% of the responding managers in the 86 companies were dissatisfied or very dissatisfied with the computer-based systems currently used in developing marketing strategy. It is also found that the four principal factors leading to manager's dissatisfaction include:

a) The individual system used is limited in support capabilities (54,3%).
b) The systems cannot couple strategic analysis with managerial judgment (53,6%).
c) The particular strategy analysis models employed are limited in function and scope (38,6%).
d) The systems cannot deal with uncertainty and ambiguity (22,9%).

In the following sections we will study several categories of intelligent decision support systems in marketing; each category is the result of integration and use of different artificial intelligence methods in the decision support systems.

4.1 ES and DSS in Marketing

4.1.1 DSS and ES Integration

The term "integration" signifies the composition of a uniform set of software, hardware, and communication capabilities either in the development level or in the application level. Integration can be either functional or physical (Turban, 1993). With functional integration, we mean that different functions-capabilities (data processing, e-mail, etc) will be provided to the user, by a single communication system under a uniform pattern. On the other hand, physical integration is related with the necessary package of software, hardware, and communication means for the realization of the functional integration (Newman, 1987).

The integration of ES and DSS is an effort to exploit the advantages of both types of systems and together to reduce their disadvantages to a minimum. As it has been pointed out already, DSSs allow the decision-maker to have full control on the acquisition and management of the information as well as in the making of the final decision. On the other hand, ESs provide the possibilities of knowledge in a certain field, the possibility to simulate the reasoning process, to infer, and to provide explanations to the derived conclusions. The goal of integration is to achieve a reconciliation of the results that are derived when ESs and DSSs work independently, in order to improve the quality of the decisions made.

Klein and Methlie (1990), draw the following points for the application of ESs' technologies in order to improve the capabilities of the DSSs:

- The integration between ESs and DSSs adds to the latter the aid of an expert, the opinion of which the user may follow. In parallel, the knowledge of the user is improved because of the augmented interaction between him and the system.
- The ES able to provide explanations on the reasoning process followed. Thus, the learning possibilities of the DSS user are expanded.
- The ESs can be used in the decision analysis methodology, as for example in the determination of the decision models or the evaluation of a probability distribution (Holtzman, 1989).
- The participation of suitable ESs provides the ability not only to receive explanations on the results of the application of a certain model but also to on the behaviour of the model with the assessment of its logical structure and of the coherence relations among its variables (King, 1986).
- Model management can be an additional application field for ES, by supporting the process of structuring a certain model (Elam and Konsynski, 1987).
- User aid with the management of statistics, operation research, and other methods. This might include the guidance of the user to the selection of the suitable tools, his training in the manipulation of these tools, and finally the discovery of the necessary data to be used by a certain tool through the entire volume of the available data (Chambers *et al.*, 1981; Hand, 1984; Hahn, 1985; Gale and Pregibon, 1983; Gale, 1986c).
- Provision of guidelines concerning the more efficient exploitation of the data, model, and knowledge bases as well as of the presentation of the various results derived by the DSS (Klein and Villedieu, 1987).

- In many cases, the user feels the need to ask for the help of an expert concerning the way that he will ask the system for something. This role can be played by a special ES that will aid the user to formulate his questions to the system in an appropriate way.

As mentioned earlier a class of intelligent systems is the result of cooperation between ESs and DSSs. Hence, their structure can be determined as combination of basic DSSs components, i.e. combination of database and model base with the basic modules of ESs, which are the knowledge base and the inference mechanism. In the above we should also consider of course the inclusion of the user interface subsystem, which is necessary in order to allow the communication and interaction of the various components as well as the facilitation of reliable communication between the user and the system.

According to Turban and Watkins (1986), the contribution of ESs and DSSs in developing intelligent DSSs includes the factors presented in *Table 6*.

Table 6. Contribution of ESs and DSSs in the development of IDSSs (*Source*: Turban and Watkins, 1986)

	ESs's contribution	DSSs's contribution
Database Management	Improve the development, operation and management of databases. Reduce the time required to access large databases. Allow the symbolic representation of data.	Introduce the use of databases.
Model base management	Improve the management of models. Assist in the selection of the most fitting model. Improve the process of sensitivity analysis. Aid in the development of alternative solutions. Aid in the consistent structuring of the problem. Support the trial and error processes.	Provide an initial structuring of the problem. Provide specific tools Provide computational capabilities.
Interface subsystem	Provide a user-friendly environment. Provide explanations. Guide the system's user.	Provide the abilities for proper presentation of results.
System's capabilities	Provide advices and estimations. Provide explanatory possibilities.	Aid the collection of appropriate data. The decision maker gains

ESs's contribution	DSSs's contribution
	experience on properly examining and analyzing the data. Provide the support that meets the preferences and decision policy of each decision maker.

4.1.2 Architecture of DSS and ES Integration

Adaptation model of ESs into DSSs' subsystems. According to this model, the partial expert systems are adapted to the various subsystems of the DSS in order to support the respective functions of the system (Turban and Watkins, 1986). An example of such model is presented in *Figure 6.*

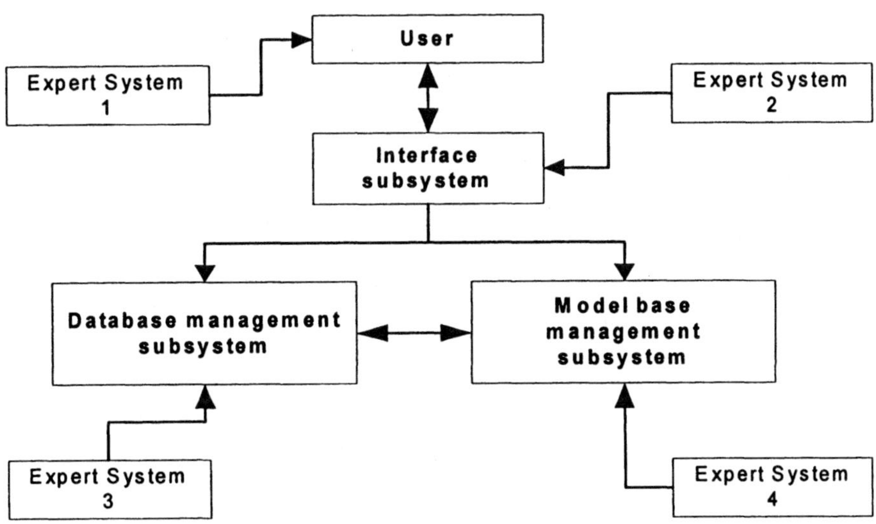

Figure 6. Adaptation of ESs into DSSs' subsystems (*Source*: Turban, 1993)

The first ES addresses to the user of the system and provides to him consultations and guidelines about the usage of the system and about the problems in which the system can be applied.

The adaptation of a second ES in the communications subsystem contributes to the improvement of the communication between the user and the system and to the augmentation of the systems' "user-friendliness".

The third ES is adapted to the data management subsystem whereas the third is adapted to the model management subsystem. The last three mentioned ESs will be examined later in more detail.

Integration model of ES as an independent subsystem. In this case, a fourth system, the ES, is added to the three classical subsystems of the DSS (*Figure 7*).

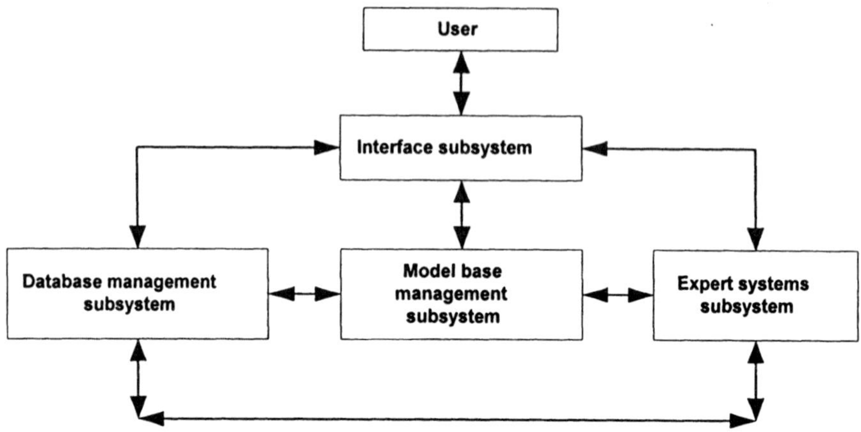

Figure 7. Adaptation of ES into DSS subsystems (*Source*: Turban, 1993)

With this type of integration, the ES subsystem is linked with the DSS according to three possible combinations, as presented in *Figure 8* (Turban and Watkins, 1986; King, 1990). According to the first type of interface, the results derived by the ES are used as input data by the DSS (Courtney *et al.*, 1987).

Another possible interconnection regards the direction of the results derived by certain tasks accomplished by the DSS into an appropriate ES (Lee and Lee, 1988).

In the third type of linkage, the results derived by the ES are transmitted as input data to a certain task of the DSS. After their processing, they are feedbacked in the input of the ES. The process is repeated until the derived results can be considered satisfactory.

Model of ES's participation in the decision making process. According to this model, the ES interfere in the decision making process by performing certain tasks. In order to accomplish its goals the ES uses the databases and probably some of the capabilities of the models contained in the DSS. The most common application of this model is in the formulation of the strategy during a decision making process (Meador *et al.*, 1984).

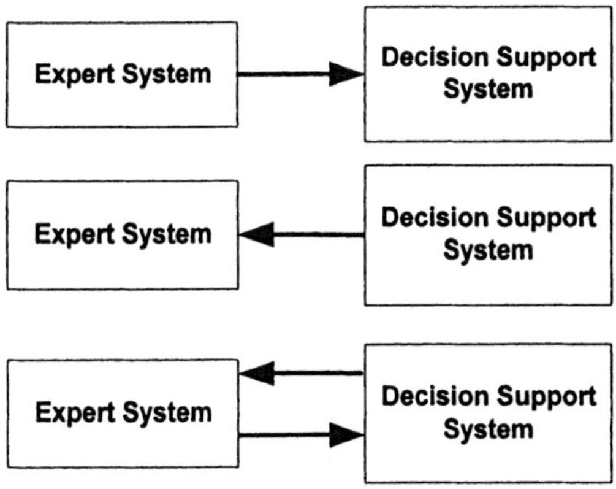

Figure 8. Possible DSSs and ESs interface

Model for the generation of alternative solutions. This model expands the possibilities of the previous one, by providing the opportunity to the user to initially formulate the set of alternative solutions, then to evaluate them, and finally to choose the most appropriate (Reitman, 1982).

Integrated model. With this model (*Figure 9*) the ES is edged into the three subsystems of the DSS, providing an intelligent way for their operation, cooperation, and management.

4.2 ES and DSS Applications in Marketing

In the following sections, some representative decision support systems that use expert systems in solving parts of marketing problems are briefly presented.

4.2.1 The INNOVATOR system

INNOVATOR supports consultants in financial service organizations in deciding whether to offer specific product innovation to their customers (Ram and Ram, 1989). The system architecture is presented in *Figure 10.* It was developed with the use of the rule-based expert system shell called Expert System Environment - ESE/VM of IBM and was implemented on an IBM4381 computer system.

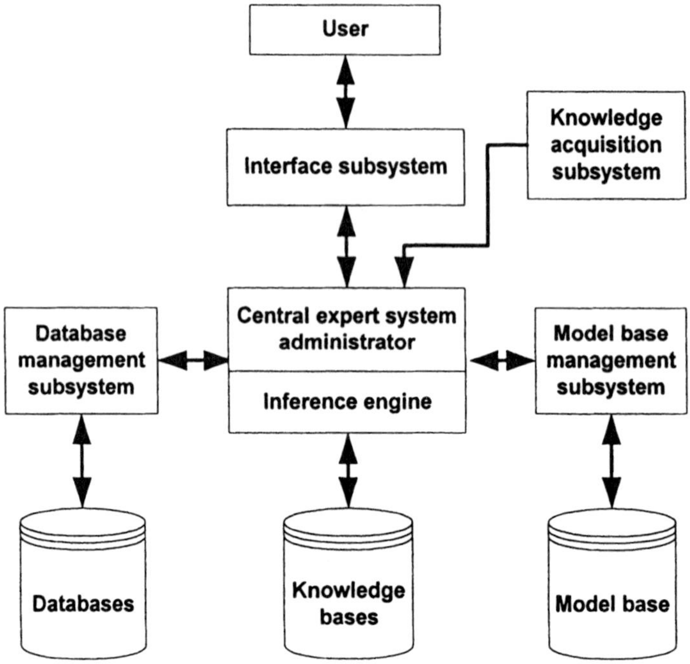

Figure 9. Integrated model (*Source*: Teng *et al.*, 1988)

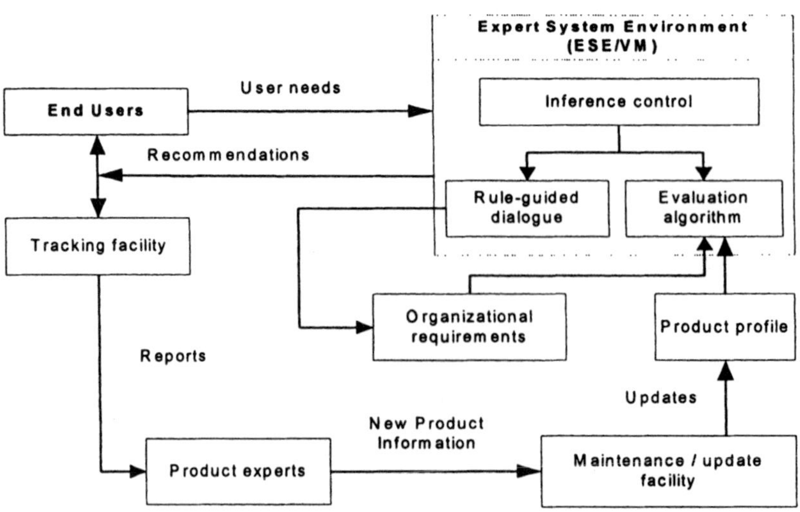

Figure 10. INNOVATOR architecture (*Source*: Ram and Ram, 1989)

The basic components of INNOVATOR architecture are the following:

1. *Inference control.* This module controls the process of user consultation. In a typical case the flow of control begins with collecting the

organizations' requirements, continues with invoking the evaluation algorithm, and concludes with presenting the results to the user.
2. *Dialog.* Dialog refers to the way in which users interact with the system. The system uses a backward chaining inference procedure to ascertain organization requirements from user based on their answers to a series of questions.
3. *Evaluation Algorithm*: Once the organizational requirements are determined, the system invokes the evaluation algorithm to determine whether the new product satisfies the organizations' requirements.
4. *Maintenance Facility.* INNOVATOR is designed for easy maintenance
5. *Tracking Facility.* The tracking facility keeps track of past recommendations made by INNOVATOR, the reasoning used in arriving at the suggestions, whether these suggestions were implemented by the organization and the outcome of the implementation.

For INNOVATOR, knowledge was elicited from the financial experts of five financial service organizations using informal initial interviews followed by in-depth interviews. Information was also collected through extensive search of secondary sources of data, such as surveys and financial data. The steps followed for the acquiring the knowledge from the domain experts were:

a) *Initial knowledge elicitation.* Initially, the experts provided a list of the major product lines that should be included in the knowledge base of INNOVATOR, such as annuities, bonds, mutual funds, etc. Then, the experts identified all possible products in each product line, and finally listed the major brands in each product category that were to be included in the knowledge base.
b) *Elicitation of attributes.* Next, the experts identified the key attributes required for evaluating a product line, a product, and a brand. A list of 20 attributes was developed and identified by the experts as the basis for deciding whether a financial service organization should add a new product line to its portfolio. These attributes were grouped into five major attribute classes: market, financial, product, corporate, and competition.
c) *Elicitation of attribute weights.* Next, the experts determined the relative importance of the attributes by assigning a numerical weight to each attribute.
d) *Determination of attribute values.* Finally, the experts rated the product lines, products, and brands on each attribute.

The knowledge base of INNOVATOR consists of facts that are acquired by interacting with the user or from external databases and rules that are pre-programmed into the system to represent human expertise.

The database of the system is divided into two parts, the organizational profile, and the product profile.

1. *Organizational profile.* The system ascertains the needs of the organization (for example profit margin expected, type of clientele served by the organization) through a dialogue process with the user and creates the organizational profile and stores it in a file.
2. *Product profile.* The profiles of product lines, products, brands, and their attribute values are stored in another database. The product profiles are used in order to determine whether the organizational requirements can be satisfied.

The evaluation algorithm that is applied during the evaluation process of a product line is as follows.

Once the user inputs attribute values into the system, the value of each attribute is multiplied by the corresponding weight. Thus, the overall score of each attribute is computed. Attribute class scores are obtained by adding the weighted scores for the attributes in each class. The scores for each attribute class (A_l) are summed up to get the overall score (S) for the product line. Formally,

$$A_l = \sum_{j=1}^{k} w_j u_j$$

where u_j is the numerical value assigned to the *j-th* attribute, w_j the weight assigned to the *j-th* attribute, and k the number of attributes in the *l-th* class.

$$S = \sum_{i=1}^{n} w_i u_i = \sum_{l=1}^{m} A_l$$

where u_i is the numerical value assigned to the *i-th* attribute, w_i the weight assigned to the *i-th* attribute, m the number of attribute classes, and n the total number of attributes.

An index of innovation acceptance is obtained for each attribute class and for the entire product line as follows:

$$I_1 = \frac{A_1}{A_l^{\max}}$$

and

$$I = \frac{S}{S^{\max}}$$

where

$$S^{\max} = \sum_{i=1}^{n} w_i u_i^{\max} = \sum_{i=1}^{m} A_l^{\max}$$

and $u_i^{\max}$ is the maximum numerical value of the *i-th* attribute.

The index of acceptance can take values between 0 and 1. The system recommendation (GO/REEVALUATE/NO GO) is made by using the following cut off values for the index:

IF $I \geq 0.85$ and $I_l \geq 0.80 \forall l$	then	GO
IF $I < 0.75$ or $\exists l$ such that $I_l < 0.70$	then	NO GO
IF $I \geq 0.75$ and < 0.85 or $\forall l$ such that $I_l \geq 0.7$ and < 0.80	then	RE-EVALUATE OR HOLD

INNOVATOR supports "what-if" analyses and also access to statistical databases. It has been validated by comparing its decisions with those of experts in the financial services domain. The validation process showed that the system has helped in speeding up the decision process.

4.2.2 The CSAS system (Liberatore and Stylianou, 1995)

The intelligent system Customer Satisfaction Assessment System - CSAS, is used for the assessment of customer satisfaction in the case of new developed products.

Knowledge was mainly acquired from informal interviews with domain experts and from experts' answers to specific questionnaires. Knowledge contained in the system's knowledge base includes the evaluation criteria and sub criteria, the factors, the weights attached to each of these, the interrelationships among them and the reasoning path for making project evaluation decisions. 185 rules were used for knowledge representation.

The system is able to encompass possible changes related with the products' attributes. Therefore, a number of databases have been included in the system in order to store the weights of the assessment criteria. Furthermore, the system contains the ability to access statistical databases. Weights can easily be changed by modifying the corresponding databases.

Changing the criteria or their interrelations require changing the rules. The expert system shell Level 5, used for system development, provides sufficient flexibility to knowledge engineer. System's knowledge base is hierarchically organized; therefore changes can be performed more easily. Experts approved the use of such a hierarchy that represents the relationships among criteria, sub criteria and value assessment scales. The system contains two main assessment sections:

- *Channel advantage.* Includes all the channel advantages through which the products will be disposed.
- *Customer assessment.* Includes the criteria that considered being very important by the end users.

CSAS uses Analytical Hierarchy Process and Discriminant Analysis as modelling and decision support methods. The flexibility of the system is enhanced by the calculation of a score for each new product development project, which enables the assessment of customer satisfaction. The system has a user-friendly interface and can be installed in any personal computer.

The results of the system include the following:

- Assessment of the customer satisfaction from the new product.
- Summary information that describes the way the system arrives at the assessments regarding the durability, the visual, the installation, the clean and maintenance.
- Explanations regarding the system's actions, the reasoning followed and the conclusions at which the system arrived.

Furthermore, CSAS supports further analyses and elaboration of the results through "what-if" analysis.

The system has been validated and evaluated by domain experts and by comparison of each performance with past, and hence known, results. The team responsible for the system evaluation concluded that it performed very well. In addition, they reached at the following results regarding the system's strong and weak points:

- The system performs very well with accurate results when a project has a clear product and market focus.
- The system has been found to be very useful in the assessment of technology and customer satisfaction for new technology projects.
- The product development process can benefit by the customer satisfaction assessment only when the change is visible to the customer.

The CSAS has been installed and operates in all the departments of Armstrong World Industries. It is used to support the customer satisfaction assessment department in all the new product development cases. Users of the system have reported their complete satisfaction by the use of the system.

4.2.3 The ADDUCE system (Burke, 1991)

The ADDUCE system is used to forecast the consumer responses to a new advertisements. The system infers the consumers' reactions in new advertisements by investigating for similar past cases and inducing the results of this investigation to the current advertisement (Carbonell, 1981; Burke, 1989). The system employs proportional logic that consists of knowledge that is conveyed by past experimental cases into new cases and which is then used to forecast the inference results into these new cases. ADDUCE requires the following input in order to forecast the consumers' reactions:

- Description of the advertisement.
- Description of the people to which the advertisement is addressed.
- Description of the advertising brand.
- Description of the market characteristics.

A prototype system has been developed in Prolog. Knowledge was acquired by published literature. Rules and frames were employed in knowledge representation. Frames are hierarchically organized in general object categories (for example object, target audience, communication) in specific examples (for example an TV advertisement for a specific brand). When a certain object is identified as case of a more abstracted object or class then this object inherits all the properties of the class (except the ones the object currently owns).

System operates as follows: Initially, a series of background questions are posted to the user, such as the brand, the advertisement and the addressed audience. This information is necessary in order to specify the similarity of current status with experiments conducted in the past and to satisfy the conditions of theoretical and empirical relations. Then the system, with the help of rules contained in its database, searches to find evidence that satisfy the conditions of the various relations. When the system accumulates sufficient evidence to make one ore more predictions of the potential consumers behaviour, displays the results to the user. The system is able to distinguish theoretical from empirical knowledge and to make the relevant operations. The interaction with the user begins with the statement of the basic characteristics of the object (brand, product category, advertisement, and a series of several other questions); also the user is asked to anticipate the response of the audience to the advertisement. The system provides the possibility to carry out "what-if" analyses. Finally, the system processes the data and displays the results.

System has been validated by comparing its results with statistical modelling techniques, such as logit and discriminant analysis, and also with previously known results.

4.2.4 The ADCAD system (Burke *et al.*, 1990)

The ADvertising Communication Approach Design – ADCAD system, supports the design of advertising strategy based on the marketing objectives and the characteristics of the specific situation. The knowledge of the system has been acquired by published literature and interviews with system users. The M.1 shell was employed for knowledge representation with the use of rules and frames. Inference is accomplished by forward or backward reasoning.

First, the system requests information regarding the name and the category of the advertised product as well as the number and names of market segments. Next, by using backward chaining, searches the rules contained in the knowledge base in order to investigate for alternative communication processes and strategies. Some variables such as the marketing objective for example are treated in a special way. ADCAD prompts the user to indicate whether the suggested marketing objectives, the communication objectives and the advantage of the product's brand are accepted. If the user rejects all the suggestions the system asks the user to input the values of these variables. In the case where variables can take more than one values the system assesses the acceptance possibility of each alternative. For variables that take a single value the system stops the search when it accumulates sufficient evidence to support the premise of this value.

In the end of the process ADCAD displays its suggestions to the user. The user may ask explanations for any of the system's suggestions. In this case, ADCAD provides its explanations in a sequence of levels. In the first level the system reports the most immediate set of conditions that led it to a certain suggestion. If the user requires the next explanation level then the system reports the conditions that directed it to derive the values of the preconditions used in the first level. The user is able also to perform sensitivity analysis by re-examining the input values of variables in order to examine their impact on the system's suggestions.

4.3 Agent-based DSS in Marketing

Recent advances in the technologies of collecting, storing and distributing information opened new perspectives in the exploitation of information to the various phases of the decision-making processes. The simultaneous progress of Artificial Intelligence technologies and the transition to Distributed Artificial Intelligence systems establishes a new DSSs generation that are based on the technology of intelligent agents. The ability to use a number of collaborating autonomous agents, which will cooperate in order to solve a large-scale problem, facilitates the handling of complex and ill-structured problems. Apparently the spread of intelligent agents and agent-based architectures in the development of intelligent DSS (Wang, 1997) could not leave the way marketing problems are managed unaffected. A perfect application area for such systems is the problem of strategic planning (Chapter 3, §6). However, the number of proposed or developed marketing decision support systems that combine distributed artificial intelligence and intelligent agents theory is relatively small. Pinson *et al.* (1997) incorporated a distributed artificial intelligence architecture into a marketing strategic DSS. The aim of this architecture is to support top-level managers in developing several scenarios of strategies. In the frame of this architecture an agent-based DSS named ARISTOT was developed. A Distributed Decision Support Systems for Real Time Supply Chain Management using Agent Technologies has been developed by Hinkkanen *et al.*, 1997 (http://cism.bus.utexas.edu/). They introduced the concept of agent organizations for developing the distributed decision support systems that control and optimise supply chain activities. An architecture for intelligent agent-assisted decision support system development has been proposed by Wang (1997). The system support the collaborative decision making process with the help of event-driven and task-driven data mining agents. An internet-based prototype has been developed in order to support marketing planning decisions. Schwartz (2000) presents the problem of information overload and decision-making complexity in marketing management. In addition, he present a blackboard-based agent architecture that allows individual agents to proceed toward their given goals yet react opportunistically to developments reported by other marketing agents. Another Web-based Decision Support Systems named TeleDSS has been proposed by Huang *et al.* (2000). It uses workflow management as a mechanism to facilitate the teamwork in an agent-based collaborative product development environment where remote TeleDSS are extensively used by team members who are geographically distributed. Product development is collaborative, involving multi-disciplinary functions and heterogeneous tools (Huang *et al.*, 2000). Matsatsinis *et al.* (1999) presented an initial approach in strategic marketing decisions, in particular in the choice of the most appropriate penetration strategy for new product launching decisions.

The framework of agent-based systems in marketing originates from the following scientific areas:

- Distributed decision making, which proposes different structures of social organization.
- Business theory, which supplies model to promote the communication of the decision makers.

- Distributed artificial intelligence and multiagent systems that study the collaboration and relations of a group of autonomous intelligent agents.

Wang (1997) argues that there is two decision making forms that should be supported by an architecture: single decision maker – multiple miners (*Figure 11*) and multiple decision makers – multiple miners (*Figure 12*)

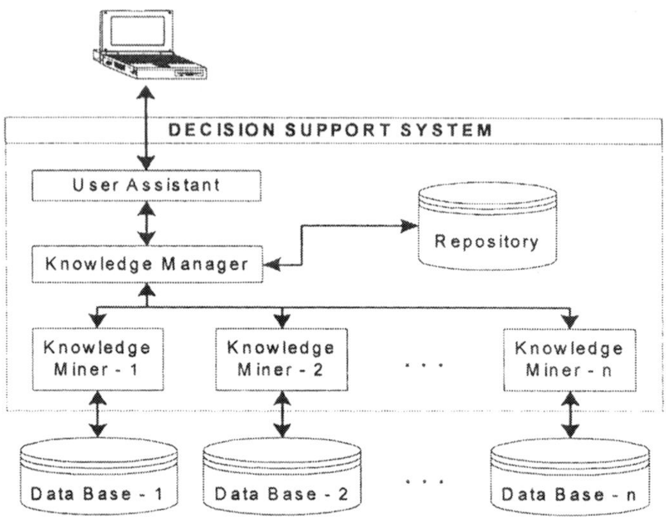

Figure 11. A multi-agent based DSS (*Source*: Wang, 1997)

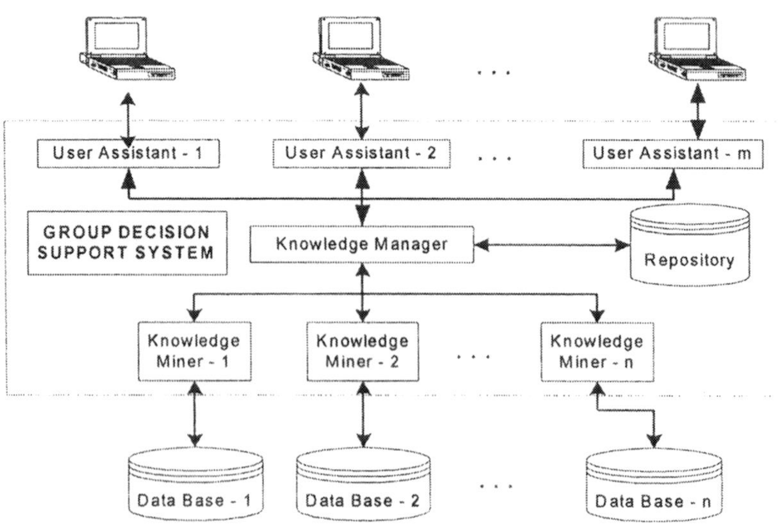

Figure 12. The Agent-based GDSS architecture (*Source*: Wang, 1997)

The architectures presented in *Figure 11* and *Figure 12* use three types of agents:

1. User assistants. These are software programs that except for their regular role carry out several other tasks (inference, collaboration proposals, etc). This significantly improves the communication of the decision makers with the core of the DSS. A factor that plays crucial role in the effectiveness and efficiency of this communication is the part of the knowledge base that is incorporated within the user assistants.
2. Knowledge manager. This agent is comprised by the decision maker's interface, the operational management, the miner interface and the knowledge base. It is the core of the system with which all the users interact through the user assistants. It contains a separate sub module for carrying out auxiliary tasks such as inference and collaboration tasks and of course a knowledge base. During the decision support process the knowledge manager plays the role of the administrator and facilitator between the decision makers, between the decision maker and the respective task driven miners and between all the system's agents and the repository where the discovered knowledge is stored in order to promote the efficient sharing of knowledge.
3. Knowledge miners. These are entities that use data mining techniques in order to find additional information and data.

4.4 Applications

In the following sections some representative agent-based DSS architectures for marketing problems will be presented.

4.4.1 The ARISTOTE system (Pinson and Moraitis, 1996)

ARISTOTE is a distributed DSS for strategic marketing decisions with architecture based on intelligent agents. System operates using a global objective that is decomposed in a set of sub objectives called scenarios. Each scenario is composed by a set of actions proposed by the system to achieve these sub objectives under economic constraints.

The system (Pinson *et al.*, 1997):

- Recommends a plan of action to be performed to achieve the global objective.
- Identifies problems, e.g. actions that are incompatible and gives relevant explanations. ARISTOTE looks for another scenario, which is proposed to the user. Either the user accepts the system's proposal and the system starts a new cycle or the user gives another global objective. The user may also stop the process.

The ARISTOTE system is based on (Pinson, Louca and Moraitis, 1997):

- The decomposition of the process in three different autonomous intelligent agents that cooperate at three different hierarchical levels (strategic, decision-centre, and specialist level).
- The separation between strategic knowledge and domain knowledge.
- A two-phase process allowing the conflict resolution mechanism to be applied.

Furthermore the system allows:

- A computer representation of a set of agents that cooperate in the problem-solving process.
- The explicit representation of communication and control between agents.
- A knowledge-driven allocation of the sub-problems to a set of agents.
- A knowledge-driven creation of elementary actions.
- The identification of incompatible actions and consequently the possibility for the user to modify the chosen global strategy.
- The solving of ill-structured problems through a trial-and-error method and by testing several alternatives in order to find a satisfactory one.
- The possibility to use qualitative knowledge.

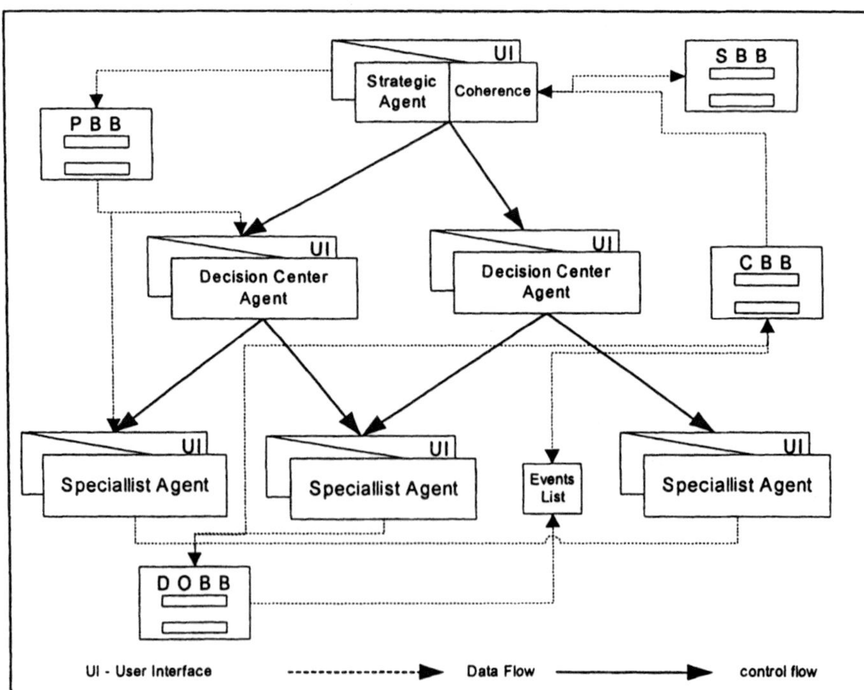

Figure 13. System architecture (*Source*: Pinson *et al.*, 1997)

Figure 13 illustrates the architecture of the system. The basic modules of the system are:

1. Agents. There are three type of agents, strategic agents (STAs), decision-centre agents (DCAs), and specialist agents (SPAs). These agents cooperate in three different hierarchical levels.
2. Blackboards. Four types of blackboard are included to allow communication between agents: the problem blackboard (PBB), the domain blackboard (DOBB), the compatibility blackboard (CBB), and the strategic blackboard (SBB).
3. Constraint base. Contains the economic and environmental constraints of the domain.

As mentioned earlier, agents collaborate at three hierarchical levels. At the strategic level, the overall goal is divided into several sub-goals to yield a scenario. The DCA level creates proposals to satisfy each sub-goal. Finally, at third and most elementary level, SPAs refine these proposals, create elementary actions and test their feasibility. At each level these proposals or elementary actions are proposed to human agents (the corresponding managers) who either accept them or modify them.

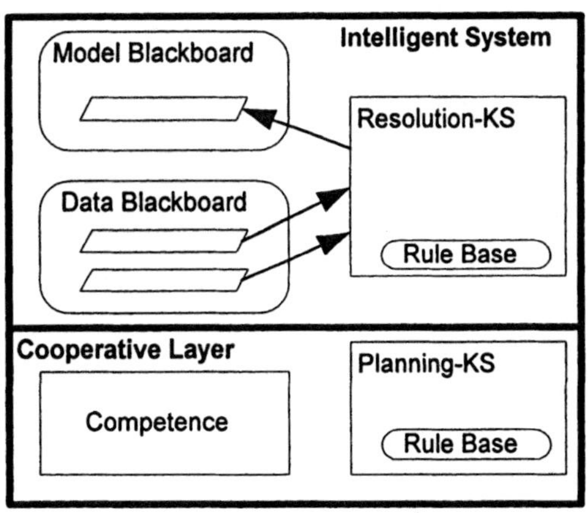

Figure 14. Architecture of ARISTOTE (*Source*: Pinson *et al.*, 1997)

The structure of agents is illustrated in *Figure 14.* Each agent is considered as having two parts:

1. The Intelligent Systems-IS. It consists of the resolution-KS (Knowledge-Source), the data-blackboard (DBB), and the model-blackboard (MBB) and is responsible for the useful work of each agent, e.g. elementary action generated for SPA agents, proposal generation for DCA agents, and skeleton plan generation for STA agents.

2. The Cooperative Layer-CL. It is responsible for cooperation with other agents and for the control of the intelligent system tasks. The planning and coordination module is a knowledge source, called Planification-KS. This knowledge source represents the knowledge about other agents of the community and the tasks that they are able to handle. It is also responsible for deciding when and how to cooperate with other agents. The Competences module supports the knowledge that the agent has about itself.

An experimental scenario on defining a new product marketing strategy is discussed in Pinson *et al.* (1997). This scenario is composed of a set of sub-goals such as product factors, distribution factors, promotion policy, and price policy. Sub-goals are stored in the DDB of the STA during the knowledge acquisition phase. During the reasoning process these sub-goals are passed to DCAs and become their local goals. Several elementary actions, defined by the SPAs and validated by low-level managers are proposed to achieve these sub-goals.

ARISTOTE is a system in prototype form and has been implemented on a SUN SPARC II workstation using SMECI, an object-oriented, multi-task platform developed by ILOG. The system uses a graphical user interface, called AIDA. It has been validated by a group of experts in a French consulting company, which concluded that the system completely satisfies the requirements of the users.

4.4.2 An agent-assisted DSS in Marketing (Wang, 1997)

The aim of the proposed agent-assisted DSS in marketing (AMDSS) (*Figure 15*) is to support a number of marketing managers in the marketing planning decision process.

The system is based on a certain architecture that is able to support two different forms of decision-making (Wang, 1997): a single decision maker with many data-mining agents, and many decision makers with many data-mining agents (*Figure 11* and *Figure 12* respectively). *Figure 16* illustrates an example of the system's application.

A prototype system has been implemented in two SUN Sparc workstations. The system's knowledge manager has been implemented using Java from Sun MicrosystemsTM and in Java RMI. The repository is a DBMS with Java Database Connectivity. The adopted knowledge representation scheme is based on the Telos knowledge representation language (Mylopoulos *et al.*, 1990). The knowledge manager and the repository lie in the same computer, which is called the host machine. Also, in the same computer there is a Microsoft Access database in which all the customers' Internet access records are stored. The sales database is stored in the second computer, which lies in a different location. The knowledge miners are implemented with Java and MLC++ (Machine Learning C++) while the user assistants are implemented with Java and HTML. The communication between the user assistant and the knowledge manager is controlled with Java RMI.

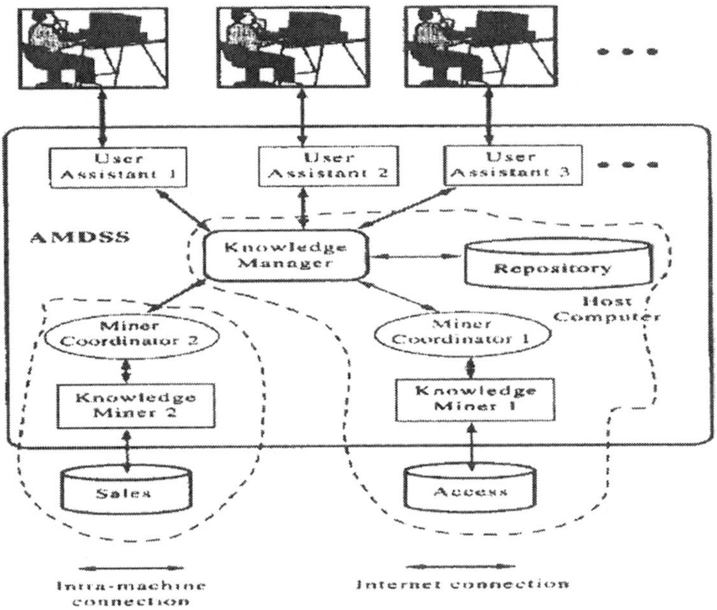

Figure 15. Architecture of the AMDSS (*Source*: Wang, 1997)

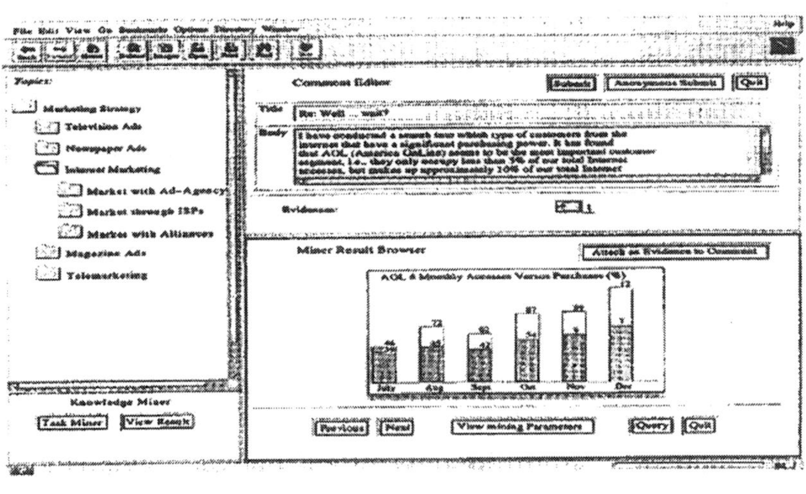

Figure 16. Knowledge discovered by knowledge miners (*Source*: Wang, 1997)

4.4.3 Concurrent marketing analysis: a multi-agent model for product, price, place and promotion (Schwartz, 2000)

The system combines the blackboard-based system architecture with the object-meta agent architecture, which provides unconstraint use of individual agents and a suitable interaction context (*Figure 17*).

The aim of the system is to implement an innovative approach, the Concurrent Marketing Analysis – CMA, in DSS and marketing. For the attainment of this goal the system allows marketing managers to conduct concurrent, interrelated analysis of their decision problems.

The basic characteristics of the system are the following:

- Decision makers communicate through the common memory (blackboard); only one decision maker at each time can write to the blackboard. The blackboard is composed of three sections: the blackboard data structure, the knowledge sources corresponding to domain experts, and a control mechanism.
- It takes into account the interdependence of the basic marketing factors (price, place, product, and promotion).
- It supports representational diversity e.g. differences in the structure and semantics of each decision maker's knowledge, and inferential diversity e.g. multiple decision models and inference methods are used.

The system architecture is determined by the four different types of interacting agents. The types of agents are determined by the four marketing factors (price, place, product, and promotion), as presented in *Figure 18.*

4.4.4 Agent –based workflow management in collaborative product development on the Internet (Huang *et al.*, 2000)

Huang *et al.* (2000) propose to use workflow management as a mechanism to facilitate the teamwork in a collaborative product development (CPD) environment where remote Web-based Decision Support Systems (TeleDSS) are extensively used by team members who are geographically dispersed. In such case, a project team is asked to develop a product. Whether geographically distributed or co-located, team members are assisted by a wide variety of Web-based DSS remotely available and accessible on the Internet. Each team member is responsible to accomplish his/her work package for which he or she is responsible, with the support of the corresponding Web-based DSS. The overall coordination, communication and organization of the tasks to be carried are accomplished by the framework agents. In addition, agents are responsible for the interaction between team members and TeleDSS and also for the workflow management. The workflow of a project is modelled as a network with nodes corresponding to the work and edges to flows of control and data

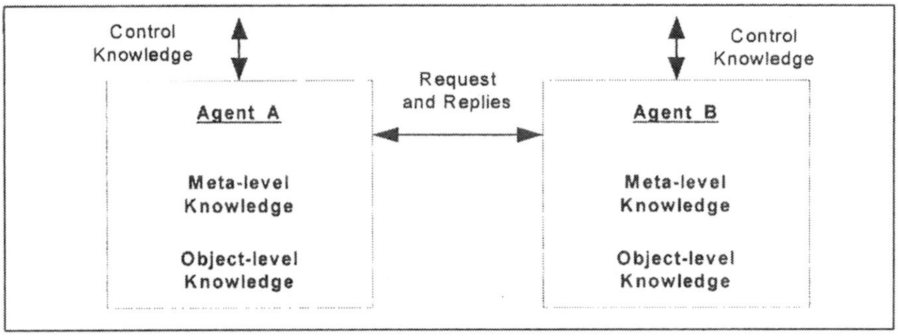

Figure 17. Object-meta agent architecture (*Source*: Schwartz, 2000)

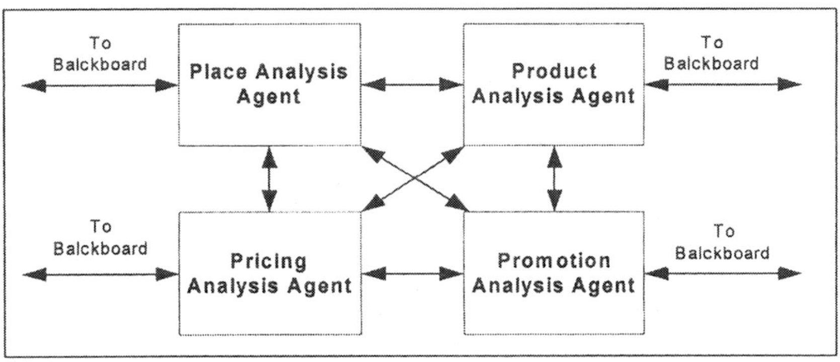

Figure 18. Interaction among marketing analysis agents (*Source*: Schwartz, 2000)

The architecture of the proposed framework, presented in *Figure 19*, is based on four different servers, namely:

- TeleDSS servers. These are DSSs in product design and manufacture that are remotely accessible on the Internet with standard Web browsers. They provide technical services relevant to the specific product development project such as manufacturing information, market surveys results, market shares, statistics, etc.
- TeleCo servers. Tele-collaboration (TeleCo) tools are utility facilities of a virtual collaborative work environment that provides teams with a group-based desktop as a place to meet and work simultaneously. Examples include whiteboard, chat, videoconference, and so on.

- WfManager server. It is responsible for the storage and processing of workflow definition and execution.
- Agents' server agentManager. It is responsible for providing services for creation, communication and or organization of the intelligent agents AgentManager maintains a database with the characteristics of the agents' population. It provides interaction services among agents and teamwork members.

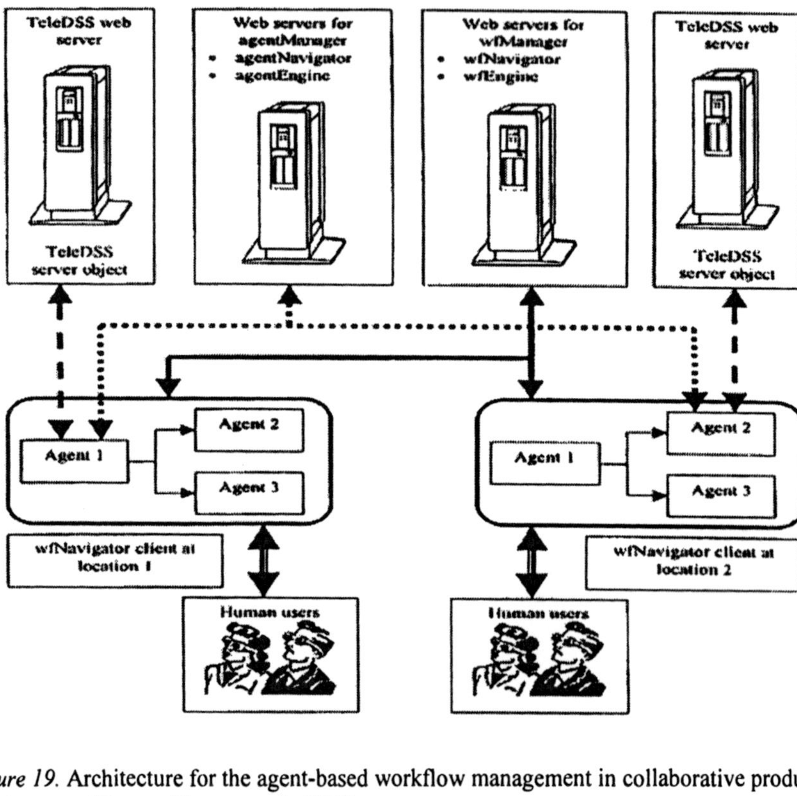

Figure 19. Architecture for the agent-based workflow management in collaborative product development (*Source*: Huang *et al.*, 2000)

4.5 ANNs – DSSs in Marketing

4.5.1 Utilization of artificial neural networks and the TD-learning method for constructing intelligent decision support systems for sales prediction (Baba and Suto, 2000)

Baba and Suto (2000) proposed an intelligent decision support system in order improve the accuracy of sales forecasting, a problem that is very significant for enterprises. The system uses artificial neural networks and the TD-Learning Method. The output of the developed neural network model gives an information concerning the increase or decrease rate of sales three months ahead/sales in the same month one year ago.

The neural network is composed of 24 input units, two hidden layers having 20 units and 15 units, and one output unit. The chosen input variables are:

- $x_1...x_8$: sales(i months ago)/sales of an electronic part in the same month one year ago ($i = 0, 1, 2, 3, 4, 6, 8, 10$).
- $x_9....x_{16}$: volume of orders (i months ago)/volume of orders of an electronic part in the same month one year ago ($i = 0, 1, 2, 3, 4, 6, 8, 10$).
- $x_{17}....x_{24}$: volume of production of portable telephones (i months ago)/volume of production of portable telephones in the same month one year ago ($i = 0, 1, 2, 3, 4, 6, 8, 10$).

The output function of each neuron is described by the formula

$$y = \frac{1 - e^{-\sigma x}}{1 + e^{-\sigma x}}$$

In order to investigate whether an appropriate sales prediction can be made by the proposed system, the authors have carried out several computer simulations. In the following, some of these simulation results are shown (*Figure 20* and *Figure 21*).

- Simulation 1. The neural network model (24 x 20 x 15 x 1) has been trained by using the data from October 1992 to March 1995. *Figure 20* illustrates predictions (during the period from April 1995 to March 1997) having been made by the trained neural network.
- Simulation 2: The authors tried to utilize the TD-Learning Method in order to enhance the performance of the proposed system. *Figure 21* illustrates predictions having been made when parameters k and a have been chosen as $k < 0$ and $a < 0.05$.

The results show that the proposed approach utilizing TD-Learning Method has made better predictions.

4.6 Case-based DSSs in Marketing

Case-based reasoning (CBR) is a computerized method that attempts to study solutions that were used to solve problems in the past in order to solve, by analogy or association, current problems (Ketler, 1993). According to Watson and Marir (1994), CBR can be presented as a cyclical process consisting of retrieving the most similar cases, reusing the cases to attempt to solve the problem, revising the proposed solution of necessary, and retaining the new solution as a part of a new case. When faced with a new problem, a

CBR system will retrieve similar cases to help solve the problem. The major issues in CBR include how to represent cases and structure relationships between cases, how to handle massive case bases and develop general adaptation heuristics for modifying previous cases.

Case-based reasoning has been proposed as an alternative approach that can overcome the weaknesses of the traditional rule-based reasoning method. CBR is more suited for unstructured and poorly understood domains.

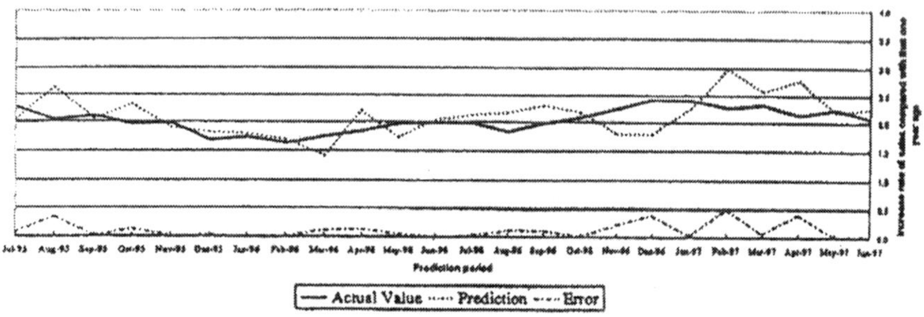

Figure 20. Predictions having been made by ANNs and the TD-Learning Method. (*Source*: Baba and Suto, 2000)

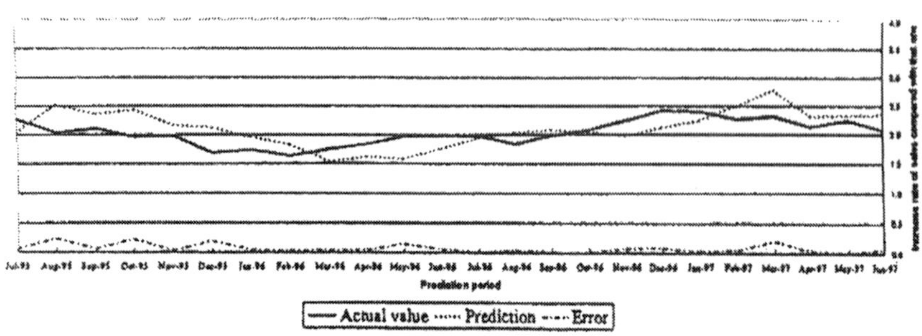

Figure 21. Predictions having been made by ANNs and the TD-Learning Method. (*Source*: Baba and Suto, 2000)

Compared to rule-based system, a case-based system is more similar to actual human decision processes. In addition, its knowledge acquisition process is easier for it is not necessary to abstract rules from the available information. Maintenance is likely to be more straightforward because it is easier to incorporate new knowledge into an existing knowledge base.

4.6.1 An intelligent case-based system for help-desk operations (CBHD system) (Chan *et al.*, 2000)

Help-desks are computer-aided environments in customer support centres that provide frontline support to external and internal customers. Chan *et al.* (2000) developed such a system based on Case-Based Reasoning CBR. The system is an automated decision support system to help call centre or customer service representatives to quickly diagnose problems in computer systems and suggest viable solutions. The system was developed for a major information technology company and system integrator in Canada and USA. The company offers a comprehensive range of solutions, services and support capabilities to customers. With the proliferation of diverse types of computer software and hardware products for personal computers, the types of products supported by the company have multiplied rapidly. There is also a high turn over rate for the company workers, which means training of new employees is critically important. If the problem of a certain customer is not solved during the first call, extra money and time is spent to subsequent calls. At the same time, customer satisfaction may be adversely affected. For these reasons the company decided to automate the process of supporting customers through the development of the system.

The basic idea of CBR is to remember and adapt solutions that were used to solve old problems and use them to solve new problems. A case is the primary knowledge-base element for a case-based reasoning application system. The description of cases is different depending on the development environments and tools

For knowledge acquisition the manual method was adopted and interviews with expert operators at the call centre were conducted. The tools adopted in the project (CBR Express Case Point 3.5 by Inference Corp. USA) required that each case should be represented with a problem statement (symptom) seeking the solution (action). Hence, a case includes a description, several questions and several actions.

The user of the CBR system first enters a case description, which is used by CBR Context Navigator (by Inference Corp. USA) to compare the search description with the descriptions of cases stored in the case base. This specific tools supports two types of features that can be chosen to represent a case: text features and symbolic features. Text features are raw text provided by the user to describe the symptoms and causes of the case whereas symbolic features represent formalized information that can offer a list of answers from which the user selects instead of having the user input the text. The system uses two matching algorithms to search for the desired case. A match score is computed for each case, indicating how closely the search description matches the case's stored description. The top scoring cases are displayed to the user. When any case achieves a score greater than the defined acceptance threshold, it will be highlighted to the user by an icon. Some informal verification and validation were conducted in the project, in which users reported that the system performed satisfactorily.

4.7 Machine Learning

A new paradigm, generally considered to be the learning approach, has attracted attention of researchers in artificial intelligence, computer science, and other functional disciplines such as engineering, medicine, multicriteria decision aid and business (Michalski, 1983; Carbonell et. al., 1983; Weiss and Kulokowski, 1991; Luger and Stubblefield, 1993). In contrast to performance systems, which acquire knowledge from human experts, learning systems acquire knowledge automatically from data, i.e. past decisions. The most frequently used techniques include symbolic, inductive learning algorithms (Quinlan, 1983) and multi-layered, feed-forward neural networks such as Back propagation networks.

Symbolic machine learning techniques, which can be classified based on such underlying learning strategies such as rote learning, learning by being told, learning by analogy, learning from examples, and learning from discovery (Carbonell et. al., 1983), have been studied extensively by AI researchers over the past two decades. Among these techniques, learning from examples, a special case of inductive learning, appears to be the most promising technique for knowledge discovery from decisions made in the past. It induces a general concept description that best describes the examples.

Inductive learning is one of the most intensively studied learning skills in machine learning research. It is described as a process of acquiring knowledge by drawing inductive inferences from facts provided by a teacher or the environment. It can be subdivided into two subclasses: supervised learning and unsupervised learning. In supervised learning, the goals for the learning process are supplied by a supervisor (in our case a decision maker or a decision analyst) along with appropriate training examples where as in unsupervised learning, the learning system itself attempts to discover what kind of goals it is looking for.

Among a lot of potential applications of inductive learning systems, one of the most promising is the automated construction of knowledge bases for expert systems. Inductive learning systems can be used as a basis for developing alternative knowledge acquisition methods to the conventional approach that involves a tedious process of formalising experts' knowledge and encoding it in some knowledge representation system, such as production rules or a semantic network (Forsyth and Rada, 1986). A less direct use of inductive learning in this area is for the refinement of knowledge bases initially developed by human experts; here, inductive learning systems could be used to detect and rectify inconsistencies, to remove redundancies, to cover gaps, and to simplify expert-derived decision rules. Other important applications of inductive learning systems are in various experimental sciences, such as biology, chemistry, psychology, medicine, genetics and marketing, in detecting interesting conceptual patterns or in revealing structure in collections of observations.

Among the various inductive learning methods, Quinlan's ID3 (Quinlan, 1993) decision-tree building algorithm and its descendants are simple and yet powerful algorithms for machine learning. In general, ID3 takes objects of known class, described in terms of a fixed collection of properties or attributes, and produces a decision tree incorporating these attributes that correctly classifies all the given objects. It uses an information-theoretic approach aimed at minimising the expected number of tests to classify an object. An important fact is that the output can be summarised in terms of production rules, which can describe in a quite simple and intelligible form the behaviour of the attributes that lead to a decision. Since it's appearance ID3 has been used successfully for various classification and prediction applications.

4.7.1 A Machine Learning MkDSS (Matsatsinis and Samaras, 1998)

In this paper, Matsatsinis and Samaras (1998) attempt to investigate a number of different approaches to apply inductive learning in data collected via market survey. The goal is to discover rules (or patterns), which could describe and in some extent explain the behaviour and the preferences of the consumers towards the selection of certain products, which form the market. Belief is that machine learning methods along with other 'traditional' methods of analysis is able to help the decision maker in the selection of the most promising penetration strategy for a new product.

A very important factor, which has not been considered yet in this decision process, is that knowledge about consumers' preferences and behaviour can be obtained directly from the available market survey data using machine-learning methods like inductive learning algorithms. As we know these methods produce 'if-then' rules, which can be very easily interpreted by the decision maker. In addition, inductive learning algorithms are able to handle almost all kind of available data including quantitative and qualitative data with discrete or continuous values.

The acquired knowledge can help the decision maker to gain more understanding concerning the preferences and the behaviour of the consumers. It is an additional tool for analysing the data and obtaining a more clear and holistic view of the market status. A rule discovering method, directly from raw data, that explain consumers' preferences should be adapted in the existing IDSS. This extension can assist the decision maker in combining experts' knowledge and knowledge about consumers' preferences in order to learn, explore and consequently result in the most promising penetration strategy.

There is no known method that can be solely used to determine the features of the new product and determine the underlying aspects of the penetration strategy to be followed. Therefore the machine-learning algorithm should be adopted in the Intelligent Decision Support System and should be used along with other scientific tools and methods. This paper describes some basic ideas on the incorporation of the ID3 algorithm (or similar inductive learning techniques) into an Intelligent Decision Support System such as the MARKEX system (Matsatsinis and Siskos, 1999). The goal is to explore the abilities of inductive learning methods in revealing consumers' preferences based on their multicriteria evaluations (figure 8.23).

The data collected through the market survey forms a significant source of information about consumers' preferences. Each multicriteria table contains, implicitly, the preferences of a particular consumer towards the examined products. The primary question is whether this information is sufficient in order to construct a model of consumers' preferences in the form of rules.

In order to examine this hypothesis the data of a market survey conducted on behalf a Greek flower mill company was used. Six products where involved in the survey with a total of 481 consumers surveyed. The consumers expressed their multicriteria preferences according to four qualitative criteria, namely quality, influence, package and image. In addition, every consumer expressed his or her order of preference by rank ordering the products.

The ID3 algorithm is employed using as attributes the criteria and as decision attribute (class) the rank order assigned by the consumers. The rules resulted from this application are in the following form:

IF

Quality	=	Unaware	AND
Influence	=	Large	AND
Package	=	Good	AND
Image	=	Unaware	

THEN

Rank = 2

The addition of a machine-learning algorithm into an Intelligent Decision Support System allows the decision maker to utilise and explore an additional very significant source of knowledge. Usually all the up to now developed Decision Support Systems in the field of marketing try to use only the knowledge of experts. By following this approach, the decision maker is also able to gain and exploit knowledge about consumers' behaviour and preferences. This type of information is very important in new product development decisions where the ultimate goal is to understand the preferences of the consumers in order to gain a share of the market.

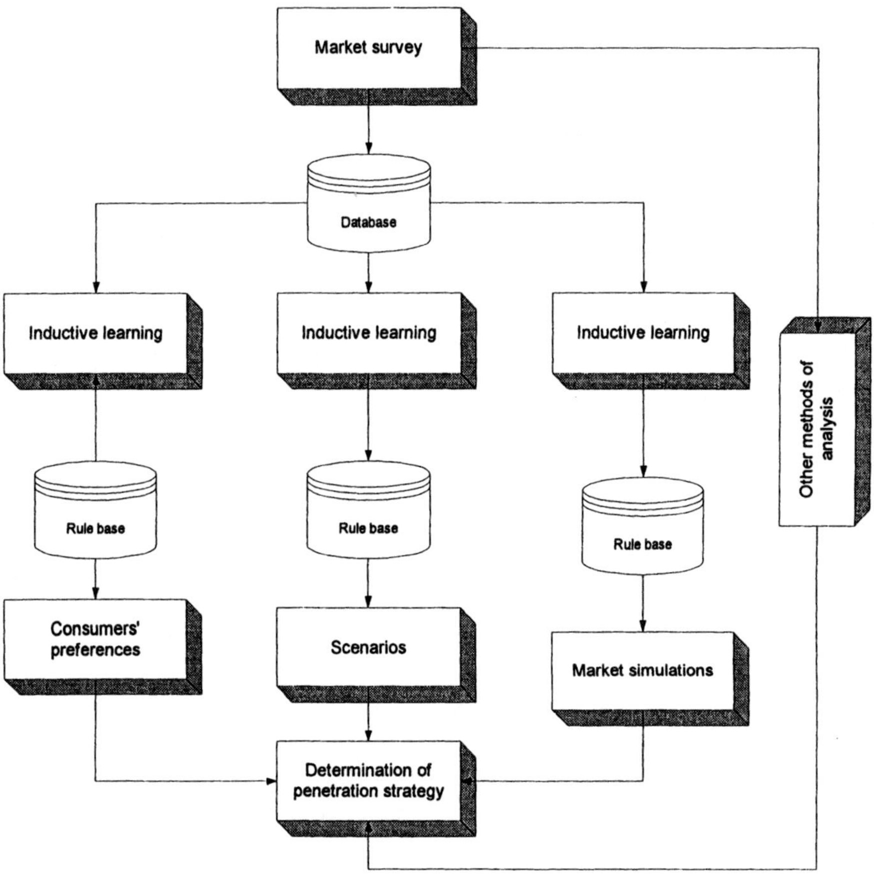

Figure 22. Overview of the proposed methodology (*Source*: Matsatsinis and Samaras, 1998)

4.8 Hybrid systems in Marketing

Hybrid systems result by the integration of several intelligent methods in the development of a single decision support system. In the following sections some examples of such systems will be presented.

4.8.1 H hybrid intelligent system for developing marketing strategies (Li, 2000a)

Having recognized the problems of existing systems (§8.5) and the principal factors that lead to managerial dissatisfaction, Li (2000a) developed a system that could effectively support the process of developing a marketing strategy. As we have already seen, several methods and techniques have been used in the development of DSSs for supporting the planning process of marketing strategies such as expert systems, fuzzy logic, neural networks, etc. However because of the complexity of the marketing strategy development and the requirements for effective support of the whole process none of these techniques is able to handle the problem on its own. Therefore, Li proposed a hybrid intelligent DSS, which combines the above support techniques (expert systems, decision support systems, fuzzy logic, and neural networks) in order to provide support in the development process of marketing strategies (Li, 1999).

The proposed hybrid DSS support the following stages of marketing strategy development process:

a) Strengths, weaknesses, opportunities and threats-SWOT analysis.
b) Portfolio summary of the current product/market status.
c) Setting marketing objectives and strategy.

To attain the above objectives the system:

- Provides a logical process for strategic analysis.
- Supports group assessment of the strategic marketing factors.
- Helps the coupling of strategic analysis with managerial judgment.
- Helps managers to handle uncertainty and fuzziness.
- Provides intelligent advices on developing the marketing strategy.

The hybrid intelligent DSS (*Figure 23*) consists of five subsystem modules that share and exchange information and undertake distinct functions to help solve parts of the problem to which they are best suited. These modules are co-ordinated by intercommunicating software control mechanisms.

1. The neural network forecasting module. The artificial neural network is developed to analyse and forecast the market growth and market shares. The forecasting results are stored in a market growth or a market share file, which is then used as information inputs to the individual/group assessment model.
2. The individual/group assessment module. The model is designed to evaluate the internal and external strategic factors based upon the judgments of an individual or a group of managers. Thus, the marketing strategy problem is decomposed into several factors, which are arranged in a hierarchic structure. Managers determine the scores and respective

weights for each factor based upon both previously made decisions and their judgment. The evaluation scores for a specific factor according to different managers are averaged, and the weights for a specific factor by individual managers are aggregated. Finally, the judgments and viewpoints of individual managers on the weight of each factor are synthesized to determine the relative importance of the strategic criteria.

3. The fuzzification component. This component is used to cope with the uncertainty and fuzziness that are inherent to strategic factors. This subsystem cooperates with the expert system in order to cope with the imprecision, the vagueness and the uncertainty in the assessment of market attractiveness and business strengths.
4. Fuzzy expert system. This subsystem is developed to represent expertise on marketing strategy development, to build the knowledge base, to provide strategic analysis guidance, and finally to generate intelligent advice or reasoned recommendations. The knowledge contained in the system was obtained from published literature, from 104 replies from a large-scale mail questionnaire survey, and from interviews with experienced managers. Also, the same sources were used for determining the general factors considered for marketing strategy. Fuzzy rules are employed for knowledge representation. The system's advices contain more than one strategy alternatives with different degrees of confidence.
5. Graphical display module. As the name implies this subsystem handles the graphical presentation of strategic positions of products and markets.
6. Database. It is used optionally to collect and provide historical records on market growth, market shares and sales history for the neural network model.

The system provides the ability to examine a wide variety of "if-then" scenarios (Li, 1999).

The system was developed by using Microsoft Visual C++ whereas specifically the EXSYS Professional expert system development package was employed to build the fuzzy logic model and the expert system model.

An initial validation of the system has been accomplished by its application in five large British companies and also by four academic experts (two information systems experts and two marketing experts). The evidence of this evaluation show that the hybrid intelligent system is helpful and useful in supporting the development process of marketing strategy.

4.8.2 A decision support system for sales forecasting through fuzzy neural networks with asymmetric fuzzy weights (Kuo and Xue, 1998)

As we have already seen, sales forecasting is a very significant and complex problem for enterprises. While several techniques have been applied in the sales forecasting problem, recently Artificial Neural Networks (ANNs) have been proposed.

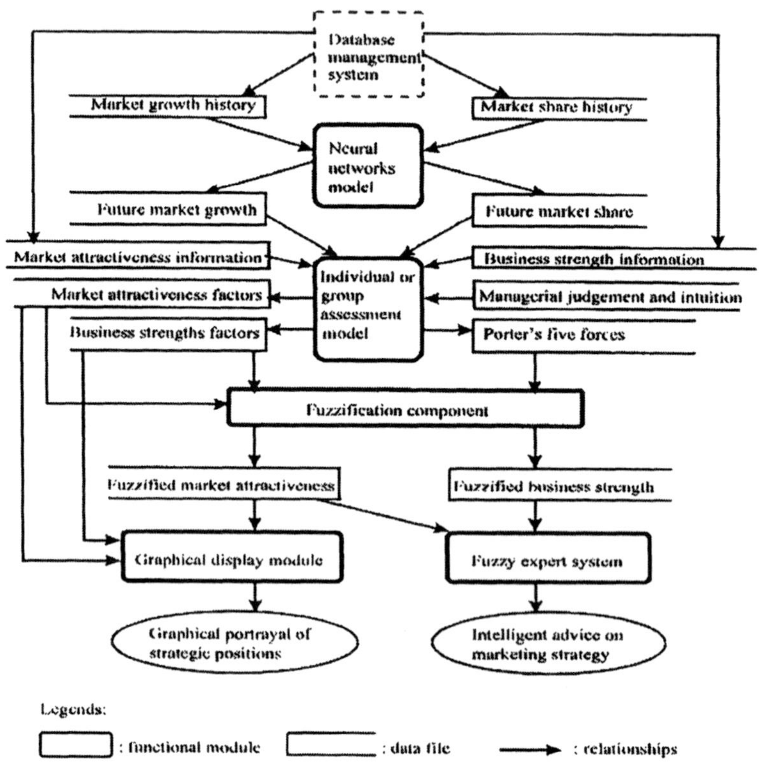

Figure 23. The architecture of the hybrid intelligent system (*Source:* Li, 2000a)

In the system (*Figure 24*), developed by Kuo and Xue (1998), the use of fuzzy neural network (FNN) is proposed. In order to improve the forecasting results ANNs were combined with Fuzzy NN. The result from FNN is further integrated with the forecast from ANN using the time series data and the promotion length through the other ANN. The results of Kuo and Xue (1998) show that the ANN gives better results than the conventional statistical methods.

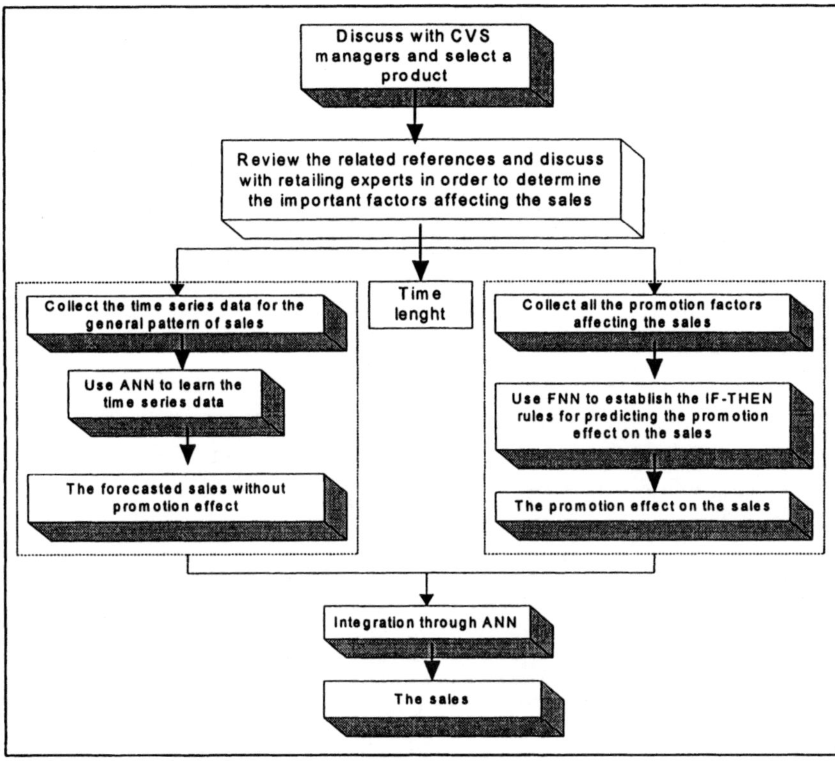

Figure 24. The architecture of the proposed sales forecasting system (*Source*: Kuo and Xue, 1998)

5. A SURVEY OF INTELLIGENT DECISION SUPPORT SYSTEMS IN MARKETING

The first studies that referred to the application of Artificial Intelligence techniques in marketing problems appeared in the middle of 80's (Mitchell *et al.*, 1984; Buyer and Keon, 1985; Schwoerer and Frappa, 1986; Choffray and Charpin, 1986; Rangaswamy *et al.*, 1987). During the following years, a new series of related studies appeared in the literature (Gaul and Shader, 1988; Moutinho and Paton, 1988; Rangaswamy *et al.*, 1989; Burke *et al.*, 1990; McCann and Gallanger, 1990; Mitchell *et al.*, 1991; Dubelaar *et al.*, 1991; Pinson *et al.* (1997); Jun Lee and Chang Lee (1999b).

The systems developed combine the possibility of handling the qualitative and quantitative data of a marketing problem by the system's marketing models. Thus, Intelligent Marketing Decision Support Systems - IMkDSS become powerful tools in the hands of the decision makers.

If we focus on the perspective that determines their application to marketing problems and on the direction that research efforts have turned to we can make the following observations. One aspect is plainly the scientific one (type of reasoning process, structure of knowledge, etc) where as the other one, which has been developed mostly, is the support of marketing decisions. Marketing problems can be classified according to the level of structure (programming). Mainly, the efforts focus on the handling of special marketing problems such as sales promotion, advertisement, competitive strategies, analysis of traceable data, input of new data, etc (Mitchell *et al.*, 1991).

Several expert systems applicable to marketing problems have been developed to date. In this section, we attempt to list the most well known systems (Decker and Gaul, 1990; Wierenga, 1992; Meyer, 1993; Matsatsinis, 1995; Vlachopoulou, 1999), which in general, follow the following conditions:

- They are the result of integration between ES and DSS.
- They are not designed to solve routine problems.
- They are cited in the international literature (papers - articles, working papers and books, www sites).

The development of the systems has been accomplished not only by using tools and techniques of AI but by also using conventional programming methods. *Table 7*, presents an attempt to record and analyse current systems, as these are cited in the published literature. We have to point out that the presented list can be considered neither exhaustive nor complete, mainly because it is very difficult to collect information on systems that actually operate within enterprises. It is even harder, to find information about systems that are in the process of design and development for private scope. Finally, it is possible that some of the Internet references have changed, since the conduction of this investigation.

Table 7. Intelligent Decision Support Systems

Index	System name/company/Authors/URL	Product description/Application scope
1.	ADCAD - Burke, Rangaswamy, Wind and Eliashbergh (1990)	Aids the planning of marketing strategy based on marketing objectives and the attributes of the examined case.
2.	ADDUCE - Burke (1991)	It used to predict the reaction of consumers to a new advertisement.
3.	ADER - Absatzwirtschaft (1989, 1990)	Consumer behaviour analysis.
4.	Advanced Software Applications - http://www.asacorp.com/product/index.html	Automated Data Analysis - On-Demand Decision Support.

Index	System name/company/Authors/URL	Product description/Application scope
5.	Agent-Assisted MkDSS - Wang (1997)	It is a prototype for supporting marketing planning decisions.
6.	ALCHEMIST™ - http://www.norkom.com/index1.htm	Improve customer and product profitability, by identifying and achieving the optimum customer-product mix. Test-drive new products and promotions though our unique scenario planner.
7.	AliahTHINK - http://aliah.pgh.pa.us/Software/Product_Sheet.htm	It facilitates strategic thinking, team decision-making, customer focus and resource allocation
8.	Allink AnalyzerTM Allink SegmentTM - http://www2.harte-hanks.com/main/dm/database_mark/data_tech/prod_serv/db_access/#ma	The application combines extensive segmentation and reporting capabilities with accelerated performance to deliver marketing results immediately in an open systems environment.
9.	AMOS – Levin *et al.*, (1995)	It is a probability-driven, customer-oriented DSS for target marketing.
10.	Aristote (Pinson, Louca, Moraitis, 1997)	A distributed agent-based DSS for strategic planning.
11.	A sales prediction system which utilizes NNs and TD-Learning - Baba and Suto (2000)	Utilization of artificial neural networks and the TD-learning method for constructing intelligent DSS for sales prediction.
12.	Assistum - http://www.assistum.com/indexp.html	Decision Making Capability.
13.	BANKSTRAT - Davies, Moutinho and Curry (1995)	It is a prototype expert system designed to advise on marketing strategy for retail banks and building societies.
14.	BEREX - Absatzwirtschaft (1989, 1990)	Sales control
15.	Blackboard expert system – Chen and Occena (2000)	The system implements a procedure for transforming the knowledge into knowledge bases as part of an approach for developing a product design blackboard system.
16.	BMA (Brand Manager's Assistant) - McCann, Lahti and Hill (1991)	Supports brand managers in reporting.
17.	BRANDFRAME - Wierenga, Dalebout, Dutta (1992)	Marketing planning and control for product management
18.	BUSINESSMAX - http://www.aimmax.com/bmax.htm	It is the fully automated software system designed to help sales and marketing plans achieve new success.
19.	Business Objects - http://www.businessobjects.com/	BusinessMiner, Web Intelligence.
20.	BUSINESS STRATEGY	Provides strategy directives.

Index	System name/company/Authors/URL	Product description/Application scope
	ADVISOR - Schuman, Congla, Lee, Sakamoto (1987)	
21.	Business Insight, Quick Insight , Plan Write for Marketing - http://www.brs-inc.com/binsight.html http://www.brs-inc.com/qinsight.html	Pricing strategy, distribution techniques, positioning within the market, competitive positioning, product/service promotion plan
22.	CAAS (Corporate Aided Advertising System) - Esch and Muffler (1989); Esch and Kroeber-Riel (1994); Kroeber-Riel (1993)	Search for creative proposals and advertisement assessment.
23.	CALEX/Rice, Department of Agronomy & Range Science, University of California - http://www.aes.ucdavis.edu/search/default.htm	An Aid to Identifying & Managing Weeds in California Rice
24.	Case-Based Reasoning System for Forecasting Promotional Sales – McIntyre, Achabal, Miller (1993)	Applying case-based reasoning to forecasting retail sales.
25.	CASPER - Absatzwirtschaft (1989, 1990)	Market shares analysis
26.	C.I.M.S. - http://www.greatlakessoftware.com/products/forecast.html	It uses artificial intelligence and powerful methodology to predict sales by customer, account group, channel, etc.
27.	CMA - Concurrent Marketing Analysis - Schwartz (2000)	It is a multi-agent DSS for concurrent marketing analysis.
28.	CMD - http://www.channelmarketing.com.au/	Channel Marketing Decisions.
29.	COLBERT - Peguin (1986)	Choice of exports strategy.
30.	COMPASS COGNOS - http://www.allegra-tech.com/index9.htm	COMPASS is designed to allow to be customised to reflect the company's data management requirements. With Cognos tools the user can deliver the power of Business Intelligence across her/his entire organization: to senior executives, production line workers, to remote sales forces and branch offices around the globe.
31.	COMPETE - Hansen and Neumann (1987)	Marketing strategy planning.
32.	COMSTRAT (Competitive Strategy) - Moutinho, Curry and Davies (1992)	Aids marketing managers in analyzing the company's niche relative to its competitors and suggests ways to improve it.

Index	System name/company/Authors/URL	Product description/Application scope
33.	CONCEPT - Walker and Miller (1987)	Model development for market analysis of consumer goods.
34.	CorWorks - http://www.norbert-tech.com/products.html	This system enables statistical modelling, data mining, and reporting to be done at any of the transaction, account, individual, or household levels.
35.	CoverStory – Little (1990); Schmitz, Armstrong and Little (1990)	It is used to find information from large volumes of data – selection of main cases and of the corresponding reasons.
36.	CSAS (Customer Satisfaction Assessement System) - Liberatore and Stylianou (1995)	It supports the strategic decisions related with new product development and allows the assessment of customer satisfaction.
37.	DANEX (Data Analysis Expert) - Böchenholt, Both and Gaul (1988, 1989)	Based on the structure of data, detects the most appropriate data analysis method in order to support market segmentation and product positioning.
38.	DataLodgic - http://www.lodgistics.com/datalodgic1.html	It is an integrated set of software tools designed using an open architecture, making them easy to link to existing marketing systems.
39.	Data Warehouse Information Center - http://pwp.starnetinc.com/larryg/market.html	Marketing and sales analysis tasks
40.	DEALMAKER - McCann and Gallagher (1990)	Aids managers in planning commercial deals. Predicts disagreements in a deal and provides explanations when the deal is not accepted.
41.	DECIBLE (an exploration support system) – Attonaty, Chatelin, Garcia, Ndiaye (1997)	Allows virtual experimentations of new crop management strategies and their implementation in practical situations.
42.	DECIDEX - Levine, Maillard, Pomerol (1987)	Support of strategic planning decisions with the help of respective scenarios; introduction strategy of new products.
43.	Decision Support Systems Ltd - http://www.decision.ie/	Red Brick Warehouse
44.	Distributed Decision Support System for Supply Chain Management - Hinkkanen, Kalakota, Saengcharoenrat, Stallaert, Whinston (1997) - http://cism.bus.utexas.edu/	A Distributed Decision Support Systems for Real Time Supply Chain Management using Agent Technologies
45.	DMAS (Development Manager's Advisory System) - Liberatore and Stylianou (1993)	Provides suitable support and the required framework for assessing new product development processes.
46.	EES (Einkaufer Experten System) - Krallmann (1986)	Support of procurement department to in choosing suppliers and optimization of orders.
47.	ESWA - Neibecker (1990)	Choice among alternative advertisement proposals

Index	System name/company/Authors/URL	Product description/Application scope
		and analysis of advertisement effectiveness.
48.	EXMAR - McDonald and Wilson (1990)	Provides support to marketing planning processes of enterprises.
49.	FastStats - http://www.smartfocus.com/	It is a specialist application with the flexibility, speed and ease of use to deliver marketing intelligence to the marketer's desktop.
50.	FLiPSiDE – Framework for Logic Programming with Distributed Execution - Schwartz (1995)	See also CMA - Concurrent Marketing Analysis.
51.	FORE - Nute, Mann and Brewer (1990)	Assists the choice of forecasting method.
52.	GENESIS - http://www.customerdevelopment.com/dss.htm http://www.customerdevelopment.com/gfunc.htm	
53.	INFER - Rangaswamy, Harlam and Lodish (1991)	Automatically analyses traceable data based on knowledge that comes form interpreting statistical analysis results.
54.	INNOVATOR - Ram and Ram (1988, 1989)	Supports consultants in financial service organizations in deciding whether to offer specific product innovation to their customers.
55.	Intelligent knowledge generator from statistical data bases - Berg and Spiegler (1992)	Uses a methodology that creates knowledge bases from statistical databases. First, the system guides the user to define her/his problem. Then, aids the user to choose data analysis method by suggesting alternatives and also assists the user in the representation of results.
56.	Intelligent forecasting system - Kuo and Xue (1998), Kuo, (2001)	A decision support system for sales forecasting through fuzzy neural networks with asymmetric fuzzy weights
57.	Intelligent model selection and forecasting system - Venkatachalam and Sohl (1999)	It is an intelligent DSS based on neural network technology for model selection and forecasting.
58.	Intelligent Miner - http://www.software.ibm.com/data/iminer/fordata/	It is a suite of tools to support the iterative process, offering data processing, statistical analysis, and results visualization to complement a variety of mining methods. Applicable to a wide range of business problems, the algorithms can be employed to facilitate decision-making in business areas such as campaign planning, customer relationship management, process reengineering, product planning and fulfilment, and fraud and abuse management.
59.	JESS – Janssen and Jager	An integrated approach to simulating behavioural

Index	System name/company/Authors/URL	Product description/Application scope
	(1999) - http://www.soc.surrey.ac.uk/JASSS/2/2/2.html	processes: A case study of the lock-in of consumption patterns
60.	KB3S (Knowledge-based system for simulation statistics) - Pierreval, Rakotomalala and Dussauchoy (1990)	Supports the user in detecting and realizing the required statistical analyses in a simulation
61.	KENS (Knowledge Enhancement System) - Hand (1987)	Aids the user in solving problems and enhance her/his knowledge on non-parametric statistics topics.
62.	KMS - http://www.dfki.uni-kl.de/~aabecker/Freiburg/Final/Pun/KBS4KM97.html	The KMS can be used as an expert system to simulate the problem-solving behaviour of an expert, can be employed as a DSS to allow scenario processing, and can be also used as a computer aided instruction system for education and training.
63.	LEVEL\5 - http://www.l5r.com	It is using Artificial Intelligence (AI) technology to solve complex data-intensive business problems.
64.	Local introduction of global brand - Mockler (1989)	Determines the local introduction strategy of a product in a global market.
65.	MARKETEER - Parker and Mokhoff (1983)	Marketing decisions – market analysis.
66.	Marketing Best Practices - http://www.marketingbestpractices.com/automation.htm#bestpracticesdesk	*Bestpracticesdesk:* A marketing sharing system designed to enable access to best practices in marketing tools and resources to improve your decisions and marketing performance. *Intellidesk:* A market intelligence and competitive intelligence sharing system for marketers to access, update and disseminate marketing intelligence for effective decisions. *Successtrack:* An automated system to successfully develop, manage, and launch new products and services.
67.	MarketMiner - http://www.abtech.com/	MarketMiner Express automatically produces a complete marketing analysis.
68.	MARKETMETRICS - McCann and Gallagher (1990)	To guide the process of analysing large volumes of data – automated modelling.
69.	MarketStrike - http://www.boostsoft.com/introduction.htm	Customer Profiling and Market Segmentation. It offers unmatched prediction results since it's based on the revolutionary fuzzy logic technology.
70.	Market Simulations via Rule Induction – Matsatsinis and Samaras (1998)	Market Simulations via Rule Induction.
71.	MARKEX – Matsatsinis and Siskos (1999)	An intelligent decision support system for product development decisions
72.	MarStra: A hybrid intelligent	The hybrid intelligent system is helpful and useful in

Index	System name/company/Authors/URL	Product description/Application scope
	system - Li, Duan, Kinman, Edwards (1999); Li (2000a; 2000b; 2000c)	supporting the development of marketing strategy.
73.	Media Planning - Mitchell (1988)	Decision support in media planning.
74.	Media Planning - Mockler (1989)	Media planning – To determine the local introduction strategy of a globally marketed new product.
75.	Meta Decision Support System - Jun Lee and Chang Lee (1999b)	A meta decision support system approach to coordinating production / marketing decisions. It is capable of providing guidance for coordinating production and marketing decisions.
76.	MEXICO - Gaul and Schader (1988); Gaul and Both, (1990)	Sales and market shares forecasting. Provides instructions for marketing planning.
77.	MicroStrategy DSS Suite - http://www.microstrategy.com/products/index.htm	It provides all the necessary tools to assure the success of data warehousing projects.
78.	MODEL 1 - http://www.unica-usa.com/products/model1.htm	It is an award-winning suite of targeted data mining solutions.
79.	ModelMAX - http://www.asacorp.com/product/index4.html	It quickly analyses data to identify individual patterns of behaviour.
80.	MORE - Cook and Schleede (1988)	Decision support for direct marketing activities.
81.	MSA – Cross, Foxman, Kishore, Sherrell (1986)	Choice of marketing strategy.
82.	MUSE - Dambroise and Massotte (1986, 1987)	Assists the user to choose a data analysis method and to interpret the results.
83.	NEGOPLAN - Kersten (1988, 1989)	Supports negotiations processes.
84.	NEGOTEX (Negotiations Expert) - Rangaswamy, Eliashbergh, Burke and Wind (1989)	Supports the preparation of international marketing negotiations.
85.	Neural Networks for Time-Series Analysis – Wierenga and Kluytmans (1996)	Prediction with neural nets in marketing time series data.
86.	One-By-One® - http://www.paragren.com/prodsvcs/obo/default.htm	It is a tool for exploration, analysis and data mining, customer acquisition and retention, real-time and one-to-one marketing.
87.	PEP - Bayer, Lawrence and Keon (1988)	Detection of sales promotion methods
88.	Pilot Decision Support Suite - http://www.pilotsw.com/products/Welcome.htm	Conduct rankings, comparisons, exceptions, and forecasts. Execute predictive modelling.

Index	System name/company/Authors/URL	Product description/Application scope
89.	PRODUCT SAFETY - Walker and Miller (1987)	Risk management in new product introduction.
90.	PROMOTER - Abraham and Lodish (1987)	An automated promotion evaluation system. Assessment of sales promotion media of commercial companies.
91.	PROMOTION ADVISOR - McCann and Gallagher (1990)	Provides guidance in product promotion based on appropriate promotion strategy.
92.	PROMOTION DEDECTIVE - McCann and Gallagher (1990)	Assesses weakly promotions; identifies promotion periods; detects and analyses problems of promotion variables.
93.	Promotion Planning System – McCann *et al.* (1991)	It is a case-based reasoning promotion planning system to support sales-promotion decisions.
94.	RAD - McCann, Tadlaoui and Gallagher (1990)	Για να σχεδιάζει εβδομαδιαία μεταφορά διαφημίσεων για προώθηση προϊόντων.
95.	RBF – Adya, Armstrong, Collopy, Kennedy (2000)	Rule-based forecasting (RBF) uses rules to combine forecasts from simple extrapolation methods.
96.	REX - Pregibon and Gale, 1984; Gale, 1986a	Guides users to carry out regression analyses by testing hypotheses and suggesting transformations when hypotheses are violated; it justifies its suggestions on user demand.
97.	ResPilot TM - http://www.tims.fr/respilot.htm Optims™ - http://www.tims.fr/optims.htm	It incorporates the highest level of expertise in operations research, forecasting and data processing.
98.	Rule-based forecasting - Collopy and Armstrong (1992)	Provides safe prediction abilities based on the characteristics of the data.
99.	SalesPartner - Schmitz (1994); http://www.infores.com/public/prodserv/NO/NPIS.iri	It is an extension of CoverStory, which has been developed to aid consumer packaged goods sales representatives in developing presentations for fact-based selling.
100.	SCAN*EXPERT - Bayer and Harter (1991)	Aids users to analyse scanner data, determine competition, explain changes in market shares, etc.
101.	SHANEX (Share Analysis Expert System) - Alpar (1991); Alpar and Dilger (1995)	Analyses market shares, their trends and their variations.
102.	SITE (Site location) - Curry and Moutinho (1991)	Aids the choice site location of stores.
103.	SIMAR - Klein (1999)	It is a KB-DSS to define and test strategic management knowledge bases.
104.	STATPATH (Statistical Pathfinder) - Portier and Lai (1983)	Assists the user to find an appropriate analysis method for the available data.

Index	System name/company/Authors/URL	Product description/Application scope
105.	STRATEX (Strategic decision making system for export firms) - Borch and Hartvigsen (1991)	Aids export companies in strategic marketing planning and in choosing market segments.
106.	STUDENT – Gale, 1986b	Aids a statistician to construct an advisory data analysis system from examples.
107.	TeleDSS – Huang, Huang, Mak (2000)	The system uses workflow management as a mechanism to facilitate the teamwork in a collaborative product development environment.
108.	TEXTBOOK PROMOTION ADVISOR - McCann and Gallagher (1990)	It is an extension of PROMOTION ADVISOR.
109.	TIMES - Girod, Orgeas and Landry (1989)	Media planning. Planning of TV campaigns.
110.	VALEX - http://www.exapps.com/product.htm	Planning, design, execution and scheduling of multi-phase marketing campaigns, profile customers, create target segments, and develop sophisticated campaigns.
111.	VPS - Plattfaut (1988)	Sales prediction and geographical sales comparison for automobile industry.
112.	XSAMPLE - Gottinger (1988)	Guides the choice of suitable problem analysis technique.
113.	XSEL - McDermontt (1982)	Customer support.
114.	XCON - Kraft (1984); Barker and O'Conner (1989)	Determination of product type according to consumers' requirements.

6. CONCLUSIONS

Unfortunately, several problems appear when one tries to collect details regarding the various systems. However, by the elaboration of the available information we may arrive to the following conclusions:

The particular application fields of the systems in marketing as well as the majority of the systems have developed for supporting either the choice of the suitable data analysis method either for supporting the elaboration of their results. The remaining systems support sales promotion, strategic issues, forecasting, advertisement and media planning, negotiations, marketing planning, new product development, market segmentation, and estimation or monitoring of market shares. Finally, a small number of systems support the analysis of market shares, data processing, problem analysis, positioning of products, simulations, stores site, market trends, and reporting.

Concerning integration issues, most of the systems are fully developed but not installed. Only a relatively small number of systems are installed and under full operation or in the phase of the testing processes. The vast majority of the systems are in the state of prototyping or in the phase of the prototype development.

By examining the knowledge acquisition sources that were used for the development of the systems, we observe that the two major knowledge sources are the international literature and the personal experience of the authors-developers-designers of the systems. In addition, surveys within experts have been used as a knowledge acquisition tool in a significant number of systems. A smaller number of systems have been developed by analysing the acquired data, using several methods. In the end, we find systems that acquire knowledge by the cooperation among the authors-developers and the experts in each time application field as well as by using informal discussions with experts and professionals. In some systems, multiple sources of knowledge were utilized. These results show a substantial deviation from the basic principle of expert systems development that the main knowledge source should stem each time from domain experts. By the available data, it seems that only in a small number of cases the "correct" knowledge acquisition method has been followed. In addition, this reveals the distance between theory and practice and may justify, in some extent, the non-satisfactory degree of expert systems acceptance by the companies. Indeed, a large number of developed systems do not posses knowledge that stems of directly from the right people (experts), but from indirect sources (literature, system developers, etc). However, in many cases, knowledge acquired from these indirect sources cannot be considered as complete because they do not contain the tacit knowledge, used by the expert to make decisions. Despite the fact, that the expert uses this knowledge in order to make decisions, it is not an easy task to elicit it and incorporate it in an expert system, because in many cases the expert cannot adequately justify his actions or decisions (Wagner and Sternberg, 1986).

From a knowledge representation method point of view, we may assert that most of the systems employ production rules. In addition, a significant number of systems use production rules with some other form of knowledge representation. Some systems use frames, heuristic knowledge, etc. In most systems, there is no reference on the form of knowledge representation used in their development.

The development of the systems has been accomplished by using, in increasing order, special tools and shells, artificial intelligence specific languages (Lisp, Prolog, etc), usual programming languages (Pascal, C, Fortran, etc), while in several cases a combination of the above has been used for developing different components of the systems. Finally, in many cases there is no evidence of the development tools.

Regarding the evaluation of the systems, a number of systems have past a certain evaluation process by domain experts. A smaller number has been evaluated based on already established results, either by actual data or by known examples from the literature. Few systems have been evaluated by their users. Finally, in the majority of the systems there is no reference on a certain evaluation procedure, mainly because most of the systems are still in the development phase and have not yet reached the evaluation phase.

Systems are mainly developed to cover the following:

- Pure research in universities and research institutes.
- Specific needs of the companies, either internal or in order to provide certain services to their customers. In this case, systems are developed either by the company itself or by its cooperation with research centres, and are applied in practice.

There is a significant divergence between the number of developed systems and the number of the systems that are known to the public and have been actually applied in practice. Most of the known developed systems are made public through publications in the international literature and come from the academic area. Their development is performed usually within the context of certain research programs, cooperation with enterprises, elaboration of master and doctoral thesis. The life cycle of these systems is usually very short, mainly because their farther development for commercial exploitation is considered unpractical due to cost, time, and work force reasons, as well as inability to provide continuous support to the systems. It is possible that the cooperation between academic institutions and companies will provide an effective solution to these problems.

III

PART III. NEW METHODOLOGY - APPLICATIONS

Chapter 9

New Product Development Methodology

1. INTRODUCTION

New products play a vital role in the successful growth of an enterprise. They consist a significant factor concerning the increase of the profits. All over the world enterprises are forced to innovation and new product development due to a variety of reasons such as the continuous changes in the consumers' preferences, the ongoing competition, the establishment of new companies therefore of new competitors, the rapid advancement of technology, the frequent changes in legislation, and the existence of different legal systems from country to country. In order to survive, companies have to develop new products. Furthermore, the life cycle of most products becomes continuously smaller because of the technological obsolescence and the rapid rate in which usually consumer's preferences change. Consequently, the need for innovation and expansion of the production lines in order to extend the life cycle of the products becomes continuously imperative for every enterprise and organization. This extension of the life cycle may be accomplished by the substitution of the product or by some changing some of its features, or by introducing a completely new product in the market.

The introduction of new products in the market is an ill-structured decision making process and exhibits several risks for the enterprise. Studies on the launch of new products have shown that 33-66% of new products fail commercially. The factors that affect the success or the failure of a new product are continuously changing. Among them, the most important are the quality of the product, the satisfaction of the customers, the time of purchase, the structural integration through marketing R&D, and the global formed strategies and alliances. According to Urban and Hauser (1993), the future trends refer to the overall generation of ideas, strategies and suitable tools in order to develop new products. The environment, in which new products are or will be developed and used, changes rapidly and thus the members of marketing departments within the companies should be trained and adopt new techniques and approaches in order to be able to respond to the rising challenges and to the newly presented opportunities. Companies that progress more quickly than their competitors in the technology level, lean on the invention of innovative ideas, and adapt more swiftly to the satisfaction of the persistently changing needs of the customers will obtain competitive advantages.

The new product development process is subdivided into various stages, according to several authors (Nylen, 1990; Urban and Hauser, 1993; Kotler, 1994). Basically, the differences among the suggested alternative processes are because of the employment of different approaches of the same process.

The new product development process, from the apprehension of a novel idea until the selection of the market penetration strategy, is a completely unstructured process and therefore it cannot be programmed in any way and requires at every turn the interference of the decision maker. On the other hand, the variety of the data used, their processing through various models as well as their interpretation is a procedure with several problems. The decision-maker has to choose among a volume of available forecasting, data analysis, brand choice, and multicriteria analysis models. The selection of the each time appropriate model lies on the decision-maker, which makes his choice based on his personal experience. Therefore, the lack of decision maker's specialized knowledge generates the imperative necessity for the presence of an expert during the new product development process.

The difficulties and problems detailed above render pivotal the presence of a tool that will be able to process the data and support the decision-maker in the selection of the suitable models. In addition, owing to the fact that experts play a vital role in the new product development process, .an intelligent decision support system with built-in knowledge and inference mechanisms could be extremely beneficial in the decision making process (Ram and Ram, 1989).

Usually the launch of a new product fails due to the inadequate analysis of the market situation or due to the lack of support in the assessment of the new product. The development and use of an intelligent DSSs in new product design and development decisions has the following effects:

- Improve the quality of the decisions concerning the new products, especially in organizations that exhibit lack of specialized knowledge in the new product design and development process.

- Preservation of the specialized knowledge of people that leave the organization.
- Support in training of new managers or decision makers; consequently the organization avoids the mistakes made by beginners, which usually have a very high cost.
- Managers are able to observe, analyze and study factors that otherwise would be overlooked.
- The time to reach a decision is considerably reduced.

In this chapter, an original new product design and development methodology (Matsatsinis and Siskos, 1999) is presented. The methodology follows a completely new philosophy by trying to support the decision-makers during the entire new product development process, to maximize the probability of success and increase of profits of the company through the satisfaction of the consumers' needs. It exploits the results of specialized market surveys in order to examine the market trends, to study the behavior of the consumers, and finally to perform market simulations, aiming at the selection of the most appropriate penetration strategy for the new product into the examined market.

Into the various stages of the proposed methodology several forecasting, data analysis, multicriteria analysis, and brand choice models are proposed. The methodology is realized through the development of an intelligent decision support system (Chapter 10). In addition to these analytical models, three partial expert systems have been integrated into the DSS, which by their intervention in the various stages of the process, aid the decision maker to:

- Choose the most appropriate data analysis method.
- Choose a suitable brand choice model.
- Assess the financial situation of the companies, whose products are considered in the market surveys.

In the remaining of this chapter, we will thoroughly present the proposed new product development methodology and its various implementation stages.

2. METHODOLOGY AND NEW PRODUCT DEVELOPMENT PROCESS

A first general view of the proposed methodology (*Figure 1*) for the analysis of the market and the design of new products is discussed in Siskos and Matsatsinis (1993). The methodology has been implemented through a decision support system and applied in a series of real world market surveys and new product design cases (Nikolaidis *et al.*, 1993; Siskos and

Matsatsinis, 1993; Baourakis *et al.*, 1993a; 1993b; 1995; 1996; Matsatsinis *et al.*, 1995; Siskos *et al.*, 1995; 2001).

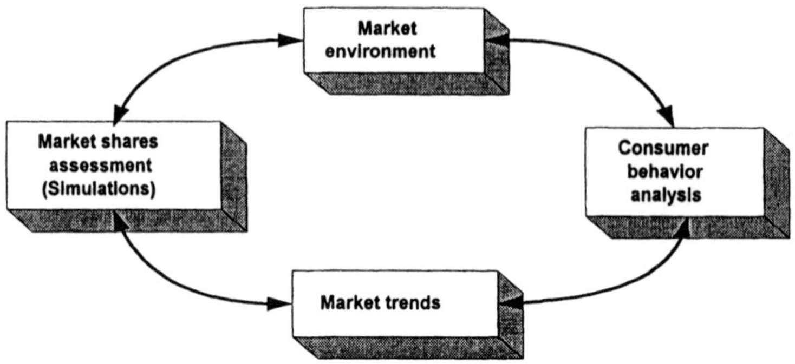

Figure 1. Market survey methodology for new product development (*Source*: Siskos and Matsatsinis, 1993)

Figure 2, presents the structure of the system from a methodological point of view, in order to render more transparent the operation and functionality of the system. According to the methodology, initially a general profile of the survey data is generated with the help of descriptive statistics. Then, by applying data analysis models, one may determine the characteristics of the consumers. The multicriteria UTASTAR method (Siskos and Yannacopoulos, 1985) is applied on the multicriteria evaluations of the consumers in order to determine their behavior. Then, by the help of brand choice models several simulations of the market are performed and the market shares of the participating products are calculated in order to select the model that best approaches the actual market shares. The most appropriate model is the one that is nearest to the actual market shares. Finally, the performances of the new product under development are introduced. This is followed by the application of various scenarios. In these scenarios, by using the selected model several simulations of the market are performed along with the calculation of the anticipated market shares, i.e. the market shares that will be obtained with the introduction of the new product. Based on the results of the application of the scenarios the selection of the most suitable penetration strategy of the new product into the market is performed.

The experience acquired by the application of the system into real world cases, its efficiency and effectiveness, some comments made by its users and several field experts led us to the revision of the above methodology. Basically, the outline of the methodology remains the same, however, it has been improved and extended (Matsatsinis and Siskos, 1999). On fact some, existing models were modified and new models were added in order to cover the possible weak points and additional needs of the proposed new product development methodology (*Figure 3*). The main idea in this new approach is to implement the methodology through a knowledge-based marketing decision support system. The second point is to develop a system that would be able to operate either as oriented to the capabilities of the system (choice of models) either as oriented to decision—maker needs (choice of the development procedure tasks) (Chapters 9, §8).

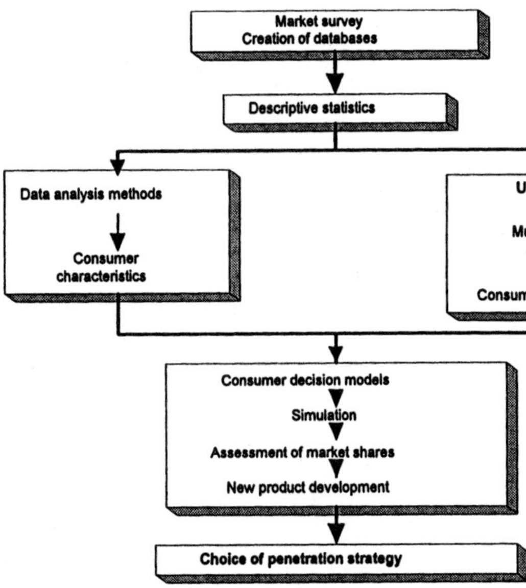

Figure 2. Structure of the system from a methodological point of view (*Source:* Siskos and Matsatsinis, 1993)

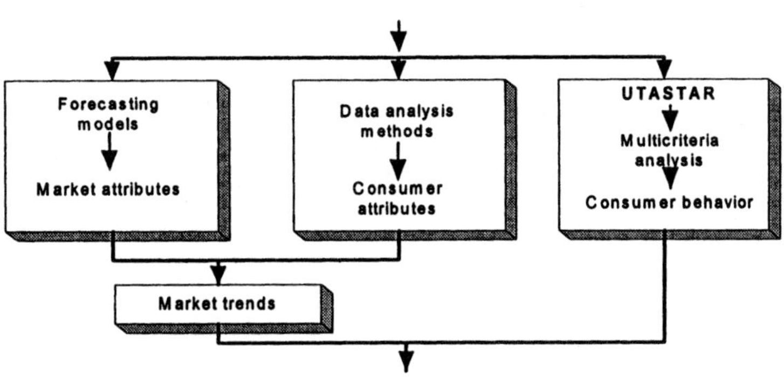

Figure 3. Structure of the revised system from a methodological point of view.

In order to implement and apply the methodology several forecasting, data analysis, multicriteria analysis, and brand choice models are used. These models comprise the model base of the system and are presented in detail in Chapter 10, §2.5.

The following sections are focused on the different parts of the methodology while the analysis, design, and development of the intelligent decision support system is presented in Chapter 10.

Figure 4 present the proposed new product development methodology, which aims at the satisfaction of decision maker's needs.

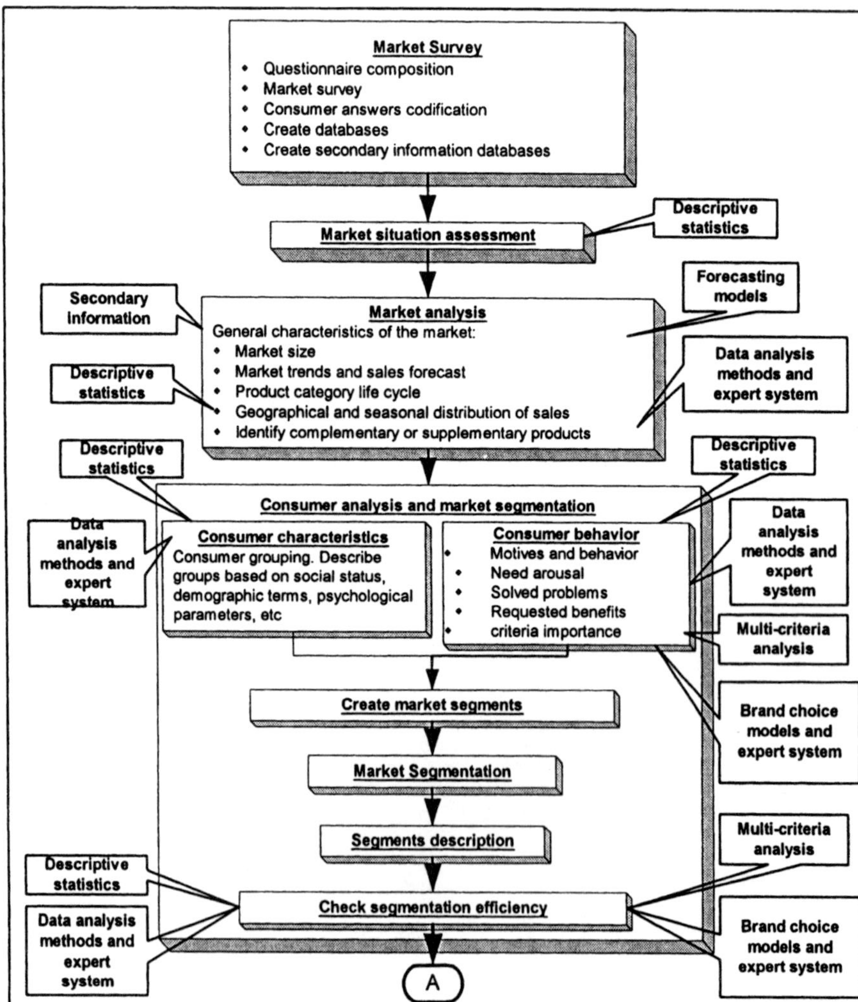

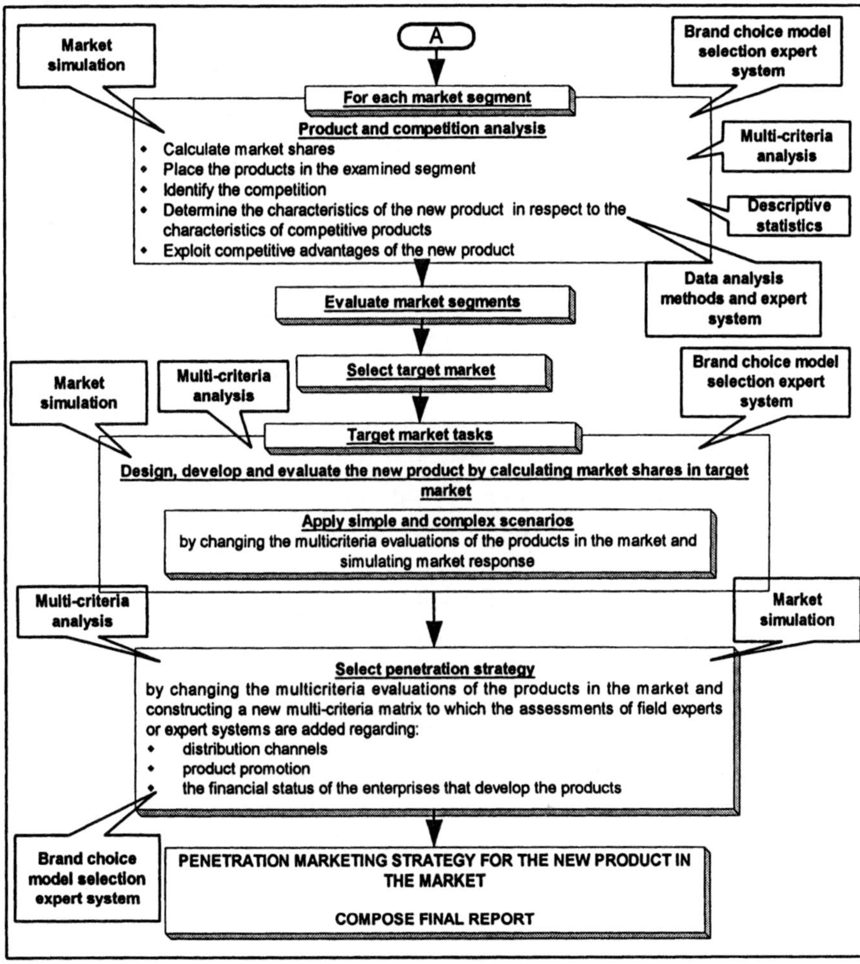

Figure 4. Proposed new product development process

3. MARKET SURVEY PROCESS

The term market survey refers to the scientific gathering, analysis, and evaluation of specific information regarding a certain marketing problem. The information should be available and its collection should be financially feasible, i.e. inexpensive. The aim of the collected data is to help the enterprises to understand more deeply the substantial need of their current or future consumers or customers (American Marketing Association, 1961; Kotler, 1994).

During the design phase of a new product, decisions related with the determination of the characteristics of the new product should be made regarding the:

- The form of the product (if it will be liquid, powder, etc).
- Its sentient characteristics like its colour, its odour, etc.
- The possible services provided with the product, like repairing guarantee, free delivery, etc.
- The characteristics that will differentiate it and will enable the product to outperform competitive products.
- The quality level of the product. With this term we consider the quality conceived by the consumers when they evaluate the reliability of the product during its intended use or operation.

These decisions require the existence of sufficient information, a fact that is considered during the development of the questionnaire.

The following activities take place during market survey stage:

- All the competitive products are recorded.
- Information regarding the production, sales, and the technical characteristics of the product that will take part in the market survey are gathered.
- The survey network is organized.
- A preliminary analysis of the consumer behavior is performed.
- The questionnaire is created.
- The actual market survey is performed.

The collection of reliable and relevant data is the leading step in the whole effort. Initially, the similar products and all the relevant information should be recorded. From secondary sources, we may collect information regarding:

- The overall size of the market, expressed in sales and money.
- The life cycle of the products.
- The seasonal and geographic distribution of sales.

The methodology proceeds with the selection of the group of products that will comprise the set that will be considered in the survey. The selection of these products makes sure that the formed "market" will be as representative as possible and that will fulfill the following requirements:

- The number of the products should be large enough so that it will represent the actual status of the market; however this number should not be very large in order to allow for the convenient completion of the questionnaires.
- The "market" should contain representative products from all the categories (leaders, challengers, followers, and nichers).

The conducting of the market survey and the formation of the required questionnaire follows the procedure shown in *Figure 5*.

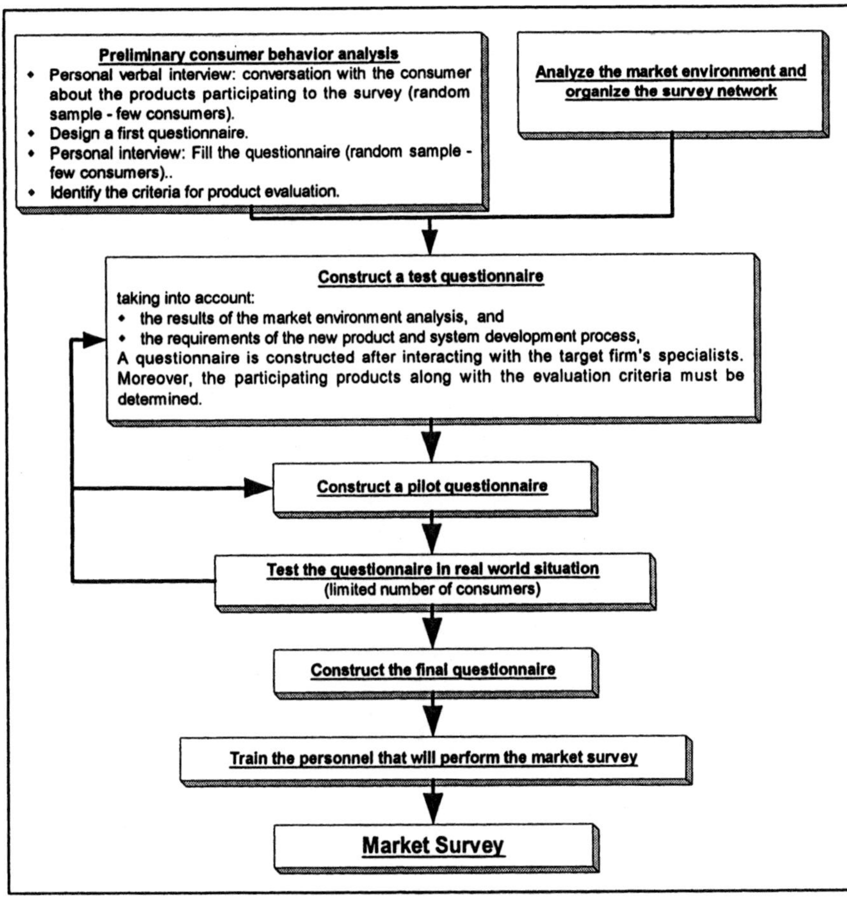

Figure 5. Structuring of the questionnaire and conduct of market survey (*Source:* ERGASYA, 1991)

During the market survey every consumer expresses his/her preferences first by evaluating the products on a consistent family of criteria (see Siskos, 1984; Roy, 1985 and chapter 1, §3.), then by ranking globally the products from the best to the worst: The ranking has the mathematical form of a weak order. Of course, in order to elicit this information, a special form of questionnaire is required (*Figure 6*).

During this process, the consumer is given the possibility to inspect or even to taste the products (e.g. juices). The ranking of the products is obtained by the following algorithmic procedure (see *Figure 5*):

- **Step 1:** The products of the "market" are presented to the consumer.
- **Step 2:** The consumer is asked to point the product (or the products) that would choose to purchase.

- **Step 3:** The selected products (or the products) are removed from the set. If the remaining set contains only one product the procedure stops; otherwise go to Step 1.

At the end of the process, the products are ranked according to the order the consumer would purchase them.

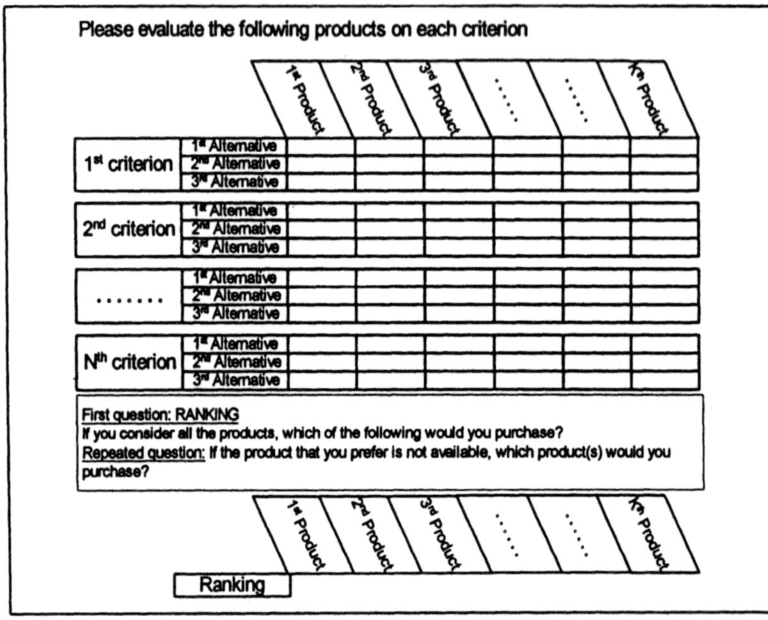

Figure 6. Questionnaire for the collection of consumers' preferential data

When the survey and the required check on the collected questionnaires are finished, the questionnaires should be codified in order to be suitable for process by the system. The type of codification should be determined during the stage of questionnaire design and not after the ending of the survey. Then, the required databases are created by entering the codified questionnaires. In addition, all the collected secondary information regarding the sales of the market products, the overall size of the market in sales and money, and the financial figures of the enterprises producing the market products are recorder into the system by creating respective databases.

By using simple descriptive statistical techniques, we obtain an initial estimation of the market status. Then, we may use advanced analysis methods (see *Table 1* and *Table 2*), in order to check:

- The general characteristics of the market.
- The size of the market.
- The development trends of the market and the sales forecast.

- The geographic and seasonal distribution of sales.
- The detection of substitute and complementary products.

In addition, from the available secondary information, the life cycle of the products should have been determined.

4. MARKET TRENDS

The study of the prevalent trends in the market under consideration turns to two directions. The first one involves the study of the trends of the general characteristics of the market such as the volume of sales of the products in quantities and money. The second mainly turns to the examination of the trends that prevail among the consumers and of their interactions with the characteristics of the market products.

With the help of the system's forecasting models (*Table 1*) the trends of the market are examined and the forecast of the evolution of sales of the products is performed. Depending on the available data, the same can also be applied to forecast the evolution of the geographic and seasonal distribution of sales. All the required data for the execution of forecasting tasks are obtained from secondary information.

Table 1. Forecasting models]

	Model
1	Linear regression
2	Exponential regression
3	Geometric regression
4	Multinomial regression

The study of the consumers' trends is accomplished by applying several data analysis methods (*Table 2* and 10 §2.5.2) to the data collected from the questionnaires. The application of data analysis methods permits us to:

- Obtain more generic information on the characteristics of the consumers and the products of the market.
- Determine the profile of the consumer that purchases each of the products of the market.
- Examine and identify the perceptions and attitudes of the consumers towards the products of the market.
- Examine the relationships among different groups of consumers and the characteristics of the products.
- Detect the products that act as complementary and substitute of other products.

With the analysis of the characteristics of the products, we attempt to determine the competitive advantages of the products. For this reason, we compare the characteristics of the product under development with those of its competitive products in order to discover its points of advantages and disadvantages.

Table 2. Data analysis methods

	Method
1	Descriptive statistics
2	Principal components analysis
3	Correspondence analysis
4	Multiple correspondence analysis
5	Simple regression
6	Multiple regression
7	Q – Analysis

Based on the results of the analyses performed, we may determine the segmentation characteristics of the market. In the case where there are no characteristics, on which valid market segmentation can be determined the market will be considered as a single segment.

The available data analysis methods (*Table 2*) are tailored, as a rule, to different analysis objectives:

1. The determination of proportions and the finding of the percentages of the alternative answers are accomplished by descriptive statistics.
2. With the application of principal components analysis we may investigate the existence of:
   - Similarities – dissimilarities among consumers.
   - Similarities – dissimilarities among characteristics-variables.
   - Strong positive or negative correlations among characteristics-variables.
   - Interactions among the characteristics-variables and the consumers.
3. Simple and multiple correspondence analysis help us to investigate the relationships and the interactions among the alternative answers given by the consumers to specific questions. In addition, we may examine the intensity of these relations.
4. Simple and multiple regression analyses allow us to investigate the rank correlation among the variables
5. Finally, the existence of groupings among consumers and characteristics is discovered either with the help of principal components analysis or with the use of Q-Analysis.

Each one of the utilized data analysis methods has certain characteristics; their application requires the fulfillment of certain conditions in order to derive valid results. Some methods require the existence of independent variables, in some methods the input data have to be qualitative; in others the input data should be quantitative, etc. Therefore, because of the assumptions required for the data analysis methods, because of the different objectives by each of these methods, as well as because the users-decision makers in the marketing field ignore, in general, the functional details of these methods, it is expected that the development of an expert system for the selection of the most suitable data analysis method for every data set will significantly alleviate the process. The expert system and the respective knowledge base are presented in chapter 10, §2.6.1.

5. CONSUMER BEHAVIOUR ANALYSIS

The objective of the behavior analysis is to investigate the way the consumer behaves at the time she/he/ purchases a certain product. We try to discover the attitudes that motivate the consumer to prefer a certain product among a set of products and in addition to find out the criteria on which his/her choice is based on. Therefore, we are able to examine the existence of groups of consumers (market segments) with similar behavior. These market segments consist of consumers that behave-act towards the products of a "market" with similar way. Based on the analysis of the consumers' characteristics we proceed to the segmentation of the market according to common characteristics and practices. These two types of analysis are complementary and not contrary.

The multicriteria analysis is the theoretical background of the attempted consumer behavior analysis (Chapter 1,§3). Consumers make decisions when they choose to purchase a product among a set of alternatives. Accordingly, if we analyze the information regarding the decisions made by a group of consumers that participate in the market survey, we may arrive at conclusions about their way of behavior and detect the criteria that play decisive role in the behavior of different groups of consumers.

The above points of consideration led us to the selection and use of the UTASTAR method (Siskos and Yannacopoulos, 1985), which is an improved variant of the original multicriteria UTA method, for the analysis of consumer behavior. An influential advantage of the UTASTAR method is that it can handle both qualitative and quantitative criteria.

Let us now define the following problem: Let,

$$A = \{\alpha_1, \alpha_2, \ldots, \alpha_m\}$$

be the set of alternatives (in our case the set of the market's products) for which a set of consumers

$$J = \{1, 2, \ldots, p\}$$

have expressed their evaluations on a consistent family of criteria

$g_1, g_2, \ldots g_n$.

Each criterion g represents a monotone qualitative or quantitative variable (the greater the evaluation of the product, the more preferable the product is). Thus, for each product $\alpha_i \in A$, the vector

$$\mathbf{g}(\mathbf{a}_i) = [\mathbf{g}_1(\mathbf{a}_i), \mathbf{g}_2(\mathbf{a}_i), \ldots, \mathbf{g}_n(\mathbf{a}_i)]$$

represents the multicriteria evaluation of the product α_i given be a consumer. In addition, the consumer has globally ordered the products according to her/his order of preference.

Based on the data that are obtained by specially designed questionnaire (*Figure 6*) a multicriteria matrix of the form shown in *Table 3* for each consumer is constructed.

Table 3. Multicriteria matrix

Products	**Ranking**	g_1	g_2	...	g_n
a_1	$r(a_1)$	$g_1(a_1)$	$g_2(a_1)$	...	$g_n(a_1)$
a_2	$r(a_2)$	$g_1(a_2)$	$g_2(a_2)$	...	$g_n(a_2)$
...	...	...	...	...	...
...	...	...	...	...	...
a_m	$r(a_m)$	$g_1(a_m)$	$g_2(a_m)$	...	$g_n(a_m)$
Worst	r_*	g_{1*}	g_{2*}	...	g_{n*}
Best	$r^* = 1$	g_1^*	g_2^*	...	g_n^*
Subintervals	$s_r = r^* - r_*$	$s_1 = g_1^* - g_{1*} + 1$	$s_2 = g_2^* - g_{2*} + 1$	...	$s_n = g_n^* - g_{n*} + 1$

For the entire set of consumers the table of initial evaluations of the consumers **EvalTable(i, j, k)** corresponding to each product and to each criterion is formed. The number of the alternative discrete evaluation values of each criterion is calculated by the formula:

$$s_j = g_j^* - g_{j^*} + 1$$

where g_j^* is the best alternative evaluation and g_{j^*} is the worst.

The aggregation rule of the n criteria in the UTASTAR method, is given by an additive value function of the form:

$$\mathrm{u}(\mathrm{g}) = u_1(g_1) + u_2(g_2) + \ldots u_n(g_n)$$

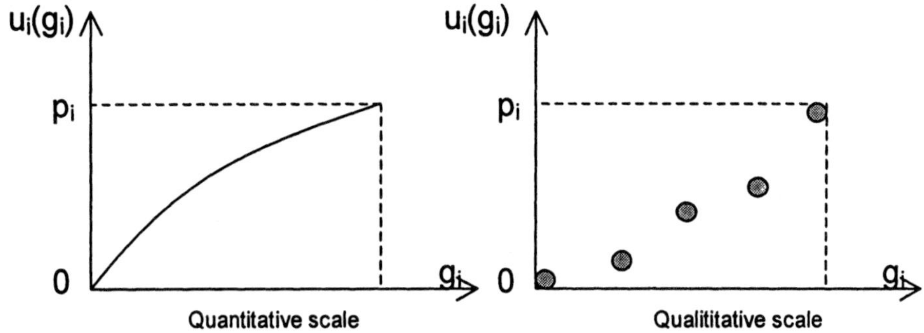

Figure 7. Quantitative and qualitative monotone variable

The UTASTAR method is applied to the table of initial evaluations in order to assess the value function of each consumer by estimating all the marginal value functions

$$u_i(g_i), \quad i = 1,2,\ldots,n.$$

By this, we create the marginal values table

MarginUtilTable(j, max s_j, k), with

$j = 1, 2, \ldots, n$
max s_j being the maximum number of intervals of all the criteria, and The
$k = 1, 2, \ldots, p$
marginal value functions are defined in the interval [0,1], since we assume that the sum of the weights p_i equals to one (see *Table 4*).

Table 4. Marginal utilities

	Marginal Utilities			
Criteria	1	2	...	Max s_j
g_1	$u_1(1)$	$u_1(2)$	...	$u_1(s_1)$
g_2	$u_2(1)$	$u_2(2)$	...	$u_2(s_2)$
...	...	...	...	
...	...	...	...	
g_n	$u_n(1)$	$u_n(2)$	...	$u_n(s_n)$

If we divide the marginal values $u_i(g_i)$ with their highest values p_i (the weight of the i-*th* criterion), then the function is normalized between 0 and 1 and the factor p_i expresses the relative weight of the criterion. Also, in order to express the weights with the form of percentages the following constraint holds:

$$\sum_{i=1}^{n} p_i = 1$$

In this way, the global value of a product $a \in A$ is calculated by the formula:

$$u\left[g(a)\right] = p_1 u_1\left[g_1(a)\right] + p_2 u_2\left[g_2(a)\right] + p_n u_n\left[g_n(a)\right]$$

The outline of the algorithmic procedure of the UTASTAR method that is then followed for each consumer separately, consists of the following steps (Jacquet-Lagrèze and Siskos, 1982; 1983; Siskos, 1982):

1. The check of the degree of consistency between the additive model and the consumer's ranking is based on:
   a) An error optimisation criterion that allows the attainment of optimal value functions through linear programming, and
   b) Kendall's τ, which takes values between −1 and 1 and measures the distance between the weak order of the reference decision and of the weak order defined a posteriori by the value function.
2. Special linear programming techniques are used in order to find global optimum solution (utility function) and stability analysis of the global optimum in order to find characteristic multiple solutions (post optimality analysis).
3. The market-forecast procedure does not rely on a single value function without the case of the sufficient stability of the model. Otherwise, as frequently occurs in marketing because of poor information, a system of functions is used that are produced by the post optimality analysis.

The solution is optimized and then post-optimized by maximizing the weight p_i of each criterion. The results of the stability analysis, which are presented below, create the matrices **PostEval (j, j, k)** and **MaxMinWeights (2, j, k)** with $j = 1, 2, \ldots, n$ and $k = 1, 2, \ldots, p$. The diagonal of the matrix contains the maximum weights of the criteria. The mean values of the criteria weights are presented for comparison purposes (*Table 5*).

The study of the consumer behaviour is performed by the help of criteria analysis. We have two possible alternatives in the criteria analysis, depending on the way that the weights of the criteria are calculated. The first approach uses the mean criteria weights whereas the second one employs the maximum weights of the criteria (*Table 2*). The following actions are completely the same no matter if we use the mean either the maximum weights of the criteria. The only difference is related with the values of the criteria weights.

Table 5. Sensitivity analysis-criteria weights: Mean and maximum weights

	g_1	g_2	...	...	g_n
Solution Type	p_1	p_2	...	...	p_n
Max p_1	$p_{1,1}$	$p_{1,2}$	...	...	$p_{1,n}$
Max p_2	p2, 1	$p_{2,2}$	...	...	$p_{2,n}$
...	...	...	...	...	...
...	...	...	...	...	...
Max p_n	$p_{n,1}$	$p_{n,2}$	...	...	$p_{n,n}$
Mean Weights	$Mw_1 = (p_{1,1}+p_{2,1}+ \ldots +p_{n,1})/n$	$Mw_2 = (p_{1,2}+p_{2,2}+ \ldots +p_{n,2})/n$	...	...	$Mw_n = (p_{1,n}+p_{2,n}+ \ldots +p_{n,n})/n$
Max Weights	$Mxw_1 = p_{1,1}$	$Mxw_2 = P_{2,2}$	...	...	$Mxw_n = p_{n,n}$

The i-*th* criterion is considered to dominate the consumer's decision when its weight exceeds an importance threshold that indicates the minimum level of the ascribed importance to a criterion. If the weight of the criterion is less than the importance threshold, it is considered that this criterion has no effect on the consumer's decision to choose a product. Respectively, all the criteria with weight greater or equal to the importance threshold are considered to play determinative roles to the consumer's decision. The algorithmic representation of the above procedure is presented below:

```
Selection of importance threshold by the user: weight threshold
For each consumer l = 1, 2, …, p
  For each criterion j = 1, 2, …, n
        If
           the weight of the criterion is greater or equal
           than the importance threshold (pj ≥ Threshold )
        then
           S(j) = S(j) + 1
  Next j
Next l
Calculation of importance
For each j = 1, 2, …, n
  S(j) = (S(j) * 100) / k
Next j
```

This procedure detects the dominant (important) and non-dominant (non-important) criteria for each consumer. By generalizing, we calculate the percentages of the consumers that seem to consider important to their decision some of these criteria, by summing each consumer for which the weights of criteria are greater or equal than the selected importance thresholds S(j).

Together, we have the ability to calculate the percentages of the consumers to which a certain combination of criteria has greater or equal values than the importance threshold. By the conclusions derived by the applications of various combinations, we may proceed to the segmentation of the market according to the behavior of the consumers. This type of market segmentation creates segments with members that show similar behaviour and react with similar way to possible variations of the characteristics of the "market's" products. The division of the market according to the type of the behavior of its members permits us to study the ways in which the market will react to the application of specific policies.

The algorithmic procedure for the production of the criteria combinations is the following:

Selection of criteria combination: The decision-maker is given the ability to consider a criterion: 1. Important, 2. Non-important, and 3. Indifferent, thus creating a table Compin(j), j = 1, 2, ..., n. The results that indicate the percentage of consumers that fulfill the specific requirements are stored in the counter CompinS. The algorithmic process is as follows:

```
For each consumer l = 1, 2, ..., p
  For each criterion j = 1, 2, ..., n
        If
            Compin(j) is 'important'
        Then
                If
                    the weight of the criterion pj < Threshold
                Then
                    Next l
        Else
                If
                    the weight of the criterion pj ≥ Threshold
                Then
                    Next l
  Next j
  CompinS = CompinS + 1
Next l
CompinS = (CompinS * 100) / k
```

If the results are not satisfactory or if the decision maker wishes to investigate additional cases then he is able to return to previous stages and select a task with mean or maximum weight, to consider another value for the importance criterion or to examine new combinations of criteria,

Based on the results derived by the study of the market trends (segmentation based on the characteristics of the consumers) and on those derived by the analysis of the consumers behaviour (segmentation based on the consumers' behaviour) we create partial market segmentation bases either using various combinations of consumers' characteristics either using combinations of the criteria that are used for the evaluation of the products.

Each one of the bases is applied to the entire market and splits it to segments. This is followed by the attempt to describe the market segments based on both the characteristics and the behaviour of the consumers that comprise the market (Nylen, 1990). Finally, the efficiency and usefulness of the particular segmentation are evaluated. If some segments are efficient then we proceed with the farther examination of each segment separately whereas if the segments are not satisfactory then we consider the entire market as a single segment.

Based on the competitive advantages that the new product presents in each of the evaluated market segment, the segments are ranked, and then the decision-maker selects one or more segments, which will constitute the target market.

6. MARKET SHARES

The primary objective of the current working phase is the selection of the specific brand choice model (*Table 6*) that best approaches and represents the underling status of the particular market segment.

Table 6. Brand choice models

Model	Formula
Luce (1959; 1977)	$P_{ij}(C) = \dfrac{U_{ij}}{\sum_{k \in C} U_{ik}}$
Lesourne (1977)	$P_{ij}(C) = \dfrac{U_{ij}^{2}}{\sum_{k \in C} U_{ik}^{2}}$

Model	Formula
Multinomial Logit Model (or McFadden-1) (1970, 1976, 1978; 1980; 1991)	$P_{ij}(C)=\frac{e^{U_{ij}}}{\sum_{k\in C} e^{U_{ik}}}$
Slightly Reinforced (or McFadden-2)	$P_{ij}(C)=\frac{e^{2U_{ij}}}{\sum_{k\in C} e^{2U_{ik}}}$
Width of Utilities-1 (Matsatsinis; 1995)	$P_{ij}(C)=\frac{U_{ij}^{\,U_{\max}-U_{\min}}}{\sum_{k\in C} U_{ik}^{\,U_{\max}-U_{\min}}}$
Width of Utilities-2 (Matsatsinis; 1995)	$P_{ij}(C)=\frac{e^{(U_{\max}-U_{\min})U_{ij}}}{\sum_{k\in C} e^{(U_{\max}-U_{\min})U_{ik}}}$
Maximum Utilities (Matsatsinis; 1995)	$P_{ij}(j\|C)=\begin{cases}\frac{1}{m} & \text{if } U_{i\max}\geq U_{ij}\geq U_{i\max}-\varepsilon_i\\ 0 & \text{else}\end{cases}$ where $\varepsilon_i=\frac{\delta_i}{n-1}$ and $\delta_i=U_{i\max}-U_{i\min}$
Equal Probabilities (Matsatsinis; 1995)	$P_j=\frac{1}{m}$, where $U_{i\max}-U_{i\min}\leq 0.1$
Heuristic (Matsatsinis and Samaras, 2000)	Heuristic algorithm

The products that took part in the survey and for which the consumers have expressed their preferences, consist the representative "market". We may introduce new products in this market provided that they are evaluated with the same criteria with those of the market survey. The preferential evaluations for the new products can be given by experts of the company or in general by field experts. The decision-maker, depending on the requirements of the tasks, may choose group of products from the market, thus formulating "new markets". The simulations or any other tasks that follow involve the products that each time are included in the "new market".

The decision-maker can chose among eight different brand choice models (*Table 6*), since the equal possibilities model is used as a heuristic model and not independently. Let us examine these brand choice models.

The model proposed by Pessemier (1966), is a generalization of the models suggested by Luce (1959; 1977) and Lesourne (1977). According to this model the According to this model the probability $P_{ij}(C)$ for consumer i to choose product j between a set of product C is given by the following formula:

$$P_{ij}(C) = \frac{U_{ij}^b}{\sum_{k \in C} U_{ik}^b},$$

where

U_{ij} is the utility that consumer i assigns to product j, and

b is a parameter that represents the distance between the most and least preferred choice.

Two assumptions should hold in order to apply this model:

a) There must be real competition among the market products.
b) The market should be stable.

Since b represents the distance between the most and least preferred choice an increase in its value tends to separate the most by the least preferred market products.

The above model has been used by Silk and Urban (1978) to develop a methodology, known as ASSESSOR, for pre-test market model in launching new products. The authors accept that the value of the parameter b remains constant after the launch of the new product, an assumption that we will also adopt. When $b=1$ we obtain, the Luce model whereas when $b=2$ we obtain the Lesourne model.

Here, in the two proposed models, the distance between the most and least preferred choice is determined by the maximum and minimum utility values, which a consumer has assigned to the market products. Each consumer evaluates the decision alternatives, i.e. the products, according to multiple criteria and implicitly assigns a utility value in each product. The distance between the maximum and minimum values of the assigned utilities determines the consumer's ability to define a well-established order of preferences and accordingly select a product (or a subset of products) as the most preferred. This range is called width of utilities, δ. Accordingly, when the value of δ is small the consumer is having difficulties in choosing a specific product. On the contrary when the width of utilities gets larger the consumer has a well-established preference on a certain product. This idea was used in the development of the heuristic model as well as in the development of the corresponding knowledge base, which will be presented in 10 §2.6.2. Thus, the parameter b is mathematically represented by the following formula

$$b = U_{i\max} - U_{i\min}:$$

The fifth model of the system is mathematically expressed as follows:

$$P_{ij}(C) = \frac{U_{ij}^{U_{i\max} - U_{i\min}}}{\sum_{k \in C} U_{ik}^{U_{i\max} - U_{i\min}}}$$

The sixth model is a modification of the multinomial logit model. The modification is related with the introduction of the width of utilities, as discussed earlier.

$$P_{ij}(C) = \frac{e^{(U_{i\max} - U_{i\min})U_{ij}}}{\sum_{k \in C} e^{(U_{i\max} - U_{i\min})U_{ik}}}$$

Assuming that consumers select only the products from which they expect to gain the maximum utility value and they reject all the rest, we build the maximum utilities model. According to this model, consumers are likely to purchase only the products that belong to the group with maximum utilities. On the contrary products that belong to other groups, have only negligible purchase probabilities, which we can consider as zero. The group with maximum utilities is defined by the products whose global utilities are within the range of maximum utilities. The range of maximum utilities is determined as follows:

For each consumer i, the global utilities that correspond to the n possible choices have been calculated. First, we calculate the distance between the maximum and minimum utility values:

$$\delta_i = U_{i\max} - U_{i\min}$$

Next, the range of the maximum utilities is calculated as

$$\varepsilon_i = \frac{\delta_i}{n-1}$$

We will consider that a product lies within the range of maximum utilities when its global utility resides in the range between

$$U_{i\max} \text{ and } U_{i\max} - \varepsilon_i$$

If the utilities of m products lie within this range then the purchase probability of each product equals

$$P_{ij} = \frac{1}{m}$$

Thus, according to the maximum utilities model the purchase probability is defined by the formula:

$$P_{ij}(j|C) = \begin{cases} \frac{1}{m} & \text{if } U_{i\max} \geq U_{ij} \geq U_{i\max} - \varepsilon_i \\ 0 & \text{else} \end{cases}$$

If the range of assigned utilities is smaller or equal to 0.1 then we can formulate another model, the model of equal probabilities. The small difference in the maximum and minimum values of the assigned utilities indicates that we are unable to determine the preferences of the consumer. In other words, the consumer by assigning indistinguishable utilities to each product expresses her/his inability to distinguish the products. Therefore, all the products share the same purchase probability. In such cases, the purchase probability for each of the m products will be calculated by the formula:

$$P_j = \frac{1}{m}, \quad j = 1, 2, \ldots, m$$

If the same brand choice model is used for all the consumers we have to assume that they all share similar attitudes and preference structures. However, the resulting utility functions reveal that this is a very strong argument, as will be explained thoroughly in Chapter 10, §2.6.2). The estimated utilities vary significantly from consumer to consumer. The distribution of the utilities and the shape of the utility function are quite different for each consumer. This implies that consumers have different preference structures and they exhibit different decision patterns. In addition, brand choice models exhibit different characteristics that render them to more efficiently represent some preference structures than others. As a conclusion due to different patterns in consumer behavior and due to different characteristics of brand choice models, the analysis would be more efficient if we could apply different models to different types of consumers. This is exactly the goal of the proposed heuristic model.

In the proposed heuristic model, a different brand choice model is used to calculate the purchase possibilities for each consumer separately. The choice of the specific model that best fits the preference structure of the consumer is carried out by the respective knowledge base.

The calculation of the market shares of the products that form the "market", based on the above models, is accomplished by the following procedure.

After the assessment of the global utilities of the products for each consumer, the purchase probability $P(a_i; A)$ of the product a_i for each consumer separately, is calculated according to the brand choice models (*Table 6*), where:

$A = \{\alpha_1, \alpha_2, \ldots, \alpha_m\}$ the set of the "market" products for which

a set of consumers $J = \{1, 2, \ldots, k\}$ have expressed their preferences.

Then for each consumer *j* and for each brand choice model, a purchase probability vector is created:

$$\left[\mathbf{P_j}(\mathbf{a_1}), \mathbf{P_j}(\mathbf{a_2}), \ldots, \mathbf{P_j}(\mathbf{a_m})\right]^{\mathbf{T}}, \quad j = 1, 2, \ldots k$$

Finally, the overall purchase probability, for the set of the consumers, of each product is calculated:

$$S_i = \sum_{j=1}^{k} \mathbf{P_j}(\mathbf{a_i}), \quad i = 1, 2, \ldots m$$

From these probabilities the market shares of the products are calculated using the formula:

$$\text{MarketShares}\left(a_i\right) = 100 * \frac{S_i}{\sum_{l=1}^{m} S_l \%}$$

The criterion on which the selection of the most suitable brand choice model is based on (see *Table 6*) is whether it approximates the actual market shares. In addition, a respective expert system has been developed that supports the decision-maker in the selection of the most appropriate brand choice model (Chapter 10, §2.6.2). If the approximation of the actual market status is not considered to be satisfactory then we should think the selection of a different market segment or the reformation of the "market" and the repetition of the above tasks, as these are described in the next section (*Figure 8*).

7. SIMULATIONS

After the selection of the brand choice model, we may launch the new product and its multicriteria evaluations into the "market". We then proceed with the execution of market simulations in order to define the design of the new product. As new product, we consider either a totally new product that is developed for the first time or an already existing product, which we wish to redesign and improve. *Figure 8* shows the flow chart of the operations that occur during the phases of market shares calculation and simulations in order to select the most appropriate penetration strategy into the market for the product under development.

With the help of the data analysis methods and also with the help of the market simulations we achieve the detection of the major competitive products of the new product and the determination of the characteristics of the new product and those of its competitors, thus finally the detection of the points where the new product presents advantages or disadvantages over the competitive ones. In addition, the decision-maker has the ability to alter the synthesis of the market and to form "markets" that consist of products that mainly antagonize the product under development.

We launch the new product in the particular "market" by determining the characteristics of the target market and those of the designed product that provide competitive advantages to it.

For each change to the evaluation criteria during the design of the product, the reactions of the consumers should be checked. The proposed methodology provides us the possibility to conduct these checks in the laboratory and consequently reduces the required cost for the development of the new product. This advantage is achieved through the ability of the decision-maker to change the multicriteria evaluations of the products that belong in the "market". When a change occurs in the multicriteria evaluations matrix the utilities of the products are re-calculated for each consumer separately and then the purchase probabilities and the market shares of the products are also recalculated according to the selected model.

We should note here that the multicriteria evaluations that appear in the final table and on which the changes on the evaluations are performed, the scenarios are applied and the simulations are tested are the mean values of the respective multicriteria evaluations for the entire set of consumers, rounded to the next integer value. In the case where some of the values of the multicriteria evaluations (e.g. price) lie in an intermediate interval of the original subdivision used for the calculation of the marginal utilities, then these utilities are assessed with lineal interpolation.

An important feature of the proposed methodology is the intrinsic flexibility to perform as many tests as we wish by adjusting the tests to the conclusions derived by the previously performed ones. In addition, a significant advantage is the fact that the reactions of the consumers to the various changes are presented directly with the form of market shares of the products.

In order to select the most suitable penetration strategy of the new product into the market we test several different scenarios. The scenarios are applied for various combinations of criteria changes and the each time market shares are evaluated. We have the ability to apply simple and complex scenarios as well as to test alternative strategies.

With simple scenarios, we examine the fluctuation of the market shares of a group of selected products when the most determinative criteria vary between predefined bounds. The application of simple scenarios helps us to resolve the situation and to limit the number of cases that will be examined next. From the examined scenarios we select those that give the desirable market shares and then those that give somewhat similar market shares but with smaller cost of implementation (*Figure 8*). The selection of the criteria on which the product development will be improved is based, among other, on:

- The dominant role of each criterion and the percentages of the consumers that consider decisive of their decision some combinations of criteria.
- The multicriteria evaluations of the consumers for the designed product.

The complex scenarios are applied over the selected simple scenarios and allow us to examine the variation of the market shares for groups of products when some selected criteria vary between predefined bounds. Complex scenarios are always examined in relation with the variation of an independent criterion. If the results derived from the application of the complex scenarios are considered satisfactory by the decision-maker then we proceed to the selection of the penetration scenarios that will be farther investigated.

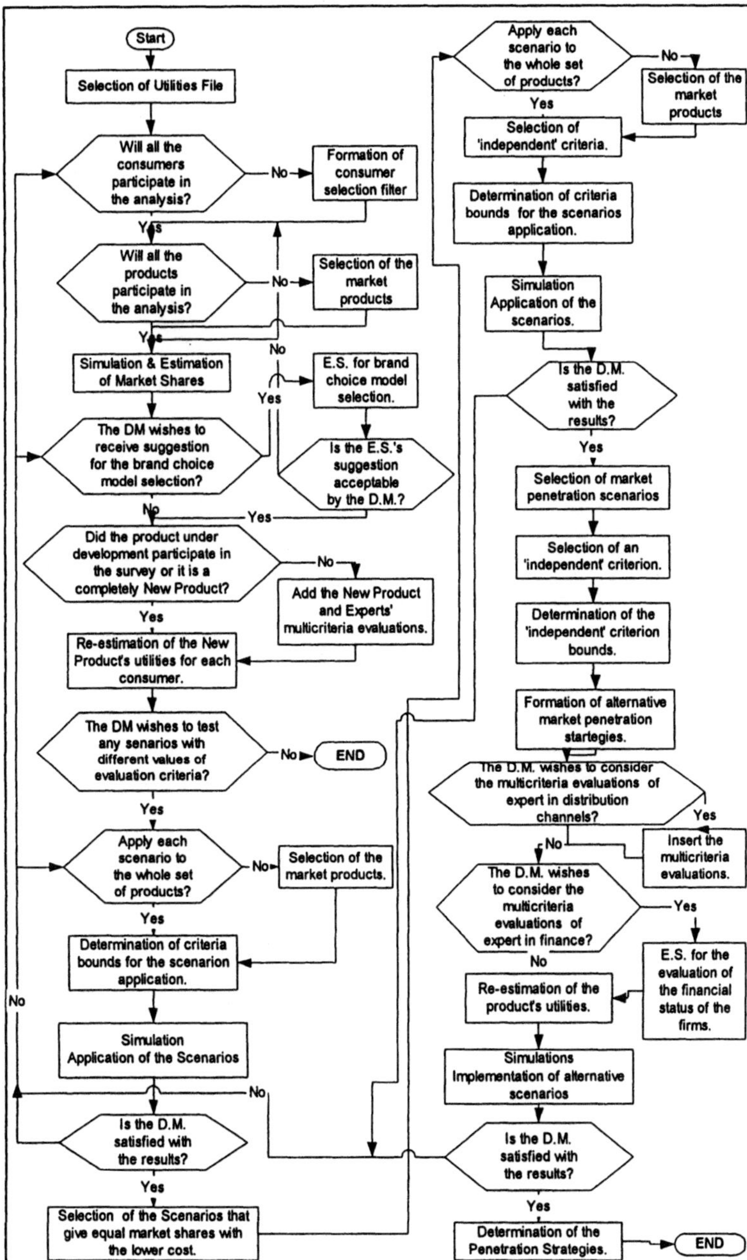

Figure 8. Required tasks for the selection of a penetration strategy

Based on the results of the various scenarios we are guided to the examination of the anticipated effects by the application of the various penetration strategies into the market. Thus, to the already existing multicriteria evaluations of the products by the consumers we add the evaluations of experts in the fields of distribution channels (Net) and the promotion strategy of each company (Adv). In addition, we introduce either by the help of a special financial analyst or by the help of an expert system for the evaluation of the financial status of companies (Matsatsinis *et al.*, 1997) the evaluations on the financial status of the companies (Fin) that produce the products under consideration. This evaluation procedure examines the possible effect of the financial status of the company that will develop the product and of its competitors on the product under development. With the introduction of the new evaluations, a new multicriteria table is created in which the evaluations of the experts and of the expert system have been added as criteria. The simulation of the market based on the final penetration strategies under consideration requires the reassessment of the utilities of the products. Consequently, before proceeding to market simulations, the UTASTAR method should be applied to the new multicriteria tables and the utilities should be reassessed. Based on the new utilities and the selected brand choice model, the market shares for each alternative penetration strategy are calculated.

In this final stage, if the decision-maker is satisfied by the results of some strategies selects the strategy that fits most to the goals and possibilities of the company. If the results are not satisfactory, the decision-maker is able to repeat some of the previous tasks or to re-evaluate the whole process. This process is repeated until we arrive to the selection of the desirable penetration strategy for the designed product.

Chapter 10

Analysis and Design of MARKEX

1. INTRODUCTION TO MARKEX

The aim of this chapter is to present a tool designed to support decision makers during the new product development process.

The main goals of the system's philosophy are:

- The support of the decision-maker during the semi-structured or unstructured marketing processes.
- The cooperation between models, databases and techniques for the presentation of the results.
- The possibility to support the decision-maker in specialized topics with the help of expert systems.
- The ability to be used even by decision makers with limited experience in computer systems.
- The possibility of continuous improvement of the decisions made by using the system.
- Its independent function for the implementation of partial tasks.
- The reliable operation of the system.
- The ability to easily and unconditionally use the data to be studied by using special filters.
- The ability to create multicriteria tables with different composition.
- The provision of a flexible and easy to use tool.
- The exploitation of the Windows environment capabilities.
- The possibility of multitasking.
- The ability to simultaneously operate several components of the system.
- The provision of a large number of models and the ability to add new ones.

- The possibility to graphically represent the results of all the tasks.
- The broad support of the decision maker in the various phases of the new product development process (Chapter 3, §3), like
  - The processing of data collected by market surveys.
  - The analysis of the market and the determination of the market's general characteristics.
  - The analysis of the characteristics of the consumers.
  - The study of consumer behaviour.
  - Product and competition analysis.
  - The segmentation of the market.
  - The design, development, and test of products through the calculation of their purchase probabilities and by the simulation of the market.
  - The examination of simple and complex scenarios.
  - The selection of the penetration strategy of the product under development through the application of alternative strategies.

The general procedure of developing an expert system, described in §4 of Chapter 7 is the one followed, in general, in the development of MARKEX. The system was developed for Windows 95 with the help of the Microsoft Professional Visual Basic 6 Enterprise edition programming language. The expert systems and the respective knowledge bases were developed with the help of the M4 expert systems development shell (Cimflex Teknowledge, 1993). The analysis and design of the system were performed by the help of the Computer Aided Software Engineering (CASE) Tool, System Architect.

2. SYSTEM'S STRUCTURE

2.1 10.2.1 System's Architecture

The general architecture of the system, which is composed by four main subsystems, is presented in *Figure 1.* The model followed for the integration of the expert systems with the decision support system is the one that supports the adaptation of the ES as independent subsystem, as described in Chapter 8, §5.1.2. We will now describe the details of the expert subsystems and in the following section we will focus on the analysis and design of MARKEX.

2.2 User

The system is designed for use by any member or members of a company's staff that is involved on the development of new products. In the process of the new product development, MARKEX aids the decision-maker to conceive more effectively the factors that enter into and affect the design process of the new product. The process is analytically described in Chapter 3, §2 and §3.

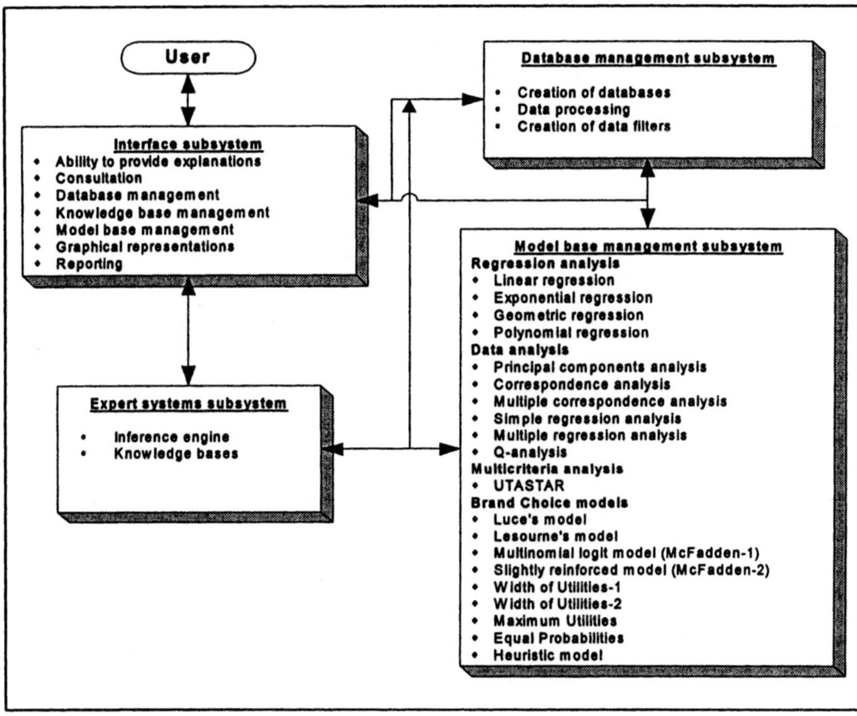

Figure 1. Structure of the system

Another usage of the system involves the carrying out of partial types of analyses such as descriptive statistics, forecasting of the evolution of historical data, other types of data analysis, calculation of products' purchasing probabilities, market shares, etc.

2.3 Interface Subsystem

The interface subsystem facilitates the interaction of the user with all the remaining subsystems. The rational planning, the simple handling, the clearness of its messages, and the possibilities of graphical presentations of its results are some of the system's characteristics. One should always bear in mind that a satisfied user is its best advertiser. The Windows environment and the Visual Basic, which was used for the development of the system, offer a friendly environment for the end-users. The use of the keyboard has been limited to a few necessary jobs because most of them are carried out with mouse clicks. In addition, graphical screens are mainly used for the presentation of the results.

The interaction of the user with the partial expert systems is realized in a different fashion for each expert system. The expert system that aids the user to choose a data analysis method triggers a special dialogue in order to facilitate its interaction with the user. On the contrary the expert system for the selection of brand choice model carries out the selection of the model automatically; no interaction with the user is necessary. The expert system informs the user about its suggestion by showing a window where the market shares, according to the proposed brand choice model, are presented. Finally, the expert system for the evaluation of the financial situation of the enterprises takes as input the respective financial data; then by looking up in the knowledge base adds the results of its evaluation in the multicriteria table.

2.4 Data Management Subsystem

The data management subsystem allows the systematic storage, request, retrieval and maintenance of all the available data. Almost all of these operations are performed in the background without the involvement of the user in the tedious details of data management. The data bases used in this system are parts of the database management system.

The role of the subsystem includes the following:

1. Creation of the required data bases like:
   - Product sales data.
   - Financial data of enterprises.
   - Questions.
   - Answers.
   - Data analyses.
   - Frequencies.
   - Multicriteria evaluations.
   - Consumer utilities.
2. Update the system databases by adding, changing, and deleting entries.
3. Offers the possibility to create special filters for the creation of multicriteria evaluation tables.
4. Offers the possibility to create special filters for the selection of group of consumers and questions that meet certain conditions.

The data obtained from the consumers' responses is entered and processed with the help of worksheets similar to those of existing professional software products. All files, except the questions' files, are ASCII files so that they can also be used by other programs and vice versa.

Filters are one of the most powerful tools of the system, since they permit the selection of any desirable subset of data for processing, such as for example the multicriteria tables.

2.5 Model Management Subsystem – Models development

A key characteristic of a Decision Support System (Chapter 5, §4), and respectively of an Intelligent Decision Support System is the availability of a set of models that are used in order to analyse an abstracted representation of the reality and not the reality itself.

The system's model base consists of twenty different models (*Figure 1*), which are grouped according to the task in which they can be used.

The first four models are used in order to forecast the trends of the market. They take as input the historical data of sales in terms of volume and money, which are retrieved by the corresponding files.

The system offers to the user seven models for data analysis. The data that will be used in any of the available data analysis methods are selected by the user from the entire set of the consumers' answers file by using special selection filters that allow the selection of particular consumers and questions.

An important problem to be solved is that the selection of the suitable data analysis method is not trivial. It is a very difficult task because of the functional details of each analysis method and in general requires the presence of a filed expert. In an effort to solve the problem, the system integrates an appropriate expert system that can easily recommend to the user the most suitable data analysis method, based on the desired goal of the analysis and the specific type of the available data.

The multicriteria UTASTAR method is used in the study of consumers' behaviour. The results of the method are then used for the calculation of purchase probabilities and market shared of the examined products, according to the eight available brand choice models. An additional expert system is used in order to support the user in the selection of the most suitable brand choice model and in execution of simulations.

2.6 Expert Systems Subsystems

The system incorporates three partial Expert Systems, which operate completely independently of each other (Chapter 10, §2.6). This type of integration provides to the user of MARKEX two major advantages

a) Complete control on the management of information and on the decision making process through the DSS.
b) The exploitation of specialized knowledge, the ability of inference, and the provision of explanations for the derived conclusions, through the available expert systems.

Expert systems communicate with the remaining components of the system through the interface subsystem. In order to facilitate the interaction of the user with the three available expert systems, the interface subsystem of MARKEX is composed of three different subsystems (Chapter. 10, §2.6.1, 2 and 3), one for each expert system. Each of them has a different way of presenting itself to the user.

The interface subsystem for the selection of the data analysis system is the most obvious one. The subsystem interacts with the user initially by requesting some information and then by presenting certain alternative actions. Finally, the subsystem proposes the suitable data analysis model.

The interface subsystem for the selection of the brand choice model presents itself only by showing on the screen the graphic illustration of the results of the application of the proposed model. The user is being informed of this recommendation by the simultaneous appearance on the screen of the market shares according to the proposed model and an auxiliary presentation giving further information on the selection. There is no other type of interaction between the user and the subsystem.

Finally, the third subsystem which handles the evaluation of the financial situation of the enterprise will appear adding its own evaluations on the financial situation of the enterprises participating with their products in the "Market", which are added to the data of the existing multicriteria table.

The interaction between expert systems subsystems and the inference engine is realized through input-output channels, which are able to transmit assignments, facts, statements, answers and messages.

Knowledge bases communicate with the inference engine, which can use either forward or backward reasoning, depending on the desired result. The data required for each knowledge base are retrieved from the respective databases.

In relation with the issues detailed in Chapter 7, §2.1, for the structure of the expert systems, *Figure 2* illustrates the structure of the three expert subsystems of MARKEX.

For the creation of knowledge bases, initially available information was collected from the international literature as well as from field experts. Then this information was codified according to the requirements and the capabilities of the kernel M4 used for the development of the expert systems. Then, the soundness of the acquired knowledge was exhaustively tested.

After the necessary corrections and improvements, the following three knowledge bases were constructed:
1. Knowledge base for the selection of data analysis method.
2. Knowledge base for the selection of market simulation model.
3. Knowledge base for the evaluation of the financial status of enterprises.

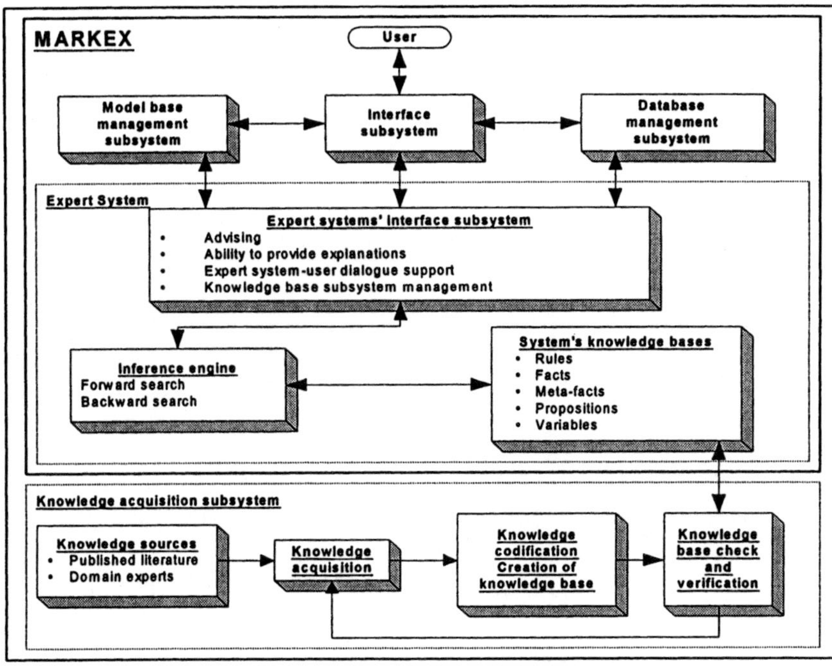

Figure 2. Structure of expert systems

The development – codification of the knowledge bases was based on rules, facts, meta-facts, propositions, and variables. The acquired knowledge is stored in the form of rules which are created, by the use of AND, OR and NOT operators (*Figure 3*). The development-codification of the knowledge bases includes rules, facts, meta-facts, propositions, and variables (Cimflex Teknowledge, 1993).

With facts we assign values to expressions, which are then used in rules. The meta-facts were used in order to provide information to the user and proper guidance concerning the required input of certain values. Thus, when the user is prompted to enter an input that will determine the next action of the system, a message with the following form is used:

question(target-data-anal) =
"What is your target?".

The user's response is assigned to the expression target-data-anal. Depending on the answer the flow of the consultation tasks is determined.

Propositions have the same form with facts. However, the veracity of propositions has to be confirmed whereas the veracity of facts does not require establishment and it is taken for granted.

In the following section, we will examine the knowledge bases available in the system.

```
rule-47: if   target-data-anal = 1 and
              nb-of-var = NVar and
              NVar > 2 and
              NVar <= 7 and
              type-of-data = 3 and
              not (transform=5 or transform=6)
         then data-anal = 'Impossible'.
```

Figure 3. General form of rules

2.6.1 Knowledge Base for the Selection of Data Analysis Method

It is commonly accepted that the choice of a certain analysis method to be applied to a set of data is not a trivial problem. It usually requires the experience and special knowledge of an appropriate field expert. On the other hand, normally the marketing decision-maker is not assumed to posses this specific knowledge in the filed of data analysis. Therefore, in order to simplify things for the user and allow him to concentrate only to his decision making task, we considered the integration of an expert system that could recommend the most suitable data analysis method, based on the task at hand, i.e. the desired goal, and the selected data set. The only information needed by the user is to define the objective of the analysis.

The knowledge base was constructed by using information acquired from the international literature (Lagarde, 1983; SAS/STAT, 1990; Hair *et al.*, 1998; Berthold and Hand, 1999; Albright *et al.*, 1999) and also by the knowledge and experience of several field experts.

The user selects a specific data set that wishes to process with an analysis method (*Table 1*), and by this actions implicitly defines the type of data that wishes to analyse. Then the user is asked to explicitly define the objective of his analysis, because as shown in *Table 2*, each objective is attained more efficiently by a specific analysis methods. The advice of the expert system is based on these two factors.

Table 1. Data analysis methods available in MARKEX

Index	Data analysis method
1	Principal components analysis
1.1	Variables correlation table
1.2	Projection of rows-variables
1.3	Projection of columns-consumers
2	Correspondence analysis
2.1	Variability table
3	Multiple correspondence analysis
3.1	Variability table
4	Simple regression
5	Multiple regression
6	Q-analysis (by row)
6.1	Q-analysis (by column)
7	Descriptive statistics

Table 2 presents the objectives of the decision-maker and the corresponding data analysis methods that satisfy these efficiently.

Table 2 Correspondence between data analysis methods and goals of the analysis

	Objectives of the analysis	Data analysis methods
1	Examination of similarities – dissimilarities among variables	Principal Components Analysis Correspondence Analysis Multiple Correspondence Analysis
2	Examination of similarities – dissimilarities among consumers	Principal Components Analysis
3	Investigation of relations between variables and consumers	Principal Components Analysis
4	Investigation of intensity relations among variables	Simple Regression Multiple Regression Variables correlation table Variability table (2,1) Variability table (3.1)
5	Examination of potential grouping of variables	Q-analysis (by column) Projection of columns-consumers
6	Examination of potential grouping of consumers	Q-analysis (by row) Projection of rows-variables
7	Determination of sizes	Descriptive statistics

In addition, the selected data set defines the type of the data that will be processed whereas the number of the selected variables affects the selection of the applicable method. The requirements for the application of the considered data analysis methods are listed in *Table 3*.

Table 3. Technical requirements for the application of data analysis methods.

	Data Analysis Method	Number of Variables	AND Number of Dependent Variables	Type of Dependent Variables	Number of Independent Variables	Type of Independent Variables
1	Principal Components Analysis	> 2	0	-	-	Quantitative
2	Correspondence Analysis	= 2	0	-	-	Order
3	Multiple Correspondence Analysis	> 2	0	-	-	Order
4	Simple Regression	= 2	1	Quantitative	= 1	Quantitative
5	Multiple Regression	> 2	1	Quantitative	> 1	Quantitative
6	Q-Analysis	> 2	0	-	-	Binary
7	Descriptive Statistics	>= 1	0	-	-	Order

The characterization of a database that consists of several types of variables depends on the number of these variables. In the development of the examined knowledge base, we have accepted that if the number of a certain type of variables is greater than the 80% of the entire set of the variables contained in the data set, and then the data set is assumed only to consists of variables of this type. In any other case, we cannot define a single type of variables (mixed case) and prior to the application of the data analysis method the user should consider an appropriate re-transformation of the variables. *Table 4* lists all the data conversion recommended by the system.

Table 4. Codification of data conversion

	Type of variables	Transitional conversion	Type of variables after conversion
1	Qualitative	None	Qualitative
1	Quantitative	Grouping	Order
1	Binary	None	Binary
1	Order	None	Order
2	Qualitative	Re-codification	Binary
2	Quantitative	None	Quantitative
2	Binary	None	Binary
2	Order	Re-codification	Binary
3	Qualitative	Split level	Binary
3	Quantitative	Split level	Binary
3	Binary	None	Binary
3	Order	Split level	Binary

2.6.2 Knowledge Base for Brand Choice Selection

The study of consumer behaviour has gained an important fraction of attention and scientific research in marketing science. A broad variety of efforts and theories that attempt to describe the factors which influence the consumers in their purchasing decisions along with models which attempt to provide an estimate of the product's purchasing probabilities have been developed. Usually, in the application of these brand choice models, it is assumed that consumers share the same type of behaviour and attitudes and in any case a single model can be used in order to derive the purchasing probabilities for the examined products. However, the study of the utility functions, estimated by the help of multicriteria analysis methods, reveals that this assumption may lead to an erroneous abstraction of the reality. The distribution of preferences, which differs from consumer to consumer, indicates that each individual shares different attitudes and types of behaviour towards the examined products. Therefore, a more realistic approach would involve the selection of the most applicable model based on the type of consumer behaviour and the inherent characteristics of the model itself. However, most decision-makers do not possess the necessary knowledge to perform this type of analysis. An approach that can actually aid the analysis is to develop a convenient and comprehensive mechanism, which matches an appropriate brand choice model to each consumer, and provides the decision maker with the most applicable brand choice model.

After the estimation of the utility function, the purchasing decisions of the consumers are modelled by using brand choice models. Brand choice models take as input the estimated utilities and provide the probability for each consumer to buy a product. A very difficult problem in marketing decision-making situations is the selection of the most suitable brand choice model for the analysis. This selection is based on one hand on the types of the consumer behaviour and on the other hand on the special characteristics of the model itself. In most cases, the decision-maker has no access to this information and he/she is unable to select the most suitable model to be used in the analysis.

Therefore, the solution that we propose is the development of a knowledge base for brand choice model selection. The developed model (rules) is based on two factors:

a) the behaviour of the consumers which is measured through the range and type of distribution of assigned utilities and,
b) the observation of the applicability of specific brand choice models on certain types of consumer behaviour.

Consumers make decisions (choices) when they decide to buy a certain product among a set of products (alternatives) that form the "market". Their decision is always based in multiple criteria. This implies that consumers always take into account multiple features of the products and use them to build into their minds a model of preferences. For example, consider a consumer who has to decide between two products. He or she will most certainly will look at the price of the products, their quality, their package, the advertisement, etc. These criteria have certain values for each product (although may be vague) in the mind of the consumer. Some criteria are considered more important than others are. For instance, price is more probably a very dominant feature for a middle class consumer where as the quality or the package of the product might be features that are more significant for a wealthy person. The values of all the criteria are synthesized and a preference structure is build. This model of preferences aggregates the values of the criteria for each product and forms an order of preferences. Based on this model the consumer finally decides which product to purchase and which products to reject.

The problem is to discover, describe, model and finally predict the various procedures or patterns used by a consumer in his/her decision making process. This problem is not a trivial one. Individual consumers (or subgroups of consumers with the same behaviour) have different attitudes and preferences and use different decision patterns in their own purchasing decisions. Since decisions are made by implicitly assigning values in multiple criteria, the goal is to describe the process and predict the outcome (the decision) when we have explicit knowledge of the multicriteria evaluations of the consumers.

The estimation of a utility function for each consumer enables the analyst to discover a model of preferences for each consumer, i.e. to discover a pattern that is followed by the consumers in their purchasing decisions. The next problem to be solved is to use the utilities, which measure and map the preferences of a consumer, in order to calculate a purchasing probability for each consumer and each product. This is accomplished by the employment of brand choice models. The problem is that if the same brand choice model is used for all the consumers we have to assume that they all share similar attitudes and preference structures. However, the resulting utility functions reveal that this is a very strong argument. The estimated utilities vary significantly from consumer to consumer. The distribution of the utilities and the shape of the utility function are quite different for each consumer (see for example *Figure 4*). This implies that consumers have different preference structures and they exhibit different decision patterns. For example in Case 1 presented in *Figure 4* the consumer assigns almost equal utility values to each alternative and thus he/she is unable to select a most preferred product and ignore the remaining ones. In contrast, Case 4 of

Figure 4 presents a very different situation where a well-established order of preferences enables the consumer to make a final decision.

In addition, brand choice models exhibit different characteristics that render them to more efficiently represent some preference structures than others. As a conclusion due to different patterns in consumer behaviour and due to different characteristics of brand choice models, the analysis would be more efficient if we could apply different models to different types of consumers. As pointed out by Lilien *et al.* (1992) consumers are different. They vary according to their personalities, values, preferences, and a range of other characteristics. These differences mean that a model that is appropriate for describing the behaviour of one particular consumer may be inadequate in explaining the behaviour of another.

If the decision maker or the analyst attempt to employ different models depending on the type of consumer preferences and the properties of the brand choice model then the problem shifts to the selection of the most suitable model. Usually, decision-makers are unaware of this type of information.

In this section, we describe a heuristic method that uses information on the distribution of utilities in order to describe different types of consumer behaviour and accordingly lead to the selection of an appropriate brand choice model to represent them. The heuristic is based on the observation that the final decision of the consumers is based on two factors. First, the range of the difference between the maximum and minimum values of the estimated utilities determine the consumer's ability to define a well-established order of preferences and accordingly select a product (or a subset of products) as the most preferred. The second factor that affects this decision is the distribution of utilities in this range; the symmetry or asymmetry of the distribution of the assigned utilities affects the partition of the products in classes of preferences.

Let

$$\delta \ (0 \le \delta \le 1)$$

be a parameter that represents the difference between the maximum and minimum values of the utilities, assigned implicitly by a consumer to the examined set of products. Thus, δ defines the range of assigned utilities,

$$\delta = U_{\max} - U_{\min})$$

Depending of the range of utilities δ, we can define four distinct cases of consumer behaviour. A typical illustrative example of each case is depicted in *Figure 4*, where the products are consecutively numbered from *1* to *n* according to increasing utility values. In each case consumers express a different type of attitude and preferences (*Table 5*).

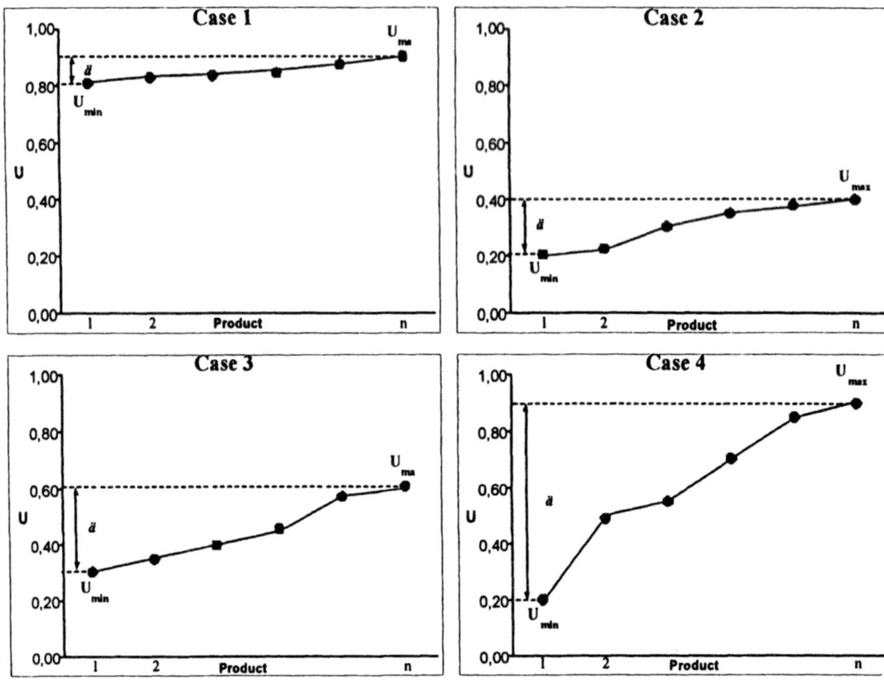

Figure 4. Examples of representative utility functions

Case 1 $(0 \le \delta \le 0.1)$. In this case, the consumers implicitly assign similar utilities to all the examined products. This means that consumers expect to retain the same level of utility despite of their final decision. They feel unable to segregate the products and they reveal their reluctance by implicitly assigning to them an equal amount of utility. The established order of preferences cannot lead to the selection of a subset of preferred products that clearly outranks the rest of the products. Imagine the situation where for example six products are assigned the following utilities: (0.9, 0.87, 0.85, 0.84, 0.83, and 0.81). Due to negligible differences in the expressed preferences between products, the consumer is unable to select a subset of products as comparatively accepted choice. In this example, all the products are equally preferred by the consumer, i.e. they are all considered to be good purchasing decisions. Consider an adverse situation where a consumer has implicitly assigned a very small utility value for each of the examined products, for example (0.20, 0.18, 0.17, 0.15, 0.14, and 0.12). In this case, the consumer expresses an aversion towards the whole set of products. All the alternative decisions are considered almost unacceptable. In both cases, the effect in the final decision is the same, i.e. the selection of the purchasing product is accomplished randomly between a set of products that share the same importance. In other words, the consumer follows a random decision making pattern.

Case 2 ($0.1 < \delta \le 0.3$). In this case, the range of utilities distribution is wider. The consumer feels that some products are more important than others but still his/her order of preferences prevent the selection of a subset of most preferred purchasing alternatives. He or she cannot observe substantial differences between the alternative decisions. Again, the consumer by assigning very close utility values to all the examined products expresses his/her difficulty to separate them into distinct classes of preferences.

Case 3 ($0.3 \le \delta \le 0.6$). Here the consumers have established a more clear order of preference. However, there is still no significant difference between the products' utility values. Thus, the consumer encounters a relative reluctance in separating the products in discrete classes of preferences.

Case 4 ($\delta > 0.6$). This is probably the clearest situation. In this case, the consumer has separated the set of products into classes of preference and he or she has a well-established strong preference over a subset of products. The difference between the assigned utility values is wide enough in order to result in some acceptable products and some unacceptable ones. The consumer express a clear preference to the products with assigned utilities closed to the maximum utility value. The difference between the class of the most preferred products and the products with a low assigned utility value is very high and consequently we have the separation of products into two major classes of preference. The first class of products i.e. products with utilities close to $U_{\max}$, have a great purchasing probability where as the purchasing probability for the rest of the products is minimum.

Table 5. Codification of the δ parameter and corresponding decision making patterns

Index	Value of δ	Segregation capability	Consumer's decision making pattern
1	$0 \le \delta \le 0.1$	None	Random choice
2	$0.1 < \delta \le 0.3$	Average	Reluctance
3	$0.3 \le \delta \le 0.6$	Efficient	Relative reluctance
4	$0.6 \le \delta \le 1$	Strong	Brand loyalty

A first partition of consumers' attitudes and decision-making patterns is achieved by considering the value of the range of utilities δ (*Table 5*). We may attempt to explore more extensively each case presented in *Table 5* by investigating the shape of the utility distribution for each value of δ and by studying the symmetry and the kurtosis of this distribution.

The range of utilities δ can be further subdivided in smaller intervals ε_i:

$$\varepsilon_i = (U_{\min} + (i-1)e, U_{\min} + ie),\ i = 1,2,\ldots,n-1,$$

with equal width ε

$$\varepsilon = \frac{\delta}{n-1}$$

where *n* is the number of the market products.

Let x_i, $i = 1,2,\ldots,n-1$ be the midpoint of each interval $[U_{\min} + i\varepsilon, U_{\min} + (i-1)\varepsilon]$ i.e.

$$x_i = U_{\min} + (2i-1)\frac{\varepsilon}{2},\ i = 1,2,\ldots,n-1$$

A graphical representation of these parameters using a sample utility function is presented in *Figure 5*.

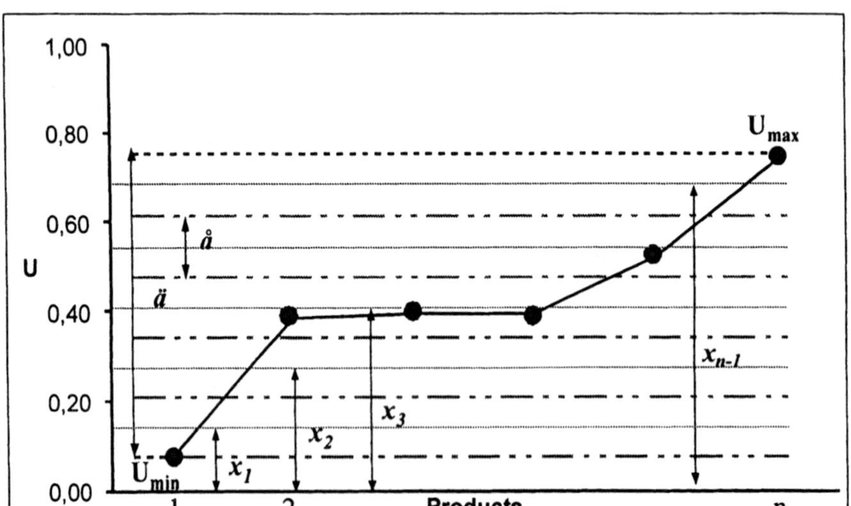

Figure 5. Graphical representation of the parameters used

Next, the number f_i of products with assigned utilities in each interval ε_i are calculated. Let μ be the mean value of the frequencies of the products

$$\mu = \frac{\sum_{i=1}^{n-1} f_i x_i}{\sum_{i=1}^{n-1} f_i}$$

The $r - th$ central moment is defined as

$$m_r = \frac{\sum_{i=1}^{n-1} f_i (x_i - \mu)^r}{\sum_{i=1}^{n-1} f_i}$$

Using these definitions we can calculate the skewness and kurtosis coefficients α_3 and α_4 respectively:

$$\alpha_3 = \frac{m_3}{\sigma^3} = \frac{m_3}{\sqrt{m_2^{\,3}}}$$

$$\alpha_4 = \frac{m_4}{m_2^{\,2}} - 3 = \frac{m_4}{\sqrt{\sigma^4}} - 3$$

Skewness characterizes the degree of asymmetry of the distribution around its mean. Positive skewness indicates a distribution with an asymmetric tail extending toward values that are more positive. Negative skewness indicates a distribution with an asymmetric tail extending toward values that are more negative. Kurtosis characterizes the relative peakedness or flatness of a distribution compared with the normal distribution. Positive kurtosis indicates a relatively peaked distribution. Negative kurtosis indicates a relatively flat distribution.

We assume that a distribution of products is symmetric when skewness takes values in the interval [-0.25, 0.25]. A negative asymmetric distribution exists when $a_3 > 0.25$ where as a value of $a_3 < -0.25$ indicates a positive asymmetric distribution of products (*Figure 6*).

In addition, when the kurtosis coefficient takes values in the interval [-0.5,0.5] we assume that the distribution of products is normal. If $\alpha_4 > 0.5$ then, the curve is high and pointed where as if $\alpha_4 < -0.5$ the curve is wide and flat (*Figure 6*).

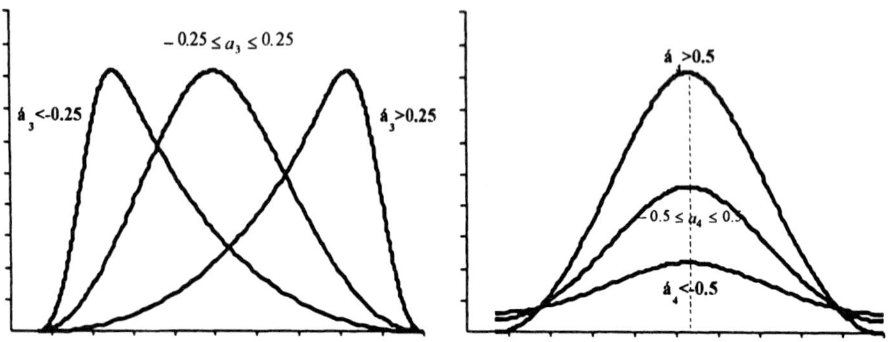

Figure 6. Shapes of distribution for different values of skewness and kurtosis coefficients

The calculation of the skewness and kurtosis coefficients permits us to define and explore different classes of consumers' behaviour within the same value of the range of utilities. The only exception lies in the first case of *Figure 6* where the range of utilities is very small i.e. there is a high density of utilities concentrated in a very small interval. In this case, we are unable to identify any further differences based on the observation of the skewness and kurtosis parameters.

Although, the investigation on the distribution of utilities permits us to define different types of consumer behaviour, it is quite difficult for a decision maker to take into account all the factors that could lead him to select the most suitable brand choice model. It would more efficient to develop simple "if...then" rules that describe the behaviour of the consumer and accordingly suggest an appropriate model. These rules could be easily adopted in a knowledge-based decision support system and form an additional tool for the best representation of the market environment. In addition, the decision-maker will be able to concentrate only to the analysis of consumer behaviour be receiving suggestions of the knowledge base without the necessity to dig into puzzling details.

Considering the issues detailed earlier we may develop rules based on two considerations:

1. The range of utilities δ consists a very dominant factor in the purchasing decision of the consumer.
2. The values of skewness and kurtosis coefficients describe different types of behaviour within the same value of δ .

Experience and extensive simulation tests have shown that the brand choice models (*Table 6*) exhibit different segregation capabilities. Each model represents in a more efficient manner specific type of consumer's attitudes. Therefore, the analysis would probably yield better results if we could apply to each consumer the brand choice model that best describes his/her type of preferences.

Table 6 presents the brand choice models in ascending order of segregation capability. The McFadden-1 model exhibits the lowest segregation capability from all the considered models in contrast with the Maximum of Utilities model, which shows the maximum segregation capabilities. Finally, the last model in *Table 6* (Equal Probabilities model) is used in order to describe certain situations where the consumer is unable to select some products.

Table 6. Codification of brand choice models in ascending segregation capability

Code	Brand choice model
1	McFadden-1
2	McFadden-2
3	Width of utilities-1
4	Width of utilities-2
5	Luce
6	Lesourne
7	Maximum Utilities
8	Equal Probabilities

Considering the values of the parameters and the different characteristics of the brand choice models a knowledge base consisting of 26 rules has been developed. The condition of each rule first examines the value of the range of utilities δ (delta), according to the codification presented in *Table 5*, and subsequently the values of the skewness and kurtosis coefficients, α_3 (Skew) and α_4 (Kurt) respectively. The result of each rule is the suggestion of a brand choice model according to the codification presented in *Table 6*.

The development of this knowledge base once again reveals that analytical models combined with concepts originating from Artificial Intelligence provide simple but vigorous tools to the decision makers. The main advantage of this approach is the fact that several types of consumers' behaviour, that are difficult to be observed by the decision-maker, are modelled with simple "if...then" rules. The analysis is encapsulated into a simple framework and the decision-maker is provided only with a simple suggestion that permits him to select the most suitable model for analysing consumer behaviour and purchasing attitudes.

However, this methodology could be further extended. The first objective is to study the behaviour of additional brand choice models in order to develop rules that could explain more efficiently the preferences of the consumers. A second objective is to develop rules that are probabilistic rather than deterministic. Probabilistic rules might exhibit a higher degree of flexibility. In the developed knowledge base each rule states that the behaviour of a consumer is explained by one and only brand choice model, in other words the behaviour of a certain consumer is explained by a certain model with a probability equal to one. The goal is to develop rules that assign probabilities to the representation potentiality of the models i.e. rules that provide the probability in which the model can describe a certain consumer. For example such rules can state that model A describes consumer x with probability P_A where as model B could describe the same consumer x with probability P_B.

In addition, we feel that is extremely important to state that these rules, regardless of their exact formation, simply form a tool, which is integrated into an Intelligent Decision Support System. The goal in decision support is not to replace the decision makers by models but rather to aid the decision making process by providing necessary and efficient tools. This implies that the developed rules will always be offered as a suggestion to the decision-maker. The decision-maker can either accept this suggestion or he/she can override it and base his analysis in his/her knowledge, intuition or personal judgments.

2.6.3 Knowledge Base for Financial Situation Estimation

The attempt of the decision-maker to select the most suitable strategy of penetration of the product to be developed requires knowledge of the financial position of the enterprises participating in the survey. Having established this knowledge, the decision-maker can examine the different scenarios with greater confidence for his final decision.

Financial problems constitute a very complex field, since many factors have to be taken into account and there is no precisely structured procedure for making these decisions. Financial analysis is based on the use of financial ratios in order to estimate the strong and weak points of an enterprise. Financial analysis usually reveals the competitive position of the enterprise within its branch and generally within a specific economy structure. This information is essential for the determination of the marketing strategy to be followed. However, the estimation of the financial position of enterprises requires special knowledge, which the normal user of MARKEX usually does not have. It was tried to satisfy this need of decision makers in the field of marketing by developing an expert system for the estimation of the financial status of enterprises (Matsatsinis, 1995; Zopounidis *et al.*, 1996; 1997). Many other researchers have also attempted to develop similar systems (see Mui and McCarthy, 1987; Sena and Smith, 1987). However, this is the first time that the estimations of such a system are introduced in a multicriteria table and are taken into account for the estimation of marketing strategies. Details of this knowledge base, which has been developed and used in MARKEX, are described below.

First, a database with financial data has to be created from the balance sheets and the commercial accounts of the enterprises taking part in the research. Thus, if the system has to express its opinion on the status of an enterprise, it retrieves the necessary information from the suitable database in the form of ratios, which then are used to express its estimation. The backbone of the knowledge base is comprised by the rules, (Newell and Simon, 1958; Rich and Knight, 1991). Each rule is a separate piece of the expert's knowledge and expertise. The adopted structure of production rules not only allows the efficient representation of the knowledge but also the check of the procedures that are followed in the search of the conclusions. From a technical point of view, the knowledge base is developed so as to represent the rules combined with the AND and OR logical operators.

In the proposed expert system, the adopted classification of financial ratios is based primarily on the methodology developed by Courtis (1978). According to this methodology, the ratios are divided into three basic categories: effectiveness, management proficiency, and solvency. Further qualitative criteria for the estimation of enterprises have been added to these ratios (Table 3).

Table 7. Financial rations and qualitative criteria of the system

Code	Ratios
	Effectiveness Ratios
A_1	Profits pro Interest Rates and Taxes / Total of Assets
A_2	Net Profits after Taxes / Own Capitals
A_3	Mixed Profits / Total of Assets
A_4	Net Profits / Mixed Profits
	Solvency Ratios
B_1	Short Term Obligations / Total Liabilities
B_2	Total of Obligations / Total of Assets
B_3	Long-term Obligations / (Long-term Obligations + Own Capital)
B_4	Circulating Assets / Short-term Obligations
B_5	(Circulating Assets - Stocks) / Short-term Obligations
B_6	Stocks *365 / Cost of Sales
B_7	(Customers + Bills to be Cashed) * 365 / Total of Net Sales
	Managerial Performance Ratios
C_1	Financial Expenses / Sales
C_2	General and Administrative Expenses / Sales
C_3	(Claims)* 365 / Yearly Sales
C_4	(Accounts to be Paid) * 365 / Purchase of Raw and Secondary Materials
	Qualitative Criteria
D_1	Administrative Experience of Managers

Code	Ratios
D_2	Position of the Enterprise in the Market
D_3	Technological Structure of the Enterprise
D_4	Organization
D_5	Specific Competitive Advantages of the Enterprise
D_6	Flexibility of the Market.

The ratios that were finally used in the development of the knowledge base are listed in *Table 7*. *Table 8* presents the threshold values of the proposed ratios of managerial performance, effectiveness, and solvency, which are the elementary rules of the knowledge base. These figures were determined by the study of the literature and by the evaluations and opinions of financial experts. The threshold values of the qualitative criteria are listed in *Table 9*.

Table 8. Threshold values of financial ratios

If	Then	Is
$A_1<10\%$	Industrial profitability	Not satisfactory
$10\%<A_1\leq20\%$	Industrial profitability	Medium
$20\%<A_1\leq30\%$	Industrial profitability	Satisfactory
$A_1>30\%$	Industrial profitability	Very satisfactory
$A_2\leq17.5\%$	Financial profitability	Not satisfactory
$17.5\%<A_2\leq20\%$	Financial profitability	Medium
$20\%<A_2\leq23\%$	Financial profitability	Satisfactory
$23\%<A_2$	Financial profitability	Very satisfactory
$A_3\leq0\%$	Gross profit/Total assets	Not satisfactory
$0\%<A_3\leq50\%$	Gross profit/Total assets	Medium
$50\%<A_3\leq75\%$	Gross profit/Total assets	Satisfactory
$A_3>75\%$	Gross profit/Total assets	Very satisfactory
$A_4\leq0\%$	Profit margin	Not satisfactory
$0\%<A_4\leq50\%$	Profit margin	Medium
$50\%<A_4\leq100\%$	Profit margin	Satisfactory
$A_4>100\%$	Profit margin	Very satisfactory
$B_1<25\%$	Short-term debt capacity	Very satisfactory
$25\%<B_1\leq50\%$	Short-term debt capacity	Satisfactory
$50\%<B_1\leq75\%$	Short-term debt capacity	Medium
$75\%<B_1\leq100\%$	Short-term debt capacity	Not satisfactory
$B_2>80\%$	Global debt capacity	Not satisfactory
$60\%<B_2\leq80\%$	Global debt capacity	Medium
$40\%<B_2\leq60\%$	Global debt capacity	Satisfactory
$B_2\leq40\%$	Global debt capacity	Very satisfactory
$B_3\leq0.5$	Long-term debt capacity	Satisfactory
$B_3>0.5$	Long-term debt capacity	Not satisfactory

If	Then	Is
$B_4 \geq 2$	General liquidity	Satisfactory
$B_4 < 2$	General liquidity	Not satisfactory
$B_5 \leq 1$	Direct liquidity	Not satisfactory
$1 < B_5 < 1.5$	Direct liquidity	Satisfactory
$B_5 \geq 1.5$	Direct liquidity	Very satisfactory
$C_1 > 5\%$	Financial expenses	Not satisfactory
$3\% < C_1 \leq 5\%$	Financial expenses	Medium
$2\% < C_1 \leq 3\%$	Financial expenses	Satisfactory
$C_1 \leq 2\%$	Financial expenses	Very satisfactory
$C_2 > 8\%$	General & administrative expenses	Not satisfactory
$6\% < C_2 \leq 8\%$	General & administrative expenses	Medium
$4\% < C_2 \leq 6\%$	General & administrative expenses	Satisfactory
$2\% < C_2 \leq 4\%$	General & administrative expenses	Very satisfactory
$C_2 \leq 2\%$	General & administrative expenses	Perfect
$C_3 > C_4$	Receiving period of accounts receivable	Not satisfactory
$C_3 \leq C_4$	Receiving period of accounts receivable	Satisfactory
C_5 increasing	Circulation of inventories	Not satisfactory
C_5 reducing or stable	Circulation of inventories	Satisfactory
$C_6 \leq C_7$	Circulation of customers and notes receivable	Satisfactory
$C_6 > C_7$	Circulation of customers and notes receivable	Not satisfactory

In order to validate the soundness of the knowledge base, repetitive tests were carried out by comparing the evaluations of financial experts with the results produced by the system. The developed knowledge base was also used as a framework for the development other systems, such as the FINEVA system (cf. Zopounidis *et al.*, 1996; Matsatsinis *et al.*, 1997).

Table 9. Threshold values of qualitative criteria

If	Is	Then
Managers' work experience	Negative experience	Not satisfactory
	No experience at all	Medium
	Positive experience up to 5 years	Satisfactory
	Positive experience 5-10 years	Very satisfactory
	Positive experience more than 10 years	Perfect
Firm's market niche/position	Strong competition, firm's weak position	Not satisfactory
	Strong competition, established and competitive firm	Medium
	Moderate competition, firm's strong position	Satisfactory
	Weak competition, firm's leadership position	Very satisfactory
	Singe position, monopoly	Perfect
Technical structure-facilities	Old an inappropriate equipment, outdated production methods	Not satisfactory

If	Is	Then
	Moderate technical structure, non-competitive production cost	Medium
	Relatively modernized equipment	Satisfactory
	Sound technical structure, full modernization scheme under way	Very satisfactory
	Excellent structure, modern production methods	Perfect
Organisation-personnel	Moderate organisation/staff hiring policy, willingness to improve	Satisfactory
	Good organisation/staff hiring policy	Very satisfactory
	Excellent organisation/staff hiring policy	Perfect
Firm's special competitive advantages	The firm does not possess expertise for its production methods	Medium
	The firm possesses a small amount of expertise for its production methods	Satisfactory
	The firm possesses a satisfactory level of expertise for its production methods	Very satisfactory
	The firm does not follow market trends, produces low-demand products	Not satisfactory
Market flexibility	The firm has a limited flexibility	Not satisfactory
	The firm has a satisfactory flexibility	Medium satisfactory
	The firm follows market trends	Very satisfactory
	The firm is a leader in its production branch activity	Perfect

3. SYSTEM ANALYSIS AND DESIGN

In this section, we will examine the details of the system's analysis and design by quoting its data flow and hierarchical diagrams and the internal representation of the files. Further details on the analysis and designs of information systems can be found on IBM, (1974), Yourdon and Constantine, (1975); Myers, (1975); DeMacro, (1978); Gane and Sarson, (1979); Alford, (1985); Ross, (1985); Yourdon, (1989); Whitten *et al.*, (1989); and Sommervill, (1992). In the analysis and design of MARKEX the representation according to Gane and Sarson (1979) has been followed.

3.1 Data flow Diagrams

The first data flow diagram (*Figure 7*), which consists the zero level of the system, shows the basic flow data in the expert marketing decision support system and all the sources if information that are used by the system. This information is processed by the various components of the system and then are either saved or directly presented to the decision-maker.

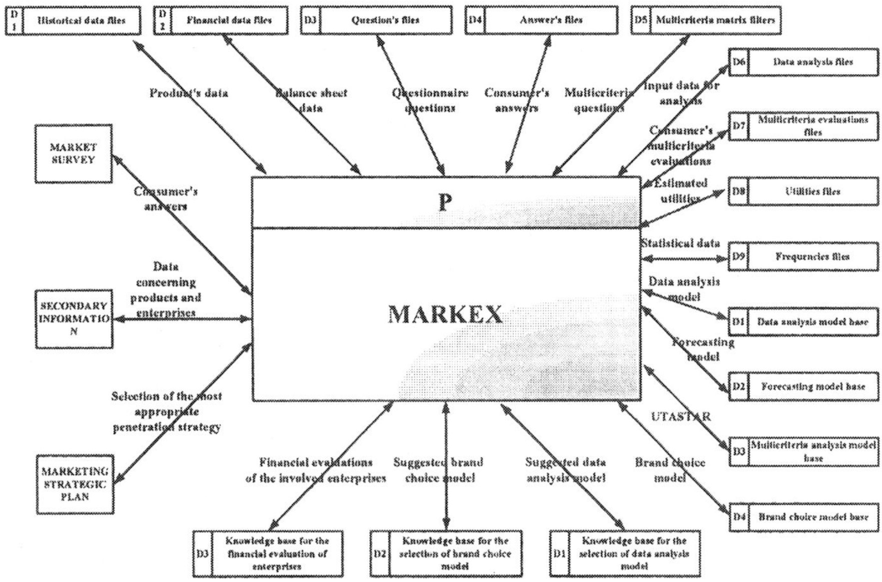

Figure 7. Data flow diagram of the marketing intelligent decision support system

There are two major sources of information:

a) The collected, through the market survey, questionnaires with the responses of the consumers.
b) All the other information collected by secondary (relevant) sources, which are related with the products and the companies that are considered in the market survey.

Input data as well as all the information derived by the processing of the original data, are stored through the database management system to the respective appropriate databases.

The main functions of the MARKEX, and the associated flow of data among them in the first level, are presented in *Figure 7*.

We will begin our examination with the functions related with the database management subsystem. Through this subsystem, the user creates the various files of the system (*Figure 8*).

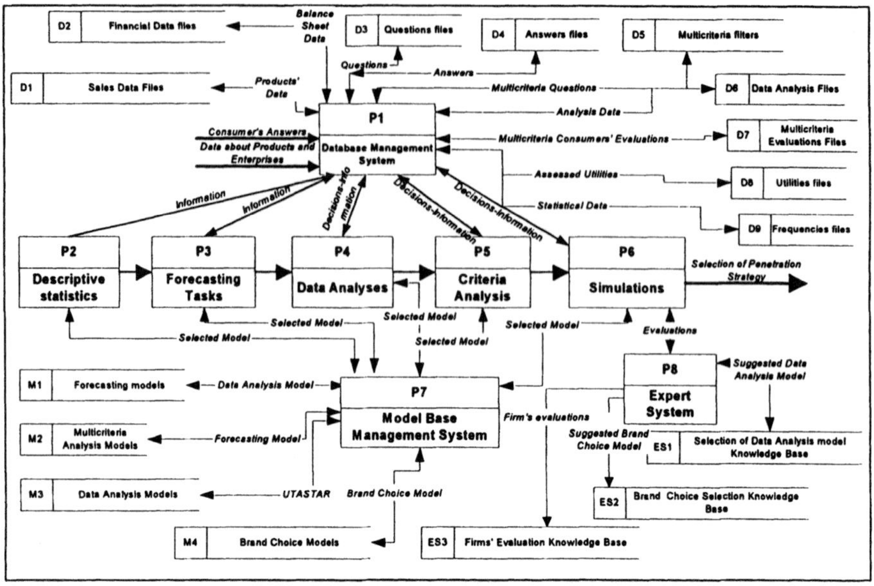

Figure 8. Data flow diagram of the main functions of MARKEX

In every case, the first files that are created are the questions files that contain the questions of the questionnaire, appropriately codified. After the creation of the questions files, the answers of the consumers are codified and entered into the system by creating the respective answers files. The questions and answers files are the two basic files of the system.

The information collected from secondary sources is related with two factors. The first involves figures related with the sales of the products whereas the second one with financial figures of the companies such as balance sheet data and profit and loss account data. This information is stored in the historical sales data files and financial data files respectively. The financial data files contains, in the form of ratios, the necessary information for the function of the expert system for the evaluation of the financial status of the participating companies.

Frequencies files are generated by the results of the descriptive statistics. Data analysis files contain the data set that will be used by a certain data analysis method. A data analysis file may contain, and respectively a data analysis method may be applied on, the complete set of questions or a subset of questions selected by the user.

The multicriteria matrix filters contain the codes of the questions that correspond with the answers of the consumers that will be used in order to construct the multicriteria matrix of each consumer. The data of the answers file pass through this filter and generate the multicriteria evaluations file, which in turn is processed by the UTASTAR method and results in the creation of the utilities file.

The statistical process of the market survey's data starts with the selection of the questions file. Then, the decision-maker selects the questions that will be processed. He is able to apply his analysis to the complete set of the consumers or to restrict his analysis to a subset of consumers by exploiting the possibilities offered by the system for the creation of consumers filters. Then, the suitable tables are created by the system and after the necessary calculations, the results are presented to the user.

The system's forecast models process the information contained in the historical sales data files. The user is prompted to enter the desired forecasting parameters.

Data analysis operations begin with the selection of the appropriate file. Again, the user may select a subset of consumers and concentrate his analysis only to them, by using the available consumer selection filters. These filters allow the inclusion to the data analysis only of those consumers with answers to specific questions within some values, determined by the decision-maker. If no filter is used, then the answers of the complete set of consumers are considered in the data analysis. After the selection of the data set, the user should select the desirable method of analysis. In this task, if he is not able to decide which model to use among the available ones, he may consult the recommendation of the respective expert system. After the selection of the method, the results can be either presented on the screen or printed.

The operation to be considered involves the study of the consumers' behaviour, through criteria analysis. First, the user selects the utilities file. Again, the user may select a subset of consumers in order to study the behaviour of specific market segments. For the chosen criteria the variance of their marginal utilities in relation with the respective percentages of consumers is presented. This allows the determination of the importance threshold for each criterion. By this threshold, the decision-maker is able to define if a criterion is determinant or non-determinant in the decision of the consumer to purchase a certain product. Thus, the marginal utilities assigned to each consumer are compared to the importance threshold. If the weight of a criterion, for a certain consumer, exceeds the importance threshold, then it is assumed that this criterion plays a decisive role in the purchase decision of the market products according to this consumer. Then for each criterion separately, the system sums up the consumers that consider this criterion determinant of their decision. By this, the system calculates the respective percentages of the consumers that consider the various criteria as determinant or non-determinant. In addition, the system is able to see these percentages for several different combinations of criteria. Based on the results of these combinations the decision-maker may detect a specific market segmentation and use it later on in the examination of various scenarios.

The determination and selection of the market segments is followed be the conduction of simulations. The flow of these tasks is analytically presented in Chapter 9, §9.7. The main functions of the simulations are:

- The selection of the simulation model.
- The determination of the "market" to be examined.
- The application of simple scenarios.
- The application of complex scenarios.
- The study of various strategies.

In the next level of analysis of the basic functions we find the selection of the simulation model, which is the first task that should be completed. First, the user selects the respective utilities file. Then, taking into account the results of the data and criteria analysis operations he uses the consumer selection filters in order to focus on a certain market segment. The system calculates the market shares of the products according to each brand choice model available in its model base. The results are presented to the decision-maker that should choose a certain model in order to be used for all the subsequent simulations. However, once again, an important question is if the decision-maker is able to select the right model. Is the normal marketing decision-maker able to take such a critical decision that will affect the entire decision making task? If the actual market shares are known, then we could assume that the decision-maker should simply select the model that goes near the actual figures. However, in most cases information on the actual market shares is not available, or it is incomplete or out of date. Therefore, we have to accept that the marketing decision-maker does not posses the knowledge and experience in order to select an applicable brand choice model. This fact joint with the importance of the selection of the simulation model in the decision task prompted us to develop and integrate into the system an expert system that acts as a consultant in the selection of the brand choice model. The developed knowledge base is grounded on the purchase intention of the survey products as these have been expressed through the consumers' answers.

If the decision-maker is not satisfied by the results, one of the possibilities offered by the system is to change the composition of the products "market". We may also use this possibility in order to introduce new products and their respective multicriteria evaluations into the analysis. In this way we are able to create whenever we believe it is necessary "New Markets" and study them. The ability to introduce and integrate into the analysis new products permits us to examine the reactions of the consumers when the characteristics of the new product are changing.

After the selection of the brand choice model, the determination of the composition of the new market, the introduction of the new product and its multicriteria evaluations, the decision maker proceeds to the application of various scenarios. With simple scenarios we are able to examine the shares of the market's products when the values of the criteria vary between specific bounds, set by the decision-maker. The order in which the multicriteria evaluations of the criteria vary is determined by which extent each criterion plays determinant role in the consumer's decisions, as described in Chapter 9, §9.5.

After the completion of simple scenarios, the decision-maker selects those scenarios that wishes to examine more exhaustively. One option is to select those scenarios that give approximate market shares with some others, but their implementation is cost is much more low. He also may fully reject either scenarios that give very small market shares or scenarios that give satisfactory shares but are associated with very high implementation cost. The results of the complex scenarios permit us to proceed with the final phase of the decision analysis task, which is the examination of different alternative strategies (Chapter 9, §9.7).

At this point the decision-maker has determined the composition of the "market" and has selected the possible development scenarios of the new product. We proceed with the selection of an independent criterion (the price of the product) and we define the bounds in which this criterion will vary. Then we determine the alternative strategies that we wish to examine when the value of the independent criterion varies between the specified limits. The decision-maker is also able to use the knowledge of experts in the sectors of distribution channels and promotion strategies. The evaluations of the experts are inserted in the existing multicriteria table. An additional, very important variable, in the selection of a penetration strategy is the evaluation of the financial status of the companies producing the products of the market. Normally, the decision-maker is unable to handle this problem. In the MARKEX system, the decision-maker is supported by the existence of the expert system used for the evaluation of the financial status of the firms. This expert system, exploiting the rules of the correspondence knowledge base, introduces its estimations in the existing multicriteria table. Then, the utilities and the market shares are re-assessed by the UTASTAR model taking into account these two additional sources of information. Thus, the decision-maker is able to examine the results of the considered strategies and finally select the most applicable penetration strategy of the new product into the market.

3.2 Hierarchical Diagrams

In this section, we will outline the structure of MARKEX by using hierarchical diagrams. The system's analysis is performed in nine levels. The main module, which is the starting section of the system's operations, is presented in the first level (*Figure 9*). Then we give the four main modules of operations 1.2-1.5 (*Figure 10-Figure 13*).

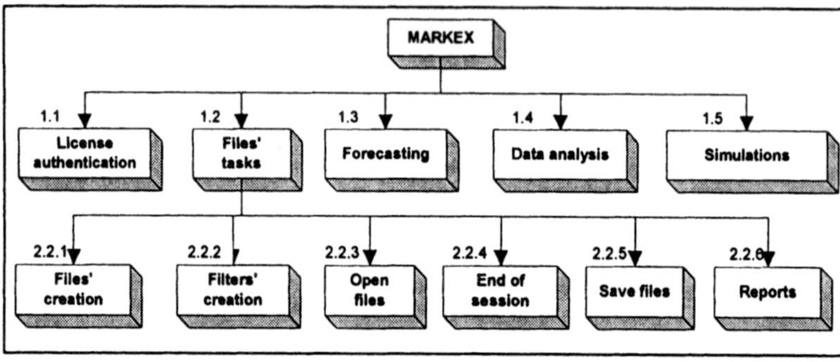

Figure 9. Hierarchical diagram of the system's main functions

A typical forecast procedure consists of the selection of the historical sales data file, the selection of the model, the input of the necessary parameters and finally the presentation of the results (*Figure 10*). In the third level of analysis, we find the available forecast models that are managed by the model base management system (3.3.2.1-3.3.2.5). *Figure 11* presents the modules that comprise the data analysis functions. In 2.4.2 we find the component that contains the interface procedures between the MARKEX and the expert system responsible for the selection of the data analysis method. Modules 3.4.3.1 through 3.4.3.7 present the components that contain the data analysis methods.

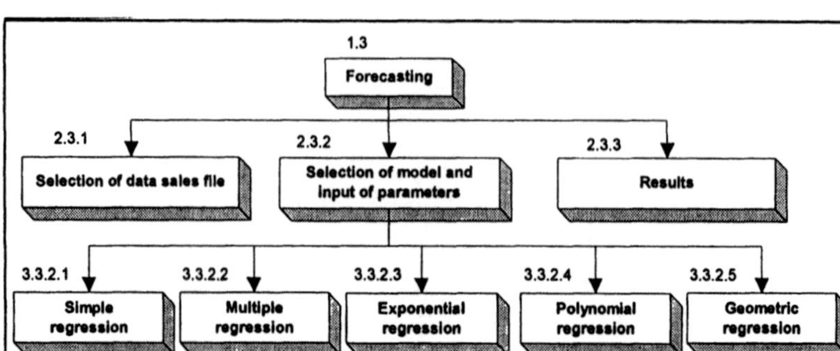

Figure 10. Hierarchical diagram of forecasting functions

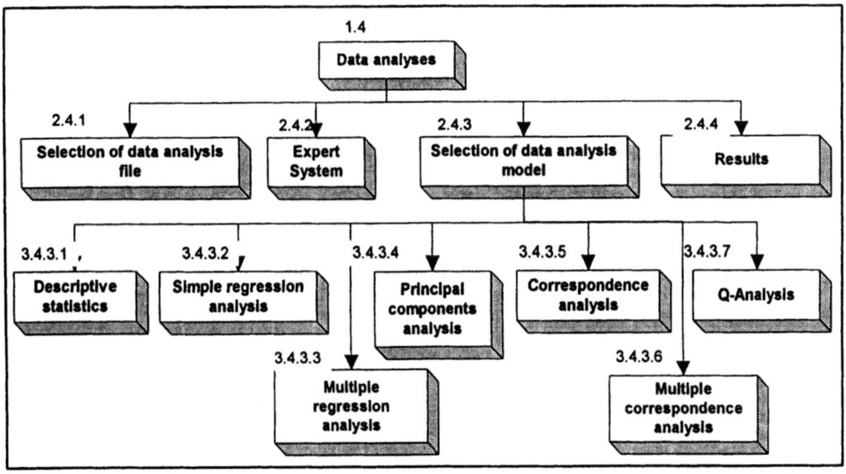

Figure 11. Hierarchical diagram of data analysis methods

Simulation tasks are presented in *Figure 12.* The main modules of simulations are located in the second level (2.5.1-2.5.6). The first task is further subdivided into two levels. Thus, the sub modules of the operations that consist the criteria importance modules are presented.

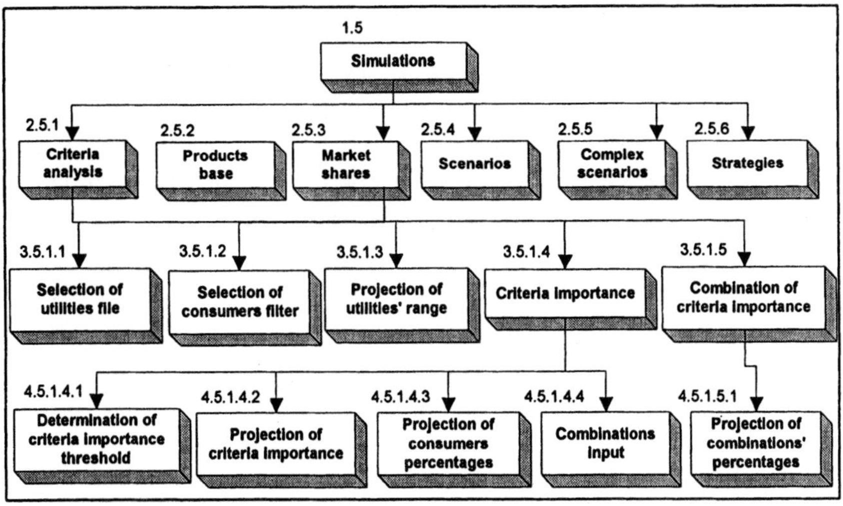

Figure 12. Hierarchical diagram of simulations

The next main module of the simulations consists of the procedures for the calculation of the market shares (*Figure 13*). The analysis at this point extends until the fifth level. The component 3.5.3.3 contains the interface operations of MARKEX with the expert system responsible for the selection of the brand choice model, presented in Chapter 10, §2.6.2. The calculation of the market shares is based on the brand choice models, the procedures of which are found in the fourth level (4.5.3.4.1-4.5.3.4.7). In the same level there are also the procedures that support the final stage of the simulation operations.

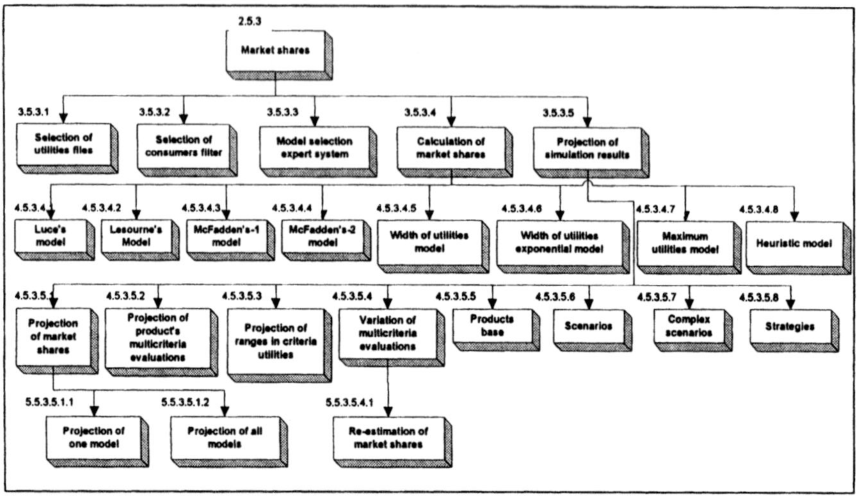

Figure 13. Hierarchical diagram of market shares

Figure 14 and *Figure 15* present the procedures that support the operations for the application of simple and complex scenarios and strategies. Also, in the strategies sections and in the fifth level of analysis there is the component that contains the interface operations of MARKEX with the expert system responsible for the evaluation of the financial status of the companies (see Chapter 10, §2.6.3).

One of the most significant modules of MARKEX is the database management system (component 1.2). File management activities are mainly located into this module. However, other procedures are carried out outside of this module as partial functions of other components.

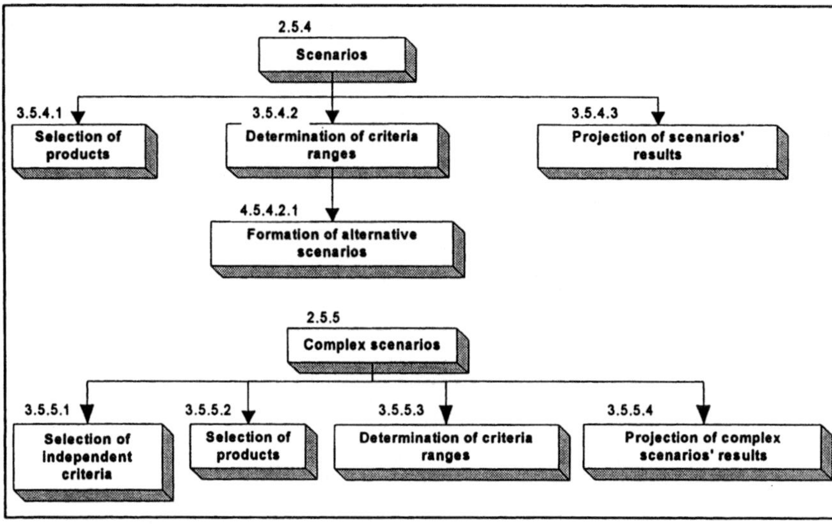

Figure 14. Hierarchical diagram of simple and complex scenarios

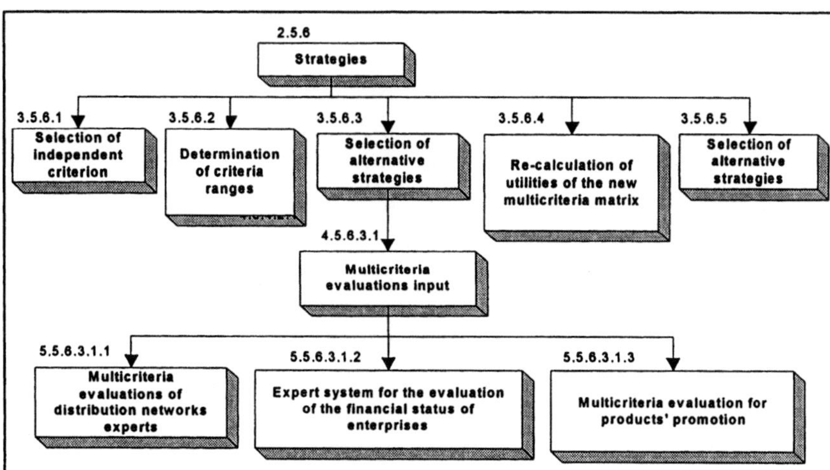

Figure 15. Hierarchical diagram of strategies

3.3 Representation of files

As illustrated in the system's data flow diagram (*Figure 7*) MARKEX uses nine types of files, the structure of which will be briefly examined in this section.

Questions file. The first file that is created with each new project and required for the creation of most of the other file types is the questions file.

It contains all the questions of the market survey questionnaire, which are codified with an appropriate format in order to optimally exploit the responses of the consumers. The questions file is used in the creation of:

- Answers file.
- Consumers' selection filters.
- Multicriteria matrix filters in order to create multicriteria evaluations files.
- Data analyses files.
- Frequencies files.

Answers file. Answers files contain the codified responses of the consumers. Prior to the creation of the answer file, the questions file should have been created. The file is in the form of a common spreadsheet with rows corresponding to consumers and columns to their responses to the questionnaire. The answers file is used jointly with the questions file in order to create the:

- Consumers' selection filters.
- Multicriteria matrix filters in order to create multicriteria evaluations files.
- Data analyses files.
- Frequencies files.

Frequencies file. They contain the results of the statistical process of the data contained in the answers files. The structure of the file is determined by the number of questions and the maximum number of alternative answers.

Data analyses files. They contain the data that are selected to be processed with a certain data analysis method. They are created by the selection of the specific questions, the answers to which we want to analyse. The structure of the file is determined by the number of consumers and the number of selected questions

Historical sales data files. In these files the historical data about the sales of the products participating in the market survey are saved. This information is used in order to form a general point of view about the market and in order to proceed with the forecast of the market trends about the examined products.

Financial data files. They are used to hold the necessary figures from the balance sheets and profits and loss accounts of the companies considered in the market survey. These figures are used in the calculation of the ratios that are introduced in the respective expert system in order to evaluate the financial status of the companies. In addition, the evaluations of the expert system are introduced into the multicriteria table during the phase of evaluating the penetration strategy for the new product.

Multicriteria matrix filters. These filters hold the codes of the questions, the answers of which will comprise the multicriteria matrix. This allows the creation of a filter, in which the answers of the consumers are channelled, and thus generate the multicriteria evaluations file. The structure of the file is determined by the dimensions of the multicriteria table that we wish to create. The number of rows depends on the number of the market survey products whereas an extra row is needed for the keeping of the criteria names. The number of fields equals to the number of criteria plus an extra field needed for the weak order of the products and another field for holding the names of the products (*Figure 16*).

Multicriteria evaluation files. These files contain the multicriteria evaluations of the consumers. The structure of the file is in the form of a three-dimensional array. The dimensions of this array are determined by the number of consumers and by the dimensions of the multicriteria table (*Figure 16*).

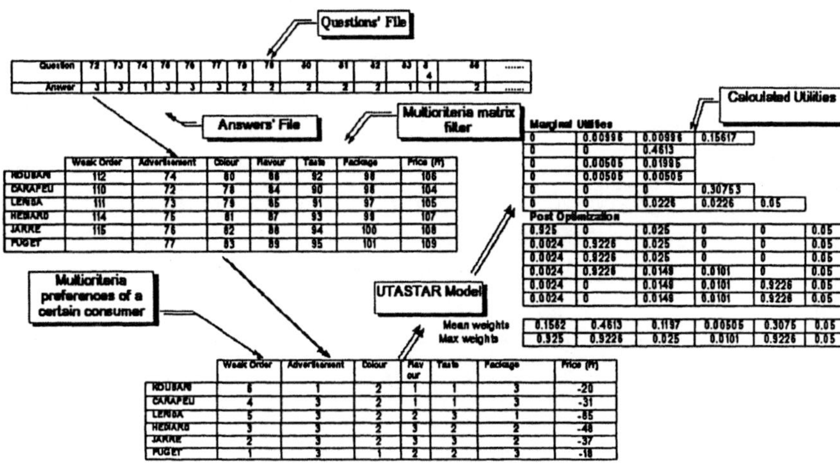

Figure 16. Creation of the utilities file

Utilities files. They are used to hold the calculated utilities. The UTASTAR method is applied to the data contained in the multicriteria evaluation file and the marginal utilities of each consumer are calculated. Then for each criterion optimality and post optimality procedures are applied. The file has a three-dimensional structure, determined by the number of the consumers and the number of the alternative evaluations of each criterion (marginal utilities × number of alternatives plus the results of post optimality analysis). The complete procedure followed for the creation of the utilities file is illustrated in *Figure 16*.

MARKEX offers the possibility to create filters in order to select specific groups of consumers with regard to their responses in combination of various questions. These filters can be applied to whichever task the decision maker wishes.

4. IMPLEMENTATION AND CONCLUSION

The phases of system's analysis and design are followed by the implementation phase. The implementation phase involves the implementation and development of the partial modules of the system by using specific software tools. In the MARKEX system, the implementation was mainly based on the top-down approach. Nevertheless, in partial modules such as the model base development, the bottom-up approach was followed. Finally, the modules related with the interface of the system with the expert systems and the knowledge bases were incorporated.

By studying the system, after the completion of its implementation, in terms of its functionality, we may refer to the most significant attempts in the classification of the decision support systems in marketing by Alter (1977), Little (1979), and Wierenga *et al.* (1994).

Alter (1977), uses a scale that groups the systems according to their capabilities in data retrieval, data analysis, simulations, and consultation. Little (1979) classifies systems according to the availability or absence of database, statistical processing, model base, and optimisation modules. Recently, Wierenga *et al.* (1997) proposed another classification that combines the views of the two earlier approaches with the characteristics of the companies that install and use the systems, in order to determine the capabilities of the systems more effectively. The proposed scale corresponds the type of the answers given by the system with its level of functionality. The scale can be extended to the evaluation of the functionality of both the decisions support systems (Wierenga *et al.*, 1994) and the intelligent marketing decision support systems.

We believe, that the issues examined within the context of this chapter, establish that MARKEX covers the four levels of the proposed scale because:

- It has the capability to manage data that are collected through market surveys as well as historic sales data.
- It supports data analysis methods.
- It is able to answer "what-if" questions, with the help of forecasting and brand choice models, which are used to perform simulations and assessment of market shares
- Finally, the system support s procedures for studying various scenarios and posing a hierarchy on the examined strategies based on an independent criterion (for example the price of the product.

According to the rules set by Jelassi (1986) the system is classified in the fifth generation of decision support systems.

Chapter 11

Applications in Marketing

1. INTRODUCTION

MARKEX has been used in the following real-world applications:

- Design of a new flour product for a Greek flourmill company (Cretan Mills - ERGASYA, 1991).
- Market survey of the Cretan olive oil in the Greek market (area of Athens) (Baourakis *et al.*, 1995).
- Market survey of the Cretan wines in the Greek market (area of Athens) (Siskos *et al.*, 1995).
- Market survey of the Cretan olive oil in the German market (Matsatsinis *et al.*, 1995).
- Market survey if the Cretan olive oil in the French market (Siskos *et al.*, 2001).

In this chapter, a real-world application of the system is presented, in order to facilitate the reader in conceiving the methodological (Chapter 9) and functional aspects of the system (Chapter 10). The application involves the development of a new extra virgin olive oil product for the French market. It was conducted by the Mediterranean Agronomic Institute of Chania (Greece) in collaboration with the Technical University of Crete (Greece), under the EU project "Marketing of Cretan Agricultural Products". The authors would like to acknowledge the LAMSADE Laboratory of the University of Paris - Dauphine for their contribution towards the realisation of the market research in Paris area. The data, the market shares, the scenarios, the strategies and in general all the results that will be presented in the following sections have been to some extent adapted in order to better support the comprehension of the system.

2. DESIGN OF AN OLIVE OIL BRAND FOR THE FRENCH MARKET

2.1 Market Environment Study

According to the methodological steps presented in chapter 9, the general environment of the olive oil market has to be studied first in EU then in France (Siskos *et al.*, 2001).

The European Community regulations for olive oil originate from the Common Market Organization (CMO) for olive oil which was established in 1966 (CEE. 136/66) for a common market for fats and oils. The role of the olive oil product within EU has been upgraded since all three main producer countries Spain, Italy and Greece are members of the Community. Olive oil production fluctuates from one crop year to another, which is mainly attributable to input factors. Among the main objectives of EU policy are restriction of production and increase in consumption over its main vegetable substitutes.

Olive oil consumption in France is very low in comparison to the one in Italy, Spain, and Greece but quite significant with respect to the rest of European countries. The French olive oil production is mainly concentrated in the southern part and the existing gap between production and consumption level has been increasing during the last years.

2.2 Questionnaire design

The survey was conducted by using a specialized questionnaire as thoroughly described in Chapter 9, §3. The questionnaire employed was designed in such a way in order to collect information of the sample's demographic characteristics, determine the oils generally used, frequency of olive oil use, type of use of the different oils and consumer perceptions with respect to attributes and factors such as health, taste, purity and pricing. Another section dealt with the size and type of packaging, brand loyalty, branding color, odor, taste, packaging and finally labeling. Through the last part of the questionnaire the aim was to identify afterwards which one of some characteristic olive oil brands the consumer would purchase in a ranking order.

Six olive oil brands were utilized: an Italian, a Spanish, a Greek and three French; all these brands were of half a liter volume, the five were virgin olive oil products, while the last was a biological product.

All the participating brands were of half a liter volume, the first five, were extra virgin olive oil products, while La Jarre d' Or was a biological olive oil product.

Carapelli being a medium quality extra virgin olive oil seems to be competitive to the Cretan olive oil. Lerida also is one of the few Spanish branded products, which are exported to France. La Jarre d'Or is available in health food stores while Hediard can be purchased only in Hediard stores, which provide products of high quality. Finally, Puget is available in almost every supermarket and is considered as the leader of the French olive oil market.

The survey was held in Paris according to the process described in Chapter 9, §3 and Figure 9.6. The respondents-consumers were arbitrarily selected. Two hundred and five olive oil consumers were interviewed in their houses. Interviews lasted approximately 45 minutes and in each single case all the examined brands were evaluated. The consumers were able to see the products in their original package or even to taste and smell all the products included in the survey. A number of districts of different socio-economic background were included in this survey.

2.3 Construction of the databases

After the completion of the market survey and of the data collection the responses of the consumers were codified in an appropriate form in order to facilitate their utilization by the system. The first file to create is the file containing the coding scheme of the questions (*Figure 1*). Several information are entered in the system like the text of the question, its type (qualitative, quantitative, order, or weak order), the number of alternative answers, the range of the acceptable values, etc. After the creation of the questions file, the file containing the responses of the consumers, the answers file, is created. The final step in the construction of the databases involves the creation of the file containing historical data concerning the sales of the products considered in the survey and the file containing the financial ratios for the financial evaluation of the enterprises.

2.4 Market Trends

The general characteristics of the market trends such as the volume of products' sales in quantities and money are studied using the forecasting models of the system (Chapter. 9, §4). With these models one is able to inspect the growth trends of the market and forecast the course of the products' sales.

In the next phase of analysis the decision maker is able to form an early outlook of the existing market situation by making use of descriptive statistics. The type of the statistical analysis to be performed is selected from the choice menu or from the large icons available on the toolbar.

Figure 2 shows the results derived by the descriptive statistics analysis. The decision maker is able to customize the statistical process and the appearance of results. There are several types of graphs available for the representation of the results; also the decision maker is able to study the results of different combinations of questions, modify the graph colors and text sizes.

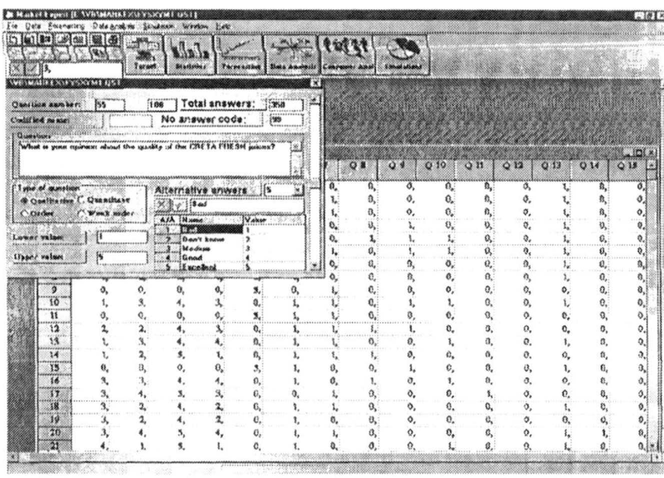

Figure 1. Input of primary data - Creation of questions and answers databases

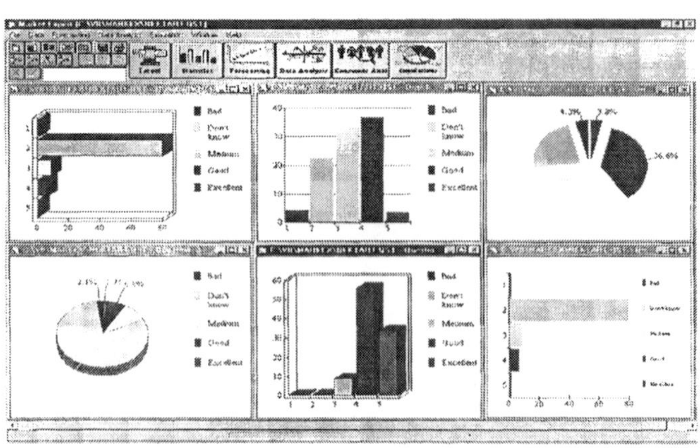

Figure 2. Window of statistical analysis results

Let us examine some of the results of the descriptive statistics analysis of the application at hand. Nearly all consumers utilize olive oil in general, 79.9% of them use sunflower oil while 50% use groundnut oil (Table 11.1). This outcome is not surprising; Pelurson (1988) argues that the spectacular increase in the world production of seed oils and the widening gaps between the prices of these and olive oil had a small impact on French olive oil consumption's levels. The frequency of olive oil use classifies the consumers into two broad categories: the regular consumers (75.1%) and the occasional consumers (24.9%).

Table 1. Oils used generally and frequency of olive oil use

Oils	%	Frequency of olive oil use	%
Olive oil	99.5	Daily	22.1
Groundnut oil	50.0	3 - 4 times/week	26.0
Sunflower oil	79.9	1 - 2 times/week	27.0
Soya oil	0.0	Every 15 days	9.8
Corn oil	16.2	Every month	15.1
Margarine	36.3		
Other oils	33.8		

Consumer behavioral analysis in French olive oil market showed that the size of container found most useful is the 1 lit (58.8%) and the 0.5 lit (38.2%). The vast majority of consumers prefers glass bottles and does not prefer plastic bottles, small cans, large cans and other kinds of containers (Table 11.2).

Table 2. Categorical analysis of type and size of container

	Frequency of use of olive oil (%)					
Purpose of use	[1]	Daily	3-4 t/week	1-2 t/week	Every 15 days	Monthly
Frying	(1)	2.94	2.94	0.98	0.49	0.00
	(2)	19.12	23.04	25.98	9.31	15.20
Cooking	(1)	13.73	14.22	9.80	2.45	3.92
	(2)	8.33	11.76	17.16	7.35	11.27
Mayonnaise	(1)	9.80	11.76	5.39	0.98	1.96
	(2)	12.25	14.22	21.57	8.82	13.24
Sauces	(1)	9.31	11.27	4.90	1.96	1.47
	(2)	12.75	14.71	22.06	7.84	13.73
Salads	(1)	22.06	25.49	26.47	9.80	13.73
	(2)	0.00	0.49	0.49	0.00	1.47
Hot dishes	(1)	17.65	16.67	14.22	1.47	3.43
	(2)	4.41	9.31	12.75	8.33	11.76

Finally, Table 11.3 shows the distributions of answers at specific attitude questions. It is important to note for instance, that French olive oil

[1] 1- Use 2- Don't use

consumers believe that olive oil is very healthy, makes food taste better but they find it considerably expensive.

Table 3. Consumer perceptions and attitudes for the olive oil product

Hypothesis	Consumers%		
	Agree	Unaware	Disagree
Olive oil is very healthy	66.2	22.5	11.3
Olive oil makes food tasty	91.7	5.4	2.9
Olive oil can be used for frying more than once	4.9	40.7	54.5
Olive oil is not fattening	25.5	34.3	42.2
Olive oil does not increase Cholesterol	30.9	46.6	22.5
Olive oil is good for the heart	40.7	49.0	10.3
Olive oil does not contain other additional substances	51.0	21.6	27.4
Olive oil is relatively expensive	92.6	0.0	7.4

2.5 Data analysis results

Prior to the execution of a certain data analysis method the user is required to create the files with the data that will be considered in the analysis. The creation of the data analysis files is accomplished by the formation of appropriate selection filters; these filters are used in order to select specific consumers and specific questions among the set of consumers and questions respectively.

With the consumers selection filter the user chooses groups of consumers (market segments) the characteristics of which she/he wishes to study. If the decision maker wishes to include the whole set of consumers in the analysis then the consumers selection filter is omitted; the user creates only a questions selection filter in order to select specific questions to be included in the analysis.

With the completion of the data selection, the first expert system of MARKEX is activated (Chapter 10 §2.6.1). MARKEX allows the user to take into account the suggestions of the expert system (Begin consultation) or to completely override the advisory process (Ignore ES) and select the desirable data analysis method (*Figure 3*). In the first case the user interacts with the expert system by responding to certain questions such as "which is the goal of the data analysis" (see *Figure 3*). The expert system replies by suggesting the most suitable method for the goal of analysis. The expert system may suggest the re-codification of certain variables-questions in the case where this is considered necessary for the proper implementation of the suggested data analysis method. This is the case when the selected set of questions includes both qualitative and quantitative data. In order to apply a certain data analysis method the existence of same type data is required. Principal Components Analysis requires the use of quantitative data. If the user has selected qualitative data then this should be transformed to quantitative values prior to the execution of the method, i.e. the user should consider revising the codification scheme of the questions.

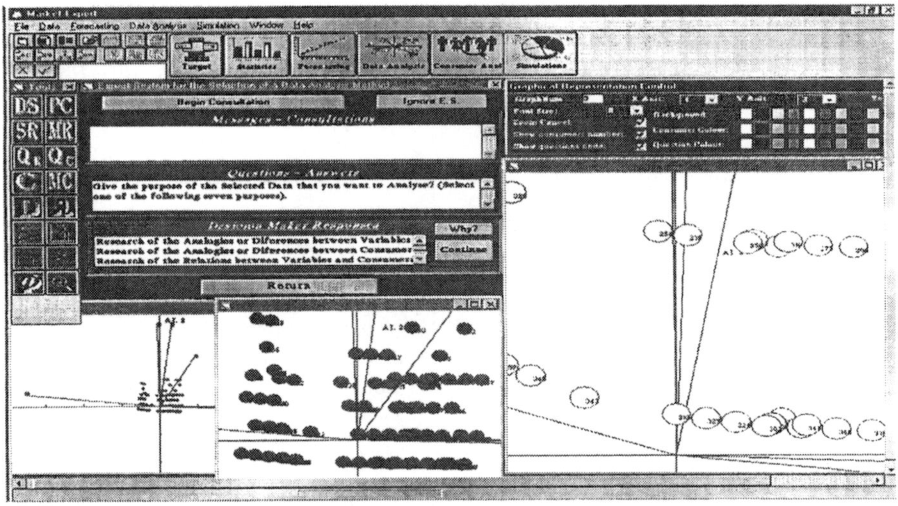

Figure 3. Expert system for the selection of a data analysis method - Data analysis: graphical representation - Graphical representation control

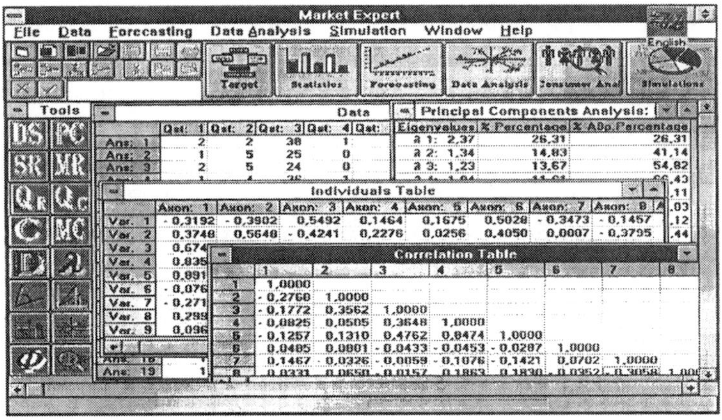

Figure 4. Data analysis results

The window of data analyses is presented *Figure 4*. On the left side there is a toolbox that contains all the available methods. The lower part of the toolbox contains the options for appearing/hiding the results of each method and other controls that handle the graphical presentation of the results such as zoom in and zoom out, rotation, axis turn, colors change, etc. The main section of the window holds the results of each selected method while at the upper right corner of the window the graphical representation control is presented.

The purpose of principal components analysis is to determine statistically whether an underlying pattern of relationships exists among the variables. In essence, such analysis searches for the possibility of reducing data by seeking a smaller set of variables that explain the variance among a larger set of variables, and determine the correlations between a product and consumer characteristics and provide a general outline of consumer perspectives and attitudes. The variables involved in the analysis are displayed as vectors, and are the questions for which the existence of correlation is expected. Consumers are displayed as dots, usually forming groups. Distances between variables are interpreted in terms of correlation. The better they fit, the better the relationship will be maintained. Distances between points (consumers) are interpreted in terms of similar pattern of response to the variables. However, a great deal of caution is needed in interpreting figures, because variables and individual points may not belong to the same space. The percentages shown on the axes define their explanatory power. They represent the proportion of the total variance that is explained by each axis.

Correspondence analysis is a data analysis method that identifies interrelations between questions and the alternative answers in each question. It examines the internal structure of the question and allows the penetration in the information received from the research. As in principal components analysis, the results of correspondence analysis are presented on graphs that represent the configurations of points in projection planes formed by the first principal axes taken two at a time.

In our market research case application interrelations among oils consumption and their main usages were examined (*Table 4*). Olive oil consumption was associated with salad dressings; these two variables had a positive correlation coefficient of +0.443. Groundnut and sunflower oils were used for all purposes as shown by the positive correlation values. Corn oil was mainly used in cooking, mayonnaise, sauces, hot-dishes and, to a much lesser extent, in frying and salads. The use of margarine was highly related to cooking (+0.775), but much less to frying, sauces and hot dishes. Margarine was not used in salads at all. The other types of oils used by consumers, were mainly related to frying, cooking, salads and hot dishes.

Table 4. Interrelations among oils consumption and their main usages

Oil Purpose	Olive Oil	Groundnut Oil	Sunflower Oil	Corn Oil	Margarine Oil	Other Oils
Frying	+0.020	+0.676	+0.407	+0.397	+0.285	+0.499

Oil Purpose	Olive Oil	Groundnut Oil	Sunflower Oil	Corn Oil	Margarine Oil	Other Oils
Cooking	+0.062	+0.494	+0.482	+0.750	+0.775	+0.523
Mayonnaise	+0.046	+0.532	+0.482	+0.517	+0.162	+0.173
Sauces	+0.045	+0.471	+0.407	+0.618	+0.346	+0.394
Salads	+0.443	+0.330	+0.312	+0.278	---	+0.486
Hot dishes	+0.075	+0.431	+0.374	+0.708	+0.316	+0.448

2.6 Consumer Behavior Analysis

Consumer behavior analysis is accomplished utilizing multicriteria preference analysis for each consumer separately in combination with data analysis methods and techniques concerning consumer profiles in general.

For each consumer a separate multicriteria table is created containing the data collected through the special questionnaire (Figure 9.6). Next the UTASTAR model (see chapter10) is applied on the consumer data preference set and the respective files are created (Figure 10.16).

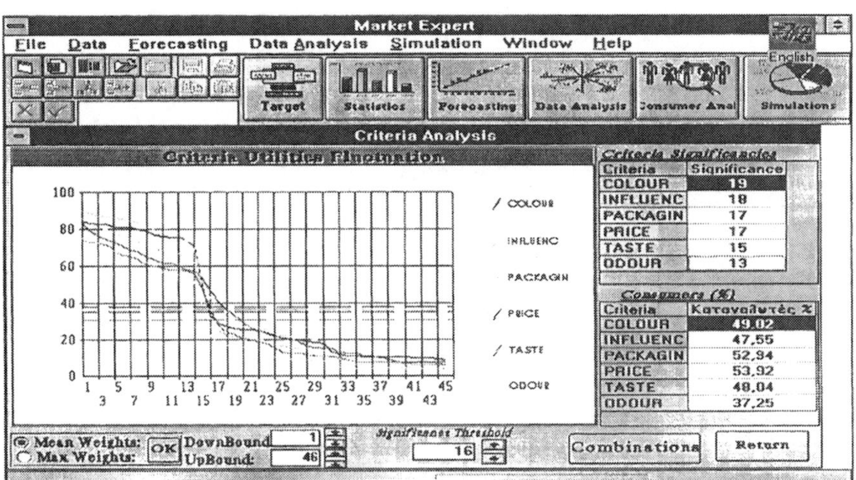

Figure 5. Criteria analysis

Preference disaggregation analysis using the UTASTAR model allows for the extraction of the criteria that appeared as determinant of each consumer preferences; a criterion is considered as a significance one when it is overcomes a significance threshold of about 10%. As significance threshold is considered the utility threshold that determines whether a criterion is important or not. Consequently, if the criterion utility is greater or equal than this significance threshold then this criterion is considered to be important in the decision of the consumer; in the opposite case the criterion is consider as non important. The decision maker is able to adjust the significance threshold. The right part of the window presented in *Figure 5* contains the significance of the criteria and the percentages of the consumers that consider each criterion as significant. The significance of the criteria is derived as the mean value of the utilities of each criterion according to the complete set of consumers. The percentage of consumers that perceive a certain criterion as significant is derived by the comparison of each criterion utility, for each consumer, with the significance threshold. When the utility of a criterion is greater than the significance threshold then this criterion is considered to be important in the decision of the consumer; in the opposite case then the criterion does not play a significant role in the decision of the consumer.

An issue of particular importance is the possibility of the decision maker to study the market segmentation for various combinations of criteria. MARKEX is able to give answers to such type of questions as for example "which is the percentage of consumers that consider the criteria price, packaging, and image as significant and also consider the color as non significant or indifferent.

Table 5 presents the percentages of consumers that considered a certain criterion as significant along with each criterions significance threshold with regard to the remaining criteria. For example the first table row shows that 77% of consumers regard as significant the color of the olive oil with a significance threshold of 19% with regard to the remaining criteria.

Table 5. Significant criteria of consumers' behavior

Criteria	Significance threshold	Consumers
Color	19%	77%
Image	18%	80%
Packaging	17%	70%
Price	17%	64%
Taste	15%	61%
Odor	13%	57%

Criteria analysis enables the rating of the criteria according to their importance as well as the calculation of consumers' percentage that regard the criteria as important. In table 11.6, 37% of consumers seem to perceive as important the company image, the price and the packaging and as indifference the criteria of color, taste and olive oil odor. Sign "+" indicates an important criterion to the consumer, "-" as a not important and the empty cell indicates indifference by the consumer.

Table 6. Market segmentation through complex criteria combinations

Color	Image	Price	Packaging	Taste	Odor	Consumers
+				+	+	34%

Color	Image	Price	Packaging	Taste	Odor	Consumers
+		+		+		29%
		+	+			46%
-	-	+	+	-	-	0%
	+	+	+			37%

The results of criteria analysis enable the decision maker to observe similarities in the behavior of consumers and split the market in appropriate market segments.

2.7 Simulating the New Product

At this point the decision maker has studied the market segmentation possibilities and has established the segmentation bases (Chapter 2). If none of the segments complies with the criteria for evaluating segments according to Nylen (1990), then the whole market is to be considered as a single segment. However if there are more than one segments then these should be studied separately. The analysis of the designed product and of the competitive products should be carried out for each segment separately in order to find certain competitive advantages for each of the segments through the calculation of market shares, the determination of the launching strategy, the detection of the main competitive products, and finally through the determination of the features of the new product.

One of the basic tools in this effort as well as in the design, development and test of the new product are the abilities of MARKEX to perform a variety of simulations.

Simulations are accomplished by the help of the available brand choice models of the system. The capabilities and the flow diagram of the penetration strategy selection process are presented in Chapter 9, §8.

The first step is to pick the model that represents more closely the behavior of the particular market segment (Chapter. 9, §2 and §6 - Chapter. 10, §2.6.2). In the case where the user has no information regarding the actual market shares she/he is able to choose the model suggested by the respective expert system. The expert system suggests the brand choice model that matches more effectively the behavior of the consumers belonging in the particular market segment. *Figure 6* presents the window used by the system in order to present the results and the suggestions of the expert system. The expert system suggests a certain brand choice model and also presents the market shares that are calculated according to the heuristic model. The user is able to accept the suggested model or ignore the suggestion of the expert system. In either case, the model that is chosen in this phase is used in the calculation of the market shares and then in the implementation of simulations.

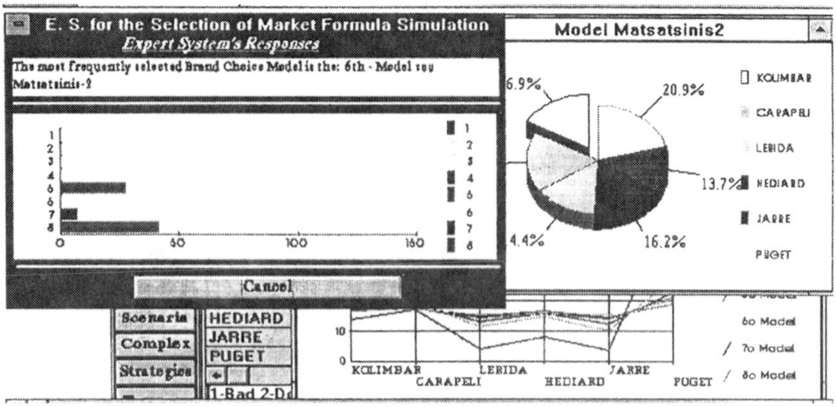

Figure 6. Expert system for the selection of brand choice model

In addition, in simulations the system informs the user on the calculated market shares according to each brand choice model (*Figure 7*). This permits the decision maker to observe the behavior of each model for the particular market segment.

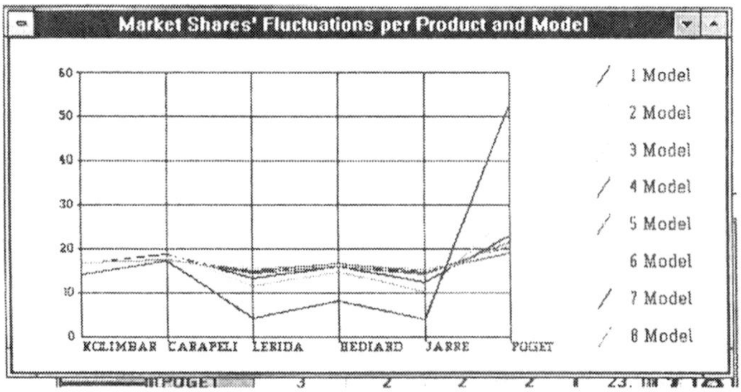

Figure 7. Market simulations

The control, choice, and execution processes of the simulations are accomplished through a main control window (*Figure 8*).

The middle section of the window holds the multicriteria table. The entries of the table are the mean values of the consumers' judgments. On the right of the table are the market shares according to the first available brand choice model, whereas at the rightmost section of the window the user is able to select any model and see the respective market shares.

The alternative values of each criterion along with their codification are shown to the decision maker below the multicriteria table. The decision maker is able to change the values of the multicriteria table and to calculate the new market shares by clicking on the command button labeled "MS Re-estimation". The original entries of the table are restores by pressing the command button labeled "Mean Estimations".

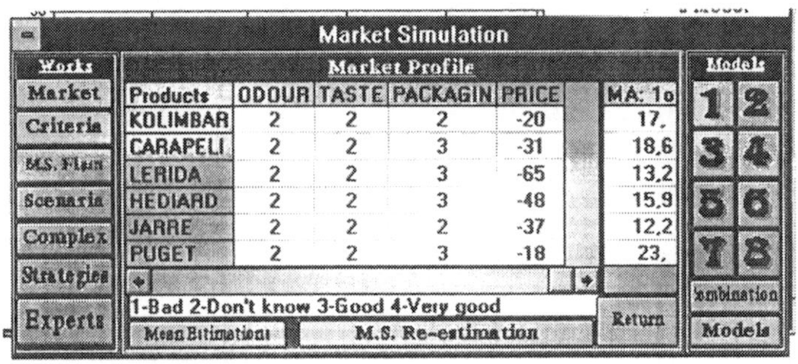

Figure 8. Control window of simulations

The leftmost section of the window has a number of command buttons that enable the execution of all the available simulation tasks and of the scenarios application.

The decision maker has the possibility to change the structure of the market by pressing the command button "Market". Through this process the decision maker may launch a new product in the market, i.e. a product that has not been considered in the market survey. The multicriteria evaluations of the new product (the values of each criterion) are given by the companies' field experts. In addition, the decision maker is able to remove certain products. In general, the decision maker can change the combination of the market and observe its behavior whenever a new product is launched.

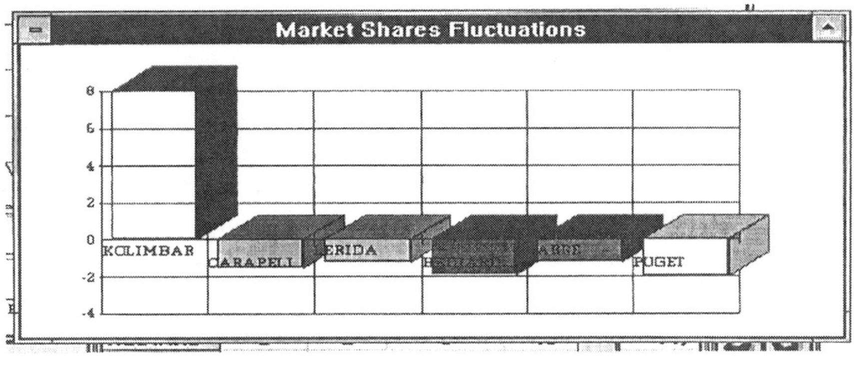

Figure 9. Changes in market shares

The decision maker has the possibility to adjust the multicriteria evaluations of each product by changing the entries of the table of *Figure 8*.

Modifications in the evaluations of the products create new market conditions, i.e. a market with different characteristics. Then the system simulates the new condition of the market by calculating the new market shares according to the already selected brand choice models. The system displays the change of each product market shares according to the newly established conditions in the environment, i.e. shows the percentage each product gains or drops from the previous market situation (*Figure 9*). In our case, KOLIMBARI gains an additional 8%, which is mainly taken from the products "CARAPELI", "HEDIARD" and "PUGET", i.e. its main competitors.

The profile of the Kolymbari olive oil brand is displayed in *Figure 10.* The new product design will mainly be based on the improvements of the determinant criteria of color, taste and packaging, while price is treated as an independent variable.

	Bad	Unaware	Good	Very Good
IMAGE	2	61.8	22.6	13.7

	Unnatural	Natural	Attractive
COLOR	16.7	70.1	13.2

	Unnatural	Natural	Pleasant
ODOUR	37.3	46.1	16.7

	Unnatural	Natural	Delicious
TASTE	25.5	39.2	35.3

	Bad	Fair	Good	Very Good
PACKAGE	15.7	47.1	32.8	4.4

PRICE (Fr)	20

Figure 10. Profile of the "KOLIMBARI" olive oil brand

The next phase of analysis involves the formation and study of simple scenarios. MARKEX uses the window shown in *Figure 11* for the creation of simple scenarios. The decision maker has the possibility to study more thoroughly the product under development along with its main competitors. We will study the market shares that result after the market simulations when the criteria values are changed according to the figures shown in *Figure 11*.

The results of the application of scenarios are derived by repetitive simulations, the results of which are presented in the window of *Figure 12.* In the right section of the window MARKEX displays all the alternative scenarios along with the respective criteria values.

The aim of the study of the simple scenarios is to pinpoint the specific scenarios that have low implementation cost and give somewhat similar market shares. This allows the decision maker to narrow the number of the scenarios that need to be studied.

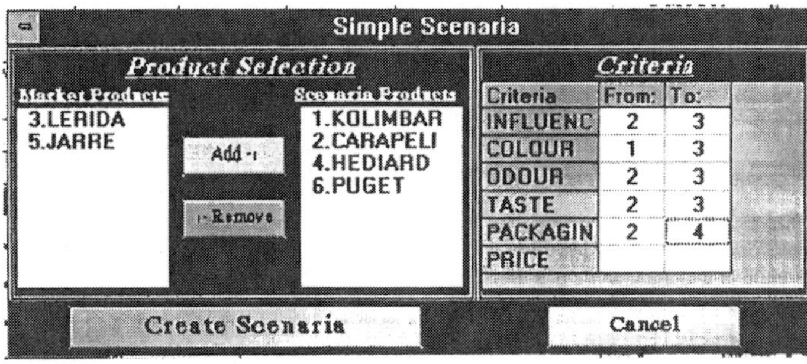

Figure 11. Formation of simple scenarios

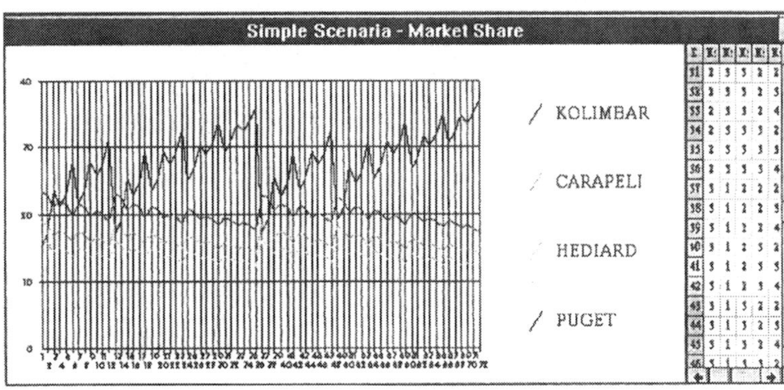

Figure 12. Market shares of simple scenarios

After deciding on which simple scenarios to study further the latter are more thoroughly examined by using complex scenarios. Complex scenarios show the changes in the market shares of each of the selected simple scenarios, with regard to the value of an independent criterion, which in the case at hand is the price of the product (*Figure 13*). In the study of a complex scenario the system asks the decision maker to choose the criterion to be considered as independent and the range within this criterion will take values. Next, the decision maker denotes the simple scenario that wishes to study and the products that should be included in the study.

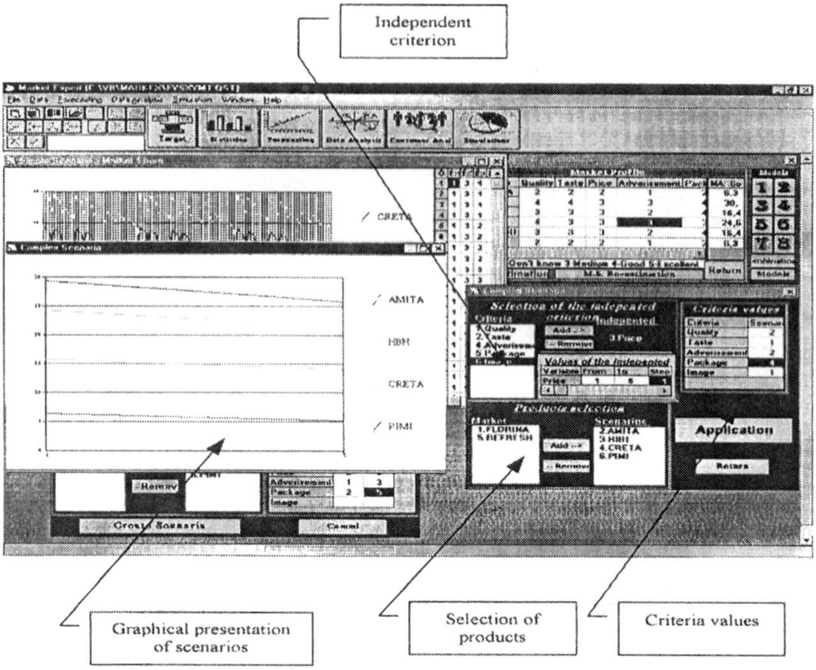

Figure 13. Formation of complex scenarios

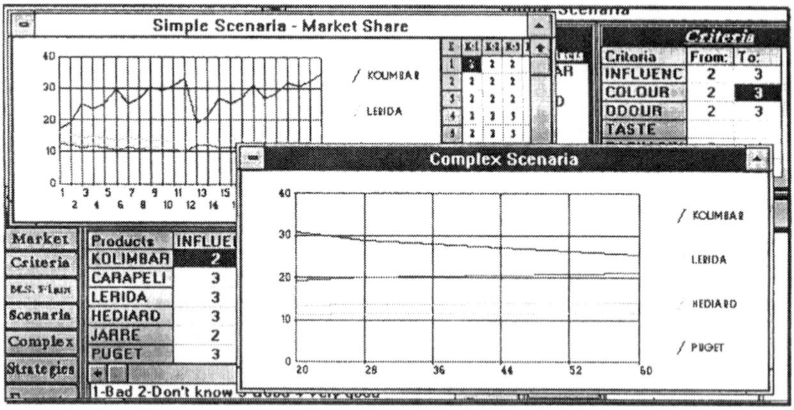

Figure 14. Results of complex scenarios

The system uses the window presented in *Figure 14* in order to display the results derived by the application of the complex scenarios. As it can be clearly observed the market shares of the product under development are shrinking as the price of the product rises. The drop in the market shares continues until the price of the product reaches 44 FF; the market shares remain the same for prices greater than 44 FF. Another remarkable observation is the fact that the market shares that are cut off from "KOLIMBARI" are gained mainly by "PUGET"; small percentages go to the other two products that are considered in this scenario. This means that as the price of "KOLIMBARI" drops, the gained market shares come mainly from the market share of "PUGET" whereas when the price of "KOLIMBARI" has a value of 18 FF the two products share equal market shares. Therefore, "PUGET" is the main competitor of "KOLIMBARI".

The results of the previous analyses draw some conclusions for the decision maker. First, the attribute of taste should be improved in the new product in order for the French consumers to have for "KOLIMBARI" the same evaluation (judgment) as for "LERIDA" and "HEDIARD". Thus, the taste of "KOLIMBARI" should be improved in order to correspond to "natural" – "excellent" evaluation. This can be accomplished by giving a bit more light taste in the new product, since consumers believe that "KOLIMBARI" tastes somewhat bitter. The color of the product should also be improved. In particular, the color of the new product should be lighter, more "natural" than the color of "KOLIMBARI". Since consumers have rated the products from dark to light ones with the order "KOLIMBARI"-"LERIDA"-"HEDIARD"-"CARAPELLI", the color of the new product should resemble the color of "LERIDA", "HEDIARD" or even of "CARAPELLI". Finally, a very critical issue is the improvement of the product's package in order to be evaluated on the average as "good", as the products "CARAPELLI" and "HEDIARD".

Consequently the design of the new product should concentrate on improvements concerning the color, taste and package of the "KOLIMVARI" olive oil. Price will be regarded as independent variable in order to chose the most appropriate penetration strategy for the new product. Thus, the strategies shown in *Figure 15* should be further examined.

The first strategy is based on the improvement of the natural characteristics of the product such as the color and taste. The second one is based on the improvement of the package whereas the third strategy is a combination of the two with improvements in all the three key attributes.

For each considered strategy the decision maker performs, with the support of the system, several repetitive market simulations. The simulations are realized by modifying the multicriteria evaluations of the consumers; the modifications involve only the features of the product that are to be examined in each scenario, i.e. color, taste, and package.

A comparison of these three different approaches (*Figure 16*) indicates that the first two provide rather similar sales revenues while the third one appears as the optimum. This was expected since all three involved criteria were improved.

	1st strategy	2nd strategy	3rd strategy
PRICE (Fr)	18 - 37	18 - 37	18 - 37
PACKAGE	Fair	Good - 3	Good - 3
TASTE	Natural - Delicious	Natural	Natural - Delicious
ODOUR	Natural	Natural	Natural
COLOUR	Natural	Natural	Natural
IMAGE	Unaware - Good	Unaware - Good	Unaware - Good

Figure 15. Alternative penetration strategies of "KOLYMBARI" in the French market

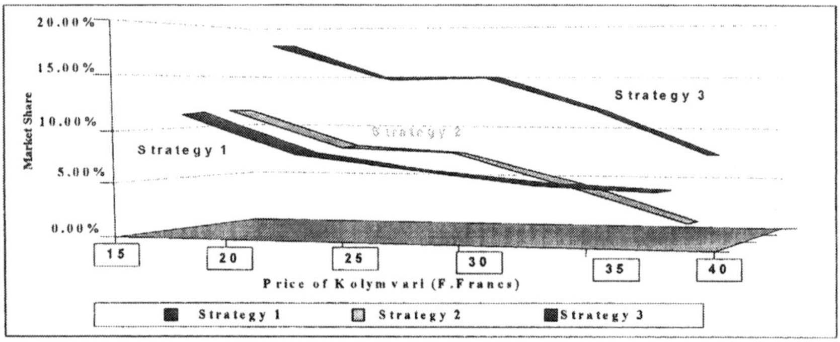

Figure 16. Market shares (sales value) of "KOLIMBARI" for the three potential marketing strategies

Concerning the price of "KOLIMBARI" it can increase from 20FF to 25FF without a significant decrease of its market share. If it approaches 31FF then it is not a competitive product since Carapelli has the same price as well. On the contrary, if its price decreases to 18FF, that of Puget's, then its market share is further increased.

The brands of La Jarre d' Or, Hediard and Lerida are not involved in these analyses since the consumers that purchase them are quite loyal. Therefore any possible change and improvement on the Kolymbari's attributes will not bring a significant impact on these three products' market shares.

At this point the decision maker has the possibility to study the market behavior and apply scenarios and strategies by introducing new information in the problem. The information regards evaluations of experts in the fields of. The third expert system of MARKEX is also used in these analyses. This expert system evaluates the financial condition of the enterprises that produce the products under examination. Thus, new multicriteria tables are created for each consumer. They contain the original judgments of the consumers along with the evaluations of the expert system and the judgments of the experts in the fields of distribution channels and product promotion. The UTASTAR method is applied on the new data set and a new set of utility values are calculated. Then the market shares are re-estimated with the selection of a certain brand choice model. Finally, scenarios – simple and complex - are applied and several penetration strategies are examined.

In conclusion, the decision maker is able to choose the most suitable strategy for the design, development, and penetration into the market of the new product, by synthesizing the partial results of all the analyses supported by MARKEX.

References

[1] Aaker, D.A. (1975), ADMOD: An advertising decision model, Journal of Marketing Research, no. 12, pp. 37-45.

[2] Aaker, D.A., J.G. Shansby (1980), Positioning your product, Business Horizons (May-June), pp. 34-42.

[3] Abdul-Gader, A.H., K.A. Kozar (1990), Discourse analysis for knowledge acquisition: The coherence method, Journal of Management Information Systems, vol. 6, no. 4, pp. 61-82.

[4] Abell, D.F. (1980), Defining the business: The starting point of strategic planning, Englewood Cliffs, N.J.: Prentice Hall.

[5] Abraham, M.M., L.M. Lodish (1987), PROMOTER: An automated promotion evaluation system, Marketing Science, vol. 6, pp. 101-123.

[6] Absatzwirtschaft, (1989), Wissen nutzen: Was leisten expertnsysteme in marketing?, ASW Report Teil 1, Absatzwirtschaft, Dezember, pp. 38-49.

[7] Absatzwirtschaft, (1990), Wissen nutzen: Was leisten expertnsysteme in marketing?, ASW Report Teil 2, Absatzwirtschaft, Januar, pp. 62-67.

[8] Ackoff, R.L. (1967), Management misinformation systems, Management Science, vol. 14, no. 4, pp. 147-156.

[9] Adams, E.W., R. Fagot (1959), A model for riskless choice, Behavioral Science, no. 4 (1-10).

[10] Addriaans, P., D. Zantige (1997), Data mining, Addison-Welsey, England.

[11] Adelman, L., M.L. Donnell (1986), Evaluating decision support systems: A general framework and case study, in: S.J. Andriole (ed.), Micro-Computer Decision Support Systems: Design,

Implementation, and Evaluation, Wellesley, MA: QED Information Sciences.

[12] Adelman, L. (1992), Evaluating decision support and expert systems, John Wiley, New York.

[13] Adetayo, J.O., S.A. Sanni, M.O. Ilori (1999), The impact of information technology on product marketing: a case study of a multinational company in Nigeria, Technovation, vol. 19, p. 691–699.

[14] Adya, M., J.S. Armstrong, F. Collopy, M. Kennedy (2000), An application of rule-based forecasting to a situation lacking domain knowledge, International Journal of Forecasting, vol. 16, pp. 477–484.

[15] Agarwal, R., M.R. Tanniru (1990), Knowledge acquisition using structured interviewing: An empirical investigation, Journal of Management Information Systems, vol. 6, no. 4, pp. 61-82.

[16] Agrawal, R., D. Bell (1990), Second international symposium on Databases in parallel and distributed systems, IEEE Computer Society Press, Los Alamitos, California.

[17] Agresti, W. (1986), New paradigms for software development, IEEE, no. 707, IEEE Press.

[18] Ahituv, N., J. Zif, I. Machlin (1998), Environmental scanning and information systems in relation to success in introducing new products, Information & Management, vol. 33, pp. 201-211.

[19] Ahuja, V. (1996), Secure Commerce on the Internet, AP Professional.

[20] Albaum, G. (1964), Horizontal information flow: An exploratory study, Academy of Management 161, vol. 7, no. 1, pp. 21-33.

[21] Albright, S.C., W.L. Winston, C. Zappe (1999), Data analysis and decision making with Microsoft Excel, Duxbury Press.

[22] Alexander, S.M., G.W. Evans (1988), The integration of multiple experts: A review of methodologies, in: E. Turban and P. Watkins (eds.), Applied Expert Systems, North-Holland.

[23] Alexis, M.H.G., L. Simon (1968), Consumer information processing: The case of women's clothing, in: Proceedings of the American Marketing Association Fall Conference, Marketing and the New Science of Planning, pp. 197-205.

[24] Alford, M. (1985), SREM at the age of eigth: The distributed computing design system, IEEE Computer, vol. 18, no. 4, pp. 36-46.

[25] Ali, A., M.U. Kalwani, D. Kovenock (1993), Selecting product development projects: Pionnering versus incremental innovation strategies, Management Science, vol. 39, no. 3, pp. 255-274.

[26] Allaire, Y. (1973), The measurement of heterogeneous semantic, perceptual and preference structures, Ph.D. thesis, MIT Camcridge.

[27] Allegayer, J, R. Jansen-Winkeln, C. Reddig, N. Reithinger (1989), Bidirectional use of knowledge in the multi-modal NL access system XTRA, in: Proceedings of IJCAI-89, Detroit, pp. 1492-1497.

[28] Allen, R.W., D.L. Madison, L.W. Porter, P.A. Renwick, B.T. Mayes (1979), Organisational Politics - Tactics and Characteristics of its Actors, California Management Review, vol. 22, no. 1, pp. 77-83.

[29] Alpar, P. (1991), Knowledge-based modeling of marketing managers: Problem solving behavior, International Journal of Research in Marketing, vol. 8, no. 1, pp. 5-16.

[30] Alpar, P., W. Dilger (1995), Market share analysis and prognosis using qualitative reasoning, Decision Support Systems, vol. 15, pp. 133-146.

[31] Alter, S. (1977), A taxonomy of decision support systems, Management Review, vol. 19, no. 1, pp. 39-56.

[32] Alter, L. (1980), Decision support systems: Current practices and continuing challenges, Addison-Wesley Publishing Company, Reading, Massachusetts.

[33] Alter, S. (1992), Why persist with DSS when the real issue is improving decision making?, in: T. Jellasi, M.R. Klein, W.M. Mayon-White (eds.), Decision support systems: Experiences and Expectations, IFIP 92, Elsevier Science Pub.

[34] Alter, S. (1992), Information systems: A management perspective, Addison-Wesley, Reading, MA.

[35] Alter, S. (1999), Information Systems: A management perspective (3rd edition), Addison-Wesley.

[36] Amaravadi, C.S., S. Samaddar, S. Dutta (1995), Intelligent marketing information systems: Computerized intelligence for marketing decision making, Marketing Intelligence & Planning, vol. 13, no. 2, pp. 4-13.

[37] Amstutz, A.E. (1969), Market-oriented management systems: The current status, Journal of Marketing Research, VI (November), pp. 481-496.

[38] Andersen, K.A., J.N. Hooker (1994), Bayesian logic, in: H. Bhargava and S. Kimbrough (eds.), Special issue on logic modelling, Decision Support Systems, vol. 11, no. 2, pp. 191-210.

[39] Andreasan, A.R. (1965), Attitudes and customer behaviour: A decision model, in: L.E.Preston (ed.), New Research in Marketing, Institute of Business and Economic Research, University of California, Berkeley.

[40] Andriole, S.J. (1982), The design of micro-computer based personal decision aiding systems, IEEE Transactions on Systems, Man and Cybernetics, SMC-12, pp. 463-469.

[41] Andriole, S.J. (1986), Micro-Computer Decision Support Systems: Design, Implementation, and Evaluation, Wellesley, MA: QED Information Sciences.

[42] Andriole, S.J. (1989), Handbook for the design, development, evaluation and application of interactive decision support systems, NJ: Petrocelli, Princeston

[43] Angehrn, A.A., H.J. Luthi (1990), Intelligent decision support systems: A visual interactive approach, Interfaces, vol. 20, no. 6, pp. 17-28.

[44] Anthony, R.N. (1965), Planning and control systems: A framework for analysis, MA: Harvard University Graduate School of Business, Cambridge.

[45] ANSI/SPARC (1975), Study group on data base management systems report, Association for Computer Machinery (ACM), vol. 7, no. 2.

[46] Applegate, L.M., B.R. Konsynski, J.F. Nunamaker (1986), Model management systems: Design for decision support, Decision Support Systems, vol. 2, no. 1, pp. 81-91.

[47] Arkinson M., P. Bailey, R. Morrison, 1983. An Approach to Persistent Programming, The Computer Journal, vol. 26, no. 4, pp. 360.

[48] Armstrong, M.P. (1992), GIS and Group Decision-Making: Problems and Prospects, GIS/LIS '92, vol. 1, pp. 20-29.

[49] Armstrong, M. (1993), Perspectives on the development of group decision support systems for locational problem-solving, Geographical Systems, vol. 1, pp. 69-81.

[50] Armstrong, M.P., P.J. Densham (1990), Database organization alternatives for spatial decision support systems, International Journal of Geographical Information Systems, vol. 3, no. 1.

[51] Armstrong, M., P. Densham (1994), Towards the development of a conceptual framework for GIS-based collaborative spatial decision making, in: Proceedings of the 3rd ACM International Workshop in GIS, pp. 4-8.

[52] Arrow, K.J. (1963), Social Choice and Individual Values, 2nd ed. Wiley, New York.

[53] Assael, H. (1987), Consumer behavior and marketing action, Boston: Kent Publishing Co.

[54] Assael, H. (1992), Consumer behavior and marketing action, 4th edition, MASS: PWS KENT Publishing Company, Boston.

[55] Assmus, G. (1975), NEWPROD: The design and implementation of a new product model, Journal of Marketing, vol. 39, pp. 16-23.

[56] Assmus, G. (1981), New product models, in: R.L. Schultz and A.A. Zoltners (eds.), Marketing Decision Models, North Holland.

[57] Attonaty, J.M., M.H. Chatelin, F. Garcia, S. Ndiaye (1997), Using extended machine learning and simulation technics to design crop management strategies, in: Kure, H., I. Thysen, A.R. Kristensen (eds.), First European Conference for Information Yechnology in Agriculture (Proceedings), The Royal Veterinary and Agricultural University, Copenhagen, Denmark, EFITA, 15-18 June.

[58] Axelrod, J.N. (1968), Attitude measures that predict purchase, Journal of advertising Research, vol. 8, pp. 3-17.

[59] Baba, N., H. Suto (2000), Utilization of artificial neural networks and the TD-learning method for constructing intelligent decision support systems, European Journal of Operational Research, vol. 122, pp. 501-508.

[60] Baker, N.R. (1974), R & D project selection models: An assessment, IEEE Transactions on Engineering Management, vol. 21, pp. 165-171.

[61] Baker, M. (1985), Globalisation vs. differentiation as international marketing strategies, Journal of Marketing Management, vol. 1, no. 2, pp. 145-156.

[62] Baker, J.M. (1990), Marketing: An Introductory Text, 4th ed., Macmillan, London.

[63] Baldwin, A.A., D. Baldwin, T.K. Sen (1991), The evolution and problems of model management research, Omega: International Journal of management Science, vol. 19, no. 6, pp. 511-528.

[64] Baourakis, G., N.F. Matsatsinis and Y. Siskos (1993a), The contribution of data analysis models in agricultural marketing, in: Janssen, J. and C.H. Skiadas, (eds), Applied Stochastic Models and Data Analysis, World Scientific, 75-93.

[65] Baourakis, G., N.F. Matsatsinis and Y. Siskos (1993b), Agricultural product design and development, in: Janssen, J. and C.H. Skiadas, (eds), Applied Stochastic Models and Data Analysis, World Scientific, 1108-1128.

[66] Baourakis, G. (1994), Agricultural product design methodology: The case of olive oil, Ph.D. Thesis, Technical University of Crete, Greece.

[67] Baourakis, G., N.F. Matsatsinis and Y. Siskos (1995), Consumer behavioural analysis for the design of Cretan olive oil brands, in: Janssen, J., C.H. Skiadas and C. Zopounidis, (eds), Advances in

Stochastic Modelling and Data Analysis, Kluwer Academic Publishers.

[68] Baourakis, G., N.F. Matsatsinis, Y. Siskos (1996), Agricultural product development using multidimensional and multicriteria analyses: The case of wine, European Journal of Operational Research, vol. 94, no. 2, pp. 321-334.

[69] Barker, V., D. O'Conner (1989), Expert systems for configuration on digital: XCON and beyond, Communications of the ACM, vol. 32, no. 3, pp. 298-318.

[70] Barr, A., E. Feigenbaum (1981), The Handbook of Artificial Intelligence, Harris Tech. Press.

[71] Barzilai, J., F.A., Lootsma (1997), Power relations and group aggregation in the multiplicative AHP and SMART, Journal of Multi-Criteria Decision Analysis, vol. 6, pp. 155-165.

[72] Bass, F.M., W.W. Talarzyk (1972), An attitude model for the study of brand preference, Journal of Marketing Research, vol. 9, pp. 93-96.

[73] Bass, F.M., A.P. Jeuland, G.P. Wright (1976), Equilibrium stochastic choice and market penetration theories: Derivation and comparisons, Management Science, vol. 22, pp. 1051-1063.

[74] Bass, F.M., M. Givon, M.U. Kalwani, D. Reibstein, G.P. Wright (1984), An investigation into order of the brand choice process, Marketing Science, vol. 3, no. 4, pp. 267-287.

[75] Bateman, I.D. (1976), Agricultural marketing: A review of the literature of marketing theory and of selected applications. Journal of Agricultural Economics, pp. 171-225.

[76] Bauer, R.A. (1967), Consumer behavior as risk taking, in: D.F. Cox (ed.), Risk Taking and Information Handling in Consumer Behavior, Boston: Harvard Business School.

[77] Bayer, J., S. Lawrence, J.W. Keon (1988), PEP: An expert system for promotion marketing, in: E. Turban and P.R. Watkins (eds.), Applied Expert System, North Holland, Amsterdam.

[78] Bayus, B.L. (1985), Word of mouth: The indirect effects of marketing efforts, Journal of Advertising Research (June/July), pp. 31-39.

[79] Bearden, W.O., M.J. Etzel (1982), Reference group influence on product and brand purchase decisions, Journal of Consumer Research, vol. 9, pp. 183-194.

[80] Bearden, W.O., J.E. Teel (1983), Selected detarminants of consumer satisfaction and complaint reports, Journal of Marketing Resarch, vol. 20, pp. 21-28.

[81] Beatty, S., L. Kahle (1988), Alternative hierarchies of the attitude-behavior relationship: The impact of brand commitment and habit, Journal of the Academy of Marketing Science, vol. 16, pp. 1-10.

[82] Bechtel, G.G. (1990), Share ratio estimation of the nested multinomial Logit model, Journal of Marketing Research, vol. 27, pp. 232-237.

[83] Bell P.C., D.C. Parker (1985), Developing a Visual Interactive Model for corporate cash management, Journal of the Operational Research Society, vol. 36, pp. 779-786.

[84] Bell, P.C. (1985), Visual Interactive Modeling in Operational Research: Successes and Opportunities, Journal of the Operational Research Society, vol. 36, pp. 975-982.

[85] Bell, P.C (1986), Visual interactive modelling: The past, the present and the prospects, European Journal of Operational Research, vol. 54, no. 3, pp. 274-286.

[86] Bell, P.C., R.M. O'Keefe (1987), Visual interactive simulation-history, recent developments and major issues, Simulation, vol.49, pp. 109-116.

[87] Bell, P.C. (1991), Visual Interactive Modeling: The Past, the Present and the Prospects Presented at Mini-Euro Conference on Visual Interactive Modeling, Warwick 1988, European Journal of Operational Research, vol. 54, pp. 307-317.

[88] Belton, V. (1985), The use of a simple multiple criteria model to assist in selection from a shortlist, Journal of the Operational Research Society, vol. 36, pp. 265-274.

[89] Belton, V., M.D. Elder (1994), Decision support systems: Learning from visual interactive modelling, Decision Support System, vol. 12, pp. 355-364.

[90] Belton, V., F., Ackermann, I., Shepherd (1997), Integrated support from problem structuring through alternative evaluation using COPE and VISA, Journal of Multi Criteria Decision Analysis, vol. 6, pp. 115-130.

[91] Ben-Akiva, M., S.R. Lerman (1985), Discrete choice analysis: Theory and application to travel demand, MIT Press, Cambridge.

[92] Benayoun, R., J., De Montgolfier, J., Tergny, O., Larichev (1971), Linear programming with multiple objective functions: Step method (STEM), Mathematical Programming, vol. 1, no. 3.

[93] Benchimol, G., P. Levine, J.C. Pomerol (1987), Developing expert systems for business, North Oxford.

[94] Benjamin, R.I., M.S. Scott Morton (1988), Information technology, integration and organizational change, Interfaces, vol. 18, no. 3, May-June, pp. 86-98.

[95] Bennett, J.L. (1977), http://www.mstnet.com/mstnet/articles/wp_sp/wp_sp.html.

[96] Bennett, J.L. (1986), Tools for building advanced user interfaces, IBM Systems Journal, no. 3/4.

[97] Berg, A., I. Spiegler (1992), Intelligent knowledge generation from statistical data bases, Journal of Information Science and Technology, vol. 2, no. 1, pp. 1-11.

[98] Berkowitz, M.K., G.H. Haines (1982), Predicting demand for residential solar heating: An attribute method, Management Science, vol. 28, no. 7, pp. 717-727.

[99] Berry, D. (1983), How marketers use microcomputers – Now and in the Future, Business Marketing, vol. 68, pp. 48-49, 52-53.

[100] Berthold, M., D.J. Hand (1999), Intelligent Data Analysis, An Introduction, Springer-Verlag.

[101] Bertino, E., B. Catania, G. P. Zarri (2001), Intelligent Database Systems, Addison-Wesley.

[102] Berzins V., M. Gray, D. Naumann, (1986). Abstraction-Based Software Development, Communications of the ACM vol. 29, no. 5, pp. 403.

[103] Bettman, J.R. (1970), Information processing models of consumer behavior, Journal of Marketing Research, no. 7, pp. 370-376.

[104] Bettman, J.R. (1974), Toward a statistics for consumer decision net models, Journal of Consumer Research, no. 1, pp. 71-80.

[105] Bettman, J.R. (1979), An information processing theory of consumer choice, Addison-Wesley Publishing Co., Inc. Reading, MA.

[106] Beuthe, M., G. Scannella (2001), Comparative analysis of UTA multicriteria methods, European Journal of Operational Research, vol. 130, no. 2, pp. 246-262.

[107] Bhargava, H.K., R. Krishnan, R. Muller (1997), Decision support on demand: Emerging electronics markets for decision technologies, Decision Support Systems, vol. 19, pp. 193-214.

[108] Bhatnagar, R.K., L.N. Kanal (1986), Handling uncertain information: A review of numeric and non-numeric methods, in: L.N. Kanal and J. Lemmer (eds.), Uncertainty in Artificial Intelligence, North-Holland.

[109] Biehal, G.J. (1983), Consumers' prior experiences and perceptions in auto repair choice, Journal of Marketing, vol. 47, pp. 82-91.

[110] Birnbaum, L., E. Horvitz, D. Kurlander, H. Lieberman, J. Marks, S. Roth (1997), Panel: Compelling Intelligent User Interfaces -- How Much AI?, in: Proceedings of the 1997 International Conference on Intelligent Interfaces, http://www.merl.com/reports/TR96-28/.

[111] Björn, H. (1996), Intelligent Software Agents on the Internet: An inventory of currently offered functionality in the information society and a prediction of (near-)future developments, Tilburg University, Tilburg, The Netherlands - http://www.hermans.org/agents.

[112] Blair, A., J. Debenham, J. Edwards (1997), A comparative study of methodologies for designing IDSSs, European Journal of Operational Research, vol. 103, pp. 277-295.

[113] Blanning, R.W. (1984), A relational framework for model bank organization, in: Proceedings of the IEEE Workshop on Languages for Automation (November), pp. 148-154.

[114] Blanning, R.W. (1987), A framework for expert model base systems, in: Proceedings of the National Computer Conference, pp. 13-17.

[115] Blanning, R.W. (1988), The application of AI to model management, Working Paper, School of Management, Vanderbilt University.

[116] Blanning, R.W. (1992), Directions in model management research, Decision Line, December/January, pp. 12-13.

[117] Blanning, R.W. (1993), Model Management Systems, Chapter 11 of Decision Support Systems: Putting theory into practice (2nd ed.), ed. By R.H. Sprague, Jr., H.J. Watson, Prentice-Hall, Englewood Cliffs, pp. 156-169.

[118] Blanning, R.W. (1993), Model Management Systems: An Overview, Decision Support Systems, no. 9, pp. 9-18.

[119] Blattberg , R.C., J. Golanty (1978), Tracker: An early test market forecasting and diagnostic model for new product planning, Journal of Marketing Research, vol. 15, pp.192 – 202.

[120] Blattberg, R.C., A.P. Jeuland (1981), A micro-modeling approach to investigate the advertising-sales relationship, Management Science, vol. 27, no. 9, pp. 988-1004.

[121] Bloom, D., M.J. Stewart (1977), An integrated marketing planning system, ESOMAR Seminar, no. 42, pp. 168-186.

[122] Bolger, F., G. Wright (1994), Assessing the quality of expert judgment: Issues and analysis, Decision Support Systems, vol. 11, no. 1, pp. 1-24.

[123] Böckenholt, I., M. Both, W. Gaul (1988), Prolog-based decision support for data analysis in marketing, in: W. Gaul, M. Schader (eds.), Data Expert Knowledge and Decisions, Springer-Verlag, Berlin.

[124] Böckenholt, I., M. Both, W. Gaul (1989), A knowledge-based system for supporting data analysis problems, Decision Support Systems, vol. 5, pp. 345-354.

[125] Bodnar, J., P. Diworth, S. Iacono (1988), Cross-sectional analysis of residential telephone subscription in Canada, Information Economics and Policy, vol. 3, pp. 359-378.

[126] Boehm, B. (1973), Quantitative Assessment, Datamation, vol. 19, no. 5, pp.49-57.

[127] Boehm, B.W. (1984), Software life cycle factors, in: C. Vick and C.V. Ramamoorthy (eds.), Handbook of Software Engineering, Van Nostrand Reinhold, New York.

[128] Boehm, B.W. (1988), A spiral model of software development and enchancement, IEEE Computer, May, pp. 61-72.

[129] Bogetoft, P., P., Pruzan (1991), Planning with Multiple Criteria, Investigation, Communication, Choice, North-Holland, Amsterdam.

[130] Bojic, P., D. Chaffey, A. Greasley, S. Hickie, D. Chaffey (1999), Business Information Systems, Prentice Hall.

[131] Bonczek, R.H., C.W. Holsapple, A.B. Whinston (1980), Future directions for developing decision support systems, Decision Sviences (October).

[132] Bonczek, R.H., C.W. Holsapple, A.B. Whinston (1981), Foundations of decision support systems, Academic Press, New York.

[133] Booch, G. (1994), Object-Oriented Analysis and Design With Applications, Addison-Wesley Publishing Company, Inc.

[134] Boon, L.E., D.L. Kurtz (1971), Marketing information systems: current status in American industry, in: Ailvine, F.C. (ed.), Marketing in Motion: Relevance in Marketing, Proceedings AMA Conference, Chicago, IL, pp. 163-167.

[135] Boose, J.H. (1985), International Journal Man-Machine Studies, vol. 23, pp. 495-526.

[136] Boose, J.H. (1986a), Expertise transfer for expert system design, Elsevier, New York.

[137] Boose, J.H. (1986b), ETS: A system for the transfer of human expertise, in: J. Kowalik (ed.), Knowledge based problem solving, Englewood Cliffs, NJ: Prentice-Hall.

[138] Boose, J.H. (1986c), Rapid acquisition and combination of knowledge from multiple experts in the same domain, Future Computer Systems, vol. 1, pp. 191-216.

[139] Boose, J.H. (1989), A survey of knowledge acquisition tools and techniques, Knowledge Acquisition, vol. 1, no. 1, pp. 3-37.

[140] Boose, J., B.R. Gaines (1990), The Foundations of Knowledge Acquisition, Academic Press, London.

[141] Booty, W.G., D.C.L. Lam, I.W.S. Wong, P. Siconolfi (2001), Design and implementation of an environmental decision support system, Environmental Modelling and Software, vol. 16, no. 5, pp. 453-458.

[142] Booz, Allen and Hamilton (1971), Management of new products, New York.
[143] Booz, Allen and Hamilton (1982), New products for the 1980's, New York.
[144] Borch, O.J., G. Hartvigsen (1991), Knowledge-based systems for strategic market planning in small firms, Decision Support Systems, no. 7, pp. 145-17.
[145] Borda, J.C. (1781), Memoire sur les Elections au scrutiny, Histoire de l'Academie Royale des Sciences, Paris.
[146] Borden, N.H. (1964), The concept of the marketing mix, Journal of Advertising Research (June), no. 4, pp. 2-7.
[147] Bostrom, R.P., R.T., Watson, S.T. Kinney (1992), Computer Augmented Teamwork: A Guided Tour, Van Nostrand Reinhold, New York.
[148] Bouyssou, D. (1984), Expected utility theory and decision aid: A critical survey, in: Hagen, O. and F. Wenstop (eds.), Progress in Utility and Risk Theory, Reidel, Dordrecht, pp. 191-216.
[149] Bouyssou, D. (1988), Building criteria: A prerequisite for MCDA, in: M. Boryczka and R. Slowinski (eds.), Derivation of optimal decision algorithms from decision tables using rough sets, Bulletin of the Polish Academy of Sciences, ser. Technical Sciences, vol. 36, pp.58-80.
[150] Bouyssou, D., T. Marchant, T. Pirlot, P. Perny, A. Tsoukias, P. Vincke (2000), Evaluation and Decision Models - A Critical Perspective, International Series in Operations Research and Management Science, vol. 32, Kluwer Academic Publishers.
[151] Boyd, H.W. Jr., S.J. Levy (1967), Promotion: A behavioral view, Englewood Cliffs, N.J.: Prentice-Hall.
[152] Brans, J.-P., B., Mareschal, Ph., Vincke (1984), PROMETHEE: A new family of outranking methods in multi-criteria analysis, in: Brans, J.-P. (Ed.), Operational Research '84, North-Holland, Amsterdam, pp. 408-421.
[153] Brans, J.P., Ph. Vincke (1985), A preference ranking organization method, Management Science, 31/6, pp. 647-656.
[154] Brans, J.P., Ph. Vincke, B. Mareschal (1986), How to rank and how to select projects: The PROMETHEE method, European Journal of Operational Research, vol. 24, pp. 228-238.
[155] Brans, J.P., B. Mareschal (1989), The PROMETHEE methods for MCDM, the PROMCALC, GAIA and Bankadviser Software, Vrije Universiteit Brussel, STOO/224.
[156] Brien, R.H., J.E. Stafford (1968), Marketing Information Systems: A new dimension for marketing research, Journal of Marketing, no. 32.

[157] Brinberg, D., L. Plimpton (1986), Self-monitoring and product conspicuousness on reference group influence, in: R. Lutz (ed.), Advances in Consumer Research, XIII.

[158] Brooks, N.A.L. (1989), Marketing technology: New marketing information systems enhance service and profitability, Bank Administration, vol. 65, no. 5, pp. 52-54.

[159] Brute, J.F., A. Blount (1989), Knowledge acquisition, McGraw-Hill, New York.

[160] Buchanan, B.G., E.H. Shortliffe (1985), Rule-based expert systems, Addison-Wesley.

[161] Buchanan, B.G., R.O. Duda (1983), Principles of rule-based expert systems, in: M.C. Yovits (Ed.), Advances in Computers, vol. 22, Academic Press, New York, pp. 164-215.

[162] Bui, T.X., M., Jarke (1986), Communications design for co-oP: A group decision support system, ACM Transactions on Office Information Systems, vol. 4, no. 2, pp. 81-103.

[163] Bui, T.X. (1987), Co-oP: A group decision support system for cooperative multiple criteria group decision making, Lecture Notes in Computer Science, No. 290, Springer, Berlin.

[164] Bui, T., J. Lee (1999), An agent-based framework for building decision support systems, Decision Support Systems, 25, 225–237.

[165] Bui, T. (2000), Building agent-based corporate information systems: An application to telemedicine, European Journal of Operational Research, vol. 122, pp. 242-257.

[166] Bunch, D.S., R.R. Batsell (1989), A Monte Carlo comparison of estimators for the multinomial logit model, Journal of Marketing Research, vol. 26, pp. 56-68.

[167] Burke, R.R., A. Rangaswamy, J. Wind, J. Eliashberg (1990), A knowledge based system for advertising design, Marketing Science, vol. 9, no. 3, pp. 212-229.

[168] Burke, R.R. (1991), Reasoning with empirical marketing knowledge, International Journal of Research in Marketing, vol. 8, no. 1, pp. 75-90.

[169] Burns, D.H., E.R. Ross (1991), Developing data bases, Bank Management, Dec., pp. 49-51.

[170] Business Week Guide (1994), The Quality Imperative, McGraw-Hill, New York.

[171] Buttery, A., R. Tamaschke (1995), Marketing decision support systems in a small trading nation: an Australian case study, Marketing Intelligence & Planning, vol. 13, no. 2, pp. 14-28.

[172] Buyer, J., J. Keon (1985), Expert systems in marketing: Developmental issues, in: R. Lusch et al. (eds.), Proceedings of the

AMA Educators' Conference, American Marketing Association, Chicago, Illinois.

[173] Byrd T. A. (1993), Experts Systems in Production and Operations Management: Results of a Survey, Interfaces, vol. 23, no. 2, pp. 118-129.

[174] Buzzell, R.D. (1964), Mathematical models and marketing management, Division of Research, Graduate School of Business Administration, Harvard University, MA: Boston.

[175] Buzzell, R.D. (1966), Competitive behavior and product life cycles, in: J.S. Wright and J.L. Goldstucker (eds.), New Ideas for Successful Marketing, Chicago: American Marketing Association.

[176] Cadbury, N.D. (1975), When, where and how to test market, Harvard Business Review (May-June), pp. 96-105.

[177] Cadotte E.R., R.B.Woodruff, R.L. Jenkins (1987), Expectations and Norms in Models of Consumer Satisfaction, Journal of Marketing Research, vol. 24, pp. 305-14.

[178] Calantone, R., R.G. Cooper (1981), New product scenarios: Prospects for success, Journal of Marketing (Spring), pp. 48-60.

[179] Calantone, R.J., C.A. Di Benedetto, J.B. Schmidt (1999), Using the Analytic Hierarchy Process in New Product Screening, Journal of Product Innovation Management, vol. 16, no. 1, pp. 65-76.

[180] Cambruzzi, T., A. Fiduccia, L. Novelli (1999), A dynamic geomonitoring system for Venetian coastal ecosystem: WATERS project, Computers, Environment and Urban Systems, vol. 23, no. 6, pp. 469-484.

[181] Canali, G. (1991), Changing meat consumption behaviours in the European community, in: Proceedings of the 25th Seminar of the European Association of Agricultural Economists, 24-26 June, pp. 245-255.

[182] Capon, N., J. Hulbert (1972), Decision systems in industrial marketing: An empirical approach, in: Proceedings of the American Institute for Decision Sciences (Nov.), pp. 112-117.

[183] Capon, N., J. Hulbert (1975), Decision systems analysis in industrial marketing, Industrial Marketing Management, no. 4, pp. 143-160.

[184] Capon, N., J.U. Farley and J. Hulbert (1975), Pricing and forecasting in an oligopoly firm, Journal of Management Studies, no. 12, pp. 133-156.

[185] Capon, N., D. Scammon (1979), Advertising agency decisions: An analytic treatment, in: J.M. Leigh and C.R. Martin, Jr. (eds.), Current Issues and Research in Advertising, Ann Arbor: University of Michigan Press.

[186] Capewell, A., J., Penn (1986), Health food marketing: The impact of changes in consumer awareness and preference on product policy, Food Marketing, vol. 2, no. 3, pp. 46-66.

[187] Carbonell, J.G., Michalski, R.S., T.M. Mitchell, (1983), An overview of machine learning, in: Michalski, R. S., Carbonell, J. G., and T. M. Mitchell (eds.), Machine Learning, an Artificial Intelligence Approach, Tioga Publishing Company, Palo Alto, CA.

[188] Carey, J. (1990), Prototyping: Alternative systems development methodology, Information and Software Technology, vol. 32, pp. 120-121.

[189] Cardelli L., P. Wegner (1985), On Understanding Types, Data Abstraction, and Polymorphism, ACM Computing Serveys vol. 17, no. 4, pp.481.

[190] Carlsson, C., D., Ehrenberg, P., Eklund, M., Fedrizzi, P., Gustafsson, P., Lindholm, G., Merkuryeva, T., Riisanen, A.G.S., Ventre (1992), Consensus in distributed soft environments, European Journal of Operational Research, vol. 61, pp. 165-185.

[191] Carroll, J.D., J.J. Chang (1964), A general index of nonlinear correlation and its applications to the interpretation of multidimensional scaling solutions, American Psychologist, vol. 19, pp. 540-549.

[192] Carver, S. (1991), Integrating multicriteria evaluation with GIS, International Journal of Geographical Information Systems, vol. 5, no. 3, pp. 321-339.

[193] Cercone, N., G. McCalba (1984), Artificial intelligence: Underlying assumptions and basic objectives, Journal of the American Society for Information Science (September).

[194] Chambers, J., J.M.E. Zayay, D. Pregibon (1981), Expert software for data analysis: An initial experiment, in: Proceedings of the 43rd Session of the International Statistics Institute, Buenos Aires, Argentina.

[195] Chan, C.W., L. Chen, L. Geng (2000), Knowledge engineering for an intelligent case-based system for help desk operations, Expert Systems with Applications, vol. 18, pp. 125-132.

[196] Chandler, A. D. (1990), The enduring logic of industrial success, Harvard Business Review, pp. 130-140.

[197] Chang, C.L., J.R. Slagle (1971), An admissible and optimal algorithm for searching AND/OR graphs, Artificial Intelligence, Vol. 2, pp. 117-128.

[198] Chapman, R.G., R. Staelin (1982), Exploiting rank ordered choice set data within the stochastic utility model, Journal of Marketing Research, vol. 19, pp. 288-301.

[199] Chart, S., R. Krishnan (1990), Towards a logical reconstruction of structured models, in: Proceedings of the 22nd Annual Hawaii International Conference on System Sciences III: Decision Support and Knowledge Based Systems Track, pp. 524-543.

[200] Chaudhuri S., U. Dayal (1997), An Overview of Data Warehousing and OLAP Technology, ACM Sigmod Record, March.

[201] Chen, C-H, L.G. Occena (2000), Knowledge decomposition for a product design blackboard expert system, Artificial Intelligence in Engineering, no. 14, pp. 71–82.

[202] Chen, K., R. Blong, C. Jacobson (2001), MCE-RISK: integrating multicriteria evaluation and GIS for risk decision-making in natural hazards, Environmental Modelling and Software, vol. 16, no. 4, pp. 387-397.

[203] Chi, R.T., E. Turban (1995), Distributed intelligent executive information systems, Decision Support Systems, vol. 14, pp. 117-130.

[204] Chisnall, P.M. (1985), Marketing: A behavioural analysis (2nd ed.), London: McGraw-Hill.

[205] Choi, H-A., E-H., Suh, C-K., Suh (1994), Analytic hierarchy process: It can work for group decision support systems, Computers and Industrial Engineering, vol. 27, no. 1-4, pp. 167-171.

[206] Choffray, J.M., B. Charpin (1986), Les systèmes experts: Outils de mise en valeur de la competence marketing, Working paper ESSEC, CERESSEC, no. 86003.

[207] Cholawsky, E.M. (1988), Beating the prototype blues, AI Expert, vol. 3, no. 12, pp. 42-49.

[208] Cimflex Teknowledge (1991), M4: Users guide, Palo Alto, CA.

[209] Clark, K.B., T. Fujimoto (1991), Product Development Performance: Strategy, Organization and Management in the World Auto Industry, Harvard Business School Press, Cambridge, MA.

[210] Clark, H. (1987), Consumer and corporate values: Yet another view of global marketing, International Journal of Advertising, vol. 6, pp. 29-42.

[211] Clark, D.N. (1992), A Literature Analysis of the Use of Management Science Tools in Strategic Planning, Journal of the Operational Research Society, vol. 43, no. 9, pp. 859-870.

[212] Clark, D., P. Krause (1993), Representing uncertain knowledge: An artificial intelligence approach, Intellect, Oxford, UK.

[213] Clarke, C. K. (1997), Getting started with geographic information systems, Prentice-Hall Inc.

[214] Clemons, E., M.C. Row (1991), Sustaining IT Advantage: The role of structural differences, MIS Quarterly, Sep., pp. 276-292.

[215] CODASYL Programming Language Committee (1971), Data Base Task Group Report, Association for Computer Machinery (ACM), Transactions on Database Systems, New York.

[216] Codd, E.F. (1970), A relational model of data for large shared data nanks, Communications of the Association for Computer Machinery (ACM), vol. 13, no. 6, pp. 377-397.

[217] Codd, E.F. (1974), Recent investigations in relational databases systems, Information Processing, vol. 74, North-Holland, pp. 1017-1021.

[218] Codd, E.F., S.B. Codd, C.T. Salley (1993), Providing OLAP (Online Analytical Processing) to user-analysts: an IT mandate, Available from: http://www.hyperion.com/downloads/OLAPCoddWP.pdf

[219] Cohen, M.D., L.S. Sproull (1991), Organization science, Special Issue on Organizational Learning, vol. 2, no. l.

[220] Cohrane, J.L., M. Zeleny (1973), Multiple criteria decision making, University of South Carolina Press, Columbia.

[221] Cole, C., S. Balasubramanian (1993), Age differeces in consumers' search for information: Public policy implications, Journal of Consumer Research, vol. 20, pp. 157-169.

[222] Coleman, R.P., L.P. Rainwater (1978), Social standing in America: New dimension of class, New York: Basic Books.

[223] Coleman, R.P. (1983), The continuing significance of social class to marketing, Journal of Consumer Research (December), pp. 265-280.

[224] Collopy, F., J.S. Armstrong (1992), Rule-based forecasting: Development and validation of an expert systems approach to combining time series extrapolations, Management Science, vol. 38, no. 10, pp. 1394-1414.

[225] Colson, G., B., Mareschal (1994), JUDGES: A descriptive group decision support system for the ranking of the items, Decision Support Systems, vol. 12, pp. 391-404.

[226] Constantine, L., E. Yourdon (1979), Structured Design, Prentice-Hall, Englewood Cliffs, New Jersey.

[227] Contini, S., F. Bellezza, M.D. Christou, C. Kirchsteiger (2000), The use of geographic information systems in major accident risk assessment and management, Journal of Hazardous Materials, vol. 78, no. 1-3, pp. 223-245.

[228] Cook, W.D., M., Kress (1985), Ordinal ranking with intensity of preferences, Management Science, vol. 31, pp. 26-32.

[229] Cook, R.L., J.M. Schleede (1988), Application of expert systems to advertising, Journal of Advertising Research, June/July, pp. 47-56.

[230] Cooke, S., A. Kauppila (1996), Tools for the internet-channeling the information tidal wave, Electronic Library, vol. 14, no. 2, pp. 129-132.

[231] Cooper, R.G. (1979), The dimensions of industrial new product success and failure, Journal of Marketing (Summer), no. 43, pp. 93-103.

[232] Cooper, R.G. (1988), The new product process: A decision guide for managers, Journal of Marketing Management, vol. 3, no. 3, pp. 238-255.

[233] Cooper, L.G., M. Nakanishi (1988), Market share analysis, Kluwer Academic Publishers, Mass.

[234] Cortes-Rello, E., F. Golshani (1990), Uncertain reasoning using the Dempster-Shafer method: An application in forecasting and marketing management, Expert Systems, vol. 7, no. 1, pp. 9-17.

[235] Cosset, J., Y. Siskos, C. Zopounidis (1992), Evaluating country risk: A decision support approach, Global Financial Journal, vol. 3, no. 1.

[236] Council Regulation -EEC (1991), No. 2092/91, Official Journal of the European Communities, 24 June.

[237] Courbon, J.C., B. Oudet, J.P. Rouet (1977), Les systemes interactifs d'aide d la decision, Informatique et Gestion, no. 89, pp. 72-77.

[238] Courbon, J.C., J. Grajew, J. Tolovi (1979), Conception et mise en oeuvre des SIAD: L' approache ivolutive, Informatique et Gestion, no. 103, pp. 51-59.

[239] Coursey, D.L. (1985), A normative model of behavior based upon an activity hierarchy, Journal of Consumer Research, June, pp. 64-73.

[240] Coursey, D.L. (1988), Preference trees, preferences hierarchies and consumer behavior, Journal of Consumer Research, vol. 15, pp. 407-409.

[241] Courtis, J.K. (1978), Modelling a financial ratios categoric framework, Journal of Business Finance and Accounting, vol. 5, no. 4, pp. 371-387.

[242] Courtney, J.F. et al. (1987), A knowledge-based DSS for managerial problem diagnosis, Decision Sciences (Summer).

[243] Courtney, J.F., D.B. Paradice (1988), Database systems for management, St. Louis: Times Mirror/Mosby College Printing.

[244] Cowen, D.J. (1988), GIS Versus CAD Versus DBMS: What Are the Differences?, Photogrammetric Engineering and Remote Sensing, vol. 54, no. 11, pp. 1551-1554.

[245] Cox, D.F., R.E. Good (1967), How to build a marketing information system, Harvard Business Review (May-June), pp. 145-154.

[246] Cox, W.E. Jr. (1967), Product life cyclesas marketing models, Journal of Business, no. 40, pp. 375-384.

[247] Cronan, T.P., L.W. Glorfeld, L.G. Parry (1991), Production system development for expert systems using a recursive partitioning induction approach: An application to mortgage, commercial and consumer lending, Decision Sciences, vol. 22, pp. 812-845.

[248] Cśaki, P., L., Csiszár, F., Fölsz, K., Keller, Cs., Méeszáros, T., Rapcsák, P., Turchányi (1995a), A flexible framework for group decision support WINGDSS Version 3.0, Annals of Operations Research, vol. 58, pp. 441-453.

[249] Cśaki, P., T., Rapcsák, P., Turchányi, M., Vermes (1995b), R and D for group decision aid in Hungary by WINGDSS, a Microsoft Windows based group decision support system, Decision Support Systems, vol. 14, pp. 205-217.

[250] Cśaki, P., F., Fölsz, T., Rapcsák, Z., Sági (1998), On tender evaluations, Journal of Decision Systems, vol. 7, pp. 179-194).

[251] Crisalli, C. (1999), User's behaviour simulation of intercity rail service choices, Simulation Practice and Theory, vol. 7, pp. 233-249.

[252] Cross, G.R., E.R. Foxman, N. Kishore, D.L. Sherrell (1986), A marketing strategy assistant, in: H. Krallmann (Hrsg.): Expertensysteme im Unternehmen: Moeglichkeiten – Grenzen – Anwendungsbeispiele, Berlin, pp. 75 – 83.

[253] Curry, B., L. Moutinho (1991), Expert systems and marketing strategy: An application to site location decisions, Journal of Marketing Channels, vol. 1, no. 1, pp. 23-37.

[254] Curry, B., L. Moutinho (1994), Intelligent Computer Models for Marketing Decisions, Management Decision, Vol. 32, No. 4, pp. 30-35.

[255] Cyert, R.M., J.G. March (1963), A behavioral theory of the firm, Englewood Cliffs, New Jersey: Prentice-Hall.

[256] Dahl O., E. Dijkstra, C. Hoare (1972), Structured Programming. London, England: Academic Press.

[257] Dalal, S.R., J.C. Lee, D.J. Sabavala (1984), Prediction of individual buying behavior: A Poisson-Bernoulli model with arbitrary heterogeneity, Marketing Science, vol. 3, no. 4, pp. 352-367.

[258] Dalal, S.R., R.W. Klein (1988), A flexible class of discrete choice models, Marketing Science, vol. 7, no. 3, pp. 232-251.

[259] Dambroise, E., P. Massotte (1986), MUSE: An expert system in statistics, COMPSTAT 86, Rizzi (ed.), Physica Verlag Heidelberg Wien, pp. 271-276.

[260] Dambroise, E., P. Massotte (1987), Mise en oeuvre d'un système expert en statistiques: MUSE, AFCET: L'aide a la décision dans l'organisation, Mars, Paris.

[261] Dando, M., P. Bennett (1981), A Kuhnian crisis in management science?, Journal of the Operational Research Society, vol. 32, pp. 91-104.

[262] David, F. (1986), Fundamentals of strategic management, Merrill Publishing Coy.

[263] Davies, G. (1990), Marketing to retailers: A battle for distribution long range planning. International Journal of Strategic Management, vol. 23, no. 6, pp. 101-108.

[264] Davies, D., L. Moutinho, B. Curry (1995), Construction and testing of a knowledge-based system in retail bank marketing, International Journal of Bank Marketing, vol. 13, no. 2, pp. 4-14.

[265] Davis, G.B. (1974), Management information systems: Conceptual foundations, structure and development, New York: McGraw-Hill.

[266] Davis, G.B., M.M. Olson (1985), Management information systems: Conceptual foundations, structure and development, McGraw Hill, New York.

[267] Davis, G. (1987), Strategies for information requirements determination, in: R. Galliers (ed.), Information Analysis: Selected readings, Addison-Wesley.

[268] Davis, A.M. et al. (1988), A strategy for comparing alternative software development life cycle models, IEEE Transactions on Software Engineering, vol. 14, no. 10, pp. 1453-1461.

[269] Davis, J.G., D. Sundaram (1995), PETAPS: A prototype decision support system for consumer product marketing and promotion, European Journal of Operational Research, vol. 87, no. 2, pp. 247 – 256.

[270] Davison, R. (1995), A survey, of group support systems: technology and operation, WP 95/02, City University of Hong Kong, Faculty of Business, Department of Information Systems.

[271] Day, R.L., E.L. Landon Jr. (1977), Toward a theory of consumer complaining behavior, in: A.G. Woodside, J.N. Sheth and P.D. Bennett (eds.), Consumer and Industrial Buying Behavior, New York: Elsevier North-Holland.

[272] Day, G.S. A.D. Shocker, R.K. Srivastava (1979), Customer oriented approaches to identifying product markets, Journal of Marketing, no. 43, pp. 8-19.

[273] Day, G.S., T. Deutscher (1982), Attitudinal predictions choices of major appliance brands, Journal of Marketing Research, vol. 19, pp. 192-198.

[274] Day, R.L. (1984), Modeling choices among alternative responses to dissatisfaction, in: T.C. Kinnear (ed.), Advances in Consumer Research, XI.

[275] Day, G. (1986), Analysis for strategic market decisions, West Publishing Company.

[276] Dean, B.V., A.K. Chaudhuri (1980), Project scheduling: A critical review, in: B.V. Dean and J. Goldhar (eds.), TIMS Studies in the Management Sciences, vol. 15, pp. 215-233, North Holland Publishing.

[277] Deb, K. (2001), Multi-Objective Optimization Using Evolutionary Algorithms, John Wiley & Sons.

[278] Decker, R., W. Gaul (1990), Einige bemerkungen ueber experten systeme fuer marketing und marktforschung, Marketing ZFP, H.4, iv.Quartal, pp. 257-271.

[279] DeMacro, T. (1978), Structured analysis and systems specification, Englewood Cliffs, N.J.: Prentice-Hall.

[280] Dempster, A.P. (1967), Upper and lower probabilities induced by a multivalued mapping, Annual Math. Statistics, no. 38, pp. 325-329.

[281] Dendy L., R. Gnanadesikan, J.R. Ketterning, J.W. Suzansky (1990), An analysis of questionnaire data on work design and job satisfaction: A case study in the use of simple graphical displays, in: S. Geisser, J.S. Hodges, S.J. Press and A. Zallner (eds), Bayesian and Likelihood Methods in Statistics and Econometrics, Elsevier Science Publishers B.V., North Holland.

[282] Deng, P.S. (1993), Automating knowledge acquisition and refinement for decision support: A connectionist inductive inference model, Decision Sciences, vol. 24, no. 2, pp. 371-393.

[283] Dennis, A.R., J.F., George, L.M., Jessup, J.F., Nunamaker, D., Vogel (1988), Information technology to support electronic meetings, MIS Quarterly, vol. 12, no. 4, pp. 591-624.

[284] Densham, P.J. (1991), Spatial Decision Support Systems, in: D.J. Maguire, M.F. Goodchild, D.W. Rhind, (eds.), Geographical Information Systems: Principles and Applications, vol.1, London: Langman, pp. 403-412.

[285] Densham, P., M., Armstrong, K., Kemp (1995), Scientific report on the specialist meeting for NCGIA Initiative 17, Santa Barbara, CA: National Center for Geographic Information and Analysis (http://www.ncgia.ucsb.edu/research/i17/I-17_home.html).

[286] Densham, P.J., M.P. Armstrong, K. K. Kemp (1995) Collaborative Spatial Decision-Making: Scientific Report for the Intitiative, 17th Specialist Meeting, Orono, Maine: National Center for Geographic Information and Analysis.

[287] Derrick, F.W., A.E. Linfeld (1980), The family life cycle: An alternative approach, Journal of Consumer Research (September), pp. 214-217.

[288] DeSalvo, D.A. (1987), Structured design of an expert system prototype at National Archives, in: B.G. Silverman (ed.), Expert systems for business, Addison-Wesley Publishing Company.

[289] DeSanctis, G., R.B., Gallupe (1987), A foundation for the study of group decision support systems, Management Science, vol. 33, pp. 589-609.

[290] DeSarbo, W.S., V.R. Rao (1986), A constrained unfolding methodology for product positioning, Marketing Science, vol. 5, no. 1, pp. 1-19.

[291] DeSarbo, W.S., D.L. Hoffman (1987), Constructing MDS joint spaces from binary choice data: A multidimensional unfolding threshold model for marketing research, Journal of Marketing Research, vol. 24, pp. 40-54.

[292] Devine, H.A., R.C. Field (1986), The Gist of GIS, Journal of Forestry, vol. 8, pp. 17-22.

[293] Dickson, G.W., R. Powers (1973), MIS Project management: Myths, opinions and realities, in: W. McFarlin et al. (eds.), Information Systems Administration, Holt, Rinehart & Winston, New York.

[294] Dickson, G.W., J.C. Wetherbe (1985), The management of information systems, McGraw-Hill, New York.

[295] Diederich, J. et al. (1987), Kriton: A knowledge acquisition tool for expert systems, Int. Journal of Man-Machine Studies, January.

[296] Dimitras, A.I., S.H. Zanakis, C. Zopounidis (1996), A survey of business failures with an emphasis on prediction methods and industrial applications, European Journal of Operational Research, vol. 90, no. 3, pp. 487-513.

[297] Dolk, D.R. (1988), Model management and structured modeling: The role of an information resource dictionary system, Communications of the ACM, vol. 31, no. 6, pp. 704-718.

[298] Donovan, J.J. (1976), Database system approach to management decision support, ACM Transactions on Database Systems, vol. 1, no. 2, pp. 344-369.

[299] Donovan, J.J., H.D. Jacoby (1977), Virtual machine communication for the implementation of decision support systems, IEEE Transactions on Software Engineering, vol. SE-3, no. 5, pp. 333-342.

[300] Dorfman, R., P.O. Steiner (1954), Optimal advertising and optimal quality, American Economic Review (December), pp. 826-836.

[301] Dos Santos, B., C.W. Holsapple (1989), A framework for designing adaptive DSS interfaces, Decision Support Systems, vol. 5, no. 1.

[302] Dos Santos, B.L., Z.T.S. Mookerjee (1993), Expert system design: Minimizing information acquisition costs, Decision Support Systems, no. 9, pp. 161-181.

[303] Douglass, S., S. Graig (1986), Global marketing myopia, Journal of Marketing Management, vol. 2, no. 2, pp. 155-171.

[304] Doukidis, G.I., E. Whitley (1988), Developing expert systems, Chartwell-Bratt.

[305] Doukidis, G.I. (1988), Decision support system concepts in expert systems: an empirical study, Decision Support Systems, vol. 4, no. 3.

[306] Doukidis, G.I., F. Land, G. Miller (1989), Knowledge based management support systems, Ellis Horwood.

[307] Doukidis, G.I., R.J. Paul (1992), Artificial intelligence in operational research, MacMillan.

[308] Doukidis, G., A. Fragopoulou, G. Anagnostopoulos (1993), EDI: The Information in the enterprises, Athens (in Greek).

[309] Doyle, J. (1979a), A glimpse of truth maintenance, in: Artificial Intelligence: An MIT Perspective, vol. 1, MIT Press, Cambridge, Mass.

[310] Doyle, J. (1979b), A truth maintenance system, Artificial Intelligence, vol. 12, no. 3.

[311] Drake, K.C., P. Hess (1990), Abduction: A numeric knowledge acquisition approach, PC AI (September-October).

[312] Drucker, P.F. (1954), The practice of management, Harper and Brothers, New York.

[313] Drucker, P.F. (1967), The effective decision, Harvard Business Review (Jan - Feb), pp. 93-105.

[314] Dubelaar, C., P.N. Finlay, D. Taylor (1991), Expert systems: The gold fusion of marketing?, Journal of Marketing Management, vol. 7, pp. 371-382.

[315] Dubin, J.A. (1986), A nested logit model of space and water heat system choice, Marketing Science, vol. 5, no. 2, pp 112-124.

[316] Duda, R.O., P.E. Hart, J. Gasschnig (1979a), Model design in the PROSPECTOR consultant system for mineral exploration, in: D. Michie (ed.), Expert Systems in the Micro-electronic Age, Edinburgh University Press.

[317] Duda, R.O., P.E. Hart, N.J. Nilsson (1979b), Subjective Bayesian methods for rule-based inference systems, in: B.L. Webber and N.J. Nilsson (eds.), Readings in Artificial Intelligence, CA: Tioga Publishing, Palo Alto.

[318] Durfee, E.H., V.R. Lesser, D.D. Corkill (1987), Coherent cooperation among communicating problem solvers, IEEE Trans. Comput., vol. 36, pp. 1275-1291.

[319] Durfee, E.H., V.R. Lesser, D.D. Corkill (1989), Trends in cooperative distributed problem solving, IEEE Transactions Knowledge Data Engineering KOE-11(1), pp. 63-83.

[320] Durkin, J. (1994), Expert Systems, Design and Development, Macmillan.
[321] Dusenbury, W. (1967), CPM for new protuct introduction, Harvard Business Review, vol. 45, no. 4, pp. 124-139.
[322] Dyer, R.F., E.H., Forman (1992), Group decision support with the analytic hierarchy process, Decision Support Systems, vol. 8, pp. 99-124.
[323] Eccles, R.G. (1991), The performance measurement manifesto, Harvard Business Review, January-February, pp. 131-137.
[324] Eck, R.D., A. Philippakis, R. Ramirez (1990), Solver representation for model management systems, in: Proceedings of the 23rd Annual Hawaii International Conference on System Sciences III: Decision Support and Knowledge Based Systems Track, pp. 474-483.
[325] Eden, C. (1990), Using cognitive mapping for strategic options development and analysis (SODA), in: Rosenhead, J. (Ed.), Rational Analysis for a Problematic World, Wiley, New York.
[326] Edwards, W. (1977), How to use multiattribute utility measurement for social decision making, IEEE Transactions on Systems Man and Cybernetics, vol. 7, pp. 326-340.
[327] Eichmann, D. (1994), Ethical Web Agents, in: Proceedings of the Second International World-Wide Web Conference, Chicago, United States.
[328] Ehrenberg, A.S.C. (1972), Repeat-buying: Theory and applications, Amsterdam, North Holland.
[329] Ehrenberg, A.S.C. (1988), Repeat buying: Facts, Theory and Data (2nd ed.), Oxford University Press, New York.
[330] Elam, J.J., B. Konsynski (1987), Using artificial intelligence techniques to enhance the capabilities of model management systems, Decision Sciences, no. 18.
[331] Eliashberg, J. (1980), Consumer preference judgments: An exposition with empirical applications, Management Science, vol. 26, no. 1, pp. 60-77.
[332] El-Swaify, S.A., D.S. Yakowitz (1998), Multiple Objective Decision Making for Land, Water and Environmental Management, Lewis Publishers.
[333] Elrod, T. (1988), Choice map: Inferring a product-market map from panel data, Marketing Science, vol. 7, no. 1, pp. 21-40.
[334] Engel, J.F., D.J. Kollatt, R.D. Blackwell (1978), Consumer behaviour, Dryden Press, New York.
[335] Engel, J.F., R.D. Blackwell, P.W. Miniard (1986), Consumer behavior (5th ed.), Chicago: Dryden Press.

[336] Enis, B.M., R. LaGarce, A.E. Prell (1977), Extending the product life cycle, Business Horizons (June), pp. 46-56.

[337] Eom, H.B. (1989), The current state of multiple criteria decision support systems, Human Systems Management, vol. 8, pp. 113-119.

[338] Eom, H.B., S.M. Lee (1990), A survey of decision support system applications (1971-1988), Interfaces, vol. 20, no. 3, pp. 65-79.

[339] Eom, H.B., S.M. Lee (1991), Decision support system applications research: A bibliography (1971-1988), European Journal of Operational Research, vol. 46, pp. 333-342.

[340] Eom, H.B., S.M. Lee, J.K. Kim (1993), The intellectual structure of decision support systems (1971-1989), Decision Support Systems, no. 10, pp. 19-35.

[341] Eom, S.B. (1999), Decision support systems research: current state and trends, Industrial Management & Data Systems, vol. 99, no. 5, pp. 213-220.

[342] Erbe, R. et al. (1980), Integrated data analysis and management for the problem solving environment, Information Systems, vol. 5, pp. 273-285.

[343] Erben, K., K. Gestren (1997), Cooperation Networks towards Virtual Enterprises, http://www.virtual-organization.net.

[344] ERGASYA (1991), Design of a new flour product for a Greek flourmill company, Technical Report, Decision Support Systems Laboratory, Technical University of Crete, Chania (in greek).

[345] Ericsson, K.A., H.A. Simon (1984), Protocol analysis: Verbal reports as data, Cambridge, MA: MIT Press.

[346] Erkes, J.W., K.B. Kenny, J.W. Lewis (1996), Implementing shared manufacturing services on the world wide Web. Communications of the ACM, vol. 39, no. 2, pp. 34–45.

[347] Ernst GW, A. Newell (1969), GPS: A case study in generality and problem solving, New York: Academic Press.

[348] Esch, F.R., T. Muffler (1989), Expertensysteme in marketing, Marketing Zeitschrift fur Forschung and Praxis, Heft 3, III.Quartal, pp. 145-152.

[349] Esch, F.R., W. Kroeber-Riel (1994), Expertnsysteme fur die Werbung/Computer Aided Advertising System, Munchen: Verlag Franz Vahlen.

[350] Escribano, B.J., S., Mili (1990), Market Research into Demand and Prices for Olive Oils in Spain, Madrid.

[351] Espinasse, B., T., Pauner (1995), NegocIAD: A multi-criteria and multi-agent system for negotiation support. International Workshop on the Design of Cooperative Systems, INRIA, Antibes-Juan-les-Pins, France.

[352] Espinasse, N., G., Picolet, E., Chouraqui (1997), Negotiation support systems: A multi-criteria and multi-agent approach, European Journal of Operational Research, vol. 103, pp. .

[353] Evans, J.P., R.E. Steuer (1973), Generating efficient extreme points in linear multiple objective programming: Two algorithms and computing experience, in: Multiple Criteria Decision Making, University of South Carolina Press, South Carolina.

[354] Evans, J.P., R.E. Steuer (1973), A revised simplex method for linear multiple objective programs, Mathematical Programming, vol. 5, no. 1, pp. 54-72.

[355] Everett, P. (1984), Operational Research in the British Airports Authority, presented at the IFORS Conference. Washington, DC.

[356] European Documentation (1987), The common agricultural policy and its reform, Office for Official Publications of the European Communities.

[357] Eisenhart, T. (1990), After ten years of marketing decision support systems, where's the payoff?, Business Marketing, June.

[358] Farley, J.U., J.A. Howard, J. Hulbert (1971), An organizational approach to an industrial marketing information system, Sloan Management Review, no. 13, pp. 35-54.

[359] Farley, J.U., J. Hulbert, D. Weinstein (1978), Industrial market planning by two European multinational companies: A study of decision process, Working Paper, Graduate School of Business, Columbia University.

[360] Fedra, K. (1997), Spatial decision support in resources management and environmental applications, in: Proceedings of the 11th Annual Symposium on Geographic Information Systems held in Vancouver, British Columbia, Canada.

[361] Feigenbaum, E. (1982), Knowledge engineering for the 1980's, Department of Computer Science, Standford University, California.

[362] Feigenbaum, E., P. McCorduck (1983), The fifth generation, Reading, MA: Addison-Wesley.

[363] Ferris, G.E. (1979), Differences between marketing information systems in the US and Australia, in: G.E. Ferris, M. Mather and P. Steidl (eds.), Regardings in Australian Marketing, Ball State University, Indiana.

[364] Fikes, R., T. Kehler (1985), The role of frame-based representation in reasoning, Communication of ACM, September.

[365] Finklin, E.F. (1983), Developing and managing new products, Journal of Business Strategy (Spring), pp. 39-46.

[366] Fishbein, M. (1963), An investigation of relationship between beliefs about an object and the attitude toward the object, Human Relations, vol. 16, pp. 233-240.
[367] Fishbein, M. (1967), Attidutes and prediction of behavior, in: M. Fishbein (ed.), Readings in Attidute Theory and Measurement, New York: John Wiley.
[368] Fishbein, M., L. Ajzen (1975), Belief, attitude, intention and behavior, Addison-Wesley, Reading, Mass.
[369] Fishburn, P.C. (1970), Utility theory for decision making, Wiley, New York.
[370] Fishburn, P.C. (1972), Mathematics of decision theory, UNESCO.
[371] Fishburn, P.C. (1977), A survey of multiattribute/multicriteria evaluation theories, in: S. Zionts (ed), Multicriteria problem solving, Springer-Verlag, Berlin.
[372] Fleck, R.A. Jr. (1973), How media planners process information, Journal of Advertising Research, no. 13, pp. 14-18.
[373] Fletcher, K. (1983), Information systems in British industry, Management Decision, vol. 21, no. 2, pp. 25-36.
[374] Fletcher, K., A. Buttery, K. Deans (1988), A structure and content of the marketing systme: A guide for management, Marketing Intelligence & Planning, vol. 6, no. 4, pp. 27-35.
[375] Fletcher, K. (1990), Marketing management & information technology, Prentice Hall International (UK).
[376] Flynn, R., R. Goldsmith (1993), Application of the personal involvement inventory in marketing, Psychology and Marketing, vol. 10, no. 4, pp. 357-366.
[377] Ford, F.N. (1985), Decision support systems and expert systems: A comparison, Information and Management, no. 8, pp. 21-26.
[378] Forsyth, R., R. Rada (1986), Machine Learning: Applications in expert systems and information retrieval, Ellis Horwood, Chichester.
[379] Fotheringham, A.S. (1988), Consumer store choice and choice set definition, Marketing Science, vol. 7, no. 3, pp. 299-310.
[380] Frank, R.E., A.A. Kuehn, W.F. Massy (1962), Quantitative techniques in marketing analysis, Homewood: Il, Irwin.
[381] Frawley, W.J., G. Piatetsky-Shapiro, C.J. Matheus (1991), Knowledge Discovery in Databases: An Overview, in: U. Fayyad, G. Piatetsky-Shapiro, P. Smyth (Eds.), Knowledge Discovery in Databases, AAAI/MIT Press, Cambridge, MA, pp. 1-27.
[382] Freeman, J.A., D.M. Skapura (1991), Neural Networks: Algorithms, Applications and Programming Techniques, Addison Wesley.
[383] Freiling, M. et al. (1985), Starting a knowledge engineering project: A step-by-step approach, AI Magazine, Fall.

[384] French, S. (1993), Decision theory: An introduction to the mathematics of rationality, Ellis Horwood, West Sussex.

[385] Frenzel, L. (1987), Crash course in AI and expert systems, H. Sams, Indianapolis.

[386] Frohn, H. (1991), Food promotion and advertising in the single European market, in: Proceedings of the 25th seminar of the EAAE, 24-26 June 1991, pp. 343-356.

[387] Gafin, A., G.W. Torrance (1981), Risk attitude and time preference in health, Management Science (April), pp. 440-451.

[388] Gaines, B.R. (1988), Knowledge acquisition: Developments and advances, in: M.D. Oliff (ed.), Expert systems and intelligent manufacturing, Elsevier Science, New York.

[389] Gaines, B.R., P.J., Compton (1992), Induction of Ripple Down Rules, in: A. Adams and L. Sterling, AI '92 Proceedings of the 5th Australian Joint Conference on Artificial Intelligence, (Hobart, Tasmania, World Scientific, Singapore, 1992), pp 349-354.

[390] Gaines, B.R, P.J. Compton, (1994), Induction of Meta-Knowledge about Knowledge Discovery, IEEE Transactions on Knowledge and Data Engineering, vol. 5, no. 6, pp. 990-992.

[391] Gale, W.A., D. Pregibon (1983), Building on Expert Interface, Technical Memorandum Bell Telephone Laboratories.

[392] Gale, W.A. (1986a), REX review, in: W.A. Gale (ed.), Artificial intelligence and statistics, Reading, MA: Addison-Wesley.

[393] Gale, W.A. (1986b), Student Phase 1: A report on work in progress, in: W.A. Gale (ed.), Artificial intelligence and statistics, Reading, MA: Addison-Wesley.

[394] Gale, W.A. (1986c), Knowledge representation in data analysis, in: Proceedings of the 4th International Symposium in Data Analysis and Informatics, Versailles.

[395] Gale, P.G. (1992), Marketing - Information: An empirical analysis, in: Proceedings of the 21st Annual Conference of the European Marketing Academy, Aarhus, Denmark, May 26-29.

[396] Galliers, J.R. (1994), A Theoretical Framework for Computer Models of Cooperative Dialogue, Acknowledging Multi-Agent Conflict. PhD thesis, Open University, Great Britain.

[397] Gane, C., T. Sarson (1979), Structured systems analysis: Tools and techniques, Prentice-Hall.

[398] Garcia-Diaz, A., W.S., Fuller, T.D., Phillips (1982), Network modelling of agricultural marketing and transportation systems, The Logistics and Transportation Review, vol. 18, no. 2, pp. 117-126.

[399] Gaul, W., A. Schader (1988), A prolog based PC implememntation for new product introduction, in: W. Gaul and M. Schader (eds.),

Data, Expert Knowledge and Decisions, Berlin: Springer-Verlag, pp. 42-53.

[400] Gaul, W., M. Both (1990), Computergestuótzes marketing, Springer-Verlag, Berlin.

[401] Gehani, N. (1982), The potential of forms in office automation, IEEE Transactions on Communications, COM-30, no. 1, pp. 120-125.

[402] Gelperin, D. (1977), On the optimality of A`, Artificial Intelligence, vol. 8.

[403] Gensch, D.H., W.W. Recker (1979), The multinominal, multiattribute Logit choice model, Journal of Marketing Research, vol. 16, pp. 124-132.

[404] Gensch, D.H., J.A. Svestka (1984), A maximum likelihood hierarchical disaggregate model for predicting choice of individuals, Journal of Mathematical Psychology, vol. 28, pp. 160-178.

[405] Gensch, D.H. (1984), Targeting the switchable industrial customer, Marketing Science, vol. 3, no. 1, pp. 41-54.

[406] Gensch, D.H. (1985), Empirically testing a disaggregate choice model for segments, Journal of Marketing Research, vol. 22, pp. 462-467.

[407] Gensch, D.H. (1987), Empirical evidence supporting the use of multiple choice models in analyzing a population, Journal of Marketing Research, vol. 24, pp. 197-207.

[408] Geoffrion, A.M., J.S. Dyer, A. Feinberg (1972), An interactive approach for multicriterion optimization with application to the operation of an Academic Department, Management Science, vol. 19, no. 4, pp.357-368.

[409] Geoffrion, A.M. (1975), A guide to computer-assisted methods for distribution systems planning, Sloan Management Review (Winter), pp. 17-41.

[410] Geoffrion, A.M. (1983), Can OR/MS evolve fast enough, Interfaces, vol. 13, pp. 10-25.

[411] Geoffrion, A.M. (1987), An Introduction to structured Modeling, Management Science, vol. 33, no. 5.

[412] Geoffrion, A.M. (1989), Computer-based Modeling Environments, European Journal of Operational Research, vol. 41, no. 33-43, North-Holland.

[413] Geoffrion, A.M. (1989), Integrated modeling system, Computer Science Economics and Management, no. 2, pp. 3-15.

[414] Geoffrion, A.M. (1992), Reusing Structured Models via Model Integration, in: B.W. Blanning and King D.R. (Ed.), Current Research in Decision Support Technology, IEEE 1992, pp.25-55.

[415] Geoffrion, A.M. (1994), Structured Modeling: Survey and Future Research Directions, ORSA CSTS Newsletter, vol. 15, no. 1.

[416] Gerson, E.M. (1976), On quality of life, American Sociology Review. 41, pp. 793-806.

[417] Gessner, G., W.A. Kamakura, N.K. Malhotra, M.E. Zmijewski (1988), Estimating models with binary dependent variables: Some theoritical and empirical observations, Journal of Business Research, vol. 16, no. 1, pp. 49-65.

[418] Gibson, M. (1989), The CASE philisophy, Byte, vol. 14.

[419] Gilbert, A. et al. (1995), The Role of Intelligent Agents in the Information Infrastructure. IBM, United States (http://activist.gpl.ibm.com:81/WhitePaper/ ptc2.htm).

[420] Gilly, M.C., R.W. Hansen (1985), Consumer complaint handling as a strategic marketing tool, Journal of Consumer Marketing, pp. 5-16.

[421] Girod, G., P. Orgeas, P.Landry (1989), Times: An expert system for media planning, in: H. Schorr and P. Landry (eds.), Innovative Applications of Artificial Intelligence, AAAI Press, Menlo Park.

[422] Givon, M., D. Horsky (1990), Untangling the effects of purchase reinforcement and advertising carryover, Marketing Science, vol. 9, no. 2, pp. 171-187.

[423] Glover, F. (1989), Tabu Search-Part I, ORSA Journal on Computing, Vol. 1, No. 3, pp 190-205.

[424] Glover, F. (1990), Tabu Search-Part II, ORSA Journal on Computing, Vol. 2, No. 1, pp 4-31.

[425] Glover, F., H.J. Greenberg (1989), New Approaches for Heuristic Search: A Bilateral Linkage with Artificial Intelligence, European Journal of Operational Research North Holland, Vol. 39 pp. 119-130.

[426] Goddard, W.E., K.A., Amuah (1989), The demand for Canadian fats and oils: A case study of advertising effectiveness, American Journal of Agricultural Economics, vol. 71, no. 3, pp. 741-749.

[427] Goicoechea, A., D.R. Hanson, L. Duckstein (1982), Multi-objective Decision Analysis with Engineering and Business Applications, John Wiley and Sons Publishers, New York.

[428] Goicoechea, A., L. Duckstein, S. Zionts (1992), Multiple Criteria Decision Making (MCDM), Applications in Industry, Business, and Government, in: Proceedings of the IX-th International Conference on MCDM, Fairfax, Virginia, August 5-8.

[429] Goicoechea, A. (1992), Does it matter which MCDM method you use? A look at experimental evaluation result of four MCDM decision support systems, in: Proceedings of the Xth International Conference on Multiple Criteria Decision Making, Taipei, Taiwan.

[430] Goldberg, D. (1989), Genetic Algorithms in Search Optimization and Machnine Learning, Addisson- Wesley.

[431] Goodman, I.R., M.M. Gupta, H.T. Nguyen, G.S. Rogers (1991), Conditional logic in expert systems, North-Holland.

[432] Gorry, G.A., and M.S. Scott-Morton (1971), A framework for management information systems, Sloan Mnagement Review, vol. 13, no. 1.

[433] Gorzalczany, M.B., Z. Piasta (1999), Neuro-fuzzy approach versus rough-set inspired methodology for intelligent decision support, Information Sciences, vol. 120, pp. 45-68.

[434] Gottinger, H.W. (1988), Statistical expert systems, Expert Systems, vol. 5, no. 3, pp. 186-196.

[435] Gottinger, H.W., P. Weimann (1992), Intelligent decision support systems, Decision Support Systems, no. 8, pp. 317-332.

[436] Goul, M., F. Tonge (1987), Project IRMA: An application of decision support system design principles to building expert-based systems, Decision Sciences, vol. 18, pp. 448-467.

[437] Goul, M., A. Philippakis, M.Y. Kiang, D. Fernandes, R. Otondo (1997), Requirements for the design of a protocol suite to automate DSS deployment on the world wide web: A client/server approach, Decision Support Systems, vol. 19, pp. 151-170.

[438] Goyal, S.K. et al. (1985), COMPASS: An expert system for telephone switch maintenance, Expert Systems, July.

[439] Grabot, B. E. Caillaud (1996), Imprecise Knowledge in Expert Systems: A Simple Shell. Expert Systems With Applications, vol. 10, no. 1, pp. 99-112.

[440] Gray, J. (1996), Data Management: Past, Present, and Future, IEEE Computer, vol. 29, no. 10, pp. 38-46.

[441] Green, P.E., V.R. Rao (1972), Applied multidimensional scaling, Holt, Rinehart and Winston, New York.

[442] Green, P.E., Y. Wind (1973), Multiattribute decisions in marketing: A measurement approach, Hinsdale, III: Dryden Press.

[443] Green, P.E., V. Srinivasan (1978), Conjoint analysis in consumer research: Issues and outlook, Journal of Consumer Research, vol. 5, pp. 103-123.

[444] Grenier, R., G. Metes (1995), Going Virtual: Moving your Organization Into the 21st Century, Prentice Hall PTR, New Jersey.

[445] Grigoroudis E., Y. Siskos (2001), Preference disaggregation for measuring and analysing customer satisfaction: The MUSA method, European Journal of Operational Research (to appear).

[446] Grigoroudis E., A. Samaras, N. F. Matsatsinis, Y. Siskos (1999a), Preference and customer satisfaction analysis: An integrated

multicriteria decision aid approach, in: Proceedings of the 5th Decision Sciences Institute's International Conference on Integrating Technology & Human Decisions: Global Bridges into the 21st Century, Athens, Greece, vol. 2, pp. 1350-1352.

[447] Grigoroudis E., J. Malandrakis, J. Politis, Y. Siskos (1999b), Customer satisfaction measurement: An application to the Greek shipping sector, in: Proceedings of the 5th Decision Sciences Institute's International Conference on Integrating Technology & Human Decisions: Global Bridges into the 21st Century, Athens, Greece, vol. 2, pp. 1363-1365.

[448] Grunert, C.S., K., Kristensen (1992), The green consumer: Some Danish evidence, in: Proceedings of the 21st Annual Conference of the European Marketing Academy, 26-29 May, pp. 529-539.

[449] Grzymala-Busse, J.W. (1991), Managing uncertainty in expert systems, Kluwer, London.

[450] Guadagni, P.M., J.D.C. Little (1983), A Logit model of brand choice calibrated on scanner data, Marketing Science, vol. 2, no. 3, pp. 203-238.

[451] Guida, M., P. Marchesi, G. Basaglia (1992), Knowledge-based decision support systems for manufacturing decision-making, Information and Decision Technologies, no. 18, pp. 347-361.

[452] Hagerty, M.R., D.A. Aaker (1984), A normative model of consumer information processing, Marketing Science, vol. 3, no. 3, pp. 227-246.

[453] Hahn, G.J. (1985), More intelligent statistical software and statistical expert systems: Future directions, The American Statistician, vol. 39, no. 1, pp. 1-16.

[454] Haines, G.H. (1974), Process models of consumer decision making, in: G.D. Hughes and M.L. Ray (eds.), Buyer/Consumer Information Processing, Chapel Hill: University of North Carolina Press.

[455] Hair, J., R. Tatham, R. Anderson, W. Black (1998), Multivariate Data Analysis, Prentice Hall.

[456] Hale, D.P., W.D. Haseman, F. Groom (1989), Integrating islands of automation, MIS Quarterly, Dec., pp. 433-445.

[457] Hamburg, M., R.J. Atkins (1967), Computer model for new product demand, Harvard Business Review (March-April).

[458] Hämäläinen, R.P., A.A., Salo, K., Pöysti (1991), Observations about Consensus Seeking in a Multiple Criteria Environment, in: Proceedings of the 25th Annual Hawaii International Conference on System Sciences, IEEE Computer Society Press, Silver Spring, MD.

[459] Hämäläinen, R.P., E., Kettunen (1994), HIPRE 3+ Group Link, User's Guide, Helsinki University of Technology, Systems Analysis Laboratory.

[460] Hämäläinen, R.P., O., Leikola (1995), Spontaneous decision conferencing in parliamentary decisions, in: Proceedings of the 28th Annual Hawaii International Conference on System Sciences, IEEE Computer Society Press, Silver Spring, MD.

[461] Hämäläinen, R.P., M., Pöyhönen (1996), On-line group decision support by preference programming in traffic planning, Group Decision and Negotiation, vol. 5, pp. 485-500.

[462] Hameri, A-P., J. Nihtila (1997), Didtributed new product development project based on internet and world-wide web: A case study, Journal of Product Innovation management, vol. 14, pp. 77-87.

[463] Hamilton, R.H. (1974), Screening business development opportunities, Business Horizons (August), pp. 13-24.

[464] Hammainen, H., R. Sulonen and C. Berard (1987), PAGES: Intelligent forms, intelligent mail and distribution, in: G. Bracchi and D. Tsicritzis (eds.), Office Systems, Elsevier Science.

[465] Hammond, K.R., R.L. Cook and L. Adelman (1977), POLICY: An aid for decision making and international communication, Columbia Journal of World Business, no. 12 (79-93).

[466] Hand, D. J. (1984), Statistical expert systems: Design, The Statistician, vol. 33, pp. 351-369.

[467] Hand, D.J. (1987), A statistical knowledge enhancement system, Journal of Royal Statistical Society, no. 150, part 4, pp. 334-345.

[468] Hansen, H., G. Neuman (1987), Beitraege zur expertensystemforschung an der Wirtschaftsuniversitaet Wien, Wien, pp. 669-672.

[469] Harmon, P., D. King (1985), Expert Systems, Wiley, New York.

[470] Harmon, P., R. Maus, W. Morrissey (1988), Expert systems, tools and applications, John Wiley.

[471] Harmon, P., B. Sawyer (1990), Creating Expert Systems for Business and Industry, John Wiley and Sons, Inc.

[472] Harshman, R.A., P.E. Green, Y. Wind, M.E. Lundy (1982), A model for the analysis of asymmetric data in marketing research, Marketing Science, vol. 1, no. 2, pp. 205-242.

[473] Hart, P.E., N.J. Nilsson, B. Raphael (1968), A formal basis for the heuristic determination of minimum cost paths, IEEE Transactions on SSC, vol. 4.

[474] Hart, P.E., N.J. Nilsson, B. Raphael (1972), Correction to 'A formal basis of the heuristic determination of minimum cost paths', SIGART Newsletter, vol. 37.

[475] Hart, A. (1986), Knowledge acquisition for expert systems, McGraw-Hill, New York.

[476] Hatzinakos, I., D. Yannacopoulos, C. Faltsetas, C. Ziourkas (1991), Application of the MINORA decision support system to the evaluation of landslide favourability in Greece, European Journal of the Operational Research, vol. 50, pp. 60-75.

[477] Hatzis, Ch. (1998), Measuring consumer satisfaction using artificial neural nets, Master Thesis, Technical University of Crete (in Greek).

[478] Hauser, J.R., G.L. Urban (1977), A normative methodology for modeling consumer response to innovation, Operations Research, vol. 25, no. 4, pp. 579-619.

[479] Hauser, J.R., G.L. Urban (1978), Consumer preference axioms: Behavioral postulates for describing and predicting stochastic choice, Management Science, vol. 24, no. 13, pp. 1331-1341.

[480] Hauser, J.R., G.L. Urban (1979), Assessment of attribute importances and consumer utility functions: von Neumann-Morgenstern theory applied to consumer behavior, Journal of Consumer Research, vol. 5, pp. 251-262.

[481] Hauser, J.R., F.S. Koppelman (1979), The relative accuracy and usefulness of alternative perceptual mapping techniques, Journal of Marketing Research, vol. 14, no. 3, pp. 495-507.

[482] Hauser, J.R., S.M. Shugan (1980), Intensity measures of consumer preference, Operations Research, vol. 28, no. 2, pp. 278-320.

[483] Hauser, J.R., J.H. Roberts and G.L. Urban (1983), Forecasting sales of a new durable, in: F.S. Zufryden (ed.), Advances and practices of marketing science management, The Institute of Management Science, Providence.

[484] Hauser, J.R. (1984), Consumer research to focus R&D projects, Journal of Product Innovation and Management, vol. 2, pp. 70-84.

[485] Hauser, J.R. (1986), Agendas and consumer choice, Journal of Marketing Research, vol. 23, pp. 199-212.

[486] Hauser, J.R., G.L. Urban (1986), The value priority hypotheses for consumer budget plans, Journal of Consumer Research, vol. 12, pp. 449-462.

[487] Hauser, J.R., B. Wernerfelt (1990), An evaluation cost model of consideration sets, Journal of Consumer Researsc, vol. 16, pp. 393-408.

[488] Hauser, J.R., G. Urban, B. Weinberg (1993), How consumers allocate their time when searching for information, Journal of Marketing Research, vol. 30, pp. 452-466.

[489] Hawgood, J. (1985), Information morphology in bureaucratic syb-systems, in: L. Methlie and R.H. Sprague (eds.), Knowledge Representation for Decision Support Systems, North Holland, Amsterdam.

[490] Hawkins, D., R. Best, K. Coney (1992), Consumer behavior: Implications for marketing strategy, 5th edition, MA: IRWIN, Boston.

[491] Hayes-Roth, F., D. Waterman, D. Lenat (1983), Building expert systems, Reading, MA: Addison-Wesley.

[492] Hayes-Roth, F. (1984), The knowledge-based expert system: A tutorial, IEEE Computer, September, pp. 11-28.

[493] Henson, S.J., J.R., Loader (1991), The implications of the single market for European food consumption and diets, in: Proceedings of the 25th Seminar of the European Association of Agricultural Economists, 24-26 June, pp. 267-282.

[494] Hayashi, K. (2000), Multicriteria analysis for agricultural resource management: A critical survey and future perspectives, European Journal of Operational Research, vol. 122, pp. 486-500.

[495] Henderson, J.C. (1987), Finding synergy between decision support systems research, Decision Sciences, no. 18, pp. 333-349.

[496] Hewson, N., W. Hewson (1994), The impact of computerized sales and marketing systems in the UK, 4th ed., HCG Publications, Buckinghamshire.

[497] Higby, M.A., B.N. Farah (1991), The status of marketing information systems, decision support systems and expert systems in the marketing functions of US forms, Information and Management, vol. 20.

[498] Hill Nigel (1996), Handbook of customer satisfaction measurement, Gower.

[499] Hinkkanen, A., R. Kalakota, P. Saengcharoenrat, J. Stallaert, A.B. Whinston (1997), Distributed Decision Support Systems for real Time Supply Chain Management using Agent Technologies, Chapter 12, R. Kalakota and A.B. Whinston (eds.), in: Readings in Electronic Commerce, Addison Wesley, http://cism.bus.utexas.edu/.

[500] Hirschman, A.O. (1970), Exit, voice and loyalty, Cabridge, Mass.: Harvard University Press.

[501] Hisrich, R.D., M.P. Peters (1984), Marketing decisions for new and mature products: Planning, Development and Control, Charles Merrill Publishing Company.

[502] Hoffman, A., P. Compton (1999), The fourth Australian Knowledge Acquisition Workshop, (Sydney, University of NSW), pp 87-101.

[503] Holland, J.H. (1975), Adaptation in natural and artificial system, Ann Arbor: University Michigan Press.

[504] Holbrook, M.B., W.L. Moore, R.S. Winer (1982), Constructing joint spaces from pick-any data: A new tool for consumer analysis, Journal of Consumer Research, vol. 9, pp. 99-105.

[505] Holsapple, C.W., A.B. Whinston (1987), Decision support systems: Theory and applications, Springer Verlag NATO ASI Series, Computer and System Science, no. 31.

[506] Holsapple, C.W., A.B. Whinston (1996), Decision support systems: A knowledge-based approach, West Publishing Company, Minneapolis.

[507] Holsheimer, M., A. Siebes (1994), Data Mining: The Search for Knowledge in Databases, Technical Report, CS-R9406, CWI.

[508] Holsheimer, M., M.L. Kersten, A.P.J.M. Siebes (1996), Data surveyor: Searching the nuggets in parallel, in: U.M. Fayyad, G. Piatetsky-Shapiro, P. Smyth, R. Uthurusamy (Eds.), Advances in Knowledge Discovery and Data Mining, MIT Press, Massachusetts Chap. 18.

[509] Holtzman, S. (1989), Intelligent decision systems, Reading MA: Addison-Wesley.

[510] Horsky, D. (1976), An empirical analysis of the optimal advertising policy, Management Science, vol. 23, pp. 1037-1049.

[511] Horsky, D. (1977), Market share response to advertising: An example of theory testing, Journal of Marketing Research, vol. 14, pp. 10-21.

[512] Horsky, D., M.R. Rao (1984), Estimation of attribute weights from preference comparisons, Management Science, vol. 30, no. 7, pp. 801-822.

[513] Howard, J.A. (1963a), Marketing: Executive and buyer behavior, New York: Columbia University Press.

[514] Howard, J.A. (1963b), Marketing management (2nd ed.), Homewood, Illinois: Richard D. Irwin.

[515] Howard, J.A., W.M. Morgenroth (1968), Information processing model of executive decisions, Management Science, vol. 14 (March), pp. 416-428.

[516] Howard, J.A., J.N. Sheth (1969), The theory of buyer behavior, New York: John Wiley & Sons.

[517] Howard, J.A., L. Ostlund (1973), Buyer behaviour: Theoretical and empirical foundations, Knopf, New York.

[518] Howard, J.A., J.M. Hulbert, J.U. Farley (1975), Organizational analysis and information system design: A decision process perspective, Journal of Business Research, no. 3, pp. 133-148.

[519] Howard, J.A. (1989), Consumer behavior in marketing strategy, Prentice-Hall.

[520] Huang, G.Q., K.L. Mak (1998), Web-based collaborative product development, Invited lecture, 1st International Seminar and Workshop on Engineering, Design in Integrated Product Development, Wroclaw, Poland, 8–10 October.

[521] Huang, G.Q., J. Huang, K.L. Mak (2000), Agent-based workflow management in collaborative product development on the Internet, Computer-Aided Design, vol. 32, pp. 133–144.

[522] Huber, J.G. (1974), Multiattribute utility models: A review of field and field-like studies, Management Science, vol. 20, no. 10, pp. 1393-1402.

[523] Huber, J.G. (1980), Organisational science contributions to the design of decision support systems, Proceedings of an international task force meeting, Pergamon Press, June 23-25.

[524] Huber, G.P. (1984), Issues in the design of group decision support systems, MIS Quarterly, vol. 8, no. 3, pp. 195-204.

[525] Huber, G.P. (1990), A theory of the effects of advanced information technologies on organization design, intelligence and decision making, Academy of Management Review, vol. 15, no. 1, pp. 41-71.

[526] Hughes, G.D. (1974), The measurement of beliefs and attitudes, in: R. Ferber (ed.), The handbook of marketing research, McGraw-Hill, New York.

[527] Hulbert, J.M. (1978), Composite forecasting systems: Avoiding the pitfalls and problems, Working Paper (December), Columbia University.

[528] Hulbert, J.M. (1981), Descriptive models of marketing decisions, in: R.L. Schultz and A.A. Zoltners (eds.), Marketing Decision Models, Elsevier Science Publishing Co., New York.

[529] Hurrion, R.D. (1978), An Investigation of Visual Interactive Simulation Methods using the Job-Shop Scheduling Problem, Journal of the Operational Research Society, vol. 29, pp. 1085-1093.

[530] Hurrion, R.D., R.J.R. Secker (1978), Visual interactive simulation: an aid to decision making, Omega, vol. 6, pp. 419-426.

[531] Hurrion, R.D. (1980a), An Interactive Visual Simulation System for Industrial Management, European Journal of the Operational Research, vol. 5, no. 86-93.

[532] Hurrion, R.D. (1985), Implementation of a Visual Interactive Consensus Decision Support System, European Journal of the Operational Research, vol. 20, pp. 138-144.

[533] Hurrion, R. D. (1986), Invited Review: Visual Interactive Modeling, European Journal of the Operational Research, vol. 54, pp. 281-287.

[534] Hurrion, R.D. (1991), Intelligent Visual Interactive Simulation, European Journal of the Operational Research, vol. 54, pp. 349-356.

[535] Hurson, Ch., C. Zopounidis (1997), Gestion de portefeuille et analyse multicritère, Economica, Paris.

[536] Hwang, Ch.-L, A.S. Masud (1979), Multiple objective decision making:Methods and Applications, Springer-Verlag, Berlin.

[537] Hwang, Ch.-L, K. Yoon (1981), Multiple attribute decision making:Methods and Applications, Springer-Verlag, Berlin.

[538] Hwang, C.L., M.J., Lin (1987), Group decision making under multiple criteria, Lecture Notes in Economics and Mathematical Systems, No. 281. Springer, Berlin.

[539] IBM Corporation (1974), HIPO: A design aid and documentation technique, GC 20-1851, IBM Corporation.

[540] IEEE/ANSI (1983), Glossary of software engineering terminology, Std-729-1983.

[541] Ince, D. (1990), Z and system specification, in: D. Ince and D. Andrews (eds), The Software Cycle, Butterworths, London, pp. 260-277.

[542] Inmon, W.H. (1996), Building the Data Warehouse (2nd Edition ed.), Wiley, New York.

[543] International Olive Oil Council (1990), Market segmentation study: The U.S. olive oil market in 1990.

[544] International Olive Oil Council (1991), Chronological statistical series, Madrid.

[545] International Olive Oil Council (1996), Chronological statistical series, Madrid.

[546] Iz, P.H. (1992), Two multiple criteria group decision support systems based on mathematical programming and ranking methods, European Journal of Operational Research, vol. 61, pp. 245-253.

[547] Iz, P., L., Krajewski (1992), Comparative evaluation of three interactive multiobjective programming techniques as group decision support tools, INFOR, vol. 30, no. 4, pp. 349-363.

[548] Iz, P., R.L., Gardiner (1993), Analysis of multiple criteria decision support systems for cooperative groups, Group Decision and Negotiation, vol. 2, no. 1, pp. 61-79.

[549] Jacquet-Lagrèze, E., J. Siskos (1982), Assesing a set of additive utility functions for multicriteria decision-making: The UTA method, European Journal of Operational Research, no. 10, pp. 151-164.
[550] Jacquet-Lagrèze, E. (1983), PREFCALC: Evaluation et decision multicriteres, Euro-Decision, Paris.
[551] Jacquet-Lagrèze, E., Y. Siskos (1983), Mèthode de dècision multicritère, Editions Hommes et Techniques, Paris.
[552] Jacquet-Lagrèze, E., Y. Siskos (2001), Preference disaggregation: 20 years of MCDA experience, European Journal of Operational Research, vol. 130, no. 2, pp. 233-245.
[553] Janca, P. (1995), Pragmatic Application of Information Agents, BIS Strategic Decisions, Norwell, United States.
[554] Jayaraman, V., R. Srivastava (1996), Expert systems in production and operations management - Current applications and future prospects, International Journal of Operations & Production Management, Vol. 16, No. 12, pp. 27-44.
[555] Jelassi, M.T. (1986), MCDM: From stand alone methods to integrated and intelligence DSS, Proceedings of the VIIth International Conference on Multiple Criteria Decision Making, vol. 1, pp. 250-262.
[556] Jelassi, M.T., R.A., Beauclair (1987), An integrated framework for group decision support systems design. Information and Management, vol. 13, no. 3, pp. 143-153.
[557] Jelassi, M.T., A., Foroughi (1989), Negotiation support systems: An overview of design issues and existing software, Decision Support Systems, vol. 5, pp. 167-181.
[558] Jelassi, T., Kersten, G., S., Zionts (1990), An introduction to group decision and negotiation support, in: C.A. Bana e Costa (Ed.), Readings in Multiple Criteria Decision Aid, Springer, Berlin.
[559] Jennings, R.N. (1996), Coordination Techniques for Distributed Artificial Intelligence, Foundations of Distributed Artificial Intelligence, Wiley-Interscience Publications, pp. 187-210.
[560] Janssen, M., W. Jager (1999), An integrated approach to simulating behavioural processes: A case study of the lock-in of consumption patterns, Journal of Artificial Societies and Social Simulation vol. 2, no. 2, http://www.soc.surrey.ac.uk/JASSS/2/2/2.html.
[561] Jarke, M. (1986), Knowledge sharing and negotiation support in multiperson decision support systems, Decision Support Systems, vol. 2, pp. 93-102.
[562] Jarke, M., M.T., Jelassi, M.F., Shakun (1987), MEDIATOR: Toward a negotiation support system, European Journal of Operational Research, vol. 31, no. 3, pp. 314-334.

[563] Jessup, L.M., J.S. Valacich (1993), Group Support Systems, New Perspectives, Macmillan, New York.

[564] Jeuland, A.P., F. Bass, G. Wright (1980), A multibrand stochastic model compounding heterogeneous erland timing and multinomial choice processes, Operations Research, vol. 28, no. 2, pp. 255-277.

[565] Jeusfeld, M.A., T.X. Bui (1997), Distributed decision support and organizational connectivity: A case study, Decision Support Systems, vol. 19, pp. 215-225.

[566] Jiang, J.J., G. Klein, R., A. Pick (1998), A marketing category management system: a decision support system using scanner data, Decision Support Systems, vol. 23, pp. 259–271

[567] Johnson, L., N.E. Johnson (1987), A knowledge elicitation method for expert systems design, System research and Info. Science, vol. 2, pp. 153-166.

[568] Johnson, E.J., J.W. Payne (1985), Effort and accuracy in choice, Management Science, vol. 31, no. 4, pp. 395-414.

[569] Johnston, S.X., S. Woodward (1988), Marketing management information systems - A review of current practice, Marketing Intelligence and Planning (U.K.), vol. 6, no. 2, pp. 27-29.

[570] Joned, A. (1979), The Object Model: A Conceptual Tool for Structuring Software, Operatimg Systems. New York, NY: Springer-Verlag.

[571] Jöreskog, K., Sörbom (1979), Advances in factor analysis and structural equation models, Abt Books, Cambridge, Mass.

[572] Joyce, J.D., N.N. Oliver (1977), Impacts of relational information system on industrial decisions, Data Base, vol. 8, no. 3, pp. 15-21.

[573] Jun Lee W., K. Chang Lee (1999a), PROMISE: A distributed DSS approach to coordinating production and marketing decisions, Computers and Operations Research, vol. 26, pp. 901-920.

[574] Jun Lee W., K. Chang Lee (1999b), A meta decision support system approach to coordinating production/marketing decisions, Decision Support Systems, vol. 25, pp. 239–250.

[575] Kahn, B.E., M.U. Kalwani, D.G. Morrison (1986), Measuring variety-seeking and reinforcement behaviors using panel data, Journal of Marketing Research, vol. 23, pp. 89-100.

[576] Kalwani, M.U., D.G. Morrison (1977), A parsimonious description of the hendry system, Management Science, vol. 23, pp. 467-477.

[577] Kalwani, M.U. (1979), The entropy concept and the hendry partitioning approach, Working Paper, Sloan School, MIT.

[578] Kapferer, J-N., G. Laurent (1993), Further evidence on the consumer involvement profile: Five antecedents of involvement, Psychology and Marketing, vol. 10, no. 4, pp. 347-355.

[579] Kaärkkaäinen, H., P. Piippo, M. Tuominen (2001), Ten tools for customer-driven product development in industrial companies, Int. J. Production Economics, vol. 69, pp. 161-176.

[580] Karmarck, A.M. (1983), Economics and the real world, Basil Blackwell, Oxford.

[581] Kassarjian, H.H., M.J. Sheffet (1981), Personality and consumer behaviot: An update, in: H.H. Kassarjian and T.S. Robertson (eds.), Perspectives in Consumer Behavior, Glenview, III.: Scott, Foresman.

[582] Katahira, H. (1990), Perceptual mapping using ordered logit analysis, Marketing Science, vol. 9, no. 1, pp. 1-17.

[583] Khoshafian S., G. Copeland (1986), Object Identity, SIGPLAN Notices vol. 21, no. 11, pp. 406.

[584] Kemble, J. (1994), Display of multi-attribute data using a presentation description language, MS Thesis, Computer Science Dept., WPI, Worcester, MA 01609, pp. 124.

[585] Keen, P.G.W., M.S. Scott-Morton (1978), Decision support systems: An organizational perspective, Reading, MA: Addison-Wesley.

[586] Keen, P.G.W. (1980), Decision support systems: A research perspective, Proceedings of an international task force meeting, Pergamon Press, June 23-25, pp. 23-43.

[587] Keen, P.G.W. (1987), Decision support systems: The next decade, Decision Support Systems, no. 3, pp. 253-265.

[588] Keeney, R., H. Raiffa (1976), Decisions with multiple objectives: Preferences and value trade-offs, Wiley, New York.

[589] Keeney, R., H. Raiffa (1993), Decisions with multiple objectives: Preferences and value trade-offs, Cambridge University Press.

[590] Keeney, R.L., G.L. Lilien (1987), New industrial product design and evaluation using multiattribute value analysis, Journal of Product Innovation Management, vol. 4, no. 3, pp. 185-198.

[591] Keeney, R.L., H., Raiffa (1991), Structuring and analyzing values for multiple-issues negotiations, in: Peyton Young, H. (Ed.), Negotiation Analysis, University of Michigan Press, Ann Arbor, MI.

[592] Keeney, R. L. (1992), Value-focused thinking: A path to creative decision making, Harvard University Press, London.

[593] Keller, K., R. Staelin (1987), Effects of quality and quantity of information on on decision effectiveness, Journal of Consumer Research, vol. 14, no. 2, pp. 200-213.

[594] Kelton, C.M.L., L.G.S. Stone (1998), Optimal television schedules in alternative competitive environments, European Journal of Operational Research, vol. 104, pp. 451-473.

[595] Kemp, D. A., (1976), The Nature of Knowledge: An Introduction for Librarians. Clive Bingley: London & Linnet: Connecticut, USA.

[596] Kersten, G.E. (1985), NEGO-group decision support system, Information and Management, vol. 8, no. 5, pp. 237-246.
[597] Kersten, G.E., T., Szapiro (1986), Generalized approach to modelling negotiations, European Journal of Operational Research, vol. 26, pp. 124-142.
[598] Kersten, G.E. (1987), On two roles decision support systems can play in negotiations, Information Processing and Management, vol. 23, no. 6, pp. 605-614.
[599] Kersten, G.E. (1988), A procedure for negotiating efficient and non-efficient compromises, Decision Support Systems, vol. 4, pp. 167-187.
[600] Kersten, G.E., W., Michalowski, S., Matwin, S., Szpakowicz (1988), Rule-based modelling of negotiation strategies, Theory and Decision, vol. 25, pp. 225-257.
[601] Kersten, G.E. et al. (1988), Representing the negotiations process with a rule-based formalism, Theory Decision, no. 22.
[602] Kersten, G.E. (1989), Expert system technology and strategic decision support, Math. Comput. Modelling, vol. 12, no. 10/11, pp. 1321-1333.
[603] Ketler, K. (1993), Case-based reasoning: an introduction, Expert Systems with Applications, vol. 6, pp. 3-8.
[604] King, W.R. (1977), Marketing management information systems, Mason Charter Publishers Inc., New York.
[605] King, W.R. (1978), Strategic planning for management information systems, MIS Quarterly, vol. 2, pp. 27-37.
[606] King, D. (1986), An explanation facility for decision support systems, Sixth Journees Internationales, Les Systéme Experts et leurs Applications, Avignon, France.
[607] King, W.R. (1988), Strategic planning for information resources: The evolution of concepts and practice, Information Resources Management Journal, vol. 1, pp. 1-8.
[608] King, D. (1990), Intelligent decision support: Strategies for integrating decision support, database management and expert system technologies, Expert Systems with Applications, vol. 1, no. 1.
[609] Kiss, L. et al. (1991), ELECALC: A DSS for modeling the decision maker's preferences, Working Paper.
[610] Kirkpatrick, P.F., P.C. Bell (1992), Visual interactive modeling in industry: Results from a survey of visual interactive model builders, Interfaces, vol. 19, no. 5, pp. 71-79.
[611] Klahr, D. (1969), A Monte Carlo invstigation of the statistical significance of Kruskal's non-metric scaling procedure, Psychometrica, vol. 34, no. 3, pp. 319-330.

[612] Klein, M., T. Villedieu (1987), A KB-DSS for financial planning, application to French municipalities, Engineering Costs and Production Economics, no. 12.

[613] Klein, M., L.B. Methlie (1990), Expert systems: A decision support approach, Addison-Wesley, England.

[614] Klein, G.A. (1990), Knowledge engineering: Beyond expert systems, Information and Decision Technologies, no. 16, pp. 27-41.

[615] Klein, M., L.B. Methlie (1991), Expert systems: A decision support approach with applications in management and finance, Addison-Wesley Publishing Company, England.

[616] Klein, M.R., B. Methlie (1995), Knowledge-Based Decision Support Systems with Applications in Business, (2nd edn. ed.), Wiley, New York.

[617] Klein, M., L.B. Methlie (1995), Expert systems: A decision support approach with applications in management and finance (2nd Ed.), Addison-Wesley Publishing Company, England.

[618] Klein, M.R. (1999), SIMAR: A software environment to define and test strategic management knowledge bases, Decision Support Systems, vol. 26, pp. 151–177.

[619] Klompmaker, J.E., G. Hughes, R.I. Haley (1976), Test marketing in new product development, Harvard Business Review (May-June), pp. 128-138.

[620] Knox, D.S., M.H., White (1991), Retail buyers and their fresh produce suppliers: A power of dependence scenario in the UK, European Journal of Marketing, vol. 25, no. 1, pp. 40-52.

[621] Kohls, L.R., N.J., Uhl (1990), Marketing of agricultural products, (7th ed.), Macmillan, New York.

[622] Kohout, L.J., J. Anderson, W. Bandler (1992), Knowledge-based systems for multiple environments, Ashgate Publishing Company.

[623] Konsynski, B. (1983), Model management in decision support systems, in: C.W. Holsapple, A.B. Whinston (eds.), Data base management: Theory and applications, D. Reidel, Dordrecht, pp. 131-154.

[624] Konsynski, B., D. Dolk (1994), Knowledge abstraction in model management, in: P. Gray (ed.), Decision Support and Executive Information Systems, Englewood Cliffs, N.J.: Prentice Hall, pp. 420-437.

[625] Korhonen, P., J. Laakso (1986a), A visual interactive method for solving the multiple criteria problem, European Journal of Operational Research, vol. 24, pp. 277-287.

[626] Korhonen, P., J. Laakso (1986b), Solving generalized goal programming problems using a visual interactive approach, European Journal of Operation Research, vol. 26, pp. 355-363.
[627] Kotler, P. (1966), A design for the firm's marketing nerve center, Business Horizons, vol. 9, no. 3, pp. 63-74.
[628] Kotler, P. (1971), Marketing Decision Making: A model building approach, Holt, Rinehart and Winston, New York.
[629] Kotler, P. (1972), A generic concept of marketing. Journal of Marketing, vol. 36, pp. 46-54.
[630] Kotler, P. (1978), Harvesting strategies for weak products, Business Horizons, no. 19, pp. 15-22.
[631] Kotler, P., M.K. Mantrala (1985), Flawed products: Consumer responses and marketer strategies, Journal of Consumer Marketing (Summer), pp. 27-36.
[632] Kotler, P., G. Armstrong (1987), Marketing: An introduction, Prinetice-Hall, Englewood Cliffs, New Jersey.
[633] Kotler, P. (1994), Marketing management: Analysis, planning, implementation and control, 8th ed., Prentice-Hall, London.
[634] Kotteman, J., D.R. Dolk (1988), Process-oriented model integration, in: Proceedings of the 21st Annual Hawaii International Conference on System Sciences III: Decision Support and Knowledge Based Systems Track, pp. 396-402.
[635] Kowalik, J.S. (1986), Coupling symbolic and numerical computing in expert systems, North Holland, Amsterdam.
[636] Kwon, O.B., S.J. Park (1996), RMT: A modeling support system for model reuse, Decision Support Systems, vol. 16, no. 2, pp. 131-154.
[637] Kraemer, K.L., J.L., King (1988), Computer-based systems for cooperative work and group decision making, ACM Computing Surveys, vol. 20, no. 2, pp. 115-146.
[638] Kraft, A. (1984), XCON: An expert configuration system at digital equipment corporation, in: P. Winston, K. Prendergast (eds.), The AI Business: the commercial uses of artificial intelligence, Cambridge, Massachusetts: The MIT Press.
[639] Krallmann, H. (1986), EES: Das expertensysteme fuer den eincauf, Betriebswirtschaftliche Forschung und praxis, no. 6, pp. 565-583.
[640] Kriketos, B.T., K.S. Pastras (1989), Expert Systems, EANT AE, Piraeus (in Greek).
[641] Krin, S., G. O'Hare (1996), Cooperative Knowledge Processing, Springer-Verlag, London, pp. 230-257.
[642] Kroeber, W., R.H. Sprague (1980), An empirical investigation and analysis of the current state of information system evolution, Information and Management, vol. 3, pp. 37.

[643] Kroeber-Riel, W., F.R. Esch (1992), Expertensysteme in marketing, in: Handbuch des Electronic Marketing, Hrsg. Hermanns, Flegel, Verlag Beck, Muenchen, pp. 249-269.

[644] Kroeber-Riel, W. (1993), Computer-Aided globalization od advertising by expert systems, in: G.J. Bamossy and W.F. van Raaij (eds.), European Advances in Consumer Research, Association of Consumer Research, vol. 1, pp. 110-117.

[645] Kroenke, D.M., K.A. Dolan (1988), Database processing (3rd ad.), Chicago: SRA.

[646] Kroenke, D.M. (1995), Database Processing Fundamentals, Design, and Implementation (5th ed. ed.), Prentice-Hall, Englewood Cliffs, NJ.

[647] Krugman, H.E. (1965), The impact of television advertising: Learning without involvement, Public Opinion Quarterly, pp. 27 - 28.

[648] Kuehn, A.A. (1962), Consumer brand choice: A learning process?, Journal of Advertising Research, vol. 2, pp. 10-17.

[649] Kunz, J.C., T.P. Kehler, M.D. Williams (1984), Applications development using a hybrid AI development system, The AI Magazine, Fall, pp. 41-54.

[650] Kuo, R.J., K.C. Xue (1998), A decision support system for sales forecasting through fuzzy neural networks with asymmetric fuzzy weights, Decision Support Systems, no. 24, pp. 105–126.

[651] Kuo, R.J. (2001), A sales forecasting system based on fuzzy neural network with initial weights generated by genetic algorithm, European Journal of Operational Research, vol. 129, pp. 496-517.

[652] Kure, H., I. Thysen, A.R. Kristensen (1997), First European Conference for Information Technology in Agriculture, in: Proceedings of EFITA - The Royal Veterinary and Agricultural University, Copenhagen, Denmark, 15-18 June.

[653] Kurstedt, H.A. (1987), Responsive decision support systems: A board view illustrates when to include expert systems, in: H.G. Sol et al. (eds.), Expert Systems and Artificial Intelligence in Decision Support Systems, D. Reidel Publishers, Dordrecht.

[654] La Barbera, P.A., D. Mazursky (1983), A longitudinal assessment of consumer satisfaction/dissatisfaction: The dynamic aspect of the cognitive process, Journal of Marketing Research (November), pp. 393-404.

[655] Lagarde, J. (1983), Initiation à l'analyse des donnèes, Bordas, Paris.

[656] Lambin, J.J., P.A. Naert and A. Bultez (1975), Optimal marketing behavior in oligopoly, European Economic Review, no. 6, pp. 105-128.

[657] Lampkin, N. (1990), Organic farming, Farming Press, Ipswich.

[658] Lancaster, K. (1966), A new approach to consumer theory, Journal of Political Economy, pp. 132-157.

[659] Latin, J.M., L. McAlister (1985), Using a variety-seeking model to identify substitute and complementary relationships among competing products, Journal of Marketing Research, vol. 22, pp. 330-339.

[660] Latin, J.M. (1987), A model of balanced choice beahavior, Marketing Science, vol. 6, no. 1, pp. 48-65.

[661] Lazinny, R. (1991), A deductive approach for problem representation and modeling support: Conceptual Schema and object-oriented models, in: Proceedings of the 24th Annual Hawaii International Conference on System Sciences III, Decision Support and Knowledge Based Systems Track, pp.291305.

[662] Leckenby, J.D., S. Kishi (1984), The Dirichlet multinomial distribution as a magazine exposure model, Journal of Marketing Research, vol. 21, pp. 100-106.

[663] LeClair, S.R. (1985), A multi-expert knowledge system architecture for manufacturing decision analysis, Unpublished Ph.D. Dissertation, Arizona State University.

[664] Lee, L.K., H. G. Lee (1988), Integration of strategic planning and short-term planning: An intelligent DSS approach by the post model analysis approach, Decision Support Systems.

[665] Lee, M., P. Compton, B., Jansen (1992), Modelling with Context-Dependant Causality, in: R. Mizoguchi, H. Motoda, J. Boose, B. Gaines, R. Quinlan, Proceedings of the Second Japanese Knowlege Acquisition for Knowledge-Based Systems Workshop, Kobe, Japan, pp. 357-370.

[666] Lee, M., P. Compton, B., Jansen (1992), Causal Explanation From Mathematical Models, in: Proceedings of AI'92, Hobart, World Scientific, pp. 38-43.

[667] Lee, M., P. Compton, B., Jansen (1992), Causal Explanation For Climate Impact Advice, in: Proceedings of AIRIES - Workshop in Artificial Intelligence Applied to Environmental Science, Monterey.

[668] Lee, J.-Y. (1981), Generic advertising, FOB price promotion, and FOB revenue: A case study of the Florida grapefruit juice industry, Southern Journal of Agricultural Economics, vol. 13, no. 1, pp. 69-78.

[669] Lee, J.-Y., G.M., Brown (1985), Coupon redemption and the demand for frozen concentrated orange juice: A switching regression analysis, American Journal of Agricultural Economics, vol. 67, no. 3, pp. 647-653.

[670] Lee, J.-Y., G.M., Brown, F.G., Fairchild (1989), Some observations on the impact of advertising on demand, Agribusiness, vol. 5, no. 6, pp. 607-618.

[671] Leeflang, P.S.H., A. Boonstra (1982), Some comments on the development and application of linear learning model, Management Science, vol. 26, no. 11, pp. 1233-1246.

[672] Leeflang P.S.H., D.R. Wittink (2000), Building models for marketing decisions: Past, present and future, International Journal of Research in Marketing, 17, 105–126.

[673] Leeflang, P.S.H., Wittink, D.R., Wedel, M. (2000), Building Models for Marketing Decisions. Kluwer Academic Publishing, Boston, MA.

[674] Leipnik, M.R., K.K. Kemp, H.A. Loaiciga (1993), Implementation of GIS for water resources planning and management, ASCE Journal of Water Resources Planning and Managemen, vol. 119, pp. 184-205.

[675] Leith, P. (1986), Fundamental errors in legal logic programming, The Computer Journal, vol. 29.

[676] Lembersky, M.R., U.H. Chi (1984), Decision simulators speed implementation and improve operations, Interfaces, vol. 14, no. 4, pp. 1-15.

[677] Lemmer, J.F., L.N. Kanal (1988), Uncertainty in artificial intelligence, North Holland.

[678] Lenard, M.L. (1987), An object-oriented approach to model management, in: Proceedings of the 20th Annual Hawaii International Conference on System Sciences I, pp. 507-515.

[679] Lenat, D.B. (1982a), Heuristics: The nature of Heuristics, Artificial Intelligence, vol. 19, no.2.

[680] Lenat, D.B. (1982b), AM: An artificial intelligence approach to discovery in mathematics as heuristic search, in: R. Davis and D.B. Lenat (ads.), Knowledge-based systems in artificial intelligence, McGraw-Hill, New York.

[681] Lenat, D.B. (1983a), Theory formation by heuristic search. The nature of heuristics II: Background and examples, Artificial Intelligence (March).

[682] Lenat, D.B. (1983b), EURISKO: A program that learns new heuristics and domain concepts. The nature of Heuristics III: Program design and results, Artificial Intelligence (March).

[683] Leoniades, J. (1986), Going global – global strategies vs. nationla strategies, Long Range Planning, vol. 19, no. 6, pp. 96-104.

[684] Lesourne, J. (1977), A theory of the individual for economic analysis, North-Holland publishing company, vol. 1, New York.

[685] Lesser, V.R., D.D. Corkill (1987), Distributed problem solving, in: S.C. Shapiro (ed.), Encyclopedia of Artificial Intelligence, Wiley, New York, pp. 245-251.

[686] Levitt, T. (1965), Exploit the product life cycle, Harvard Business Review (November/December), pp. 81-94.

[687] Levitt, T. (1966), Innovative imitation, Harvard Business Review (September-October), pp. 63-70.

[688] Levitt, T. (1972), Industrial purchasing behavior: A Bayesian reanalysis, Journal of Business Administration, no. 4, pp. 79-81.

[689] Levine, P., J.Ch. Maillard, J. Pomerol (1987), DECIDEX: A multi-expert system for strategic decisions, in: H.G. Sol et al. (eds.), Expert Systems and Artificial Intelligence in Decision Support Systems, Reidel, pp. 247-255.

[690] Levin, I., G. Gaeth (1988), How consumers are affected by the framing of attribute information before and after consuming the product, Journal of Consumer Research, vol. 18, no. 1, pp. 63-70.

[691] Levin, N.; J. Zahavi, M. Olitsky (1995), AMOS - a probability-driven, customer-oriented decision support system for target marketing of solo mailings, European Journal of Operational Research, vol. 87, no. 3, pp. 708-721.

[692] Lewandowski, A. (1989), SCDAS-decision support system for group decision making: Decision theoretic framework, Decision Support Systems, vol. 5.

[693] Lewis, B. (1990), Marketing Success in the 1990's: Characteristics of the intelligent corporation, Information Management Review, 5(4), pp. 15-22.

[694] Liang, T.P., E. Turban (1993), Case-based reasoning, Special issue of Expert Systems with Applications, January.

[695] Liang T-P., J-S. Huang (1998), An empirical study on consumer acceptance of products in electronic markets: A transaction cost model, Decision Support Systems, vol. 24, pp. 29–43.

[696] Liberatore, M.J., A.C. Stylianou (1993), The development manager's advisory system: A knowledge-based DSS tool for project assessment, Decision Sciences, vol. 24, no. 5, pp. 953-976.

[697] Liberatore, M.J., A.C. Stylianou (1995), Expert support systems for new product development decision making, in: A modeling framework and applications, Management Science, vol. 41, no. 8, pp. 1296-1316.

[698] Li, E.Y. (1995), Marketing information systems in the top U.S. companies: A longitudinal analysis, Information & Management, vol. 28, pp. 13-31.

[699] Li, E.Y., McLeod, R. Jr., J.C. Rogers (1993), Marketing information systems in the Fortune 500 companies: Past, Present and Future, Journal of Management Information Systems, vol. 10, no. 1, pp. 165-192.

[700] Li, S., Y. Duan, R. Kinman, J. S. Edwards (1999), A framework for a hybrid intelligent system in support of marketing strategy development, Marketing Intelligence and Planning, vol. 17, no. 4, pp. 209-216.

[701] Li, S. (1999), Computer-based support for marketing strategy development: investigation of managers' needs for support, current provision, and hybrid intelligent support systems, PhD Thesis, University of Luton, England.

[702] Li, S. (2000a), The development of a hybrid intelligent system for developing marketing strategy, Decision Support Systems, vol. 27, pp. 395–409.

[703] Li, S. (2000b), Computer-based support for marketing strategy development, European Journal of Marketing, vol. 34, pp. 551-575.

[704] Li, S. (2000c), Developing marketing strategy with MarStra: the support system and the real-world tests, Marketing Intelligence & Planning, vol. 18, no. 3, pp. 135-143.

[705] Liang, T.P., J.S. Chandler, I. Han (1990), Integrating statistical and inductive learning methods for knowledge acquisition, Expert Systems with Applications, vol. 1, pp. 391-401.

[706] Liebowitz, J. (1984), Determining functional requirements for NASA Goddard's command management system software design using expert systems, Washington, D.C.: George Washington University, Ph.D. dissertation, December.

[707] Liebowitz, J. (1998), Expert systems: An integral part of knowledge management, Kybernetes, vol. 27, no. 2, pp. 170-175.

[708] Lilien, G.L. (1974a), A modified linear learning model of buyer behavior, Management Science, vol. 20, pp. 1027-1036.

[709] Lilien, G.L. (1974b), An application of a modified linear learning model of buyer behavior, Journal of Marketing Research, vol. 11, pp. 279-285.

[710] Lilien, G.L. (1979), ADVISOR 2: Modeling the marketing mix for industrial products, Management Science, vol. 25, no. 2, pp. 191-204.

[711] Lilien, G.L., P. Kotler (1983), Marketing Decision Making: A model building approach, Harper and Row.

[712] Lilien, G.L., P. Kotler, K.S. Moorthy (1992), Marketing Models, Prentice-Hall Inc., New Jersey.

[713] Lin, C.T., C.S.G. Lee (1996), Neural Fuzzy Systems, Prentice Hall.

[714] Lindholm, E. (1992), A world of CASE tools, Datamation, vol. 38, no. 1, pp. 31-45.

[715] Lindblom, C.E. (1959), The science of muddling through, Public Administration Review, no. 19, pp. 79-99.

[716] Lindblom, C.E. (1965), The intelligence of Democracy, New York: Free Press.

[717] Linneman, E.R., L.J.J. Stanton (1991), Making niche marketing work, McGraw-Hill, New York.

[718] Little, J.D.C., L. Lodish (1969), A media planning calculus, Operation Research, vol. 17, no. 1, pp. 1-35.

[719] Little, J.D.C. (1970), Models and managers: The concept of a decision calculus, Management Science, vol. 16, B466-B485.

[720] Little, J.D.C. (1975a), BRANDAID: A marketing-mix model – Part 1: Structure, Operations Research, vol. 23, no. 4, pp. 628 - 655.

[721] Little, J.D.C. (1975b), BRANDAID: A marketing-mix model – Part 2: Implementation, calibration and case study, Operations Research, vol. 23, no. 4, pp. 656 - 673.

[722] Little, J.D.C. (1979), Decision support systems for marketing managers, Journal of Marketing, vol. 43, no. 3, pp. 9–27.

[723] Little, J.D.C. (1990), Information technology in marketing, Working Paper, Sloan School of Management, MIT.

[724] Liu, J.D., D.O., Forker (1988), Generic fluid milk advertising, demand expansion, and supply response: The case of New York City, American Journal of Agricultural Economics, pp. 229-236.

[725] Liu, J.I., D.Y.Y. Yen, G. Klein (1990), An agent for intelligent model management, Journal of Management Information Systems, vol. 7, no. l, pp. 101-122.

[726] Lodish, L.M. (1971), CALLPLAN: An interactive salesman's call planning system, Management Science, Part II, vol. 18, no. 4, pp. 25-40.

[727] Lofti, V., Th. Stewart, St. Zionts (1992), An aspiration-level interactive model for multiple criteria decision making, Computers and Operations Research, vol. 19, no. 7, pp. 671-681.

[728] Long, J.S. (1983), Confirmatory factor analysis, Quantitative Applications in the Social Sciences, Series no. 33, Sage Publications, Beverly Hills, Calif.

[729] Lootsma, F.A. (1993), Scale sensitivity in the multiplicative AHP and SMART, Journal of Multi-Criteria Decision Analysis, vol. 2, pp. 87-110.

[730] Louviere, J.J., D.A. Hensher (1983), Using discrete choice models with experimental design data to forecast consumer demand for a

unique cultural event, Journal of Consumer Research, vol. 10, pp. 348-361.

[731] Louviere, J.J., G. Woodworth (1983), Design and analysis of simulated consumer choice or allocated experiments: An approach based on aggregate data, Journal of Marketing Research, vol. 20, pp. 350-367.

[732] Lowen, R., M. Roubens (1993), Fuzzy logic: State of the art, Kluwer, England.

[733] Lucas, H.C. (1981), Implementation: The key to successful information systems, Columbia University Press, New York.

[734] Lucas, P., L. van der Gaag (1991), Principles of expert systems, Addison-Wesley, Reading, MA.

[735] Luconi, F.L., T.W. Malone, M.S. Scott-Morton (1986), Expert systems: The next challenge for managers, Sloan Management Review, no. 27, pp. 3-14.

[736] Luce, R. (1959), Individual choice behaviour, John Wiley and Sons, New York.

[737] Luce, R. (1977), The choice axiom after twenty years, Journal of Mathematical Psychology, no. 15, pp. 215-233.

[738] Luger, G.F., Stubblefield, A.W. (1993), Artificial Intelligence: Structures and strategies for complex problem solving (2nd ed.), The Benjamin/Cummings Publishing Company, Inc.

[739] Lunn, J.A. (1971), Review of consumer decision process models, ESOMAR, Helsinki.

[740] Lutz, R.J., J.R. Bettman (1977), Multiattribute models in marketing: A bicentennial review, in: A. Woodside, J. Sheth and P. Bennett (eds.), Consumer and industrial buying behavior, North-Holland, New York.

[741] Lynch, J.G. Jr. (1985), Uniqueness issues in the deco positional modeling of multiattribute overall evaluations: An information integration perspective, Journal of Marketing Research, vol. 22, pp. 1-19.

[742] Magill, E.G.W., S.A. Leech (1991), Uncertainty techniques in expert systems software, Decision Support Systems, no.7, pp. 55-65.

[743] Maguire J. D., F. M. Goodchild, W. D. Rhind (1991), Geographic Information Systems, Longman Scientific and Technical.

[744] Mahajan, V., E. Muller, S. Sharma (1984), An empirical comparison of awareness forecasting models of new product acceptance, Marketing Science, vol. 3, pp. 179-197.

[745] Malhotra, N.K. (1987), Validity and structural reliability of multidimensional scaling, Journal of Marketing Research, vol. 24, pp. 164-173.

[746] Mandell, S.L. (1979), Computers and data processing: Concepts and application, St. Paul, Minn.: West Publishing.
[747] Manrai, A.K., P. Sinha (1989), Elimination by cutoffs, Marketing Science, vol. 8, no. 2, pp 133-152.
[748] Manrai, A.K. (1995), Mathematical models of brand choice behavior, European Journal of Operational Research, vol. 82, pp. 1-17.
[749] Maslow, A.H. (1954), Motivation and personality, New York, McGraw-Hill.
[750] Marakas, G.M. (1999), Decision Support Systems in the 21st century, Prentice Hall Inc., New Jersey.
[751] Marcot, B. (1987), Testing your knowledge base, AI Expert, August.
[752] Marshall, K.P., S.W. Lamotte (1992), Marketing information systems: A marriage of systems analysis and marketing management, Journal of Applied Business Research, vol. 8, no. 3, pp. 61-73.
[753] Marshall, W.D., B.D., Rodriquez, J., Curvall (1992), Food provisioning and Spanish attitudes (from a UK perspective), in: Proceedings of the 21st Annual Conference of the European Marketing Academy, 26-29 May, pp. 821-835.
[754] Marshall, K.P. (1996), Marketing information systems, International Thomson Publishing Inc, USA.
[755] Marschner, D.C. (1967), Theory vs. Practice in allocating advertising money, Journal of Business, no. 40, pp. 286-302.
[756] Marsden, J.R., D.E. Pingry (1988), The intelligent organization: Some observations and alternative views, in: Proceedings of the 21 st Annual Hawaii International Conference on System Sciences III, Decision Support and Knowledge Based Systems Track, pp. 19-24.
[757] Martinez, I.J., A.J., Quelch (1991), David Del Curto S.A., in: Quelch, A.J., Buzzell, D.R., Salama, R.E. (Eds.), The Marketing Challenge of Europe 1992, Addison-Wesley, Reading, MA.
[758] Martell, D. (1988), Marketing and information technology, European Journal of Marketing, vol. 22, no. 9, pp. 16-24.
[759] Martelli, A. (1977), On the complexity of admissible search algorithms, Artificial Intelligence, vol. 8.
[760] Martinsons, M.G. (1995), Knowledge-based systems leverage human resource management expertise, International Journal of Manpower, vol. 16, no. 2, pp. 17-34.
[761] Masud, A., C.L., Hwang (1981), Interactive sequential goal programming, Journal of Operational Research Society, vol. 32, no. 5.
[762] Massy, W.F., J.D. Savvas (1964), Logical flow models for marketing analysis, Journal of Marketing, no. 28, pp. 30-37.

[763] Massy, W.F., D.B. Montgomery, D.G. Morrison (1970), Stochastic models of buying behavior, M.I.T. Press, Cambridge.

[764] Matsatsinis, N.F. (1995), A marketing intelligent decision support system: Support methodology and integrated architecture, PhD Dissertation, Technical University of Crete, Crete (in Greek).

[765] Matsatsinis, N.F., E. Avgerinopoulos, G. Baourakis (1995), Data analysis methods applied to agricultural marketing, in: Janssen, J., C.H. Skiadas and C. Zopounidis, (eds), Advances in Stochastic Modelling and Data Analysis, Kluwer Academic Publishers.

[766] Matsatsinis, N.F., A.P., Samaras (1997), Aggregation and disaggregation of preferences for consensus seeking in group decisions, Paper presented at the 46th Meeting of the European Working Group 'Multicriteria Aid for Decisions', Bastia, France, pp. 23-25 October.

[767] Matsatsinis, N.F., M. Doumpos, C. Zopounidis (1997), Knowledge acquisition and representation for expert systems in the field of financial analysis, Expert Systems with Applications, vol. 12, no. 1, pp. 247-262.

[768] Matsatsinis, N.F., A.P. Samaras (1998), Market Simulations via Rule Induction: A Machine Learning Approach, in: Managing in Uncertainty: Theory and Practice, Zopounidis C. and Pardalos P.M, (eds.), Kluwer Academic Publishers.

[769] Matsatsinis, N., P. Moraïtis, V. Psomatakis, N. Spanoudakis (1999), Intelligent Software Agents for Products Penetration Strategy Selection, in: Proceedings of MAAMAW'99 (posters), Valencia, Spain, 30/6 – 2/7.

[770] Matsatsinis, N.F., Y. Siskos (1999), MARKEX: An intelligent decision support system for product development decisions, European Journal of Operational Research, vol. 113, no. 2, pp. 336-354.

[771] Matsatsinis, N.F., A.P. Samaras (2000), Brand Choice Model Selection Based on Consumers' Multicriteria Preferences and Experts' Knowledge, Computers and Operations Research, vol. 27, pp. 689-707.

[772] Matsatsinis, N.F., A.P. Samaras (2001), MCDA and preference disaggregation in group decision support systems, European Journal of Operational Research, vol. 130, no. 2, pp. 414-429.

[773] Matwin, S., S., Szpakowicz, Z., Koperczac, G.E.,Kersten, W., Michalowski (1989), NEGOPLAN: An expert system shell for negotiation support, IEEE Expert, vol. 4, no. 4, pp. 50-62.

[774] Mazis, M.B., O.T. Ahtola (1975), A comparison of four multiattribute model in the prediction of consumer attitudes, Journal of Consumer Research, vol. 2, pp. 38-52.
[775] McAlister, L. (1979), Choosing multiple items from a product class, Journal of Consumer Research (December), pp. 213-224.
[776] McAlister, L. (1982), A dynamic attribute satiation model of variety-seeking behavior, Journal of Consumer Research, vol. 9, pp. 141-150.
[777] McAlister, L., E. Pessemier (1982), Variety seeking behavior: An interdisciplinary review, Journal of Consumer Research, vol. 9, pp. 311-322.
[778] McCann, J.M., J.P. Gallagher (1990), Expert systems for scanner data environments, Kluwer Academic Publishers, Boston.
[779] McCann, J.M., A. Tadlaoui, J.P. Gallagher (1990), Knowledge systems in merchandising: Advertising design, Journal of Retailing, vol. 66, no. 3, pp. 257-277.
[780] McCann, J.M., W.G. Lahti, J. Hill (1991), The brand manager's assistant: A knowledge-based system approach to brand management, International Journal of Research in Marketing, vol. 8, no. 1, pp. 51-74.
[781] McCann, J.M., J. Hill, D. McCullough (1991), The application of marketing experiences via case-based reasoning, Working Paper, Fuqua School of Business, Duke University.
[782] McCarthy, J. (1963), Situation, actions, and causal laws, Tech. Res. Memo 2, Stanford Artificial Intelligence Project.
[783] McCarthy, J., P.J. Hayes (1969), Some philosophical problems from the standpoint of artificial intelligence, in: B. Meltzer, D. Michie (Eds.), Machine Intelligence, vol. 4, pp. 463-502.
[784] McCarthy, J. (1977), Epistemological problems of artificial intelligence, in: Proceedings of the Fifth International Joint Conference on Artificial Intelligence, Cambridge, MA, pp. 1038-1044.
[785] McCarthy, J. (1980), Circumscription: A form of non-monotonic reasoning, Artificial Intelligence, vol. 13.
[786] McCarthy, J. (1995), What has AI in Common with Philosophy?, in: Proceedings of the Fourteenth International Joint Conference on Artificial Intelligence, Morgan Kaufmann, August 20-25, pp. 2041-2044.
[787] McCarthy, E.J., W.D. Perreault Jr. (1990), Basic Marketing, Homewood IL: Richard D. Irwin.
[788] McCusker, T. (1991), Tools to manage big projects, Datamation, vol. 37, pp. 71-82.

[789] McDermott, D., J. Doyle (1980), Non-monotonic logic I, Artificial Intelligence, vol. 13.

[790] McDermontt, J. (1982), XSEL: A computer sales person's assistant, in: J.E. Hayes, D. Michie, Y.H. Pao (eds.), Machine Intelligence 10, Ellis Horwood, Chichester, pp. 325-337.

[791] McDonald, M.H.B., H.N. Wilson (1990), State of the art developments in expert systems and strategic marketing planning, British Journal of Management, vol. 1, pp. 159-170.

[792] McDonald, M. (1996), Strategic marketing planning, Kogan Page, London.

[793] McDonald, C., P. Ellison (1994). Knowledge Acquisition from Domain Literature. In *AI and Natural Resource Management*: A Workshop in Conjunction with AI'94, University of New England, 22 November 1994, Armidale, Australia, pp. 83-91.

[794] McFadden, D. (1970), Conditional Logit analysis of qualitative choice behavior, in: P. Zarembka (ed.), Frontiers in Econometrics, Academic Press, New York.

[795] McFadden, D. (1976), Quintal choice analysis: A survey, Annals of Economic and Social Measurement, May, pp. 363-369.

[796] McFadden, D. (1978), Modelling the choice of residential location, in: A. Karlquist (ed.), Spatial Interaction Theory and Residantial Location, North-Holland, Amsterdam.

[797] McFadden, D. (1980), Econometric models for probabilistic choice among products, Journal of Business, vol. 53, no. 3, pp. 513-530.

[798] McFadden, D. (1991), Advances in computation, statistical methods and testing of discrete choice models, Marketing Letters, vol. 2, no. 3, pp. 215-230.

[799] McGovern, J., D. Samson, A. Wirth (1991), Knowledge acquisition for intelligent decision systems, Decision Support Systems, no. 7, pp. 263-272.

[800] McGraw, K.L., B.K. Harbison (1989), Knowledge acquisition, principles and guidelines, Englewood Cliffs, NJ: Prentice-Hall.

[801] McIntyre, S., D.D. Achabal, C.M. Miller (1993), Applying case-based reasoning to forecasting retail sales, Journal of Retailing, vol. 69, no. 4, pp. 372-398.

[802] McKay, D.B., J.L. Zinnes (1986), A probabilistic model for the multidimensional scaling of proximity and preference data, Marketing Science, vol. 5, no. 4, pp. 325-344.

[803] McKeen, J.D. (1983), Successful Development Strategies for Business Applications Systems, MIS Quarterly, vol. 7, no 2, pp. 47-59.

[804] McKinney, D.C., D.R. Maidment (1993), Expert Geographic Information System for Texas Water Planning, ASCE Journal of Water Resources Planning and Management, vol. 119, pp. 170-183.

[805] MacLean, R.F. (1986), User-System interface requirements for decision support systems, in: S.J. Andriole (ad.), Micro-Computer Decision Support Systems: Design, Implementation, and Evaluation, Wellesley, MA: QED Information Sciences.

[806] McLeod, R. Jr., J.C. Rogers (1985), Marketing information systems: Their current status in Fortune 1000 companies, Journal of Management Information Systems, vol. 1, pp. 57-75.

[807] McLeod, D., R. Sacks-Davis, H. Schek (1990), Sixteenth International Conference on Very Large Databases, Morgan Kaufmann Pub., Brisbane, Australia.

[808] McLeod, R. (1993), Management information systems, 5th Edition, Mcmillan Publishing Company, New York.

[809] McLeod, R. (1997), Management Information Systems, Prentice Hall.

[810] Meador, C.L., M.J. Guyote, P.G.W. Keen (1984), Setting Priorities for DSS Development, MIS Quarterly, vol. 8, no. 2, pp. 117-129.

[811] Menkhaus, J.D., D.G., Whipple, J.S., Torok, A.R., Field (1988), Developing a marketing strategy for branded, low fat, fresh beef, Agribusiness, vol. 4, no. 1, pp. 91-103.

[812] Mennecke, B. (1997), Understanding the role of geographic information technologies in business: Applications and research directions, Journal of Geographic Information and Decision Analysis, vol. 1, no. 1, pp. 44-68, (http://www.geog.uwo.ca/gimda/journal/vol1.1/Mennecke/Mennecke.htm).

[813] Mentzer, J.T., C.P. Schuster, D.J. Roberts (1987), Microcomputers versus mainframe usage by marketing professionals, Journal of the Academy of Marketing Science, vol. 15, pp. 1-9.

[814] Meredith, J.R. (1981), The implementation of computer-based systems, Journal of Operational Management, October.

[815] Meulenberg, G.M. (1986), The evolution of agricultural marketing theory: Towards better coordination with general marketing theory. Netherlands Journal of Agricultural Science, vol. 34, pp. 301-315.

[816] Meulenberg, G.T.M., M.B.E.J., Steenkamp (1991), The role of store image in food store patronage behaviour, in: Proceedings of the 25th Seminar of the European Association of Agricultural Economists, 24-26 June, pp. 307-318.

[817] Meyer, R.J., A. Sathi (1985), A multiattribute model of consumer choice during product learning, Marketing Science, vol. 4, no. 1, pp. 41-61.

[818] Meyer, G.G. (1993), Marketing research and sales forecasting at Schlegel Corporation, Journal of Business Forecasting, vol. 12, no. 2, pp. 22-23.

[819] Meyer, D.W. (1996), Essays on Quality and Product Differentiation, PhD Thesis, The University of Michigan.

[820] Meyers-Levy, J., D. Maheswaran (1991), Exploring differences in males' and females' processing strategies, Journal of Consumer Research, vol. 18, no. 1, pp. 63-70.

[821] Meziane, F., S. Vadera, K. Kobbacy, N. Proudlove (2000), Intelligent systems in manufacturing: Current developments and future prospects, Inyegrated Manufacturing Systems, vol. 11, no. 4, pp.218-238.

[822] Michalewicz, Z. (1996), Genetic Algorithms + Data Structures = Evolution Programs, Springer-Verlag, 3rd Edition.

[823] Michalski, R.S. (1983), A theory and methodology of inductive learning, in: Michalski, R. S., J.G., Carbonell, T. M. Mitchell (eds.), Machine Learning, an Artificial Intelligence Approach, Tioga Publishing Company, Palo Alto, CA.

[824] Michalski, R.S., J.G. Carbonell, T.M. Mitchell (1983), Machine Learning: An Artificial Intelligence Approach, vol. II, Morgan Kaufmann, Los Altos, California.

[825] Michalski, R.S., J.G. Carbonell, T.M. Mitchell (1986), Machine Learning: An Artificial Intelligence Approach, vol. II, Morgan Kaufmann, Los Altos, California.

[826] Michie, D. (1984), Introductory readings in expert systems, Gordon & Breach, New York.

[827] Miettinen, K., P., Salminen, J., Hokkanen (1997), Acceptability analysis for multicriteria problems with multiple decision-makers, Report 2/1997, University of Jyväskylä, Department of Mathematics, Laboratory of Scientific Computing, Jyväskylä.

[828] Mihelis G., E. Grigoroudis, Y. Siskos, Y. Politis, Y. Malandrakis (2001), Customer satisfaction measurement in the private bank sector, European Journal of Operational Research, vol. 130, no. 2, pp. 347-360.

[829] Miller, D.R., M.K. Starr (1969), Executive decisions and operations research, Prentice-Hall, Englewood Cliffs, N.J.

[830] Millet, I., et al. (1991), Executive Information Systems, DSS 91 Transactions, Zigurs, I.(ed.), Providence, RI: The Institute of Management Science.

[831] Millet, I., C.H. Mawhinney (1992), Executive Information Systems, Information Management, vol. 23.

[832] Miniard, P.W., J.B Cohen (1981), An examination of the Fishbein-Ajzen behavioral-intentions model's: Concepts and measures, Journal of Experimental Social Psychology (May), pp. 309-339.

[833] Mintzberg, H. (1971), Managerial work: Analysis from observation, Management Science, October.

[834] Mintzberg, H. (1975), Impetiments to the use of management information, National Assotiation of Accountants, New York.

[835] Mitchell, A. (1983), The nine American life styles, New York: Macmillan.

[836] Mitchell, A., A. Sathi, C. Spaulding, A. Sitole (1984), Prospects of expert systems in marketing, in: Proceedings of the Marketing Science Conference, Chicago, Illinois.

[837] Mitchell, A.A. (1988), The development of a knowledge based media planning systems, in: W. Gaul and M. Schader (eds.), Data, Expert Knowledge and Decisions, Springer-Verlag, Berlin.

[838] Mitchell, A.A., J.E. Russo, D.R. Wittink (1991), Issues in the development and use of expert systmes for marketing decisions, International Journal of Research in Marketing, vol. 8, no. 1, pp. 41-50.

[839] Mitrakas, A., (1996), Changes in the Interchange Agreements, in: Electronic Commerce Current Research Issues and Applications, N. Adam & Yel. Yesha (eds.), Springer Verlag.

[840] Mittal, S. (1985), Knowledge acquisition from multiple experts, AI Magazine, Summer.

[841] Mockler, R.J. (1989), Knowledge-based systems for management decisions, Prentice-Hall, Englewood Cliff, New York.

[842] Móhlemann, S. (1995), Das verschóttete Kapital. Spezial /Wissensmanagement, BILANZ, 1:76-80.

[843] Montgomery, D.B. (1969), A stochastic response model with application to brand choice, Management Science, vol. 15, pp. 323-337.

[844] Montgomery, D.B., G.L. Urban (1969), Management science in marketing, Englewood Cliffs, Prentice Hall.

[845] Montgomery, D.B., G.L. Urban (1970), Marketing decision information systems: An emerging view, Journal of Marketing Research, vol. VII, pp. 226-234.

[846] Montgomery, D.B. (1975), New product distribution: An analysis of supermarket buyer decisions, Journal of Marketing Research, no. 12, pp. 255-264.

[847] Montgomery, D.B., C. Weinberg (1979), Toward strategic intelligence systems, Journal of Marketing, no. 43, pp. 41-52.

[848] Moorman, C. (1990), The effects of stimulus and consumer characteristics on the utilization of nutrition information, Journal of Consumer Research, vol. 17, pp. 362-374.

[849] Moormann, J., M. Lochte-Holtgreven (1993), An approach for an integrated DSS for strategic planning, Decision Support Systems, vol. 10, pp. 401-411.

[850] Moore, J.H., M.G. Chang (1980), Design of decision support systems, Data Base, vol. 12, no. 1 and 2.

[851] Moore, W.L., R.S. Winer (1987), A panel-data based method for merging joint space and market response function estimation, Marketing Science, vol. 6, no. 1, pp. 25-42.

[852] Moore, J.S. (1992), A prototype expert decision support system for the market appraisal of the single family residence, Decision Sciences, vol. 23, pp. 1408-1421.

[853] Moriarty, R.T., G.S. Swartz (1989), Automation to boost sales and marketing, Harvard Business Review, January-February, pp. 100-108.

[854] Morin, W.T. (1963), Practical media decisions and the computer, Journal of Marketing (July), pp. 26-30.

[855] Morgan, E.R., G., Sarris (1991), The international marketing of Cyprus wines: A case example - the UK market, International Journal of Wine Marketing, vol. 4, no. 1, pp. 44-63.

[856] Morrison, D.G., A. Perry (1970), Some data based models for analyzing sales fluctuations, Decision Sciences, vol. 1, pp. 258-274.

[857] Morrison, D.G., D.C. Schmittlein (1988), Generalizing the NBD model for customer purchases: What are the implications and is it worth the effort?, Journal of Business and Economic Statistic, vol. 6, no. 2, pp. 145-159.

[858] Moschis, G. (1985), The role of family communication in consumer socialization of children and adolescents, Journal of Consumer Research (March), pp. 898-913.

[859] Moutinho, L., R. Paton (1988), Expert systems: A new tool in marketing, Quarterly Review of Marketing, vol. 13, no. 4, pp. 5-12.

[860] Moutinho, L., B. Curry, F. Davies (1992), The COMSTRAT model: Development of an expert system in strategic marketing, in: Academy of Marketing Science Annual Conference Proceedings, San Diego, California.

[861] Muhanna, W.A. (1993), An Object-Oriented Framework for Model Management and DSS Development, Decision Support Systems, vol. 9, no. 2, pp. 217-229.

[862] Muhanna, W.A. (1994), SYMMS: A Model Management System that supports model reuse, sharing, and integration, Decision Support Systems, vol. 10, no. 2, pp. 214-242.

[863] Mui, G., W.E. McCarthy (1987), FSA: Applying AI techniques to the familiarization phase of financial decision making, IEEE Expert, pp. 33-41.

[864] Myers, J.H., M.L. Alpert (1968), Determinant buying attitudes: Meaning and measurement, Journal of Marketing (October), pp. 13-20.

[865] Myers, G. (1975), Reliable software through composite design, New York: Petrocelli-Charter.

[866] Myers, J.H., M.L. Alpert (1976), Semantic confusion in attitude research: Salience vs. Importance vs. Determinance, in: Advances in Consumer Research, Proceedings of the 7th Annual Conference of the Association of Consumer Research.

[867] Myers, J., S. Greyser, W. Massy (1979), The effectiveness of marketing R&D for marketing management, Journal of Marketing, vol. 43, pp. 17-29.

[868] Mylopoulos, J. et al. (1990), Telos: A language for representing knowledge about information systems, ACM Transactions on Information Systems, vol. 8, no. 1, pp. 325-362.

[869] Naert, P.A., P.S.H. Leeflang (1978), Building implementable marketing models, Martinus Nijhoff, Leiden/Boston.

[870] Nakanishi, M., J.R. Bettman (1974), Attitude models revisited: An individual level analysis, Journal of Consumer Research, vol. 1, pp. 20-21.

[871] Narasimhan, C., S. Sen (1983), New product models for test market data, Journal of Marketing (Winter), no. 47, pp. 11-24.

[872] Narayana, C.L., R.J. Markin (1975), Consumer behavior and product performance: An alternative conceptualization, Journal of Marketing, vol. 32, pp. 1-6.

[873] Naylor, C. (1983), Build your own expert system, Sigma Tech. Press.

[874] Naylor, C. (1993), Build your own Expert System, Sigma.

[875] Neal, W.D. (1980), Strategic product positioning: A step by step guide, Business (May-June), pp. 34-42.

[876] Neat, S., K.L. Traunik (1986), Database management systems in business, Englewood Cliffs, NJ: Prentice-Hall.

[877] Neal, J. G., S. C. Shapiro (1991), Intelligent Multi-Media Interface Technology, in: Sullivan J. W. and Tyler S. W (eds.), Intelligent User Interfaces, Frontier Series, New York, ACM Press, pp. 11-43.

[878] Neapolitan, R.E. (1987), Models for reasoning under uncertainty, Applied Artificial Intelligence, no. l, pp. 337-366.

[879] Nebendahl, D. (1988), Expert Systems, John Willey & Sons.

[880] Neibecker, B. (1990), Werbewirkungsanalyse mit Expertensysteme, Heidelberg: Physica Verlag.

[881] Ness, R.M. (1986), Product positioning using quantitative research: A strategic perspective, Food Marketing, vol. 2, no. 3, pp. 145-162.

[882] Newell, A., H.A. Simon (1958), Elements of a theory of human problem solving, Psychological Review, no. 65, pp. 151-166.

[883] Newell, A., C. Shaw, H.A. Simon (1962), The process of creative thinking. in: H.E. Grubert, W. Wertheimer (Eds.), Contemporary approaches to creative thinking, New York: Atherton Press.

[884] Newell, A., H.A. Simon (1972), Human problem solving, NJ: Prentice-Hall, Englewood.

[885] Newell, A. (1991), Unified theories of cognition, Harvard University Press, Cambridge MA.

[886] Newman, W.M. (1987), Designing integrated systems for the office environment, New York: McGraw-Hill.

[887] Ngwenyama, O.K., N., Bryson, A., Mobolurin (1996), Supporting facilitation in group support systems: Techniques for analyzing consensus relevant data, Decision Support Systems, vol. 16, pp. 155-168.

[888] Nguyen, T.A. et al. (1987), Knowledge base verification, AI Magazine, Summer.

[889] Nicosia, F.M. (1968), Advertising management, consumer behaviour and simulation, Journal of Advertising Research, vol. 8, no. 1.

[890] Nigay, L., Coutaz, J. (1993), A Design Space for Multimodal Systems: Concurrent Processing and Data Fusion, in: Procideengs InterCHI'93 (Amsterdam), ACM Press, pp. 172-178.

[891] Nii, P. (1986), Blackboard systems: The blackboard model of problem solving and the evolution of blackboard architectures, AI Magazine, vol. 7, no. 2.

[892] Nii, H.P. (1989), Blackboard Systems: The Handbook of Artificial Intelligence, Vol. IV, Addison-Wesley, New York.

[893] Nikolaidis, A., G. Baourakis, P. Dardabounis, N. Matsatsinis, Y. Siskos, C. Xigaki (1993), Production and marketing of Cretan olive oil and wine, in: J.D. van der Ploeg (ed.), Options Méditerranéennes, Strengthening endogenous development patterns in European agriculture, no. 23, pp. 233-243.

[894] Nilsson, N.J. (1971), Problem solving methods in artificial intelligence, McGraw Hill.

[895] Nonaka, I., F.M. Nicosia (1979), Marketing management: Its environment and information processing, Journal of Business Research, vol. 7, no. 4, pp. 277-301.

[896] Noori, H. (1995), The design of an integrated group decision support system for technology assessment, R&D Management, vol. 25, no. 3, pp. 309-322.

[897] Norman, R., J.F. Nunamaker (1989), CASE productivity perceptions of software engineering professionals, Communications of the ACM, vol. 32, pp. 1102-1108.

[898] Norris, M., P. Rigby (1992), Software engineering explained, John Wiley and Sons.

[899] Norton, J.A., F.M. Bass (1992), Evolution of technological generations: The law of capture, Sloan Management Review, vol. 33, no. 2, pp. 66-77.

[900] Nunamaker, J.F., A.R., Dennis, J.S., Valacich, D.R., Vogel, J.F., George (1991), Electronic meeting systems to support group work, Communications of the ACM, vol. 34, no. 7, pp. 40-60.

[901] Nute, D., R.I. Mann, B.F. Brewer (1990), Controlling expert system recommendations with defeasible logic, Decision Support Systems, no. 6, pp. 153-164.

[902] Nuzzolo, A., F. Russo, U. Crisalli, G. Beltrami (1995), SASM: A DSS for the operative marketing of the Italian railways, in: Proceedings of Third EURO Working Group on Transportation, Barcelona, Spain.

[903] Nwana, H.S. (1996), Software Agents: An Overview, Intelligent Systems Research AA&T, BT Laboratories, Ipswich, United Kingdom.

[904] Nylen, D.W. (1990), Marketing decision-making handbook, Prentice-Hall Inc, New Jersey.

[905] Oasis, J. (1989), A report on the management of marketing information, Organisation and System Innovations Limited (In association with the U.K. Institute of Marketing), Berkshire, U.K.

[906] O'Brien, T.V., D.D. Schoenbachler, G.L. Gordon (1995), Marketing information systems for consumer products companies: A management review, Journal of Consumer Marketing, vol. 12, no. 5, pp. 16-36.

[907] O'Connor, P. (1986), New product ventures to spell success for industrial firms, Marketing News, vol. 20, pp. 1-12.

[908] O'Keefe, R.M., O. Balci, E.P. Smith (1987), Validating expert system performance, IEEE Expert, Winter.

[909] O'Hare, G.M.P., N.R. Jennings (1996), Foundations of Distributed Artificial Intelligence, Wiley, pp. 211-229.

[910] Olshavsky, R.W., J.A. Miller (1972), Consumer Expectations, Product Performance and Perceived Product Quality, Journal of Marketing Research, vol. 9, pp. 19-21.

[911] O'Meara, J.T. (1961), Selecting profitable products, Harvard Business Review (January-February), pp. 83-89.

[912] Ophuis, O. (1991), The importance of health and environment as product attributes for foods, in: Proceedings of the 25th seminar of the EAAE, 24-26 June 1991, pp. 295-306.

[913] Ophuis, O., K.Y., Van Dam, J.M.A., Lamer (1992), Relative importance of health aspects and environmental issues for food consumption: Product attributes of lettuce, in: Proceedings of the 21st Annual Conference of the European Marketing Academy, 26-29 May, pp. 929-947.

[914] Oren, S.S., R.G. Schwartz (1988), Diffusion of new products in risk-sensitive markets, Journal of Forecasting, vol. 7, pp. 273-287.

[915] Ovum Consultancy London, (2000), Business-to-Business Electronic Commerce: Opening the Market, Intelligent Agents, the new software revolution - A Planning Sciences International Limited White Paper - http://www.ovum.com/.

[916] Papakonstantinou, Y., H. Garcia-Molina, J. Widom (1995), Object exchange across heterogeneous information sources, Proceedings of the 11th International Conference on Data Engineering, Taipei, Taiwan, pp. 251-260.

[917] Parker, R., N. Mokhoff (1983), An expert for every office, Computer Design, pp. 37-46.

[918] Parnas, D. (1985), Software aspects of strategic defence systems, Datamation, vol. 28, no. 12.

[919] Parsaye, K. (1988), Acquiring and verifying knowledge automatically, AI Expert, May.

[920] Parsaye, K., M. Chignell, S. Khoshafian, H. Wong (1989), Intelligent databases: Object-Oriented, Deductive hypermedia technologies, Wiley.

[921] Parsons, L.J., R.L. Schultz (1976), Marketing models and econometric research, North-Holland, New York.

[922] Pascoe, G. (1987), Elements of Object-Oriented Programming, in: Tutorial: Object-Oriented Computing (Concepts), Computer Society Press of the IEEE, Washington.

[923] Patridge D., K. M. Hussain (1994), Knowledge-based Information Systems.

[924] Patsis, G.P. (1988), Publicity and prices of olive oil and its substitutes, Olivae, no. 21, pp. 22-24.

[925] Pawlak, Z. (1982), Rough sets, International Journal of Information and Computer Sciences, vol. 11, no. 5, pp. 341-356.

[926] Pawlak, Z. (1991), Rough sets; theoritical aspects of reasoning about data, Kluwer Academic Publisher, Dordrecht.

[927] Pawlak, Z. (1997), Rough set approach to knowledge-based decision support, European Journal of Operational Research, vol. 99, pp. 48-57.

[928] Payne, J.W., E.K. Ragsdale (1978), Verbal protocols and direct observation of supermarket shopping behavior: Some findings and a discussion of methods, in: Proceedings of the Association for Consumer Research, Advances in Consumer Research, no. 5, pp. 571-577.

[929] Pearl, J. (1984), Heuristics: Intelligent search strategies for computer problem solving, Reading, MA: Addison-Wesley.

[930] Peguin, D. (1986), COLBERT: Systeme expert en strategie export pour PME – Les lecons d'une experience, in: Proceedings of the Itac International Conference on Economics and Artificial Intelligence, Aix-en-Provence, pp. 243-258.

[931] Pereira, J.M., L. Duckstein (1993), A multiple criteria decision-making approach to GIS-based land suitability evaluation, International Journal of Geographical Information Systems, vol. 7 5, pp. 407-424.

[932] Pessemier, E. (1966), New product decisions: An analytical approach, McGraw Hill, New York.

[933] Petroni, G. (1991), New directions for food research - long range planning, International Journal of Strategic Management, vol. 24, no. 1, pp. 40-51.

[934] Pfeffer, J. (1981), Power in organizations, Pitman, Marshfield, Mass.

[935] Pfeifer, R., H.J. Luthi (1987), Decision support systems and expert systems: A complementary relationship, in: H.G. Sol et al. (eds), Expert Systems and Artificial Intelligence in Decision Support Systems, D. Reidel Publishers, Dordrecht.

[936] Piercy, N.F. (1980), Marketing information systems: Theory vs. Practice, Quarterly Review of Marketing, vol. 6, no. 1, pp. 16-24.

[937] Piercy, N.F. (1983), A social psychology of marketing information, Journal of Market Research Society, vol. 24, no. 2, pp. 103-119.

[938] Piercy, N.F., M. Evans (1983), Managing marketing information, Croom Helm.

[939] Pierreval, H., M. Rakotomalala, A. Dussauchoy (1990), Integration of statistical methods in a knowledge based environment for assisting discrete simulation, Operational Research, pp. 659-673.

[940] Pinson S.D, P. Moraitis (1996), An intelligent distributed system for strategic decision making, Group Decision and Negotiation, no. 6, pp. 77-108.

[941] Pinson S.D, J.A. Louca, P. Moraitis (1997), A distributed decision-support system for strategic planning, Decision Support Systems, vol. 20, no. 1, pp.35-52.

[942] Plattfaut, E. (1988), DV: Unterstuetzung strategischer Unternehmensplanung – Beispiele und Expertensystemeinsatz, Berlin, Heidelberg, New York, pp. 88-133.

[943] Powers, J.N. (1989), A study of demand response to grocery advertising of fresh California-Arizona navel oranges, Agribusiness, vol. 5, no. 5, pp. 423-435.

[944] Porter, K. (1991), Visual Interactive Simulation as a Communication Tool: A Case Study, Presented at a Mini-Euro Conference on Visual Interactive Modeling, Warwick 1988, European Journal of Operational Research, vol. 54, pp. 287-292.

[945] Portier, K.M., P-Y. Lai (1983), A statistical expert system for analysis determination, in: Proceedings of the ASA statistical computing section, pp. 309-311.

[946] Preece, J. (1993), A guide to usability: Human factors in computing, Addison Wesley.

[947] Pregibon, D., W.A. Gale (1984), REX: An expert system for regression analysis, in: T, Havránek, Z. Sidák and M. Novák (eds.), Proceedings in Computational Statistics, Vienna: Physica-Verlag.

[948] Pressman, R.S. (1997), Software engineering (4th ed.), McGraw Hill.

[949] Price, L.L., L.F. Feick (1984), The role of interpersonal sources in external search: An informational perspective, in: T.C. Kinnear (ed.), Advances in Consumer Research, XI.

[950] Price, C.J. (1990), Knowledge engineering tool kits, Englewood Cliffs, NJ: Prentice-Hall.

[951] Pringle, L.G., R.D. Wilson, E.I. Brody (1982), NEWS: A decision-oriented model for new product analysis and forecasting, Marketing Science, vol. 1, no. 1, pp. 1-29.

[952] Proctor, R.A. (1991), Marketing information systems, Management Decision, vol. 29, no. 4, pp. 55-60.

[953] Punj, G.N., R. Staelin (1978), The choice for graduate business schools, Journal of Marketing Research, vol. 15, pp. 588-598.

[954] Quaddus, M.A., D.J. Atkinson, M., Levy (1992), An application of decision conferencing to strategic planning for a voluntary organization, Interfaces, vol. 22, no. 6, pp. 61-71.

[955] Qualls, W., R. Olsharsky, R. Michaels (1981), Shortening of the PLC: An empirical test, Journal of Marketing, vol. 45, no. 4, pp. 76-80.

[956] Quelch, J., E. Hoff (1986), Customising global marketing, Harvard Business Review, May/June, pp. 59-68.

[957] Quinlan, R. (1979), Discovering Rules from Large Collections of Examples: A Case Study, Edinburg University Press, Edinburg, Scotland.

[958] Quinlan, J.R. (1983), Learning efficient classification procedures and their application to chess end games, in: R.S. Michalski, J.G. Carbonell and T.M. Mitchell (ads), Machine Learning: An Artificial Intelligence Approach, val. I, Tioga Publishing Co., Palo Alto, California.

[959] Quinlan, J.R. (1984), Inductive inference as a tool for the construction of high performance programs, in: R.S. Michalski, J.G. Carbonell and T.M. Mitchell (ads), Machine Learning: An Artificial Intelligence Approach, vol. I, Tioga Publishing Co., Palo Alto, California.

[960] Quinlan, R. (1983), Learning Efficient Classification Processors and Their Applications to Chess and Games, in: J.G. Carbonell and T.M. Mitchell, (Eds.), Machine Learning: An Artificial Intelligence Approach (Tioga), pp. 463-482.

[961] Quinlan, J.R. (1986), The effect of noise on concept learning, in: R.S. Michalski, J.G. Carbonell, T.M. Mitchell (ads), Machine Learning: An Artificial Intelligence Approach, vol. II, Morgan Kaufmann, Los Altos, California.

[962] Quinlan, R. (1986), Induction of Decision Trees, Machine Learning, vol. 1, no. 1, pp. 81-106.

[963] Quinlan, R. (1987a), Simplifying Decision Trees, International Journal of Man-Machine Studies, Vol. 27, pp. 221-234,.

[964] Quinlan, R. (1987b), Decision Trees as Probabilistic Classifiers, in: Proceedings of Fourth International Workshop on Machine Learning, Morgan-Kaufman Press, Los Altos, CA, pp. 31-37.

[965] Quinlan, J.R. (1993), C4.5: Programs for Machine Learning. Morgan Kaufmann, San Mateo, CA.

[966] Rados, D.L. (1970), Simulation of the selection of an item for a grocery ad, British Journal of Marketing, no. 4, pp. 70-79.

[967] Rados, D.L. (1972), Selection and evaluation of alternatives in repetitive decision making, Administrative Science Quarterly, no. 17, pp. 196-206.

[968] Ram, S., S. Ram (1988), INNOVATOR: An expert system for new product launch decisions, Applied Artificial Intelligence, no. 2, pp. 129-148.

[969] Ram, S., S. Ram (1989), Expert systems: An emerging technology for selecting new product winers, Journal of Product Innovation Management, vol. 6, pp. 89-98.

[970] Rangaswamy, A., R.R. Burke, J. Eliashberg, J. Wind (1986), Expert systems for marketing, Working Paper 86-036R, Marketing Department, The Wharton School, University of Pennsylvania.

[971] Rangaswamy, A., R.R. Burke, J. Eliashberg, J. Wind (1987), Expert systems for marketing, Working Paper 86-036R, Marketing Department, The Wharton School, University of Pennsylvania.

[972] Rangaswamy, A., J. Eliashberg, R.R. Burke, J. Wind (1989), Developing marketing expert systems: An application to international negotiations, Journal of Marketing, vol. 53, pp. 23-39.

[973] Rangaswamy, A., B.A. Harlam, L.M. Lodish (1991), INFER: An expert system for automatic analysis of scanner data, International Journal of Research in Marketing, vol. 8, no. 1, pp. 29-40.

[974] Rangaswamy, A., G.R. Shell (1997), Using computers to realize joint gains in negotiations: Toward an electronic bargaining table, Management Science, vol. 43, no. 8.

[975] Rao, A.G., G.L. Lilien (1972), A system of promotional models, Management Science, vol. 19, no. 2, pp. 152-160.

[976] Rao, A.G., P.B. Miller (1975), Advertising/Sales response functions, Journal of Advertising Research, vol. 15, no. 2, pp. 7-15.

[977] Rao, A.S., M.P. Georgeff (1993), A model-theoretic approach to the verification of situated reasoning systems, in: Proceedings of IJCAI-93, Chambery, France.

[978] Rauscher, H. M., W.J. Dale (1993). Managing the Global Climate Change Knowledge Base, AI Applications, vol. 7, no. 4.

[979] Reeves, C.R. (1995), Modern Heuristic Techniques for Combinatorial Problems, McGraw-Hill Co.

[980] Reinfrank, M., J. de Kleer, M.L. Ginsberg, E. Sandewall (1989), Non-monotonic reasoning, Springer-Verlag.

[981] Reiter, R. (1978), On reasoning by default, TINLAP (July).

[982] Reiter, R. (1980), A logic for default reasoning, Artificial Intelligence, vol. 13 (April).

[983] Reitman, W. (1982), Applying artificial intelligence to decision support, in: M.J. Ginberg, W. Reitman and E. Stohr (eds.), Decision Support Systems, North Holland, Amsterdam.

[984] Rentsch, T. (1997), Object-Oriented Programming, in: Tutorial: Object-Oriented Computing (Concepts), pages 5-8. Computer Society Press of the IEEE, Washington, pp. 5-8.

[985] Rich, E. (1983), Artificial Intelligence, McGraw-Hill.

[986] Rich, E., K. Knight (1991), Artificial intelligence (2nd ed.), McGraw-Hill, New York.

[987] Riedel, S.L., G.F. Pitz (1986), Utilization-Oriented evaluation of Decision Support Systems, IEEE Transactions on Systems, Man and Cybernetics, SMC-16, pp. 980-996.

[988] Ries, A., J. Trout (1980), Positioning: The battle for your mind, New York: McGraw-Hill Book Co.

[989] Ritson, C. (1986), Marketing and agriculture, Discussion Paper, Department of Agricultural Economics Food Marketing, University of Newcastle upon Tyne.

[990] Ritson, C., R.K. Hutchins (1991), The consumption revolution, Paper presented at the National Food Survey, in: Proceedings of the 50th Anniversary Symposium, Royal Society, London.

[991] Roberts, J.H., G.L. Urban (1988), Modeling multiattribute utility: Risk and belief dynamics for new consumer durable brand choice, Management Science, vol. 34, no. 2, pp. 167-185.

[992] Roberts, J.H., J.M. Lattin (1991), Development and testing of a model of consideration set composition, Journal of Marketing Research, vol. 28, pp. 136-145.

[993] Robinson, P.V., C.W. Faris, Y. Wind (1967), Industrial buying and creative marketing, Boston: Allyn and Bacon.

[994] Rockart, J.F. (1979), Chief Executives Define Their Own Data Needs, Harvard Business Review, vol. 57, no. 2, pp. 81-93.

[995] Rockart, J.F., D. DeLong (1988), Executive Support Systems, Homewood, IL: Dow Jones-Irwin.

[996] Rogers, E. (1983), Diffusion of innovations, 3rd edition, The Press

[997] Rogers, M., M. Bruen, L-Y. Maystre (2000), ELECTRE and Decision Support: Methods and Applications in engineering and infrastructure investment, Kluwer Academic Publishers.

[998] Romei, L. (1989), Desktop publishing: What's the outlook?, Modern Office Technology, vol. 34, pp. 100-105.

[999] Romei, L. (1992a), Fax integration: More uses, less equipment, Modern Office Technology, vol. 37 (Feb), pp. 38-39.

[1000] Romei, L. (1992b), Telecommuting: A workstyle revolution?, Modern Office Technology, vol. 37 (May), pp. 38-40.

[1001] Rook, P. (1986), Controlling software projects, Software Engineering Journal, January, pp. 7-16.

[1002] Ross, D. (1985), Applications and extensions of SADT, IEEE Computer, vol. 18, no. 4, pp. 25-34.

[1003] Ross, D. (1996), Fuzzy Logic with Engineering Applications, McGraw- Hill.

[1004] Rossiter, J.R., L. Percy (1987), Advertising and promotion management, McGraw-Hill, New York.

[1005] Rothman, J. (1986), Experimental designs and models (3rd ed.), in: R.M. Worcester and J. Downham (eds.), Consumer Market Research Handbook, European Society for Opinion and Marketing Research (ESOMAR), McGraw-Hill, London.

[1006] Rothman, P. (1988), Knowledge transformation, AI Expert, November.

[1007] Rothschild, W.E. (1979), Competitor analysis: The missing link in strategy, Management Review (July), pp. 22-39.

[1008] Rouse, W.B. (1986), Design and evaluation of computer-based decision support systems, in: S.J. Andriole (ed.), Micro-Computer Decision Support Systems: Design, Implementation, and Evaluation, Wellesley, MA: QED Information Sciences.

[1009] Roy, B. (1968), Classement et choix en presence de points de vue multiples (la methode ELECTRE), Revue Informatique et Research Operationelle, 2e Annee, no. 8, pp. 57-75.

[1010] Roy, B., P. Bertier (1971), La methode ELECTRE II: Une methode de classement en presence de criteres multiples, SEMA (Metra International), Direction Scientifique, Note de Travail, no. 142, Paris, 25p.

[1011] Roy, B., P. Bertier (1973), La methode ELECTRE II: Une application au media-planning, in: M. Ross (ed.), Operational Research, North-Holland Publishing Company, pp. 291-302.

[1012] Roy, B. (1975), Vers une méthodologie générale d'aide à la Décision, Revue Metra, vol. XIV, no. 3.

[1013] Roy, B. (1976), From optimization to multicriteria decision aid: Three main operational attitudes, in: Thiriez, H. and S. Zionts (eds.), Multiple Criteria Decission Making, Springer-Verlag, 130, pp. 1-32.

[1014] Roy, B. (1978), ELECTRE III: Un algorithm de classements fonde sur une representation floue des preferences en presence de criteres multiples, Cahiers de CERO, vol. 20, no. 1, pp. 3-24.

[1015] Roy, B., J-C. Hugonnard (1982), Classement des prolongements de lignes de metro en banlieue parisienne (presentation d'une methode multicritere originale), Cahiers du CERO, vol. 24, no. 2-3-4, pp. 153-171.

[1016] Roy, B., Ph. Vincke (1984), Relational systems of preference with one or more pseudo-criteria: Some new concepts and results, Management Science, vol. 30, no. 11, pp. 1323-1335.

[1017] Roy, B. (1985), Méthodologie multicritère d'aide à la Décision, Economica, Paris.

[1018] Roy, B., J.M. Skalka (1985), ELECTRE IS: Aspects methodologiques et guide d'utilisation, Document de LAMSADE, no. 30, Université de Paris-Dauphine, 125p.

[1019] Roy, B. (1989), The outranking approach and the foundations of ELECTRE methods, Document du LAMSADE, no. 53, Université de Paris-Dauphine.

[1020] Roy, B. (1990), Decision aid and decision making, European Journal of Operational Research, vol. 45, pp. 324-331.

[1021] Roy, B. and D. Bouyssou (1993), Aide multicritère à la Décision: Méthodes et Cas, Economica, Paris.

[1022] Roy, B. (1996), Multicriteria methodology for decision aiding, Nonconvex Optimization and Its Applications, vol. 12, Kluwer Academic Publishers, The Netherlands.

[1023] Royce, W.W. (1970), Managing the development of large software systems: Concepts and Techniques, Proc. IEEE WES CON, August, pp. 1-9.

[1024] Russ, F.A. (1971), Consumer evaluation of alternative products models, Carnegie-Mellon University.

[1025] Ruttman, L. (1980), Planning useful evaluations: Evaluability assessments, Beverly Hills, CA: Sage.

[1026] Sääksjärvi, M.V.T., J.M. Talvinen (1993), Integration and effectiveness of marketing information systems, European Journal of Marketing, vol. 27, no. 1, pp. 64-79.

[1027] Saaty, T.L. (1980), The analytic hierarchy process, Decision Support Systems, vol. 8, pp. 343-359.

[1028] Saaty, T.L. (1990), How to make a decision: The analytic hierarchy process, European Journal of Operational Research, vol. 48, pp. 9-26.

[1029] Sage, A.P. (1986), An overview of contemporary issues in the design and development of microcomputer decision support systems, in: S.J. Andriole (ed.), Micro Computer Decision Support Systems: Design, Implementation, and Evaluation, Wellesley, MA: QED Information Sciences.

[1030] Sage, A.P. (1991), Decision Support Systems Engineering, Wiley, New York.

[1031] Sagle, J., M. Wick (1988), A method for evaluating candidate expert systems application, AI Magagine, Winter.

[1032] Salo, A.A. (1995), Interactive decision aiding for group decision support, European Journal of Operational Research, vol. 84, pp.134-149.

[1033] Samuel, A. (1963), Some studies in machine learning using the game of checkers, in: E. Feigenbaum and J. Feldman, Editors, Computers and Thought, McGraw-Hill, New York, pp. 71-109.

[1034] Sanchez-Sinencio, E., C. Lau (1992), Artificial Neural Networks, IEEE Press.

[1035] SAS/STAT (1990), User's guide, version 6, Fourth Edition, Vol. 1, SAS Institute, Cary, NC, USA.

[1036] Savage, L.J. (1954), The foundations of statistics, Wiley, New York.

[1037] Saurais, O., J. Siskos (1980), L'approche multicritère: Application au lancement d'un nouveau jeu de plage, in: Cahiers: Mèthodologie de la Recherche en Marketing, ADETEM et FNEGE (eds.), Lille.

[1038] Sauter, V. L. (1997), Decision Support Systems, John Wiley & Sons.

[1039] Schewe, C.D., R.M. Smith (1980), Marketing: Concepts and Applications, McGraw Hill, New York.

[1040] Schiffman, L.G., L.L. Kanuk (1983), Consumer behavior (2nd ed.), Englewood Cliffs, N.J.: Prentice-Hall.

[1041] Schiffman, L., L. Kanuk (1994), Consumer behavior, 4th edition, Englewood Cliffs, NJ: Prentice Hall.

[1042] Schoonderwoerd, R., O.E. Holland, J.L. Bruten, L.J.M. Rothkrantz (1997), Ant-based Load Balancing in telecommunications Networks, Adaptive behavior, vol. 5., no. 2., pp 169-207.

[1043] Schultz, R.L., A.A. Zoltners (1981), Marketing decision models, New York: North Holland.

[1044] Schultz, S.R., S.R. Rao (1986), Product life cycles of durable goods for the home, Journal of the Academy of Marketing Science, no. 14, pp. 7-12.

[1045] Schuman, M., P.A. Congla, K.S. Lee, J.G. Sakamoto (1987), Business strategy advisor: An expert system implementation, Paper, IBM Los Angeles Scientific Center.

[1046] Schmittlein, D.C., D.G. Morrison (1983), Prediction of future random events with the condensed negative binomial distribution, Journal of the American Statistical Association, vol. 78, pp. 449-456.

[1047] Schmittlein, D.C., D.G. Morrison, R. Colombo (1987), Counting your customers: Who are they and what will they do next?, Management Science, vol. 33, no. 1, pp. 1-24.

[1048] Schmitz, J.D., G.D. Armstrong, J.D.C. Little (1990), COVERSTORY: Automated news finding in marketing, Interfaces, no. 20, pp. 29-38.

[1049] Schmitz, J.D. (1994), Expert systems for scanner data in practice, in: R.C. Blattberg, R. Glazer, J.D.C. Little, (Eds.), The Marketing Information Revolution, Harvard Business School Press, Boston, MA, pp. 102-119.

[1050] Schwartz, D.G. (1995), Cooperating Heterogeneous Systems, Kluwer International Series in Engineering and Computer Science, Kluwer Academic Publishers, Boston.

[1051] Schwartz, D.G. (2000), Concurrent marketing analysis: a multi-agent model for product, price, place and promotion, Marketing Intelligence and Planning, vol. 18, no. 1, pp. 24-29

[1052] Schwoerer, J., J.P. Frappa (1986), Artificial intelligence and expert systems: Any applications for marketing and marketing research?, European Research, vol. 14, no. 4, pp. 510 – 524.

[1053] Segal, D., P.E. Bonzon, A Reflective Architecture for Implementing Decision Support Agents, http://isdss97.unil.ch/isdss97/.

[1054] Segev, A., J. Porra, M. Roldan (1997), Internet-based EDI strategy, Decision Support Systems, vol. 21, pp. 157-170.

[1055] Selly, M.A., E.H. Forman (1986), Expert Choice: Decision Support Software, Inc., 4922 Ellsworth Avenue, Pittsburgh, PA 16213.

[1056] Sena, J.A., L.M. Smith (1987), A sample expert system for financial statement analysis, Journal of Accounting and EDP, Summer, pp. 15-22.

[1057] Senauer, B. (1989), Major consumer trends affecting the US food system, Staff-paper, in: Department of Agricultural and Applied Economics, University of Minnesota, vol. 89, no. 16, pp. 1-23.

[1058] Sen, A.K. (1970), Collective Choice and Social Welfare, Holden-Day, San Francisco, CA.

[1059] Senn, J. (1984), Analysis and design of information systems, New York, McGraw-Hill.

[1060] Shannon, C.E. (1950), Programming a computer for playing chess, Philosophical Magazine, series 7, vol. 41.

[1061] Shafer, G. (1976), A mathematical theory of evidence, Princeston University Press.

[1062] Shafer, D. (1981), Constructive probability, Syntheses, no. 48, pp. 1-60.

[1063] Shafer, D. (1986), Probability judgment in artificial intelligence, in: L.N. Kanal and J.F. Lemmer (eds.), Uncertainty in Artificial Intelligence, Amsterdam: North-Holland.

[1064] Shafer, D. (1987), Belief functions and possibility measures, in: J.C. Bezdek (ed.), Analysis of Fuzzy Information, CRC Press, New York.

[1065] Shanteau, J. (1986), Psychological characteristics of expert decision makers, in: Proceedings of the Symposium on Expert Systems and Audit Judgment, School of Accounting, University of Southern California, Los Angeles.

[1066] Shooman, M.L., M.L. Bolsky, (1975), Types Distribution, and Test and Correction Times for Programming Errors, International Conference on Reliable Software Proceedings, Los Angeles, California, pp. 347-357.

[1067] Shakun, M.F. (1988), Evolutionary systems design. Policymaking Under Complexity and Group Decision Support Systems, Holden-Day, San Francisco, CA.

[1068] Shakun, M.F. (1990), Group decision and negotiation support in evolving, nonshared information contexts, Theory and Decision, vol. 28, pp. 275-288.

[1069] Shakun, M.F. (1991), Airline buyout: Evolutionary systems design and problem restructuring in group decision and negotiation, Management Science, vol. 37, no. 10, pp. 1291-1303.

[1070] Shaw, M. (1984), Abstraction Techniques in Modern Programmng Languages, IEEE Software vol. 1, no. 4, pp. 10.

[1071] Shaw, M.L.G., B.R. Games (1986), Interactive elicitation of knowledge from experts, Future Computing Systems, vol. l, no. 2, pp. 151-190.

[1072] Sheth, J.N. (1974), An investigation of relationships among evaluative beliefs, affect, behavioral intention and behavior, in: J.U. Farley, J.A. Howard and L.W. Ring (eds.), Consumer Behavior: Theory and Application, Boston: Allyn & Bacon.

[1073] Shocker, A.D., V. Srinivasan (1979), Multi-attribute approaches for product concept evaluation and generation: A critical review, Journal of Marketing Research, vol. 16, pp. 159-180.

[1074] Shocker, A.D., M.Ben-Akira, B. Boccara, P. Nedungadi (1991), Consideration set influences on consumer decision making and choice: Issues, models and suggestions, Marketing Letters, vol. 2, no. 3, pp. 181-198.

[1075] Shortliffe, E. (1976), Computer-based medical consultations: MYCIN, Elsevier, New York.

[1076] Shortliffe, E.H., B.G. Buchanan, E.A. Feigenbaum (1979), Knowledge engineering for medical decision making: A review of computer-based clinical decision aids, in: Proceedings of the IEEE, vol. 67, pp. 1207-1224.

[1077] Shortliffe, E. (1984), Rule-based expert systems: The MYCIN experiments of the Stanford heuristics programming project, Addison-Wesley.

[1078] Silk, A.J., G.L. Urban (1978), Pre-Test-Market evaluation of new packaged goods: A model and measurement methodology, Journal of Marketing Research, vol. 15, pp. 171-191.

[1079] Silverman, B.G. (1984), Chapter one: Nature of an expert's knowledge, Institute for artificial intelligence technical report, Washington, D.C.: George Washington University.

[1080] Silverman, B.G. (1985), Software cost and productivity improvements: An analogical view, IEEE Computer Society, May.

[1081] Silverman B.G. (1987), Expert systems for business, Addison-Wesley Publishing Company.
[1082] Simon, H. (1960), The new science of management decision, Harper and Row, New York.
[1083] Simon, H.A. (1981), The sciences of the artificial (2nd ed.), MIT Press, Cambridge, Mass.
[1084] Simonovic, S.P. (1993), Flood control management by integrating GIS with expert systems: Winnipeg City case study, in: K. Kovar, H. P. Nachtnebel, HydroGIS93: Application of Geographic Information Systems in Hydrology and Water Resources, IAHS Publication no. 211.
[1085] Simonson, I. (1990), The effect of purchase quantity and timing on variety-seeking behavior, Journal of Marketing Research, vol. 27, pp. 150-162.
[1086] Singh, J. (1988), Consumer complaint intentions and behavior: Definitional and taxonomical issues, Journal of Marketing, vol. 52, pp. 93-107.
[1087] Singh, H.S. (1998), Data warehousing: Concepts, Technologies and Management, Prentice Hall.
[1088] Sintos, I. (1996), Development of an Information System using Machine Learning Methods, Master Thesis, Technical University of Crete, Crete (in Greek).
[1089] Siskos, J. (1982), Le processus d'évaluation du réseau de distribution d'un nouveau produit, Revue Française du Marketing, no. 2, pp. 71-89.
[1090] Siskos, J. (1982), A way to deal with fuzzy preferences in multicriteria decision problems, European Journal of Operational Research, vol. 10, pp. 314-324.
[1091] Siskos, J. (1984), Le traitement des solutions quasi-optimales en programmation linéaire continue: Une synthèse, RAIRO Recherche Opérationnelle, no. 18, pp. 382-401.
[1092] Siskos, Y. (1985). Analyses de régression et programmation linéaire, Révue de Statistique Appliquée XXXII, pp. 41-55.
[1093] Siskos, Y., D. Yannacopoulos (1985), UTASTAR: An ordinal regression method for building additive value functions, Investigaçao Operacional, vol. 5, no. 1, pp. 39-53.
[1094] Siskos, Y., C. Zopounidis (1987), The evaluation criteria of the venture capital investment activity: An interactive assessment, European Journal of Operational Research, vol. 31, pp. 304-313.
[1095] Siskos, Y., D. Despotis (1989), A DSS oriented method for multiobjective linear programming problems, Decision Support Systems, vol. 5, pp. 47-55.

[1096] Siskos, Y., N.F. Matsatsinis (1993), A DSS for market analysis and new product design, Journal of Decision Systems, vol. 2, no. 1, pp. 35-60.

[1097] Siskos, Y., A. Spyridakos, D. Yannacopoulos (1993), MINORA: A multicriteria decision aiding system for discrete alternatives, Journal of Information Science and Technology, vol. 2, no. 2, pp. 136-149.

[1098] Siskos, Y., C. Zopounidis, A. Pouliezos (1994), An integrated DSS for financing firms by an industrial development bank in Greece, Decision Support Systems, vol. 12, pp151-168.

[1099] Siskos, Y., G. Baourakis, E. Grigoroudis, N.F. Matsatsinis (1995), Preference disaggregation analysis in agricultural product consumer behaviour, in: P.M. Pardalos, Y. Siskos and C. Zopounidis (eds.), Advances in Multicriteria Analysis, pp. 185-202, Kluwer Academic Publishers.

[1100] Siskos, Y., N.F. Matsatsinis and G., Baourakis, (1996), Agricultural product development using multidimensional and multicriteria analyses: The case of wine, European Journal of Operational Research, vol. 94, no. 2, pp. 321-334.

[1101] Siskos, Y., E. Grigoroudis, C. Zopounidis, O. Saurais (1998), Measuring customer satisfaction using a collective preference disaggregation model, Journal of Global Optimization, vol. 12, pp. 175-195.

[1102] Siskos, Y., A. Spyridakos (1999), Intelligent multicriteria decision support: Overview and perspectives, European Journal of Operational Research, vol. 113, no. 2, pp. 236-246.

[1103] Siskos, Y., A. Spyridakos, D. Yannacopoulos (1999), Using artificial intelligence and visual techniques into preference disaggregation analysis: The MIIDAS system, European Journal of Operational Research, vol. 113, no. 2, pp. 281-299.

[1104] Siskos Y., Y. Politis, G. Kazantzi (2000a), Multicriteria methodology for the evaluation of higher education systems: The case of an engineering department, European Journal of Operational Research (to appear).

[1105] Siskos Y. E. Grigoroudis, Y. Politis, Y. Malandrakis (2000b), Customer satisfaction evaluation: Some real experiences, EURO-MCDA 25th anniversary book (to appear).

[1106] Siskos Y., E. Grigoroudis (2000), Measuring customer satisfaction for various services: The role of multicriteria analysis, in Book honouring Bernard Roy, D. Bouyssou, and R. Slowinski (eds.), Kluwer Academic Publishers, Dordrecht (to appear).

[1107] Siskos, Y., N.F. Matsatsinis, G. Baourakis (2001), Multicriteria analysis in agricultural marketing: The case of French olive oil market, European Journal of Operational Research, vol. 130, no. 2, pp. 315-331.

[1108] Sisodia, R.S. (1992), Marketing information systems and decision support systems for services, The Journal of Services Marketing, vol. 6, no. 1, pp. 51-64.

[1109] Sissors, J.Z., E.R. Petray (1976), Advertising Media Planning, Chicago, Illinois: Crain Books.

[1110] Siomkos, G. (1994), Consumer behavior aand Marketing strategy, Stamoulis, Athina (in Greek).

[1111] Skalka, J.-M., D. Bouyssou, D. Valée (1992), ELECTRE III et IV: Aspects méthodologiques et guide d'utilisation, Document du LAMSADE, no. 25, Université de Paris-Dauphine.

[1112] Skyrme, D. (1997), Virtual Teaming and Virtual Organizations, http://www.skryme.com/ updates/u11.htm.

[1113] Slowinski, R. (1992), Intelligent decision support, Kluwer Academic Publishers, The Netherlands.

[1114] Slowinski, R., C. Zopounidis (1995), Application of the rough set approach to evaluation of bankruptcy risk, International Journal of Intelligent Systems in Accounting, Finance and Management, vol. 4, pp. 27-41.

[1115] Smith, J.M. (1986), Expert database systems: A database perspective, in: Proceedings from the First International Workshop Expert Database Systems, Menlo Park CA: Benjamin Cummings.

[1116] Smith, D.L. (1988), Implementing real world expert systems, AI Expert, December.

[1117] Snaprud, M., H. Kaindl (1994), Types and inheritance in hypertext, International Journal of Human Computer Studies, vol. 41, no. 1/2, pp. 223-241.

[1118] Sommervill, I. (1992), Software engineering, Addison-Wesley.

[1119] Spyridakos, A., Y. Siskos, D. Yannacopoulos, A. Skouris (2001), Multicriteria job evaluation for large organizations, European Journal of Operational Research, vol. 130, no. 2, pp. 375-387.

[1120] Sprague, R.H. (1980), A framework for the development of decision support systems, MIS Quarterly, vol. 4, no. 4.

[1121] Sprague, R.H., E.D. Carlson (1982), Building effective decision support systems, Prentice-Hall, Englewood Cliffs, N. J.

[1122] Srinivasan, V., P.V. Abeele, I. Butaye (1989), The factor structure of multidimensional response to marketing stimuli: A comparison of two approaches, Marketing Science, vol. 8, no. 1, pp. 78-88.

[1123] Sriram, D., R. Logcher, S. Fukuda (1989), Computer aided cooperative product development Berlin: Springer.

[1124] Staelin, R., R.E. Turner (1973), Error in judgment sales forecasts: Theory and results, Journal of Marketing Research, no. 10, pp. 10-16.

[1125] Stahl, B. (1986), The trouble with application generators, Datamation, vol. 1, pp. 93-94.

[1126] Stanulov, N. (1994), Expert knowledge and computer-aided group decision-making: Some pragmatic reflections, Annals of Operations Research, vol. 51, pp. 141-162.

[1127] Stanulov, N. (1995), A parsimonious outranking method for individual and group decision making and its computerized support, IEEE Transactions on Systems Man and Cybernetics, vol. 25, no. 2, pp. 266-276.

[1128] Stark, J. (1992), Engineering Information Management Systems, Van Nostrad Reinhold, New York, NY.

[1129] Starr, M.K., M. Zeleny (eds.) (1977), Multiple criteria decision making (TIMS Studies in the Manegement Sciences, vol. 6), Amsterdam: North-Holand.

[1130] Stefik, M., D. Bobrow (1986), Object-Oriented Programming: Themes and Variations, AI Magazine vol. 6, no. 4, pp 41.

[1131] Stevenson, H. (1976), Defining corporate strengths and weaknesses, Sloan Management Review (Spring), pp. 51-68.

[1132] Steuer, R.E. (1986), Multiple criteria optimization: Theory, computation and application, Krieger Publishing, Melbourne, Florida.

[1133] Stewart, T.J. (1992), A critical survey on the status of multiple criteria decision making theory and practice, OMEGA, vol. 20, no. 5, pp. 569-586.

[1134] Stewart, T.C., R.C. van den Honert (1998), Trends in Multicriteria Decision Making, in: Proceedings of the 13th International Conference on Multiple Criteria Decision Making, Cape Town, South Africa, 1997, Springer-Verlag, Berlin, Heidelberg.

[1135] Steuer, R.G., E.U., Choo (1983), An interactive weighted tchebycheff procedure for multiple objective programming, Mathematical Programming, vol. 26, pp. 326-344.

[1136] Swan, J., D. Rink (1982), Fitting marketing strategy to varying product life cycles, Business Horizons, Jan./Feb., pp. 72-76.

[1137] Swanson, E.B. (1988), Information system implementation, Homewood, IL: Richard D. Irwin.

[1138] Sycara, K.P. (1990), Negotiation planning: An AI approach, European Journal of Operational Research, vol. 46, pp. 216-234.

[1139] Sycara, K.P. (1991), Problem restructuring in negotiation, Management Science, vol. 37, no. 10, pp. 1248-1268.

[1140] Sycara, K., D. Zeng (1994), Towards an intelligent electronic secretary, in: Proceedings of the CIKM-94 (International Conference on Information and Knowledge Management) Workshop on Intelligent Information Agents, National Institute of Standards and Technology, Gaithersburg, Maryland.

[1141] Sycara, K., D. Zeng (1996), Multi-agent integration of information gathering and decision support, in Proceedings of 12th European Conference on Artificial Intelligence – ECAI96, John Wiley & Sons Ltd.

[1142] Sullivan, J.W., S.W. Tyler (1991), Intelligent User Interfaces, Frontier Series. New York, ACM Press.

[1143] Takeuchi, H., I. Nonaka (1986), The new product development game, Harvard Business Review (January - February), pp. 137-146.

[1144] Tang, Y., S. Lee, C. Suen (1996), Automatic document processing: A survey, Pettern Recognition, vol. 29, no. 12, pp. 1931-1952.

[1145] Tang, C., L.D. Xu, S. Feng (2001), An agent-based geographical information system, Knowledge-Based Systems, vol. 14, no. 5-6, pp. 233-242.

[1146] Tauber, E.M. (1977), Forecasting sales prior to test market, Journal of Marketing (January), no. 41, pp. 80-84.

[1147] Taylor, J.W. (1974), The role of risk in consumer behavior, Journal of marketing (April), pp. 54-60.

[1148] Taylor, J.W. (1984), Planning profitable new product strategies, Modern Business Reports, NY: Alexander Hamilton Institute Inc.

[1149] Teng, J.T.C. et al. (1988), A unified architecture for intelligent DSS, in: Proceedings of the 21st Annual Hawaii International Conference on System Sciences, Los Alamitos, CA: January.

[1150] Teng, J.T.C., K., Ramamurthy (1993), Group decision support systems: Clarifying the concept and establishing a functional taxonomy, INFOR, vol. 31, no. 3, pp. 166-185.

[1151] Teich, J.E., H. Wallenius, M. Kuula, S. Zionts (1995), A decision support approach for negotiation with an application to agricultural income policy negotiations, European Journal of Operational Research, vol. 81, pp. 76-87.

[1152] Terveen, L. - http://www.cs.wpi.edu/Research/airg/IntInt/intint-outline.html - http://www.cs.wpi.edu/Research/airg/IntInt/intint-bibliog.html

[1153] Thierauf, R.J. (1988), User-oriented decision support systems, Englewood Cliffs, N.J.: Prentice Hall.

[1154] Thuraisingham, B. (1989), Rules to frames and frames to rules, AI Expert (October).

[1155] Tietz, R., O.J. Barbos (1983), Balancing of aspiration levels as fairness principle in negotiations, in: Tietz, R. (Ed.), Aspiration Levels in Bargaining and Economic Decision Making, Springer, Berlin.

[1156] Tkach, R.J., S.P. Simonovic (1997), A New approach to multi-criteria decision making in water resources, Journal of Geographic Information and Decision Analysis, vol. 1, no. 1, pp. 25-43.

[1157] Triantaphyllou, E. (2000), Multi-Criteria Decision Making Methods: A Comparative Study, Kluwer Academic Publishers, Boston.

[1158] Tricker, R.I. (1971), Ten myths of management information, Management Accounting, August, pp. 231-233.

[1159] Tse, D.K., P.C. Wilton (1988), Models of consumer satisfaction formation: An extension, Journal of Marketing Research, vol. 25, pp. 204-212.

[1160] Tsichritzis, D., A. Klug (1978), The ANSI/X3/SPARC DBMS framework, AFIPS Press.

[1161] Tsichritzis, D. (1982), Form management, Communications of ACM, vol. 25, no. 7, pp. 453-478.

[1162] Tsichritzis, D., E. Fiume, S. Gibbs, O. Nierstraz (1987), KNOs: Knowledge acquisition, dissemination and manipulation objects, ACM Transactions on Office Information System, vo. 5, no. 1, pp. 96-112.

[1163] Tufte, E.R. (1992), The Visual Display of Quantitative Information, Graphics Press.

[1164] Tung, L., R.G. Ramariz, R.D. St. Louis (1991), Model integration in an object-oriented model management system, in: Proceedings of the 24th Annual Hawaii International Conference on System Sciences III, Decision Support and Knowledge Based Systems Track, pp. 284-290.

[1165] Tuorila, H. (1987), Selection of milks with varying fat contents and related overall liking, attitudes, norms and intentions, Appetite, vol. 8, pp. 1-14.

[1166] Turban, E., P. Watkins (1986), Integrating expert systems and decision support systems, MIS Quarterly, vol. 10, no. 2, pp. 121-136.

[1167] Turban, E. (1988), Decision support and expert systems, New York, Macmillan.

[1168] Turban, E., H. Watson (1989), Integrating expert systems, executive information systems and decision support systems, DSS Transactions, June, pp. 74-82.

[1169] Turban, E. (1992), Expert systems and applied artificial intelligence, New York: Macmillan.

[1170] Turban, E. (1993), Decision support and expert systems: Management support systems, 3rd ed., Macmillan, New York.
[1171] Turban E., E. Mclean, J. Wetherbe (1996), Information technology for management: Improving quality and productivity, John Wiley & Sons, New York.
[1172] Tuthill, G.S. (1990), Knowledge engineering, Blue Ridge Summit, PA: TAB Books.
[1173] Tversky, A. (1972), Elimination by aspects: A theory of choice, Psychological Review, vol. 79, pp. 281-299.
[1174] Tybout, A.M., B.J. Calder, B. Sternthal (1981), Using information processing theory to design marketing strategies, Journal of Marketing Research (February), pp. 73-79.
[1175] Tzafestas, S. (1988), Introduction to Artificial Intelligence and Expert Systems, National Technical University of Athens, Athens (in Greek).
[1176] Urban, G.L. (1970), SPRINTER mod III: A model for the analysis of new frequently purchased consumer products, Operations Research, vol. 18, no. 5, pp. 805-853.
[1177] Urban, G.L. (1975), PERCEPTOR: A model for product positioning, Management Science, vol. 21, no. 8, pp. 858-871.
[1178] Urban, G.L., J.R. Hauser (1993), Design and marketing of new products (2nd ed.), New Jersey: Prentice Hall.
[1179] Uhl, N.J. (1991), Comparison of food marketing systems in the EC and the USA: The market convergence hypothesis, in: Proceedings of the 25th seminar of the EAAE, 24-26 June 1991, pp. 23-36.
[1180] Vallèe, D (1994), ELECTRE III-IV – Aspects Méthodologiques, Université de Paris DAUPHINE, LAMSADE, Document no. 85.
[1181] Vallèe, D., P. Zielniewicz (1994), ELECTRE III-IV, version 3x – Aspects méthodologiques, Université de Paris Dauphine, Document du LAMSADE, no. 85.
[1182] Van Bruggen, G.H. (1992), Performance effects of a marketing decision support system: A laboratory experiment, in: Proceedings of the 21st Annual Conference of the European Marketing Academy, AARHUS.
[1183] Van Bruggen G.H., A. Smidts, B. Wierenga (1996), The impact of the quality of a marketing decision support systems: An experimental study, International Journal of Research in Marketing, 13, 331–343.
[1184] Van Bruggen G.H., B. Wierenga (2000), Broadening the perspective on marketing decision models, International Journal of Research in Marketing, vol. 17, no. 159–168.

[1185] Vandermerwe, S., W. Carney (1987), Integrating computers and marketing management: A European overview, European Management Journal, vol. 6, no. 1, pp. 10-15.
[1186] Van Horn, M. (1986), Understanding expert systems, Toronto: Bantam Books.
[1187] Van Nee, K.M., A. Lapinsky (1988), OR and AI approaches to Decision Support Systems, Decision Support Systems, vol. 4, no. 4, pp. 447-459.
[1188] Van Nee, K.M., L.J. Somers, M. Voorhoeve (1991), A modeling environment for decision support systems, Decision Support Systems, vol. 7, no. 3, pp 241-251.
[1189] Van Weelderen, J.A. (1991), MEDESS: A methodology for designing expert support systems, Ph.D. Dissertation, Technical University of Delft.
[1190] Van Weelderen, J.A., H.G. Sol (1993), MEDESS: A methodology for designing expert support systems, Interfaces, no. 23, pp. 51-61.
[1191] Vári, A., J. Vescenyi (1992), Experiences with decision conferencing in Hungary, Interfaces, vol. 22, no. 6, pp. 72-83.
[1192] Venkatachalam, A.R., J.E. Sohl (1999), An intelligent model selection and forecasting system, Journal of forecasting, no. 18, pp167-180.
[1193] Venugopal, V., W. Baets (1995), Intelligent support systems for organizational learning, The Learning Organization, vol. 2, no. 3, pp. 22–34.
[1194] Vetchera, R. (1991), Integrating databases and preference evaluations in group decision support: A feedback-oriented approach, Decision Support Systems, vol. 7, pp. 67-77.
[1195] Vincke, P. (1985), Multiattribute utility theory as a basic approach, in: G. Fandel and J. Spronk (eds), Multiple Criteria Decision Methods, Springer-Verlag, Berlin.
[1196] Vincke, P. (1992), Multicriteria decision-aid, John Wiley and Sons, West Sussex.
[1197] Vlachopoulou, M. (1999), E-marketing: Information systems – New technologies in marketing, Rosili, Athens (in greek).
[1198] Von Hippel, E. (1982), Get new products from customers, Harvard Business Review (March-April), pp. 117-122.
[1199] Von Hippel, E. (1985), Learning from lead users, in: R.D. Bussell (ed.), Marketing in an Electronic Age, Cambridge Harvard Business School Press, pp. 308-317.
[1200] Von Neumann, J., O. Morgestern (1947), Theory of games and economic behavior, Princeton University Press, Princeton, N.J.

[1201] Von Winterfeldt, E., W. Edwards (1993), Decision analysis and behavioural research, Cambridge University Press, Cambridge.

[1202] Voorbraak., F. (1996), Probabilistic belief expansion and conditioning, Research Report LP-96-07 Institute for Logic, Language and Computation (ILLC), University of Amsterdam.

[1203] Wagner, U., A. Taudes (1986), A multivariate polya model of brand choice and purchase incidence, Marketing Science, vol. 5, no. 3, pp. 219-244.

[1204] Wagner, R.K., R.J. Sternberg (1986), Tacit knowledge and intelligence in the everyday world, in: R.J. Sternberg and R.K. Wagner (eds.), Practical Intelligence: Nature and origins of competence in the everyday world, Cabridge University Press, New York.

[1205] Walker, T.C., R.K. Miller (1987), Expert system 1987: An assessment of technology and applications, SEAI Technical Publications, Madison.

[1206] Walker, A. (1996), Knowledge Systems: Principles and practice, McGraw-Hill.

[1207] Walsh, M.R. (1993), Toward spatial decision support systems in water resources, ASCE Journal of Water Resources Planning and Management, vol. 119, pp. 158-169.

[1208] Wang (1997), Intelligent Agent-Assisted DSS: Integration of Knowledge Discovery, Knowledge Analysis and Group Decision Support, Expert Systems with Applications, vol. 12, no. 3, pp. 323-335.

[1209] Wasserman, P.D. (1989), Neural Computing: Theory and Practice, Van Nostrand Reinhold.

[1210] Wasson, C.R. (1976), The importance of the product life cycle to the industrial marketer, Industrial Marketing Management, vol. 5, pp. 299-308.

[1211] Waterman, D., A. Newell (1976), PASII: An interactive task-free version of an automatic protocol analysis system, IEEE Transactions on Computers, no. 25, pp. 402-413.

[1212] Waterman, D.A. (1985), A guide to expert systems, Reading, Ma: Addison-Wesley.

[1213] Waterman, D.A. (1986), How do expert systems differ from conventional programs?, Expert Systems (January).

[1214] Watkins, C.J., P. Dayan (1992), Technical note: Q-learning, Machine Learning, vol. 8, pp. 3-4.

[1215] Watkins, D.W., D.C. McKinney, D.R. Maidment, M.D. Lin (1996), Use of geographic information systems in ground-water flow modelling, ASCE Journal of Water Resources Planning and Management, vol. 122, pp. 88-96.

[1216] Watson, I., F. Marir (1994), Case-based reasoning: a review, The Knowledge Engineering Review, vol. 9, no. 4, pp. 327-354.

[1217] Watson, H.J., G. Houdshel, R.K. Rainer (1997), Building executive information systems and other decision support applications, John Wiley & Sons, Inc.

[1218] Weber, E.S., Y.I. Liou, M. Chen, J.F. Nunamaker, Jr. (1990), Toward more intelligent organizations, in: Proceedings of the 23rd Annual Hawaii International Conference on System Sciences IV: Emerging Technologies and Applications Track, pp. 290-299.

[1219] Weber, J.A., U. Dholakia (1998), Planning Market Share Growth in Mature Business Markets, Industrial Marketing Management, vol. 27, pp. 401–428.

[1220] Webster, F.E., Y. Wind (1972a), A general model for understanding organizational buying behavior, Journal of Marketing, vol. 36, pp. 12-19.

[1221] Webster, F.E., Y. Wind (1972b), Organizational buying behavior, Englewood Cliffs, N.J.: Prentice Hall.

[1222] Weiss, S.M., C.A. Kulikowski (1984), A practical guide to designing expert systems, Rowman and Allanheld Publishers, USA.

[1223] Wellan, D.M., A.S.C. Ehrenberg (1990), A case of seasonal segmentation, Marketing Research, June, pp. 11-13.

[1224] Welz, G. (1995), New Deals, Internet World, June.

[1225] Westbrook, R.A. (1987), Product consumption-based affective responses and postpurchase processes, Journal of Marketing Research, vol. 24, pp. 258-270.

[1226] Wielinga, B., J. Boose, B. Gaines, G. Schreiber, M. Someren (1990), Current trends in knowledge acquisition, IOS Press, Amsterdam.

[1227] Wiener, N. (1948), Cybernetics, or Control and Communication in the Animal and the Machine, MIT Press, Cambridge, MA, USA.

[1228] Wierzbicki, A.P. (1982), A mathematical basis for satisfying decision making, Mathematical Modelling, vol. 3, pp. 391-405.

[1229] Wierzbicki, A.P. (1986), On the completeness and constructiveness of parametric characterizations of vector optimization problems, OR-Spectrum, vol. 8, pp. 73-87.

[1230] Wilkie, W.L., E.A. Pessemier (1973), Issues in marketing's use of multiattribute model, Journal of Marketing Research, vol. 10, pp. 428-441.

[1231] Wilson, D.T., H.L. Matthews, J.W. Harvey (1975), An empirical test of the Fishbein behavioral intention model, Journal of Consumer Research, vol. 1, pp. 39-8.

[1232] Wilson, H., M. McDonald (1994), Critical problems in marketing planning: the potential of decision support systems, Journal of Strategic Marketing, vol. 2, pp. 249-269.

[1233] Winblad, A.L. *et al.* (1990), The Future of Object-Oriented Programming, in: Object-Oriented Software, Addison-Wesley Publishing Company, Inc.

[1234] Winston, P.H. (1979), Artificial Intelligence, Adelson - Wesley.

[1235] Winston, P.H., S.A. Shellard (eds.) (1990), Artificial intelligence at MIT expanding frontiers, vol. 1 and 2, MIT Press, Cambridge.

[1236] Whinston (1997), Intelligent agents as a basis for decision support systems, DSS, vol. 20.

[1237] White, J.E. (1994), Telescript technology: The foundation for the electronic marketplace, White paper, General Magic Inc.

[1238] Whitten, J.L., L.D. Bentley, V.M. Barlow (1989), Systems analysis and design methods (2nd ed.), Irwin, Boston.

[1239] Wierenga, B. (1974), An investigation of brand choice processes, Rotterdam University Press, Rotterdam.

[1240] Wierenga, B. (1980), Multidimensional models for the analysis of consumers' perceptions and preferences with respect to agricultural and food products, Journal of Agricultural Economics, vol. 31, no. 1, pp. 83-97.

[1241] Wierenga, B. (1992), Knowledge-based systems in marketing: Purpose, performance, perceptions and perspectives, in: K. Grunet, D. Fuglede (eds.), Marketing for Europe Marketing for the Future, Proceedings of the 21st Annual Conference of the European Marketing Acadmy, Aarhus, Denmark, May, pp. 1197-1217.

[1242] Wierenga, B., A. Dalebout, S. Dutta (1992), BRANDFRAME: A Knowledge-based system for the brand manager, Advances and Practices in Marketing Science, in: Proceedings of the Marketing Science Conference, London Business School.

[1243] Wierenga, B., J. Kluytmans (1996), Prediction with neural nets in marketing time series data, Management Report Series, no. 258, Rotterdam School of Management, Erasmus University Rotterdam.

[1244] Wierenga, B., P.A.M. Oude Ophuis, K.R.E. Huizingh, P.A.F.M. Campen (1994), Hierarchical scaling of marketing decision support systems, Decision Support Systems, vol. 12, no. 3, pp. 219-231.

[1245] Wierenga, B., P.A.M. Oude Ophuis (1997), Marketing decision support systems: Adoption, use and satisfaction, International Journal of Research in Marketing, vol. 14, pp. 275-290.

[1246] Wierenga, B., G.H. Van Bruggen (2000), Marketing Management Support Systems: Principles, Tools and Implementation, Kluwer Academic Publishing, Boston, MA.

[1247] Wil, U. and J. Leggett (1997), Hyperform: A hypermedia system development environment, ACM Transaction on Information Systems, vol. 15, no. 1, pp. 1-31.

[1248] Wirth, N. (1971), Program development by stepwise refinement, ACM, vol. 14, no. 4, pp. 221-227.

[1249] Wiseman, C., I. Macmillan (1984), Creating a competitive weapon from information systems, Journal of Business Strategy, vol. 5, no. 2, pp. 42-49.

[1250] Wittink, D.R., M.J. Addona, W.J. Hawkes, J.C. Porter (1988), SCAN*PRO: The estimation, validation and use of promotional effects based on scanner data, Working Paper, February.

[1251] Wolfgram, D.D., *et al.* (1987), Expert systems, John Wiley & Sons, New York.

[1252] Wong, S.T.C. (1994), Preference-based decision making for cooperative knowledge-based systems, ACM Transactions on Information Systems, vol. 12, no. 4, pp. 407-435.

[1253] Wong, K., H. Saiedian (1996), Intelligent forms, ACS SIGICE Bulletin, vol. 21, no. 3, pp. 20-27.

[1254] Wooldridge, M., N.R. Jennings (1995), Intelligent agents: Theory and practice, The Knowledge Engineering Review, vol. 10, no. 2, pp. 115-152.

[1255] Wright, G., P. Ayton (1987), Eliciting and modeling expert knowledge, Decision Support Systems, no. 3, pp. 13-26.

[1256] Xu, X.M. (1999), The strategic orientation of marketing information systems - an empirical study, Marketing Intelligence & Planning, 17/6, pp. 262-271.

[1257] Yager, S. (1997), Everything's Coming Up Virtual, http://www.acm.org/crossroads/xrds4-1/organ.html.

[1258] Yager, R.R., L.A. Zadeh (1992), An introduction to fuzzy logic: Applications in intelligent systems, Kluwer, London.

[1259] Yakowitz, D.S. (1997), Multiple Objective Decision Making for Land, Water, and Environmental Management, IPublisher: St Lucie.

[1260] Yao, S., A. Henever, Z. Shi, D. Luo (1984), FORMANAGER: An office forms management system, ACM Transactions on Office Information Systems, vol. 2, no. 3, pp. 235-262.

[1261] Yen, J. (2000), Special issue of decision supports systems, intelligent agents and digital community, Decision Support Systems, vol. 28, pp. 217–218.

[1262] Yntena, D.B., W.S. Torgerson (1961), Man-computer cooperation in decision requiring common sense, IRE Transactions on Human Factors in Electronics, HFE-2, pp. 20-26.

[1263] Yourdon, E., I. Constantine (1975), Structured Design, New York: Yourdon Press.

[1264] Yourdon, E. (1989), Modern structured analysis, Englewood Cliffs, NJ: Yourdon Press.

[1265] Yu, W. (1992), ELECTRE Tri: Aspects methodologiques et manual d'utilisation, Document du LAMSADE, no. 74, Universite Paris-Dauphine, 80p.

[1266] Zadeh, L.A. (1965), Fuzzy sets, Information and Control, no. 8, pp. 338-353.

[1267] Zadeh, L.A. (1968), Probability measures of fuzzy events, Journal of Math. Analyses and Applications, vol. 23, pp. 421-427.

[1268] Zadeh, L.A. (1971), Similarity relations and fuzzy orderings, Information Science, vol. 3, pp. 177-200.

[1269] Zadeh, L.A. (1975), Calculus of fuzzy restrictions, in: L.A. Zadeh, K.S. Fu, K. Tanaka and M. Shimura (eds.), Fuzzy sets and their applications to cognitive and decision processes, Academic Press, pp. 1-39.

[1270] Zadeh, L.A. (1978), Fuzzy sets as a basis for a theory of possibility, International Journal for Fuzzy Sets and Systems, vol. l, no. l, pp. 3-28.

[1271] Zadeh, L.A. (1979), Fuzzy sets and information granularity, in: M.M. Gupta, R.K. Ragade and R.R. Yager (eds.), Advances in fuzzy set theory and applications, North-Holland.

[1272] Zaltman, G., M. Wallendorf (1983), Consumer behavior: Basic findings and management implications, New York: John Wiley & Sons.

[1273] Zanakis, S.H., J.R. Evans (1981), Heuristic optimization: Why, when and how to use it, Interfaces, October 1981.

[1274] Zanakis, S.H., Evans J.R., A.A. Vazacopoulos (1989), Heuristic Methods and Applications: A Categorized Survey, European Journal of Operational Research, North Holland, Vol. 43, pp. 88-110.

[1275] Zannetos, Z.S. (1968), Toward intelligent management information systems, Industrial Management Review, vol. 9, no. 3, pp. 21-38.

[1276] Zave, P. (1984), The operational versus the lonventional approach to software development, ACM, vol. 27, no. 2, pp. 104-118.

[1277] Zeleny, M. (1974), Linear multiobjective programming, Springer-Verlag, New York.

[1278] Zeleny, M. (1982), Multiple Criteria Decision Making, Springer-Verlag, New York.

[1279] Zimmermann, H.J. (1995), Fuzzy Set Theory and its Applications, Kluwer Academic Publishers.

[1280] Zionts, S. (1978), Multiple criteria problem solving, New York: Springer-Werlag.

[1281] Zoltners, A.A., P. Sinha, C. Chong (1978), An optimal algorithm for sales representative time management, Management Science, vol. 25, no. 12, pp. 1197-1207.

[1282] Zoltners, A.A., P. Sinha (1980), Integer programming models for sales resource allocation, Management Science, vol. 25, no. 12, pp. 242-260.

[1283] Zoltners, A.A. (1981), Normative marketing models, in: R.L. Schultz and A.A. Zoltners (eds.), Marketing Decision Models, Elsevier Science Publishing Co., New York.

[1284] Zopounidis, C., N.F. Matsatsinis, M. Doumpos (1996), Developing a multicriteria knowledge-based decision support system for the assessment of corporate performance and viability: The FINEVA system, Fuzzy Economic Review, vol. 1, no. 2, pp. 35-53.

[1285] Zopounidis C., M. Doumpos, N.F. Matsatsinis (1997), Application of the FINEVA multicriteria knowledge-based decision support system to the assessment of corporate failure risk, Foundations of Computing and Decision Sciences, vol. 21, no. 4, pp. 233-251.

[1286] Zopounidis C., M. Doumpos (1998), Developing a multicriteria decision support system for financial classification problems: The FINCLASS system, Optimization Methods and Software, vol. 8, pp. 277-304.

[1287] Zufryden, F.S. (1978), An empirical evaluation of a composite heterogeneous model of brand choice and purchase timing, Management Science, vol. 24, pp. 761-773.

Index

Agricultural
  CAP- Common Agricultural Policy 78
  distribution 77
  marketing mix 75
  price formation of agricultural products 76
  product characteristics 75
  promotion of agricultural products 76
  research methodologies in agricultural marketing 79

Alternatives
  Evaluation 10, 13, 17, 30, 35, 49, 359

Aggregation – Disaggregation 12, 17, 18, 38, 52, 163, 177, 185, 188, 352, 411

Agent-based DSS 304
  ARISTOTE system 307
  AMDSS system 310
  CMA system 312
  Marketing 304
  TeleDSS system 312

Artificial Intelligence 96, 114, 142, 148, 160, 181, 183, 221,
  Evolution 222
  Techniques 224, 289

Artificial Neural Network 96, 156, 260, 324
  Decision support systems 314
  DSS for sales prediction 314
  Marketing 159, 314

Behaviour
  Consumer 321, 351, 357, 377, 385
  models 12, 102
  purchase 41, 385

Brand choice models 54, 340, 342, 357, 377, 398, 413, 414

Business Information Systems 160

Case-based
  Marketing decision support systems 159, 315
  reasoning systems 201, 317, 328, 333

Communication Systems 99, 115
  Types 126

Computer-based Information Systems 88, 94
  strengths and weaknesses 156

Consumers
  attitudes 34, 37, 39, 40, 55, 80, 349
  behavior analysis 31
  behavior involvement 38
  behavior factors 34, 39
  behavior survey 42
  behavior theory 44
  decision making model 44
  decision making 32
  involvement 37
  needs 21, 31, 48, 56, 63, 65, 71, 75

post-purchase behavior 36
requirements 48, 50, 71

Criteria 10, 11, 14, 16, 17, 19, 35, 43, 52, 57, 71, 163, 171, 347, 352, 378, 387, 411

Customers
Perception 39, 47, 48, 404
Satisfaction – dissatisfaction 21, 35, 48, 50, 167
Satisfaction measurement 47, 49, 52, 54, 166, 199

Data
Analysis 31, 79, 82, 102, 141, 149, 198, 206, 211, 218, 282, 326, 330, 342, 350, 374, 392, 397, 408
External-internal 23, 25, 205
Management 93, 114, 122, 134, 136, 165, 273, 290, 295, 370

Data Bases
management system 136, 137, 287, 370
systems 138
topology 140

Data Mining 160, 263, 290, 305

Data Warehouses 213, 264

Decision
Alternatives 3, 10, 12, 19, 30, 143, 144, 189, 359
Problems 9, 23, 30, 96, 185, 312
Purchasing 31, 32, 33, 377
structured, semi structured and unstructured 4, 5, 7, 96, 116, 156
variables 143,

Decision Science 3

Decision alternatives 3, 10, 12, 19, 30, 31, 115, 143, 189, 198, 359

Decision Making
choice phase 5, 7, 113
design phase 5, 7, 93, 113, 152, 346
implementation phase 5, 9, 153, 402
intelligence phase 5, 6, 113
marketing 22, 25, 27, 28, 100
process 4, 5, 6, 10, 11, 179, 186, 188, 205, 207, 209, 280, 296, 305, 339, 372

Decision Support
Case-based 315, 317
Development process 149
Framework 7
Intelligent 221, 273, 284
systems analysis 149, 151
systems architecture 117
systems architecture advantages–disadvantages 120
systems assessment needs 150
systems characteristics 112, 116
systems compound 122
systems components 114, 117, 123
systems framework 7, 121, 147, 148
systems interface 124
systems knowledge-based 186, 274
systems technology levels 154
systems components 112, 114, 123
systems design 152
systems development stages 152
systems development process 154
systems documentation 154
systems implementation 153
systems improvements 154
systems integration 153
systems maintenance 154
systems prototype 153
systems structure 122
systems user 124
Technology levels 154

Descriptive models
Search 8, 126

Development process 63

Distributed
Artificial Intelligence 181, 266, 304
data bases 140
decision making 74, 179, 305,
decision support systems 163, 179, 181, 305, 329,
problem solving 183

Electronic Commerce 104, 180, 271

Electronic Data Interchange 105, 180

Executive Information Systems 96, 97, 156, 202
Advantages – disadvantages 205
Factors 204

Executive Support Systems 202

Expert support systems 273, 292
  Architecture 295
  Integration 296
  Marketing 292
  INNOVATOR system 297
  CSAS system 301
  ADDUCE system 303
  ADCAD system 304

Expert Systems 96, 113, 159, 223, 224
  Application areas 226, 227
  Application problems 246
  Backward reasoning or chaining 246
  Forward reasoning or chaining 245
  Development 246
  Development process 246
  Development rate
  Formal logic 226, 227
  Inference 241
  Inference engine 244
  Integration 234
  Knowledge acquisition 233
  Knowledge bases 250, 274
  Knowledge engineering 223, 231
  Knowledge elicitation 234
  Knowledge representation 235
  Non monotonic reasoning 239
  Production rules 224, 237
  Reasoning under uncertainty 240
  Structure 228
  Tools 251
  Working Memory 230, 231

Fuzzy Logic 156, 241, 263,

Fuzzy Sets 263, 292

Geographic Information Systems 206, 210
  Conceptual Model 211
  Functions and Applications 210
  Structure 209

Graphical User Interfaces 127

Group decision support systems 185
  Taxonomy 186, 226

Hybrid systems 251
  Marketing 321

Heuristics 8, 31, 148, 230, 243, 316

Human Computer Interaction 125, 126,

Inference
  Best-first search 244
  Branch and bound search 243
  Breadth-first search 242
  Depth-first search 242
  Heuristic search 243
  Strategies 244
  Backward reasoning or chaining 246
  Forward reasoning or chaining 246

Information Systems 23, 85
  Analysis 93
  Computer-Based 84
  categories 91
  life cycle 91
  Marketing 98
  Framework 99
  Strategic role 89
  Structure 90

Information resources management 87

Intelligent Agents 97, 181, 184, 266, 268,
  Ability 271
  Applications 307
  Characteristics 268
  Coordination 270
  RETSINA 270
  Decision support systems 304

Intelligent
  Case-based system 159, 201, 265, 315, 317, 328
  Data bases management subsystems 287
  Decision support methods 221
  Decision support systems 273, 276, 284, 292, 314, 325, 326
  Interfaces 284
  Marketing decision support systems 160, 325, 402
  Model bases 291
  Support Systems 97, 276

Intelligent Decision Support Systems
  Design and Development 275

Development problems 282
Interfaces 284
Marketing 273
MARKEX 320, 331, 367
Model Bases 291, 294,
Survey 283, 291, 325
System development tools 280

Interactive Decision Support Systems 171

Internet 104, 160, 180, 183, 212, 305, 310, 312, 326

Knowledge acquisition 230, 233
Phases 234
Process 233

Knowledge bases 122, 182, 250, 274, 278, 289, 318, 327, 330, 368, 372, 373,
data analysis 374
brand choice selection 377
financial status of enterprises 386

Knowledge elicitation 232
Methods 234, 254, 299

Knowledge engineering 223, 231,

Knowledge representation 116, 224, 233, 235, 238, 241, 253, 257, 266, 275, 280, 291, 301, 310, 318, 323, 335,
Methods 236,

Machine Learning 96, 253, 264, 291, 311
rule induction process 254
Marketing DSS 318, 319

Management Information Systems 87, 95, 97, 98, 103, 113, 116, 117, 215, 264, 274

Management Support Systems 158, 159, 273

Management science 3, 7, 28, 112, 113

Marketing
agricultural 75, 78, 79, 81
agricultural marketing mix 75
case-based reasoning systems 159
decisions 21, 22, 27, 29, 44, 61, 73, 155, 163, 305, 307, 326, 328, 332
decision making 22, 25, 26, 28, 100
decision support systems 28, 100, 114, 157, 158, 160, 305, 325, 402
decision support systems software 160
expert systems 159,
information systems 22, 87, 98, 99, 100, 101, 114, 156, 158, 160, 292
information systems components 100
information systems framework 99
information systems strategic-oriented 157, 158
Intelligent decision support systems 273
knowledge-based systems 159
management 74, 99, 115, 158, 305
management support systems 158, 159
mix 63, 67, 70, 71, 75, 160
models 27, 28, 44, 51, 100, 115, 141, 158, 159, 325
neural networks 159
problems 22, 25, 26, 27, 158, 160, 297, 305, 307, 325, 326
situation analysis 43, 67, 70
strategy 46, 65, 67, 73, 79, 215, 292, 310, 322, 323, 326, 328, 332, 386

Market
survey questionnaire 400
shares 22, 23, 27, 29, 51, 56, 89, 101, 108, 132, 160, 215, 276, 313, 322, 323, 328, 332, 333, 334, 342, 357, 362, 363, 364, 369, 372, 394, 395, 397, 403, 413, 414, 415, 417, 419, 420
segments 55, 70, 77, 304, 334, 351, 357, 393, 408, 413
surveys 27, 51, 54, 65, 86, 100, 102, 114, 115, 203, 313, 341, 368, 402
survey process 345
trends 101, 215, 265, 334, 341, 349, 400, 405

Metadata 215, 217

Method
Correspondence analysis 350, 375, 376, 410
Data analysis 31, 79, 82, 92, 102, 141, 149, 150, 198, 206, 211, 218, 219, 282, 326, 329, 330, 334, 340, 341, 344, 349, 350, 369, 371, 373, 374, 375, 392, 393, 397, 400, 408, 409, 411
Disaggregation 18
Multiple correspondence analysis 350, 375, 376

Multiple regression 81, 350, 375, 376
MUSA 160, 162, 163
Outranking 16
Principal components analysis 176, 178, 350, 375, 376, 408, 410
Q – Analysis 350
Simple regression 350, 375, 376
UTASTAR 18, 172, 178, 199, 342, 351, 352, 353, 366, 371, 393, 395, 401, 411, 421

Models
brand choice 54, 59, 132, 340, 342, 344, 357, 359, 360, 362, 370, 372, 377, 385, 394, 398, 413, 414, 416
brand awareness 57
descriptive 8, 26, 29, 30, 102, 144
Forecasting 29, 81, 87, 101, 128, 144, 156, 162, 262, 265, 282, 314, 322, 324, 328, 334, 340, 344, 349, 369, 393, 396, 405
information integration 35,
mathematical programming 12
normative 29, 30
individual awareness 35
optimization 31, 81, 148, 329
OR and Management Science 7, 28
Stochastic 34, 56, 59,
Theoretical 29, 159,

Model Base Management 141, 152, 209, 291, 294, 396

Modelling process 143, 172, 282

Multiagent Systems 266, 270, 306

Multiattribute utility theory 13, 192, 194

Multiple Criteria
decision analysis 9, 19
decision making 10, 187, 188
decision support systems 96, 171, 177
disaggregation approaches 18
evaluations 36, 59, 132, 320, 342, 363, 364, 366, 370, 378, 392, 394, 395, 400, 401, 415, 419
evaluation table 12
models 201
multiattribute utility theory 13, 194
multiobjective mathematical programming 12
outranking methods 16, 17, 172, 176, 190, 197, 199
satisfaction analysis 163

Multiobjective mathematical programming 12

Multimedia – Hypertext 132

Negotiation Support System 187, 190, 191, 195, 199, 200

New Products
adoption process 69,
design 7, 23, 63, 65, 70, 313, 341, 346, 363, 366, 403, 404, 413, 416, 419
development process 63
development methodology 339
dissemination and acceptance processes 68
examination of the ideas 66
failure 65
generation-birth of a new idea 65
introduction 333
launching 68, 305, 359
methodology 341, 342
product life cycle 71, 72
market survey 86, 342, 345, 347, 403
tests & pre-tests 67

Neural Networks 96, 98, 148, 159, 224, 260, 265, 314, 318, 322, 324, 327
Training 262

Office Automation Systems 96, 97, 98

On Line Analytical Processing 218
OLAP systems 213, 217

Optimization Search 148

Outranking methods 16

Questionnaires 44, 52, 102, 234, 301, 346, 348, 391

Positioning 32, 63, 67, 70, 157, 162, 328, 334

Rough Sets 256

Scenarios 12, 132, 143, 145, 146, 148, 162, 191, 219, 305, 307, 323, 329, 342,

364, 365, 366, 368, 386, 395, 398, 399, 402, 403, 415, 416, 417, 418, 420, 421

Service
  Behavioral Gap 48
  Perception Gap 48
  Procedural Gap 48
  Promotional Gap 48
  Understanding Gap 48

Simulation 68, 115, 128, 130, 132, 144, 147, 158, 163, 315, 331, 334, 341, 359, 363, 366, 368, 373, 385, 394, 397, 402, 413, 414, 419

Spatial Decision Support Systems 96, 206

Strategic
  Application 157
  marketing decisions 60, 73, 305, 307
  marketing planning 31, 74, 115, 334
  marketing process 62, 156
  market planning process 61
  planning 63, 64, 71, 73, 115, 193, 305, 327

Systems
  ADELAIS 175
  AIM 176
  COPE 200
  ELECALC 177
  ELECTRE 16, 17, 172, 175, 177, 190, 199
  EXPERT CHOICE 161, 178
  FINCLAS 179
  FINEVA 178
  Group Work Environment 197
  HIPRE 198
  JUDGES 194
  MARKEX 320, 331, 367, 390, 399
  MIIDAS 179
  MINORA 172
  MEDIATOR 190
  MUSA 163
  MUSTARD 175
  NegocIAD 201
  NEGOPLAN 200, 332
  NEGOTIATION ASSISTANT 199
  NTech-GDSS 197
  PERSUADER 201
  PLEXSYS 191
  PREFCALC 175
  PROMCALC 176
  PROMETHEE 175
  RAMONA 195
  SCDAS 191
  UNIDAS 197
  VIDMA 177
  WINGDSS 196
  life cycle 90, 91
  Analysis 90, 91, 92
  Design 90, 92, 100, 114
  Implementation 92, 114
  Types 88, 90, 94, 97, 98, 113, 117, 156, 158, 174

Target markets 23

Transaction Processing Systems 97, 98

Utility
  Functions 13, 15, 173, 175, 191, 199, 361, 377, 380,
  Global 175, 361
  Marginal 15, 175, 191

Visual Interactive Modeling 128

Virtual Enterprises 104, 107

Virtual Reality 133, 134

Web Based
  decision support systems 179, 305, 312

World Wide Web 105, 180, 181, 213

Printed in the United Kingdom
by Lightning Source UK Ltd.
131492UK00001BB/70/P